VISUAL QUICKSTART GUIDE

Photoshop CS

FOR WINDOWS AND MACINTOSH

Elaine Weinmann
Peter Lourekas

 Peachpit Press

For our mothers, Bert Weinmann & Theodora Lourekas

Visual QuickStart Guide
Photoshop CS for Windows and Macintosh
Elaine Weinmann and Peter Lourekas

Peachpit Press
1249 Eighth Street
Berkeley, CA 94710
510/524-2178
800/283-9444
510/524-2221 (fax)

Find us on the World Wide Web at: http://www.peachpit.com

Visual QuickStart Guide is a trademark of Peachpit Press, a division of Pearson Education

Cover design: Peachpit Press
Interior design: Elaine Weinmann
Production: Elaine Weinmann and Peter Lourekas
Illustrations: Elaine Weinmann and Peter Lourekas, except as noted

Colophon
This book was created with QuarkXPress 5 on a Power Macintosh G4 and G5. The primary fonts used were New Baskerville and Myriad from Adobe Systems Inc.

Notice of Rights

Notice of Liability

ISBN 0-321-21353-X
9 8 7 6 5

Printed and bound in the United States of America

The story behind the book

Sometime in the mid-'80s, a smart guy in Berkeley, California, by the name of Ted Nace got a brainstorm. He decided to start up a computer book publishing company, which he called Peachpit Press (how he came up with the name is another story). The books he published were innovative and user-friendly and offered a fresh approach to learning computer graphics. I (Elaine) found myself teaching a course in QuarkXPress not long thereafter, and I yearned for a book that would offer steps, like a recipe book, for learning various techniques. If nothing else, I thought, it would make my job easier. Then I got a brainstorm of my own. "What the heck, I have nothing to lose," I said to Peter, and made a cold call to Ted. I'd never written anything longer than a shopping list before, but I had an art background, teaching and practical experience under my belt, and enthusiasm in abundance, and Ted, bless him, let me take the plunge.

Ted supported innovation, not just in content, but also in production. He figured since many of his authors were writing about desktop publishing programs, why not let them put words into action and typeset and illustrate their own books (what is known in the trade as book packaging)? The rabbit was already on the cover of the Visual QuickStart Guide series, but the thumb tabs, tips, numbered steps, and other design features that you see in our books were my innovations, fine-tuned with Ted's feedback. I invited my husband, Peter, to come on board for the second book (Photoshop 2.5: Visual QuickStart Guide), and our 24/7 partnership continues today.

Who does what

What started out as a serendipitous idea turned into a career. We write, rewrite, design, typeset, illustrate, and test all of our books, and when we're done sweating over all the nitpicky details and are ready to up the prescription on our reading glasses, we hand the electronic files off to Peachpit Press's production department for a final prepress check.

The first book (QuarkXPress 3.1: Visual QuickStart Guide), nicknamed by Peter "the little book that could," was 200 pages long. As features are added to the software, revised editions of the books swell accordingly. Some things are easier now than in the old days, such as storing files and sending them hither and thither, but we still rely on other people to help us get the job done.

In 1996, Ted Nace handed the baton to his hand-picked successor, Nancy Aldrich-Ruenzel, who took the baton and ran with it. Under her energetic leadership, Peachpit Press continues to be a thriving and dynamic company.

And then there's Cary Norsworthy, our editor at Peachpit Press, who is always there when we need her. Victor Gavenda, our technical editor at Peachpit, tests the book in Windows and is an indispensible member of our team. Lisa Brazieal, our production coordinator, spearheads the prepress production and then sends the files off to Malloy Lithographing. Peachpit Press is also lucky to have Editor-in-Chief Nancy Davis, Executive Editor Marjorie Baer, publicist Gary-Paul Prince, and associate publisher Keasley Jones on staff, as well as other terrific people who now number too many to mention.

In our writing, testing, and book packaging "department," Jeff Seaver helped us revise some chapters, Heidi Jonk-Sommer and Tim Plumer did a bit of technical editing, Rebecca Pepper did the copy editing, Leona Benten did the final proofreading, and Steve Rath generated the index.

Hats off also to the Adobe Photoshop CS beta team, innovators in their own right.

On the home front, we'd like to thank our wonderful family of friends (you know who you are) for helping to give our lives whatever semblance of balance it has. And the biggest thanks of all go to our kids, simply for being there (you make it all worthwhile).

Elaine Weinmann & Peter Lourekas

The artists

Clifford Alejandro
voice 201-451-0441
www.oldtin.com
(color section)

Marty Blake
Box 266
2043 Jamesville Terrace
Jamesville, NY 13078
voice 315-492-1332
fax 315-469-5907
mblake01@twcny.rr.com
www.martyblakedesign.com
(color section)

Nina Fuller
www.ninafuller.net
(page 256)

Wendy Grossman
www.rosebudstudios.com
(pages 82, 264)

David Humphrey
represented by
Brent Sikkema Gallery, NYC
aikenhump@aol.com
(page 158)

John Kachik
7540 Main St., Suite 11C
Sykesville, MD 21784
voice 410-552-1900
fax 410-552-6645
kachik@adelphia.net
www.johnkachik.com
(color section)

William Low
voice/fax 631-421-5859
info@williamlow.com
www.williamlow.com
(color section)

Paul Mirocha
425 East 17th St.
Tucson, AZ 85701
voice/fax 520-623-1515
paul@paulmirocha.com
www.paulmirocha.com
(color section)

Bert Monroy
11 Latham Lane
Berkeley, CA 94708
voice 510-524-9412
fax 510-524-2514
bert@bertmonroy.com
www.bertmonroy.com
(color section)

Keri Smith
voice 519-924-3535
info@kerismith.com
www.kerismith.com
(color section)

Mick Wiggins
Mick Wiggins Illustration
www.mickwiggins.com
(color section)

PHOTO CREDITS
Nolan Hester, *page 255;* **Nadine Markova** *(Mexico City), pages 33, 173;* **Paul Petroff** *(Seattle, Washington), pages 127, 156, 173, 175, 226, 373;* **Cara Wood** *(Poughkeepsie, NY), page 389;* **PhotoDisc,** *pages v, 1, 2, 30, 36, 38, 57, 58, 101, 103, 110, 123, 128, 131, 133, 136, 138, 148, 157, 164, 165, 174, 179, 189, 194, 195, 207, 230, 232, 234, 242, 246, 249, 251, 253, 265, 266, 270, 291, 295, 314, 351, 374, 375, 388, 471, 472, 488, 515, 533;* **Corel Professional Photos,** *pages 228, 274, 465.* All other images are owned by the authors.

TABLE OF CONTENTS

Note: New or substantially changed features are identified by this symbol: ■

1/THE BASICS

Launch Photoshop in Windows 1
Launch Photoshop in Macintosh 1
The Photoshop screen in Macintosh 2
The Photoshop screen in Windows 3
The menus ....■ 4
Using the Toolbox ....■ 6
The Toolbox 7
Options bar 11

The palettes
How to use the palettes 12
Create a custom workspace 13
Delete any or all custom workspaces 13
Actions palette 14
Brushes palette 15
Channels palette 16
Character palette 17
Color palette 18
File Browser ....■ 19
Histogram palette ....■ 20
History palette 20
Info palette ....■ 21
Layer Comps palette ....■ 22
Layers palette 23
Navigator palette 24
Paragraph palette 24
Paths palette 25
Styles palette 26
Swatches palette 27
Tool Presets palette 28
Mini-glossary 29
Production techniques ....■ 31

2/PHOTOSHOP COLOR

Pixels 33
RGB vs. CMYK color 33
Channels 34
Image modes 35
The blending modes 38
Color management 43
Calibrate your monitor in Macintosh 44
Calibrate your monitor in Windows 46
Choose a predefined color management setting ...48
Customize your color management policies 51
Customize your conversion options 52
Change or delete a document's color profile 54
Convert a document's color profile 54
Proof colors using preset settings 55
Proof colors using custom settings 56

3/STARTUP

Where images come from 57
Scanning 57
Desktop scanning software basics 58
16-bits-per-channel mode 60
Scan into Photoshop 61
Calculate the proper resolution for print output 62
File storage sizes of scanned images 63
Potential gray levels at various output
     resolutions and screen frequencies 63
Using the status bar 64
Find out an image's storage size 64
Create a new image ....■ 65
Create a document preset ....■ 67
Using the File Browser
Open the File Browser ....■ 68
The File Browser palette ....■ 69

Customize the File Browser .... ■ 70

Th File Browser menus .... ■ 71

Open files via the File Browser .... ■ 72

Flag files .... ■ 73

Rotate a thumbnail .... ■ 73

Search for a file using the File Browser .... ■ 74

Arrange thumbnails manually .... ■ 75

Apply a sorting method .... ■ 75

Create a custom ranking system .... ■ 75

Rename a file via the File Browser 76

Create a folder via the File Browser .... ■ 76

Delete a file via the File Browser 76

Export a File Browser cache .... ■ 77

Delete the cache files .... ■ 77

Other ways to open files

Use the Open command 78

Switch between open documents .... ■ 78

Open a Photoshop image from Windows Explorer ..79

Open a Photoshop image from the Finder
 in Macintosh 79

Create image thumbnails 79

Open an EPS, PDF, or Illustrator file as a
 new image .... ■ 80

Paste from Illustrator 81

Place an EPS, PDF, or Adobe Illustrator image
 into a Photoshop image 82

Saving files

Save an unsaved image 83

Saving layers, vectors, and effects 84

Save an already saved image 84

Revert to the last saved version 84

Save a new version of an image 85

Navigating

Change the zoom level using the Navigator
 palette 86

Change the zoom level using the Zoom tool 87

Move an image in its window 88

Change the screen display mode .... ■ 88

Display one image in two windows .... ■ 89

Scroll or zoom in multiple windows .... ■ 89

Ending a work session

Close an image 90

Exit/quit Photoshop 90

4/PIXEL BASICS

Changing dimensions and resolution

Change an image's pixel dimensions for
 onscreen output .... ■ 91

Change an image's dimensions for print output .. ■ 92

Change an image's resolution 93

Resize an image to fit a specific width or height 94

Resize an image automatically 95

Apply the Unsharp Mask filter 96

Changing the canvas

Change the canvas size .... ■ 98

Crop an image using a marquee .... ■ 99

Specify dimensions and resolution as you
 crop an image .... ■ 100

Enlarge the canvas area using the Crop tool 101

Crop an image using the Crop command 102

Crop an image using the Trim command 102

Flip an image 103

Rotate an image by a preset amount 104

Rotate an image by specifying a number 104

5/LAYER BASICS

Layer basics 105

Create a new layer 106

Turn a selection into a layer 107

Duplicate a layer in the same image 107

Hide or show layers 108

Flip a layer 109

Delete a layer 109

Rename a layer or layer set 109

Managing layers

Restack a layer 110

Convert the Background into a layer 111

Convert a layer into the Background 111

Move layer pixels 112

Activate a layer using the Move tool 112

Create a layer set 113

Lock a layer or layer set 113

Create a fill layer 114

Tools and layers 115

Lock transparent pixels 115

Copy layers

Save a copy of a layer or layer set to a
new document 116

Drag-and-drop a layer to another image using
the Layers palette 117

Drag-and-drop a layer to another image using
the Move tool 118

Merge and flatten layers

Merge two layers together 120

Merge multiple layers 121

Other merge commands 121

Flatten layers 122

6/SELECT

Creating selections

Select an entire layer 123

Create a rectangular or elliptical selection 124

Create a freeform selection 125

Create a polygonal selection 125

Select by color using the Magic Wand tool 126

Select using the Magnetic Lasso tool 128

Magnetic Lasso tool options bar 129

Use the Color Range command to create
a selection 130

Create a border selection manually 131

Create a border selection by using a dialog box . . .131

Working with selections

Deselect a selection 132

Reselect the last selection 132

Delete selected pixels 132

Move a selection marquee 133

Smooth a selection 133

Switch the selected and unselected areas 134

Hide a selection marquee 134

Transform a selection marquee 135

Modify a selection marquee via a menu
command 135

Add to a selection 136

Subtract from a selection 136

Select the intersection of two selections 136

Vignette an image 137

Mask a shape using the Extract command 138

7/COMPOSITING

Moving

Move a selection's contents 141

Align a layer or layers to a selection marquee 142

Copying

Drag-copy a selection 142

Clipboard basics 143

Copy and paste a selection 144

Drag and drop a selection between images 145

Paste into a selection 146

Paste into a smaller image 147

Sharpening and blurring

Sharpen or blur edges 148

Using rulers and guides

Hide or show rulers 149

Change the rulers' zero origin .149

Use the Snap feature 150

Hide or show the grid 150

Create a guide 151

Place a guide at a specific location 151

Remove guides 151

Use the Measure tool 152

Cloning

Clone areas in the same image 153

Use the Pattern Stamp tool 155

Clone from image to image 156

Feather a selection 157

Defringe a layer 158

8/HISTORY

Using the History palette

Linear and nonlinear 159

Revert to a prior history state .161

Duplicate a state 161

Delete a state 161

Using snapshots

Create a snapshot of a history state 162

Make a snapshot become the latest state 163

Delete a snapshot 163

Create a new document from a history state
or snapshot 163

Restoring and erasing
Use the History Brush tool 164

Fill a selection or a layer with a history state 165

Use the Art History Brush tool 166

9/ADJUSTMENTS
Adjustment basics 167

Adjustment layers
Create an adjustment layer 168

Modify an adjustment layer 168

Choose blending options for an adjustment
layer (or any layer) 169

Choose a different command for an
adjustment layer 170

Merge an adjustment layer 170

Ways to use adjustment layers 171

Adjustment commands
Apply the Auto Contrast command 172

Invert lights and darks 173

Make a layer high contrast 173

Posterize 174

Use the Brightness/Contrast command 175

Adjust brightness and contrast using Levels 176

Screen back a layer 177

Lighten using the Dodge tool or darken
using the Burn tool 178

Restrict an adjustment layer's effect using
a mask 179

Make a layer grayscale using the Channel Mixer ...180

Using the Histogram palette
Update the Histogram palette ....■ 181

Reading the histogram 182

10/CHOOSE COLORS
Foreground and Background colors 183

Choose a color using the Color Picker 184

Choose a custom color 185

Choose a color using the Color palette 186

Swatches palette
Choose a color from the Swatches palette 187

Add a color to the Swatches palette 187

Delete a color from the Swatches palette 187

Save an edited swatches library 188

Replace or append a swatches library 188

Load a swatches library 188

Restore the default Swatches palette 188

Using the Eyedropper tool
Choose a color from an image using the
Eyedropper tool 189

Copy a color as a hexadecimal value 190

11/RECOLOR
Adjustment basics 191

Fill a selection or a layer with a color, a pattern,
or imagery 193

Apply a stroke to a selection or a layer 195

Adjust a color image using Hue/Saturation 196

Using the Color Sampler tool
Place color samplers on an image 198

Move a color sampler 199

Using the Info palette with the Color
Sampler tool 199

Remove a color sampler 199

Adjustment techniques
Colorize or color-correct using Color Balance 200

Saturate or desaturate colors using the
Sponge tool 201

Heighten color or silhouette color areas on black ..202

Convert a layer or the Background to grayscale 203

Convert a color layer to grayscale and
selectively restore its color 203

Levels and Curves
Adjust individual color channels using the
Levels command 204

Apply Auto Color Correction options 205

Adjust color or values using the Curves
command 206

Spot color channels
Create a spot color channel 208

Paint on a spot color channel 209

Convert an alpha channel into a spot
color channel 209

Spot color channel basics 210

Printing spot color channels 210

12/PAINT

Getting started
Use the Brush tool 211

Make temporary changes to a brush preset .....■ 212

Brushes palette
Use the Brushes palette 213

Edit a brush preset ....■ 214

Choose variation options 218

Working with presets
Save a new preset 220

Save brush presets in a new library 220

Load a brush preset library 221

Restore the default brush presets 221

Make a brush into a tool preset 222

Save tool presets to a library 223

Create a brush preset from an image 224

Delete a brush preset 224

Other painting techniques
Smudge colors 225

Fill an area using the Paint Bucket tool 226

Apply tints to a grayscale image 227

Erasing
Erase part of a layer 228

Use the Background Eraser tool 229

Use the Magic Eraser tool 231

13/PHOTOGRAPHY

Camera Raw ....■ 233

Open a Camera Raw file ....■ 234

Change views in the preview window ....■ 235

Change the image attributes for a Camera
Raw file ....■ 235

Change a Camera Raw image's basic settings ...■ 236

Make global color adjustments to a Camera
Raw fle ....■ 237

Make detail adjustments to a Camera Raw file ..■ 239

Adjust Camera Raw's built-in camera profiles ...■ 240

Camera Raw versus JPEG ....■ 241

Shadow and highlight adjustment
Apply the Shadow/Highlight command ....■ 242

Colored lens effect
Apply the Photo Filter command ....■ 244

Lens Blur
Apply the Lens Blur filter ....■ 245

Replace colors
Use the Replace Color command 248

Use the Color Replacement tool ....■ 250

Make repairs
Repair areas using the Healing Brush tool 252

Use the Patch tool 254

Photomerge
Collect images for Photomerge ....■ 256

Create a Photomerge montage ....■ 257

14/GRADIENTS

Apply a gradient as a fill layer 259

Apply a gradient using the Gradient tool 261

Create or edit a gradient preset 262

Save the current gradients presets to a file 264

Use alternate gradient preset libraries 264

Restore the default gradient presets 265

Change the opacity of gradient colors 265

Create a multicolor wash 266

Apply a gradient map to a layer 267

15/LAYERING LAYERS

Layer opacity and fill
Change a layer's opacity or fill percentage ......■ 269

Blending layers
The layer blending modes 270

Fine-tune the blending between two layers 271

Choose a knockout option for a layer 273

Blend a modified layer with the original layer 274

Layer Comps
Create a layer comp ....■ 275

Apply a layer comp to an image ....■ 276

Restore the last document state ....■ 276

Update a layer comp ....■ 276

Respond to a layer comp warning ....■ 276

Table of Contents

Change which characteristics a layer
  comp applies .... ■ 277

Output layer comps as a multipage PDF .... ■ 277

Delete a layer comp .... ■ 277

Layer masks
Create a layer mask 278

Reshape a layer mask 279

Move layer pixels or a layer mask independently ..280

Duplicate a layer mask 280

Choose layer mask display options 280

Fill type with imagery using a layer mask 281

Temporarily deactivate a layer mask 282

Apply or discard the effects of a layer mask 282

Clipping masks
Create a clipping mask 283

Release a layer from a clipping mask 284

Release an entire clipping mask 284

Linking layers
Link layers (and move them as a unit) 285

Align two or more linked layers 285

Align the pixel edge of a layer with a selection 286

Distribute three or more linked layers 286

Transform layers
Transform a layer using its bounding box 287

Free-transform a layer 289

Transform a layer by entering numeric values 290

16/LAYER EFFECTS

Layer effects 291
Applying layer effects 292

Remove a layer effect 293

Copy layer effects from one layer to another 293

Apply the Drop Shadow or Inner Shadow effect ...294

Transform a Drop Shadow effect 295

Create a drop shadow without using an effect 296

Apply an Outer or Inner Glow effect 296

Apply the Bevel or Emboss effect 298

Change the profile of a contour 300

Apply the Satin effect 301

Apply the Color Overlay effect 302

Apply the Gradient Overlay effect 302

Apply the Pattern Overlay effect 303

Apply a Stroke effect 304

Other effects commands 305

17/MASKS

Chapter overview 307

Alpha channels
Save a selection to a channel using the current
  options settings 308

Choose options as you save a selection to
  a channel 308

Display a channel selection 309

Load a channel selection onto an image using
  the current options 309

Choose options as you load a channel
  selection onto an image 309

Save Selection Operations 310

Load Selection Operations 310

Rename an alpha channel 311

Reverse the black and white areas in an
  alpha channel 311

Delete a channel 311

Duplicate a channel 311

Reshape an alpha channel mask 312

Quick Masks
Reshape a selection using Quick Mask mode 313

Create a Quick Mask without using a selection 314

Choose Quick Mask options 314

18/PATHS/SHAPES

Chapter overview 315

Creating paths
Convert a selection into a path 316

Draw a path using the Pen tool 317

Draw a magnetic Freeform Pen path 318

The Freeform Pen Options pop-up palette 319

Draw a path using the Freeform Pen 320

Working with paths
Move a path 320

Add to an existing, open path 321

Transform an entire path 321

Transform points on a path 321

Copy a path in the same image 322

Copy a path outline under the same name 322

Drag-and-drop a path to another image 322

Save a work path 322

Display a path 323

Hide a path 323

Select anchor points on a path 323

Reshape a path 324

Delete a path 325

Deselect a path 326

Convert a path into a selection 326

Export a path to Illustrator or FreeHand 327

Vector masks

Create a vector mask 328

Combine a new path with an existing path 329

Reshape a vector mask 329

Reposition a vector mask 330

Duplicate a vector mask 330

Deactivate a vector mask 330

Reverse the visible and hidden areas in a
vector mask 331

Discard a vector mask 331

Convert a layer mask into a vector mask 332

Create an adjustment layer that uses a
vector mask 332

Create a vector mask from type 333

Shapes

Create a shape layer 334

Create a work path using a shape tool 336

Create a geometric area of pixels 337

Choose geometric options for a shape tool 338

Move a shape layer's vector mask 338

Transform a shape layer 339

Modify the contour of a shape layer 339

Deactivate a shape layer's vector mask 339

Paste a path object from Illustrator into
Photoshop as a shape layer .340

Use the pathfinder options to add to or
subtract from a shape 340

Save a shape as a preset 341

Change the fill contents of a shape layer 341

Rasterize a shape layer 342

19/TYPE

Creating type

Different kinds of type 343

Create an editable type layer .344

Add type on or inside a path . . . .■ 346

Editing text

Select all or some characters on a type layer 346

Convert paragraph type to point type 347

Convert point type to paragraph type 347

Resize type by choosing a value 348

Resize type manually 348

Apply kerning 349

Apply tracking 349

Adjust leading in horizontal type 350

Change type orientation 351

Style type using the Character palette 352

Shift characters above or below the normal
baseline 353

Paragraph settings

Set paragraph alignment and justification for
horizontal type 354

Adjust paragraph indents and spacing for
horizontal type 355

Fine-tune paragraph settings .356

Special effects with type

Transform a type bounding box and the type
inside it 357

Transform a type bounding box but not the type . .357

Warp type on an editable layer 358

Move a type layer 359

Rasterize type into pixels 359

Screen back an image behind type 360

Screen back type 361

Create fading type 362

Apply layer effects to semitransparent type 362

Apply a stroke to type 363

Using the type mask tools

Create a type selection 363

Move a type selection 364

Create a type mask for an adjustment layer 365

Type in a spot channel
Create type in a spot channel .366

Word processing
Find and replace text 367

Check spelling 368

20/FILTERS

Filter basics
How filters are applied 369

Use the Filter Gallery . . . . ■ 370

Individual filter dialog boxes 371

Lessening a filter's overall effect 372

Restricting the area a filter affects 373

Making filter effects look less artificial 374

Maximizing a filter's effect 374

Texture mapping using a filter 374

All the filters illustrated
Artistic filters 375

Blur filters 377

Brush Strokes filters 378

Distort filters 379

Noise filters 380

Pixelate filters 381

Render filters 382

Sharpen filters 382

Sketch filters 383

Stylize filters 385

Texture filters 386

Filters in action
Apply a texture using a layer mask 387

Turn a photograph into a painting or a drawing . . .388

Our watercolor filter 388

Apply a motion blur to part of an image 389

Lighting Effects
Cast a light on an image 390

Pattern Maker
Generate a pattern 393

Navigate through pattern tiles 396

Delete a pattern tile 396

Save a tile as a pattern preset 396

21/LIQUIFY

Chapter overview 397

Apply distortion using the Liquify command . . . .■ 398

Display the Liquify mesh 401

Remove all distortion from the preview 402

Reverse distortion in all unfrozen areas 402

Return individual unfrozen areas to their
    initial state 402

22/AUTOMATE

Chapter overview 403

Actions
Record an action . . . .■ 404

Create an actions set 405

Insert a stop in an action 406

Insert a menu item in an action 407

Insert a path in an action 408

Exclude a command from playback 409

Play back an action on an image 409

Add commands to an action .410

Delete a command from an action 410

Play an action on a batch of images . . . .■ 411

Choose file naming options for batch
    processing . . . .■ 412

Create a droplet for an action 413

Add a modal control to an action 414

Change the order of commands 414

Rerecord an action using different dialog box
    settings 415

Rerecord a single command in an action 415

Duplicate an actin 415

Delete an action 415

Save an actions set to a file 416

Load a set onto the Actions palette 416

Replace the current actions set with a
    different set 416

Run one action in another action 417

Other Automate commands
Perform a conditional image mode change 418

Create a contact sheet . . . .■ 419

Fit an image to width and/or height dimensions . . .420

Convert a multi-page PDF to Photoshop format . . .421

Create a picture package . . . .■ 422

Create a Web gallery . . . .■ 424

23/PREFERENCES

Chapter overview 427

General Preferences 428

File Handling Preferences 430

Display & Cursors Preferences 431

Transparency & Gamut Preferences 432

Units & Rulers Preferences 433

Guides, Grid, & Slices Preferences 434

Plug-ins & Scratch Disks Preferences 435

Memory & Image Cache Preferences 436

File Browser Preferences . . . .■ 437

Managing Presets

Use the Preset Manager 438

Save selected presets to a new library 439

Reset or replace presets 439

Save the presets in the current picker to a
   new library 440

24/PRINT

Printing from Photoshop 441

Choose a paper size and orientation 442

Print using the basic Print command 443

Print using the Print with Preview command . . . .■ 444

Print using color management . . . .■ 446

Apply trapping 450

Prepare a file for an IRIS or dye sublimation
   printer, or an imagesetter .451

Preparing files for other applications

Photoshop to QuarkXPress 452

Photoshop to InDesign 452

Photoshop to After Effects 452

Photoshop to Illustrator 453

Photoshop to CorelDRAW 11 454

Save an image as an EPS 455

Save an image in DCS 2.0 format 457

Save an image as a TIFF 458

Save an image as a PDF 459

Producing duotones

Produce a duotone 460

Print a grayscale image using a PANTONE tint 461

Color reproduction basics

Enter custom CMYK settings .462

Save a Color Setting preset with your custom
   CMYK settings 463

Create a custom proof setup .464

Correct out-of-gamut colors .465

Color correction: A first glance 466

25/WEB/IMAGEREADY

The basics 467

Image size 469

Compression 470

GIF 471

Color depth 472

JPEG 472

PNG-8 and PNG-24 473

Dithering 474

Anti-aliasing 475

The ImageReady Toolbox . . . .■ 476

Optimize an image in the GIF or PNG-8 format . .■ 477

Create a master palette for optimized images
   in ImageReady 480

Apply a master palette to an image 481

Use weighted optimization 481

Use the ImageReady previews 482

Edit in . . . .■ 482

Quick-optimize 483

Create and apply a droplet 483

Optimize an image in the JPEG or PNG-24 format . .484

Make flat-color areas Web-safe 486

Preview potential browser dither in an
   optimized image 487

Controlling dithering 487

Preview Windows and Mac gamma values 488

Change the gamma for an optimized file 488

Preview an optimized image in a browser on
   your system 489

Table of Contents

Save a file in ImageReady 490

Save an optimized file in ImageReady 490

Update an HTML file 491

Change a Web page title and embed metadata .■ 492

Create type in ImageReady 493

Creating display type for Web pages 493

Slicing

Slice an image using a command 495

Slice an image manually 496

Create a layer-based slice 497

Convert an auto slice or a layer-based slice
into a user slice 497

Delete slices 497

Use the Table palette . . . .■ 497

Resize user slices 498

Slice an image into multiple links 499

Change the stacking position of a slice 500

Align user slices along a common edge 500

Evenly distribute user slices along a common axis . .501

Create a layer-based image map 501

Create a tool-based image map 502

Change an image map from layer-based to
tool-based 503

Hide/show image maps 503

Select an image map 504

Delete an image map 504

Align tool-based image maps along a
common edge 504

Evenly distribute tool-based image maps
along a common axis 504

Optimize an individual slice .505

Copy optimization settings from one slice
to another 505

Link slices 506

Unlink slices 506

Attach an Alt tag to a slice or to an entire image . . .507

Rollovers

Create a rollover for a slice 508

Create a rollover using a layer effect 511

Create a layer-based rollover .512

Use the Unify buttons to apply changes from
the active layer 512

More rollover ideas 513

Preview a rollover in ImageReady 514

Preview a rollover in a Web browser 514

Create a remote rollover 515

Create a button for a Web page . . . .■ 516

Add rollover states to the buton 516

Use the Move tool modifiers .516

GIF animations 517

Move layer imagery across an image
via animation 518

Make imagery fade in or out .520

Choose a delay value for a frame 521

Preview an animation 521

Create a rocking animation 522

Make further pixel edits to an animation object . . .523

Layers palette edits and animations 523

Make an existing animation reverse itself to
the first frame 523

Apply a second animation effect to an
existing animation 524

Make a rollover trigger an animation sequence 525

Create a warped type animation 526

Remove or adjust warped type 527

Save a GIF animation 527

Optimize an animation 528

Ways to slim an animation down 528

Save animation frames as layers . . . .■ 528

Other layer features in ImageReady 529

Applying styles

Apply a style to a layer 530

Save a layer effect as a style .531

Background tiling

Create a tile for an HTML background 532

Preview an image as a tiled background 533

Use Photoshop's Save for Web dialog box 534

KEYBOARD SHORTCUTS 535

INDEX 553

Table of Contents

THE BASICS 1

Welcome to Photoshop 8—Er...CS!

In this chapter (which is more of a read than a do), you'll learn how to launch Photoshop and get acquainted with the Photoshop interface—menus, palettes, and whatnot. You can use this chapter as a reference guide as you work. The next chapter, which is an introduction to color in Photoshop, is more theory than technique, too. From Chapter 3 onward, though, it's nonstop action.

To launch Photoshop in Windows:

In Windows 2000 or XP, click the Start button on the taskbar, choose All Programs, then click Adobe Photoshop CS **1**.
or
Open the C:\Program Files\Adobe\ Photoshop CS folder in My Computer, then double-click the Photoshop application icon **2**.
or
Double-click a Photoshop file icon.

To launch Photoshop in Macintosh:

In Mac OS X, click the Photoshop icon in the Dock **3**. (If you don't have an icon there yet, open the Adobe Photoshop CS folder in the Applications folder, then drag the Adobe Photoshop CS application icon into the Dock.)
or
Open the Adobe Photoshop CS folder in the Applications folder, then double-click the Adobe Photoshop CS application icon.
or
Double-click any Photoshop file icon.

1 *In Windows, click* **Adobe Photoshop CS.**

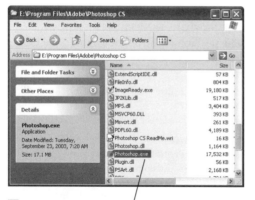

2 *In Windows, double-click the Photoshop* **application** *icon.*

3 *In Mac, click the* **Adobe Photoshop CS** *icon in the Dock.*

Launch Photoshop

The Photoshop screen in Macintosh

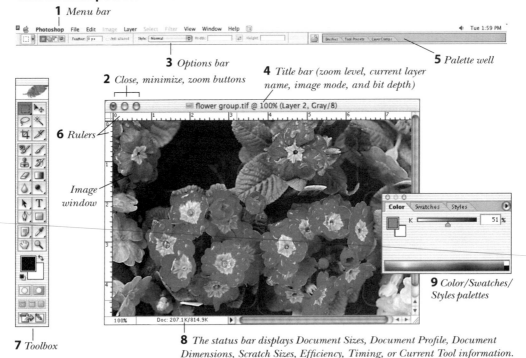

1 *Menu bar*

2 *Close, minimize, zoom buttons*

3 *Options bar*

4 *Title bar (zoom level, current layer name, image mode, and bit depth)*

5 *Palette well*

6 *Rulers*

Image window

9 *Color/Swatches/ Styles palettes*

7 *Toolbox*

8 *The status bar displays Document Sizes, Document Profile, Document Dimensions, Scratch Sizes, Efficiency, Timing, or Current Tool information.*

Key to the Photoshop screen: Macintosh and Windows features

1 *Menu bar*
Press any menu heading to access dialog boxes, submenus, and commands.

2 *Close, minimize, and zoom buttons*
To close a file or a palette, click its close (red) button. Click the minimize (yellow) button to stow it in the Dock. Click the zoom (green) button to enlarge a window to maximum size, or on a palette to show/hide extra options.

3 *Options bar*
Use to choose settings for the current tool.

4 *Title bar*
Displays the image's title, zoom level, current layer (or the Background), image mode, and bit depth.

5 *Palette well*
Use to store and open palettes.

6 *Rulers*
Choose View > Show Rulers to display rulers. The position of the pointer is indicated by a mark on each ruler.

7 *Toolbox*
Press Tab to show/hide the Toolbox and all open palettes.

8 *Status bar*
The status bar displays Document Sizes, Document Profile, Document Dimensions, Scratch Sizes, Efficiency (the percentage of time Photoshop is processing edits, as opposed to writing to the scratch disk), Timing, or Current Tool information. To reset the timer, choose Timing with Alt/ Option held down.

9 *Palettes*
There are 19 movable palettes. Click a tab (palette name) in a palette group to bring that palette to the front of its group.

The Photoshop screen in Windows

4 *Application close button*

3 *Application maximize button*

1 *Application Control menu*   *Menu bar*   *Options bar*   **2** *Application minimize button*

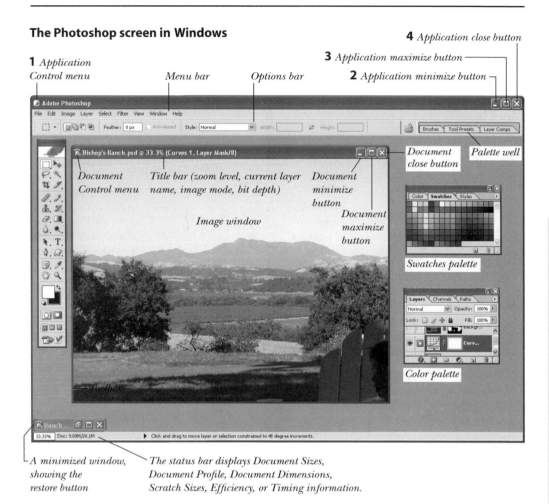

Document close button

Palette well

Document Control menu   *Title bar (zoom level, current layer name, image mode, bit depth)*   *Document minimize button*

Document maximize button

Image window

Swatches palette

Color palette

Toolbox

A minimized window, showing the restore button

The status bar displays Document Sizes, Document Profile, Document Dimensions, Scratch Sizes, Efficiency, or Timing information.

Key to the Photoshop screen: Windows-only features

1 *Application (or document) Control menu*
The application Control menu commands are Restore, Move, Size, Minimize, Maximize, and Close. The document Control menu commands are Restore, Move, Size, Minimize, Maximize, Close, and Next.

2 *Application (or document) minimize button*
Click the application minimize button to shrink the document to an icon in the taskbar. Click the icon on the taskbar to restore the application window to its previous size.

Click the document minimize button to shrink the document to an icon at the lower left corner of the application window. Click the restore button to restore the document window to its previous size.

3 *Application (or document) maximize/restore button*
Click the application or document maximize button to enlarge a window to its largest possible size. Click the restore button to restore a window to its previous size. When a window is at the restored size, the restore button turns into the maximize button.

4 *Application (or document) close button*
Closes the application (or image).

The menus

Menus

File menu

Use commands on the File menu to create, open, close, save, place, scan, import, export, and print images; open the File Browser; automate operations; and exit Photoshop. Use the Jump To submenu to switch to a helper application, such as Adobe Illustrator or GoLive. (In Mac, the Quit Photoshop command is on the Photoshop menu.)

Edit menu

The Edit menu is a storehouse of image-editing commands that copy, transform, and paste imagery; apply fills and strokes; and create custom brushes, patterns, and shapes. Fade lessens the effect of the last edit; the Purge commands free up memory. Also found here are commands for word processing, for managing presets, and for customizing shortcuts. (In Mac, the Preferences and Color Settings commands are on the Photoshop menu.)

Image menu

An image can be converted to any of eight image (color) modes via the Mode submenu. The Adjustment commands modify an image's hue, saturation, brightness, contrast, etc. The Image Size command modifies an image's file size, dimensions, or resolution. The Canvas Size dialog box is used to add or subtract from an image's live canvas area. Other commands rotate, crop, or trim the canvas.

Layer menu

Layer menu commands create, duplicate, delete, apply styles to, rasterize, arrange, align, distribute, merge, and flatten layers. Other commands add, remove, or disable layer, vector, and clipping masks. Some of these commands can also be chosen from the Layers palette menu.

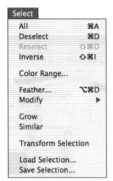

Select menu

The All command on the Select menu selects an entire layer. Deselect deselects all selections, Reselect restores the last deselected selection, and Inverse swaps the selected and unselected areas. The Color Range command creates a selection based on image color. Other Select menu commands enlarge, contract, smooth, or feather selection edges, as well as save selections to and from channels.

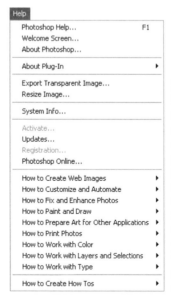

Filter menu

Filters, which perform a wide range of image-editing functions, are organized into submenu groups. Extract allows you to make complex silhouettes, the Filter Gallery allows you to apply multiple filters, Liquify pushes pixels around, Pattern Maker creates seamless patterns from selections, and Digimarc embeds a copyright watermark.

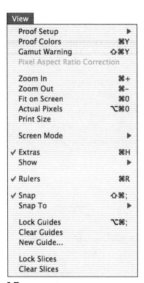

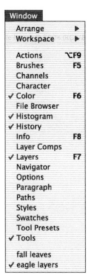

Window menu

The Window menu is used primarily for showing and hiding the 19 palettes. Open images can also be activated via this menu and arranged via Arrange submenu commands. Workspace commands allow you to customize your workspace. In Windows, the Status Bar command for showing/hiding the status bar is also found on this menu.

View menu

Commands on the View menu control what features are visible onscreen. Use this menu to show/hide rulers, grids, guides, slices, selection edges, the currently selected (target) path, or annotations, or to change the current zoom level or screen mode. The Proof Setup commands allow you to see how your image will look in different output color spaces, and the Gamut Warning highlights colors that won't print on a four-color press.

Help menu

Use Help menu commands to access Photoshop onscreen help, get the latest news from Adobe, connect to Adobe Online, or perform automated tasks via onscreen prompts. (Not all the commands shown here are available in Mac.)

Menus

Using the Toolbox

To **choose** a tool whose icon is currently visible, click once on its icon. Click the itty bitty arrowhead next to a tool icon to choose a related tool from a pop-out menu.

Or even better, choose a tool using its shortcut (try to memorize the boldface letters on the next three pages). If you forget a tool's shortcut, just leave the cursor over the tool icon for a moment, and the tool tip will remind you 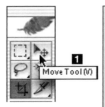. To cycle through hidden, related tools on a pop-out menu that also share the same shortcut, press **Shift** plus the shortcut key. You could also Alt-click/Option-click the currently visible tool icon. *Note:* If Use Shift Key for Tool Switch is unchecked in Edit (Photoshop, in Mac) > Preferences > General, you can just press the letter without using Shift.

Attributes are chosen for each tool (e.g., blending mode, opacity percentage) from the **options bar** at the top of the screen (read more about the options bar on page 11) **3**. Features on the bar change depending on which tool is selected.

Options bar settings remain in effect for an individual tool until they're changed or the tool is reset. You can save settings as presets in the Tool Preset palette (see page 28). To reset a tool to its defaults, right-click/Control-click the tool thumbnail on the options bar, then choose **Reset Tool** from the context menu **2**. Or to reset all tools, choose **Reset All Tools** from the same menu.

If you try to use a tool **incorrectly,** a cancel icon ⊘ will appear. Click in the image window to make an explanation appear.

TIP Choose whether tool pointers look like their Toolbox icon or a crosshair in Edit (Photoshop, in Mac) > Preferences > Display & Cursors.

Tool tips

Rest the pointer on a tool icon—without clicking or pressing the mouse button—to learn that tool's name or shortcut **1**. Use the same method to learn the function of a palette or options bar feature **3**. Check **Show Tool Tips** in Edit (Photoshop menu, in Mac) > Preferences > General to enable this feature.

Tool shortcuts

Hide/show the Toolbox and all open palettes	Tab
Cycle through hidden, related tools on the same pop-out menu	Shift plus shortcut key* or Alt-click/Option-click the currently visible tool
Cycle through blending modes for the current editing tool or layer	Shift-+ (plus) or Shift- - (minus)

*If Use Shift Key for Tool Switch is checked in Edit (Photoshop, in Mac) > Preferences > General

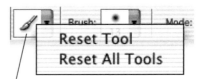

2 *To access the* **Reset Tool** *command for an individual tool or the* **Reset All Tools** *command for all tools, right-click/Control-click the tool thumbnail on the options bar.*

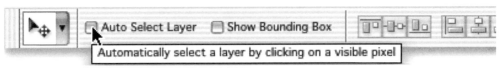

3 *Choose options for the current tool from the* **options bar** *at the top of your screen.*

Using the Toolbox

The Toolbox

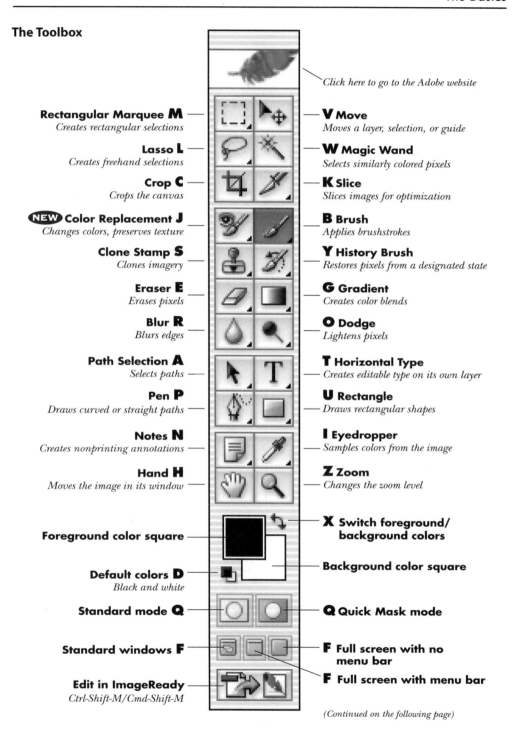

Click here to go to the Adobe website

Rectangular Marquee M
Creates rectangular selections

V Move
Moves a layer, selection, or guide

Lasso L
Creates freehand selections

W Magic Wand
Selects similarly colored pixels

Crop C
Crops the canvas

K Slice
Slices images for optimization

NEW Color Replacement J
Changes colors, preserves texture

B Brush
Applies brushstrokes

Clone Stamp S
Clones imagery

Y History Brush
Restores pixels from a designated state

Eraser E
Erases pixels

G Gradient
Creates color blends

Blur R
Blurs edges

O Dodge
Lightens pixels

Path Selection A
Selects paths

T Horizontal Type
Creates editable type on its own layer

Pen P
Draws curved or straight paths

U Rectangle
Draws rectangular shapes

Notes N
Creates nonprinting annotations

I Eyedropper
Samples colors from the image

Hand H
Moves the image in its window

Z Zoom
Changes the zoom level

Foreground color square

X Switch foreground/
background colors

Default colors D
Black and white

Background color square

Standard mode Q

Q Quick Mask mode

Standard windows F

F Full screen with no
menu bar

Edit in ImageReady
Ctrl-Shift-M/Cmd-Shift-M

F Full screen with menu bar

(Continued on the following page)

Toolbox

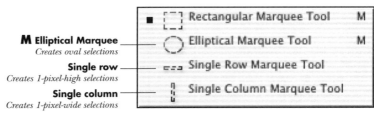

M Elliptical Marquee
Creates oval selections

Single row
Creates 1-pixel-high selections

Single column
Creates 1-pixel-wide selections

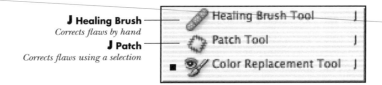

L Polygonal Lasso
Creates polygonal selections

L Magnetic Lasso
Creates snap-to freehand selections

J Healing Brush
Corrects flaws by hand

J Patch
Corrects flaws using a selection

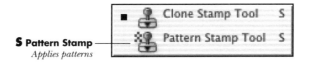

S Pattern Stamp
Applies patterns

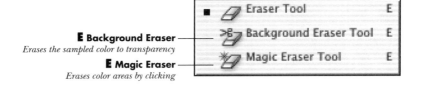

E Background Eraser
Erases the sampled color to transparency

E Magic Eraser
Erases color areas by clicking

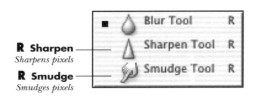

R Sharpen
Sharpens pixels

R Smudge
Smudges pixels

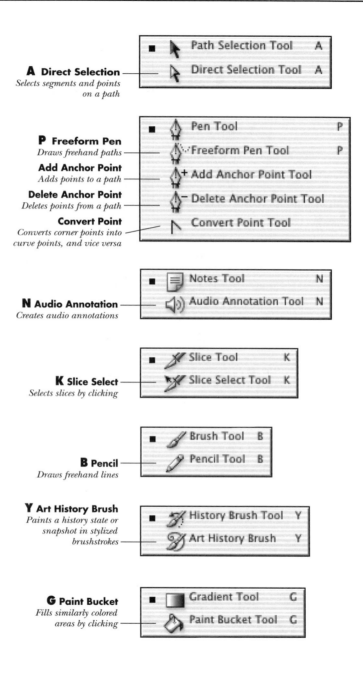

A **Direct Selection**
*Selects segments and points
on a path*

P **Freeform Pen**
Draws freehand paths

Add Anchor Point
Adds points to a path

Delete Anchor Point
Deletes points from a path

Convert Point
*Converts corner points into
curve points, and vice versa*

N **Audio Annotation**
Creates audio annotations

K **Slice Select**
Selects slices by clicking

B **Pencil**
Draws freehand lines

Y **Art History Brush**
*Paints a history state or
snapshot in stylized
brushstrokes*

G **Paint Bucket**
*Fills similarly colored
areas by clicking*

Tool Pop-Out Menus

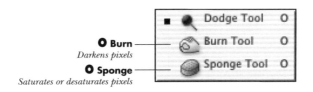

O Burn — *Darkens pixels*

O Sponge — *Saturates or desaturates pixels*

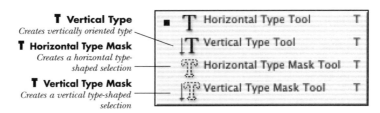

T Vertical Type — *Creates vertically oriented type*

T Horizontal Type Mask — *Creates a horizontal type-shaped selection*

T Vertical Type Mask — *Creates a vertical type-shaped selection*

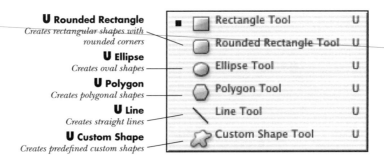

U Rounded Rectangle — *Creates rectangular shapes with rounded corners*

U Ellipse — *Creates oval shapes*

U Polygon — *Creates polygonal shapes*

U Line — *Creates straight lines*

U Custom Shape — *Creates predefined custom shapes*

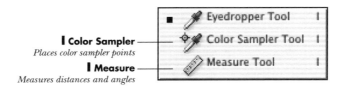

I Color Sampler — *Places color sampler points*

I Measure — *Measures distances and angles*

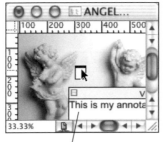

1 *An **annotation** created using the **Notes** tool*

Annotate

The **Notes** tool creates nonprinting Acrobat-compatible notes, which can be used for communicating with a client, output service, etc. **1** When you click a note icon, a note window containing the message opens. The **Audio Annotation** tool creates audio notes.

Options bar

The options bar is used to choose settings for each tool (e.g., Opacity, Flow, blending Mode). Options on the bar change depending on which tool is currently chosen, and your choices remain in effect until you change them. Like the palettes, the options bar can be dragged to a different part of your screen. Double-click the left edge of the options bar to collapse/expand it.

The palette well on the options bar is discussed on page 12.

*Click the Brush arrowhead to open the **Brush Preset picker** (it's a pop-up palette).*

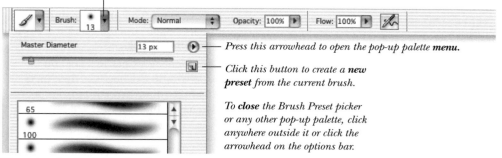

Master Diameter   13 px

— *Press this arrowhead to open the pop-up palette **menu**.*

— *Click this button to create a **new preset** from the current brush.*

*To **close** the Brush Preset picker or any other pop-up palette, click anywhere outside it or click the arrowhead on the options bar.*

*The options bar for the **Brush** tool*

*The options bar for the **Rectangular Marquee** tool*

*The options bar for the **Gradient** tool*

*The options bar for the **Pen** tool*

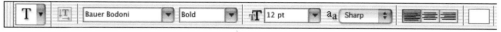

*The options bar for the **Type** tool*

The palettes

How to use the palettes

Many Photoshop operations are triggered by choosing commands on movable palettes. To save screen space, the palettes are joined into default **groups,** such as History/Actions and Color/Swatches/Styles.

To **open** a palette, choose its name from the Window menu. The palette will appear in front within its group.

Press Tab to **show/hide** all open palettes, including the Toolbox. Press Shift-Tab to show/hide all open palettes except the Toolbox.

To **display** an open palette at the front of its group, click its tab (palette name).

You can **separate** a palette from its group by dragging its tab **1–2.** You can **add** a palette to any group by dragging the tab into the group. If you need to widen a palette to make additional tabs visible, drag the palette's **resize** box (lower right corner). Most of the palettes are resizable.

You can **dock** (store) palettes in the palette well on the right side of the options bar,

either by dragging the palette into the well **3** or by choosing Dock to Palette Well from the palette menu.

If the current tool uses a particular palette (e.g., the Pencil tool uses the Brushes palette, the type tools use the Character palette), you can click the **Toggle** palette button 📄 on the options bar to show/hide that palette.

To **shrink/expand** a palette, double-click its tab. In Windows, you can also click the palette minimize/maximize button. If the palette isn't at its default size, click the minimize box/zoom (green) button once to restore its default size, then click it a second time to shrink the palette.

TIP Quick-change: Click in a field on a palette or in a dialog box, then press the up or down arrow on the keyboard to change that value incrementally.

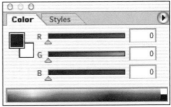

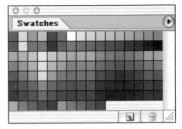

2 *The Swatches palette is now going solo.*

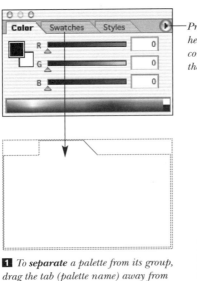

*Press this arrow-head to choose commands from the **palette menu.***

1 *To **separate** a palette from its group, drag the tab (palette name) away from the palette group.*

Use Palettes

Change your values

You can change most numerical values simply by **NEW** clicking the option name and **dragging** to the left or the right. Examples of options that this works for are the Width and Height values in dialog boxes, Opacity and Fill on the Layers palette, Feather on the options bar, Input Levels and Output Levels in the Levels dialog box, and Fuzziness in the Color Range dialog box.

There are two ways to use a **pop-up slider** ■: Either press an arrowhead and drag the slider in one move, or click the arrowhead and then drag the slider. To close a slider, click anywhere outside it or press Enter/Return. If you click the arrowhead to open a slider, pressing Esc will restore its last setting.

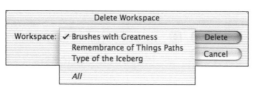

1 *A pop-up slider on the options bar.*

2 *In the **Delete Workspace** dialog box, choose a workspace name, or choose All.*

If **Save Palette Locations** is checked in Edit (Photoshop, in Mac) > Preferences > General, palettes that are open when you exit/quit Photoshop will reappear in their same location when you relaunch the program.

To further customize your onscreen working environment, you can set up special configurations of palettes and dialog boxes for different kinds of tasks and save them as **workspaces.** For example, you might want to keep the Character and Paragraph palettes open any time you're working on a text-intensive document, or create a workspace in which the Brushes, Color, and Swatches palettes are open and accessible for use when painting.

To create a custom workspace:

1. Display whichever palettes you want open and accessible, and arrange them on the screen as you like.

2. Choose Window > Workspace > Save Workspace.

3. Enter a descriptive Name for the new workspace, then click Save. The new workspace is now accessible on the Window > Workspace submenu.

To delete any or all custom workspaces:

1. Choose Window > Workspace > Delete Workspace.

2. Choose the name of the workspace you want to get rid of, or choose All **2**.

3. Click Delete, then click Yes.

TIP To restore the palettes' default groupings and locations at any time, choose Window > Workspace > Reset Palette Locations.

Workspaces

Actions palette

You can record a series of commands in an action, and then replay that action on one image or on a batch of images. The Actions palette is used for recording, storing, editing, and replaying actions.

The game plan

The palettes are illustrated in alphabetical order, starting on this page except, that is, for the indispensible Toolbox, which is illustrated on pages 7–10, and the options bar, which is illustrated on page 11.

Actions Palette

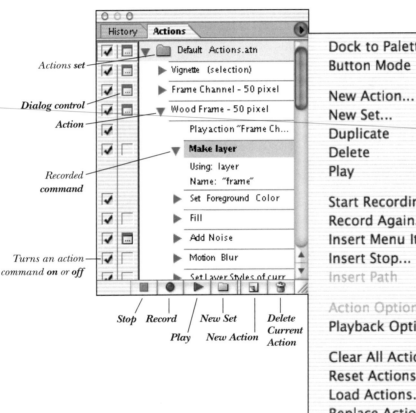

Actions set

Dialog control

Action

Recorded command

Turns an action command on or off

Dock to Palette Well
Button Mode

New Action...
New Set...
Duplicate
Delete
Play

Start Recording
Record Again...
Insert Menu Item...
Insert Stop...
Insert Path

Action Options...
Playback Options...

Clear All Actions
Reset Actions
Load Actions...
Replace Actions...
Save Actions...

Commands
Frames
Image Effects
Production
Text Effects
Textures

Stop *Record* *New Set* *Delete Current Action*

Play *New Action*

Brushes palette

The Brushes palette is used for customizing brush tips for the Brush, Pencil, History Brush, Art History Brush, Clone Stamp, Pattern Stamp, Eraser, Background Eraser, Blur, Sharpen, Smudge, Dodge, Burn, and Sponge tools. Options on the palette are organized into categories, such as Shape Dynamics, Scattering, Texture, and Color Dynamics. You can also use the Brushes palette to choose options for a stylus or for an airbrush input device.

TIP The numeral under a brush tip icon is the diameter of the tip, in pixels.

Picker or palette?

Brush tips for the painting and editing tools can be chosen either from the **Brushes palette** (illustrated below) or from the **Brush Preset picker** **1**, a pop-up palette that you open from the options bar. To close the Brush Preset picker, click outside it or click the Brush arrowhead again. To hide the Brushes palette (but keep it open), dock it into the palette well on the options bar; to redisplay it, click the palette tab in the well.

Commands for **loading, appending,** and **saving** brushes and brush libraries can be chosen from the Brushes palette menu or the Brush Preset picker menu (click the palette menu button ▶ on the right side).

1 *Click here to open the **Brush Preset picker**.*

*Brush **tips***

Brush editing categories

Individual brush options

Brush stroke preview

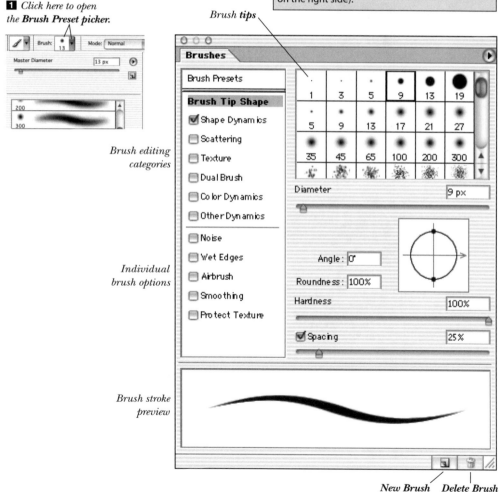

New Brush *Delete Brush*

Brushes Palette

Channels palette

The Channels palette is used for displaying
one or more of the color channels that make
up an image. It is also used for creating and
displaying alpha channels, which are used
for saving selections, and spot color channels,
which are used for producing individual spot
color plates.

Channels Palette

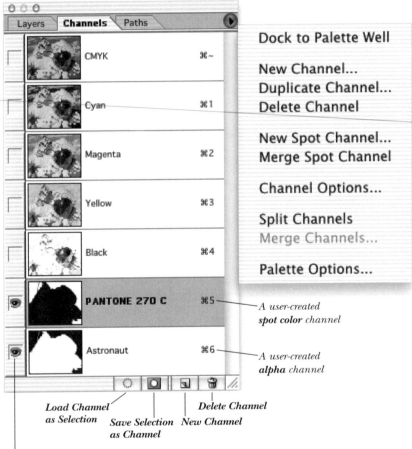

Dock to Palette Well

New Channel...
Duplicate Channel...
Delete Channel

New Spot Channel...
Merge Spot Channel

Channel Options...

Split Channels
Merge Channels...

Palette Options...

A user-created
spot color *channel*

A user-created
alpha *channel*

**Load Channel
as Selection**   **Save Selection   New Channel**
as Channel

Delete Channel

*The eye icon indicates that this channel is
currently **visible**. To display a channel by
itself in the image window, click its name
or use the keystroke listed on the palette.*

Character palette

When a type tool is chosen, type attributes can be chosen via the Character palette, illustrated below, or from the options bar.

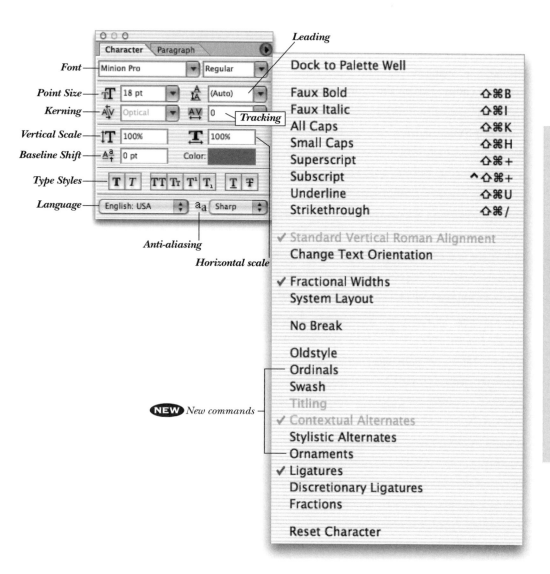

Font — Minion Pro · Regular

Point Size — 18 pt · Leading

Kerning — Optical · Tracking

Vertical Scale — 100% · Horizontal scale — 100%

Baseline Shift — 0 pt · Color:

Type Styles

Language — English: USA · Anti-aliasing — Sharp

Dock to Palette Well	
Faux Bold	⇧⌘B
Faux Italic	⇧⌘I
All Caps	⇧⌘K
Small Caps	⇧⌘H
Superscript	⇧⌘+
Subscript	^⇧⌘+
Underline	⇧⌘U
Strikethrough	⇧⌘/
✓ Standard Vertical Roman Alignment	
Change Text Orientation	
✓ Fractional Widths	
System Layout	
No Break	
Oldstyle	
Ordinals	
Swash	
Titling	
✓ Contextual Alternates	
Stylistic Alternates	
Ornaments	
✓ Ligatures	
Discretionary Ligatures	
Fractions	
Reset Character	

NEW *New commands*

Color palette

The Color palette is used for mixing and choosing colors. Colors are applied with a painting or editing tool, or via a command such as Fill or Canvas Size. Choose a color model for the palette from the palette menu. Mix a color using the sliders, or quick-select a color by clicking on the color bar at the bottom of the palette.

To open the Color Picker, from which you can also choose a color, click once on the Foreground or Background color square if it's already active, or double-click the square if it's not active.

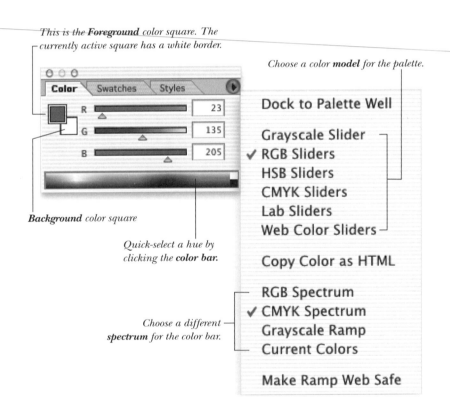

This is the Foreground color square. The currently active square has a white border.

Choose a color model for the palette.

Background color square

Quick-select a hue by clicking the color bar.

Choose a different spectrum for the color bar.

Dock to Palette Well

Grayscale Slider
✓ RGB Sliders
HSB Sliders
CMYK Sliders
Lab Sliders
Web Color Sliders

Copy Color as HTML

RGB Spectrum
✓ CMYK Spectrum
Grayscale Ramp
Current Colors

Make Ramp Web Safe

Color Palette

File Browser palette

The File Browser enables you to search for, open, sort, batch-process, move, rename, and delete Photoshop files. Images in the currently selected folder are represented by image thumbnails in the main window. The File Browser in Photoshop CS boasts a number of new features, such as buttons at the top of the palette, palettes on the left side, and menus that let you activate many commands.

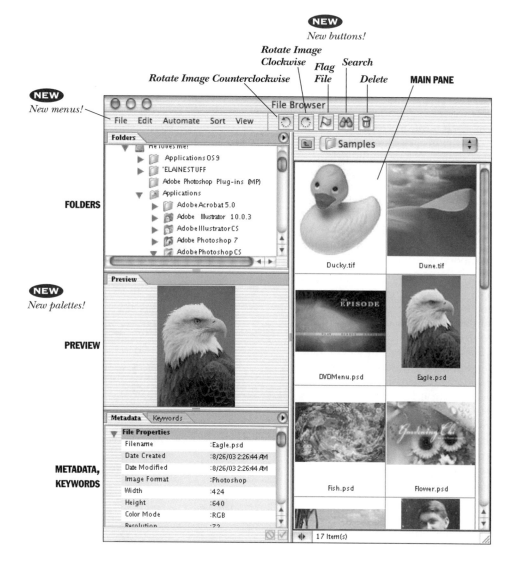

NEW
New buttons!

Rotate Image Clockwise

Flag File

Search

Delete

MAIN PANE

Rotate Image Counterclockwise

NEW
New menus!

FOLDERS

NEW
New palettes!

PREVIEW

METADATA, KEYWORDS

File Browser Palette

NEW Histogram palette

The Histogram palette (formerly a dialog box) diagrams the current light and dark values of an image, or its before and after light and dark values as it's being edited or while an adjustment dialog box is open. Via the Channel pop-up menu, you can choose to have the palette display information about the combined channels or about just one channel. You can also expand the palette to display histograms for every channel. The screenshot at right shows the palette in Expanded View (the other display options are Compact View and All Channels View).

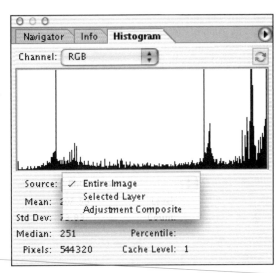

History palette

The History palette is used to selectively undo one or more previous steps in a work session. Each brushstroke, filter application, or other image-editing command is listed as a separate state on the palette, with the bottommost state being the most recent. Clicking on a prior state restores the document to that stage of the editing process. What happens to the document when you click on a prior state depends on whether the palette is in linear or non-linear mode.

In linear mode, if you click back on and then delete a state or resume image editing from an earlier state, all subsequent states (dimmed, on the palette) will be deleted. In non-linear mode, you can click back on an earlier edit state or delete a state without losing subsequent states. This option is turned on or off via the Allow Non-Linear History check box in the History Options dialog box (choose History Options from the palette menu). You can switch between linear and non-linear modes at any time during editing.

The New Snapshot command creates a state that stays on the palette until the image is closed. The History Brush tool restores an image to a designated prior state where the brush is dragged in the image window. The Art History Brush does the same thing, but in stylized strokes.

*The current source for the **History Brush***

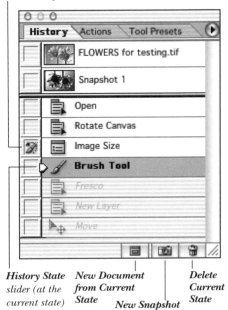

History State slider (at the current state)   **New Document from Current State**   **New Snapshot**   **Delete Current State**

*This is the **History** palette in **linear** mode. Note that some steps are dimmed.*

Info palette

The Info palette displays a color breakdown of the pixel that's currently under the pointer 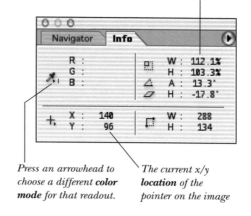. The palette will also show readouts for up to four color samplers, if they're placed on the image ②. If a color adjustment dialog box is open, the palette will display before and after color readouts. The Info palette also shows the *x/y* location of the pointer on the image.

Other information may display on the palette, depending on which tool is being used, such as the distance between points when a selection is moved, a shape is drawn, or the Measure tool is used; the dimensions of a selection or crop marquee; or the width, height, and angle of a selection as it's being transformed ③.

Press one of the tiny arrowheads to choose a color mode for that readout (it can be different from the current image mode): Actual Color (the current image mode), Proof Color, Grayscale, RGB Color, Web Color, HSB Color, CMYK Color, Lab Color, Total Ink, the current layer Opacity, or 16-bit. **NEW**

To do this via a dialog box, choose Palette Options from the palette menu, then change the mode for the First and Second Color Readouts. You can also change the unit of measurement for the palette (Mouse Coordinates), and for an image in 16-bit mode, you can check Show 16 bit values ④. **NEW**

TIP If an exclamation point appears next to a color readout, it means that color is outside the printable, CMYK gamut.

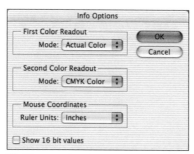

④ *Choose options for different areas of the Info palette via the **Info Options** dialog box.*

1 *Color breakdown for the pixel that's currently under the pointer*

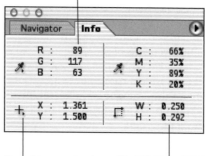

Press this arrowhead to choose a different unit of measurement for the palette (and the rulers).

*The **Width** and **Height** of the current **selection***

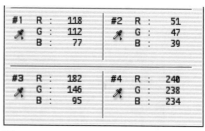

2 *#1, #2, #3, and #4 color readouts on the Info palette from four **color samplers** that were placed on the image*

3 *During a **transform** operation, the width (W), height (H), angle (A), and horizontal skew (H) or vertical skew (V) of the transformed layer, selection, or path are shown in this area.*

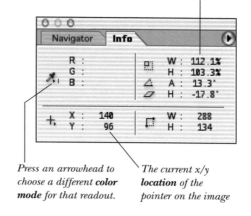

*Press an arrowhead to choose a different **color mode** for that readout.*

*The current x/y **location** of the pointer on the image*

Info Palette

NEW **Layer Comps palette**

A layer comp (short for "composition") is a set of layer characteristics, including visibility, position, and appearance (layer styles). The purpose of layer comps is to enable multiple versions of the same image to coexist in one Photoshop or ImageReady file, and to provide a convenient palette mechanism for displaying them. This can be useful when you need to present design variations to a client.

Layer comps are saved to the Layer Comps palette with the image in which they're created and are applied to a whole image simply by clicking the comp name on the palette. Whereas histories affect all editing done to an image (and can't be saved), layer comps remember and apply only specific layer options and settings.

Layer Comps Palette

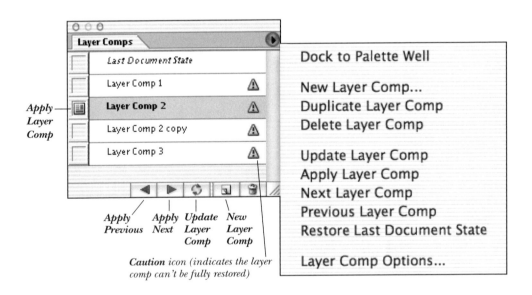

Apply Layer Comp

Apply Previous   Apply Next   Update Layer Comp   New Layer Comp

Caution icon (indicates the layer comp can't be fully restored)

Dock to Palette Well

New Layer Comp...
Duplicate Layer Comp
Delete Layer Comp

Update Layer Comp
Apply Layer Comp
Next Layer Comp
Previous Layer Comp
Restore Last Document State

Layer Comp Options...

Layers palette

Each new image starts out with a Background, which can be a solid color or transparent. Using the Layers palette, you can add layers on top of the Background, that you can show/hide, duplicate, group, link, delete, or restack. Each layer can be assigned its own blending mode, opacity, and fill opacity without affecting the other layers.

In addition to standard layers, you can also create three other kinds of layers: adjustment layers, which are used for applying temporary color or tonal adjustments to the layers below it; editable type layers, which are created automatically when the Horizontal Type or Vertical Type tool is used; and shape layers, which contain vector shapes with a color or pattern fill. If you apply a layer effect to a layer (e.g., Inner Glow or Drop Shadow), a layer effect icon and pop-up menu will appear next to the layer name. You can also attach a mask to a layer.

Only the current (or "active") layer can be edited. To choose a layer, click next to its name or click its thumbnail.

Starting out transparent

To have the bottommost tier of a new image be a layer with transparency instead of an opaque Background, in the File > New dialog box, click **Contents: Transparent.**

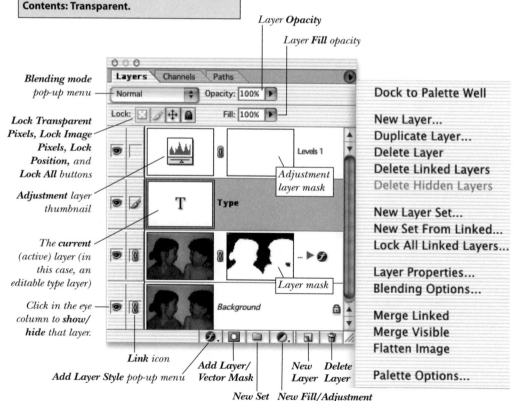

Navigator palette

The Navigator palette is used for moving an image in its window and for changing the zoom level of an image.

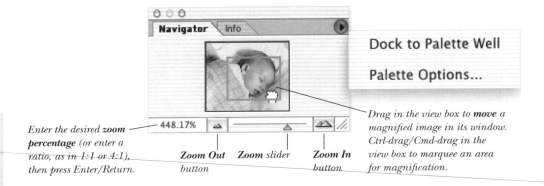

*Enter the desired **zoom percentage** (or enter a ratio, as in 1:1 or 4:1), then press Enter/Return.*

***Zoom Out** button*

***Zoom** slider*

***Zoom In** button*

*Drag in the view box to **move** a magnified image in its window. Ctrl-drag/Cmd-drag in the view box to marquee an area for magnification.*

Paragraph palette

The Paragraph palette is used to apply paragraph-wide attributes to type, including horizontal alignment, indentation, space before, space after, and auto hyphenation.

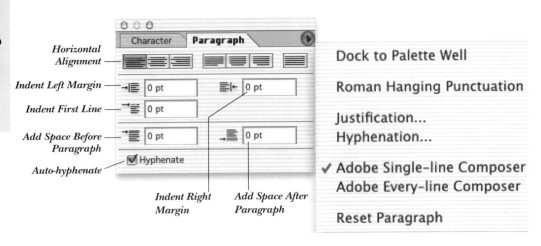

Horizontal Alignment

Indent Left Margin

Indent First Line

Add Space Before Paragraph

Auto-hyphenate

Indent Right Margin

Add Space After Paragraph

Paths palette

A path is a vector shape that's composed of curved and straight line segments connected by anchor points. A path can be drawn directly with a shape tool or a pen tool, or you can start by creating a selection and then convert the selection into a path. To create a precisely drawn selection, you can draw a path and then convert it into a selection.

Once a path is drawn, you can apply a fill or stroke color to it or use the Pen tool or any of its relatives—the Add Anchor Point, Delete Anchor Point, or Convert Point tool—to reshape it. Paths are saved, activated, duplicated, and deleted via the Paths palette.

TIP While a shape layer or an image layer that has a vector mask is selected, the path for that vector mask will be listed on the Paths palette.

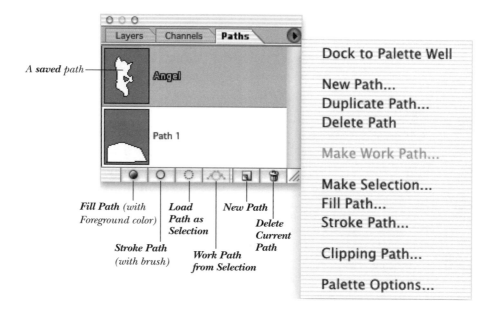

A saved path

Fill Path (with Foreground color)

Stroke Path (with brush)

Load Path as Selection

Work Path from Selection

New Path

Delete Current Path

Dock to Palette Well

New Path...
Duplicate Path...
Delete Path

Make Work Path...

Make Selection...
Fill Path...
Stroke Path...

Clipping Path...

Palette Options...

Styles palette

The Styles palette is used to save and apply previously saved individual layer effects or combinations of effects. Custom style libraries can be loaded, appended, and saved using commands on the Styles palette menu.

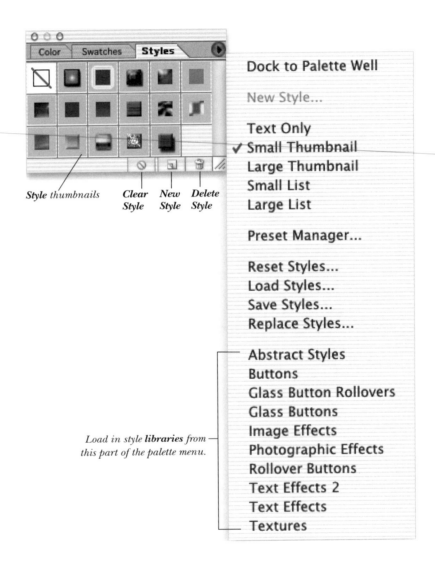

Style thumbnails   **Clear Style**   **New Style**   **Delete Style**

Dock to Palette Well

New Style...

Text Only
✓ Small Thumbnail
Large Thumbnail
Small List
Large List

Preset Manager...

Reset Styles...
Load Styles...
Save Styles...
Replace Styles...

Abstract Styles
Buttons
Glass Button Rollovers
Glass Buttons
Image Effects
Photographic Effects
Rollover Buttons
Text Effects 2
Text Effects
Textures

*Load in style **libraries** from this part of the palette menu.*

Styles Palette

Swatches palette

The Swatches palette is used for saving and choosing already mixed colors. Individual swatches can be added to or deleted from the palette. Custom swatch libraries can also be loaded, appended, and saved using commands on the Swatches palette menu.

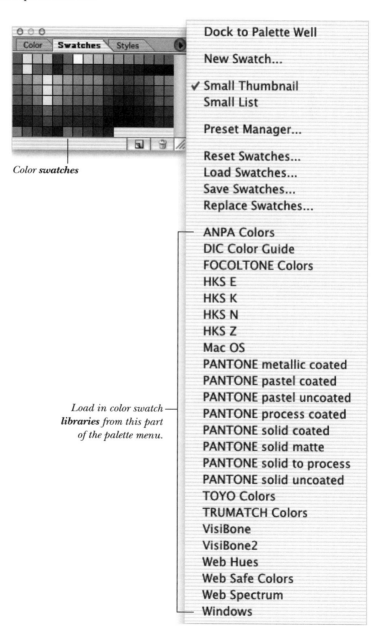

*Color **swatches***

*Load in color swatch **libraries** from this part of the palette menu.*

Tool Presets palette

You can save and reuse tool settings, just as you can any other type of preset. Say, for example, you frequently resize and crop images to a particular set of dimensions. If you create a preset with the width, height, and resolution parameters you need, the next time you perform the cropping operation, instead of having to type in the numbers, all you have to do is choose the tool preset from the Tool Presets palette or pop-up palette.

You can also save presets for type (complete with font, point size, and color attributes),

and for selection tools, brushes, gradients, patterns, shapes, contours, and styles.

The Tool Presets palette is used for managing saved tool presets. To have the palette list the presets for only the current tool, check Current Tool Only.

Tool presets are also accessible from this pop-up palette, which opens if you click the tool's thumbnail on the options bar.

*Click a tool **preset** to make it the current tool, complete with its saved settings.*

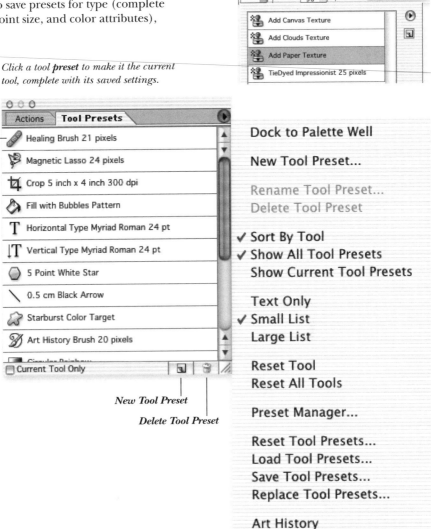

Tool Presets Palette

New Tool Preset

Delete Tool Preset

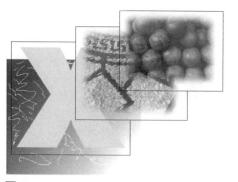

1 *Layers are like clear acetate sheets: **opaque** where pixels are present, **transparent** where there are none.*

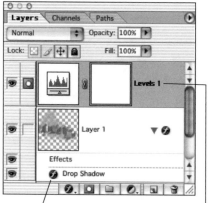

*A **layer effect***   **2** *The Levels command, applied via an **adjustment layer***

3 *Individual **pixels** are discernible in this image because it is shown at 500% view.*

Mini-glossary

Layer

An image can have just a Background (no layers), or it can have multiple layers **1**. Only the currently active layer can be edited. Individual layers can contain layer effects; they can be restacked and moved; you can choose blending options for them; and you can assign masks to them. They are transparent where there are no pixels.

Adjustment layer

Unlike a standard layer, modifications made to an adjustment layer don't alter actual pixels until the layer is merged with the layers below it **2**. You can use them to try out color and tonal adjustments without having to commit to those changes immediately.

Pixels

Pixels are dots that are used to display a bitmapped image in a grid onscreen **3**.

Vector

In addition to pixel imagery, you can also create paths, shapes, and editable type in Photoshop, each of which automatically appears on its own mathematically defined vector layer **4**. Vector elements print at the printer resolution, not the file resolution.

Foreground and Background colors

The current Foreground and Background colors are shown in the Foreground and Background color squares on the Toolbox and on the Color palette. The Foreground color is applied when you use a painting tool, create type, or use the Stroke command. The Background color is applied when you apply a transformation command

(Continued on the following page)

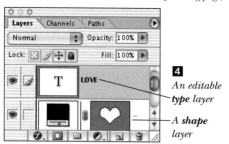

4
*An editable **type** layer*

*A **shape** layer*

Mini-Glossary

to, or move a selection on, the Background using the Move tool.

Selection

A selection is an area of an image that's isolated via a "marching ants" marquee; the unselected area is protected from editing . A selection can be created by using a selection tool (e.g., Lasso), by using a command (e.g., Color Range), by converting a path into a selection, or by loading an alpha channel mask as a selection. Another way to protect part of an image is by using a mask.

Preset

Saved type, gradient, pattern, shape, contour, style, or tool settings.

History

Every change that's made to an image is saved on the History palette as a separate state. While an image is still open, it can be restored to any prior state that's listed.

Layer effects

Photoshop has ten effects (e.g., Drop Shadow, Outer Glow, Gradient Overlay) that can be applied to any layer and are fully editable (and removable). A style is a saved effect or combination of multiple effects.

Pixel dimensions, resolution

The pixel dimensions value is the number of pixels an image contains. The resolution is the density of pixels per unit of measure (usually per inch) 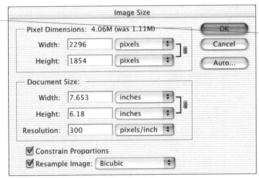.

Brightness, hue, saturation

Brightness is a color's lightness 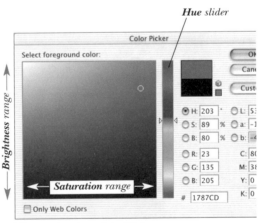; its hue is the wavelength of light that gives the color its name, such as red or blue; saturation is its degree of purity (amount of gray).

Optimization

Optimization is the preparation of an image for Web output, and it involves choosing file format, color, and size parameters. By using slices, you can apply differing optimization settings to various areas of an image.

Rollover

A rollover is a change on a Web page (e.g., the temporary appearance of supplemental text or a picture) that occurs when the user's mouse is over or clicks on a designated area.

1 *A selected area of an image*

2 *The Image Size dialog box is used for changing an image's pixel dimensions and/or resolution.*

3 *The Photoshop Color Picker*

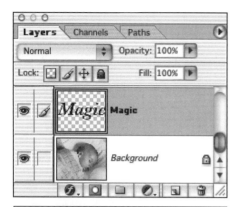

Build your image using layers

You can work on one layer at a time without affecting the other layers, and discard any layers you don't need. You can conserve memory when you're working on a large image by merging two or more layers together periodically.

Using a **layer mask** or a **vector mask,** you can temporarily hide pixels on select areas of a layer. When you're finished using the mask, you can either discard it or permanently apply its effect to the layer.

Quick on the redraw

To speed performance, choose Palette Options from the Layers, Channels, or Paths palette menu, then click the smallest **Thumbnail Size.**

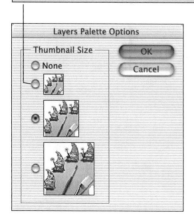

Production techniques

Keep these ideas in mind for future reference (don't worry, we'll explain them later!):

- To undo the last modification, choose Edit > **Undo** (Ctrl-Z/Cmd-Z) (*Note:* Some commands can't be undone.) To undo multiple steps, click a prior state on the **History** palette or use the **History Brush** tool to restore selective areas.

- Drag across an option name (e.g., **NEW** "Opacity" on the Layers palette) to the left or right to change a value without having to type it in the field.

- Use the **File Browser** to search for, sort, open, move, rename, and delete files, and to activate Automate commands. **NEW**

- Periodically click the **New Snapshot** button at the bottom of the History palette to save temporary versions of your image. Click a snapshot thumbnail to revert to that version.

- Use **adjustment layers** to try out tonal and color adjustments, and then later merge them downward to apply the effect, or discard them to remove the effect. Use the Layers palette Opacity slider to lessen the impact of an adjustment layer.

- Use Edit > **Fade** (Ctrl-Shift-F/Cmd-Shift-F) to lessen the last applied filter, adjustment command, or tool edit without having to undo and redo—and choose an opacity and blending mode for the command while you're at it.

- Memorize as many **keyboard shortcuts** as you can. Start by learning the shortcuts for choosing tools. Use onscreen tool tips to refresh your memory, or refer to pages 7–10 or our shortcuts appendix. Shortcuts are included in most of the instructions in this book.

- Choose the **lowest** possible resolution and dimensions for your image, given your output requirements. Note that vector layers (editable type, shapes, and vector masks) print at the printer resolution— not at the file resolution.

(Continued on the following page)

Production Techniques

...en redraw after executing... pplying a filter by ...t tool or command.

...nce of commands that you ...tly in an **action** so it can be ... quickly and easily to any image.

...play your image in **two windows** simultaneously, one at a larger zoom level than the other, so you don't have to constantly change zoom levels.

■ Save any complex selection to its own grayscale channel, called an **alpha channel,** which can be loaded and reused on any image whenever you like. Or even better, create a **path** or a **vector mask,** which occupies significantly less storage space than an alpha channel and can be converted into a selection at any time.

■ Use **Quick Mask** mode to turn a selection into a mask, which will cover the protected areas of the image with transparent color and leave the unprotected area as a cutout, and then modify the mask contour using a painting tool. Turn off Quick Mask mode to convert the cutout area back into a selection.

■ CMYK files process more slowly than RGB files. You can work in RGB Color mode, using View > Proof Setup > **Working CMYK** to preview your image as CMYK Color mode, and wait until it's done to convert it to the "real" CMYK Color mode.

■ Try to allot at least 50% of available **RAM** (at least 128 MB) to Photoshop, or four times an image's RAM document size.

■ Choose the Edit > **Purge** submenu commands periodically to regain RAM that was used for the Clipboard, the Undo command, the History palette, or All (of the above) **1**. The Purge commands can't be undone.

1 Use the **Purge** submenu commands to free up memory.

Context menus save time

To choose from an onscreen **context menu,** right-click/Control-click a Layers, Channels, or Paths palette thumbnail, name, or feature **2**. Or choose general commands or options for the current tool by right-clicking/Control-clicking in the image window **3**–**4**.

2 You can choose some **palette** commands via context menus.

3 Right-click/Control-click with a **type** tool to choose from a list of type commands.

4 Right-click/Control-click with a **selection** tool to choose from yet another list of commands.

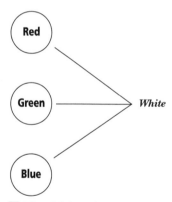

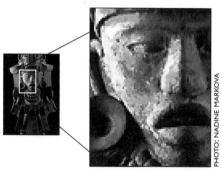

1 *A close-up of an image, showing individual* **pixels**

PHOTO: NADINE MARKOVA

2 *The* **additive primaries** *on a computer monitor*

3 *The* **subtractive primaries** *(printing inks)*

THIS CHAPTER consists of an introduction to color basics (color models, image modes, and blending modes), and also to Photoshop's color management features.

Color basics

Pixels

Onscreen, your Photoshop image is a bitmap—a geometric arrangement (mapping) of a layer of dots of different shades or colors on a rectangular grid. Each dot, or pixel, represents a color or shade. If you drag with a painting tool across an area of a layer, pixels under the pointer are recolored. By magnifying an area of an image, you can edit pixels individually **1**. Images can originate from scans, from another application, or entirely within Photoshop using painting tools and editing commands. Bitmap programs like Photoshop are ideal for producing painterly, photographic, or photorealistic images that contain subtle gradations of color. (Don't confuse Bitmap image mode with the term "bitmap.")

RGB vs. CMYK color

Red, green, and blue (RGB) lights are used to display a color image on a monitor. When these additive primaries in their purest form are combined, they produce white light **2**. The primary inks used in four-color process printing are cyan (C), magenta (M), yellow (Y), and black (K) **3**.

The display of color on a computer monitor is highly variable and subject to the whims of ambient lighting, monitor temperature, and room color. What's more, many colors that are seen in nature can't be printed, some colors that can be displayed onscreen can't be printed, and some printable colors

(Continued on the following page)

can't be displayed onscreen. All monitors display color using the RGB model; CMYK colors are merely simulated. If your image is going to be output to the Web or to a film recorder, keep it in RGB Color mode.

TIP For most desktop ink-jet printers, especially those that use six or more ink colors, you'll achieve the best results by leaving the file in RGB Color mode and allowing the printer's driver to perform the conversion to CMYK.

An exclamation point will appear on the Color palette if you choose a nonprintable (out-of-gamut) color ◼1. Exclamation points will also display on the Info palette if the color currently under the pointer is out of gamut ◼2. Using Photoshop's Gamut Warning command, you can display non-printable colors in your image in gray, and then, using the Sponge tool, you can desaturate them to bring them into gamut.

You can use the grayscale, RGB (red-green-blue), HSB (hue-saturation-brightness), CMYK (cyan-magenta-yellow-black), or Lab (lightness, a-component, and b-component) color model when you choose colors in Photoshop via the Color Picker or Color palette.

Channels

Every Photoshop image is a composite of one or more semitransparent, colored-light overlays called channels. For example, an image in RGB Color mode has three channels: red, green, and blue. To illustrate, open a color image, then click Red, Green, or Blue on the Channels palette to display only that channel. Click RGB (Ctrl-~/ Cmd-~) to restore the full channel display. (If the channels don't display in color, go to Edit [Photoshop, in Mac] > Preferences > Display & Cursors, and check the Color Channels in Color box.)

Color adjustments can be made to an individual channel, but normally modifications are made and displayed in the multichannel, composite image (the topmost channel name on the Channels palette), and affect

Web graphics

If you're creating an image for a website, use the RGB color model. Bear in mind that RGB colors—or colors from any other color model, for that matter— may not match the color palette of your Web browser (see page 492). For dependable results, load one of the Web or Visibone palettes onto the Swatches palette and choose **Web Color Sliders** and **Make Ramp Web Safe** from the Color palette menu.

Default channels per image mode

One	Three	Four
Bitmap	RGB	CMYK
Grayscale	Lab	
Duotone	Multichannel	
Indexed Color		

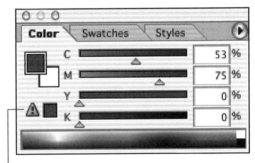

◼1 *Out-of-gamut indicator on the Color palette*

◼2 *Out-of-gamut indicator on the Info palette*

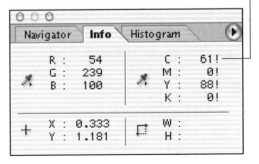

Channels

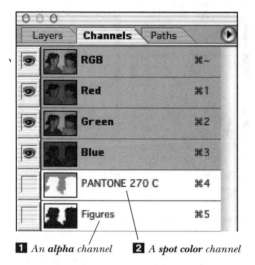

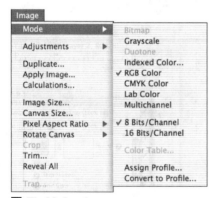

1 *An* **alpha** *channel*   **2** *A* **spot color** *channel*

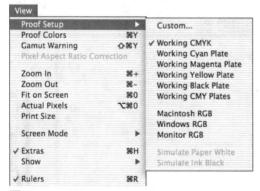

3 *The* **Mode** *submenu*

4 *The* **Proof Setup** *submenu*

all of an image's channels at once. Special grayscale channels that are used for saving selections as masks, called alpha channels, can be added to an image **1**; you can also add channels for individual spot colors **2**. Only the currently highlighted channels can be edited.

The more channels an image contains, the larger its file storage size. The storage size of an image in RGB Color mode, which has three channels (Red, Green, and Blue), will be three times larger than the same image in Grayscale mode, which has one channel. The same image in CMYK Color mode will have four channels (Cyan, Magenta, Yellow, and Black), and will be even larger.

Image modes

An image can be converted to, displayed in, and edited in any one of eight image modes: Bitmap, Grayscale, Duotone, Indexed Color, RGB Color, CMYK Color, Lab Color, or Multichannel. Simply choose the mode you want from the Image menu > Mode submenu **3**. To access a mode that's unavailable (its name is dimmed), you must first convert your image to a different mode as an intermediate step. For example, to convert an image to Indexed Color mode, it must be in RGB Color or Grayscale mode.

Some mode conversions cause noticeable color shifts. For example, dramatic changes may occur if an image is converted from RGB Color mode to CMYK Color mode because in this case, printable colors will be substituted for rich, glowing RGB colors. Color accuracy may diminish if an image is converted back and forth between RGB and CMYK Color modes too many times.

Medium- to low-end scanners usually produce RGB scans. If you're creating an image that's going to be printed, for faster editing and to access all the filters, edit it in RGB Color mode and then convert it to CMYK Color mode when you're ready to imageset it. You can use View > Proof Setup **4** in conjunction with View > Proof Colors (Ctrl-Y/Cmd-Y) to preview an image in

(Continued on the following page)

Image Modes

CMYK Color mode without actually changing its mode. You can preview your image in CMYK in one window and open a second window to display the same image without the preview.

Some conversions cause layers to be flattened, such as a conversion to Indexed Color, Multichannel, or Bitmap mode. For other conversions, you'll have the option to click Don't Flatten if you want to preserve layers.

Images that are saved by high-end scanners in CMYK Color mode should be kept in that mode to preserve their color data. Photoshop CS can handle large scans, even those that are saved with a pixel depth of 16 bits per channel.

Some output devices require that an image be saved in a particular image mode. The availability of some commands and tool options in Photoshop may also vary depending on an image's current mode.

These are the image modes, in brief:

In **Bitmap** mode , pixels are 100% black or 100% white only, and layers, filters, and adjustment commands (except for the Invert command) aren't available. An image must be in Grayscale mode before it can be converted to Bitmap mode.

In **Grayscale** mode , pixels are black, white, or up to 254 shades of gray (for a total of 256). If an image is converted from a color mode to Grayscale mode and then saved and closed, its luminosity (light and dark) values will remain intact, but its color information will be deleted and can't be restored.

Images in **Indexed Color** mode have one channel and a color table that contains a maximum of 256 colors or shades (8-bit color). It's often helpful to reduce images to 8-bit color for use in multimedia applications. You can also convert an image to Indexed Color mode to create arty color effects. An image that's been reduced to 8-bit color for Web output should be optimized in the GIF format (see Chapter 25).

1 *Bitmap* mode, Method: Diffusion Dither   **2** *Grayscale* mode

*The **Channels** palette for an image in various modes*

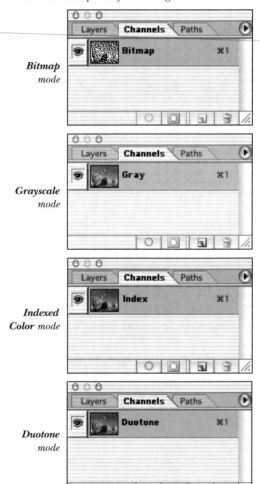

Bitmap mode

Grayscale mode

Indexed Color mode

Duotone mode

*The **Channels** palette for an image in various modes*

RGB Color mode

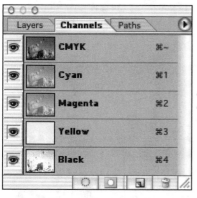

CMYK Color mode

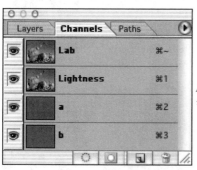

Lab Color mode

Multichannel mode

RGB Color is the most versatile mode of all because it's the only mode in which all of Photoshop's tool options and filters are accessible. It's also the mode of choice for onscreen output and for export to many video and multimedia applications.

Photoshop is one of the few programs in which images can be displayed and edited in **CMYK Color** mode. You can convert your image to CMYK Color mode when you're ready to color-separate it, export it to a page layout application, or output it on a composite color printer.

Lab Color is a three-channel mode that was developed for the purpose of achieving consistency among various devices, such as printers and monitors. The channels represent lightness, the colors green to red, and the colors blue to yellow. PhotoCD images can be converted to Lab Color (or RGB Color) mode in Photoshop. In Lab Color mode, an image's luminosity and color values can be edited independently of one another.

Duotone is a printing method in which two or more plates are used to add richness and tonal depth to a grayscale image.

Multichannel images are composed of multiple, 256-level grayscale channels. This mode is used for some grayscale printing situations. It can also be used for assembling individual channels from several images as an intermediary step; the composite image can then be converted to another color mode. If you convert an image from RGB Color to Multichannel mode, its Red, Green, and Blue channels will be converted to Cyan, Magenta, and Yellow. As a result, the image may become lighter and its contrast may be diminished. This mode preserves spot color and alpha channels.

Image Modes

Blending Modes

The blending modes

You can choose from a list of blending modes on the options bar for many tools, on the Layers palette, in the Layer Style dialog box, and in the Fill, Stroke, Fade, or Fill Path dialog box, among other places. The mode you choose for a tool or a layer affects how that tool or layer modifies underlying pixels (the "base color" in the descriptions below). The "blend layer" is the color applied via a layer or tool for which a mode is chosen.

Note: If the Lock Transparent Pixels button ⊠ is selected on the Layers palette for the target layer, only pixels—not transparent areas—can be recolored or otherwise edited.

> ## Opacities add up
> When you choose a mode and an opacity for a **tool**, be sure to factor in the mode and opacity of the current **layer** you're working on. For example, if you choose 60% opacity for the Paintbrush tool on a layer that has 50% opacity, your resulting brush stroke will have an opacity of 30%.

Note: In the illustrations on this page through page 41, a dark color was used on the left and a light color was used on the right. And except for Dissolve, the blend layer always has an opacity of 100%.

NORMAL

All base colors are modified. *Note:* When an image is in Bitmap or Indexed Color mode, Normal mode is called Threshold.

DISSOLVE

Creates a chalky, dry brush texture with the paint or blend layer color. The higher the pressure or opacity, the more solid the stroke.

DARKEN

Base colors that are lighter than the paint or blend layer color are modified; base colors that are darker than the paint or blend layer color are not. Use with a paint color that is darker than the base colors you want to modify.

MULTIPLY

A dark paint or blend layer color removes the lighter parts of the base color to produce a darker base color; a light paint or blend layer color darkens the base color less. Good for creating semitransparent shadows.

COLOR BURN

A dark paint or blend layer color darkens the base color by increasing the layer's contrast; a light paint or blend layer color slightly tints the base color.

COLOR DODGE

A light paint or blend layer color lightens the base color by decreasing the layer's contrast; a dark paint or blend layer color slightly tints the base color.

LINEAR BURN

A dark paint or blend layer color darkens the base color by decreasing the layer's brightness; a light paint or blend layer color slightly tints the base color.

LINEAR DODGE

A light paint or blend layer color lightens the base color by increasing the layer's brightness; a dark paint or blend layer color slightly tints the base color.

LIGHTEN

Base colors that are darker than the paint or blend layer color are modified; base colors that are lighter than the paint or blend layer color are not. Use with a paint color that is lighter than the base colors you want to modify.

SCREEN

A light paint or blend layer color removes the darker parts of the base color to produce a lighter, bleached base color; a dark paint or blend layer lightens the base color less.

OVERLAY

Multiplies (darkens) dark areas and screens (lightens) light base colors while preserving luminosity (light and dark) values. Black and white aren't changed, so details are maintained.

PIN LIGHT

The blend color replaces the colors in the base color, depending on their relative brightness. If the blend color is lighter than 50% gray, pixels darker than the blend color are replaced; if the blend color is darker than 50% gray, pixels lighter than the blend color are replaced. Good for creating special effects.

SOFT LIGHT

Lightens the base color if the paint or blend layer color is light; darkens the base color if the paint or blend layer color is dark. Preserves luminosity values in the base color. Creates a soft, subtle lighting effect.

HARD LIGHT

Screens (lightens) the base color if the paint or blend layer color is light; multiplies (darkens) the base color if the paint or blend layer color is dark. Contrast is increased in the base color and layer color. Good for painting glowing highlights and creating composite effects.

HARD MIX NEW

Posterizes the base color to five or six shades. A dark paint or blend layer color reduces the base color to dark shades; a light blend layer color reduces the base color to light shades.

LINEAR LIGHT

Burns (darkens) the base color by decreasing its brightness if the paint or blend layer color is dark; dodges (lightens) the base color by increasing its brightness if the paint or blend layer color is light.

VIVID LIGHT

Burns (darkens) the base colors by increasing the contrast if the paint or blend layer color is dark; dodges (lightens) the base color by decreasing the contrast if the paint or blend layer color is light.

DIFFERENCE

Creates a color negative effect on the base color. When the paint or blend layer color is light, the negative (or invert) effect is more pronounced. Produces noticeable color shifts.

EXCLUSION

Grays out the base color where the paint or blend layer color is dark; inverts the base color where the paint or blend layer color is light.

HUE

The blend color's hue is applied. The saturation and luminosity values aren't changed in the base color.

SATURATION

The blend color's saturation is applied. The hue and luminosity values aren't changed in the base color.

COLOR

The blend color's saturation and hue are applied. The base color's light and dark (luminosity) values aren't changed. Details are preserved, making this a good mode to use for tinting.

LUMINOSITY

The base color's luminosity values are replaced by luminosity values from the blend color, but hue and saturation values in the base color aren't changed.

BEHIND

On a layer for which Lock Transparent Pixels is off, only transparent areas are modified, not existing base color pixels, producing an effect like painting on the reverse side of clear acetate. Good for creating shadows. This mode can't be used on the Background.

CLEAR

Makes the base color transparent where strokes are applied (turn off Lock Transparent Pixels). Available only for a multilayer image when using the Paint Bucket tool; the Line tool with the Fill Pixels button clicked; or the Fill, Stroke, or Fill Path command. This mode can't be chosen for a layer or used on the Background.

Cycling through

To cycle through the **blending modes** for the current tool, press Shift - + (plus) or Shift - – (minus).

*This alert dialog box may open when Photoshop is launched if the current color settings have been modified in another Adobe program (e.g., Illustrator CS). Click **Synchronize** to have Photoshop's color settings match (be synchronized with) the color settings from the other program. In Mac OS X, both Photoshop and the other Adobe program must be installed at the same user level for them to be aware of each other's color settings.*

Color management

Problems with color can creep up on you when various hardware devices and software packages you use treat color differently. If you opened an image in several different imaging programs and in a Web browser, the colors in the image might look completely different in each case, and thus may not match the color of the picture you originally scanned in on your scanner. Print the image, and you will probably find that your results are different yet again. In some cases, you might find these differences to be slight and unobjectionable, but in other cases, such color changes can wreak havoc with your design and turn a project into a disaster.

A color management system can solve most of these problems by acting as a color interpreter. Such a system knows how each device and program understands color, and adjusts colors so your images look the same as you move them from one program or device to another. This is achieved by using color profiles, which are mathematical descriptions of each device's color space. Both Illustrator and Photoshop use the standardized ICC (International Color Consortium) profiles to tell your color management system how specific devices use color.

You can find most of Photoshop's color management controls in the Color Settings dialog box, which is accessed from the Edit menu in Windows, the Photoshop menu in Mac. This dialog box gives you access to predefined management settings for various publishing situations, including prepress output and Web output.

Photoshop also supports color management policies for RGB and CMYK color files, for files that use spot colors, and for grayscale files. These color management policies govern how Photoshop deals with color when opening images that do or don't have an attached color profile.

TIP Consult with your prepress service provider, if you're using one, about color

(Continued on the following page)

management to ensure that your color management workflows work together smoothly.

TIP If you're planning to use the same image for multiple purposes, such as for the Web and for print, you may benefit from using color management.

Calibration

The first step toward achieving color consistency is to calibrate your monitor by adjusting the contrast and brightness, gamma, color balance, and white point. The Adobe Gamma utility is installed with the Windows version of Photoshop CS, whereas the Macintosh version relies on the operating system's monitor calibration utility in the Displays option in System Preferences **1**.

Both the Adobe Gamma and Displays control panels generate an ICC profile that Photoshop can use as its working RGB space in order to display the colors in your artwork accurately.

You have to **calibrate** your **monitor** and save the settings as an ICC profile only once; thereafter, the profile will be available to all applications. *Note:* The calibration utility in Mac OS 10.3 or later will look different than in these illustrations, but the basic steps will be similar.

To calibrate your monitor in Macintosh:

1. Let the monitor warm up for 30 minutes so the display will stabilize, and establish a level of room lighting that will remain constant (paint your windows black, ha-ha). Make the desktop pattern light gray.

2. Choose Apple > System Preferences, click Displays, click the Color tab, then click Calibrate.

Click the right arrow to advance to the next options pane.

Note: In the following procedure, some options may not be available for LCD (flat-panel) monitors.

3. *Optional:* Check Expert Mode to access advanced options.

Finding the calibration utility

In Windows, choose Start Menu > Control Panel > Adobe Gamma, or run the Adobe Gamma.cpl utility from C:\Program Files\Common Files\Adobe\Calibration.

In Mac, choose Apple > System Preferences, click Displays, then click the Color tab in the Displays pane.

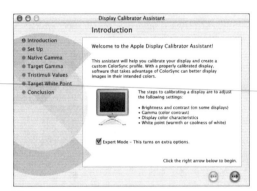

1 *This is the starting point for calibrating your monitor in Mac OS X.*

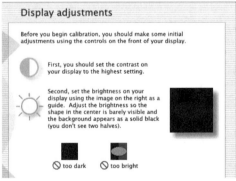

2 *The first step in calibrating your monitor is to set the **contrast** and **brightness** to the proper values (this is for CRT displays only).*

Determine your display's current gamma

Your display's actual gamma is affected by contrast and brightness settings and other characteristics of your display.

Move the slider until the grey shape in the middle blends in with the background as much as possible. It may help to squint or step back from the display.

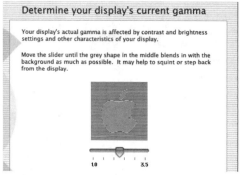

1 *Drag the slider to make the gray apple fade into the background (for CRT displays only).*

Select a target gamma

Select the gamma setting you want for your display. (Watch the picture on the right to see the effect as you click the different options.)

○ 1.8 Standard Gamma
  This is the traditional setting for Mac OS computers.

○ 2.2 Television Gamma
  You may want to select this setting if you are working with images to be displayed on television or PC–compatible computers.

○ No Correction (native)

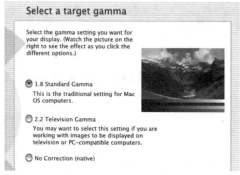

2 *Choose a **gamma** setting (this is non-Expert mode).*

Select a target white point

Select the white point setting you want for your display.

○ D50 Warm yellowish lighting – standard for graphic arts work.

◉ D65 Cooler – equivalent to midday sunlight.

○ 9300 Coolest – the default white point of most displays and televisions.

○ None No white point correction performed.

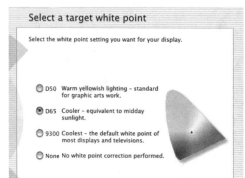

3 *Choose the **target white point** that's appropriate for the type of work you do (this is non-Expert mode).*

4. For "Display adjustments," leave your monitor's contrast at the maximum setting, and adjust the brightness until the light gray oval is barely visible and the background looks like solid black (**2**, previous page). Click the right arrow to proceed.

5. For "Determine your display's current gamma," the gray square represents a combined grayscale reading of your monitor **1**. To adjust the gamma, move the slider below the square until the solid gray apple shape matches the surrounding, stripey box (it helps to squint). If you checked Expert Mode earlier, you'll have separate adjustments to make for Red, Green, and Blue; this is for CRT (non-flat panel) displays only. Click the right arrow.

6. For "Select a target gamma," choose the gamma you want your display to use: 1.8 Standard Gamma for Mac, 2.2 Television Gamma for Windows, or No Correction (native) to leave the display in its native gamma **2**. If you chose Expert Mode, you'll be able to choose a gamma setting via a spectrum slider here. Click the right arrow.

7. For a CRT display, under "Select your display's color characteristics," choose your display type from the scroll list. If it isn't listed there, choose the type or brand that most closely matches yours. Click the right arrow.

8. For "Select a target white point," choose a target white point based on the kind of work you'll be doing **3**. If you checked Expert Mode, you will have a continuous range of white point settings from which to choose. Click the right arrow.

9. Finally, name the profile, then click Create. It will automatically be saved in Users/[User Name]/Library/ColorSync/Profiles, and can be accessed via the RGB pop-up menu in the Working Spaces area of the Color Settings dialog box (see page 49).

Calibration in Mac

_nitor in Windows:

_s for the monitor to
_he display to stabilize, and
_evel of room lighting that
_n constant.

_he desktop pattern light gray.

_ose Start menu > Control Panel,
_hen open the Adobe Gamma utility.

4. Click Step by Step (Wizard), which will
walk you through the process 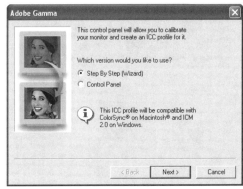.
or
Click Control Panel to choose settings
from a single dialog box without expla-
nations. (If the Adobe Gamma dialog
opens directly, you can skip this step.) **2**

Note: If you're using the Wizard, click
Next to advance to the next dialog box.

5. Leave the default monitor ICC profile
as is.
or
Click Load and choose a profile that
more closely matches your monitor.

6. Turn up your monitor's brightness and
contrast settings. Leave the contrast at
the maximum; adjust the brightness
until the alternating gray squares in the
top bar are very dark, but not black,
while keeping the lower bar bright white.

7. For Phosphors, choose your monitor
type, or choose Custom and enter the
Red, Green, and Blue chromaticity
coordinates that are specified by your
monitor's manufacturer.

8. For Gamma, the gray square represents
a combined grayscale reading of your
monitor. Adjust the gamma using this
slider until the smaller, solid-color box
matches the outer, stripey box (it helps
to squint). You might find it easier to
uncheck View Single Gamma Only and
make separate adjustments based on
the readings for Red, Green, and Blue.

9. For Desired, choose Windows Default
(value of 2.2), if available.

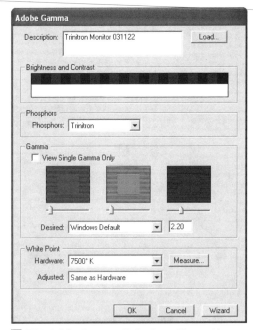

1 *This is the **Adobe Gamma** dialog box, set for the
Step by Step calibration method.*

2 *This **Adobe Gamma dialog** box will open if you
choose the Control Panel option. With **View Single
Gamma Only** unchecked, adjustments can be made
to the individual Red, Green, and Blue components.*

Calibration in Windows

10. For White Point: Hardware, choose the white point the monitor manufacturer specifies, or click Measure and follow the instructions.

11. For Adjusted, choose Same as Hardware, or, if you know the color temperature at which your image will ultimately be viewed, you can either choose it from the pop-up menu or choose Custom and enter it there. *Note:* This option isn't available for all monitors.

12. Close the Adobe Gamma dialog box and save the profile in WindowsXP > system32 > spool > drivers > color, with the .icm extension. Photoshop can use this profile as its working RGB space in the Color Settings dialog box (see the next page).

Note: If you adjust your monitor's brightness and contrast settings or change the room lighting, you'll need to recalibrate your monitor. Also, keep in mind that what we've outlined here is a basic calibration method. Professional-level calibration requires more precise monitor measurement using expensive hardware devices, such as colorimeters and spectrophotometers (what?).

Calibration in Windows

To choose a predefined color management setting:

1. Choose Edit (Photoshop, in Mac) > Color Settings (Ctrl-Shift-K/Cmd-Shift-K).

2. Choose a configuration option from the Settings pop-up menu:

Color Management Off emulates the behavior of applications that don't support color management. This is a good choice when preparing projects for video or onscreen presentation.

ColorSync Workflow (Mac only) manages color using the ColorSync color management system. Profiles are based on those in the ColorSync control panel (including any monitor profile you may have created using the Apple Display Calibrator utility). This setting is a good choice if you need to keep color consistent between Adobe and non-Adobe applications.

Emulate Acrobat 4 uses Acrobat 4.0's color handling. To access this setting, Acrobat must first be installed.

> ### Point and learn
>
> The **Description** area **1** at the bottom of the Color Settings dialog box provides valuable information about whichever option the pointer is currently over. You can use these tool tips to learn about the various Color Settings features.

North American General Purpose Defaults tries to keep colors consistent among Adobe products.

Emulate Photoshop 4 uses the same color workflow used by the Mac OS version of Photoshop 4 and earlier versions. This setting doesn't recognize or save color profiles.

Photoshop 5 Default Spaces uses the same working spaces as the default settings found in Photoshop 5.

U.S. Prepress Defaults manage color using settings based on common press conditions in the U.S. In the European and Japanese prepress settings, the CMYK working space is changed to a press that's standard for that region.

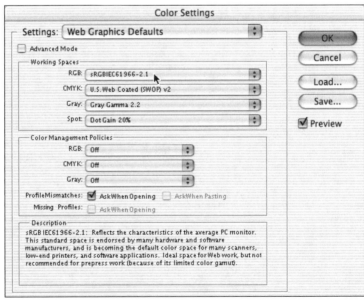

1 *The Color Settings dialog box, with the Web Graphics Defaults setting chosen*

Document-specific color

Photoshop supports **document-specific color,** which means each open document keeps its own profile for controlling how it previews and how its color is managed on output. The current working space is used to create previews for documents that lack an embedded profile.

Web Graphics Defaults manage color for content that's going to be published on the Web.

At this point you can click OK to accept the predefined settings or you can proceed with step 3 to choose custom settings.

3. Next, you can choose color working spaces, which define how RGB and CMYK color will be treated in your document. For CMYK settings, you should ask your output service provider which working space to choose. You can also specify a dot gain value or gamma setting for grayscale images and a dot gain value for spot colors.

The following RGB settings are available:

Monitor RGB [current monitor name]: This choice sets the RGB working space to your monitor's profile, and is useful if you know that other applications you'll be using for your project don't support color management. Keep in mind, however, that if you share this configuration with another user, the configuration will use that user's monitor profile as the RGB working space, and color consistency may be lost.

ColorSync RGB: (Mac OS X only) Use this color space to match Photoshop's RGB space to the space specified in the Apple ColorSync 3.0 (or later) control panel. This can be the profile you created using System Preferences > Displays. If you share this configuration with another user, it will utilize the ColorSync space specified by that user.

Adobe RGB (1998): This color space produces a wide range of colors, and is useful when converting RGB images to CMYK images, but it's not a good choice for Web work.

Apple RGB: This space is useful for files that you plan to display on Mac monitors, as it reflects the characteristics of

(Continued on the following page)

Color Settings

the older standard Apple 13-inch monitors. It's also a good choice for older desktop publishing files (e.g., Adobe Photoshop 4.0 files).

ColorMatch RGB: This space produces a smaller range of color than the Adobe RGB (1998) model, but it matches the color space of Radius Pressview monitors and is useful for print production work.

sRGB IEC61966-2.1: This is a good choice for Web work, as it reflects the settings on the average computer monitor. Many hardware and software manufacturers are using it as the default space for scanners, low-end printers, and software. It shouldn't be used for prepress work; use Adobe RGB or ColorMatch RGB instead.

4. Click OK.

You can choose a **customized** color management policy that will tell Photoshop how to deal with artwork that doesn't match your current color settings.

To customize your color management policies:

1. Choose Edit (Photoshop, in Mac) > Color Settings (Ctrl-Shift-K/ Cmd-Shift-K).

2. From the Settings pop-up menu, choose any predefined setting other than Color Management Off or Emulate Photoshop 4, or chose your own custom Working Spaces settings.

3. From the pop-up menus in the Color Management Policies area **1**:

   If you choose **Off,** Photoshop won't color-manage color files that are imported or opened.

   Choose **Preserve Embedded Profiles** if you think you're going to be working with both color-managed and non-color-managed documents. This will tie each color file's profile to the individual file. Remember, in Photoshop, each open document can have its own profile.

   Choose **Convert to Working…** if you want all your documents to reflect the same color working space. This is usually the best choice for Web work.

   For Profile Mismatches, check **Ask When Opening** to have Photoshop display a message if the color profile in a file you're opening doesn't match your selected working space. If you choose this option, you can override your color management policy when opening documents.

   Check **Ask When Pasting** to have Photoshop display a message when color profile mismatches occur as you paste color data into your document. If you choose this option, you can override your color management policy when pasting.

   For files with Missing Profiles, check **Ask When Opening** to have Photoshop display a message offering you the opportunity to assign a profile.

4. Click OK.

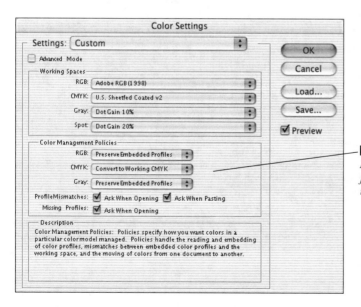

1 *Color Management Policies options are chosen from the middle portion of the Color Settings dialog box.*

To customize your conversion options:

1. Choose Edit (Photoshop, in Mac) > Color Settings (Ctrl-Shift-K/Cmd-Shift-K).

2. Check Advanced Mode **1**.

3. Under Conversion Options, choose a color management Engine to be used to convert colors between color spaces: **Adobe (ACE)** uses Adobe's color management system and color engine; both **Apple ColorSync** and **Apple CMM** use Apple's color management system; and **Microsoft ICM** uses the system provided in the Windows 98 and later systems. Other color engines can be chosen to fit into color workflows that use specific output devices.

4. Choose a rendering Intent to determine how colors will be changed as they're moved from one color space to another:

Perceptual changes colors in a way that seems natural to the human eye, even though the color values actually do change. It's appropriate for continuous-tone images.

Saturation changes colors with the intent of preserving vivid colors, although it compromises the accuracy of the color; it's good for charts and business graphics.

Absolute Colorimetric keeps colors that are inside the destination color gamut unchanged, but the relationships among colors outside this gamut are changed in an attempt to maintain color accuracy.

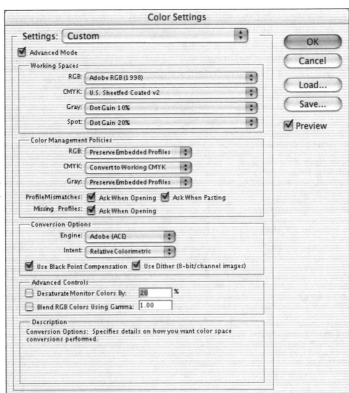

1 *When **Advanced Mode** is checked in the Color Settings dialog box, the **Conversion Options** become available.*

Conversion Options

Saving settings

■ To save your custom settings for later use, click **Save** in the Color Settings dialog box. If you want your custom file name to display on the Settings pop-up menu in Windows, save it in the default location: Program Files/Common Files/Adobe/Color/Settings. To do the same thing in Mac, save the file in User/[CurrentUser]/Library/Application Support/Adobe/Color/Settings.

■ When you're ready to reuse the saved settings, choose the file name from the Settings pop-up menu. To locate a settings file that isn't saved in the Settings folder (and thus isn't on the Settings menu), click **Load** in the Color Settings dialog box.

■ In the Save As dialog box, when you save a file in a format that supports embedded profiles, such as Photoshop or Photoshop PDF, you can check **Embed ICC Profile** in Windows or **Color Profile** in the Mac to embed a profile with the document, if one has been assigned.

Relative Colorimetric, the default intent for all predefined settings options, is the same as Absolute Colorimetric, except it compares the white point, or extreme highlight, of the source color space to the destination color space and shifts all colors accordingly. The accuracy of this intent depends on the accuracy of white point information in an image's profile.

Note: Differences between rendering intents are visible only on a printout or upon a conversion to a different working space.

Check **Use Black Point Compensation** if you want adjustments to be made for differences in black points between color spaces. When this option is chosen, the full dynamic range of the source color space is mapped into the full dynamic range of the destination color space. If you don't choose this option, your blacks may appear as grays. We recommend that you check this option for a RGB-to-CMYK conversion, but consult your print shop before checking it for a CMYK-to-CMYK conversion.

Check **Use Dither (8-bit/channel images)** if you want Photoshop to dither colors when converting 8-bits-per-channel images between color spaces. Sometimes when an image is converted from one color space to another, colors that don't exist in the target space are lost, resulting in banding or undesirable color artifacts (extraneous pixels). With this option checked, Photoshop will mix blocks of similar colors to simulate a missing color, thus achieving smoother overall continuous tones.

We recommend keeping Use Dither (8-bit/channel images) checked when converting between RGB and CMYK spaces for print, but turning it off when preparing graphics for the Web. The Save for Web dialog box provides more precise controls for dithering images.

5. Click OK.

Conversion Options

You may decide later that you want to change or remove a document's color profile. For example, when preparing a document for a specific output device, you may need to switch profiles. You also may need to switch profiles if you change your mind about your color management settings. The **Assign Profile** command reinterprets the color data directly in the color space of the new profile (or lack thereof), and visible shifting of colors can be the result. When you use the Convert Profile command, however, the color numbers are recalculated before the new profile is applied, in an effort to preserve the document's appearance. In either case, keep Preview checked so you know what you're getting into!

To change or delete a document's color profile:

1. Choose Image > Mode > Assign Profile **1**.

2. Click **Don't Color Manage This Document** to remove the color profile.
   or
   Click **Working** (plus the document color mode and the name of the working space you're using) to assign that particular

working space to a document that doesn't use a profile or that uses a profile that's different from the working space.
or
Click **Profile** to reassign a different profile to a color-managed document; choose a profile from the pop-up menu.

3. Click OK.

   Note: If you save a file in (or export a file to) a format that supports embedded profiles, you'll have the choice to select or deselect the Embed ICC Profile option. You should keep this option checked unless you have a specific reason to uncheck it.

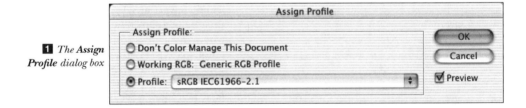

1 *The Assign Profile dialog box*

To convert a document's color profile:

1. Choose Image > Mode > Convert to Profile (**1**, next page).

2. From the Destination Space: Profile pop-up menu, choose the space that you want to convert the document to. It doesn't have to be the current working space.

   For information on the Conversion Options, see "To customize your conversion options" on page 52.

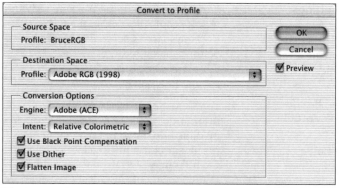

1 *The Convert to Profile dialog box*

Specifying a color management setup is all well and good, but sometimes what you need is to get an idea of how a document is going to look when it's printed or on a website. You can do this by **soft-proofing** your colors. Although this method is less accurate than actually making a print or viewing your Web artwork on different monitors, it can give you a general idea of how your work will look in different settings. You can either choose a preset proof setup or choose custom settings.

To proof colors using preset settings:

1. From the View > Proof Setup submenu, choose which one of these output display types you want Photoshop to simulate:

    Working CMYK to soft-proof colors using the CMYK working space as defined in the Color Settings dialog box.

    Working Cyan Plate, Working Magenta Plate, Working Yellow Plate, Working Black Plate, or **Working CMY Plates** to soft-proof specific ink colors as defined by the current CMYK working space.

    Macintosh RGB or **Windows RGB** to soft-proof colors using a Mac or Windows monitor profile as the proofing space you want to simulate.

    Monitor RGB to use your monitor profile as the space for proofing.

2. View > Proof Colors will be checked automatically so the soft proof can be previewed. Uncheck it at any time to turn off proofing.

To proof colors using custom settings:

1. From the View > Proof Setup submenu, choose Custom. The Proof Setup dialog box opens, allowing you to create a proofing method for a specific output device ◼.

2. Check Preview, then from the **Profile** pop-up menu, choose the color profile for your desired output device.

3. Check or uncheck **Preserve Color Numbers,** if this option is available. If checked, Photoshop will simulate how the colors will appear if they're not converted to the proofing space. If unchecked, Photoshop will simulate how the colors will appear if they are converted, and you'll need to specify a rendering intent, as described in "To customize your conversion options" on page 52.

Note: Preserve Color Numbers is available only if the color mode of the output device that you chose from the Profile pop-up menu matches that of the current file (e.g., if the chosen proofing profile is RGB and the document color mode is also RGB).

4. For the **Profile,** choose Working CMYK to soft-proof colors using the CMYK working space as defined in the Color Settings dialog box.

For the Use Black Point Compensation option, see page 53.

5. For **Simulate,** check Paper White to preview the shade of white of the print medium as defined in the document's profile, or check Ink Black to preview the full range of gray values as defined in the document's profile.

6. Click OK. View > Proof Colors will be checked automatically so the soft proof can be previewed. Uncheck it at any time to turn off proofing.

TIP To save a custom proof setup, click Save in the Proof Setup dialog box. Saved proof setups are listed at the bottom of the Proof Setup submenu and on the Setup pop-up menu.

TIP To learn how to use the color management features in the Print with Preview dialog box, see pages 446 and 447.

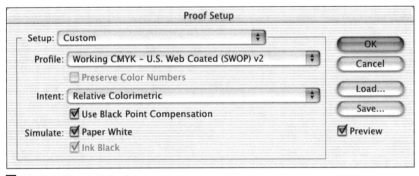

◼ *The **Proof Setup** dialog box*

```
✓ Photoshop
  BMP
  CompuServe GIF
  Photoshop EPS
  JPEG
  PCX
  Photoshop PDF
  Photoshop 2.0
  Photoshop Raw
  PICT File
  PICT Resource
  Pixar
  PNG
  Scitex CT
  Targa
  TIFF
  Photoshop DCS 1.0
  Photoshop DCS 2.0
```

1 *Files can be saved in any of these **formats** in Mac.*

```
Photoshop (*.PSD;*.PDD)
BMP (*.BMP;*.RLE;*.DIB)
CompuServe GIF (*.GIF)
Photoshop EPS (*.EPS)
Photoshop DCS 1.0 (*.EPS)
Photoshop DCS 2.0 (*.EPS)
JPEG (*.JPG;*.JPEG;*.JPE)
PCX (*.PCX)
Photoshop PDF (*.PDF;*.PDP)
Photoshop Raw (*.RAW)
PICT File (*.PCT;*.PICT)
Pixar (*.PXR)
PNG (*.PNG)
Scitex CT (*.SCT)
Targa (*.TGA;*.VDA;*.ICB;*.VST)
TIFF (*.TIF;*.TIFF)
```

2 *Files can be saved in any of these **formats** in Windows.*

IN THIS CHAPTER you'll learn how to scan images; create new images; create document presets; open and place images into Photoshop; use the ever evolving File Browser to manage files; and save, copy, and close images. And then, to get comfortable working with image windows, you'll learn how to change the zoom level of an image, move an image in its window, switch screen display modes, and open a second window for an image. We'll also tell you how to close up shop.

Note: If you haven't yet launched Photoshop, see page 1!

Where images come from

An image can be created, opened, edited, and saved in over a dozen different file formats in Photoshop **1**–**2**. Of this large selection, most likely you'll use only a handful on a regular basis (e.g., TIFF, GIF, JPEG, EPS, Photoshop PDF, and PSD, the native Photoshop file format). There's also a new native format, Large Document format, or PSB (nicknamed "Photoshop Big"), which is designed for large—no, make that huge—files.

Because Photoshop accepts so many formats, imagery can be gathered from many sources, such as scanners, drawing applications, digital cameras, PhotoCDs, and video captures. Images can also be created entirely within Photoshop using brushes, filters, and commands, or by collaging or assembling imagery from multiple files. In this chapter, we'll focus on scanning and managing files. As you progress through the book, you'll learn a host of image-editing techniques.

Scanning

Using a scanning device and scanning software, slides, flat artwork (e.g., drawings), and photographs can be digitized (translated

(Continued on the following page)

into numbers) so they can be read, displayed, edited, and printed by a computer. You can scan directly into Photoshop, or you can use other scanning software and save the scan in a file format that Photoshop opens.

To produce a high-quality scan for print output, start with as high-quality an original as you can get your hands on. Some scanners will compress an image's dynamic range and increase its contrast, so starting off with a photograph with good tonal range is an important first step. If you're going to scan the photo yourself, set the scanning parameters carefully.

The quality of a scan is partially determined by the quality of the device being used. If you're going to dramatically transform the image in Photoshop (e.g., by applying filters or performing drastic color adjustments), you can get away with using an inexpensive flatbed scanner, which will produce an RGB scan. If you need more accurate color and crisper details, you could scan a transparency using a slide scanner.

For professional-quality print output, a better bet is to have your artwork scanned by an output service provider on either a high-resolution CCD scanner (e.g., the Scitex Smart-Scanner) or a drum scanner. These devices capture a wider dynamic range of color and shade and can optically distinguish subtle differences in luminosity, even in those hard-to-capture shadow areas. High-end scanners usually produce CMYK scans, as well as larger file sizes.

Desktop scanning software basics

Scanning software usually offers most of the options that are discussed below, although the terms may vary from one product to another. The quality and file storage size of a resulting scan can be controlled somewhat by several factors under your control, such as the mode, resolution, scale, and crop size.

Preview: Place your artwork in the scanner, then click Preview, PreScan, or an equivalent button.

3 *300 ppi*

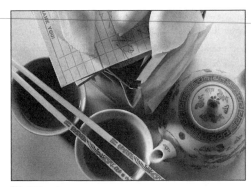
2 *150 ppi*

1 *72 ppi*

Scanning Basics

Scan mode: Choose Black-and-White Line Art (no grays), Grayscale, or Color (choose millions of colors, if available). An image scanned in Color will be approximately three times larger in file size than the same image scanned in Grayscale.

Resolution: Scan resolution is measured in pixels per inch (ppi) (**1**–**3**, previous page). You should choose the minimum resolution necessary to obtain the desired output quality from your target output medium without going overboard, keeping in mind the inherent limitations of that medium. High-resolution images contain more pixels, and thus greater detail, but also have larger file sizes. Large images take longer to render onscreen, require more processing time for edits, and take longer to print or display on the Web. On the other hand, an image with too low a resolution will look coarse and jagged, and will lack sufficient detail.

Before selecting a resolution for print output, ask your print shop what printer or imagesetter resolution and halftone screen frequency they're going to use. (The scan resolution is different from the resolution of the output device.) As a general rule, for a grayscale image, the resolution should be one-and-a-half times the halftone-screen frequency (lines per inch) of your target output device, or twice the halftone-screen frequency for a color image. Use a high scanning resolution (600 ppi or higher) for line art. For example, if your commercial printer is going to use a 133-line screen for black-and-white printing, enter 200 ppi as your scan resolution. To calculate the appropriate file size for a scan, see page 63.

If you're using an ink-jet printer, make the scan resolution 200 ppi or higher.

Cropping: If you're planning to use only part of an image, reposition the handles of the bounding box in the preview area to reduce the scan area. Cropping can significantly reduce the storage size of a scan.

Scale: To enlarge an image's dimensions, choose a scale percentage above 100%.

(Continued on the following page)

Scanning Basics

Bear in mind, though, that enlarging an image or increasing its resolution in Photoshop or any other software program may make it look blurry because the program uses mathematical "guesswork" (interpolation) to fill in additional information. An image's original information is only recorded at the time of scanning!

Scan: Click Scan and choose a location in which to save the file.

16-bits-per-channel mode

Run-of–the-mill, average-quality scanners can capture 10 bits of accurate data per channel from an image, whereas high-end scanners can capture up to 16 bits of accurate data per channel. Scanners that can capture a wide dynamic color range and have a good optical density (at least 3.3) produce scans with finer subtleties of color and shade—even in those tricky shadow areas. Starting off with those extra pixels of data can help mitigate the slight reduction in quality that images suffer when they're edited in Photoshop.

Photoshop can open CMYK or RGB files that contain up to 16 bits per channel (a total of 64 bits for an image that contains four channels); the image's original pixel information is preserved. Except for the restrictions listed below, such images can be edited and adjusted in Photoshop.

- Most of the filters on the Blur, Noise, Sharpen, Stylize, and Other submenus on the Filter menu are available, whereas filters on the other submenus are not.

- The Art History brush isn't available (sorry, Van Gogh wannabes).

- **NEW** 16-bits-per-channel files can be saved in only these formats: Photoshop (.psd), Large Document (.psb), Photoshop PDF (.pdf), Photoshop RAW (.raw), PNG (.png), TIFF (.tif), and Cineon (.cin, .sdpx, .dpx, .fido).

Note: For print output, find out if your output service provider needs you to convert your 16-bit image into an 8-bit image (Image > Mode > 8 Bits/Channel).

16-Bit Mode

Scanning into ImageReady

The first time you choose a scanning module from the File > Import submenu in ImageReady, choose **Twain Select,** choose a Twain device (the scanner), click OK, then choose Twain Acquire.

Thereafter, to access the scanning software, just choose File > Import > **Twain Acquire** directly. For information about scanning modules, see Photoshop Help.

To **scan** into Photoshop, the scanner's plug-in or Twain module must first be installed in your system. For installation instructions, see the documentation that came with your scanner. If your scanner doesn't have a Photoshop-compatible scanner driver, you can scan your image outside Photoshop instead, save it as a TIFF, and then open it in Photoshop as you would any other image.

To calculate the proper resolution for a scan, follow the instructions on the next page.

To scan into Photoshop:

1. Choose File > Import, then choose a scanning module or a Twain scanning device.

2. Click Prescan or Preview **1**.

3. Following the guidelines outlined on the previous two pages, choose a scan mode and a resolution. Other options may be available, depending on the scanning software you're using.

4. *Optional:* Choose a different scaling or magnification percentage and/or manually crop the image preview.

5. Click Scan. The scanned image will appear in a new, untitled window.

6. Save the image (see pages 83–85). If it requires color correction, see pages 462–466. If it needs to be straightened out, see the tip on page 104. Also read about the Crop and Straighten Photos command on page 99.

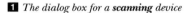
1 *The dialog box for a **scanning** device*

Scan into Photoshop

The **resolution** of a Photoshop image, like that of any bitmapped image, is independent of the monitor's resolution, so it can be customized for a particular output device, with or without modifying its file storage size.

Note: It's always best to scan an image at or very close to the size and resolution required for your target output device.

To calculate the proper resolution for print output:

1. Create a new document (File > New), enter the target Width and Height dimensions, choose 72 pixels/inch for the image Resolution, choose RGB Color Mode, then click OK. (Stay tuned: The resolution will be readjusted in step 5.)

2. Choose Image > Image Size.

3. Click Auto on the right side of the dialog box. The Auto Resolution dialog box opens **1**.

4. Enter the Screen frequency of your target output device, that is, the lpi, or lines per inch setting to be used by your desktop or commercial printer.

5. Click Quality: Draft (1x screen frequency), Good (1½x screen frequency), or Best (2x screen frequency).

6. Click OK.

7. Jot down the Document Size: Resolution value. That's the value you should enter when you scan your image. *Note:* If you're going to scale the image up or down in Photoshop, multiply the resolution by that scale factor to arrive at the proper resolution for scannning (e.g., if you're going to shrink the image by half, divide the resolution value by 2). You don't need to multiply the resolution if you're going to scale the original image when you scan it.

8. Now that you've gotten the information you need, click Cancel.

TIP An image whose resolution is greater than the monitor's resolution will appear larger than its print size when displayed in Photoshop at 100% view.

Resolution for Web graphics

When creating an image for Web output, you need to estimate how large your user's browser window is likely to be, and then figure out how much of that window you want your image to cover. Nowadays, most viewers are likely to have their browser window open to around 800 x 600 pixels. After subtracting the space taken up by menu bars, scroll bars, and other controls that are part of the browser interface, you're left with a "canvas" of approximately 740 x 460 pixels, at most. Given that for most viewers the browser window doesn't fill the entire screen, you can count on only about **660 x 420** pixels.

You might find it helpful to create a blank document at a 660 x 420-pixel size (and a resolution of 72 pixels per inch) to use as a template. Keep it in the background while you work, so as you create the actual images for your Web page, you can see what portion of the screen they'll cover. (Don't fret over the inch equivalent for pixels—onscreen imagery is measured in pixels.)

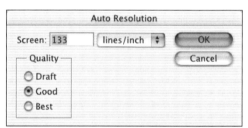

1 *Use the **Auto Resolution** dialog box to have Photoshop calculate the appropriate resolution for an image based on your chosen print output parameters.*

File storage sizes of scanned images

Size (In inches)	PPI (Resolution)	Black/White 1-Bit	Grayscale 8-Bit	RGB Color 24-Bit
2 x 3	150	17 KB	132 KB	436 KB
	300	67 KB	528 KB	1.66 MB
4 x 5	150	56 KB	440 KB	1.39 MB
	300	221 KB	1.72 MB	5.44 MB
8 x 10	150	220 KB	1.72 MB	5.44 MB
	300	879 KB	6.87 MB	21.64 MB

Note: These file storage sizes are for a one-layer TIFF file with no alpha channels.

Potential gray levels at various output resolutions and screen frequencies (print output)

Output Resolution (dpi)	Screen Frequency (lpi)				
	60	85	100	133	150
300	26	13			
600	101	51	37	21	
1270	256*	224	162	92	72
2540		256*	256*	256*	256*

Note: Ask your commercial printer what screen frequency (lpi) you will need to specify when imagesetting your file. Also ask your output service provider what resolution (dpi) to use for imagesetting. Some imagesetters can achieve resolutions above 2540 dpi. Note that as the line screen frequency (lpi) goes up at a constant dpi, the number of gray levels goes down.

*PostScript Level 2 printers produce a maximum of 256 gray levels, whereas PostScript Level 3 printers can produce more.

Status Bar; Storage Size

Using the status bar

In Windows, choose Window > Status Bar to display or hide the status bar.

In Windows and Mac:

When **Document Sizes** is chosen from the status bar pop-up menu at the bottom of the application/image window, the status bar displays the file storage size for the flattened file (the first amount) and the file storage size for the layered file (the second amount) .

When **Document Profile** is chosen, the embedded color profile is listed; the words "Untagged [RGB or CMYK]" appear when no profile is present.

When **Document Dimensions** is chosen, the dimensions of the image are displayed, in the currently selected units.

When **Scratch Sizes** is chosen, the bar displays the amount of storage space Photoshop is using for all currently open pictures (on the left) and the amount of RAM currently available to Photoshop (on the right). When the first amount is greater than the second amount, it means Photoshop is currently using virtual memory on the scratch disk.

When **Efficiency** is chosen, the bar displays the percentage of processing time that's currently being devoted to actual program operations in RAM. A percentage below 100 indicates the scratch disk is being used.

When **Current Tool** is chosen, the name of the currently chosen tool displays.

Press and hold on the status bar to display the page **preview,** which is a thumbnail of the image relative to the current paper size (including custom printing marks, if any).

To find out an image's storage size:

In Windows, use Windows Explorer to locate the file you're interested in, and look in the Size column 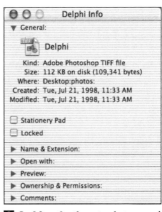. Or for a more accurate figure, right-click the file icon and click Properties.

In Mac, look at the file information in the Finder. Or for a more accurate figure, click once on the file icon in the Finder, then choose File > Get Info (Cmd-I) .

Do this any time

Regardless of which option is chosen from the status bar pop-up menu, you can Alt-press/Option-press on the status bar to display the image's dimensions, number of channels, mode, and resolution.

1 *The status bar with **Document Sizes** chosen: The figure on the left is the RAM required for the flattened image with no extra channels; the figure on the right is the RAM required for the image with layers and extra channels, if any. Note: If the status bar isn't visible, make the image window wider; it should appear.*

2 *In Windows, image sizes are listed in the **Size** column.*

3 *In Mac, for the actual **storage size** of an image, use **Get Info** (Cmd-I).*

To create a new image:

1. Choose File > New (Ctrl-N/Cmd-N).

2. Enter a name in the Name field **1**.

3. Choose a unit of measure from the pop-up menu next to the Width field; the **NEW** same unit will be chosen automatically for the Height. Or hold down Shift while choosing a unit to change the value for that dimension only. Next, enter Width and Height values; or position the **NEW** pointer over the word "Width" and drag to the left or right to choose a value, then do the same for the Height.

   or

   NEW To choose a preset size, choose from the Preset pop-up menu. The Default Photoshop Size is illustrated below. The preset sizes are grouped as follows: paper sizes for print, print sizes for photos, monitor sizes (in pixels), video output sizes, and European print sizes. For more about the presets, see page 67.

4. Enter the Resolution required for your target output device—whether it's an imagesetter or the Web (resolution issues are discussed on pages 59 and 62). **NEW** You can position the pointer over the word "Resolution," then drag to the left or right to choose a value.

5. Choose an image mode from the Color **NEW** Mode pop-up menu, then, from the adjacent pop-up menu, choose 8 bit or 16 bit for the color depth. You can convert the image to a different mode later (see "Image modes" on pages 35–37).

6. Note the Image Size listed on the right side of the dialog box. If you need to reduce that size, you can choose smaller dimensions, a lower resolution, or a lower bit depth.

7. For the Background of the image, choose Background Contents: White or Background Color. To choose a Background color, see pages 183–187. Or choose Transparent if you want the bottommost tier of the image to be a layer. **NEW**

8. *Optional:* When you click the Advanced arrowhead, the Color Profile pop-up menu becomes available. You can assign a Color Profile here and now, or you can do it later via Image > Mode > Assign

(Continued on the following page)

1 *In the **New** dialog box, enter a Name and choose a Preset size or enter Width, Height, and Resolution values. Also choose a Color Mode and your Background Contents.*

Create a New Image

Profile. The available profiles will vary depending on which Color Mode you've chosen. For more about color profiles, see pages 49–50 and 54.

For Web or print output, choose Square as the Pixel Aspect Ratio; for video output, choose one of the other options. For more information, see Photoshop Help.

9. Click OK. An image window will appear onscreen ◼▬◼.

TIP To have the New dialog box settings **NEW** match those of another open document, with the New dialog box open, from the bottom of the Preset pop-up menu, choose the name of the image that has the desired dimensions.

TIP If the current Clipboard contents originated from Photoshop or Illustrator, the New dialog box will automatically display its dimensions. Another way of getting those dimensions to show up in the New **NEW** dialog box is by choosing Clipboard from the Preset pop-up. If you want to prevent those dimensions from displaying, hold down Alt/Option as you choose File > New.

Photoshop Big **NEW**

In Photoshop, you can create and save files as large as 300,000 x 300,000 pixels, or over 2 gigabytes (GB), and files can contain up to 56 user-created channels. Huge files can be saved in the **Large Document** (.psb) format, a new format that's specially designed to handle large documents. Images in this format can be opened and edited only in Photoshop CS.

So what are we supposed to do with these files, we ask? Well, as Victor, our technical editor, points out, 30,000 x 30,000 pixels is the largest file size that can be printed. So if you have the space to store and work with PSB files, great, but you'll have to drastically lower the resolution in order to output them (copy the file first, of course!).

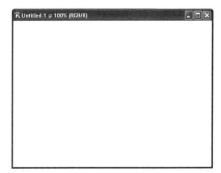

◼ *A **new**, untitled image window in Windows*

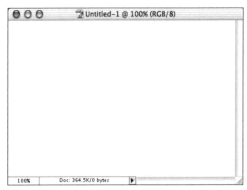

◼ *A **new**, untitled image window in Mac*

If you tend to use certain document sizes, color modes, or other settings repeatedly, it's worth your while to create **document presets** that contain those settings. This will lessen your startup time when you create new files.

To create a document preset: NEW

1. Open the New dialog box (Choose File > New or press Ctrl-N/Cmd-N).

2. Choose the desired settings in the dialog box, such as width, height, resolution, color mode, bit depth, background contents, and profile. For any setting that you don't want included in the preset, simply don't choose a value for it; you'll be able to exclude it from the preset in step 5.

3. Click Save Preset. The New Document Preset dialog box opens **1**.

4. Enter a name in the Preset Name field.

5. In the Include In Saved Settings area, uncheck the New dialog box settings you *don't* want included in the preset.

6. Click OK. The preset will appear on the Preset pop-up menu in the New dialog box.

TIP To delete a user-created preset, choose it from the Preset pop-up menu, click Delete Preset, then click Yes (this can't be undone).

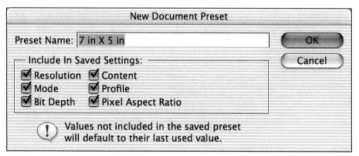

1 *Use the* **New Document Preset** *dialog box to control which of the current settings in the New dialog box will be saved in your preset.*

Create Document Presets

Using the File Browser

The File Browser enables you to view, rotate, and open your Photoshop files using thumbnails instead of just file names **1**. You can also use this palette to locate, learn about, sort, rename, move, batch-process, and delete files. In the beefed up File **NEW** Browser in Photoshop CS, you'll see some new buttons, a menu bar, and four palettes. (The File Browser pane in the Preferences dialog box also has some new options.) With its new bells and whistles, the File Browser is a powerhouse tool and should be your primary vehicle for opening files.

To open the File Browser:

Choose Window > File Browser.
or
Choose File > Browse (Ctrl-Shift-O/ Cmd-Shift-O).
or
Click the File Browser button on the **NEW** options bar. You can toggle the File Browser open and closed by clicking this button.

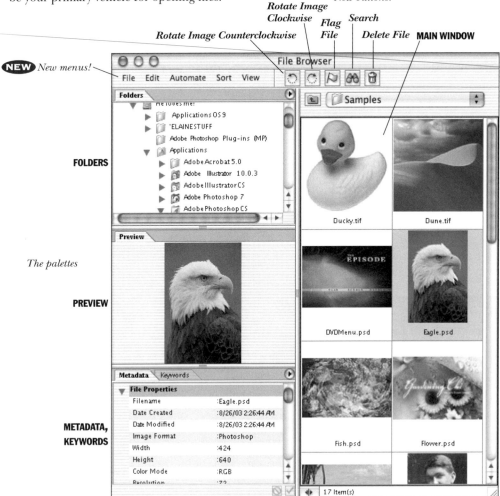

1 *You can use the **File Browser** to locate, sort, open, move, rename, and even delete files.*

The File Browser palettes

On the left side of the File Browser are four palettes, each with its own folder tab. (Adobe calls them palettes, so we are too, even though they don't behave quite like the other palettes in Photoshop.) The main window, where multiple image thumbnails are displayed, is on the right side.

The **Folders** palette contains a scroll window with a hierarchical listing of the top-level and nested folders on your hard drive.

The **Preview** palette displays a preview of the currently selected file thumbnail.

The **Metadata** palette has three sections. **NEW** The File Properties section lists such info as the currently selected image name, date created, format, color mode, and resolution.

The Description, Author, and Copyright fields in the IPTC section are editable (note the pencil icon). When you enter or modify file description information here, it updates in the Description and Origin panels of the File Info dialog box, and vice versa.

If a file was imported from a digital camera, the Camera Data (Exif) section will list image information recorded by the camera.

For more information about the Metadata palette, see Photoshop Help.

Using the **Keywords** palette, you can catego- **NEW** rize images by assigning keywords to them. Then you'll be able to display image thumbnails based on keywords (see the sidebar on page 77 and the Photoshop Help file).

TIP You can't drag any of the palettes (Folders, Preview, Metadata, or Keywords) out of the File Browser.

The **main** window on the right side of the File Browser displays image thumbnails as well as any nested folders within the currently selected folder. Choose a thumbnail size from the View menu in the upper left corner of the File Browser. In Details view (**1**, next page), for example, you'll see an image thumbnail and some of the metadata information for each image in the selected folder.

Choose Folders from the View menu in the File Browser to have both images and folders display in the main window; turn this option off to display only image thumbnails (no folders). To reveal the contents of a nested folder, double-click its thumbnail.

TIP To learn more about an image, rest the pointer over its thumbnail—a tool tip will appear **1** (not available in Details view).

1 *Rest the pointer over a thumbnail to learn more about that image, such as its path, file format, etc.*

You can **customize** the File Browser palette to your liking—a little more of this, a little less of that.

NEW **To customize the File Browser:**

Do any of the following:

- Double-click the Folder, Preview, Metadata, or Keywords folder tab to minimize/redisplay that palette.

- Change the palette groupings by dragging any folder tab.

- Drag a horizontal bar to make a palette taller or shorter. The other palettes will resize automatically.

- Drag the vertical bar to the left or right to adjust the width of all the palettes **1**.

- To have the main window fill the entire File Browser, click the Toggle Expanded View button at the bottom of the File Browser. Click the button again to redisplay the palettes.

> ## Custom custom
> The current sizes of the File Browser palettes and of the overall File Browser window can be saved as an individual **workspace** so you don't have to set them up all over again each time you launch Photoshop. See page 13.

Customize the File Browser

The main window is being displayed in Details view.

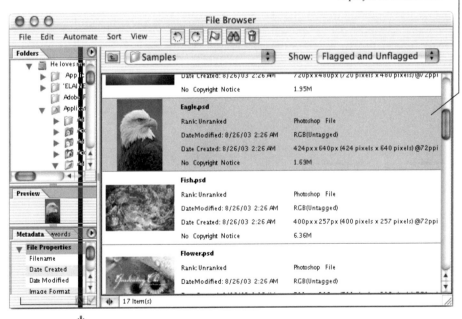

1 *The vertical bar is being moved to the left to **enlarge** the main window.*

Open/close the File Browser (NEW)

To bring the File Browser to the front of all open image windows, click in the File Browser window or the File Browser button 🖳 on the options bar **1**. Click the button again when you're ready to close the File Browser.

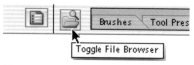

1 *You can open and close the File Browser by clicking this button on the options bar.*

2 *File menu*

The File Browser menus (NEW)

At the top of the File Browser are five menus. Some of the commands on these menus are also found on Photoshop's main menu, and some are unique to the File Browser.

- Use File menu **2** commands to search for, access File Info for, open, delete, and cache files. You can use File Browser > File > Edit in ImageReady to open a selected file directly into that program.

- Use Edit menu **3** commands to select, rotate, or assign flags or ranking categories to thumbnails, and to specify preferences for the File Browser panes.

- Use the Automate menu **4** to access some of the commands that are also found on the File > Automate submenu in Photoshop (see Chapter 22).

- Choose a Sort menu command **5** to control the order in which thumbnails display in the main window.

- Use View menu commands **6** to control whether flagged or unflagged files display in the main window, to control the size of thumbnails in the main window, and to update the palette.

Menus in the File Browser

3 *Edit menu*

4 *Automate menu*

5 *Sort menu*

6 *View menu*

The number of images that can be **open** at a time depends on currently available RAM and scratch disk space.

To open files via the File Browser:

1. Locate an image file by using the Folders palette in the File Browser. You can scroll upward or downward, expand or collapse any folder using the arrowheads or by double-clicking, or open a folder by clicking its icon.

To move up in the folder hierarchy, click the Up One Level button or use the location pop-up menu at the top of the main window.

2. Click a thumbnail for an image file. A blue frame will appear around it. Its preview will appear on the Preview palette, and file data will appear on the Metadata and Keyword palettes. If you need to dig down one more level, click a folder icon in the main window, then click an image thumbnail.

or

Ctrl-click/Cmd-click multiple nonconsecutive thumbnails **1**. Or click the first thumbnail in a series of consecutive thumbnails, then Shift-click the last.

3. Double-click a thumbnail (or one of several selected thumbnails).

or

Press Ctrl-O/Cmd-O.

or

Choose Open from the File menu in the File Browser.

TIP By default, the File Browser stays open even after it's used for opening a file. To have the palette close when you open a file, Alt-double-click/Option-double-click the image thumbnail.

TIP If you move, add, or rename files in the Finder, you can update the current listing of files and folders in the File Browser by choosing Refresh (F5) from the Folders palette menu or from the View menu in the File Browser. The File Browser also updates automatically if you close and then reopen it.

> ### The real thing
> To locate an "actual" file in the Explorer/Finder, click a thumbnail in the File Browser, then choose **Reveal Location in Explorer/Reveal Location in Finder** from the View menu in the File Browser. The file's folder will open as a window in Explorer/Finder; in Mac, the icon will also be highlighted.

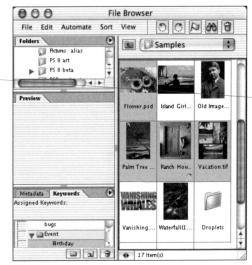

1 *Ctrl-click/Cmd-click to select nonconsecutive multiple thumbnails.*

Playing favorites

If you return to the same folder again and again, you can access it quickly by adding it to a list of favorites. Locate the folder via the Folders palette or via the location pop-up menu in the main window, then choose File > **Add Folder to Favorites** in the File Browser (if the command is dimmed, it means the folder was already designated as a favorite). The folder will be listed in the Favorite Folders section of the location pop-up menu and in the Favorites section on the Folder palette.

To remove a selected folder from the list, choose **Remove Folder from Favorites.**

bald eagle.psd

Rank: nature

1 *A* **flag** *appears in the lower right corner of the thumbnail.*

bald eagle.psd

Rank: nature

2 *Be careful what you ask for.*

You can **flag** files to quickly sort them into two groups.

To flag files: **NEW**

1. Select one or more thumbnails in the main window. Ctrl-click/Cmd-click multiple nonconsecutive thumbnails or click the first thumbnail in a series of consecutive thumbnails, then Shift-click the last.

2. Click the Flag File button 🏴 at the top of the main window (or uncheck the button to unflag the file).
   or
   Press Ctrl-'/Cmd-'. This command toggles the flag on and off.

   A flag icon appears in the bottom right corner of all flagged thumbnails **1**.

3. From the View menu at the top of the File Browser or the Show pop-up menu on the upper right side of the File Browser, choose Flagged Files, Unflagged Files, or Flagged and Unflagged Files, depending on what you want to display.

TIP From the Edit menu in the File Browser, choose Select All Flagged (Ctrl-Shift-A/Cmd-Shift-A) to select all flagged files in the current folder. (Select All selects all files in the folder, flagged and unflagged.)

If you **rotate** a thumbnail in the File Browser, Photoshop will rotate the image when it opens the file!

To rotate a thumbnail:

1. Click a thumbnail.

2. Click the Rotate Counter-Clockwise button 🔄 or Rotate Clockwise button 🔄 at the top of the File Browser.
   or
   From the Edit menu in the File Browser, **NEW** choose Rotate 180°, Rotate 90° CW (Ctrl-]/Cmd-]), or Rotate 90° CCW (Ctrl-[/Cmd-[).

3. If a warning prompt appears, click OK. If the prompt irritates you, also click "Don't Show Again." **2**

4. *Optional:* Choose Edit > Apply Rotation **NEW** if you want to apply the rotation to the actual image without opening it.

NEW **To search for a file using the File Browser:**

1. Choose File > Search in the File Browser.
   or
   Click the Search button 👓 (cute!) at the top of the File Browser.

2. In the Search dialog box **1**, choose a folder to search through from the "Look in" pop-up menu. If you need to navigate to a different folder, click Browse, locate the folder, then click Choose. Check Include All Subfolders to search all subfolders within the designated folder, or uncheck this option to search only the current folder.

3. From the pop-up menus in the Criteria area, choose search criteria (e.g., date created, file type, flag, rank), and enter data in the adjoining field(s). If you need additional criteria fields, click the plus sign button. ⊕

4. Click Search. The results will display on the Folders palette in a temporary folder called Search Results, which will remain there until either another search operation is conducted or you exit/quit Photoshop.

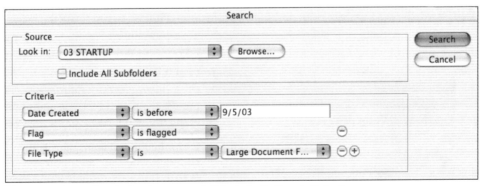

1 *Choose a Source (location) and enter search Criteria in the **Search** dialog box.*

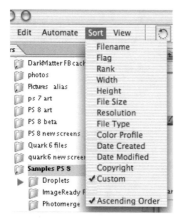

1 *Choose a sorting method from the* **Sort** *menu in the File Browser.*

2 *Type a numeral, letter, or word in the* **Rank** *field below a thumbnail.*

3 *To apply a category to multiple selected thumbnails at once, type a numeral, letter, or word in the* **Rank Files** *dialog box.*

There are several ways that thumbnails can be sorted or **rearranged** in the main window. This is especially important if you use batch or automate operations, as these commands process files based on the current order of the thumbnails. First, the straightforward, manual approach.

To arrange thumbnails manually: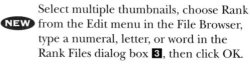

Drag a thumbnail or thumbnails to any location in the main window. The thumbnails will remain in the new order unless you perform a sorting operation.

Choosing an appropriate **sorting** order (Date Created, Date Modified, etc.) can help you locate the image you need, especially when fishing through a lot of files.

To apply a sorting method:

1. Select a folder in the File Browser that contains images.

2. Choose a sorting method from the Sort menu in the File Browser **1**. Also decide whether you want to leave Ascending Order checked on this menu. With this option unchecked, files will be sorted in descending order.

If you want to prioritize the order in which files display in the File Browser, try creating your own **ranking** system.

To create a custom ranking system:

1. Make sure Large Thumbnail is chosen from the View menu in the File Browser, then choose Show Rank from the same menu.

2. Click next to the term "Rank:" below a thumbnail, then type a numeral, letter, or word (e.g., "roughs," "finals," "Web") **2**. To accept the entry, press Enter/Return or click elsewhere in the File Browser.
   or
   Select multiple thumbnails, choose Rank from the Edit menu in the File Browser, type a numeral, letter, or word in the Rank Files dialog box **3**, then click OK.

(Continued on the following page)

Arrange, Sort, Rank in File Browser

3. To activate your custom ranking method, choose Rank from the Sort menu. Categories display in alphanumeric order. (Choose Show Rank from the View menu if you want to turn it off.)

To rename a file via the File Browser:

1. Click a file name below a thumbnail. The text to the left of the period will become highlighted automatically.

2. Enter a new name **1**. Don't try to delete the extension (it won't go away). To accept the entry, press Enter/Return or click outside the name field.

TIP To quickly move from one file name (or rank) field to the next, press Tab.

To create a folder via the File Browser:

1. Open the desired drive or folder that you want the new folder to appear in.

2. Choose New Folder from the File menu in the File Browser, type a name, then press Enter/Return.

TIP You can drag a file from the main window into the Folders palette to move it to another folder or to the Desktop. Alt-drag/Option-drag a thumbnail to add a copy of the file to another folder.

To delete a file via the File Browser:

1. Drag a thumbnail to the Delete File button at the top of the File Browser palette.
   or
   Click a thumbnail, then press Backspace/Delete or click the Delete File button. (Or to delete multiple files, Ctrl-click/Cmd-click multiple thumbnails first; or click the first in a series of thumbnails, then Shift-click the last in the series.)

2. Click Yes.

TIP You can also delete a file or files by choosing File > Delete in the File Browser. Snore.

TIP You can't delete a folder that contains files, but you can delete an empty one.

Drop in!
You can drag and drop an image thumbnail from the File Browser into an open **email** message or attachment window!

1 *In the File Browser, you can change a file's **name** but not its extension.*

Assigning keywords NEW

Keywords are names that are used to categorize picture content. They are used by file search programs to locate files and by file management programs to organize them. You can assign keywords to a file using the **Keywords** palette in the File Browser.

A few default categories are already listed on the palette, but you're by no means limited to what's there. You can create your own keyword line or keyword grouping (called a "set") by using commands on the Keywords palette menu. Then, to assign a keyword to an image, click an image thumbnail and click next to a keyword category to make a check mark appear.

You can use the Rename command on the Keywords palette menu to rename a keyword category, or use the Delete command to remove a category.

TIP If you select multiple image thumbnails in the main window, any keywords that you check on the Keywords palette (and any data that you enter into the editable IPTC fields on the Metadata palette) will be applied to all the selected images.

When a folder is displayed in the File Browser, a separate **cache** file is created containing information (e.g., thumbnail data, metadata, rank, rotation) about all the files in that folder. This helps to speed up the redisplay of thumbnails if you redisplay the folder later on.

In Windows, the cache files are stored in C:\Document and Settings\[user]\Application Data\Adobe\FileBrowser\Photoshop CS.

In Mac, the cache files are stored in Users/[username]/Library/Application Support/Adobe/FileBrowser/Photoshop CS.

To export a File Browser cache:

1. Use the File Browser to open the folder that contains the images in question and customize any of the thumbnails (e.g., flag, rotation, rank, metadata).

2. Choose Export Cache from the File menu in the File Browser. Three cache files—named AdobePS8M.md0 (a metadata cache) and AdobePS8P.tb0 and Adobe P8T.tb0 (thumbnail caches)—will be placed into whichever folder is currently selected in the File Browser. When you copy image files to removable disks or to a shared folder on a network, copy the cache files, too, to help speed up the display of thumbnails.

   Note: The cache files are visible in Explorer in Windows and in the Finder in Mac OS X, but not in Photoshop.

The **Purge** commands delete ranking, flag, and thumbnail information (the data that's used for generating image thumbnails in the File Browser).

To delete the cache files:

To remove the three caches from the current folder, choose File > Purge Cache in the File Browser.
or
To remove all caches from all folders in the location listed above, choose File > Purge Entire Cache in the File Browser.

File Browser Cache

Other ways to open files

With the File Browser now taking center stage, the **Open** command is relegated to being a bit player, for occasional use only.

To use the Open command:

1. Choose File > Open (Ctrl-O/Cmd-O).

2. Locate the file you want to open (Win) **1**/(Mac) **2**. Choose a specific format from the Files of type/Show drop-down menu, or choose All Formats/All Readable Documents.

Note: If the name of the file you want to open isn't available on the scroll list, it may be because the plug-in module for its format isn't installed in the Photoshop Plug-Ins folder. Install the plug-in, then try again.

Once opened, an image can be resaved in any of the available formats in Photoshop.

3. Click the file name, then click Open.
or
Double-click the file name.

Got a profile mismatch? See page 51.

For some file formats, a further dialog box will open. For example, if you open an EPS, Adobe Illustrator, or PDF file that requires a conversion from vector to bitmap, the Rasterize Generic [　] Format dialog box will open; follow steps 3–8 on pages 80–81.

TIP To open an Adobe Illustrator file in Photoshop, follow the instructions on page 80 or 82.

TIP Special plug-in modules must be used to open images in some file formats, such as Scitex CT or PICT Resource (access them via File > Import).

To switch between open documents:

Click in a document window.
or
NEW Choose a document name from the bottom of the Window menu.
or
To cycle among open documents, press Ctrl-Tab/Control-Tab.

1 *Double-click a file name in* **Windows.**

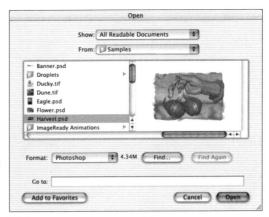

2 *Double-click a file name in* **Mac.**

Open Command; Switch Between Documents

Do it again

To reopen a file that was recently worked on and then closed, choose that file's name from the File > **Open Recent** submenu.

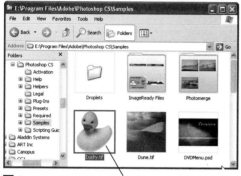

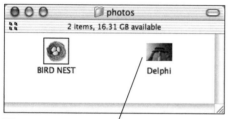

1 *Double-click a Photoshop file icon in **Windows**.*

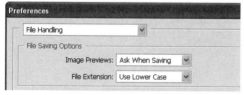

2 *Double-click a Photoshop file icon in **Mac**.*

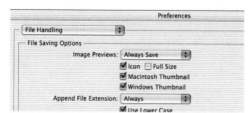

3 *In **Windows**, in Preferences > File Handling, choose **Image Previews: Always Save**.*

4 *In **Mac**, in Preferences > File Handling, choose **Image Previews: Always Save** or **Ask When Saving**.*

To open a Photoshop image from Windows Explorer:

Double-click a Photoshop image file icon in Windows Explorer **1**. Photoshop will launch if it hasn't already been launched.

To open a Photoshop image from the Finder in Mac:

Double-click a Photoshop image file icon in the Finder **2**. Photoshop will launch if it hasn't already been launched.

To create image thumbnails:

In Windows, to create image icons for Windows Explorer that will display when the Views menu is set to Large Icon, click the Save Thumbnail check box for individual files as you save them. To create thumbnails of all subsequently saved images for display in the Open dialog box, choose Edit > Preferences > File Handling, then choose Image Previews: Always Save **3**. A thumbnail icon will appear only for images that have a .psd, .psb, .jpg, .png, or .tif file extension.

In Mac, to have Photoshop create an icon automatically for each image for display in the Finder, choose Photoshop > Preferences > File Handling, choose Image Previews: Always Save, then check Icon **4**.

Or in Windows and Mac, you can choose Image Previews: Ask When Saving instead to create icons on a file-by-file basis (Image Preview check boxes will display at the bottom of the Save and Save As dialog boxes). To create image icons for display in the Open dialog box, check Macintosh Thumbnail and/or Windows Thumbnail.

Open File from Explorer, Finder; Create Thumbnails

When an EPS or Adobe Illustrator file is opened or placed in Photoshop, it is rasterized, meaning it's converted from its native vector format into Photoshop's pixel format. Follow these instructions to **open** an EPS or Illustrator file as a new file, or follow the instructions on page 82 to place an EPS file into an existing Photoshop file.

Note: To open a single-page PDF file in Photoshop, you can use the Open command (this page) or the Place command (page 82). To open a multipage PDF as multiple images in the Photoshop format, choose File > Automate > Multi-Page PDF to PSD (see page 421).

In Photoshop CS, Illustrator 9, 10, and CS files are listed as Generic PDF format, not as EPS.

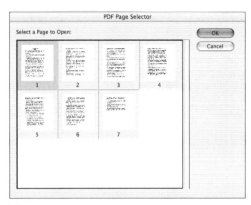

1 *In the* **PDF Page Selector** *dialog box, locate and select the thumbnail for the page you want to open, then click OK.*

To open an EPS, PDF, or Illustrator file as a new image:

1. Open the File Browser, locate the image you want to open, then double-click its thumbnail.
or
Choose File > Open (Ctrl-O/Cmd-O), locate and highlight the file to be opened, then click Open. *Note:* If the file name isn't listed, in Windows, try choosing All Formats from the Files of type drop-down menu; in Mac, choose Show: All Readable Documents.

2. *Note:* If you're opening a PDF that contains more than one page, the PDF Page Selector dialog box will open **1**. Locate and select the thumbnail for the page that you want to open, then click OK.

3. *Optional:* In the Rasterize Generic EPS (or PDF) Format dialog box, check Constrain Proportions to preserve the file's width-to-height ratio **2**.

4. *Optional:* Choose a unit of measure from the pop-up menus next to the Height and Width fields, and enter new dimensions.

5. In the Resolution field, enter the final resolution required for your target

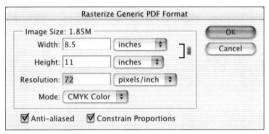

2 *Check Constrain Proportions in the* **Rasterize Generic PDF Format** *dialog box to preserve the file's width-to-height ratio.*

Open EPS, PDF, Illustrator File

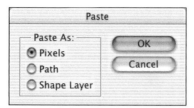

1 *When you paste an object from Illustrator into Photoshop, the **Paste** dialog box opens automatically.*

output device. Entering the correct final resolution now, before the image is rasterized, will produce the best rendering of the image.

6. Choose an image mode from the Mode pop-up menu. (See "Image modes" on pages 35–37.)

7. Check Anti-aliased to reduce jaggies and soften edge transitions.

8. Click OK.

TIP If the PDF contains security settings, those settings must be disabled via Adobe Acrobat before the file can be opened.

TIP PDF and EPS files open with a transparent background. To create a white background for a newly opened file, create a new layer, choose white (or another color) for the Background color, then choose Layer > New > Background From Layer.

To paste from Illustrator

You can copy an object in Adobe Illustrator and then paste it into a Photoshop image; the **Paste** dialog box will open automatically. Click Paste As: Pixels, Path, or Shape Layer **1** (shapes are discussed in Chapter 18). If you choose the Shape Layer option, the resulting vector shape will be editable in Photoshop—not so if you use the Open or Place command to get the object into Photoshop.

Note: For the Paste dialog box to display, in Adobe Illustrator, open the Preferences dialog box, navigate to the File Handling & Clipboard pane, check the Copy As: PDF and AICB options, and also click Preserve Appearance and Overprints.

When you **place** an object-oriented (vector) image into a Photoshop image, it becomes bitmapped, and it's rendered in the resolution of the Photoshop image. The higher the resolution of the Photoshop image, the better the rendering.

Note: Alternatively, you can drag a path from an Illustrator image window into a Photoshop image window; it will appear on a new layer.

To place an EPS, PDF, or Adobe Illustrator image into a Photoshop image:

1. Open a Photoshop image.

2. Choose File > Place.

3. Locate and click the file that you want to open. To place a PDF that contains multiple pages, choose a page, then click OK (see page 80).

4. Click Place. A box will appear in the image window. Pause, if necessary, to allow the image to draw inside it.

5. *Perform any of these optional steps (use the Undo command to undo any of them):*

To resize the placed image, drag a handle of the bounding box. Shift-drag to preserve the proportions of the placed image as you resize it.

To move the placed image, drag inside the bounding box.

To rotate the placed image, position the pointer outside the bounding box (curved pointer ↰), then drag. You can move the center point to rotate the image from a different axis.

6. To accept the placed image, press Enter/Return or double-click inside the bounding box. The placed image will appear on a new layer **1**.

TIP To remove the placed image, press Esc before or while it's rendering. If the image is already rendered, drag its layer into the trash on the Layers palette. Easy come, easy go.

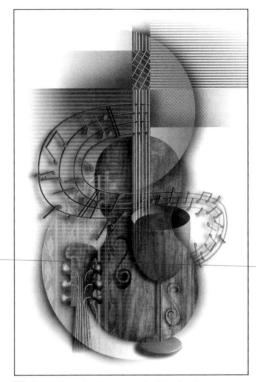

1 *To produce this image, artist **Wendy Grossman** created the musical notes and other shapes in Illustrator and then imported them into Photoshop.*

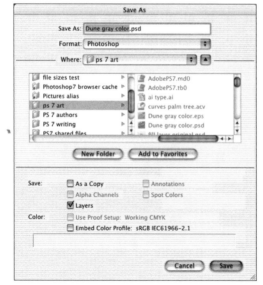

1 *The **Save As** dialog box in **Windows***

2 *The **Save As** dialog box in **Mac OS X***

Saving files

If you're not sure which format to choose when **saving** your file, start with the native Photoshop format, PSD. In Chapter 24, you'll find specific instructions for saving files in the EPS, DCS, PDF, and TIFF formats; in Chapter 25, you'll find information about the GIF, JPEG, and PNG formats.

To save an unsaved image:

1. Choose File > Save (Ctrl-S/Cmd-S).

2. Type a name in the File name **1**/ Save As **2** field.

3. Choose a location for the file.

   In Windows, to locate another folder or drive, click the pop-up menu at the top of the dialog box.

   In Mac, to locate a drive, scroll as far left as possible in the window, then click a drive. To locate a Favorite or Recent folder, use the Where pop-up menu or scroll in the window.

4. Choose a file format from the Format pop-up menu. Only the native Photoshop (PSD), Large Document (PSB), TIFF, and Photoshop PDF formats can save files that contain multiple layers.

5. Check any options in the Save area of the dialog box (except the As a Copy option, which is discussed on page 85). Don't worry, these features are discussed later in the book. You can also check Color: Embed Color Profile: [ ] if the file contains an embedded profile and the format you're saving to supports embedded profiles (see page 54).

6. Click Save.

TIP In Mac, to have a three-character file extension be appended automatically to your files, go to Photoshop > Preferences > File Handling and choose Append File Extension: Always or Ask When Saving. This is essential when exporting Mac OS X files to the Windows platform.

Saving layers, vectors, and effects

Photoshop (PSD), Large Document (PSB), TIFF, and **Photoshop PDF** are the only formats in which the following are preserved:

■ Multiple layers and layer transparency

■ Adjustment layers

■ Editable type layers

■ Layer effects

■ Grids and guides

■ ICC color management profiles (actually, the PICT, JPEG, Photoshop DCS, and Photoshop EPS formats preserve these profiles, too)

■ Lab Color image mode (the Photoshop EPS and Photoshop DCS formats also preserve this mode)

Note: An image in Duotone color mode can be saved only in the native Photoshop, Large Document, Photoshop EPS, or Photoshop PDF formats.

If you're going to export a file to another application, be sure to save a flattened copy of it in another format, as few applications can read Photoshop's layer transparency.

TIP Flatten a copy of a layered image instead of the original (see the following page). That way, you'll preserve your option to rework the original layers later.

The prior version of a file is overwritten each time you choose the **Save** command.

To save an already saved image:

Choose File > Save (Ctrl-S/Cmd-S).

The simple Revert command restores a document to its last-saved version, whereas the History palette, which we discuss in Chapter 8, is a full-service multiple undo feature. Its partner, the History Brush tool, can be used to selectively revert a portion of an image. Revert does show up as a state on the History palette, so you can undo it if need be by clicking an earlier history state.

To revert to the last saved version:

Choose File > Revert.

PSD file compatibility

If, in Edit (Photoshop, in Mac) > Preferences > File Handling, you choose **Maximize PSD File Compatibility: Always,** a flattened version will be saved with each layered image. This is helpful when exporting images to applications that don't read layers. If you prefer to decide on a file-by-file basis whether to have the extra image save with your file, choose Ask from the pop-up menu instead. Each time you use the Save or Save As command, an alert dialog box will appear, and you can decide on the spot whether or not you want the extra image to be included.

What is the Duplicate command?

The Image > **Duplicate** command copies an image and all its layers, layer masks, and channels into currently available memory, but a permanent copy of the file isn't saved to disk unless you then choose File > Save. With Duplicate, you can try out variations without altering the original file, but if an application freeze or a system crash occurs, you'll lose whatever's currently in memory, including your duplicate image! We think it's better to use File > Save As.

1 *The Save As dialog box in Windows*

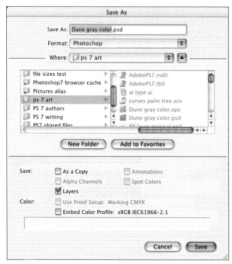

2 *The Save As dialog box in Mac*

Using the **Save As** command, you can save a copy of an image in a different image mode (e.g., save a copy in CMYK Color mode and keep the original version in RGB Color mode). Or you can use Save As to spawn off a design or some other kind of variation.

To save a new version of an image:

1. Choose File > Save As (Ctrl-Shift-S/ Cmd-Shift-S).

2. Change the name in the File name **1**/ Save As **2** field.

3. Choose a location in which to save the new version, using the Save in pop-up menu in Windows or the Where pop-up menu and scroll windows in Mac.

4. *Optional:* Choose a different file format from the Format pop-up menu. Only formats that are available for the current image (color) mode will be available.

   Beware! If the chosen format doesn't support multiple layers, the Layers option will automatically become dimmed, an alert icon will display, and the saved file will be flattened.

5. Check any available options in the Save area, as desired, and also check Embed Color Profile: [profile name], if that option is available (see page 54).

   TIP Check As a Copy to have the copy remain closed and the original stay open. Or leave this option unchecked to do the opposite: have the original close and the new version stay open.

6. Click Save. For an EPS file, follow the instructions on pages 455–456. For a TIFF or PDF file, follow the instructions on pages 458–459. For other formats, see Photoshop Help.

   TIP If you don't change the file name and you click Save, an alert dialog box will appear. Click Replace to save over the original file, or click Cancel to return to the Save As dialog box.

   TIP Explore layer comps on pages 275–277.

Save As

Navigating

In this section you'll learn how to change the zoom level for an image; move an image in its window; switch screen display modes; and display, scroll, or change the zoom level for an image in more than one window.

You can display an entire image in its window or magnify part of an image to work on a small detail. The **zoom level** is indicated as a percentage in three locations: on the image window title bar, in the lower left corner of the application/image window, and in the lower left corner of the Navigator palette. The zoom level of an image has no effect on its output size.

*A portion of the image is **magnified**.*

*If the image is magnified, you can drag the view box on the thumbnail to **move** the image in its window. Ctrl-drag/ Cmd-drag across part of the thumbnail (as in this illustration) to marquee the area you want to **magnify**.*

To change the zoom level using the Navigator palette:

*Enter the desired **zoom percentage** (or ratio, as in 1:1 or 4:1), then press Enter/Return. To zoom to a percentage and keep the field highlighted, press Shift-Enter/Shift-Return.*

Thumbnail

View box

155.34%

*Click the **Zoom out** button to zoom out.*

*Move the **Zoom slider** to change the zoom level.*

*Click the **Zoom in** button to zoom in.*

TIP You can also change the zoom level by double-clicking the zoom percentage field in the lower left corner of the application/image window, typing the desired zoom percentage, and then pressing Enter/Return.

TIP Photoshop trivia: To change the outline color of the view box on the Navigator palette, choose Palette Options from the palette menu, then choose a preset color from the Color pop-up menu, or click the color swatch and choose a color from the Color Picker.

Change Zoom Levels

1 *Choose settings on the Zoom tool options bar.*

Zoom shortcuts

WINDOWS

Zoom in (window doesn't resize)	Ctrl +
Zoom out (window doesn't resize)	Ctrl –
Zoom in (window resizes)	Ctrl Alt +
Zoom out (window resizes)	Ctrl Alt –
Actual pixels/100% view	Ctrl Alt 0
Fit onscreen	Ctrl 0 (zero)

MACINTOSH

Zoom in (window resizes)	Cmd +
Zoom out (window resizes)	Cmd –
Zoom in (window doesn't resize)	Cmd Option +
Zoom out (window doesn't resize)	Cmd Option –
Actual pixels/100% view	Cmd Option 0
Fit onscreen	Cmd 0 (zero)

2 *Click on the image with the Zoom tool to zoom in. Note the plus sign in the pointer.*

3 *Alt-click/Option-click on the image with the Zoom tool to zoom out. Note the minus sign in the pointer.*

To change the zoom level using the Zoom tool:

1. Choose the Zoom tool (Z).

2. *Optional:* On the Zoom tool options bar **1**, uncheck Resize Windows To Fit to prevent the image window from resizing as you zoom in or out. With this option checked, you can check Ignore Palettes to allow the image window to enlarge all the way to the right edge of your screen (palettes will be on top), or uncheck this option to keep the window from enlarging all the way.

3. To **zoom in,** click in the image window **2**, or drag a marquee across an area to magnify that area.
   or
   To **zoom out,** Alt-click/Option-click in the image window **3**.
   or
   To view the image at actual pixel size, click **Actual Pixels** on the options bar. *Note:* The zoom level will equal the actual print size only when the display ratio is 100% and the image resolution is the same as the monitor resolution.
   or
   To display the entire image at the largest possible size that can fit on your screen/ application window, click **Fit On Screen** on the options bar (Ctrl-0/Cmd-0).
   or
   Click **Print Size** on the options bar to display the image at its print size.

   TIP Hold down Ctrl-Spacebar/Cmd-Spacebar and click or drag to zoom in when another tool is chosen or when a dialog box with a Preview option is open. Alt-Spacebar-click/Option-Spacebar-click to zoom out. To have the window resize automatically whenever the zoom level is changed using a keyboard shortcut, check Zoom Resizes Windows in Edit (Photoshop, in Mac OS) > Preferences > General, or uncheck this option to prevent the window from resizing.

Zoom In or Out

To move an image in its window:

Click outside, or drag, the view box on the Navigator palette .

or

Click the up or down scroll arrow on the image window. Or to move the image more quickly, drag a scroll box.

or

Choose the Hand tool (H), ✋ then drag in the image window ❷.

Note: If the scroll bars aren't active, it means the entire image is displayed, and it can't be moved.

TIP Other shortcuts for moving an image in its window are listed on page 542.

To change the screen display mode:

Click the Standard Screen Mode button in the lower left corner of the Toolbox (F) ❸ to display the image, menu bar, and palettes, and the scroll bars on the image window.

or

Click the Full Screen Mode with Menu Bar (middle) button (F) ❹ to display the image at its full size without scroll bars, but with the menu bar and palettes visible. The area around the image will be gray ❻.

or

Click the Full Screen Mode (rightmost) button (F) ❺ to display the full-size image, palettes, and options bar (and also rulers, if they're showing) but not the menu bar or scroll bars. The area around the image will be black (trés dramatique).

TIP Press Tab to show/hide the Toolbox and any open palettes. Or press Shift-Tab to show/hide just the palettes, leaving the Toolbox open.

TIP You can use the Hand tool (H) or the Navigator palette to reposition the **(NEW)** onscreen image when either of the full-screen modes are in effect. (Hold down the Spacebar to use a temporary Hand tool while another tool is selected.)

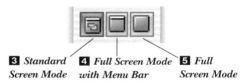

❶ *Click outside, or drag, the view box on the **Navigator** palette to move an image in its window.*

❷ *Or move an image in its window using the **Hand** tool.*

❸ *Standard Screen Mode* ❹ *Full Screen Mode with Menu Bar* ❺ *Full Screen Mode*

*Keep pressing **F** to cycle through the screen modes.*

❻ *Full screen mode with menu bar*

1 *An image displayed in **two windows** simultaneously: one at a low zoom level for previewing, the other at a higher zoom level for editing.*

You can open the same image in **two windows** simultaneously. "Why?" you ask. Well, you could choose a high zoom level, such as 400%, for one window to edit a small detail, and choose a lower zoom level, such as 100%, for the other in order to view the overall image. Or you could leave the image in RGB Color mode in one image window and choose View > Proof Setup > Working CMYK for the same image in the second window. That way, you get the best of both worlds (er, windows). Listings on the History palette will be identical for both windows.

To display one image in two windows:

1. With an image open, choose Window > **NEW** Arrange > New Window for [file name]. The same image will appear in a second window **1**.

2. *Optional:* Move either (or both) windows by dragging the title bar, and/or resize either window by dragging its lower right corner.

This method for **scrolling** or **zooming** is a great time saver when you have several documents open (tiled) or have created multiple windows for the same document.

To scroll or zoom in multiple windows: **NEW**

Hold down Shift while scrolling with the Hand tool or while zooming with the Zoom tool to scroll (or zoom) all open Photoshop document windows.
or
Check Scroll All Windows on the options bar before using the Hand tool, or check Zoom All Windows on the options bar before using the Zoom tool.

TIP If two or more image windows are open, you can choose Window > Arrange > Match Zoom to force all the windows to match the zoom level of the currently active image; or choose Match Location to synchronize the position of all the images in their windows; or choose Match Zoom & Location to perform both functions at once.

One Image, Two Windows; Scroll/Zoom Windows

Ending a work session

To close an image:

Click the Close button in the upper right corner of the image window (Win) **1**/upper left corner of the image window (Mac) **2**.
or
Choose File > Close (Ctrl-W/Cmd-W).

If you attempt to close an image that was modified since it was last saved, a warning prompt will appear **3**. Click Don't Save to close the file without saving; or click Save to save the file before closing; or click Cancel to cancel the close operation.

To exit/quit Photoshop:

Windows: Choose File > Exit (Ctrl-Q) or click the application windows's close box.

Mac: Choose Photoshop > Quit Photoshop (Cmd-Q).

All open Photoshop files will close. If any changes were made to any open file since it was last saved, a prompt will appear **4**. Click Don't Save (or press D) to close the file without saving; or click Save to save the file before exiting/quitting; or click Cancel to cancel the exit/quit operation altogether.

1 *In Windows, click the* **Close** *button in the upper right corner of the image window.*

2 *In Mac, click the* **close** *(red) button in the upper left corner of the image window.*

Victor's tip

Mac users are familiar with the traffic light buttons in the title bar of every window: Red means close, yellow means minimize (to the Dock), and green means zoom (to full size). One of the more obscure features of OS X is a little **dot** that appears in the close button of an image window if the file has been **modified** since it was **last saved.** (From Victor Gavenda, our eagle-eyed technical editor.)

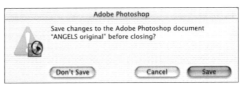

3 *If you attempt to close an image that was modified since it was last saved, this prompt will appear.*

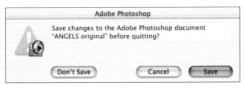

4 *If you exit/quit Photoshop and changes were made to any open file since it was saved, this prompt will appear.*

PIXEL BASICS 4

Copy cat NEW

In dialog boxes that have Width and Height fields, if you choose a unit of measure from the pop-up menu next to the Width field, the same unit will be chosen automatically for the Height, and vice versa. If you want to prevent this from happening, hold down Shift as you choose a unit; the unit will change just for that dimension.

I N THIS CHAPTER you'll learn how to change an image's overall dimensions or resolution; sharpen the image afterward; change an image's canvas size; and crop, flip, and rotate an image.

Changing an image's **dimensions** in Photoshop while preserving its current **resolution** (leaving the Resample Image box checked) involves a process known as resampling, which degrades image quality. To minimize resampling, it's best to scan or create an image at or close to the desired output size, and then if you have to resample, apply the Unsharp Mask filter afterward to resharpen (see pages 96–97).

Changing dimensions and resolution

To change an image's pixel dimensions for onscreen output:

1. Choose Image > Image Size.

2. Make sure Resample Image is checked **1**, then choose an interpolation method from the pop-up menu. The Bicubic methods degrade the image the least but also take longer to process. Bicubic **NEW** Smoother and Bicubic Sharper are new.

3. To preserve the image's width-to-height ratio, leave Constrain Proportions checked.

4. Set the Resolution to 72 pixels/inch (or "ppi" for short).

5. At the top of the dialog box, enter new Pixel Dimensions: Width and/or Height values.

6. Check or uncheck Scale Styles to control **NEW** whether applied styles in the image will be scaled to fit the image's new pixel count (see Chapter 16). Styles are saved combinations of layer effects.

7. Click OK.

1 *The **Image Size** dialog box*

Change Print Dimensions

To change an image's dimensions for print output:

1. Choose Image > Image Size.

2. To preserve the image's width-to-height ratio, check Constrain Proportions; or to modify the image's width independently of its height, uncheck Constrain Proportions.

3. *Optional:* To preserve the image's resolution, check Resample Image, and from the adjacent pop-up menu, choose Nearest Neighbor, Bilinear, Bicubic, **NEW** Bicubic Smoother, or Bicubic Sharper as the interpolation method. The Bicubic methods cause the least degradation in image quality but also take the longest to process.

4. Choose a unit of measure from the pop-up menu next to the Document Size: **NEW** Width field; the same unit will be chosen automatically for the Height. Or to choose two different units instead, hold down Shift as you choose each unit.

5. Enter new Document Size: Width and/or Height values corresponding to the physical dimensions you've chosen for the printed image. The Resolution will change if Resample Image is unchecked.

6. Check or uncheck Scale Styles to control **NEW** whether applied styles (layer effects) in the image will be scaled.

7. Click OK.

TIP To restore the original Image Size settings while the dialog box is still open, Alt-click/Option-click Reset.

TIP You can also use File > Print with Preview to resize or rescale an image's print dimensions, but this command won't preserve the image resolution.

Previewing the print

To preview the image size relative to the paper size, press and hold on the status bar at the bottom of the image window **1**; or choose File > **Print with Preview,** then click Cancel.

To display the image onscreen at the size it will print, choose View > **Print Size.** The onscreen size of an image is determined by the image's pixel dimensions and the monitor size and resolution, whereas the display of an image's print size is determined by its pixel dimensions and resolution, that is, the number of pixels viewed per unit of printed length (usually inches). So for a high-resolution image at a 100% zoom level, choosing View > Print Size will display the image at an approximation of its actual printout size, not necessarily its actual, physical printout size.

1 *To preview the image size relative to the **paper size,** press and hold on the status bar at the bottom of the image window.*

Cash in on a high resolution

An image contains a given number of pixels after scanning, and its Document Size attributes (width, height, and resolution) are interdependent. If an image's Document Size is changed with **Resample Image** unchecked in Image > Image Size, the file's total pixel count is preserved. If you increase an image's pixels-per-inch resolution, its width or height dimensions will shrink, and similarly, if you lower the resolution, the width and height will increase.

If your file's resolution is higher than needed (more than twice the screen frequency), you can allocate the extra resolution to the Document Size by unchecking Resample Image (the width, height, and resolution are now interdependent), and then lowering the resolution to twice the screen frequency. The width and height values will automatically increase, and the file storage size and pixel dimensions will remain constant—no pixels will be added or deleted from the image.

If you must further enlarge the Document Size, check Resample Image, then change the Width value. The Height will change proportionally, and the file storage size and pixel dimensions will increase. The image will be resampled, though, so after clicking OK, apply the Unsharp Mask filter to resharpen.

If you increase an image's **resolution** (resample up) with Resample Image checked, pixels will be added to the image, its file storage size will increase, and its sharpness will diminish. If you decrease an image's resolution (downsample), information will be deleted from the file that can be retrieved only by clicking the initial state on the History palette before closing the image. Blurriness caused by resampling may not be evident until the image is printed; it may not be discernible onscreen. Just one more reason to scan or create an image at the proper resolution. Follow the instructions on pages 96–97 to resharpen a resampled image. (See also pages 59 and 62.)

To change an image's resolution:

1. Choose Image > Image Size.

2. To preserve the image's Document Size (Width and Height), check Resample Image **1** and choose an interpolation method from the pop-up menu.
   or
   To preserve the image's Pixel Dimensions (total pixel count), uncheck Resample Image. The Width and Height dimensions will change in order to preserve the current pixel count.

3. Enter a Resolution value.

4. Click OK.

TIP The History Brush tool won't work on an image that's been resampled (new dimensions chosen with Resample Image checked); you'll be able to set the source for the History Brush tool from only the current state forward.

1 *Check **Resample Image** in the Image Size dialog box to allow resampling, or uncheck this option to prevent resampling.*

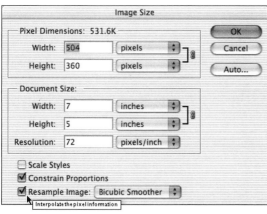

Change Resolution

The **Fit Image** command has no effect on an image's resolution—it only changes its width and height. Use this command to make an image smaller.

To resize an image to fit a specific width or height:

1. Choose File > Automate > Fit Image 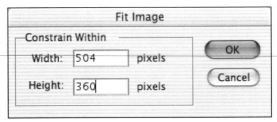.

2. Enter a Width or Height value in pixels. The other field will automatically adjust *after* you click OK, so the width-to-height ratio will stay the same.

3. Click OK.

1 *Use the* **Fit Image** *command to change an image's width and height dimensions while preserving its resolution.*

1 *Click **Print** or **Online**.*

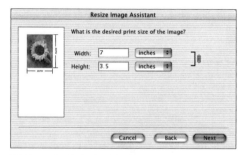

2 *Enter the desired **print size**.*

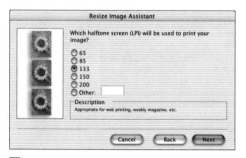

3 *Click or enter the **lpi** that your print shop specifies.*

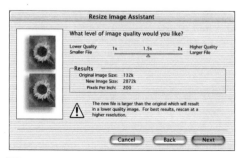

4 *Move the slider to the desired image **quality**.*

The **Resize Image** command duplicates an image and resizes the duplicate automatically. All you have to do is respond to a sequence of dialog boxes—Photoshop will figure out the math for you.

To resize an image automatically:

1. Choose Help > Resize Image.

2. Click Print or Online **1**, then click Next.

3. Enter the desired output dimensions **2**, then click Next. If you chose Online in the previous step, click Finish now. For print output, follow the remaining steps.

4. As per instructions from your commercial printer, either click the appropriate lpi (lines per inch setting) or click Other and enter the desired lpi **3**, then click Next.

5. Move the image quality slider **4**, then note the final image size in the Results area. If a message appears below the Results area, read that as well. If you want to proceed, click Next.

6. Click Finish **5**, and then save the new duplicate, resized image.

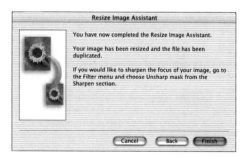

5 *Click **Finish**.*

Resize Image

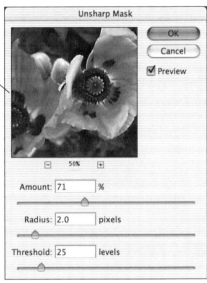

If you change an image's dimensions or resolution with Resample Image checked, convert it to CMYK Color mode, or transform it, blurring may occur due to resampling. You can help correct this by applying the **Unsharp Mask** filter. Despite its name, this filter produces a focusing effect by increasing the contrast between adjacent pixels that already have some contrast. You can specify the amount of contrast to be added (Amount), the number of surrounding pixels that will be modified around each pixel that requires more contrast (Radius), and determine which pixels the filter affects or ignores by specifying the minimum contrast (Threshold).

1 *The original 240 ppi image—a bit blurry*

Note: The Unsharp Mask effect may be more noticeable onscreen than on high-resolution print output.

To apply the Unsharp Mask filter:

1. Choose Filter > Sharpen > Unsharp Mask **1**.

2. Choose an Amount for the percentage increase in contrast between pixels **2**. Use a low setting (less than 50) for figures or natural objects; use a higher setting if the image contains sharp-edged objects. Too high a setting will produce noticeable halos around high-contrast areas (**1**, next page). The larger the image, the less sharpening may be required. For a high-resolution image (say, 250 ppi and higher), try using an Amount between 150 and 200 percent.

3. To choose an appropriate Radius value —which is a bit trickier—you need to factor in the final size, the resolution, and the subject matter of the image. The Radius (0.1–250) controls the number of pixels surrounding high-contrast edges that will be modified (**2**, next page). Try between 1 and 2 pixels. A higher value could produce too much contrast in areas that are already high in contrast.

The higher the resolution of the image, the more pixels there are, and thus the

If you click on the image, that area will display here in the preview window.

2 *When using the **Unsharp Mask** dialog box, start off with conservative Amount, Radius, and Threshold settings.*

1 *After Unsharp Masking with a **high Amount** (160), Radius 1.5, and Threshold 0: Note the halos around the edges and centers of the flowers.*

2 *After Unsharp Masking with a **high Radius** (6.0), Amount 130, and Threshold 0: The soft gradations have become choppy and the image has an unnatural contrast and sharpness.*

3 *After Unsharp Masking with a **high Threshold** (15), Amount 160, and Radius 1.5: Even with the same Amount setting as in the top image, the soft gradations in the petals and the background are preserved.*

higher the Radius setting required. Try a high Radius setting for a low-contrast image and a lower Radius setting for an intricate, high-contrast image.

Note: The higher the Radius setting, the lower the Amount setting can be, and vice versa.

4. Choose a Threshold value (0–255) for the minimum amount of contrast an area must have before it will be modified **3**. At a Threshold value of 0, the filter will be applied to the entire image. A Threshold value above 0 will cause sharpening along already high-contrast edges, less in low-contrast areas. If you raise the Threshold value, you can then increase the Amount and Radius values to sharpen the edges without oversharpening areas that don't require it. To prevent noise from distorting skin tones, specify a Threshold value between 8 and 20.

5. Click OK.

TIP To soften a grainy scan, apply Filter > Blur > Gaussian Blur at a low setting (less than 1), and then apply Filter > Sharpen > Sharpen Edges once or twice afterward to resharpen.

TIP To avoid waiting for the Unsharp Mask effect to preview on a full-screen image, first get close to the desired settings using just the preview window with Preview unchecked; then check Preview to preview the results on the full screen; and finally, readjust the settings if needed.

TIP Try applying the Unsharp Mask filter to one or two individual color channels (for example, just the Red or Green channel in an RGB image). If you sharpen two separate channels, use the same Radius value for both. You can also convert an image to Lab Color mode and then apply the filter to the L channel to sharpen luminosity without affecting any color pixels.

Apply Unsharp Mask

Changing the canvas

The **Canvas Size** command changes the live, editable image area.

Note: If you want to enlarge the canvas area using a marquee, use the Crop tool instead (see page 99). You can also use the Crop command to reduce the image size.

To change the canvas size:

1. Choose Image > Canvas Size ■–■.

2. *Optional:* Choose a different unit of measure from the Width pop-up menu; **NEW** the same unit will be chosen automatically for the Height. Or to choose two different units instead, hold down Shift as you choose each one. If you choose "columns," the current Column Size: Width setting in Edit (Photoshop, in Mac) > Preferences > Units & Rulers will be used as the increment.

3. Enter new Width and/or Height values. Changing one dimension has no effect on the other dimension.
   or
   Check Relative, then enter the amount by which you want to increase each dimension. Enter a negative value to decrease a dimension.

4. *Optional:* To reposition the image on its new canvas, click any arrow in the Anchor diagram. The white (Win)/ gray (Mac) square represents the existing image area.

5. From the Canvas extension color pop-up **NEW** menu, choose a color for the added pixels (see page 183). Or to choose a color from the Color Picker, choose Other or click the color square (see page 184). If the image doesn't have a Background (look for it on the Layers palette), this option won't be available.

6. Click OK. Any added canvas area will automatically be filled with the color you chose in the previous step, unless the bottommost tier of the image is a layer with transparency, in which case the added canvas area will be transparent ■.

■ *The original image*

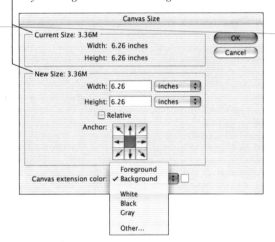

■ *Compare the **Current Size** with the **New Size** as you change the Width and Height values.*

■ *The same image with **added** canvas pixels*

Change the Canvas Size

Crop and straighten NEW

The File > Automate > **Crop and Straighten Photos** command is an action that searches for straight edges and rectangular areas in an image, copies each rectangular section that it finds into a new document window, and rotates each image, if necessary, to square it off. You can scan more than one image at a time and let the command sort the images into individual documents.

If you think Crop and Straighten Photos sounds too good to be true, you're partially correct. For one thing, it may take a while to process. And for another, the feature isn't as smart as you are, so it can be fooled. For example, it may mistake a shadow that the scanner detects around the actual photo for the edge of the image. Also, the images may end up being slightly off square. To help the command do its job properly, don't overlap pictures in the scanner or let them hang off the side.

1 *Marquee the portion of the image you want to* ***keep.***

A whole image can be cropped using the Crop tool, the Crop command, or the Trim command. First, the **Crop tool.**

To crop an image using a marquee:

1. Choose the Crop tool (C).
2. Drag a marquee over the portion of the image that you want to keep **1**.
3. Do any of the following on the Crop tool options bar:

   If you're cropping a layer (not the Background), you can either click **Cropped Area: Delete** to have the cropped-out areas be deleted or click **Hide** to have those areas save with the file but extend outside the visible canvas area. (You can use the Move tool later to move hidden pixels back into view.)

   Check **Shield** if you want the area outside the crop marquee to be darkened by a cropping shield (this helps you see what will remain after cropping) **2**. Click the Color swatch if you want to change the shield color; you can also change its Opacity percentage.

   For the Perspective option, see Photoshop Help.

4. Do any of these optional steps:

   To resize the marquee, drag any handle (double-arrow pointer). Shift-drag a corner handle to preserve the marquee's proportions. Alt-drag/Option-drag a handle to resize the marquee from its center.

   To reposition the marquee, position the pointer inside it, then drag.

   To rotate the marquee, position the cursor outside it (curved arrow pointer), then drag in a circular direction. To change the axis point around which the marquee rotates, drag the circle away from the center of the marquee before

(Continued on the following page)

2 *The* ***Crop*** *tool options bar* ***after*** *drawing a marquee with the tool*

Crop Tool

rotating. (The crop marquee can't be rotated for an image in Bitmap mode.)

5. Press Enter/Return .
   or
   Double-click inside the marquee.
   or
   Right-click/Control-click the image and choose Crop.

   If you rotated the marquee, the rotated image will be squared off in the image window.

TIP To cancel the cropping process before accepting it, press Esc, or click the ⊘ button on the options bar.

To specify dimensions and resolution as you crop an image:

1. Choose the Crop tool (C). 🔲

2. On the Crop options bar, enter **Width** and **Height** values for the final image **2**.
   NEW (You can click the Swap Width and Height button ⇄ to reverse the values.)
   or
   If you want to crop using the Width, Height, and Resolution values from another image, click in that other image, click **Front Image** on the options bar, then click back in the image to be cropped.

3. *Optional:* Modify the **Resolution.** If, after clicking Front Image, you change the Resolution value, the image will be resampled after cropping.

   (To empty the Width, Height, and Resolution fields, click Clear.)

4. Drag a crop marquee on the image. (The values you entered in step 2 were for the final image size, not the marquee size.)

5. To accept the crop, double-click inside the marquee; or press Enter/Return; or right-click/Control-click the image and choose Crop.

TIP To resharpen an image after cropping, apply the Unsharp Mask filter (see pages 96–97).

Unsnap

Normally, when resizing a crop marquee, if View > Snap To > **Document Bounds** is on, the crop edges will snap to the edge of the image. To override this snap function (let's say you want to crop slightly inside the edge of the image), turn the Snap To > Document Bounds feature off; or start dragging a marquee handle, then hold down Ctrl-Shift/Cmd-Shift as you drag the handle near the edge of the image.

1 *The **cropped** image*

If you change the Resolution, Width, and Height values on the Crop options bar and then use the tool to crop the image, the image will be resampled as a result.

| 🔲 ▾ | Width: 500 px | ⇄ Height: 400 px | Resolution: 144 | pixels/inch ⬍ | Front Image | Clea |

2 *The options bar **before** drawing a marquee with the **Crop** tool*

Crop Tool

Crop one image to fit inside another

Open both images, activate the target image, choose the Crop tool (C), click **Front Image** on the Crop options bar, activate the image you want to crop, then draw a marquee. After cropping, Shift-drag-and-drop the layer from the Layers palette or copy and paste the layer onto the target image. The resolution will adjust automatically.

Cropping with a marquee that's larger than the image effectively **increases** the image's canvas size.

To enlarge the canvas area using the Crop tool:

1. Enlarge the image window so the work canvas (gray area) around the image is showing.

2. Choose the Crop tool (C). 🔳

3. Draw a crop marquee within the image.

4. Drag any of the handles of the marquee into the work canvas **1**–**2**. If areas of the image originally extended outside the canvas border, those areas can now be included.

5. Double-click inside the marquee.
   or
   Press Enter/Return.
   or
   Right-click/Control-click the image and choose Crop.

   If there were no hidden pixels and if the image has a Background (Layers palette), the added canvas area will be filled with the current Background color. If the bottommost tier is a layer or if the image has only one layer and no Background, the added canvas area will be filled with transparency.

1 *Drag any of the crop marquee handles **outside** the canvas area into the work canvas.*

2 *Our newly **cropped** image has new proportions. In our example, the added pixels filled automatically with black, which was our current Background color, because the default Background wasn't changed (Layers palette).*

The **Crop** command is simple and straight-forward, but it's useful only if you don't need any of the options that the Crop tool provides. You'll start by drawing a selection marquee.

To crop an image using the Crop command:

1. Choose the Rectangular Marquee tool (M or Shift-M). [ ]
2. Draw a marquee over the part of the image you want to keep.
   or
   To control the size of the marquee, use the Style: Fixed Aspect Ratio or Fixed Size options on the Rectangular Marquee tool options bar, then click on the image.
3. Choose Image > Crop, then deselect (Ctrl-D/Cmd-D).

You can use the **Trim** command to quickly trim away any excess transparent or solid color areas, such as a frame or border, from around an image.

To crop an image using the Trim command:

1. Choose Image > Trim.
2. Click a Based On option 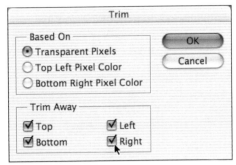:

   Transparent Pixels trims away any extra transparency at the edges of the image, while preserving all image pixels. If the image doesn't contain any transparent pixels, this option won't be available.

   Top Left Pixel Color removes any border areas that match the color of the uppermost-left pixel in the image.

   Bottom Right Pixel Color removes any border areas that match the color of the lowermost-right pixel in the image.

3. Check which areas of the image you want the command to Trim Away: Top, Bottom, Left, or Right.
4. Click OK.

1 *The* **Trim** *command removes excess transparent areas or color areas, depending on which Based On option you click.*

1 *The original image*

The Rotate Canvas > **Flip Canvas Horizontal** and **Flip Canvas Vertical** commands flip all the layers in an image, creating a mirror image. (To flip just one layer at a time, use Edit > Transform > Flip Horizontal or Flip Vertical instead.)

To flip an image:

To flip the image from left to right, choose Image > Rotate Canvas > Flip Canvas Horizontal **1**–**2**.

or

To flip the image upside-down, choose Image > Rotate Canvas > Flip Canvas Vertical **3**.

2 *The image **flipped horizontally***

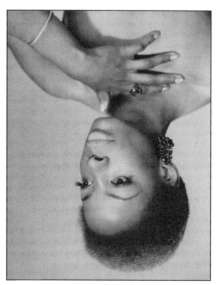

3 *The original image **flipped vertically***

Flip Image

The **Rotate Canvas** commands rotate all the layers in an image. (To rotate one layer at a time, use a rotate command from the Edit > Transform submenu instead.)

To rotate an image by a preset amount:

Choose Image > Rotate Canvas > 180°, 90° CW (clockwise), or 90° CCW (counter-clockwise).

TIP You can also use the File Browser to rotate an image or images (see page 73).

To rotate an image by specifying a number:

1. Choose Image > Rotate Canvas > Arbitrary.

2. Enter an Angle between −359.99° and 359.99° 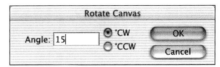.

   TIP To straighten out a crooked scan, measure the angle using the Measure tool (see page 152), then enter that angle here.

3. Click °CW (clockwise) or °CCW (counterclockwise).

4. Click OK –**3**.

1 *You can enter a custom angle in the **Rotate Canvas** dialog box.*

2 *The original image*

3 *The image **rotated 180°**; compare with the flipped images on the previous page.*

LAYER BASICS 5

In this chapter

Create a new layer
Turn a selection into a layer
Duplicate a layer
Hide/show layers
Flip a layer
Delete a layer
Rename a layer
Restack a layer
Convert the Background into a layer
Convert a layer into the Background
Move or activate a layer
Create a layer set
Lock a layer or layer set
Create a new fill layer
Lock transparent pixels
Drag-and-drop/copy a layer to another image
Merge and flatten layers
For additional layer topics, see Chapters 15 & 16

IF YOU CHOOSE Background Contents: White or Background Color for a new image in File > New, the bottommost tier of the image will be the Background, which isn't a layer. If you choose Contents: Transparent, the bottommost tier of the image will be a layer. Layers can be added to an image at any time, but an image can contain only one Background.

Layer basics

Unlike the Background, layers are like clear acetate sheets—opaque where there's imagery and transparent where there's none. To each layer you can assign a different opacity and mode to control how it blends with the layers below it. You can also hide/show, flip, duplicate, change the stacking order of, or assign a layer mask to any layer. By using layers, you can easily single out one part of an image for editing while preserving the rest. For added control, you can also use selections or masks on a layer.

Layers are listed on the **Layers palette** from topmost to bottommost, with the Background, of course, at the bottom of the list. Click a layer (or the Background) to activate it. The name of the currently active layer is listed on the title bar of the image window.

Layers Palette

*The currently **active** layer has a brush icon.*

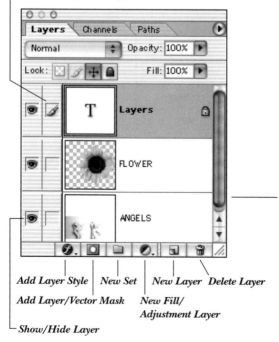

Add Layer Style   New Set   New Layer   Delete Layer
Add Layer/Vector Mask   New Fill/
                         Adjustment Layer
Show/Hide Layer

The composite image, with all three layers visible

If you've already learned how to paste a
selection or create type, you know that both
operations **create** a new **layer** automatically.
In this chapter, you'll learn the layer basics.
In Chapter 9, you'll learn about a special
variety of layers called adjustment layers,
which are used for previewing color adjustments on underlying layers.

An image can contain as many layers as
available memory and storage will allow.
However, because the pixel areas on a layer
occupy storage space, when you finish a
large image, you can merge or flatten its
layers together to reduce its storage size **1**.

Beware! If you save your image in any format
except Photoshop (.psd), PSB, PDF, or layered TIFF (.tif), all layers will be flattened
and any transparency in the bottommost
layer will become opaque white. Also, if you
change image modes (e.g., from RGB to
CMYK), remember to click Don't Flatten or
Don't Merge if you want to preserve layers.

To create a new layer:

1. To create a layer with 100% opacity
and Normal mode, click the New Layer
button at the bottom of the Layers
palette and skip the remaining steps.
or
To choose options for the new layer as
it's created, press Ctrl-Shift-N/Cmd-
Shift-N; or choose New Layer from the
Layers palette menu; or Alt-click/
Option-click the New Layer button
at the bottom of the palette. Follow the
remaining steps.

2. *Do any of the following optional steps:*
Change the layer **Name 2**.

Check **Use Previous Layer to Create
Clipping Mask** to make the new layer a
part of a clipping mask (see page 283).

Choose a **Color** for the area on the
Layers palette behind the layer's eye
and brush/link icons (see the sidebar).

Choose a different blending **Mode** or
Opacity (both can easily be changed
later).

Dress it up

To help you identify layers quickly (and to make
your Layers palette look "purty"), right-click/
Ctrl-click in the eye column and choose a color.

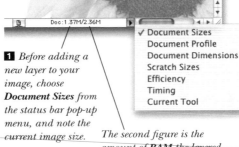

1 *Before adding a
new layer to your
image, choose
Document Sizes from
the status bar pop-up
menu, and note the
current image size.*

*The second figure is the
amount of **RAM** the layered,
unflattened file is utilizing.
Note how much the file's storage
size increases when you add a
new layer. The image in this
illustration contains two layers.*

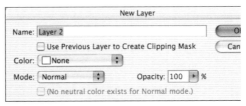

2 *Enter a name and choose options for a layer in the
New Layer dialog box.*

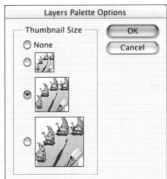

3 *Click a different
Thumbnail Size in
the **Layers Palette
Options** dialog box.*

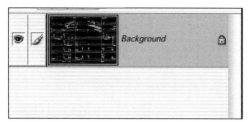

1 *A detail of the Layers palette, showing the original* **Background**

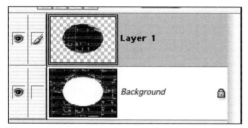

2 *The* **Layer Via Cut** *command cuts the current selection from the Background and places it onto a new layer.*

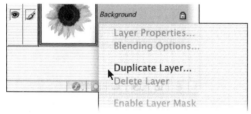

3 *Right-click/Ctrl-click a layer name, then choose* **Duplicate Layer** *from the context menu.*

4 *The* **duplicate** *layer appears on the palette.*

3. Click OK. The new layer will appear directly above the previously active layer.

TIP To choose a different size for the Layers palette thumbnails, choose Palette Options from the Layers palette menu, then click a thumbnail size (**3**, previous page).

To turn a selection into a layer:

1. Choose a layer or the Background, then create a selection.

2. To place a **copy** of the selected pixels on a new layer and leave the original layer as is, right-click/Ctrl-click and choose Layer Via Copy (Ctrl-J/Cmd-J).
or
To place the selected pixels on a new layer and **remove** them from the original layer, right-click/Ctrl-click and choose Layer Via Cut (Ctrl-Shift-J/Cmd-Shift-J) **1**–**2**.

3. *Optional:* Click the eye icon for the original layer to temporarily hide it from view.

To duplicate a layer in the same image:

To create a new layer with a generic name, drag the name of the layer you want to duplicate over the New Layer button ▣ at the bottom of the Layers palette. The duplicate layer will appear above the original layer, and it will be the active layer.
or
To name the duplicate as you create it, right-click/Ctrl-click the name of the layer you want to duplicate and choose Duplicate Layer, or Alt-drag/Option-drag the layer over the New Layer button. Type a name for the duplicate layer in the "As" field, then click OK **3**–**4**.

By **hiding** layers you're not currently working on, you remove them as a visual distraction. Hiding layers also boosts Photoshop's performance.

There are a couple of things you should keep in mind when hiding layers. Only visible layers can be merged (you'll learn about merging and flattening at the end of this chapter). Be especially careful when using the Flatten Image command, as it discards hidden layers! Also, if you're going to be printing your image, remember that only visible layers will print.

To hide or show layers:

Click the eye icon on the Layers palette for any individual layer you want to hide **1**–**3**. Click in the eye column again to redisplay the layer.

or

Drag upward or downward in the eye column to hide or show multiple layers.

or

Alt-click/Option-click an eye icon to hide all the layers except the one you're clicking on (including the Background). Alt-click/Option-click the remaining eye icon again to redisplay all layers.

or

Right-click/Ctrl-click in the eye column and choose "Hide this layer" or "Show/Hide all other layers" from the context menu **4**.

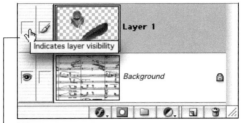

1 *Click the **eye** icon to **hide** a layer. Click in the eye column again to redisplay it.*

2 *Layer 1 **hidden***

3 *Layer 1 **redisplayed***

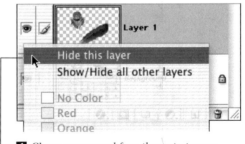

4 *Choose a command from the context menu.*

Hide/Show Layers

1 *The original image*

2 *Layer 1 flipped horizontally*

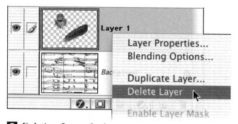

Layer Properties...
Blending Options...

Duplicate Layer...
Delete Layer

Enable Layer Mask

3 *Deleting Layer 1 via a context menu command*

4 *After deleting Layer 1*

To flip a layer:

1. On the Layers palette, choose the layer that you want to flip. Any layers that are linked to this active layer are also going to flip.

2. Choose Edit > Transform > Flip Horizontal **1**–**2** or Flip Vertical.

To delete a layer:

On the Layers palette, click the layer you want to delete. Next, click the Delete Layer 🗑 button and click Yes, or Alt-click/Option-click the Delete Layer button to bypass the prompt.
or
Right-click/Ctrl-click the layer you want to delete, choose Delete Layer from the context menu, then click Yes **3**–**4**.

TIP Change your mind? No problem. Choose Edit > Undo or click a prior state on the History palette.

To rename a layer or layer set:

1. Double-click a layer or layer set name on the Layers palette.

2. Type a new name **5**.

3. Press Enter/Return.

5 *Renaming a layer*

Managing layers

To restack a layer:

1. On the Layers palette, click the name of the layer you want to restack.

2. Drag the layer name upward or downward on the palette, and release the mouse when a dark horizontal line appears in the desired location **1**–**4**.

TIP You can also restack an active layer by choosing Layer > Arrange > Bring to Front, Bring Forward, Send Backward, or Send to Back, or by using any of the shortcuts listed in the sidebar. You can't stack a layer below the Background.

TIP To move the Background upward on the list, it must first be converted into a layer (see the following page).

1 *The original image*

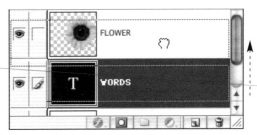

2 *Dragging the WORDS layer* **upward**

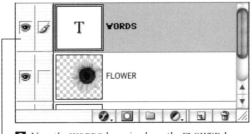

3 *Now the WORDS layer is above the FLOWER layer.*

Restack an active layer

Windows

Bring Forward	Ctrl-]
Bring to Front	Ctrl-Shift-]
Send Backward	Ctrl-[
Send to Back	Ctrl-Shift-[

Macintosh

Bring Forward	Cmd-]
Bring to Front	Cmd-Shift-]
Send Backward	Cmd-[
Send to Back	Cmd-Shift-[

4 *Here's the result.*

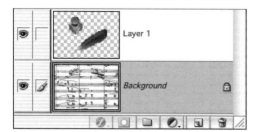

1 *Double-click the **Background**.*

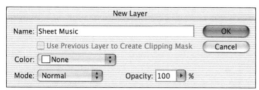

2 *Name the layer.*

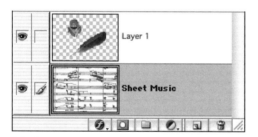

3 *The former Background is now a **layer**.*

There are some things that you can do to a layer that you can't do to the Background, such as move it upward or downward in the layer stack, choose a blending mode or opacity for it, or create a layer mask for it. You can, however, **convert** the **Background** into a **layer,** and it will then function like any other layer.

To convert the Background into a layer:

Double-click the Background on the Layers palette **1**, type a new Name **2**, choose a Mode and Opacity for the layer, then click OK **3**.

or

Alt-double-click/Option-double-click the Background on the Layers palette to bypass the dialog box.

If you need to **create** a **Background** for a file that doesn't have one, you can convert an existing layer into the Background.

To convert a layer into the Background:

1. Choose or create a layer.

2. Choose Layer > New > Background From Layer (at the top of the Layer menu). The new Background will appear at the bottom of the stack on the Layers palette.

Follow these instructions to **move** one layer. To move multiple layers in unison, see page 285.

To move layer pixels:

1. On the Layers palette, choose the layer you want to move.

2. Choose the Move tool (V) ⊹ or hold down Ctrl/Cmd if any other tool is chosen.

3. Drag in the image window. The entire layer will move ■–■. If pixels are moved beyond the existing edge of the image, don't worry—they'll be saved with the image, and you can always move them back into view.

TIP Press an arrow key with the Move tool chosen to nudge an active layer one pixel at a time. Press Shift-arrow to move a layer 10 screen pixels at a time. (Don't use Alt-arrow/Option-arrow— that shortcut duplicates the layer.)

TIP For faster previewing of high-resolution images when using the Move tool, choose Edit (Photoshop, in Mac) > Preferences > Display & Cursors, then check Use Pixel Doubling. Pixels will temporarily double in size while you drag (they'll be half their normal resolution).

To activate a layer using the Move tool:

Right-click/Ctrl-click in the image window and choose a layer from the context menu ■. (Ctrl-right-click/Cmd-Ctrl-click with any other tool selected.) Only layers containing nontransparent pixels under the pointer will appear on the context menu.

or

Ctrl-click/Cmd-click an object in the image window to activate that object's layer. In Mac, you can Cmd-Option-Ctrl-click if another tool is chosen.

or

Check Auto Select Layer on the Move tool options bar, then click any visible pixels in the image window. *Note:* The layer won't become selected if the pixels you click on have an opacity below 50%.

1 *The original image*

2 *After **moving** the type layer with the **Move** tool*

3 *Choosing a layer from a context menu*

Getting out of a set

To **move** a layer out of its set, but keep the set, drag the layer name over the current set name, or over another set name, or above or below any layer that's outside the set.

To **delete** a set, but not the layers inside it, click a set name (not the layer), click the Delete Layer button at the bottom of the palette, then click Set Only in the alert dialog box. (If you click Set and Contents, both the set and any layers inside it will be deleted!)

1 *Click the triangle to expand or contract the **layer set** list.*

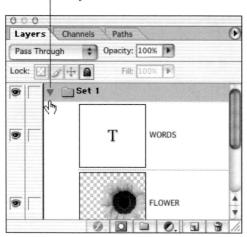

2 *The WORDS and FLOWER layers were dragged into the Set 1 folder.*

3 *Lock Position   Lock All*

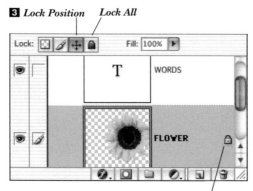

*The **lock icon** appears next to the layer **name**.*

Layer sets are to layers what folders are to files: they allow you to collect, label, and organize multiple layers. By using layer sets, you can avoid having to do a lot of scrolling up and down on the Layers palette and you can keep the palette neat and tidy. On the Layers palette, you can display just the name of a set or you can click the arrow to reveal the layer names inside the set **1**. Sets can be nested inside other sets, up to five levels.

Another reason for using sets is to restrict the effect of layer blending modes and adjustment layers. Adjustment layers and blending modes (except for Pass Through) that are applied to layers within a set will affect only layers within the set. When a layer mask or vector mask is applied to a set, it affects all the layers in the set, as well as any sets nested inside it.

To create a layer set:

1. Click the New Set button ▢ at the bottom of the Layers palette.
or
Choose Layer > New > Layer Set, change the Name, Color, blending Mode, or Opacity setting for the new set, if desired, then click OK.

2. On the Layers palette, drag each layer you want to include in the set onto the set's folder icon **2**.

Use the **Lock** feature to prevent inadvertent edits.

To lock a layer or layer set:

1. On the Layers palette, choose the layer or set you want to lock.

2. Click the Lock Position button **3** ✛ to lock only the layer's location. Now the layer can't be moved, but its pixels can still be edited.
or
Click the Lock All button ▣ to protect the layer or set from being moved or edited.

TIP To learn about the Lock Transparent Pixels button on the Layers palette, see page 115.

Fill layers function like adjustment layers, in that they can be edited or removed without affecting any other layers, except in this case they contain a solid color, gradient, or pattern. (Read about adjustment layers on pages 168–171.)

To create a fill layer:

1. On the Layers palette, activate the layer that you want the fill layer to appear above (you can restack it later).

2. Choose Solid Color, Gradient, or Pattern from the New Fill/Adjustment Layer pop-up menu ⬤ at the bottom of the Layers palette **1**.

or

To choose options for the fill layer as you create it, choose Layer > New Fill Layer > Solid Color, Gradient, or Pattern, then do any of the following: change the layer Name; choose a Color for the area on the Layers palette behind the layer's eye and brush/link icons; choose a different Mode or Opacity percentage; or check Use Previous Layer to Make Clipping Mask to make the new layer a part of a clipping mask (see page 283). Click OK. All of these options can be changed later.

3. For a **Solid Color** layer, choose a color from the Color Picker, then click OK.

For a **Gradient** layer, choose a preset from the Gradient Preset picker, choose a Style, and choose Angle and Scale values. (For the Reverse, Dither, or Align with layer options, see page 260).

For a **Pattern** layer, choose a preset from the Pattern Preset picker and choose a Scale percentage (1–1000) **2**.

Optional: Uncheck Link with Layer to keep the pattern stationary if the layer is moved; click Snap to Origin to make the pattern snap to the current ruler origin (where the zeros on the horizontal and vertical rulers meet); or click the New Preset button ⬛ to create a preset.

4. Click OK.

TIP Adjust the mode or opacity of the fill layer by using the Layers palette.

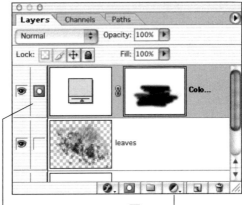

—*The adjustment layer for a **Solid Color** fill (with a modified layer mask)*

1 *Choose **Solid Color, Gradient,** or **Pattern** from the **New Fill/Adjustment Layer** pop-up menu.*

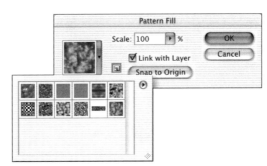

2 *Choose options for a pattern fill layer in the **Pattern Fill** dialog box.*

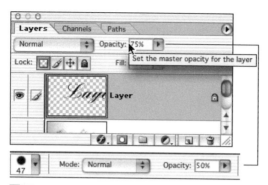

1 *This **layer** opacity is 75% (Layers palette) and the Paintbrush **tool** opacity is 50% (options bar): the opacity of the resulting stroke will be 37%.*

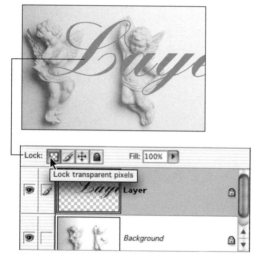

2 *A rasterized type layer is recolored with **Lock Transparent Pixels** on.*

3 *Only the **type** is recolored—not the transparent pixels.*

Tools and layers

Keep in mind as you use painting and editing tools that in addition to the blending mode, opacity, and fill settings chosen for your **tool** from the options bar, the blending mode, opacity, and fill of the currently active **layer** will also contribute to the tool's effect **1**. (Learn more about the Opacity and Fill settings on page 269.)

For example, if a layer has a 60% opacity, a painting or editing tool with an opacity of 100% will work at a maximum opacity of 60% on that layer, or at an even lower opacity if the tool opacity is below 100%.

With **Use All Layers** checked on the options bar for the Blur, Sharpen, Smudge, Paint Bucket, Magic Eraser, Magic Wand, Healing Brush, or Clone Stamp tool, the tool will sample pixels from all the currently visible layers. Whether Use All Layers is on or off, pixels can be modified only on the currently active layer.

Lock transparent pixels

With the **Lock Transparent Pixels** button ▦ activated on the Layers palette, only **non-transparent** pixels on a layer can be edited or recolored **2**–**3**; blank areas will remain transparent. Turn this option off if you want to **create** visible pixels. It can be turned on or off for individual layers.

Transparent pixels on editable type layers are always locked, whereas for rasterized type layers, the Lock Transparent Pixels option can be turned on or off.

Note: If you use the Eraser tool with Lock Transparent Pixels on, you will recolor visible pixels with the current Background color rather than remove them.

TIP Press / to toggle the Lock Transparent Pixels option on or off.

You can change the size or color of the checkerboard pattern that's used to represent transparent areas on a layer, or turn off the checkerboard pattern, in Edit (Photoshop, in Mac) > Preferences > Transparency & Gamut (Ctrl-K/Cmd-K, then Ctrl-4/Cmd-4). (Grid Size: None turns it off.)

Copy layers

Let's say you're about to perform an operation that requires or causes your file to become flattened, such as converting it to Indexed Color mode (which doesn't support multiple layers), or saving it to a format other than Photoshop (.psd), TIFF, or PDF. If you want to preserve a **copy** of some of the layers from the file before flattening, the following instructions will come in handy. You can save individual layers to a new document or to any existing, open document.

To save a copy of a layer or layer set to a new document:

1. On the Layers palette, choose the layer or layer set that you want to save a copy of.

2. Right-click/Ctrl-click that layer or set and choose Duplicate Layer from the context menu.

3. Choose Destination Document: New ■.

4. In the As field, enter a name for the layer or set to appear in the new file.

5. In the Destination: Name field, enter a name for the new file.

6. Click OK. A new image window will appear onscreen.

7. Save the new document.

Save Layer in Separate Document

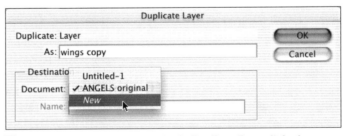

■ *Choose a Destination Document in the **Duplicate Layer** dialog box.*

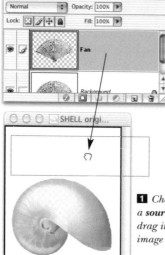

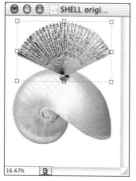

1 *Choose a layer in a **source** image, then drag it into the **target** image window.*

There are two methods for **drag-copying** layers between images. Choose your method based on how much of each layer you need to copy (area-wise) and whether you want to copy linked layers. If you drag a layer from the Layers palette to the target image window, any areas that extend beyond the edge of the image boundary will be copied along with it. This method is described in the instructions below. To copy linked layers, follow the instructions on the next page instead. Or to trim any overhanging areas as you copy a layer, follow the instructions on page 144.

To drag and drop a layer to another image using the Layers palette:

1. Open both the image that contains the layer you want to copy (the "source" image) and the image the layer will be copied to (the "target" image), and make sure the two windows don't completely overlap.

2. Click in the source image window.

3. On the Layers palette, click the layer you want to copy (you can also copy the Background) **1**. It doesn't matter which tool is chosen.

4. Drag the layer from the Layers palette into the target image window, and release the mouse when the darkened border is in the desired spot. The added layer will be stacked above the previously active layer in the target image, but of course it can be restacked **2**. If you copied the Background, it will show up as a layer in the target image.

Note: If you copy a layer between an 8-bits-per-channel image and a 16-bits-per-channel image, a prompt will alert you that the image quality may be diminished due to the difference in pixel depths. Click Yes to accept the drop, or click No to cancel.

TIP Shift-drag a layer to have the copy appear in the center of the target image.

2 *The target image after adding the SHELL layer*

Drag and Drop a Layer

Use this method to copy individual layers or a series of **linked** layers from one file to another.

To drag and drop a layer to another image using the Move tool:

1. Open the image that contains the layer(s) that you want to copy (the "source" image) and the image to which the layer(s) are to be copied (the "target" image).

2. On the Layers palette, click the layer that you want to copy.
   or
   To move multiple layers, make sure they're linked (see page 285).

3. *Optional:* Click in the target image window, then click the name of the layer on the Layers palette above which you want the added layer to appear.

4. Choose the Move tool (V).

5. Click in the source image window. Drag the active layer from the source image window into the target image window 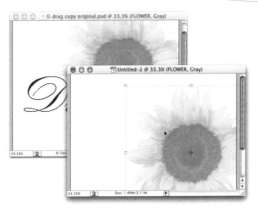. The new layer(s) will be positioned where you release the mouse, above the currently active layer in that file 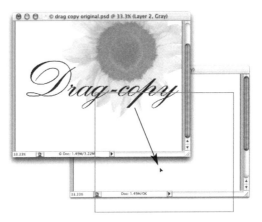.

   Note: If you copy a layer between an 8-bits-per-channel image and a 16-bits-per-channel image, a prompt will alert you that the image quality may be diminished due to the difference in pixel depths. Click Yes to accept the drop or click No to cancel.

6. *Optional:* Use the Move tool to reposition the layer(s) in the target image window.

7. *Optional:* Restack the new layer or layers (drag them upward or downward on the Layers palette).

TIP Shift-drag a layer to have the copy appear in the center of the target image.

1 *The flower layer is dragged from the **source** image window into the **target** image window.*

2 *The new layer appears in the **target** image.*

Merge and flatten layers

The sad truth is, most file formats other than Photoshop (.psd), Photoshop PDF (.pdf), and layered TIFF (.tif) don't support multiple layers. In order to export your file to another application, it's going to have to get flattened. We think the best way to do this is to save a flattened copy of it using File > **Save as** with **As a Copy** checked (the layered version will remain open). This way, the layered version will be preserved so you can overwork it to death at some later date.

If you're the cocky sort and you're positive your image is totally and completely done, *finis,* you can flatten it down into the Background yourself using the **Flatten Image** command (see page 122). Actually, because flattened files are smaller than layered files, flattening the stuff you're done with is a good way to free up storage space —if you happen to need storage space. (My, how times have changed. We had to save our first book, QuarkXPress layout, illustrations, and all, onto 12 floppy disks!)

Whereas the Flatten Image command is used when a file is complete, the two merge commands, **Merge Down** and **Merge Visible,** are normally used periodically while an image is still being edited. Using either of these commands, you can merge two or more layers together on a case-by-case basis, while leaving the remaining layers intact.

(Continued on the following page)

Merge and Flatten Layers

To merge two layers together:

1. Click the top layer of the two layers you want to merge 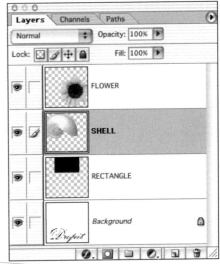.

   Rules and restrictions: Either layer can have a layer mask or be an adjustment layer. The topmost layer can be a shape layer or an editable type layer, but the bottom layer can't. And finally, if you choose a layer set, all the layers in the set will be merged into one layer.

2. Choose Merge Down from the Layers palette menu, or for a layer set, choose Merge Layer Set. The same shortcut, Ctrl-E/Cmd-E, works for both commands. The active layer will merge into the layer directly below it 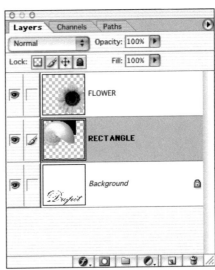.

   If the underlying layer contains a mask, an alert dialog box will appear 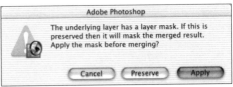; click Preserve or Apply, whichever you prefer.

1 *The SHELL layer is chosen.*

2 *After choosing the **Merge Down** command*

3 *This prompt will appear if the underlying layer being merged contains a **layer mask.***

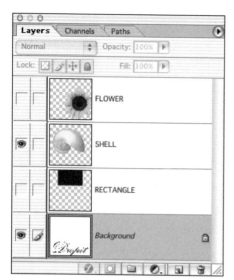

1 *The SHELL layer and Background are visible and the Background is chosen; the FLOWER and RECTANGLE layers are hidden.*

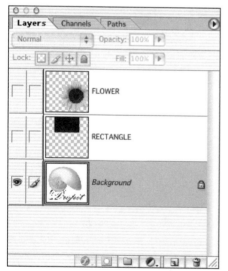

2 *After choosing the **Merge Visible** command, the SHELL layer merges into the Background. The FLOWER and RECTANGLE layers stay as they are.*

The **Merge Visible** command merges all the currently visible layers into the active layer and *preserves* hidden layers.

To merge multiple layers:

1. Make sure only the layers you want to merge are visible (all should have eye icons on the Layers palette) and *hide* any layers you *don't* want to merge. They don't have to be consecutive. Hide the Background if you don't want to merge layers into it.

2. Activate any one of the layers to be merged. *Beware!* If you merge an editable type layer or an adjustment layer, it will cease to be editable.

3. Choose Merge Visible (Ctrl-Shift-E/Cmd-Shift-E) from the Layers palette menu **1**–**2**.

Other merge commands

To merge linked layers, choose **Merge Linked** (Ctrl-E/Cmd-E) from the Layers palette menu or the Layer menu. This command discards hidden, linked layers, and it ignores nonlinked layers and layers in a clipping mask. To merge layers in a set to other layers inside or outside the set, link just the layers that you want to merge—not the whole set—and have a layer (not a set) active when you choose the command. To merge all the layers within a set, click the set, then choose **Merge Layer Set.**

To merge a **copy** of the pixels on the currently visible layers or layer sets into the active layer (which can be a new layer that you create just for this purpose), hold down Alt/Option and choose **Merge Visible** from the Layer menu or Layers palette menu. Use Alt/Option plus Merge Linked to merge a copy of linked layers. Alt/Option plus Merge Down leaves upper layers intact but copies pixels to the layer below the current layer.

To merge layers in a clipping mask, click the layer with the underlined name, then choose **Merge Clipping Mask** (Ctrl-E/Cmd-E) from either the Layers palette menu or the Layer menu. Any hidden layers in the clipping mask will be discarded. See page 283.

The **Flatten Image** command merges the currently displayed layers into the bottom-most visible layer and *discards* hidden layers.

To flatten layers:

1. Make sure all the layers you want to flatten are visible (have eye icons) **1**. It doesn't matter which layer is currently active.

2. Choose Flatten Image from the Layers palette menu. If the file contains any hidden layers, you'll get a warning prompt; click OK **2**. If there were any transparent areas in the bottommost layer, they will become white.

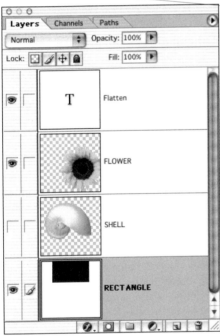

1 *Before choosing the Flatten Image command, make sure all the layers you want to merge are* ***visible!***

2 *The* ***Flatten Image*** *command flattens all the* ***visible*** *layers into the bottommost visible layer. In this case, Photoshop discarded the SHELL layer, because it was hidden.*

Flatten All Layers

SELECT 6

Stick with the Background

If you're not comfortable working with layers, for the instructions in this chapter, instead of choosing a layer, just work with the pixels on the Background.

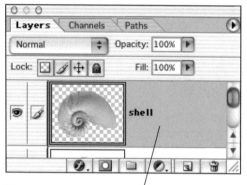

1 *Ctrl-click/Cmd-click a layer to select **all** the opaque pixels on that layer.*

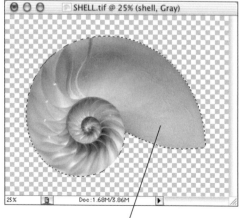

2 *Opaque pixels—not transparent areas—are selected on this layer.*

WHEN A LAYER OR part of a layer is selected, only that area is editable —the rest of the image is protected. Selection borders have a "marching ants" marquee. In this chapter, you'll learn how to create selections using the Rectangular Marquee, Elliptical Marquee, Single Row Marquee, Single Column Marquee, Lasso, Polygonal Lasso, Magic Wand, and Magnetic Lasso tools, as well as the Color Range and Extract commands. You'll also learn how to create selections of various shapes; deselect, reselect, invert, or delete selected pixels; move, transform, or hide a selection marquee; add to or subtract from a selection; and create a vignette.

Creating selections

A selection contains pixels from whichever layer is currently active. If you move a selection on the Background of an image using the Move tool, the current Background color is applied automatically to the exposed area. If you move a selection on a layer using the Move tool, the exposed area becomes transparent.

TIP A selection can be converted into a path for precise reshaping, and then converted back into a selection (see pages 316 and 326). Quick Masks, which function like selections but can be painted on an image, are covered in Chapter 17.

To select an entire layer:

Click a layer or the Background on the Layers palette, then choose Select > All (Ctrl-A/Cmd-A). A marquee will surround the entire layer.
or
To select only opaque pixels—not any transparent areas—on a layer, Ctrl-click/Cmd-click the layer on the Layers palette **1**–**2**. Or right-click/Ctrl-click a layer thumbnail and choose Select Layer Transparency.

To create a rectangular or elliptical selection:

1. Choose a layer.

2. Choose the Rectangular Marquee or Elliptical Marquee tool (M or Shift-M). Or to create the thinnest possible selection, choose the Single Row Marquee or Single Column Marquee tool .

3. *Optional:* To specify the exact dimensions of the selection, with the Rectangular or Elliptical Marquee tool highlighted choose Fixed Size from the Style pop-up menu on the options bar , then enter Width and Height values. Remember, though, you're counting pixels based on the file's resolution, not the monitor's resolution, so the same Fixed Size marquee will appear larger in a low-resolution file than in a high-resolution one.

   Or to specify the width-to-height ratio of the selection (3-to-1, for example), choose Fixed Aspect Ratio from the Style pop-up menu, then enter Width and Height values. Enter the same value in both fields to create a circle or a square.

4. *Optional:* To soften the edges of the selection, enter a Feather value above zero on the options bar . Also, the Anti-aliased option can be checked on or off for the Elliptical Marquee tool.

5. If you specified Fixed Size values (or are using the Single Row Marquee or Single Column Marquee tool), click on the image. For any other style, drag diagonally –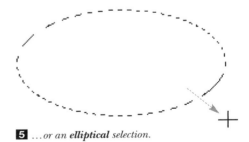. A marquee will appear. To create a square or circular selection for the Normal style, start dragging, then finish the marquee with Shift held down.

   Hold down the Spacebar to move the marquee while drawing it. To move the marquee after releasing the mouse, drag inside it.

TIP As you drag the mouse, the dimensions of the selection will be indicated in the W and H areas on the Info palette.

TIP To add to or subtract from a selection, see page 136.

see page 136.

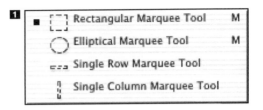

2 *Instead of drawing a marquee manually, you can choose **Fixed Size** from the Style pop-up menu on the options bar and enter exact Width and Height dimensions.*

3 *Enter a **Feather** value to soften the edges of the selection.*

4 *Drag diagonally to create a **rectangular** selection…*

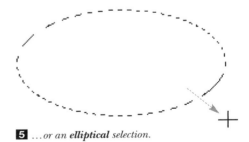

5 *…or an **elliptical** selection.*

Anti-aliasing

Check **Anti-aliased,** if available, on the options bar before using a selection tool to create a selection with a softened edge that fades gradually to transparency. Or uncheck Anti-aliased to create a crisp, hard-edged selection.

 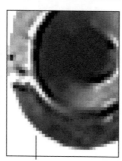

Aliased   *Anti-aliased*

1 *A hand-drawn **Lasso** tool selection*

2 *A straight-edged **Polygonal Lasso** tool selection*

Deleting Polygonal Lasso corners

As you're creating a selection with the Polygonal Lasso tool, you can press Backspace/Delete (keep the mouse button down) to erase the last-created corner. Keep pressing Backspace/Delete if you want to erase multiple corners.

TIP As it's difficult to precisely reselect an area (unless you save your selection in an alpha channel or as a path), try to refine your selection before you deselect it.

TIP If the shape you want to select isn't too complex, use the Pen or Freeform Pen tool to trace it (and then convert the path into a selection; see page 326) instead of using the Lasso—you'll get a smoother selection. You can also convert a selection into a path for precise reshaping.

To create a freeform selection:

1. Choose a layer.

2. Choose the Lasso tool (L or Shift-L).

3. *Optional:* Enter a Feather value above zero on the Lasso tool options bar to soften the edges of the selection.

4. Drag around an area of the layer **1**. When you release the mouse, the open ends of the selection will join automatically.

TIP To feather a selection after it's created, use the Select > Feather command (Ctrl-Alt-D/Cmd-Option-D).

TIP To create a straight side using the Lasso tool, with the mouse button still down, press Alt/Option, and click to create corners. Drag, then release Alt/Option to resume drawing a freehand selection.

To create a polygonal selection:

1. Choose a layer.

2. Choose the Polygonal Lasso tool (L or Shift-L).

3. To create straight sides, click to create points **2**. To join the open ends of the selection, click on the starting point (a small circle will appear next to the pointer). Or Ctrl-click/Cmd-click or double-click anywhere on the image to have the selection close automatically.

   Alt-drag/Option-drag to draw a curved segment as you create a polygonal selection. Release Alt/Option to resume drawing straight sides.

Lasso; Polygonal Lasso

If you click on a layer pixel with the **Magic Wand** tool, a selection will be created that includes adjacent pixels of a shade, color, or transparency level similar to the one you clicked on. You can then add similarly colored, nonadjacent pixels to the selection using the Similar command, or add non-similar colors by Shift-clicking.

To select by color using the Magic Wand tool:

1. Choose a layer.

2. Choose the Magic Wand tool (W).

3. Check **Contiguous** on the Magic Wand tool options bar **1** to limit the selection to areas that are connected to the first pixel you click on, or uncheck this option to select noncontiguous areas.

4. On the Magic Wand options bar, check **Use All Layers** to sample colors in all the currently displayed layers in order to create the selection. Only pixels on the current layer can be edited, but you can apply changes within the same selected area through successive layers.
   or
   Uncheck Use All Layers to sample colors only on the current layer.

   Also, check Anti-aliased, if desired, to create a smoother selection edge.

5. Click a shade or color in the image window.

6. *Do any of these optional steps:*

   To enlarge the selection based on the current Tolerance value on the Magic Wand tool options bar, choose Select > **Grow** as many times as you like (use a low Tolerance value). You can also access this command by right-clicking/ Ctrl-clicking in the image window.

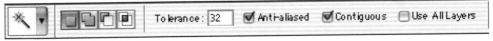

1 *The **Magic Wand** tool options bar*

Magic Wand

PHOTO: PAUL PETROFF

*A selection created using the **Magic Wand** with a **Tolerance** value of **10***

*A selection created using the **Magic Wand** with a **Tolerance** value of **40**: At the higher Tolerance value, more pixels are selected.*

To select additional, noncontiguous areas of similar color or shade based on the current Tolerance value on the Magic Wand tool options bar, choose Select > **Similar.** You can also access this command by right-clicking/Ctrl-clicking in the image window.

To change the range of shades or colors within which the Magic Wand tool selects, enter a **Tolerance** value (0–255) on the Magic Wand tool options bar, then click on the image again. For example, at a Tolerance value of 32, the Magic Wand will select within a range of 16 shades below and 16 shades above the shade it's clicked on. Enter zero to select only one color or shade.

To gradually expand or narrow the range of shades or colors the Magic Wand tool selects, modify the Tolerance value between clicks. The higher the Tolerance value, the broader the range of colors it will select.

TIP Choose Edit > Undo (Ctrl-Z/Cmd-Z) to deselect the last-created selection area.

TIP To add to or subtract from a selection, see page 136.

TIP To Expand or Contract a selection by a specified number of pixels, choose either command from the Select > Modify submenu.

TIP To remove a flat background color from around a shape, click the background of the image using the Magic Wand tool, then press Backspace/Delete.

Magic Wand

In creating the **Magnetic Lasso** tool (and the Extract command, discussed on page 138), Adobe has tried to make the difficult task of selecting irregular shapes and furry or fuzzy edges a little easier. Neither technique solves the problem completely, but they're useful tools nevertheless.

The Magnetic Lasso tool creates a freeform selection automatically as you move or drag the mouse. It snaps to the nearest distinct shade or color that defines the edge of a shape. *Note:* This tool utilizes a lot of processing time and RAM. If you move or drag the mouse quickly, the tool may not keep pace with you.

To select using the Magnetic Lasso tool:

1. Choose the Magnetic Lasso tool (L or Shift-L).
2. *Optional:* Change any of the tool's options bar settings. See "Magnetic Lasso tool options bar" on the next page.
3. Click on the image to establish a fastening point. Move the mouse, with or without pressing the mouse button, along the edge of the shape that you want to select **1**. As you move or drag the mouse, the selection line will snap to the edge of the shape. The temporary points that appear will disappear when you close the selection.
4. If the selection line starts to follow adjacent shapes that you don't want to select, click on the edge of the shape that you *do* want to select to add a fastening point manually, then continue to move or drag the mouse to complete the selection.
5. To close the selection line: **2**

   Double-click anywhere over the shape.
   or
   Click the starting point (a small circle will appear next to the Magnetic Lasso tool pointer).
   or
   Press Enter/Return.
   or

Make your life easier
To temporarily heighten the contrast in an image in order to enhance the Magnetic Lasso tool's effectiveness, choose **Brightness/Contrast** from the New Fill/Adjustment Layer pop-up menu ⬤. at the bottom of the Layers palette, move the Contrast slider to the right (and also the Brightness slider, if necessary), then click OK. Delete this adjustment layer when you're done using the Magnetic Lasso.

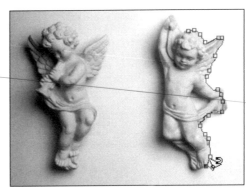

1 *Move the mouse **slowly** around a shape.*

2 *After **closing** the selection*

Magnetic Lasso

Ctrl-click/Cmd-click.

or

Alt-double-click/Option-double-click to close the selection with a straight segment.

6. Choose a layer to be edited using the selection.

TIP Alt-click/Option-click to use the Polygonal Lasso tool temporarily while the Magnetic Lasso tool is selected, or Alt-drag/Option-drag to use a temporary Lasso tool.

| | Feather: 0 px | ☑ Anti-aliased | Width: 10 px | Edge Contrast: 10% | Frequency: 57 | ☑ Pen Press |

1 *The **Magnetic Lasso** tool options bar*

2 *When **Other Cursors: Precise** is chosen in Edit (Photoshop, in Mac) > Preferences > **Display & Cursors,** the pointer will be a circle with a crosshair in the center, and the current Lasso Width will be its diameter. To use a temporary Precise pointer, press Caps Lock.*

Magnetic Lasso tool options bar **1**

The **Feather** amount is the softness of the edges of the selection.

The **Width** (1–256 pixels) is the size of the area in pixels under the pointer that the tool considers when it places a selection line **2**. Use a wide Width for a high-contrast image that has strong edges. Use a narrow Width for an image that has subtle contrast changes or small shapes that are close together; the selection will be more precise and the line won't flip-flop back and forth across the edge.

TIP To decrease the Width setting by one pixel as you create a selection, press "[". To increase the width, press "]".

Edge Contrast (1–100%) is the degree of contrast needed between shapes for the tool to consider it an edge. Use a low Edge Contrast for a low-contrast image.

TIP If you enter a low or high Width, do the same for the Edge Contrast.

Frequency (0–100) controls how often fastening points are placed as a selection is made. The lower the Frequency, the less frequently points are placed. Use a high Frequency to select an irregular contour.

Magnetic Lasso

Using the **Color Range** command, you can select areas based on colors in the image or based on a luminosity or hue range.

To use the Color Range command to create a selection:

1. Choose a layer. The Color Range command samples colors from all the currently visible layers, but only the current layer will be available for editing. You can limit the selection range by creating a selection first.

2. Choose Select > Color Range.

3. Choose from the Select pop-up menu. You can limit the selection to a preset color range (e.g., Reds, Yellows), to a luminosity range (Highlights, Midtones, or Shadows), or to Sampled Colors (shades or colors you'll click on with the Color Range eyedropper). The Out of Gamut option can be used only on an image that's in Lab Color or RGB Color mode. If you choose a preset color range and the image contains only light saturations of that color, an alert dialog box will warn you that the selection marquee will be present but invisible.

4. Choose a Selection Preview option for previewing selection areas on the image.

5. To preview the selection, click the Selection button; to redisplay the whole image, click the Image button. Or hold down Ctrl/Cmd with either option chosen to toggle between the two. If the image extends beyond the edges of the image window, use the Image option; the entire image will be displayed in the preview box to facilitate sampling.

6. If you chose Sampled Colors in step 3, choose the eyedropper 🖋 in the dialog box, then click or drag in the preview box or in the image window to sample colors in the image.

7. *Optional:* Move the Fuzziness slider to the right to expand the range of colors or shades selected, or move it to the left to narrow the range.

8. *Optional:* If you chose Sampled Colors for step 3, Shift-click in the image window or in the preview box to add more colors or shades to the selection; Alt-click/ Option-click to remove colors or shades from the selection. Or click the 🖋 or 🖋 eyedropper in the dialog box, then click on the image or in the preview box without holding down Shift or Alt/Option.

9. Click OK.

*Choose a color or a luminosity range from the **Select** pop-up menu; or choose **Sampled Colors**, then sample colors from the image using the Color Range eyedropper.*

*Move the **Fuzziness** slider to the left to reduce the range of selected colors, or to the right to expand the range of selected colors.*

*Choose a **Selection Preview** method for the image in the image window.*

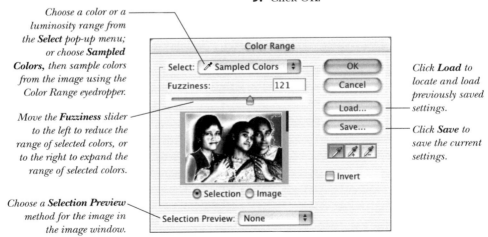

*Click **Load** to locate and load previously saved settings.*

*Click **Save** to save the current settings.*

1 *A **frame** selection created using the Rectangular Marquee tool*

2 *Here's another option. We used the Rectangular Marquee tool to select the center area, then chose Select > Inverse to reverse the selected and nonselected areas. We also used the Levels command to screen back the selected area (the outer area).*

In the first set of instructions on this page, you'll create a **border selection** by dragging with a selection tool. In the second set of instructions, you'll create a border by specifying a value in a dialog box.

To create a border selection manually:

1. Choose a layer.

2. Choose the Rectangular or Elliptical Marquee tool (M or Shift-M).

3. Drag to create a selection, or choose Select > All (Ctrl-A/Cmd-A).

4. Alt-drag/Option-drag a smaller selection inside the first selection **1**. To subtract from a selection using another method, see page 136. See also **2**.

To create a border selection by using a dialog box:

1. Create a selection.

2. Choose Select > Modify > Border.

3. Enter the desired Width (1–200 pixels) for the border **3**.

4. Click OK. The new selection will evenly straddle the edge of the original selection **4**.

3 *Enter a Width in the **Border Selection** dialog box.*

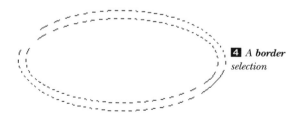

4 *A **border** selection*

Working with selections

To deselect a selection:

With any selection tool chosen, right-click/
Ctrl-click the image and choose Deselect.

or

With any tool chosen, press Ctrl-D/Cmd-D
(or if you want to be slow about it, choose
Select > Deselect).

or

Click inside the selection with any selection
tool **1**.

Note: If you click *outside* the selection with the
Magic Wand, Polygonal Lasso, or Magnetic
Lasso tool, you will create a new selection.

TIP It's difficult to reselect the same area
twice, so deselect a selection only when
you're sure you've finished using it. If
you unintentionally deselect, choose
Undo immediately. If you think you
might want to reuse a selection, save
it as a path or in an alpha channel.

To reselect the last selection:

With any selection tool chosen, right-click/
Ctrl-click on the image and choose Reselect.

or

With any tool chosen, press Ctrl-Shift-D/
Cmd-Shift-D (or choose Select > Reselect).

TIP If you click a prior state on the History
palette that involved a selection, the
Reselect command will reselect the
selection from that prior state.

If you **delete** a selection from a layer, the
original selection area will become transparent **2**. If you delete a selection from the
Background, the selection area will fill with
the current Background color **3**.

To delete selected pixels:

Press Backspace/Delete.

or

Choose Edit > Clear.

or

Choose Edit > Cut (Ctrl-X/Cmd-X) to place
the selection on the Clipboard.

Deselect, Reselect, Delete Selected Pixels

1 *Click **inside** a selection to **deselect** it.*

PHOTO: PAUL PETROFF

2 *A selection deleted from a **layer***

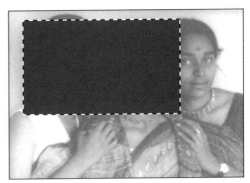

3 *A selection deleted from the **Background***

1 *Moving a marquee*

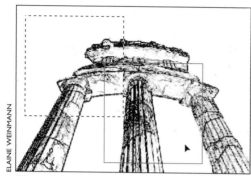

2 *The original Magic Wand tool selection*

3 *After applying the **Smooth** command*

Follow these instructions to move only the selection **marquee**—not its contents.

To move a selection marquee:

1. *Optional:* To aid in positioning the marquee, choose View > Show > Grid or drag a guide or guides from the horizontal or vertical ruler. Also, turn on View > Snap To > Guides and/or View > Snap To > Grid.

2. Choose any selection tool.

3. Drag inside an existing selection **1**. Hold down Shift after you start dragging to constrain movement to a multiple of 45°.
or
Press any arrow key to nudge the marquee one pixel at a time.

TIP You can drag a selection marquee from one image window into another image window using a selection tool.

TIP If you drag a selection on a layer using the Move tool, the selection's pixel contents will be cut from that layer and the empty space will be replaced by layer transparency. If a selection is moved on the Background, on the other hand, the empty space will be filled with the current Background color.

The **Smooth** command adds unselected pixels to or removes unselected pixels from a selection within a specified radius. It's a good way to eliminate extraneous selection areas, particularly after using the Magic Wand tool.

To smooth a selection:

1. Choose the Magic Wand tool, then use the tool to select part of a layer **2**.

2. Choose Select > Modify > Smooth.

3. Enter a Sample Radius value (1–100 pixels). If most pixels within the specified radius are selected, any unselected pixels within that radius will be added to the selection; if most pixels are unselected within the specified radius, any selected pixels will be removed from the selection.

4. Click OK **3**.

To switch the selected and unselected areas:

With any selection tool chosen, right-click/ Ctrl-click the image and choose Select Inverse.

or

With any tool chosen, press Ctrl-Shift-I/ Cmd-Shift-I (or choose Select > Inverse) **1**–**2**.

Choose the same command or shortcut again to switch back to the original selection.

TIP Here's an easy way to select a shape on a solid color background: Choose the Magic Wand tool, enter 10 or less in the Tolerance field on the Magic Wand tool options bar, click the solid color background to select it entirely, then choose Select > Inverse.

Sometimes selection edges ("marching ants") can be annoying or distracting. To hide them temporarily, follow the instructions below. You can even **hide selection edges** while some Image menu and Filter menu dialog boxes are open.

To hide a selection marquee:

Choose View > Show > Selection Edges to uncheck the command. The selection will remain active.

To redisplay the selection marquee, choose View > Show > Selection Edges (it should have a check mark).

The Ctrl-H/Cmd-H shortcut hides/shows whichever options are currently available on the Show submenu. The Show Extras Options dialog box **3** (View > Show > Show Extras Options) controls what options are listed on the Show submenu.

TIP To verify that a selection is still active, press on the Select menu. Most of the commands on the menu will be available if a selection is active.

1 *The original selection: The **angels** are selected.*

2 *After inverting the selection: now the **background** is selected.*

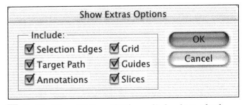

3 *In the **Show Extras Options** dialog box, check the onscreen features you want the Ctrl-H/Cmd-H shortcut to show and hide.*

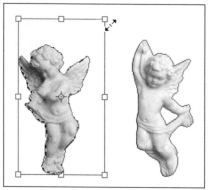

1 *Scaling a selection marquee*

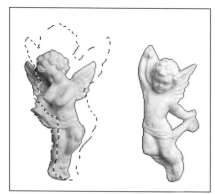

2 *The marquee is enlarged—not its contents.*

3 *You can use any of the **Select** > **Modify** submenu commands to modify an existing selection.*

The **Transform Selection** command affects only the selection marquee—not its contents. (To transform selected pixels, you can either use a command on the Edit > Transform submenu or manipulate the bounding box of the selection; see page 287.)

To transform a selection marquee:

1. With any selection tool chosen, right-click/Control-click the image and choose Transform Selection from the context menu.
or
With any tool chosen, choose Select > Transform Selection.

2. Follow the instructions on pages 287–289 to perform a flip, rotate, scale, or other transformation **1**–**2**.

To modify a selection marquee via a menu command:

Choose Select > Modify > Smooth (see page 133) **3**.
or
Choose Select > Modify > Expand or Contract, enter a value, then click OK.
or
Choose Select > Grow or Similar. These two commands use the current Magic Wand Tolerance setting (see pages 126–127). You can repeat either command to further expand the selection.
or
Choose the Magic Wand tool, then right-click/Ctrl-click the image and choose Grow or Similar.

Transform, Modify Selection Marquee

To add to a selection:

Choose any selection tool other than the Magic Wand, click the Add to Selection button on the options bar **1**, choose other options bar settings for the tool, if desired, then drag across the area to be added **2**–**3**. Or without clicking the Add to Selection button, position the cursor over the selection, then Shift-drag over the area to be added.

or

Choose the Magic Wand tool, click the Add to Selection button on the options bar, then click outside the selection. Or without clicking the Add to Selection button, Shift-click outside the selection.

TIP If the additional selection overlaps the original selection, it will become part of the new, larger selection. If the addition doesn't overlap the original selection, a second, separate selection will be created.

To subtract from a selection:

Choose any selection tool other than the Magic Wand, click the Subtract from Selection button on the options bar **1**, choose other options bar settings, if desired, then drag around the area to be subtracted. Or without clicking the Subtract from Selection button, Alt-drag/Option-drag around the area to be subtracted.

or

Click the Magic Wand tool, click the Subtract from Selection button on the options bar, then click inside the selection. Or without clicking the Subtract from Selection button, Alt-click/Option-click inside the selection.

To select the intersection of two selections:

1. With a selection present, choose a selection tool.

2. Click the Intersect with Selection button on the options bar **1**, then create a new selection that overlaps the current selection **4**–**5**. Or without clicking the button, Alt-Shift-drag/Option-Shift-drag.

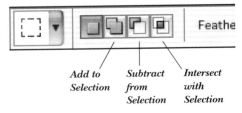

Add to   Subtract   Intersect
Selection   from   with
     Selection   Selection

1 *Use any of these buttons on the options bar to amend a selection, then click the New Selection (first) button to restore the tool's normal function.*

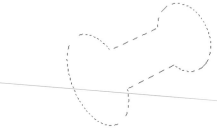

2 *The original selection*

3 *After **adding** a new area to the selection*

4 *A circular selection is drawn over an existing selection with **Alt/Option** and **Shift** held down.*

5 *As a result, only the **intersection** of the two selections remains selected.*

Add to or Subtract from a Selection

1 *First create a feathered-edge selection.*

2 *The vignette*

3 *The original image (Peter's relatives—no joke)*

To vignette an image:

1. For a multilayer image, choose a layer that contains pixels, and turn off Lock Transparent Pixels. The vignette you create is going to appear to fade into the layer or layers below it.

   For an image with a Background only, choose a Background color (see pages 183–186) to be used for the area around the vignette.

2. Choose the Rectangular Marquee or Elliptical Marquee tool (M or Shift-M), or the Lasso tool (L or Shift-L).

3. Enter 15 or 20 px in the Feather field on the options bar. You can also feather the selection after it's created (after step 4), using Select > Feather.

4. Create a selection **1**.

5. With the selection tool still chosen, right-click/Ctrl-click on the image and choose Select Inverse.

6. Press Backspace/Delete.

7. Right-click/Ctrl-click on the image and choose Deselect **2**–**5**.

4 *The vignette*

5 *For this image, we applied the Glass filter after step 5.*

If you've ever torn your hair out trying to mask a shape with an irregular edge (a figure with curly hair or an animal in a landscape), you'll appreciate the **Extract** command. The nicest thing about this feature is that you'll create the mask on a full-size preview right in the dialog box , so you can tweak it until you're certain you've got it just right. When you click OK, the masked area will be preserved, and the remaining areas will be erased to transparency.

To mask a shape using the Extract command:

1. *Note:* For safety's sake, work on a copy of the image—or at least on a duplicate layer. You could also make a snapshot of the original image.

   Choose the layer from which you want to extract imagery.

2. Choose Filter > Extract (Ctrl-Alt-X/Cmd-Option-X). A large, resizable dialog box will appear.

3. You'll use the Edge Highlighter to mask the object border first, and then click on the interior with the Fill tool to define the fill.

   Choose the **Edge Highlighter** tool from the toolbox in the dialog box (B) 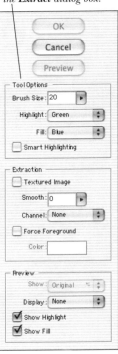.
   and
   In the Tool Options area , enter or choose a **Brush Size** (1–999 pixels) for the marker. The sharper the edge of the object you're going to extract, the smaller the brush you can use. Use a large brush if the shape has wide, choppy edges.
   and
   Choose Red, Green, or Blue as the **Highlight** color for the mask. Or choose Other and choose a color from the Color Picker.

4. *Optional:* If you're going to trace a crisp-edged shape (e.g., a geometric shape), check Smart Highlighting. The highlight will be the minimum width necessary to cover the edge of the

1 *After outlining the chimp with the **Edge Highlighter** tool and filling the interior of the chimp with the **Fill** tool*

2 *Tools and tool shortcuts in the **Extract** dialog box*

3 *Choose **Tool Options** on the right side of the **Extract** dialog box.*

Channel it

To make the marker highlight conform to the shape of a selection, create a selection, choose Select > Modify > Border (Width about 12 pixels), then click OK. Inverse the selection, and save the selection in an alpha channel (see page 308). Choose Filter > Extract, then choose that alpha channel from the Extraction: Channel pop-up menu. Finally, click with the Fill tool (G) inside the highlighted area.

shape, regardless of the current brush size.

5. Drag around the border of the area of the image you want to extract. Complete the loop to make a closed shape. Drag right along the object's border so as to catch any frizz or fringe. You don't need to drag along the edge of the canvas area if the imagery extends that far.

6. *Optional:* In the Extraction area, check **NEW** Textured Image to include a few background pixels with the extracted imagery, for a sort of bas relief look. The higher the Smooth value (0–1000), the more extraneous pixels are eliminated.

7. Choose the **Fill** (second) tool (G) from the toolbox in the dialog box.
   and
   Choose Red, Green, or Blue as the Fill color for the mask. Or choose Other and choose a color from the Color Picker.
   and
   Click on the area of the image that you want to extract. (Click again to unfill.)

   Note: To extract pixels of one color, instead of using the Fill tool, check Force Foreground, choose the **Eyedropper** tool in the dialog box (I), then click a color in the preview window. Or click the Color swatch and choose a color from the Color Picker.

8. Use the **Eraser** tool (E) from the dialog box if you need to unmask any masked areas. Choose a Brush Size for the Eraser in the Tool Options area of the dialog box.

   TIP To zoom in on the preview, press Ctrl-+/Cmd-+ (plus). To zoom out, press Ctrl--/Cmd-- (minus). You could also use the **Zoom** tool in the dialog box (Alt-click/Option-click to reduce the view).

   TIP If the preview is greater than 100% view, you can use the **Hand** tool from the dialog box (H) to move the

(Continued on the following page)

preview in the window (press the Spacebar to access the Hand tool temporarily).

9. Click Preview, then in the Preview area of the dialog box, do any of the following:

Choose **Show:** Extracted to toggle to the extracted image view; choose Original to toggle back to the original image.

Choose **Display:** None to display the background as transparent; choose Black Matte, Gray Matte, or White Matte to display the extracted shape on a background of black, gray, or white, respectively; choose Other to choose a custom color; or choose Mask to display the discarded area as black and the protected area as white.

Check **Show Highlight** and/or **Show Fill.**

10. To refine the mask further, do any of the following:

Use the **Cleanup** tool (C) to gradually subtract opacity. (Alt-drag/Option-drag to restore opacity.)

Use the **Edge Touchup** tool (T) to gradually sharpen edges.

Change the Smooth value.

11. Click OK. If you want to restore lost areas now, use the History Brush tool **1**–**2** (see pages 164–165). Or to erase further by hand, use the Background Eraser (see pages 229–230).

*The **Extract** command overdid it in these areas.*

1 *After extracting (chimp not in the mist)*

2 *This is after using the **History Brush** tool to restore areas of the chimp's face and arm. The Cleanup tool could have been used instead (see step 10).*

Extract

COMPOSITING 7

THIS CHAPTER covers methods for composing image elements: the Clipboard commands (Cut, Copy, Paste, and Paste Into), drag-and-drop, cloning, and pattern stamping. Also covered are techniques for precisely positioning and aligning image elements and smoothing the seams between them.

Moving

In these instructions and in the "drag-copy" instructions on the next page, you'll be **moving** actual image **pixels**. (To move just a selection marquee without moving its contents, see page 133.)

To move a selection's contents:

1. *Optional:* To help you position the selection, choose View > Show > Grid (Ctrl-'/Cmd-') or drag a guide or guides from either ruler, and turn on both View > Snap To > Guides and View > Snap To > Grid.

2. If the selection is on the Background, choose a Background color (see page 183). The area exposed by the moved selection will fill with this color automatically. If the selection is on a layer, the exposed area will become transparent.

3. Choose the Move tool (V). (You can use Ctrl/Cmd to access the Move tool when most other tools are chosen.)

4. Position the pointer over the selection (the pointer will have a scissors icon), then drag. The selection marquee and its contents will move together **1**–**3**.

   Beware! When you deselect a selection, its pixel contents drop back into its original layer, in its new location, regardless of which layer is currently active.

TIP With the Move tool chosen, press an arrow key to nudge a selection marquee one pixel at a time.

1 *If you move a selection on a **layer**...*

2 *...a **transparent** hole is left behind.*

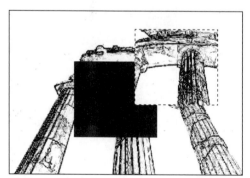

3 *If you move a selection on the **Background**, the exposed area fills with the current **Background color**.*

141

The **Align To Selection** commands align
layer pixels to a selection marquee. If you
need to align areas from different layers, you
can align each one individually to the same
marquee, or you can link them first (see
page 285) and then align them all at once.

To align a layer or layers to a selection marquee:

1. Create a selection. *Note:* The Align To
   Selection command affects only pixels
   that have an opacity of 50% or greater.

2. Choose a layer or one layer in a set of
   linked layers.

3. Choose the Move tool (V), then
   click an Align button on the Move tool
   options bar **1**.
   or
   Choose Layer > Align To Selection >
   Top Edges, Vertical Centers, Bottom
   Edges, Left Edges, Horizontal Centers,
   or Right Edges.

   The layer pixels will align to the edges
   or center of the selection marquee,
   depending on which alignment option
   you chose.

Copying

To drag-copy a selection:

Choose the Move tool (V), then
Alt-drag/Option-drag the selection you
want to copy. The copied pixels will remain
selected **2**–**3**.
or
Without choosing the Move tool, Ctrl-Alt-
drag/Cmd-Option-drag the selection you
want to copy.

TIP Press Alt-arrow/Option-arrow with the
Move tool chosen to offset a copy of a
selection by one pixel from the original.
Press Alt-Shift-arrow/Option-Shift-arrow
to offset a copy by 10 pixels.

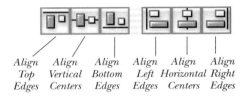

Align Top Edges   *Align Vertical Centers*   *Align Bottom Edges*   *Align Left Edges*   *Align Horizontal Centers*   *Align Right Edges*

1 *The* **Align** *buttons on the* **Move** *tool options bar*

2 *Alt-dragging/Option-dragging a selection*

PHOTO: ELAINE WEINMANN

3 *A* **copy** *of the selected pixels is moved.*

Purge thy Clipboard

If the current selection on the Clipboard is large, the remaining available memory for other processing functions is reduced. To empty the Clipboard and reclaim memory, choose Edit > **Purge** > **Clipboard,** then click OK. This can't be undone.

Clipboard basics

You can use the Edit > **Cut** or **Copy** command to save a selection to a temporary storage area called the Clipboard, and then use Edit > **Paste** or **Paste Into** to paste the Clipboard pixels onto another layer in the same image or in another image. The Cut, Copy, and Paste Into commands are available only while a selection is active.

If you create a selection and choose Edit > Cut, the selection will be placed on the Clipboard. (The Clear command doesn't use the Clipboard.) If you Cut or Clear a selection from the Background, the exposed area will be filled with the current Background color. If you remove a selection from a layer, the area left behind will be transparent.

TIP For a soft transition between pasted imagery and a layer, check Anti-aliased on the options bar for your selection tool (if available) before you use it.

The Edit > Paste command automatically pastes the Clipboard contents into a new layer. If you paste into a smaller size document, any pasted pixels that extend beyond the canvas area will be preserved, and can be moved into view using the Move tool. Pixels outside the canvas area will save with the document, so you don't have to worry about losing them. If you subsequently crop the layer, however, and you don't want the extended pixels to be discarded, click Cropped Area: **Hide** on the Crop options bar.

You can paste the same Clipboard contents an unlimited number of times. If **Export Clipboard** is checked in Edit (Photoshop, in Mac) > Preferences > General, the Clipboard contents will be stored in temporary system memory even if you exit/quit Photoshop. Only one selection can be stored on the Clipboard at a time, and the Clipboard contents are replaced whenever the Cut or Copy command is chosen.

TIP The dimensions in the New dialog box automatically match the dimensions of the current contents of the Clipboard.

Before using either the **Clipboard** commands (Cut, Copy, or Paste) or the drag-and-drop method to copy imagery, compare the dimensions of the source image with the dimensions of the target image. If the selection being copied is larger than the target image, some of the copied pixels will extend beyond the canvas area when they're pasted or dropped, and they'll be hidden from view. You can move the layer with the Move tool to bring the hidden pixels into view.

There's another reason why the size of a selection may change when it's pasted or dropped: it's rendered in the resolution of the target image. If the resolution of the target image is higher than that of the source imagery, the copied image will appear smaller when it's pasted or dropped. Conversely, if the resolution of the target image is lower than that of the source image, the source imagery will look larger when it's pasted or dropped.

TIP If you want the imagery to stay the same size, before copying it, make the resolution (and dimensions, if desired) of the source and target images the same using Image > Image Size. To paste into a smaller image, see page 147.

To copy and paste a selection:

1. Select an area on a layer or on the Background. *Optional:* To feather the selection, right-click/Ctrl-click and choose Feather, enter a Feather Radius value, then click OK.
   or
   To copy and paste only the visible part of a layer (when displayed at 100% view) and not any areas that extend beyond the canvas area, on the Layers palette click the layer you want to copy, then choose Select > All (Ctrl-A/Cmd-A).

2. Choose Edit > Copy **1** (Ctrl-C/Cmd-C) (or Edit > Cut to cut the selection).

3. Click in any image window.

4. Choose Edit > Paste (Ctrl-V/Cmd-V) **2**. The pasted pixels will appear in a new layer. The layer can be restacked using

1 *An area of the Background is placed on the **Clipboard** via Edit > **Copy**.*

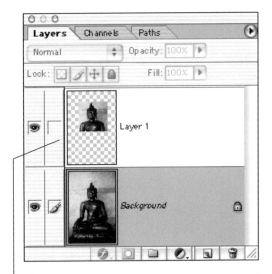

2 *When the **Paste** command is chosen, the Clipboard contents automatically appear in a new layer.*

1 *A selection is dragged from the* **Background***. The exposed area* **temporarily** *fills with the Background color.*

the Layers palette, moved using the Move tool, or defringed (see page 158).

TIP To turn a selection into a new layer, right-click/Ctrl-click and choose Layer Via Copy or Layer Via Cut (see page 107).

If you **drag and drop** selected pixels from one image to another, presto, a copy of those selected pixels will appear on a new layer in the target image. This method bypasses the Clipboard, so it both saves memory and preserves the current contents of the Clipboard. If your monitor is too small to display two image windows simultaneously, use the copy-and-paste method instead, as described on the previous page.

To drag and drop a selection between images:

1. Open the source and target images, and arrange them so their windows don't completely overlap.

2. In the source image, select an area on a layer or on the Background.

3. Choose the Move tool (V). ⊹ (You can use Ctrl/Cmd to access the Move tool when most other tools are chosen.)

4. *Optional:* Check Show Bounding Box on the Move options bar to make the selection's bounding box visible.

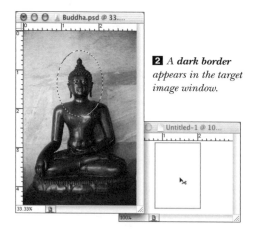

2 *A* **dark border** *appears in the target image window.*

5. Drag the selection into the target image window, and release the mouse where you want the pixels to be dropped **1**–**3**. The copied imagery will automatically appear on a new layer. You can reposition it using the Move tool.

TIP Shift-drag with the Move tool to drop the selection in the exact center of the target image. You can release the mouse button anywhere inside the target image window.

TIP To drag and drop a whole layer to another image, including any pixels outside the canvas area, see pages 117–118.

TIP Drag-and-drop is the only way to copy a shape layer from one image to another.

3 *The mouse is released, and the copied pixels appear in the* **target** *image window. The source image is unchanged.*

If you use the **Paste Into** command to paste the Clipboard contents inside a selection, a new layer will be created automatically and the active marquee will become a layer mask. The pasted imagery can then be repositioned within the layer mask, or the mask itself can be reshaped to reveal more or reveal less.

To paste into a selection:

1. Select an area of a layer. *Optional:* Right-click/Ctrl-click and choose Feather, enter a value, then click OK.

2. Choose Edit > Copy to copy pixels from the active layer only, or choose Edit > Copy Merged (Ctrl-Shift-C/Cmd-Shift-C) to copy pixels within the selection area from all the currently visible layers.

3. Leave the same layer active, or choose a different layer, or choose a layer in another image.

4. Select the area (or areas) that you want to paste the Clipboard contents into.

5. Choose Edit > Paste Into (Ctrl-Shift-V/ Cmd-Shift-V). A new layer and layer mask will be created **1**–**3**.

6. *More options:*

   The entire Clipboard contents were pasted onto the layer, but the layer mask is probably hiding some of those pixels. To **move** the layer **mask** relative to the layer, choose the Move tool (V), click the layer mask thumbnail (the thumbnail on the right), then drag in the image window. Or to **move** the layer **contents,** click the layer thumbnail, then drag in the image window.

   Click the layer mask thumbnail, then paint on the layer mask in the image window with white to **expose** more of the image or with black to **hide** more of the image.

   To move the layer and layer mask in **unison,** click between the layer and layer mask thumbnails to link the two layer components together, choose the Move tool, then drag in the image window. Click the link icon 🔗 to unlink.

1 *To create this effect in one image, first a music layer was selected and copied. In another image, the type layer was Ctrl-clicked/Cmd-clicked, then Edit > **Paste Into** was chosen. A new layer resulted.*

2 *The layer contents can be repositioned within the layer mask because the two thumbnails aren't linked together. For this image, the music layer thumbnail was activated and then the layer contents were moved upward using the Move tool.*

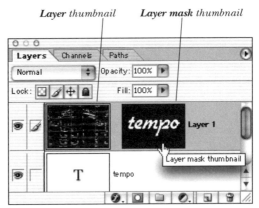

Layer *thumbnail*   Layer mask *thumbnail*

3 *When the **Paste Into** command is chosen, the pasted image appears on a new layer, and a layer mask is created automatically for it. The pasted image (the music) is visible only within the white areas in the layer mask (the letter shapes).*

Off the edge

- To remove pixels that extend beyond the edge of a layer, make sure the layer is active, choose Select > All, then choose Image > Crop. Trimming off the extra pixels will reduce the file's storage size.

- If pixels extend off the edge of a layer and the layer is merged into the Background, the hidden pixels will be trimmed away.

- If you apply an image-editing command, such as a filter, to a whole layer, any pixels beyond the edge of the layer will also be modified.

- To enlarge the canvas to include hidden pixels, use Image > Canvas Size.

- To select all the pixels on a layer, including any pixels beyond its edge, Ctrl-click/Cmd-click the layer name on the Layers palette. Don't use Select > All.

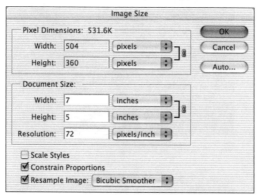

1 *Use the **Image Size** dialog box to change an image's resolution and/or dimensions.*

Normally, in Photoshop, if you move a large selection or layer, or **paste** a layer **into** another image, all the moved or pasted pixels on a layer are preserved, even if they extend beyond the visible edge of the layer. If you want the imagery to be trimmed as it's pasted, follow these instructions, but read page 144 first.

To paste into a smaller image:

1. Click in the target image window, then Alt-press/Option-press and hold on the status bar at the bottom of the image window. Note (or jot down) the image's width, height, and resolution.

2. Click in the source image window, choose Image > Duplicate, then click OK.

3. With the duplicate image window active, choose Image > Image Size.

4. Check Resample Image, and change the resolution to the same value as that of the target image **1**. In the Document Size: Width or Height field, enter a smaller number than the dimensions that you noted for step 1, then click OK.

5. In the source image, choose the layer you want to copy.

6. Choose Select > All (Ctrl-A/Cmd-A) to select the layer, choose Edit > Copy, click in the target image, then choose Edit > Paste.
   or
   Shift-drag the source layer name into the target image window.

7. Close the duplicate image. Save the original image, if desired.

TIP In lieu of steps 3 and 4 above, you can choose File > Automate > Fit Image and enter the desired pixel dimensions for the width or the height (from step 1). Note that the Fit Image action won't change the image resolution. Instead, the copied or dragged layer will adopt the resolution of the target file.

Sharpening and blurring

The **Blur** tool decreases contrast between pixels and is used to soften edges between shapes. The **Sharpen** tool increases contrast between pixels and is used to delineate edges between shapes. Neither tool can be used on an image in Bitmap or Indexed Color mode.

To sharpen or blur edges:

1. Choose the Blur tool 🖌 or the Sharpen tool 🖌 (R or Shift-R). Each tool keeps its own options bar settings.

2. On the Sharpen or Blur tool options bar **1**, do all of the following:

   Click the Brush Preset picker arrowhead, then click a hard-edged or soft-edged **brush**.

   Choose a blending **Mode.** Normal sharpens/blurs pixels of any shade or color; Darken sharpens/blurs only pixels that are darker than the Foreground color; Lighten sharpens/blurs only pixels that are lighter than the Foreground color; Hue and Color cause a slight buildup of complementary colors; Saturation causes a buildup of existing colors; and Luminosity intensifies the existing luminosity (more about the blending modes on pages 38–42). You'll see a greater distinction between modes when using the Sharpen tool than when using the Blur tool.

   Choose a **Strength** percentage. Try a low setting at first (oh, say around 30%).

3. *Optional:* Check Use All Layers on the options bar to pick up pixels from other visible layers under the pointer to place onto the active layer (see the sidebar).

4. Drag across an area in the image window to sharpen or blur pixels **2**–**3**. To intensify the effect, drag again.

TIP To avoid creating an overly grainy texture when using the Sharpen tool, choose a medium Strength setting and drag only once on a given area.

Sharpen or Blur

Use all ya got

With **Use All Layers** unchecked on the options bar for the Magic Wand, Smudge, Sharpen, Blur, Healing Brush, Magic Eraser, Paint Bucket, or Clone Stamp tool, you will sharpen, blur, etc. using data sampled from the currently active layer only. With Use All Layers checked, you will sharpen, blur, etc. using sampled data from all the currently visible layers under the pointer. With this option on, try applying pixels with a new layer as the active layer.

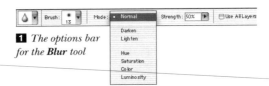

1 *The options bar for the **Blur** tool*

2 *The original image*

3 *After using the **Sharpen** tool on the strawberry in the center to bring it into sharper focus, and the **Blur** tool on the rest of the image to make it recede*

1 *The **location** of the **pointer** is indicated by a dotted marker on each ruler.*

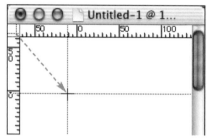

2 *Dragging the **ruler origin***

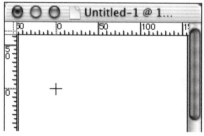

3 *A new location for the **ruler origin***

Using rulers and guides

Grids, rulers, and guides can help you position objects more precisely than you can do "by eye."

To hide or show rulers:

Choose View > Rulers (Ctrl-R/Cmd-R); when the rulers are visible, the command has a check mark. Rulers will appear on the top and left sides of the image window, and the current position of the pointer will be indicated by a dotted marker on each ruler **1**. Move the pointer, and you'll see what we mean. To hide the rulers, choose View > Rulers again.

TIP To change the ruler units quickly, right-click/Ctrl-click either ruler and choose a unit from the context menu. Or to change units via the Units & Rulers Preferences dialog box, double-click either ruler.

The **rulers' zero origin** is the point from which a selection or object's location is measured.

To change the rulers' zero origin:

1. *Optional:* To make the new ruler origin snap to a gridline, first display the grid by choosing View > Show > Grid (Ctrl-'/ Cmd-'). Then you can choose View > Snap To > Grid.

   To make the ruler origin snap to a guide, choose View > Snap To > Guides, then drag a guide into the image window, if you haven't already done so.

   See also "To use the Snap feature" on the following page.

2. Drag from the intersection of the rulers in the upper left corner of the image window diagonally into the image **2**–**3**. Note where the zeros are now located on the rulers.

   TIP To reset the ruler origin, double-click the square in the upper left corner of the image window where the rulers intersect.

Rulers

The **Snap** feature works like an electronic "tug." When View > Snap is on, as you move a selection border, slice, drawing tool pointer, path, or shape, that item will snap to the nearest guide, grid, slice, or document edge, depending on which of those options is chosen on the View > Snap To submenu.

To use the Snap feature:

1. Choose View > Snap To > Guides, Grid, Slices, Document Bounds, All [of the above], or None.

   Note: To turn on the Snap To > Grid function, the grid must be showing (View > Show > Grid).

2. Make sure View > Snap is on (has a check mark) (Ctrl-Shift-;/Cmd-Shift-;).

The **grid** is a nonprinting framework that can be used to align image elements. Guides are individual guidelines that you drag into the image window yourself. With View > Snap To > Guides turned on, a selection or tool pointer will snap to a guide if it's moved within eight screen pixels of the guide. Ditto for View > Snap To > Grid.

To hide or show the grid:

Choose View > Show > Grid (Ctrl-'/Cmd-') **3**. To hide the grid, choose the command again. The grid can be turned on or off for individual files. (To change the appearance of the grid, see page 434.)

Show or snap all

Show or hide Selection Edges, the Target Path, Grid, Guides, Slices, Annotations, or all of the above via the View > **Show** submenu **1** (or via the View > Show > Show Extras Options dialog box). The **Extras** command (Ctrl-H/Cmd-H) shows/hides the items that are currently enabled on the Show submenu.

Turn on the snap feature for Guides, Grid, Slices, Documents Bounds, or all of the above via the View > **Snap To** submenu **2**. The **Snap** command turns all of the current chosen Snap To options on and off.

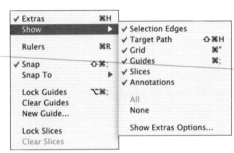

1 *The **Extras** command shows/hides all the currently enabled items on the **Show** submenu.*

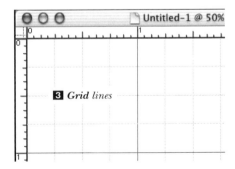

2 *The **Snap** command turns all the currently enabled commands on the **Snap To** submenu on or off.*

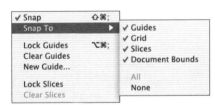

3 *Grid lines*

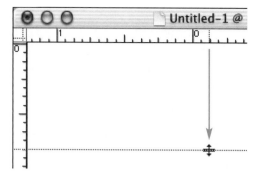

1 *A **guide** is dragged downward from the horizontal ruler.*

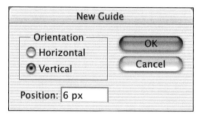

2 *Use the **New Guide** dialog box to place a new guide at a specific location.*

To create a guide:

Make sure the rulers are displayed, then drag from the horizontal or vertical ruler into the image window **1**.

If View > Snap is checked, you can Shift-drag to snap the guide to a ruler increment. If the grid is displayed and View > Snap To > Grid is on, the guide can be snapped to a grid line. A guide can also be snapped to a selection marquee.

TIP Alt-drag/Option-drag as you create a guide to switch its **orientation** from vertical to horizontal (or vice versa).

TIP To **move** an existing guide, drag it using the Move tool (make sure the guides aren't locked). Guides will keep their relative positions if you resize the image —provided they're not locked.

TIP To **lock** all guides so they *can't* be moved using the Move tool, choose View > Lock Guides (Ctrl-Alt-;/Cmd-Option-;).

TIP You can choose a new guide **color** or **style** in Edit (Photoshop, in Mac) > Preferences > Guides, Grid & Slices. To quickly open that dialog box, double-click a guide with the Move tool (this works only if guides aren't locked).

To place a guide at a specific location:

1. Choose View > New Guide.

2. Click Orientation: Horizontal or Vertical **2**.

3. Enter a Position in any measurement unit used in Photoshop.

4. Click OK.

To remove guides:

To remove one guide, choose the Move tool (V), then drag the guide out of the image window (this works only if guides aren't locked).

or

To remove all guides, choose View > Clear Guides.

Create, Place, Remove Guide

To use the Measure tool:

1. Choose the Measure tool (I or Shift-I). It's on the Eyedropper tool pop-out palette.

2. Display the Info palette (F8).

3. Drag in the image window . The angle (A) and distance (D) of the measure line will be displayed on the Info palette **2**. Shift-drag to constrain the angle to a multiple of 45°.

4. *Optional:* After dragging with the Measure tool, Alt-drag/Option-drag from either end of the line to create a protractor **3**. The angle (A) formed by the two lines will display on the Info palette **4**. You can readjust the angle at any time by dragging either end of the line.

5. Choose another tool when you're finished using the Measure tool. If you choose it again, the measure line will redisplay.

   To remove a measure line, drag it off the image using the Measure tool or click Clear on the Measure tool options bar.

TIP You can drag a measure line or protractor to another area of the image using the Measure tool. Drag any part of the line except an endpoint, unless you want to change its angle.

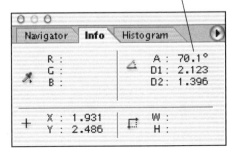

1 *If you drag in the image window using the **Measure** tool...*

2 *...**angle** (A) and **distance** (D) readouts will appear on the **Info** palette.*

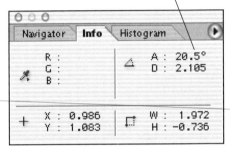

3 *With the **Measure** tool, Alt-drag/Option-drag from the end of the first line to form a protractor.*

4 *If you create a **protractor**, its **angle** (A), as well as the **distance** (D1 and D2), or length, of each line from the point where they meet will be displayed on the **Info** palette.*

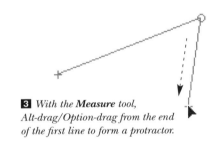

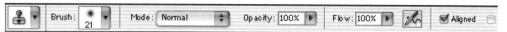

1 *The options bar for the **Clone Stamp** tool*

2 *Drag the mouse where you want the clone to appear. To produce this illustration, the **Aligned** option was turned on for the Clone Stamp tool.*

3 *Uncheck the **Aligned** option for the Clone Stamp tool to create multiple clones from the same source point.*

Cloning

The **Clone Stamp** tool can be used to clone imagery from one **layer** to another within the same image (as in these instructions), or to clone imagery from one image to another (as in the instructions on page 156).

To clone areas in the same image:

1. Choose the Clone Stamp tool (S or Shift-S).

2. On the Clone Stamp tool options bar **1**, do all of the following:

   Click the Brush Preset picker arrowhead, then click a **brush** that has an appropriate size for the area you want to clone.

   Choose a blending **Mode.**

   Choose an **Opacity** percentage.

   Choose a **Flow** percentage to control the rate of application.

   Check **Aligned** to create a single, uninterrupted clone from the same source point, even if you release the mouse between strokes or switch modes or brushes between strokes **2**. Uncheck Aligned to create repetitive clones from the same source point; in this case, the crosshair pointer will return to the same source point each time you release the mouse **3**.

   Check **Use All Layers** to sample pixels from all currently visible layers that you Alt-click/Option-click over. Or uncheck Use All Layers to sample pixels from the current layer only.

3. *Optional:* To apply the cloned imagery in an airbrush style, click the Airbrush button.

(Continued on the following page)

Clone Areas in the Same Image

4. If Use All Layers is unchecked on the options bar, then on the Layers palette, choose the layer that you want to clone pixels from.

5. In the image window, Alt-click/Option-click the area of the layer you want to clone from, to establish a source point. Don't click a transparent part of the layer—there won't be anything to clone.

6. On the same layer, drag the mouse back and forth where you want the clone to appear.
or
Choose or create another layer, then drag the mouse.

Two pointers will appear on the screen: a crosshair pointer over the source point and a Clone Stamp pointer (or Brush Size pointer) where you drag the mouse. Imagery from the source point will appear where the mouse is dragged, and it will replace any underlying pixels.

Note: If Lock Transparent Pixels is enabled on the Layers palette when you use the Clone Stamp tool, the cloned imagery will replace only existing pixels; it won't fill transparent areas.

7. *Optional:* To establish a new source point to clone from, Alt-click/Option-click a different area in the source image.

TIP You can change options bar settings for the Clone Stamp tool between strokes.

TIP To create a double-exposure effect, choose a low Opacity percentage so the underlying pixels will partially show through the cloned pixels .

TIP To paint areas from earlier stages of the same editing session, use the History Brush tool.

1 *An **Opacity** of 50% was chosen for the **Clone Stamp** tool to create this double-exposure effect.*

IT GIVES US GREAT PLEASURE to present the fresh, juicy bumper crop of images that you see in these color pages.

The work is, as they say in the art world, painterly. Even artists who had intially been leery of (or downright resistant to) anything digital have found a way to produce sensuous textures, soft brushstrokes, and realistic shadows using Photoshop. In exchange for giving up the tactile quality of traditional media, they've gained access to an ever expanding range of image-editing commands and features, such as transparency, blending modes, filters, feathering, defringing, cloning, transforming, adjusting, gradients, masking, layer effects, patterns, paths, shapes, type, distortion—not to mention brushes and pens. If you're new to Photoshop, skim through our table of contents (Egads!). Artists are developing their own methods, employing the features and commands that suit them. Some create montages from scanned imagery, some work entirely from memory or imagination, some pin a photograph to their copystand and reinterpret it "by eye."

Don't get us wrong. We love—and will always love—oil painting, drawing, printmaking, paper collage, and other traditional media, not to mention crafts and anything homey and handmade. But having the ability to transfer files almost instantaneously to clients, prepare images for print or web output, and output duplicates on archival paper isn't just an added incentive for artists to use Photoshop—nowadays it's often a requirement. Like it or not, folks, this is the digital age.

Using Photoshop, artists also enjoy being able to undo or partially undo edits, using the Undo and Fade commands, the History palette, and tools such as the Eraser and the History Brush. These features are the electronic equivalent of scrubbing down a canvas with a turpentine-soaked rag, minus the smell. As one artist said, working in Photoshop has enabled him to take more artistic "chances" with his work, and he's delighted with the results.

Artists are a solitary and idiosyncratic lot, but they don't work in a vacuum. They've always inspired and learned from one another—and always will. We're grateful to the artists who contributed to this collection of images. We hope you'll enjoy looking at it as much as we enjoyed gathering it together.

Bert Monroy

©*Bert Monroy*

All of Bert Monroy's digital paintings were created entirely in Adobe Illustrator and Photoshop without the use of scans.

Bert Monroy

Bert Monroy

Bert Monroy

Bert Monroy

Clifford Alejandro

Clifford Alejandro

Clifford Alejandro

Clifford Alejandro

William Low

William Low

William Low

William Low

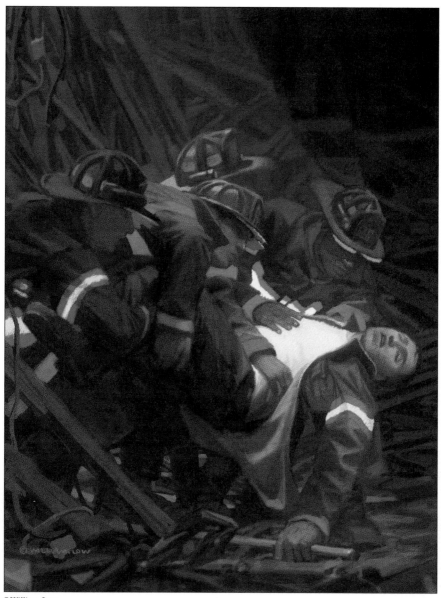

Marty Blake

Marty Blake

©Marty Blake

Marty Blake

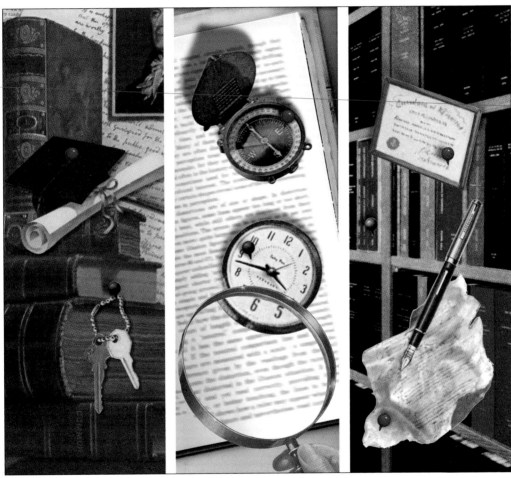

Marty Blake

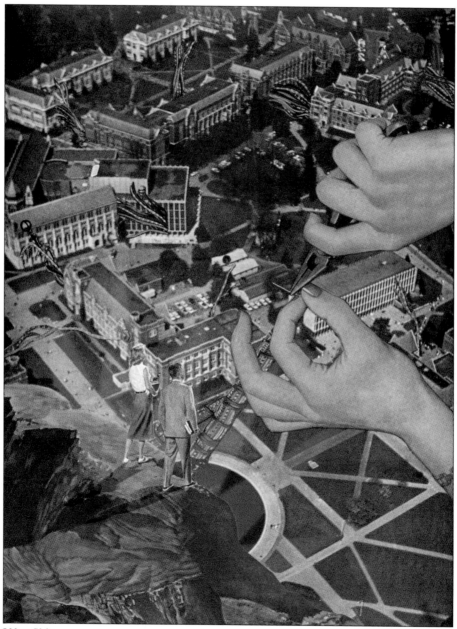

Mick Wiggins

Mick Wiggins

©Mick Wiggins

Mick Wiggins

John Kachik

John Kachik

John Kachik

Keri Smith

Keri Smith

Keri Smith

Paul Mirocha

Paul Mirocha

©Paul Mirocha

©Paul Mirocha

Paul Mirocha

To use the Pattern Stamp tool:

1. To create a custom pattern, choose the Rectangular Marquee tool ⬚ (M or Shift-M), select an area of an image to become a tile **1**, choose Edit > Define Pattern, type a Name, click OK, then deselect (Ctrl-D/Cmd-D).

2. Choose the Pattern Stamp tool (S or Shift-S). 🖫

3. On the Pattern Stamp tool options bar, choose options as per steps 2–3 on page 153. Check Aligned to stamp pattern tiles in a perfect grid, regardless of how many separate strokes you use; or uncheck Aligned if you don't need the tiles to align perfectly.

   Click the Pattern Preset picker arrowhead or thumbnail, then click a pattern on the picker **2**. Your custom pattern from step 1 will be the last pattern on the picker.

4. *Optional:* Check Impressionist to apply a blurry, fragmented version of the pattern.

5. Drag on a layer in the same image or in another image to stamp the pattern **3**. No source point is required for this tool.

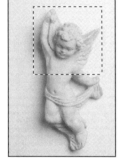

1 *Select an area of an image, then choose Edit > **Define Pattern.***

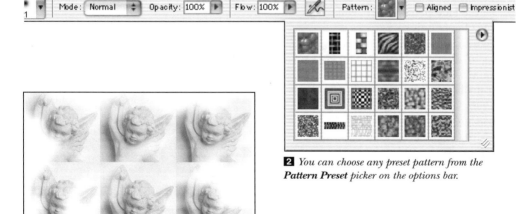

2 *You can choose any preset pattern from the **Pattern Preset** picker on the options bar.*

3 *You can apply the pattern in another image with various opacities chosen for the **Pattern Stamp** tool.*

Pattern Stamp

1 The options bar for the **Clone Stamp** tool

1 The options bar for the **Clone Stamp** tool

You can use the **Clone Stamp** tool to clone imagery from one **image** to another. Try using it to gather imagery from several open images into one final image. To create a brush stroke version of an image or images, using a soft brush, clone to a new document that has a white or solid-colored background.

2 Alt-click/Option-click on the **non-active** (source) image to establish a **source** point…

To clone from image to image:

1. Open two images, and position the two windows side by side.

2. If they're both color images, choose the same image mode for both. You can also clone between a color image and a grayscale image. *Note:* Choose the Don't Flatten option to preserve layers.

3. Choose the Clone Stamp tool (S or Shift S).

4. On the Clone Stamp tool options bar **1**, do all of the following :

   Click the Brush Preset picker arrowhead, then click a **brush.**

   Choose a blending **Mode.**

   Choose an **Opacity.**

   Set the **Flow** percentage to control the rate of application.

   Check **Aligned** to reproduce a continuous area from the source point even if you release the mouse between strokes, or uncheck Aligned to produce multiple clones from the source point.

3 …then drag back and forth in short strokes on the **active** (target) image to make the **clone** appear.

5. *Optional:* To apply cloned imagery in an airbrush style, click the Airbrush button.

6. Click in the image window that you want to clone to, and choose a layer.

7. Alt-click/Option-click the area of the source (nonactive) image that you want to clone from **2**.

8. Drag back and forth on the target (active) image to make the clone appear **3**–**4**.

4 To create this effect, an image was cloned to a new document with a white background.

1 *The original image, with a feathered selection*

2 *After inversing the selection and pressing Delete*

Use the **Feather** command to fade the edge of a selection by a specified number of pixels inward and outward from the marquee. A feather radius of 5, for example, would create a feather area 10 pixels wide.

Note: The feather won't be visible until the selection is modified with a painting tool, copied/pasted, moved, or filled, or a filter or Image menu command is applied to it.

To feather a selection:

1. With a selection active, right-click/ Ctrl-click and choose Feather, or choose Select > Feather, or press Ctrl-Alt-D/ Cmd-Option-D.

2. Enter a Feather Radius value (.2–250 pixels). The feather width is affected by the image resolution. The higher the image resolution, the wider you need to make the feather radius.

3. Click OK **1**–**2**. *Note:* If the feather radius is too wide for the selection area, the message "No pixels are more than 50% selected…" will appear.

TIP To specify a feather radius before creating a selection, choose a Marquee or Lasso tool, then enter a Feather value on the options bar.

TIP Read about the Smooth command for smoothing selections on page 133.

Feather

To eliminate a noticeable seam after pasting or moving layer pixels, use the **Defringe** command. It recolors pixels on the edge of a selection within a specified radius using pixel colors from just inside the edge.

Note: If the imagery you moved or pasted was originally on a black background and was selected with the anti-aliased option on, you can try using the Layer > Matting > Remove Black Matte command to remove unwanted remnants from the black background. Or choose Layer > Matting > Remove White Matte command if the imagery was originally on a white background. Feathered selections are more noticeably affected by the Matting commands.

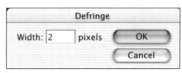

1 *Use the* **Defringe** *command to make montaged imagery look more seamless.*

To defringe a layer:

1. With a layer that was created via the Paste command chosen or with a selection of moved pixels still active, choose Layer > Matting > Defringe.

2. Enter a Width for the Defringe area (1–200) pixels **1**. Try a low number first (1, 2, or 3 pixels) so your edges won't lose definition. Some non-edge areas may also be affected.

3. Click OK.

To produce this image, entitled **Physique Medley,** *David Humphrey composited scans of embroidery and his own charcoal drawings and photographs, among other things. He then adjusted the luminosity levels of the various components on individual layers using blending modes (Darken, Multiply) and the Eraser and Burn tools.*

Defringe

HISTORY 8

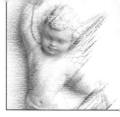

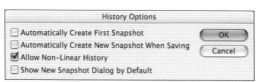

1 *Allow Non-Linear History and other options are turned on or off in the* **History Options** *dialog box.*

I N THIS CHAPTER you'll learn how to use the History palette to selectively undo up to 1,000 previous stages (called "states") of a work session. You'll also learn how to preserve states using snapshots, and how to restore selective areas to a prior state by using the History Brush or Art History Brush tool, or by filling a selection with a history state.

The **History palette** displays a list of the most recent states (edits) that were made to an image, with the bottommost state being the most recent. Clicking on a prior state restores the image to that stage of the editing process. What happens to the image when you do this depends on whether the palette is in linear or nonlinear mode, so the first step is to learn the difference between these two modes.

Using the History palette

Linear and nonlinear

There are two ways in which the History palette can be used: linear mode or non-linear mode. To toggle between modes, choose History Options from the palette menu, then in the History Options dialog box, check or uncheck **Allow Non-Linear History** **1**. You can switch between these two modes at any time during an editing session.

In **linear** mode, if you click back on an earlier state and resume image editing from that state or delete it, all subsequent (dimmed) states will be discarded **2**.

In the History palette's **nonlinear** mode, if you click back on or delete an earlier state, subsequent states won't be deleted (or dimmed). If you then resume image editing while that earlier state is selected, the new edits will show up as the latest states on the palette and earlier states will be preserved.

(Continued on the following page)

Source for the
History Brush *tool*   *The current history* **state**

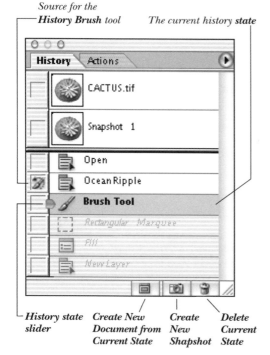

History state slider   Create New Document from Current State   Create New Snapshot   Delete Current State

2 *This is the* **History** *palette in* **linear** *mode. Note that all the steps below the current state are grayed out. The figure on the next page shows the palette in nonlinear mode.*

If you delete an earlier state and then click on the latest state, the deleted edits will still remain in the actual image. Nonlinear is the more flexible of the two modes **1**.

When would you want to work in nonlinear mode? When you need flexibility. Let's say you apply paint strokes to a layer, try out different blending modes for that layer, and then settle on a mode that you like. If you want to reduce the number of states on the palette, you can then delete any of the other blending mode states, whether they're before or after the one you've settled on. You can pick and choose.

When would you want to work in linear mode? If you find nonlinear mode confusing or disorienting, or if you want the option to revert back to an earlier state with a nice, clean break.

As long as **Automatically Create First Snapshot** is checked in the History Options dialog box, the History palette will automatically make a snapshot of the original state of the image each time the image is opened (see page 162). This is a good option to use in case you edit and save the document and then want to restore the original file.

To specify the number of states that can be listed on the palette for an editing session, go to Edit (Photoshop, in Mac) > Preferences > General, then enter a **History States** value (1–1000). If the maximum number of history states is exceeded during an editing session, earlier steps will automatically be removed to make room for the new ones. *Note:* The maximum number of states may be limited by various factors, including the image size, the kind of edits that are made to the image, and currently available memory. Each open image keeps its own list of states.

Clearing your palette

To deliberately clear the History palette for all currently open images in order to free up memory, choose Edit > Purge > **Histories,** then click OK.

To clear the History palette for just the current document, choose **Clear History** from the History palette menu. The Purge commands can't be undone, whereas the Clear History command can.

1 *This is the **History** palette in **nonlinear** mode. All the of the states are available, even those below the current state.*

History Snapshot; History States

History shortcuts

Step Forward one state   Ctrl-Shift-Z/Cmd-Shift-Z

Step Backward one state   Ctrl-Alt-Z/Cmd-Option-Z

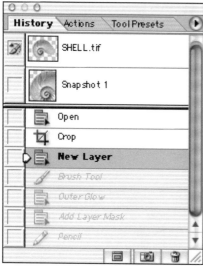

1 *After clicking a prior state with the* **History** *palette in* **linear** *mode*

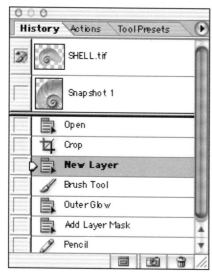

2 *After clicking a prior state with the* **History** *palette in* **nonlinear** *mode*

If the palette is in linear mode (Allow Non-Linear History is off), the **states** below the one you **click on** will become dimmed. If you delete the state you click on or edit the image at that state, all the dimmed states will be *deleted*. If you change your mind, choose Undo immediately to restore them. If the palette is in nonlinear mode, you can restore the document to the latest stage of editing by clicking the bottommost state.

To revert to a prior history state:

Click a prior state on the History palette **1**–**2**.
or
Choose Step Forward or Step Backward from the palette menu (see the shortcuts at left).
or
On the left side of the palette, drag the slider upward or downward to the desired state.

To duplicate a state:

Alt-click/Option-click a state. The duplicate will be listed as the latest (bottommost) state.

If Allow Non-Linear History is checked and you **delete** a state, *only* that state will be deleted. If Allow Non-Linear History is unchecked and you delete a state, *all* subsequent states will be deleted, too (you can choose Edit > Undo to restore them).

To delete a state:

Drag the name of the state that you want to delete over the Delete Current State button 🗑 on the History palette.
or
Alt-click/Option-click the Delete Current State button (and keep clicking) to delete consecutive states from the current state backward.

TIP When File > Revert is chosen, as with other commands, it becomes a state on the History palette, and all the states preceding it are retained. So you can restore an image to a state before the Revert command was invoked (or restore a state selectively with the History Brush).

Revert to Prior, Duplicate, Delete State

Using snapshots

A snapshot is like a copy of a history state, with one major difference: unlike a state, a snapshot will stay on the palette—even if the state from which it was created is deleted due to the maximum number of history states being reached or the palette being cleared or purged. It's a good idea to create a snapshot before performing a long series of editing steps or running an action on an image. Beware, though: all snapshots are deleted when an image is closed.

To have a snapshot created automatically each time a file is opened, check **Automatically Create First Snapshot** in History Options. To have a snapshot created each time a file is saved, check **Automatically Create New Snapshot When Saving**.

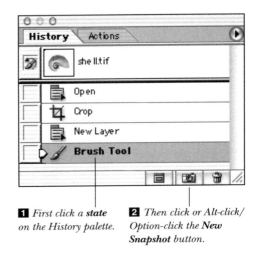

1 *First click a* **state** *on the History palette.* **2** *Then click or Alt-click/ Option-click the* **New Snapshot** *button.*

To create a snapshot of a history state:

1. Click the state that you want to create a snapshot of **1**.

2. Click the New Snapshot button **2**. If Show New Snapshot Dialog by Default is unchecked in History Options, a new snapshot thumbnail will appear at the top of the palette, and you can ignore the remaining instructions. If this option is checked, the New Snapshot dialog box will open; follow the remaining steps.
   or
   To choose options for the snapshot as you create it, choose New Snapshot from the palette menu; or Alt-click/Option-click the New Snapshot button; or right-click/Control-click the state and choose New Snapshot from the context menu.

3. Type a Name for the snapshot **3**.

4. Choose From: Full Document to make a snapshot that preserves all the layers on the Layers palette at that state; or choose Merged Layers to create a snapshot that merges all layers on the Layers palette at that state; or choose Current Layer to make a snapshot of only the currently active layer at that state.

5. Click OK **4**.

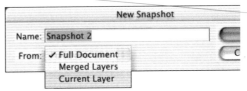

3 *In the* **New Snapshot** *dialog box, enter a name and choose which part of the image you want the snapshot to be created from.*

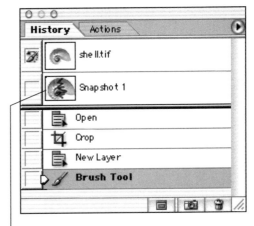

4 *A thumbnail for the new snapshot appears on the History palette.*

Create Snapshot

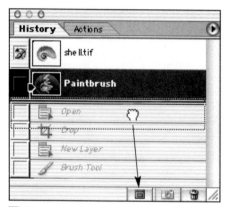

1 *Drag a snapshot or state over the **New Document from Current State** button.*

2 *A **duplicate** of the snapshot appears in a new document.*

To make a snapshot become the latest state:

Click a snapshot thumbnail. If the Allow Non-Linear History option is off and edits were made to the image since that snapshot was taken, the document will revert to the snapshot stage of editing and all the states will be dimmed. If you then resume editing, all dimmed states will be deleted. If Allow Non-Linear History was on, subsequent states will remain on the palette.
or
With either History option chosen, Alt-click/Option-click a snapshot thumbnail. The other states will remain available and that snapshot will become the latest state. This is a very useful option.

To delete a snapshot:

Click the snapshot thumbnail, choose Delete from the palette menu or click the Delete Current State button, 🗑 then click Yes.
or
Drag the snapshot to the Delete Current State button. 🗑

If you turn a history snapshot or state into a **new document,** you'll have a sort of freeze insurance—something to fall back on in the event of a system or power failure. Only one history state can be copied at a time.

To create a new document from a history state or snapshot:

Drag a snapshot or a state over the New Document from Current State button **1**. 🖼
or
Click a snapshot or a state, then click the New Document from Current State button.
or
Right-click/Control-click a snapshot or a state, then choose New Document from the context menu.

A new image window will appear, bearing the title of the snapshot or state from which it was created, and "Duplicate State" will be the name of the starting state for the new image **2**. Save this new image!

1 *Choose settings from the **History Brush** tool options bar.*

Restoring and erasing

You can select any snapshot or state on the History palette to use as a source of earlier pixel data for the **History Brush** tool. Dragging with the brush restores pixels from that prior state of editing.

Note: The History Brush tool can't be used on an image if you've changed its pixel count since it was opened (e.g., by resampling or cropping, or by changing the image mode or canvas size).

To use the History Brush tool:

1. Choose the History Brush tool (Y or Shift-Y).

2. On the History Brush tool options bar **1**:

   Choose a blending **Mode, Opacity** percentage, and **Flow** percentage. Click the Airbrush button, too, if you like.

   Click the Brush Preset picker arrowhead, then click a **brush** on the picker.

3. On the History palette, click in the leftmost column for the state or snapshot that you want to use as a source for the History Brush tool (the history source icon appears).

4. Choose the layer that you want to restore pixels on, and turn off Lock Transparent Pixels.

5. Draw strokes on the image. Pixel data from the prior state of that layer will replace the current pixel data where you draw strokes **2**–**3**.

TIP Here's an example of how the History Brush tool could be used to restore an earlier stage of an image. You add brushstrokes to a layer and then decide several editing steps later that you want to remove them. Clicking the state prior to the brushstrokes state could cause

Snapshot as History Brush source

Modify a layer (e.g., apply an adjustment command, a filter, or paint strokes), take a snapshot of the current state, and then delete that state. Set the **History Source** icon to the snapshot, then stroke with the History Brush tool on the part of the layer that you modified, to selectively restore it.

2 *The original image*

3 *After applying the Graphic Pen filter, positioning the **History Source** icon at a prior state, and then painting on parts of the image using the **History Brush** tool at 95% opacity*

1 *The original image*

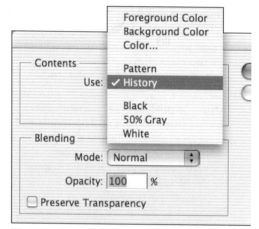

2 *Choose* **Use: History** *in the* **Fill** *dialog box.*

3 *We applied the Glass filter to a layer, selected the area around the tree, and then filled the selection with an earlier history state (Use: History) option. Try doing the same thing using the Distort > Wave or Ripple filter or an Artistic or Sketch filter.*

other edits to be deleted. Instead, click in the box next to any state prior to the state in which the strokes were added to set the source for the History Brush tool, click the layer on the Layers palette to which the brushstrokes were added, choose the History Brush tool (Y or Shift-Y), then paint out the added strokes.

TIP When restoring from a snapshot, you can choose a layer if the snapshot you're using as a source was created with the Full Document or Merged Layers option on. If the Current Layer option was chosen, you will paint on the layer that was preserved in the snapshot.

Note: The **Fill > Use: History** command can't be used on an image if you've changed its pixel count since it was opened (e.g., by resampling or cropping or by changing its image mode or canvas size). Furthermore, you can't restore deleted or modified layer effects or vector data layers (type or shapes) using the History Brush tool, or restore a vector mask on an image layer that's been modified.

To fill a selection or a layer with a history state:

1. Choose a layer that contains pixels **1**.

2. *Optional:* Create a selection.

3. On the History palette, click in the left-most column for the state you want to use as a fill (the History Source icon will appear where you click).

4. Choose Edit > Fill (Shift-Backspace/ Shift-Delete or Shift-F5).

5. Choose Use: History **2**.

6. Choose a Blending Mode and an Opacity percentage.

7. *Optional:* Check Preserve Transparency to replace only existing pixels. Leave this option unchecked to allow pixels to appear anywhere on the layer.

8. Click OK **3**.

Using the **Art History Brush** tool, you can paint a designated history state or snapshot back onto an image in an assortment of different-shaped strokes (actually, in our humble opinion, all the brush choices—Tight Long, Loose Curl, etc.—look like worms). Adjacent colors are blended to produce a painterly effect, and those colors will vary depending on the current Tolerance setting for the Art History Brush tool. If you have a stylus, go ahead and use it.

To use the Art History Brush tool:

1. Perform some edits on a layer, if you haven't already done so, to create states on the History palette **1**.

   TIP If you're working on the Background, before using the Art History Brush tool, fill the layer with white or a solid color to create a clean background to apply the Art History strokes to.

2. On the History palette, click in the leftmost column for the state or snapshot that you want to use as the source for the tool. The history source icon appears.

3. Choose the Art History Brush tool (Y or Shift-Y).

4. On the Art History Brush tool options bar **3**, do all of the following:

   Click the Brush Preset picker arrowhead, then click a small **brush** in the picker.

   Choose a **Mode** and an **Opacity.**

   Choose a painting style from the **Style** pop-up menu.

   Choose an **Area** (0–500 pixels) for the size of the area the strokes can cover.

   Choose a **Tolerance** value (0–100%). At a low tolerance, strokes will appear anywhere in the image; at a high tolerance, strokes will appear only over pixels that differ markedly from the source color.

5. Choose a layer, then draw strokes in the image window **2**. The longer you keep the mouse button down in the same spot, the more the colors will blend.

   TIP For a more handmade look, try switching stroke shapes and other parameters on the Art History Brush tool options bar between strokes, or choose different source states on the History palette. Or for your brush preset, create variations via the Shape Dynamics, Scattering, Texture, Color Dynamics, or Other Dynamics panes on the Brushes palette.

1 *A photograph, after applying Photoshop's Find Edges filter*

2 *After clicking in the leftmost column on the History palette at a prior state and then adding brushstrokes here and there using the **Art History Brush** tool (Darken mode, Style: Loose Long, Tolerance 0%)*

3 *The **Art History Brush** tool options bar*

ADJUSTMENTS 9

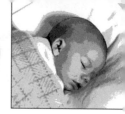

In this chapter

Creating and using adjustment layers

Auto Contrast

Invert

Threshold

Posterize

Brightness/Contrast

Levels

Screen back a layer

Dodge and Burn tools

Channel Mixer

Histogram palette

To use Hue/Saturation, Desaturate, Replace Color, and other commands on the Image > Adjustments submenu to perform color adjustments, see Chapter 11, Recolor. For the Shadow/Highlight command, see pages 242–243. For the Gradient Map command, see pages 267–268.

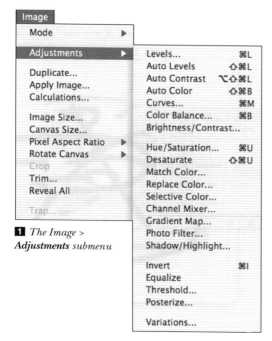

1 *The Image > Adjustments submenu*

THIS **CHAPTER** covers many methods for adjusting an image's light and dark values. First, we'll show you how to create adjustment layers—a great way to apply adjustment commands. Then you'll learn how to use adjustment commands **1** to make simple adjustments, such as inverting a layer to make it look like a film negative or posterizing it to reduce its luminosity levels to a specified number. You'll also learn how to use such features as the Levels dialog box to make more precise lightness or contrast adjustments to a layer's highlights, mid-tones, or shadows; and on a smaller scale, how to use the Burn and Dodge tools to make adjustments by hand. Finally, we'll show you how to use the Histogram palette to gauge the effectiveness of your work.

Adjustment basics

Before delving into the individual adjustment commands, review these general pointers:

■ For flexibility in editing, use **adjustment layers** (see the following page).

■ To restrict an adjustment command's effect to a specific area of a layer, create a **selection** before choosing the command.

■ To **reset** the settings in a dialog box, hold down Alt/Option and click Reset.

■ Check **Preview** in an adjustment dialog box to see how the adjustment will affect the image.

■ To reduce an adjustment command's effect, choose Edit > **Fade** (Ctrl-Shift-F/ Cmd-Shift-F), move the Opacity slider, then click OK.

■ To have the **last-used** settings display when you open an adjustment dialog box instead of the default settings, hold down Alt/Option while choosing the command, or include Alt/Option if you use a shortcut to invoke the command.

Adjustments Basics

167

Adjustment layers

There are two ways to apply adjustment commands: They can be applied directly to the current layer (or to a selection on the current layer), or they can be applied via an adjustment layer. We prefer the latter method because it offers the most flexibility.

Unlike a normal layer, an adjustment layer affects all the visible layers below it—not just the current layer. But the beauty of an adjustment layer is that it doesn't actually change pixels until it's merged with the layer below it (Ctrl-E/Cmd-E), so you can use it to try out various effects. We use adjustment layers to test out various color and tonal adjustments.

On this page and the following three pages we explain how to **create** and use adjustment layers. If you prefer, you can skip ahead and read about the individual adjustment commands first (starting on page 172), and return to these pages later.

To create an adjustment layer:

1. Choose the layer above which you want the adjustment layer to appear.

2. Choose an adjustment command from the New Fill/Adjustment Layer pop-up menu ⊘. at the bottom of the Layers palette **1**–**2**.
   or
   Choose a command from the Layer > New Adjustment Layer submenu, then click OK.

3. Make the desired adjustments, then click OK.

To modify an adjustment layer:

1. On the Layers palette, double-click the adjustment layer thumbnail (the thumbnail on the left).
   or
   The slow way: Click the adjustment layer name, then choose Layer > Layer Content Options.

2. Make the desired changes in the adjustment dialog box, then click OK.

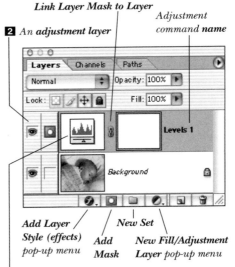

1 *Choose an **adjustment** command from this portion of the pop-up menu.*

Link Layer Mask to Layer

*Adjustment command **name***

2 *An **adjustment layer***

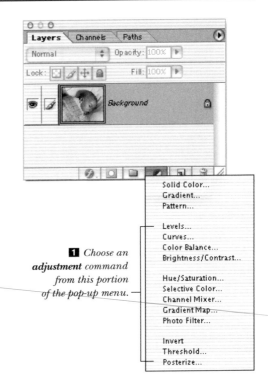

Add Layer Style (effects) pop-up menu

Add Mask

New Set

New Fill/Adjustment Layer pop-up menu

*The top part of the **adjustment** command thumbnail is the icon for that command (each command has its own symbol). If the thumbnail has a slider icon, it means that command is editable and changeable.*

File to file

To copy an adjustment layer from one image to another, **drag and drop** it from the Layers palette in the source image into the target image window.

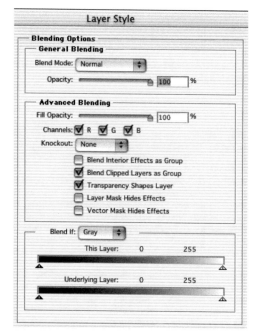

 *Choose **Blending Options** for an adjustment layer in the **Layer Style** dialog box.*

You can control how an adjustment layer **blends** with underlying layers. This is accomplished via the Layer Style dialog box.

Note: You can also make blending mode, opacity, and fill opacity adjustments via an adjustment layer. See page 171.

To choose blending options for an adjustment layer (or any layer):

1. On the Layers palette, double-click the blank area to the right of an adjustment layer (or ordinary layer) name.

2. Make sure Blending Options is chosen on the left side of the Layer Style dialog box.

3. Change the **General Blending: Blend Mode** and/or **Opacity** settings **1**.

4. Change any of these **Advanced Blending** options:

   Uncheck any **Channels** you want to exclude from blending with the underlying layer. To set the blend range for each channel one at a time, choose a channel from the Blend If pop-up menu; or to work on all the channels simultaneously, leave Gray as the choice on that pop-up menu. The current image mode (e.g., RGB Color, CMYK Color) determines which channels are available.

   Move the leftmost Blend If: **This Layer** slider to the right to remove shadow areas from the active layer. Move the rightmost This Layer slider to the left to remove highlights from the active layer.

   Move the leftmost **Underlying Layer** slider to the right to restore shadow areas from the layer directly below the active layer. Move the rightmost Underlying Layer slider to the left to restore highlights from the layer directly below the active layer.

   (To read about Knockout and the two "Blend..." check boxes, see pages 270–273.)

5. Click OK.

You can keep an adjustment layer right where it is but **change** which adjustment **command** it contains (e.g., Levels to Curves or Hue/Saturation to Color Balance).

To choose a different command for an adjustment layer:

1. Click an adjustment layer on the Layers palette.

2. Choose the command you want to switch to from the Layer > Change Layer Content submenu.

3. Make the desired adjustments, then click OK.

TIP To discard an adjustment layer, drag it to the Delete Layer button. 🗑

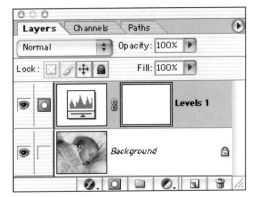

1 *An adjustment layer is chosen.*

When you **merge down** an adjustment layer, the adjustments become permanent for the image layer below it, so be certain you want the effect to become permanent before you perform another operation. Well, it's sort of permanent. If you change your mind, you can choose Edit > Undo or click the prior state on the History palette.

To merge an adjustment layer:

1. Choose the adjustment layer you want to merge downward **1**.

2. Choose Merge Down from the Layers palette menu (Ctrl-E/Cmd-E) **2**.

   Note: Adjustment layers don't contain pixels, so you can't merge them with each other. What you can do is merge multiple adjustment layers into an image layer (or layers) by using either the Merge Visible or the Flatten Image command (see pages 119–122).

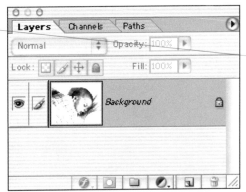

2 *After applying the **Merge Down** command, the Levels values from the adjustment layer are permanently applied to the layer below it (in this case, the Background).*

1 *Choose a **blending mode** for an adjustment layer.*

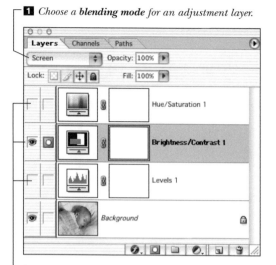

2 *Show/hide adjustment layers to compare their effects.*

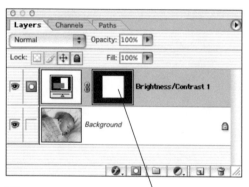

3 *Create a **selection** before choosing an adjustment layer command.*

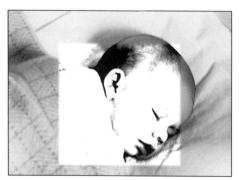

4 *In this case, a Brightness/Contrast adjustment affected only the rectangular selection area.*

Ways to use adjustment layers

Click an adjustment layer, then choose a **blending mode** from the pop-up menu on the Layers palette **1**. Changing an adjustment layer's blending mode can dramatically change how it affects underlying layers. Try Overlay mode to heighten contrast, Multiply mode to darken the image, or Screen mode to lighten the image. Or try stacking several adjustment layers, then hide, or lower the opacity of, each layer to see how the underlying image is altered **2**.

To **compare** different settings for the same adjustment command, create multiples of the same adjustment layer (e.g., Levels), hide all the adjustment layers, and then show/hide them one at a time. You can also restack adjustment layers among themselves or place them at different locations within the overall layer stack.

To **prevent** an underlying layer from being affected by an adjustment layer, restack it so it's above the adjustment layer.

To limit the area an adjustment layer affects, create a **selection** before you create it. The selection area will be shown in white on the layer mask thumbnail **3**–**4**.

You can also **paint** or **fill** with black on an adjustment layer to remove the adjustment effect, or with white to reveal the adjustment effect. The strokes will display on the layer mask thumbnail. To read more about adjustment layer masks, see page 179.

Normally, an adjustment layer will affect all the currently visible layers below it, but you can use a **clipping mask** to limit an adjustment layer's effect to only the layer or layers it's grouped with (see pages 283–284). If you choose a command from the Layer > New Adjustment Layer submenu, you can also create a mask by checking Use Previous Layer to Create Clipping Mask in the New Layer dialog box.

Using Adjustment Layers

Adjustment commands

Next we'll show you how to use the individual commands on the Image > Adjustments submenu. They can be applied to a layer directly or via an adjustment layer. Try applying the adjustment commands to a grayscale image first to learn how they work, then use them on color images.

Once you get used to the adjustment commands, you can explore the Histogram palette, which is discussed on pages 181–182. This palette displays before and after diagrams of the light and dark values of the image while it's being edited. Some dialog boxes also have a histogram built into them.

We'll begin with the simple, one-step **Auto Contrast** command, which turns the almost-lightest pixels in an image white and the almost-darkest pixels black, and then redistributes the gray levels in between.

To apply the Auto Contrast command:

1. Choose a layer or the Background.

2. Choose Image > Adjustments > Auto Contrast (Ctrl-Alt-Shift-L/Cmd-Option-Shift-L) **1**–**2**.

1 *The original image*

2 *After applying* **Auto Contrast**

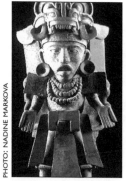

PHOTO: NADINE MARKOVA

1 *The original image*

2 *The image **inverted***

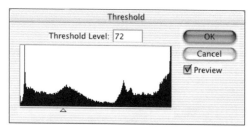

PHOTO: PAUL PETROFF

3 *The original image*

4 *Move the **Threshold** slider to control the cutoff point for black and white values.*

5 *After applying the **Threshold** command*

Choose the **Invert** command to make a layer or the Background look like a film negative. Each pixel is replaced with its opposite brightness and/or color value. You can also use this command to make a negative look like a positive, though this may not be the most exacting way to do it, at least from a photographer's point of view.

To invert lights and darks:

1. Choose a layer or the Background.

2. Choose Image > Adjustments > Invert (Ctrl-I/Cmd-I) **1**–**2**. You can use the same shortcut again to reverse the command.
   or
   Choose Invert from the New Fill/ Adjustment Layer pop-up menu 🄸, at the bottom of the Layers palette.

The **Threshold** dialog box makes the current layer or the Background high-contrast by converting color or gray pixels into pure black and white pixels.

To make a layer high contrast:

1. Choose a layer or the Background **3**.

2. Choose Image > Adjustments > Threshold.
   or
   Choose Threshold from the New Fill/ Adjustment Layer pop-up menu 🄸, at the bottom of the Layers palette.

3. Move the slider to the right to increase the number of black pixels **4**, or to the left to increase the number of white pixels.
   or
   Enter a value (1–255) in the Threshold Level field. Pixels lighter than the value you enter will become white; pixels darker than the value you enter will become black.

4. Click OK **5**.

Invert; Threshold

Use the **Posterize** command to reduce the number of color or value levels in the current layer or the Background to a specified number. We love the arty effects that this simple command can produce. It's also useful for reducing the number of colors in an image prior to optimizing it as a GIF for Web output.

To posterize:

1. Choose a layer or the Background 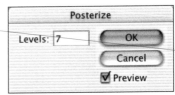, then choose Image > Adjustments > Posterize.

   or

   Choose Posterize from the New Fill/ Adjustment Layer pop-up menu , at the bottom of the Layers palette.

2. Make sure Preview is checked, then enter the desired number of Levels (2–255) . To make the layer look like a poster or silkscreen, try a Levels value between 4 and 8.

3. Click OK .

TIP If the number of shades in an image is reduced using the Posterize command (or any other tonal adjustments are made, for that matter), without using an adjustment layer, and then the image is saved and closed, the original shade information will be permanently lost.

TIP Create a gradient using two or more colors, then create a Posterize adjustment layer above the gradient layer. The gradient will have obvious color bands.

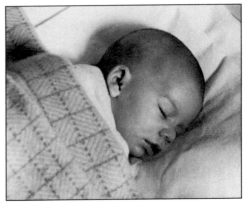

1 *The original image*

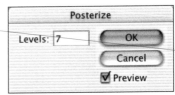

2 *Enter the desired number of color or value levels in the* **Posterize** *dialog box.*

3 *Posterized*

PHOTO: PAUL PETROFF

1 *The original image*

2 *Move the Brightness and/or Contrast sliders in the* **Brightness/Contrast** *dialog box.*

3 *The Brightness slider moved to the right*

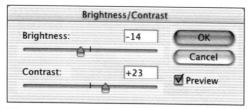

4 *The brightness and contrast adjusted*

The **Brightness/Contrast** command, discussed below, is easy to use, but it's also limited in scope. If you want to adjust the shadows, midtones, and highlights in an image individually and with more precision, use the Levels dialog box instead (see the following page).

To use the Brightness/Contrast command:

1. Choose a layer **1**, then choose Image > Adjustments > Brightness/Contrast.
   or
   Choose Brightness/Contrast from the New Fill/Adjustment Layer pop-up menu ⬤, at the bottom of the Layers palette.

2. To lighten the layer, move the Brightness slider to the right **2**.
   or
   To darken the layer, move the Brightness slider to the left.
   or
   Enter a Brightness value (–100 to 100).

3. To intensify the contrast, move the Contrast slider to the right.
   or
   To lessen the contrast, move the Contrast slider to the left.
   or
   Enter a Contrast value (–100 to 100).

4. Click OK **3**–**4**.

Brightness/Contrast

Use the **Levels** dialog box to make fine
adjustments to a layer's highlights, midtones,
or shadows. We use this dialog box, day in
and day out, for most of our adjustments.

To adjust brightness and contrast using Levels:

1. Choose a layer **1**, then choose Image >
   Adjustments > Levels (Ctrl-L/Cmd-L).
   or
   Choose Levels from the New Fill/
   Adjustment Layer pop-up menu ⊘.
   at the bottom of the Layers palette.

2. Do any of the following **2**:

   To brighten the highlights and intensify
   the contrast, move the **Input highlights**
   slider to the left. The midtones (middle)
   slider will move along with it. Readjust
   the midtones slider, if necessary.

   To darken the shadows, move the **Input
   shadows** slider to the right. The midtones slider will move along with it.
   Readjust the midtones slider, if necessary.

   To adjust the midtones independently,
   move the **Input midtones** slider.

   To decrease contrast and lighten the
   image, move the **Output shadows** slider
   to the right.

   To decrease contrast and darken the
   image, move the **Output highlights** slider
   to the left.

   Note: You can enter values in the Input
   Levels or Output Levels fields instead of
   moving the sliders.

3. *Optional:* To save the current settings,
   click Save. (Use Load to apply the saved
   settings to other images.)

4. Click OK **3**–**4**.

TIP To adjust levels automatically, choose
Image > Adjustments > **Auto Levels**
(Ctrl-Shift-L/Cmd-Shift-L) or click Auto
in the Levels dialog box. For the Auto
Color Correction options, see page 205.

1 *The original image*

2 *The five sliders in the* **Levels** *dialog box*

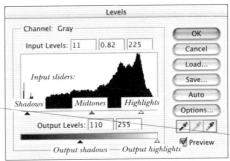

3 *After* **Levels** *adjustments*

PHOTO: PAUL PETROFF

4 *To produce this image, an area of the image was*
selected *before the Levels adjustment layer was made.*

Levels

1 *The original image*

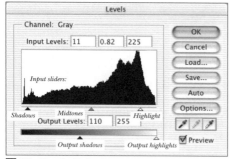

2 *The **Levels** dialog box*

3 *The music layer **screened back***

4 *The Output slider positions reversed*

This is another way to use the **Levels** command.

To screen back a layer:

1. Choose a layer or the Background **1**, then choose Image > Adjustments > Levels (Ctrl-L/Cmd-L).
or
Choose Levels from the New Fill/ Adjustment Layer pop-up menu *🖋*, at the bottom of the Layers palette.

2. To reduce contrast, move the Input highlights slider slightly to the left **2**.
and
Move the Output shadows slider to the right.

3. To lighten the midtones, move the Input midtones slider to the left.

4. Click OK **3**, **5**–**6**.

TIP To make a layer look like a film negative, reverse the position of the two Output sliders **4**. The farther you move them apart, the more the brightness and contrast attributes will be reversed. Or try the Invert command for a similar effect.

PHOTO: PAUL PETROFF

5 *The original image*

6 *The **screened-back** version*

Screen Back a Layer

177

To lighten pixels by hand in small areas, use the **Dodge** tool; to darken pixels, use the **Burn** tool. You can choose separate brushes and options bar settings for each tool.

To lighten using the Dodge tool or darken using the Burn tool:

1. Choose a layer. *Note:* The Dodge and Burn tools can't be used on a image in Bitmap or Indexed Color mode.

2. Choose the Dodge 🔍 or Burn 🖑 tool (O or Shift-O).

3. On the tool's options bar, do all of the following :

   Click the Brush Preset picker arrowhead, then click a hard-edged or soft-edged brush. A large, soft brush will produce the smoothest result. You can also choose a brush from the Brushes palette.

   Choose Shadows, Midtones, or Highlights from the **Range** pop-up menu to dodge or burn only pixels in that value range.

   Choose an **Exposure** setting between 1% (low intensity) and 100% (high intensity). Try a low exposure first (20%–30%) so the tool won't bleach or darken areas too quickly.

   Click the **Airbrush** button, 🖋 if desired.

4. Stroke on any area of the layer. Pause between strokes, if necessary, to allow the screen to redraw **2**–**3**. To dodge or burn in a straight line, click on the image, move the pointer, then Shift-click on the image again.

TIP If you dodge or burn an area too much, choose Edit > Undo or use the History palette to remove those states. Don't use the opposite tool to fix it—it will end up looking blotchy.

TIP To create a smooth, even highlight or shadow line, dodge or burn a path using the Stroke Path command with the Dodge or Burn tool chosen (see the sidebar on page 325).

1 *Choose settings for the **Dodge** or **Burn** tool from the options bar.*

2 *The **Dodge** tool with **Shadows** chosen from the options bar was used to eliminate dark spots in the background of this image.*

3 *After **dodging***

Dodge or Burn

Layer mask shortcuts

For the following shortcuts, repeat the same command to toggle the feature off:

View the mask in the image window	Alt-click/Option-click adjustment layer mask thumbnail
View the mask in a **rubylith** color (red) thumbnail	Alt-Shift-click/Option-Shift-click adjustment layer mask
Deactivate/activate the mask for an adjustment layer	Shift-click adjustment layer mask thumbnail
Convert nonmasked area into a **selection**	Ctrl-click/Cmd-click adjustment layer mask thumbnail

1 *We painted with black on the left side of the **Threshold** adjustment layer. The Threshold effect is visible only in the areas we didn't paint on.*

2 *In this image, the adjustment layer's **opacity** was lowered to 60%, which caused the Threshold effect to blend with the original underlying image.*

There are two ways to **restrict** an **adjustment layer** effect to a portion of an image. One way is to create a selection before you create the adjustment layer. Another way is to create a selection or paint with black on the adjustment layer after it's created, which we discuss below.

To restrict an adjustment layer's effect using a mask:

1. Choose an adjustment layer, and choose black as the Foreground color. The Color palette will reset automatically to the Grayscale model.

2. To mask the adjustment layer effect:

Create a selection using any selection tool (e.g., Rectangular Marquee, Lasso, or Magic Wand), choose Edit > Fill (Shift-Backspace/Shift-Delete), choose Use: Foreground Color, then click OK. *or*
Choose the Brush tool (B or Shift-B), choose Mode: Normal and Opacity 100% from the options bar, then paint on the image **1**. Or to partially mask the adjustment layer effect, choose a lower opacity for the Brush tool.

3. *More options:*

To restore the adjustment layer effect, paint or fill with white.

To reveal just a small area of the adjustment effect, fill the entire layer with black and then paint with white over some areas.

To make the adjustment effect visible on the entire image, fill the whole adjustment layer with white.

TIP To diminish the adjustment layer's effect over the entire layer by a percentage, lower the opacity of the adjustment layer via the Opacity slider on the Layers palette **2**.

TIP By default, adjustment layers contain a pixel-based layer mask. To create a vector mask for an adjustment layer, see page 328.

To make a layer grayscale using the Channel Mixer:

1. Choose a layer or the Background, then choose Image > Adjustments > Channel Mixer.

   or

   To apply the command via an adjustment layer, choose Channel Mixer from the New Fill/Adjustment Layer pop-up menu ⊘, at the bottom of the Layers palette.

2. Check Monochrome **1**. The layer or image will become grayscale and Gray will be the only choice on the Output Channel pop-up menu.

3. Move any of the Source Channels sliders to control how much that color channel is used as a source for the luminosity levels in the grayscale image. Drag a slider to the left to decrease the amount of that color in the output channel, or to the right to increase the amount of that color.

4. Move the Constant slider to the left to add black or to the right to add white.

5. Click OK. Despite the layer's appearance, the image is still in its original color mode. If you like, you can now convert it to Grayscale mode via the Image > Mode submenu.

TIP If you apply the Channel Mixer to a layer, you can choose a different layer opacity or blending mode for the layer.

TIP To add a color tint to a layer, check Monochrome in the Channel Mixer dialog box, then uncheck it to restore the color Output Channels. Choose an Output Channel and move the Source Channels sliders to produce a different color tint. Repeat for any other Output Channel(s).

TIP Have the Histogram palette open while using the Channel Mixer command so you can see how settings in the dialog box affect the tonal and color distribution of pixels in the image.

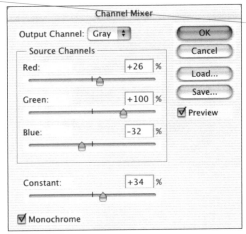

1 *Check* **Monochrome** *in the* **Channel Mixer** *dialog box to make the layer grayscale.*

Using the Histogram palette NEW

The Histogram palette (formerly a dialog box) displays up-to-the-minute before and after diagrams of the light and dark tonal values of an image while the image is being edited or an adjustment dialog box is open. The horizontal axis represents the gray or color levels between 0 and 255; the number of pixels in each level are stacked in bars on the vertical axis. Shadow areas are on the left, highlights on the right. The Histogram palette and palette options are accessible while adjustment and adjustment layer dialog boxes are open.

This palette is useful for judging whether a good scanning job was done on a continuous-tone photograph. The histogram for an image that has been overly manipulated and thus lacks tonal details in the shadows, mid-tones, or highlights will have gaps between the vertical lines and noticeable spikes (like teeth on a comb). That doesn't mean the image isn't pleasing, though. Many intentional edits that are made to an image, such as applying various filters, can produce a lousy-looking histogram, but it may be just the effect you're aiming for.

Via the Histogram palette menu, you can choose from three views for the palette: Compact View **1**; Expanded View to view palette display information about the combined channels or just one channel at a time **2**; or All Channels View to display a histogram for each and every channel.

While a large file is being edited, Photoshop maintains the redraw speed of the Histogram palette by reading from the cache data for the histogram—not actual data. When this happens, the Cached Data Warning icon ⚠ appears on the palette. Be sure to keep updating the palette so it reflects the current tonal values in the image. You can choose a Cache Levels setting (2–8) in Preferences > Memory & Image Cache; relaunch Photoshop to activate the new setting.

To update the Histogram palette: NEW

Double-click anywhere on the histogram.
or
Click the Cached Data Warning icon. ⚠
or
Click the Uncached Refresh button. 🔄

The black areas on the Histogram palette represent the tonal and color distribution changes being made to image pixels; the gray areas represent the tonal and color distribution of pixels in the original image.

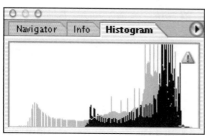

1 *The **Histogram** palette in **Compact View***

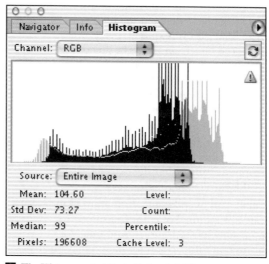

2 *The **Histogram** palette in **Expanded View***

NEW Reading the histogram

A histogram is a visual display of the distribution, or tonal range, of pixels in an image. Shadow pixels are on the left, midtone pixels in the middle, and highlight pixels on the right. An image with a wide tonal range has a fairly even distribution of pixels in the shadow, midtone, and highlight areas. When an image lacks pixels in any of those areas, the result is a loss of image detail. Learning how to read a histogram can help you evaluate the quality of a scan, and it can also help you judge the effect of any tonal and color adjustments made to the image in Photoshop.

Images fall loosely into three categories, based on their overall tonal range. For a dark (low-key) image, such as a night scene, pixels will be clustered primarily on the left side of the histogram; for an image with both light and dark areas (average-key), you'll see a more even distribution of pixels across the histogram; and for a light image with little or no shadow areas (high-key), such as a polar bear romping in the snow, pixels will be clustered mostly on the right side of the histogram.

If your image is average-key but underexposed, pixels will be clustered mostly on the left side of the histogram, indicating that the image lacks detail in the highlights **1**. If an image is overexposed, pixels will be clustered mostly on the right side of the histogram, indicating that the image lacks detail in the shadows **2**. A scan with a good tonal range will have a mostly solid histogram with a smooth contour **3**.

If an area of pixels rises sharply upward off the left or right edge of the histogram **4**, it means pixels were clipped (detail was stripped) from either the extreme shadow or the extreme highlight areas.

Small gaps or spikes in a histogram **5** indicate abrupt tonal or color transitions (or even some posterization). And finally, a histogram with a comb formation may mean the image has been manipulated either in Photoshop or by the scanner software.

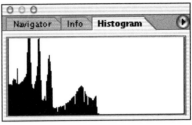

1 *Histogram for an* ***underexposed*** *image*

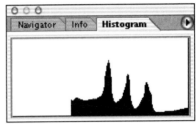

2 *Histogram for an* ***overexposed*** *image*

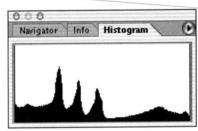

3 *Histogram for an image that has* ***good tonal range***

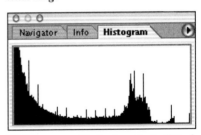

4 *Histogram with* ***shadow pixels clipped***

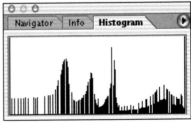

5 *Histogram with* ***gaps*** *and* ***spikes***

Histogram Palette

CHOOSE COLORS 10

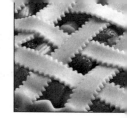

*Click the **Switch Colors** button (X) to swap the Foreground and Background colors.*

Foreground 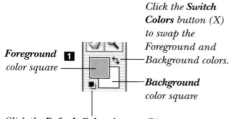 color square

Background color square

*Click the **Default Colors** button (D) to make the Foreground color **black** and the Background color **white**.*

The currently active square has a double border. This is the **Foreground** *color square.*

2 **Background** color square

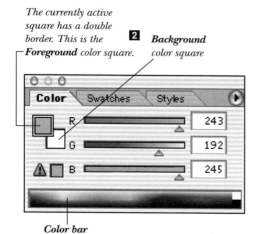

Color bar

IN THIS CHAPTER, you will learn how to choose the colors that are applied by Photoshop's commands and tools. In the next chapter, you'll learn how to apply colors using various painting and editing tools, as well as some commands.

Foreground and Background colors

When you use a painting tool, create type, or use the Stroke command, the current **Foreground** color is applied.

When you use the Eraser tool on the Background or on a layer with Lock Transparent Pixels on, or when you apply a transformation command to or move a selection on the Background using the Move tool, the hole that's left behind is automatically filled with the current **Background** color. With the Gradient tool, you can produce blends using the Foreground and/or Background colors.

The Foreground and Background colors are displayed in the Foreground and Background color squares on the Toolbox **1** and on the Color palette **2**. (When written with an uppercase "F" or "B," these terms refer to those two colors, not the foreground or background areas of a picture.)

The methods for choosing a Foreground or Background color are described on the following pages. In brief, you can:

- Enter values in fields or click the large color square in the **Color Picker.**
- Choose a premixed color from a matching system using the **Custom Colors** dialog box.
- Enter values in fields or move sliders on the **Color** palette.
- Click a swatch on the **Swatches** palette.
- Pluck a color from an image using the **Eyedropper** tool.

Next, we'll get into specifics.

To choose a color using the Color Picker:

1. Click the Foreground or Background color square on the Toolbox.
   or
   Click the Foreground or Background color square on the Color palette, if it's already active (has a double border).
   or
   Double-click the Foreground or Background color square on the Color palette, if it's not active.

   Note: If the color square you click on is a Custom color, the Custom Colors dialog box will open. Click Picker to open the Color Picker dialog box.

2. *Optional:* In the Photoshop Color Picker, check Only Web Colors to make only Web-safe colors available.

3. Click a color on the vertical color slider to choose a hue **1**, then click a variation of that hue in the large square **2**.
   or
   To choose a specific process color for print output, enter percentages from a printed color matching system swatch-book in the C, M, Y, and K fields.
   or
   For onscreen output, enter a value (0–255) for the R, G, and B components. When all these components are set to 0, black is produced; when all three are set to 255, white is produced. You could also enter numbers in the HSB or Lab fields.

4. Click OK. The color will appear in the Foreground or Background color square on both the Toolbox and the Color palette. To save it to the Swatches palette for future use, see page 187.

TIP To make the Photoshop Color Picker available, choose Edit (Photoshop, in Mac) > Preferences > General (Ctrl-K/Cmd-K), then choose Color Picker: Adobe. You can choose the Windows/Apple color picker from the same pop-up menu. Only one color picker is accessible at a time.

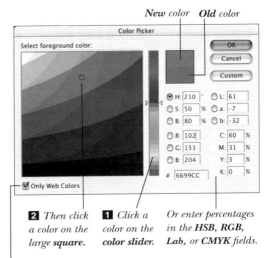

New color *Old* color

2 *Then click a color on the large* **square.** **1** *Click a color on the color slider.* *Or enter percentages in the* **HSB, RGB, Lab,** *or* **CMYK** *fields.*

Check **Only Web Colors** *in the* **Color Picker** *to make only Web-safe colors available.*

⚠ or ⬡

This icon ⚠ in the Color Picker or on the Color palette indicates that there is no ink combination for the color you chose—meaning it's outside the **printable gamut.** If you're planning to print your image, change it to an in-gamut color or click the exclamation point to have Photoshop substitute the closest printable color (shown in the swatch next to or below the exclamation point). If you convert your image to CMYK Color mode, the entire image will be brought into printable gamut. The out-of-gamut range is defined by the CMYK output profile currently chosen in Edit (Photoshop, in Mac) > Color Settings.

This icon ⬡ in the Color Picker indicates that the chosen color isn't **Web-safe.** Click the swatch under the cube to have Photoshop substitute the closest Web-safe color to yours.

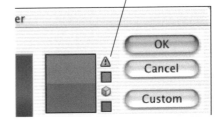

Color Picker

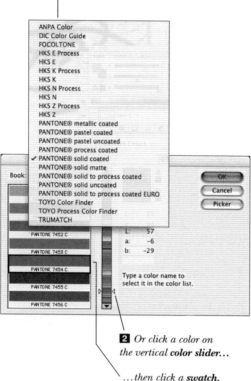

1 *Choose a matching system from the **Book** pop-up menu, then type a **number**.*

2 *Or click a color on the vertical **color slider**...*

*...then click a **swatch**.*

By default, Photoshop separates all colors in an image into the four process colors, regardless of whether they are process or spot colors. If you want to output a spot color to a separate plate from Photoshop, you must create a spot color channel for it (see page 208).

Note: Don't rely on your monitor to represent **matching system** colors accurately—you must choose them from a printed PANTONE, TRUMATCH, TOYO, DIC, FOCOLTONE, or ANPA Color swatch book. But before you do so, find out which brand of ink your printer is planning to use.

For online output, you can choose hexadecimal colors (HKS E, HKS K, HKS N, or HKS Z).

To choose a custom color:

1. Click the Foreground or Background color square on the Toolbox.
   or
   Click the Foreground or Background color square on the Color palette, if it's already active (has a double border).
   or
   Double-click the Foreground or Background color square on the Color palette, if it's not active.

   Note: If the color square you click on isn't a custom color, the Color Picker dialog box will open. Click Custom to open the Custom Colors dialog box.

2. Choose a matching guide system from the Book pop-up menu **1**.

3. Type a number—that swatch will become selected.
   or
   Click a color on the vertical color slider, then click a swatch on the left side of the dialog box **2**.

4. *Optional:* Click Picker to return to the Color Picker.

5. Click OK.

TIP To load a matching system library onto the Swatches palette, see page 188.

Custom Colors

To choose a color using the Color palette:

1. Click the Foreground or Background color square, if it isn't already active █.

2. From the Color palette menu, choose a color model for the sliders █.

3. Move any of the sliders █.
   or
   Click on or drag across the color bar.
   or
   Enter values in the fields.

TIP Right-click/Control-click the color bar to choose a different spectrum style for the color bar from a context menu.

TIP Alt-click/Option-click the color bar to choose a color for whichever color square isn't currently selected.

TIP Colors inside the slider bars will update as you drag a slider. To turn this feature off, uncheck Dynamic Color Sliders in Edit (Photoshop, in Mac) > Preferences > General.

TIP In the RGB model, white (the presence of all colors) is produced when all the sliders are in their rightmost positions, black (the absence of all colors) is produced when all the sliders are in their leftmost positions, and gray is produced when all the sliders are vertically aligned in any other position.

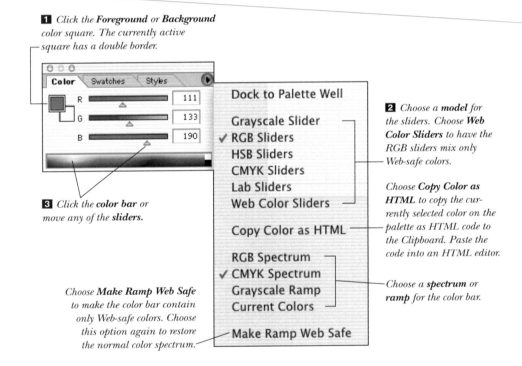

█ *Click the **Foreground** or **Background** color square. The currently active square has a double border.*

█ *Click the **color bar** or move any of the **sliders**.*

█ *Choose a **model** for the sliders. Choose **Web Color Sliders** to have the RGB sliders mix only Web-safe colors.*

*Choose **Copy Color as HTML** to copy the currently selected color on the palette as HTML code to the Clipboard. Paste the code into an HTML editor.*

*Choose a **spectrum** or **ramp** for the color bar.*

*Choose **Make Ramp Web Safe** to make the color bar contain only Web-safe colors. Choose this option again to restore the normal color spectrum.*

Color Palette

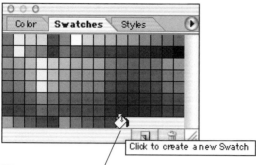

1 *Click in the blank area below the swatches to **add** a color to the palette.*

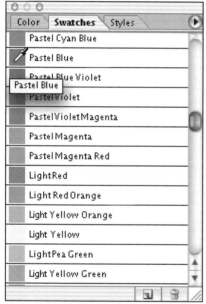

2 *The Swatches palette in **Small List** mode*

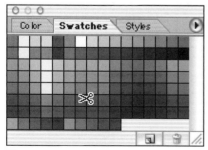

3 *Alt-click/Option-click a swatch to **delete** it.*

Swatches palette

TIP Detach the Swatches palette from the Color palette group before proceeding with these instructions.

To choose a color from the Swatches palette:

To choose a color for the currently active color square, click a color swatch.
or
To choose a color for the square that isn't currently active, Ctrl-click/Cmd-click a color swatch.

TIP To load or append a different set of swatches to the palette, see the instructions on the following page.

To add a color to the Swatches palette:

1. Mix a Foreground color using the Color palette or the Color Picker.

2. Show the Swatches palette.

3. Click in the blank area below the swatches on the palette (paint bucket pointer) **1** or right-click/Ctrl-click any existing swatch and choose New Swatch. Enter a Name, then click OK.
   or
   To create a new swatch without entering a custom name, click the New Swatch of Foreground Color button 🔲 at the bottom of the Swatches palette.

   Regardless of which method you use, the new swatch will appear as the last swatch on the palette.

TIP To rename a swatch, double-click it, change the name, then click OK. To see the swatch name, choose Small List **2** from the palette menu or use tool tips.

To delete a color from the Swatches palette:

Alt-click/Option-click the swatch to be deleted (scissors pointer) or right-click/Control-click a swatch and choose Delete Swatch **3**. This can't be undone.

Note: If you edit the Swatches palette, exit/quit Photoshop, and then relaunch, your edited palette will redisplay.

To save an edited swatches library:

1. Choose Save Swatches from the Swatches palette menu.
2. In the File Name/Save As field, enter a name for the edited library 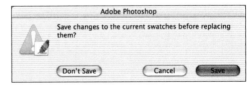.
3. Choose a location in which to save the library. For locations, see the sidebar.
4. Click Save.

Onto the Swatches palette, you can **load** any of the preset color swatch libraries that are supplied with Photoshop or any swatch library that you've created. You can either replace the existing preset library with the new one or append (add) the additional library to the existing swatches.

To replace or append a swatches library:

1. Choose a library name from the bottom of the palette menu.
2. Click Append to add the new library swatches to the current palette.
   or
   Click OK to replace the current palette with the new library swatches, then respond to the prompt, if it appears 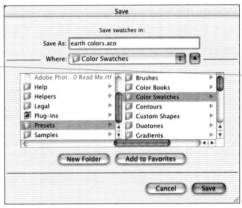.

TIP To enlarge the palette to display the loaded swatches, drag the palette resize box or click the palette zoom button.

You'll need to follow the instructions below only if the swatches library you want to open isn't in the **default** location listed in the sidebar.

To load a swatches library:

1. Choose Load Swatches from the Swatches palette menu.
2. Locate and highlight the swatches library you want to open.
3. Click Load. The loaded swatches will appear below the existing swatches on the Swatches palette.

To restore the default Swatches palette:

Choose Reset Swatches from the Swatches palette menu, then click OK.

Finding defaults

- In Windows, the swatches libraries are stored in Program Files\Adobe/Photoshop CS\Presets\ Color Swatches.

- In the Mac, the swatches libraries are stored in Applications/Adobe Photoshop CS/Presets/Color Swatches, or in the Adobe Photoshop Only folder in the Color Swatches folder.

1 *Enter a **Name** and open the **Color Swatches** folder.*

2 *This prompt will appear if you decide to **replace** your current Swatches palette colors with a new library, and the current swatches haven't yet been saved.*

(sidebar) Save, Replace, Load, Reset Swatches

1 *Sampling a color from an image using the **Eyedropper** tool*

2 *Choose a **Sample Size** for the **Eyedropper** tool from the options bar.*

Using the Eyedropper tool

To choose a color from an image using the Eyedropper:

1. Decide whether you want to choose a Foreground or Background color, then click that color square if it's not already active.

2. Choose the Eyedropper tool (I or Shift-I).

3. Click a color in any open image window **1**.

or

Drag in any open image window (the currently active color square will update continuously on the Toolbox and Color palette), and release the mouse when the pointer is over the desired color.

TIP If you want to choose a color based on its color components, note the color percentages on the Info palette as you drag with the Eyedropper tool. You could also move the mouse with the button up, noting the color percentages, then click when the pointer is over the desired color.

TIP To change the area within which the Eyedropper tool samples, from the Eyedropper options bar, choose Sample Size: Point Sample (the exact pixel that's clicked on), or 3 by 3 or 5 by 5 Average (an average within a 3-by-3-pixel or 5-by-5-pixel square) **2**. Or right-click/ Control-click the image with the Eyedropper and choose a Sample Size from the context menu. (For the Copy Color as HTML option, see the next page.)

TIP Alt-click/Option-click or drag in the image window with the Eyedropper tool to choose a Background color when the Foreground color square is active, or to choose a Foreground color when the Background color square is active.

Eyedropper

Colors can be copied as **hexadecimal values** from a file in Photoshop or ImageReady and then pasted into an HTML file for Web output. There are two methods for doing this.

To copy a color as a hexadecimal value:

Method 1

1. Choose the Eyedropper tool (I or Shift-I).

2. In Photoshop: Right-click/Ctrl-click a color in the image window, then choose Copy Color as HTML.
   or
   In ImageReady: Click the color that you want to copy in the image window (it will become the Foreground color). Then, with the Eyedropper tool still over the image, right-click/Control-click and choose Copy Foreground Color as HTML.

   The selected color will be copied to the Clipboard as a hexadecimal value.

3. To paste the color into an HTML file, display the HTML file in your HTML-editing application, then choose Edit > Paste. You can insert the code for any HTML element that allows a color property.

Method 2

1. Choose a Foreground color via the Color palette, Color Picker, or Swatches palette.

2. In Photoshop or ImageReady: Choose Copy Color as HTML from the Color palette menu.
   or
   In ImageReady: Choose Edit > Copy Foreground Color as HTML.

   The Foreground color will be copied to the Clipboard as a hexadecimal value.

3. To paste the color into an HTML file, open the destination application, display the HTML file, then choose Edit > Paste.

Copy Color as HTML

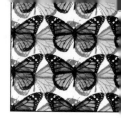

RECOLOR 11

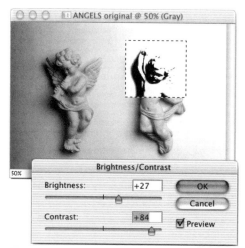

1 *Changes preview in the image window or a selection only when **Preview** is checked.*

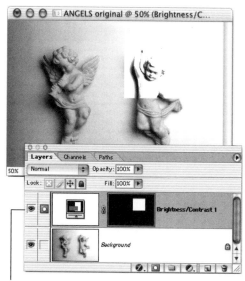

2 *For more flexibility, try out adjustments via an adjustment layer.*

I **N THIS CHAPTER,** you'll learn to fill a selection with color, a pattern, or imagery; apply a stroke to a selection or a layer; adjust a color image using the Hue/Saturation, Color Balance, Curves, and Levels commands; use the Color Sampler tool to get multiple color readouts; strip color from a layer; saturate or desaturate colors using the Sponge tool; use a neutral color layer to heighten color; tint a gray-scale image; and create, edit, and print spot color channels.

Note: Make sure your monitor is calibrated before performing color adjustments! See pages 44–47.

Adjustment basics

Every Image > Adjustments submenu dialog box has a **Preview** option. Changes preview in the image or selection when Preview is checked **1**.

TIP While an adjustment dialog box is open, you can Ctrl-Spacebar-click/Cmd-Spacebar-click to **zoom in;** or hold down Spacebar and Alt-click/Option click to **zoom out;** or press Spacebar to **move** a magnified image around in the image window.

In addition to the standard method for applying adjustment commands, many of those commands can also be applied via an **adjustment layer 2**. Unlike the standard method, which affects only the currently active layer, the adjustment layer affects all the currently visible layers below it, but doesn't actually change pixels until it's merged with the layer below it. Adjustment layers are used in this chapter, but to learn how to create and use them, follow the instructions on pages 168–171. Similarly, for added flexibility, you can use a **fill layer**

(Continued on the following page)

to apply a solid color, gradient, or pattern (see pages 193–194).

You can use the **Save** command in the Levels, Curves, Replace Color, Selective Color, Hue/Saturation, Channel Mixer, or Variations dialog box to save color adjustment settings. You can then apply those settings to another layer or to another image via the **Load** button in the same dialog box. And for even greater efficiency, you can record and apply Adjustments submenu commands via **actions.**

Some adjustment commands, such as Variations, Color Balance, and Brightness/Contrast, produce broad, overall changes. Other commands, such as Levels, Curves, Hue/Saturation, Replace Color, Selective Color, and Channel Mixer, offer more control, but are a little trickier to use. Which command you decide to use will depend on the type of imagery you're working with and whether it will be color-separated or output online. For example, a color cast (e.g., too much blue or too much magenta) will be most noticeable in flesh tones, so this kind of imagery would require careful color adjustment.

TIP To restore the original settings to any Adjustments dialog box while it's still open, hold down Alt/Option and click Reset (Cancel becomes Reset).

TIP For up-to-the-minute feedback, display the Info palette and/or Histogram palette and leave either or both palettes open while you use any of the adjustment command dialog boxes.

Adjustment Basics

Fill selection or layer

Windows

Fill with Foreground color, 100% opacity	Alt-Backspace
Fill with Background color, 100% opacity	Ctrl-Backspace
Fill visible pixels (not transparent areas) with the Foreground color	Alt-Shift-Backspace
Fill visible pixels (not transparent areas) with the Background color	Ctrl-Shift-Backspace

Mac

Fill with Foreground color, 100% opacity	Option-Delete
Fill with Background color, 100% opacity	Cmd-Delete
Fill visible pixels (not transparent areas) with the Foreground color	Option-Shift-Delete
Fill visible pixels (not transparent areas) with the Background color	Cmd-Shift-Delete

1 *Select an area to use as a **tile** for a pattern.*

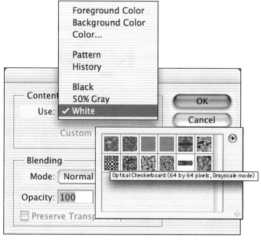

2 *Choose options in the **Fill** dialog box.*

To fill a selection or a layer with a color, a pattern, or imagery:

1. To fill with a solid Foreground or Background **color,** choose a color from the Color or Swatches palette.
or

To fill with **history,** click in the box next to a state on the History palette to establish a source for the History Brush.
or

To tile an area using a **pattern** preset, you don't need to do anything. Or if you'd like to create a custom pattern now, select an area on a layer in any open image using the Rectangular Marquee tool (no feathering) **1**, choose Edit > Define Pattern, enter a Name, click OK, then Deselect (Ctrl-D/Cmd-D).

2. Choose a layer. To fill only non-transparent areas on the layer, turn on Lock Transparent Pixels ▨ on the Layers palette; or to fill the entire layer, click that option off.

To restrict the fill area, create a selection using any selection method (no feathering).

3. Choose Edit > Fill (Shift-Backspace/Shift-Delete).
or

If a selection is active, you can right-click/Control-click in the image window and choose Fill.

4. From the Use pop-up menu, choose what you want to fill the selection or layer with: **2**

Foreground Color, Background Color, Black, 50% Gray, or **White.**

Color, then choose a color from the **NEW** Color Picker, then click OK.

Pattern, then click the Custom Pattern Preset picker thumbnail or arrowhead, and click a pattern in the picker. Peter piper picked...

History to fill the selection or layer with imagery from the active layer at the state that you chose as a source.

(Continued on the following page)

5. Choose a blending Mode and an Opacity percentage.

6. *Optional:* If you forgot to click the Lock Transparent Pixels button on the Layers palette, you can check Preserve Transparency here instead.

7. Click OK **1**–**2**.

TIP If you dislike the new fill color, choose Edit > Undo now so it won't blend with your next color or mode choice.

TIP To fill a layer using a layer effect, double-click next to the layer name, then, in Layer Style, click Color Overlay, Gradient Overlay, or Pattern Overlay. The Gradient Preset Picker is accessible in the Gradient Overlay pane, the Pattern Preset picker in the Pattern Overlay pane. Adjust the settings, then click OK. You can apply one, two, or all three of the Overlay effects to the same layer (see pages 302–303).

Working with patterns

Using the **presets** feature in Photoshop CS, it's easy to save patterns for future use. To learn about presets, see pages 438–440. Even so, for safekeeping, you should hold onto the files that you've used as sources for pattern tiles in case the presets are inadvertently deleted.

You're not limited to the Fill command as a way to apply patterns. You can also apply patterns using the **Pattern Stamp** tool (see page 155) or the **Paint Bucket** tool (see page 226).

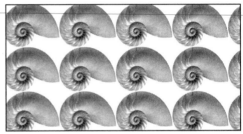

1 *The tile shown on the previous page used as a **fill pattern** in another image*

2 *To produce this image, we duplicated a pattern layer, lowered the opacity of the duplicate to 43%, changed its blending mode to Multiply, and offset the duplicate layer from the original.*

Fill

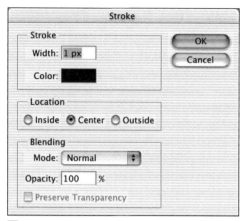

1 *Choose options in the* **Stroke** *dialog box.*

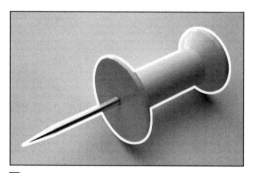

2 *We applied a white* **stroke** *to this pushpin.*

To apply a stroke to a selection or a layer:

1. *Optional:* If you'd rather choose a stroke color by using the Color palette or Swatches palette than by using the Color Picker, do so now. If you want to use the Color Picker, you can access it when you get to the Stroke dialog box in step 5.

2. Click a layer. If you don't want the stroke to extend into transparent areas on the layer, click the Lock Transparent Pixels button ▦ on the Layers palette now, and for step 6, below, don't click the Location: Outside option.

   Optional: Select an area on the layer.

3. Choose Edit > Stroke.
   or
   If a selection is active (and the Magic Wand tool isn't selected), you can right-click/Control-click in the image window and choose Stroke.

4. Enter a Width (1–250 pixels) **1**.

5. If you didn't choose a stroke color for step 1, click the Color swatch, choose a color from the Color Picker, then click OK.

6. Click Location: Inside, Center, or Outside for the position of the stroke on the edge of the selection or layer imagery.

7. Choose a Blending Mode and an Opacity.

8. *Optional:* If you forgot to click the Lock Transparent Pixels button on the Layers palette, you can check Preserve Transparency here instead.

9. Click OK **2**.

TIP To apply a stroke as a layer effect, double-click next to any layer name, check Stroke in the Layer Style dialog box, adjust the settings, then click OK. The Stroke layer style ignores the Lock Transparent Pixels setting.

TIP To apply a stroke to path, see the sidebar on page 325.

Stroke

To adjust a color image using Hue/Saturation:

1. Choose a layer. *Optional:* Select an area of the layer to adjust only that area.

2. Choose Image > Adjustments > Hue/Saturation (Ctrl-U/Cmd-U).
   or
   Choose Hue/Saturation from the New Fill/Adjustment Layer pop-up menu ◑. at the bottom of the Layers palette.

3. From the Edit pop-up menu, choose Master to adjust all the image colors at once, or choose a preset range to adjust only colors within that range **1**.

4. Make sure Preview is checked.

5. Do any of the following:
   Move the **Hue** slider **2** to the left or the right to shift colors to another part of the color bar.

   Move the **Saturation** slider to the left to decrease saturation or to the right to increase saturation. *Note:* If the image is going to be printed and colors are oversaturated, the conversion to CMYK Color mode will desaturate colors so as to bring them into the printable gamut.

   To lighten the image or layer, move the **Lightness** slider to the right. To darken the image or layer, move it to the left.

   TIP To add Color Sampler points while the Hue/Saturation dialog box is open, choose Edit: Master, then Shift-click on the image (see pages 198–199).

6. When a color range is chosen from the Edit pop-up menu (step 3, above), the adjustment slider and color selection droppers become available **3**. You can use the adjustment slider to narrow or widen the range of colors in the layer that the Hue, Saturation, and Lightness sliders will affect. By default, the slider covers 90° of the color bar (think color wheel): the areas to the left and right of the vertical bars (the fall-off) each occupy 30°, and the center area between the vertical bars (the color range) occupies 30°.

Hue/Saturation *(side tab)*

Colorize a color or grayscale image

Check **Colorize** in the Hue/Saturation dialog box to tint the current layer. Move the Hue slider to apply a different tint; move the Saturation slider to reduce or increase the tint color intensity; or move the Lightness slider to lighten or darken the tint (and the image or layer). The Edit pop-up menu defaults to Master when the Colorize option is on. To tint a grayscale image using this method, convert it to RGB Color or CMYK Color mode first. To produce a duotone, see page 460.

1 *From the Edit pop-up menu, choose Master or choose a preset color range…*

2 *…then adjust the Hue, Saturation, and Lightness sliders.*

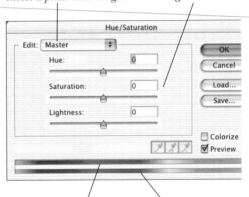

The reference color bar won't change.

Color adjustments will be displayed in this color bar.

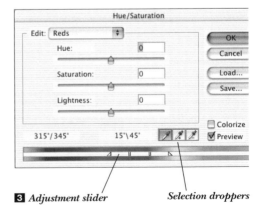

3 *Adjustment slider*

Selection droppers

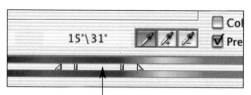

1 *The adjustment slider is moved into a different range.*

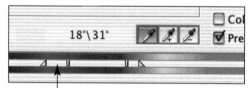

2 *The vertical gray bar is moved inward to **narrow** the **color range** (the center area) that the feature affects.*

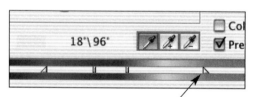

3 *The outer area (the fall-off) is moved outward to **widen** the **color range** (the center area). The fall-off is unchanged.*

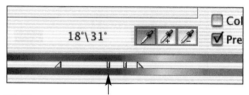

4 *The triangle is moved outward to **widen** the **fall-off**, alllowing changes to adjacent colors. The color range isn't changed.*

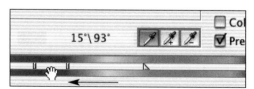

5 ***Ctrl-drag/Cmd-drag** a color bar to change where colors display on the color bars.*

Do any of the following to the adjustment slider:

Drag the center area to move the whole slider, as is, to a new spot on the color bar, thus making a different range of colors available for editing **1**. The Edit pop-up menu will update to reflect your new color range choice.

Drag either or both of the vertical bars on the slider to narrow or expand the color range **2**.

Drag either or both of the areas outside the vertical bars to widen or narrow that range without altering the fall-off area **3**.

Drag the outer triangles on the slider to control how much the current edits will affect adjacent colors **4**. Drag outward to increase this "fall-off" or inward to decrease it. *Note:* A very short fall-off may produce dithering in the image.

Ctrl-drag/Cmd-drag either color bar to move different colors onto the bar **5**. Colors wrap from one edge to the other. This won't affect the image.

If you alter the slider for any of the six preset color ranges, that current color adjustment will become the new listing on the Edit pop-up menu. For example, if you move the preset Reds range slider so it enters the Yellows range, Yellows and Yellows 2 will be on the menu, but Reds will be removed from the menu because the Yellows range now includes Reds.

Click a color in the image window— related colors will be adjusted. Or use the Add to Sample eyedropper 🖌 or Subtract from Sample 🖌 eyedropper to add to or subtract from the current color range by clicking on the image.

TIP Hold down Shift with the first dropper chosen to make it function temporarily like an Add to Sample eyedropper; or hold down Alt/Option to make it function temporarily like a Subtract from Sample eyedropper.

7. Click OK.

TIP To restore the original dialog box settings, Alt-click/Option-click Reset.

Using the Color Sampler tool

Instead of using the Eyedropper tool to get a color readout from one spot, you can use the **Color Sampler** tool to place up to four color readout markers, called color samplers, on an image. As you perform color and shade adjustments, before and after color breakdown readouts taken from the sampler locations will display on the Info palette. You can also add color samplers while a color adjustment dialog box is open (Shift-click on the image). Color samplers save with the file in which they're created.

To place color samplers on an image:

1. Choose the Color Sampler tool (I or Shift-I).

2. Click up to four locations on the image to position color samplers ■. You might want to place a sampler in a highlight area, a midtone area, and a shadow area, and perhaps the fourth sampler on a color that you want to monitor closely.

   Note: If you choose a tool other than the Color Sampler, the Eyedropper, or a painting or editing tool, the samplers will disappear from view. To redisplay them, choose one of the above-mentioned tools or open a dialog box from the Adjustments submenu. To deliberately hide them, choose Color Samplers from the Info palette menu to uncheck that command.

TIP You can also add samplers by Alt-Shift-clicking/Option-Shift-clicking with the Eyedropper tool.

TIP Color samplers gather data from the topmost visible layer that contains pixels in the spot where the sampler is located. If you hide a layer from which a sampler is reading, the sampler will then read from the next layer down that contains visible pixels in that location. The Info palette will update if you hide a layer from which it was reading sampler data.

TIP Samplers will move if a layer is flipped or if the whole canvas is rotated.

■ *Click on an image with the **Color Sampler** tool to create up to four sampler locations.*

Color Sampler Tool

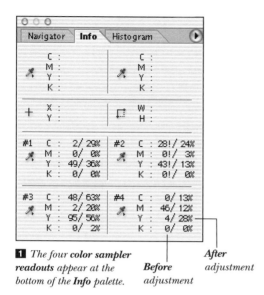

1 *The four **color sampler** readouts appear at the bottom of the **Info** palette.*

***Before** adjustment*

***After** adjustment*

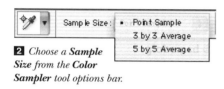

2 *Choose a **Sample Size** from the **Color Sampler** tool options bar.*

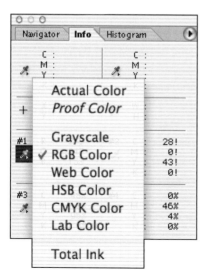

3 *A different **color model** can be chosen for each color sampler.*

To move a color sampler:

Choose the Color Sampler tool (I or Shift-I), then drag a color sampler.
or
Choose the Eyedropper tool (I or Shift-I), then Ctrl-drag/Cmd-drag a color sampler.

Using the Info palette with the Color Sampler tool

The Info palette displays before-adjustment (and after-adjustment) color breakdowns of the pixel or pixel area under each color sampler **1**. The size of the sample area depends on which **Sample Size** setting is chosen on the Color Sampler options bar **2**. Choose Point Sample to sample only the pixel under the pointer; or choose 3 by 3 Average or 5 by 5 Average to sample an average color from a 3- or 5-pixel-square area. If you change the Sample Size for the Color Sampler tool, that setting will also change for the Eyedropper, and vice versa.

To choose a **color model** (Grayscale, RGB Color, etc.) for a section of the Info palette, click the tiny arrowhead next to a dropper icon on the palette, then choose from the pop-up menu **3**. Actual Color is the image's current color mode; Proof Color is the color profile mode currently chosen in View > Proof Setup; and Total Ink is the total percentage of CMYK under the pointer based on the current settings in CMYK Setup (in Color Settings). The model you choose for the Info palette doesn't have to match the current image mode. You can also choose color models in the Info Options dialog box (choose Palette Options from the Info palette menu).

To remove a color sampler:

Choose the Color Sampler tool, then Alt-click/Option-click a sampler (the pointer will become a scissors icon) or drag the sampler out of the image window. That sampler's readout area will be removed from the Info palette.
or
Choose the Eyedropper tool, then Alt-Shift-click/Option-Shift-click a sampler.

Adjustment techniques

You can use the **Color Balance** dialog box to apply or correct a warm or cool cast in a layer's highlights, midtones, or shadows. Color adjustments are easiest to see in an image that has a wide tonal range. (When you're ready to do finer adjustments with greater control, use the Curves command; see pages 206–207).

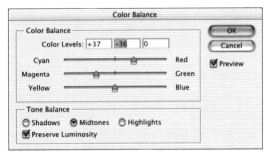

1 In the **Color Balance** dialog box, click Tone Balance: Shadows, Midtones, or Highlights, then move any of the sliders.

To colorize or color-correct using Color Balance:

1. Make sure the composite color image is displayed (Ctrl-~/Cmd-~). In other words, all the channels on the Channels palette should have eye icons, including the topmost one. To colorize a Grayscale image, first convert it to a color image mode.

2. Choose a layer or the Background.

3. Choose Image > Adjustments > Color Balance (Ctrl-B/Cmd-B).
   or
   To apply the command via an adjustment layer, choose Color Balance from the New Fill/Adjustment Layer pop-up menu ⊘ at the bottom of the Layers palette.

4. At the bottom of the dialog box, click the tonal range you want to adjust: Shadows, Midtones, or Highlights **1**.

5. *Optional:* Check Preserve Luminosity to preserve lightness values as you make corrections.

6. Move a slider toward any color you want to add more of. Cool and warm colors are paired opposite each other. Pause to preview.

   TIP Move sliders toward related colors to make an image warmer or cooler. For example, move sliders toward Cyan and Blue to produce a cool cast.

7. *Optional:* Repeat the previous step with any other Tone Balance button selected.

8. Click OK.

1 *The **Sponge** tool options bar*

2 *Using the **Sponge** tool to desaturate colors in an image*

Use the **Sponge** tool to make color areas on the current layer more or less saturated. (The Sponge tool is also discussed on page 465, where it's used to bring colors into the printable gamut.) This tool can't be used on a Bitmap or Indexed Color image.

To saturate or desaturate colors using the Sponge tool:

1. Choose the Sponge tool (O or Shift-O). 🌑 It's on the Burn tool pop-out menu.

2. On the Sponge tool options bar: **1**

   Click the Brush Preset picker arrowhead, then click a **brush.** A soft brush will produce the smoothest result. You can also choose a brush from the Brushes palette.

   Choose **Mode:** Desaturate or Saturate.

   Choose a **Flow** percentage between 1% (low intensity) and 100% (high intensity). Try a lowish Flow percentage first (20%–30%) so the tool won't saturate or desaturate areas too quickly.

   TIP Press a single number on the keyboard to get a Flow percentage of 10 times that number (e.g., press "4" to get 40 percent). Or press two numbers to enter an exact percentage.

3. Choose a layer or the Background.

4. Stroke on any area of the layer **2**. Pause to allow the screen to redraw, if necessary. Stroke again on the same area to intensify the effect.

   TIP If you Saturate or Desaturate an area too much, choose Edit > Undo or click an earlier state or snapshot on the History palette. Don't try to use the tool with its opposite setting to fix it—the results will be patchy and uneven.

   TIP You can also make color saturation adjustments by using the Image > Adjustments > Hue/Saturation or Replace Color command.

Sponge Tool

These instructions describe how to paint shades of gray on a special **neutral** black or white layer in Color Dodge or Color Burn mode in order to heighten or lessen color in the underlying layer. Feel free to try out other layer modes.

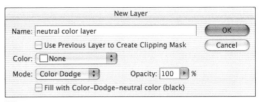

1 *Choose a* **Mode** *in the* **New Layer** *dialog box.*

To heighten color or silhouette color areas on black:

1. Convert the image to RGB Color mode, and activate the layer that you want to affect.

2. Alt-click/Option-click the New Layer button on the Layers palette.

3. Type a name for the layer.

4. Choose a Mode. We chose Color Dodge mode for our illustration **1**, but you can choose any mode other than Normal, Dissolve, Hard Mix, Hue, Saturation, Color, or Luminosity.

5. Check "Fill with [mode name]-neutral color [color name]," then click OK. Our layer was filled with black.

6. Choose the Brush tool (B or Shift-B). On the options bar, choose a brush preset, and make the Opacity and Fill 100%.

7. Choose Grayscale Slider from the Color palette menu.

8. Paint with a 60–88% gray. You'll actually be changing the neutral black on the layer. Areas you stroke over will become much lighter.

   If you're displeased with the results, paint over areas or fill the entire layer again with black to remove all the changes, and start over. Repainting or refilling with black will remove any existing editing effects while preserving pixels in the underlying layers.

9. To heighten the color effect, you can choose another mode from the Layers palette for the neutral layer. We chose Color Burn mode. Your image strokes will be silhouetted against black **2**–**5**.

   Or to restore more of the original color, paint with a medium to light gray.

2 *The original image*

3 *After painting on the Color Dodge mode layer, choosing Color Burn as the layer mode, and painting medium-gray strokes on the Color Burn mode layer*

4 *The original image*

5 *After choosing Overlay mode, checking the "Fill with…" option for the neutral layer, and applying Dodge and Burn strokes to the neutral layer to heighten the highlights and shadows*

Combining grays with color

Duplicate a color layer, choose Image > Adjustments > **Desaturate** (Ctrl-Shift-U/Cmd-Shift-U), choose Layer > Add Layer Mask > Hide All to create a layer mask for the duplicate layer, then paint with white to reveal parts of the grayscale layer above the color layer. You can gradually reshape the mask this way, alternately painting with black to add to the mask or with white to remove parts of the mask.

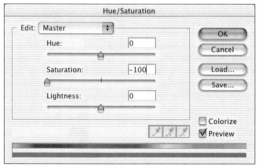

1 *In the **Hue/Saturation** dialog box, move the **Saturation** slider all the way to the left to remove color from the layer.*

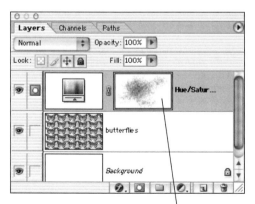

2 *Brushstrokes are applied to an **adjustment layer's** mask.*

You can use the **Desaturate** command to strip color from a layer (convert it to grayscale) without having to change the color mode for the whole image.

To convert a layer or the Background to grayscale:

1. Choose a layer or the Background.
2. Choose Image > Adjustments > Desaturate (Ctrl-Shift-U/Cmd-Shift-U).

To convert a color layer to grayscale and selectively restore its color:

1. Choose a layer in a color image. Layers below this one will be affected by the adjustment layer you're about to create.
2. Create an adjustment layer by choosing Hue/Saturation from the New Fill/ Adjustment Layer pop-up menu ⊘, at the bottom of the Layers palette.
3. Move the Saturation slider all the way to the left (to –100) **1**.
4. Click OK.
5. Set the Foreground color to black.
6. With the adjustment layer chosen, paint across the image where you want to restore the original colors from the underlying layers **2**. Paint with white to restore grayscale areas.

   You can also restack a layer above the adjustment layer to fully restore that layer's color.

TIP Try any of these mode and opacity combinations for the adjustment layer: Dissolve with a 40%–50% opacity to restore color with a chalky texture; Multiply with a 100% opacity to restore subtle color in the shadow areas; Color Dodge at 60% opacity to lighten and intensify color; Color Burn to darken and intensify color; or Vivid Light or Linear Light to heighten contrast.

TIP To limit the adjustment layer effect to just the layer directly below it, Alt-click/ Option-click the line between them on the Layers palette. This creates a clipping mask.

Convert to Grayscale, Then Restore Color

Levels and Curves

When you use the **Levels** or Curves command to make color or tonal adjustments, you should adjust the overall tone of the image first (the composite channel), then adjust individual color channels, if necessary (a bit more cyan, a bit less magenta, etc.).

To adjust individual color channels using the Levels command:

1. Display the Info palette.

2. Choose Image > Adjustments > Levels (Ctrl-L/Cmd-L).
   or
   Create an adjustment layer by choosing Levels from the New Fill/Adjustment Layer pop-up menu ⊘, at the bottom of the Layers palette.

3. Check Preview.

4. If there's an obvious predominance of one color in the image (e.g., too much red or green), choose that channel from the Channel pop-up menu **1**.

   Follow any of these steps for an **RGB** Color image (*Note: The sliders will have the opposite effect in a CMYK image!*):

   To decrease the amount of that particular color, move the black or gray Input Levels slider to the right. The black triangle affects the shadows in the image, the gray triangle affects the midtones.
   or
   To increase the amount of that color, move the gray or white Input Levels slider to the left. The white slider affects the highlights.
   or
   To tint the image with the chosen channel color, move the black Output Levels slider to the right. To lessen the chosen channel color, move the white Output Levels slider to the left. The Output sliders are very effective for adjusting skin tones in a photograph.

   Repeat these steps for any other channels that need adjusting, bearing in mind that adjusting one channel may cause another channel to need adjustment.

Use the Histogram ⬤NEW

You can show and use the **Histogram** palette while the Levels or Curves dialog box is open. If you're adjusting a layer in a multilayer image and you want to see the overall effect of the adjustment on pixels in the entire image—not just the current layer—choose Expanded from the Histogram palette menu and choose Entire Image from the Source pop-up menu. To learn more about the Histogram palette, see pages 181–182.

1 *Choose an individual **channel**, if desired.*

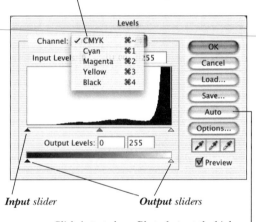

Input slider   *Output sliders*

*Click **Auto** to have Photoshop set the highlight and shadow values in an image and redistribute the midrange color values. Individual channel curves will be altered.*

Levels

Auto Color Correction algorithms

- **Enhance Monochromatic Contrast** moves the black and white input sliders inward, resulting in lighter highlights and darker shadows. The sliders are moved by the same amount for each channel, so color relationships among the channels are preserved. (The Auto Contrast command uses this option.)

- **Enhance Per Channel Contrast** moves the input sliders inward by a different amount for each channel, resulting in more noticeable changes in contrast and color (color casts). (The Auto Levels command uses this option.)

- **Find Dark & Light Colors** finds the average darkest and lightest pixels in the image and uses those values to position the black and white input sliders in each channel. The result is increased contrast. (The Auto Color command uses this option.)

Note: The Auto Color Correction options can also be accessed in Image > Adjustments > Curves. In the Curves dialog box, the curve for each channel will be adjusted using the same options, but no change will be seen on the curve for the composite channel.

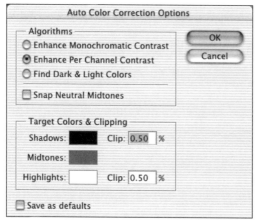

1 *The **Auto Color Correction Options** dialog box*

5. Click OK.

TIP With the dialog box still open, hold down Alt/Option and click Reset to restore the last-used settings.

TIP Shift-click the image to place Color Sampler points while the Levels dialog box is open.

The **Auto Color Correction Options** command can be used to automatically adjust the color, tonal range, and contrast in an image and establish target values for shadows, midtones, and highlights. We recommend using these auto correction options as a starting point for correcting an image.

To apply auto color correction options:

1. With a pixel (nonvector) layer chosen, choose Image > Adjustments > Levels.

2. Click the Options button. Move the Auto Color Correction Options dialog box so you'll be able to see the Levels histogram readjust as options are chosen, and also display the Histogram palette.

3. Click one of the Algorithms (see the sidebar) **1**.

4. *Optional:* Check Snap Neutral Midtones to have Photoshop adjust image colors that are close to neutral to match the Midtones target color swatch in the dialog box.

5. *Optional:* To alter the target value that was assigned to the shadow, midtone, or highlight areas of the image, click that swatch. In the Color Picker, drag the small circle upward or downward along the left edge of the large square. Note how the histogram shifts to the left or right on the Histogram palette, remapping image pixels based on the chosen color.

6. Click OK to close the Color Picker, Auto Color, and Levels dialog boxes.

TIP To see how adjustments affect an individual channel, choose that channel on the Histogram palette.

Using the **Curves** command, you can correct a picture's highlights, quarter tones, midtones, three-quarter tones, or shadows individually. You can even use multiple adjustment layers to do this. Use one adjustment layer for the composite channel first and then use an adjustment layer for each individual channel to fine-tune the color. You can experiment with the adjustment layer opacity or paint on its layer mask to remove or lessen the effect in specific areas.

To adjust color or values using the Curves command:

1. Display the Histogram palette, and choose Expanded View from the palette menu.

2. Choose Image > Adjustments > Curves (Ctrl-M/Cmd-M).
   or
   Create an adjustment layer by choosing Curves from the New Fill/Adjustment Layer pop-up menu ⊘, at the bottom of the Layers palette.

3. Move the pointer over the grid. The default Input and Output readouts in the lower left corner of the dialog box represent either the brightness values for RGB Color mode or the percentage values for CMYK Color mode. Click the gradient bar below the grid to switch between the two readouts ■.

4. *Optional:* Choose a Channel to adjust it separately.

5. If your image is in CMYK Color mode and the gradient on the gradient bar is white on the left side, drag the part of the curve you want to adjust upward to darken or downward to lighten the entire image or the chosen channel. (Click the double arrow in the middle of the gradient bar to reverse the curve.) Reverse this instruction if your image is in RGB Color mode.
   and/or
   For more precise adjustments, click on the curve to create additional points (up to 14), then drag the segment between

> ## Changing channels
> If you adjust an individual color channel, keep in mind that **color opposites** (cyan and red, magenta and green, yellow and blue) work in tandem. Lowering cyan, for example, adds more red; lowering red adds more cyan. In fact, you'll probably need to adjust more than one channel to remove an undesirable color cast. If you overzealously adjust only one channel, you'll throw off the color balance of the whole image.

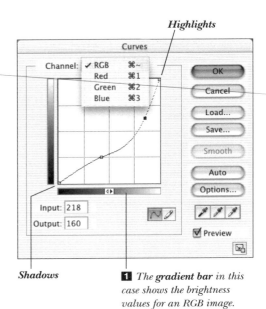

Highlights

Shadows

■ *The **gradient bar** in this case shows the brightness values for an RGB image.*

Get real

Read David Blatner and Bruce Fraser's *Real World Adobe Photoshop CS* (Peachpit Press) for in-depth real-world information on scanning, tonal adjustments, color correction, output, and other topics that are beyond the scope of this QuickStart Guide.

1 *The original image*

2 *After a* **Curves** *adjustment*

any pair of points to make subtle adjustments. (To remove a point, click on it and press Backspace/Delete; or Ctrl-click/Cmd-click on it.)

You can also move the extreme end of the curve to reduce absolute black to less than 100%, or absolute white to greater than 0%.

Note: Once you've added a point, you can enter numbers in the Input and/or Output fields for that point.

6. Click OK **1**–**2**.

TIP For an image in RGB Color mode, click on the image to see that pixel's placement on the curve; Ctrl-click/Cmd-click on the image to place a point on the curve. For a CMYK Color image, you can choose an individual C, M, Y, or K channel from the Channel pop-up menu to show that pixel's placement on the curve (this won't work on the composite CMYK channel).

TIP Alt-click/Option-click the grid in the Curves dialog box to toggle between a grid spacing of 4 by 4 and 10 by 10.

TIP Shift-click on the image to place Color Sampler points while the Curves dialog box is open.

TIP Click the Auto button to have Photoshop reset the highlight and shadow values in the image and redistribute the midrange color values. Individual channel curves will be altered.

TIP Click the button in the lower right corner of the Curves dialog box to expand the dialog box, in case you need to adjust your curve more precisely. Click the button again to restore the dialog box to its original size.

TIP Custom curves drawn with the pencil tool in the Curves dialog box tend to be bumpy and may produce abrupt color transitions in the image.

Curves

Spot color channels

A spot color can be placed in its own separate channel. Then, when the image is color-separated, this **spot color channel** will appear on its own plate.

To create a spot color channel:

1. Display the Channels palette, and drag it away from the Layers palette so you can see both palettes at once.

2. Choose New Spot Channel from the Channels palette menu.

3. Click the Color swatch, **1** and if necessary, click Custom to open the Custom Colors dialog box.

4. Choose a Pantone or other spot color matching system name from the Book pop-up menu, choose a color, then click OK.

5. *Optional:* To change the way color in the spot channel is simulated onscreen, enter a new Ink Characteristics: Solidity percentage. At 100%, it will display as a solid color; at a lower percentage, it will appear more transparent.

6. Click OK. The new spot color channel will appear on the Channels palette, with the color you chose as its name **2**. Any stroke that's applied or image element that is created while the spot color channel is active will appear in that color (see the following page). The spot color won't appear as a new layer on the Layers palette.

TIP To change the spot color in a channel, double-click next to the channel name, then follow steps 3–6, above. The channel will automatically be renamed for the new color, and all the pixels on the channel will display in that new color.

Copy to a spot color channel

■ To copy imagery to a spot color channel, first make a selection on a layer. Then, with the selection active, create a new spot color channel using the Channels palette; or choose an existing spot color channel and fill the selection with black.

■ To copy an image's light and dark values to a spot color channel as shades of the spot color, create a selection, copy it to the Clipboard, create or choose a spot color channel, then paste onto that channel.

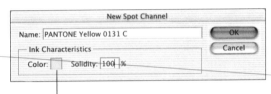

1 *Click the **Color** swatch in the New Spot Channel dialog box.*

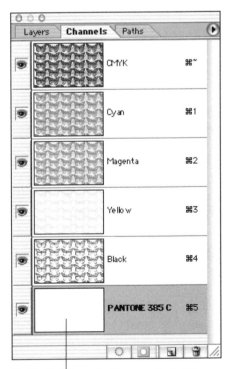

2 *The **spot channel** appears on the palette.*

Lighten/darken spot channel tint

Click the spot channel on the Channels palette, then choose Image > Adjustments > Levels. To darken the tint, move the black Input slider to the right; to lighten the tint, move the black Output slider to the right. Position the pointer over the image so you can get an opacity readout on the Info palette (choose Actual Color mode for the readout). Readjust either slider, if desired.

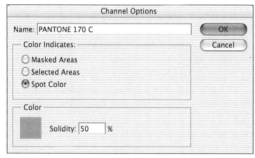

1 *Click Spot Color in the **Channel Options** dialog box.*

To paint on a spot color channel:

1. Create a spot color channel (instructions on the previous page).

2. Double-click the spot color channel, enter 90 as the Solidity value, then click OK.

3. Choose the Brush tool. (The Color palette will display in Grayscale mode while the spot color channel is active.) Choose black as the Foreground color.

4. On the Brush tool options bar, choose Normal as the painting Mode, and choose an Opacity percentage to establish the tint percentage for the spot color ink on the spot color plate.

5. Make sure the spot color channel is still active, then paint on the image.

TIP The color that displays on a spot color channel is merely a simulation of how that color will appear in the printed image, so don't concern yourself with how it looks onscreen. Just create and apply the colors where you want them to appear on the spot color channel and be on your merry way.

Another way to create a spot color channel is by converting an **alpha channel.**

To convert an alpha channel to a spot color channel:

1. Double-click an alpha channel on the Channels palette.

2. Choose Color Indicates: Spot Color **1**.

3. Click the Color swatch. If the Custom Colors dialog box isn't showing, click Custom. Choose a spot color, then click OK.

4. Click OK. Former nonwhite (black or gray) areas on the channel will now display in the chosen spot color.

Spot color channel basics

To display a spot color channel along with all the main image channels, make sure an **eye** icon is present for both the spot color channel and the topmost (composite) channel on the Channels palette. To display the spot channel by itself, hide the composite channel by clicking its eye icon.

If you want to know the **opacity** of a spot color area, choose the spot color channel, choose Actual Color mode for the K (grayscale) readout on the Info palette, move the pointer over the image, and then note the K percentage on the Info palette.

While a spot color channel is active on the Channels palette, only that spot channel can be edited—not any layers. To resume editing the most recently active layer, click the topmost (composite) channel.

To add **type** to a spot color channel, see page 366.

If a color image that contains a spot color channel (or an image in Duotone mode) is converted to Multichannel mode, any spot colors in the image (or duotone) will be placed in separate spot channel(s) without any preexisting spot color channels being discarded. To **tint** an entire image with a spot color, convert the image to Duotone mode and specify the desired spot color as the monotone color (see page 461).

To **export** a file that contains spot color channels, save it in the DCS 2.0 format (make sure Spot Colors is checked in the options pane). Each spot color channel will be preserved as a separate file, along with the composite DCS file. Let Photoshop assign the spot color channel name for you so other applications will recognize it as a spot color. The Photoshop PDF and TIFF formats also support spot colors, but DCS is the most reliable format for exporting and printing spot colors.

Printing spot color channels

Spot color channel colors **overprint** all other image colors. The stacking order of spot color channels on the Channels palette controls the order in which spot colors overprint each other. To prevent a spot color from overprinting, you must manually knock out (delete) any areas from other channels that fall beneath the spot color shapes (read more about this in the Photoshop documentation). Talk with your print shop, though, to see if this step is necessary.

Choosing **Merge Spot Channel** (Channels palette menu) merges any spot colors into the existing color channels and flattens all layers, so a composite (single-page) proof can be printed on a color printer. If you don't merge spot channels, they'll print as separate pages. Merging a spot color channel into the other color channels changes the actual spot color, because CMYK inks can't exactly replicate spot color inks. When a spot color channel is merged into other color channels, its Solidity value determines the tint percentage of the merged spot color. The lower the Solidity value, the more transparent the newly merged color will be. All image layers are flattened when spot channels are merged.

TIP Use the Solidity option in the Spot Channel Options dialog box to produce an onscreen simulation of the ink opacity for the spot color plate. For an opaque ink, such as a metallic ink, use a Solidity value of 90%. For a transparent, clear varnish, use a Solidity value of 0%. This value has no effect on output.

TIP Custom colors that are applied to standard or shape layers will be converted to process colors on output. Only color areas on spot color channels will separate to spot color plates.

PAINT 12

Tool shortcuts

These shortcuts work with any tool for which the option or feature is available (e.g., Brush, Paint Bucket, Pencil, Smudge, Dodge, Burn).

Cycle through the blending modes on the options bar	Shift + or Shift -
Decrease/increase a brush preset's master diameter	[or]
Change opacity, exposure, or strength percentage* (Shift-press a number to change the flow level)	0 through 9 on the keypad (e.g., 2 = 20%) or quickly type a percentage (e.g. "38")

*If the Airbrush option is on, pressing a keypad number changes the flow percentage and Shift-pressing a keypad number changes the opacity percentage.

*Click in either of these two spots to open the **Brush Preset** picker.*

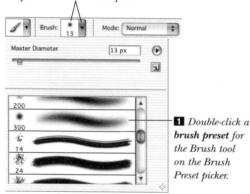

1 *Double-click a* **brush preset** *for the Brush tool on the Brush Preset picker.*

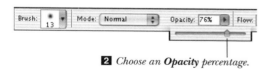

2 *Choose an* **Opacity** *percentage.*

IN THIS CHAPTER, you'll learn how to use the Brush, Smudge, Paint Bucket, Eraser, Background Eraser, and Magic Eraser tools to embellish or edit a scanned image or paint a picture from scratch. You'll also learn how to use the Brushes palette to save and load brush preset libraries, and how to create, edit, and save custom brush and tool presets.

Getting started

First, just to get started, let's get acquainted with the **Brush** tool. In these instructions, you will choose an existing brush preset (brush tip) for the Brush tool, and then choose various options bar settings to customize how the tool applies pigment. In the next section, starting on page 213, you will learn how to customize a brush preset using a wide assortment of options on the Brushes palette.

To use the Brush tool:

1. Choose a layer. *Optional:* Create a selection on the layer if you want to restrict the brush strokes to that area.

2. Click the Brush tool (B or Shift-B).

3. Choose a Foreground color (see pages 183–186).

4. On the options bar, do the following:

   Click the **Brush Preset** picker arrowhead or thumbnail, then double-click a preset **1**.

   Choose a blending **Mode** (see "Blending modes" on pages 38–42).

   Choose an **Opacity** percentage **2**. At 100%, the stroke will completely cover underlying pixels.

   Choose a **Flow** percentage to control how fully and smoothly the paint is applied.

(Continued on the following page)

Master Diameter

5. *Optional:* Turn on the Airbrush option to have the tool continue to dispense paint for as long as you hold down the mouse button, simulating traditional airbrushing **1**–**2**.

6. Drag across any area of the picture. If you press and hold on a spot when the Airbrush option is on, the paintdrop will gradually widen (up to the brush's maximum diameter) and become more dense and opaque.

Note: Click the Lock Transparent Pixels button on the Layers palette to have the tool recolor only nontransparent areas, not any fully transparent areas.

Each brush preset has its own built-in **Master Diameter** and **Hardness** settings, but you can make temporary changes to either setting via a context menu or the options bar.

To make temporary changes to a brush preset:

1. Choose any tool that uses brush presets (e.g., the Brush, Pencil, Dodge, Burn, or Eraser tool).

2. Right-click/Ctrl-click in the image window, then change the Master Diameter and/or Hardness setting **3**.

3. Press Enter/Return or click in the image window. This setting will remain in effect only until you choose a different preset.

TIP To draw a straight stroke, click once to begin the stroke, then Shift-click or Shift-drag in a different location to complete the stroke.

TIP Alt-click/Option-click in any open image to sample a color while a painting tool is chosen (this is a temporary Eyedropper).

Airbrushing

The **Airbrush** function can be turned on or off for the Brush tool via a button on the options bar. This option is also available for the Clone Stamp, Pattern Stamp, History Brush, Eraser, Dodge, Burn, and Sponge tools.

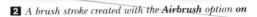

1 *A brush stroke created with the **Airbrush** option **off***

2 *A brush stroke created with the **Airbrush** option **on***

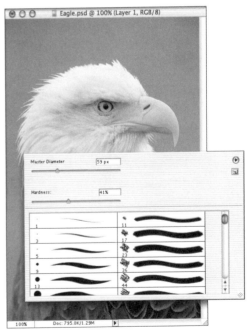

3 *Via the context menu, you can change the **Master Diameter** and **Hardness** for a preset on the fly.*

Dock it

If the Brushes palette is displayed and your monitor is wide enough to display the **palette well** at the right side of the options bar, drag the Brushes palette tab into the well or choose Dock to Palette Well from the Brushes palette menu. Thereafter, to display the palette, just click its tab in the well. To access the palette menu when the palette is docked, click its tab, then click the arrowhead on the tab. `Brushes ▸`

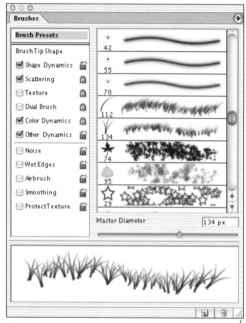

1 *The Brushes palette*

Drag the lower right corner of the palette to change its shape from horizontal to vertical, or vice versa.

Using the Brushes palette

The **Brushes palette** offers a myriad of options for customizing brush presets for the Brush, Pencil, History Brush, Art History Brush, Clone Stamp, Pattern Stamp, Eraser, Blur, Sharpen, Smudge, Dodge, Burn, and Sponge tools. The options are organized into categories, such as Shape Dynamics, Scattering, Texture, and Color Dynamics. Settings for a stylus or an airbrush input device can also be chosen from the palette.

The first step is to get acquainted with the palette. This is **Brushes Palette 101.**

To use the Brushes palette:

1. Choose any of the tools listed in the introductory paragraph above.

2. To display the Brushes palette **1**:
   Choose Window > Brushes (F5).
   or
   Click the Brushes palette button toward the middle of the options bar.

3. If you don't see a list of categories on the left side of the palette, choose Expanded View from the palette menu. And if the palette is just a bar, double-click the bar.

4. Check the box for any of the first six categories to activate the features for that category. If a category is dimmed, it means it's not available for that tool. The categories are discussed in depth in the next set of instructions.

5. To display the pane for a category, click the category name. The options below the horizontal line can only be switched on or off; there are no settings to adjust.

6. To choose a different display option for the palette, from the palette menu, choose Text Only, Small Thumbnail, Large Thumbnail, Small List, Large List, or Stroke Thumbnail. The Small options compact the list; the Large options allow you to see the brush tips more clearly. (The arrowhead for accessing the palette menu is on the palette tab if the palette is in the Dock; it's on the right side of the palette if the palette isn't in the Dock.)

Brushes Palette

Given the enormous range of options on the Brushes palette, your choices are endless. For example, you can make subtle adjustments to a hard-edged brush or create a simulation of a natural-media bristle brush. Start by editing the **preset** brushes that are supplied with Photoshop. Later, you'll learn how to save your customized presets as well as create brand new brushes.

Steps 3 through 11 in the following instructions are optional—you can pick and choose among them. And remember, when we talk about applying "pigment," the brushes are used with many other tools besides the Brush.

Note: A preset's settings remain in effect until they're changed.

To edit a brush preset:

1. Choose a tool that uses brush presets, and display the Brushes palette.

2. Click **Brush Presets** ◼1 in the upper left corner of the Brushes palette, then click a preset. Use the scroll arrows to scroll down the list, if necessary

3. To change any of the basic shape or size settings for the preset, click **Brush Tip Shape** at the top of the list ◼2, then watch the brush preview at the bottom of the palette as you make any of these changes:

For the brush size, enter a **Diameter** value (1–2500 pixels) or move the slider. If the preset was originally created from a selection, you can check Use Sample Size to make the preset the same size as the original selection (see "To create a brush preset from an image" on page 224.)

Enter a new **Angle** or drag the arrowhead around the circle to alter the brush slant.

Enter a new **Roundness** value (0–100%) or drag one of the two tiny dark circles inward to make the brush tip more elliptical, less round ◼3.

Change the **Hardness** value (0–100%) to feather or sharpen the edge of the brush (not available for all brush tips) ◼4.

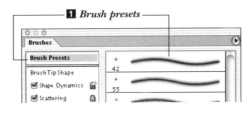

◼1 *Brush presets*

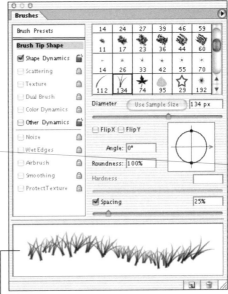

◼2 *You can watch the preset **preview** at the bottom of the **Brushes** palette as you change settings.*

100% Roundness

100% Hardness

◼3 *20% Roundness*

◼4 *3% Hardness*

◼5 *25% Spacing*

150% Spacing: Brush tips are evenly spaced.

A slow stroke (top) and a fast stroke (bottom) with Spacing unchecked: brush tips are unevenly spaced.

Edit Brush Preset

1 *100% **Size Jitter**, 25% spacing*

0% Size Jitter

2 *0% Scatter, 100% Spacing*

*500% Scatter, **Both Axes** option **checked***

*500% Scatter, **Both Axes** option **unchecked***

3 *0% **Count Jitter**, 100% Spacing*

*100% **Count Jitter**: The Count varies randomly from 1% to 100% of the Count value.*

4 *Painting with a **texture** preset with **Pen Pressure** chosen as the Opacity Jitter Control (see the following page).*

To control the distance between brush tips within the stroke, check Spacing, then enter or choose a value (1–1000%) (**5**, previous page).

4. To control how much variation is allowable in the brush tip shape, click **Shape Dynamics** (click the words—the box will become checked automatically), then do any of the following:

   Change the **Size Jitter** **1**, **Angle Jitter,** and **Roundness Jitter** values to establish variation parameters for those attributes. ("Jitter" is the amount of random variation allowable for that option.)

   From the **Control** pop-up menus, choose a stylus feature to directly control that option's variation (see pages 218–219). Variations occur even with Off chosen.

   Change the **Minimum Diameter** value for the brush size variations.

   Change the **Minimum Roundness** value.

5. To control the placement of pigment in the stroke, click **Scattering**, then do any of the following:

   Change the **Scatter** value **2** to control how far pigment can veer off the path drawn by the mouse. The lower the Scatter value, the more solid the stroke.

   Check **Both Axes** to allow pigment to be scattered both along and perpendicular to the path. Uncheck Both Axes to have strokes be scattered perpendicular to, but not along, the path. Also choose a Control option, if desired.

   Change the **Count** value to control the stroke's overall density (the amount of pigment).

   Change the **Count Jitter** value **3** to control how much the Count (density) can vary.

6. To use the texture from a pattern in a brush stroke, click **Texture** **4**, then do any of the following:

   Click the **Pattern Preset** arrowhead, then choose a texture from the picker.

   (Continued on the following page)

Check **Invert** to swap the light and dark areas in the pattern.

Change the texture's **Scale** (1–1000%).

Check **Texture Each Tip** to allow the Depth (see below) to vary within each stroke. Uncheck this option to have the Depth value remain constant.

Choose a blending **Mode** to control how the texture mixes with the brush stroke.

Choose a **Depth** value ▮ to control how deeply paint sinks into the texture. At a high Depth value, paint will be applied only to the high points in the texture, and the texture will look more prominent. Choose a Minimum Depth to keep a texture from appearing too flat. Some brushes reveal texture more than others.

Choose a **Depth Jitter** value to control how much the Depth can vary. Choose an option from the Control pop-up menu to specify if and how the brush stroke can fade (see page 218).

7. As an added bonus to make the brush preset more interesting, add another tip to it. Click **Dual Brush** ▮; click a tip; choose a Mode to control how the two tips interact with each other; then choose Diameter, Spacing, Scatter, and Count values.

8. To control how much the color can vary as you use the brush, click **Color Dynamics,** then do any of the following:

Enter a **Foreground/Background Jitter** value ▮ for the amount of variation between the Foreground and Background colors. Choose an option from the Control pop-up menu to specify if and how colors can fade.

Enter **Hue Jitter, Saturation Jitter,** and **Brightness Jitter** values to establish variation parameters for those attributes.

Enter a **Purity** value to control how much of the Foreground color can appear in the stroke. The lower the Purity, the grayer the stroke.

Edit Brush Preset

1 *50% Texture Depth*

100% Texture Depth

2 *Primary brush tip*

Secondary brush tip

Tips combined using **Dual Brush** *option with Linear Burn mode*

3 *0% Foreground/ Background Jitter*

100% Foreground/ Background Jitter

4 *0% Opacity Jitter*

100% Opacity Jitter

5 *100% Opacity Jitter,* **Control** *off: the Opacity varies randomly from 1% to 100%.*

0% **Opacity Jitter,** *Control set to* **Pen Pressure:** *the Opacity is controlled by the amount of pressure on the tablet stylus.*

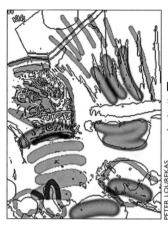

1 *Strokes created with the Brush tool with **Wet Edges** checked*

PETER LOUREKAS

2 *More **Wet Edges***

PETER LOUREKAS

3 *Wet Edges unchecked*

4 *Wet Edges checked*

5 *Smoothing is off: straight segments and corners are visible in this rapidly drawn stroke.*

6 *Smoothing is on: this stroke was drawn as quickly as the one at left, but it's smooth and has no corners.*

9. To control how randomly the overall stroke opacity can vary as you paint, click **Other Dynamics,** then do any of the following:

Change the **Opacity Jitter** (**4**–**5**, previous page) for the amount the opacity can vary. Choose a Control option to control fading.

Change the **Flow Jitter** to control how smoothly the pigment is applied. A high Flow Jitter makes for a blotchy stroke, but that may be what you're aiming for. Choose a Control option.

10. And last but not least (you're almost done!), check any or all of these options:

Noise to add random grain to brush strokes to make them look rougher.

Wet Edges to simulate the buildup of pigment at the edges of brush strokes, as in traditional watercolors **1**–**4**.

Airbrush to allow a stroke to build up for as long as the mouse button is held down in the same spot. You can also press the ✎ button on the options bar.

Smoothing 5–**6** to convert straight segments into smooth curves.

To apply the same texture pattern and scale to other brushes that currently use a texture option, or to which you add a texture option, check **Protect Texture.** This method will create a uniform surface texture for the entire canvas.

11. *Optional:* Click an open lock icon 🔓 **NEW** next to any category name to make the current settings for that category uneditable. The locked settings will be applied (but not saved) to any other preset you choose. Click a closed lock icon 🔒 to make those settings editable again.

12. To save your custom preset, click the New Brush button 📄 at the bottom of the palette or choose New Brush Preset from the palette menu, enter a name, then click OK.

Edit Brush Preset

If you want to make your brush strokes look more painterly, or to take advantage of the capabilities of a pressure-sensitive tablet, you can specify how gradually you want some or all of a brush preset's attributes to vary (e.g., opacity, size, texture).

Some of the **variation** options work only with certain kinds of graphics tablets. For example, some tablet models may not sense the tilt of the stylus (Pen Tilt) or support airbrush devices. The Fade, Initial Direction, and Direction options, on the other hand, work with a mouse or with any other input device.

To choose variation options:

1. Choose a tool that uses the Brushes palette.

2. Display the Brushes palette.

3. Click any of these categories:

   Shape Dynamics to choose variation controls for Size Jitter, Angle Jitter, or Roundness Jitter.

   Scattering to choose variation controls for Scatter or Count Jitter.

   Texture to choose variation controls for Depth Jitter.

   Color Dynamics to choose variation controls for Foreground/Background Jitter.

   Other Dynamics to choose variation controls for Opacity Jitter and Flow Jitter.

4. For any option that offers variation controls, choose one of these options from the Control pop-up menu (not all of these options will be available for every attribute) 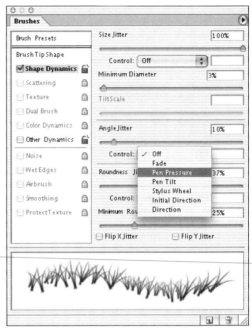:

   Off prevents fading.

   Fade decreases the attribute over the length of the stroke, using the number of steps you specify.

   Pen Pressure varies the attribute based on how hard you press with a stylus on a pressure-sensitive tablet.

   Pen Tilt varies the attribute based on the angle at which you hold a stylus.

1 *Choose a method from the **Control** pop-up menu below any option.*

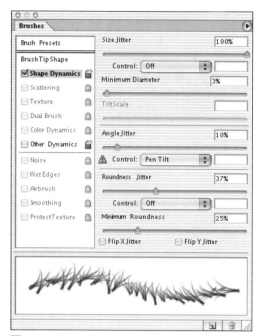

1 *If you choose a Control pop-up menu option that isn't supported by any of the graphics tablet devices that you have connected, this warning icon will appear:* ⚠️ *If you think an option should work, double-check that the tablet device is on the tablet and that its driver software is set up correctly.*

Stylus Wheel lets you control the brush attribute using the wheel found on a stylus input device (this is available for some pressure-sensitive tablets).

Initial Direction sets the angle of an option based on the direction in which you first drag the brush.

Direction sets the angle of an option based on the direction the mouse is dragged.

5. *Optional:* Click an open lock icon 🔓 **NEW** next to any category name to make the current settings for that category uneditable, even if you change presets. Click a closed lock icon 🔒 to make those settings editable again. (To unlock all locked settings, choose Reset All Locked Settings from the palette menu.)

TIP If you have a pressure-sensitive graphics tablet, keep an eye out for Jitter and Scatter attributes on the Brushes palette **1**. To have an attribute vary randomly as you paint with a stylus or other tablet device, choose an option from the Control pop-up menu below any Jitter or Scatter attribute. For example, to allow the stylus to control opacity, choose an option from the Control pop-up menu below Opacity Jitter in the Other Dynamics pane.

TIP To copy the currently chosen texture and texture settings to all the non-painting tools that have a texture option, check the Texture box, then choose Copy Texture to Other Tools from the Brushes palette menu.

TIP Choose Clear Brush Controls from the Brushes palette menu to temporarily turn off all the Brush Tip Shape options for the current preset. If you want to restore the preset's default settings, reselect the preset—bearing in mind that any custom settings that weren't saved as a preset will be lost.

Variation Options

Working with presets

To summarize (and drive a point home), when you modify an existing brush preset via the Brushes palette, you're modifying an unsaved copy of the preset—not the original brush that's in the current library. If you want to preserve a new preset variation that you've created, make a **new brush preset** from it.

Go to the manager

Brush libraries can be organized, appended, replaced, and reset using the **Preset Manager.** This dialog box controls which library will display in each of the 8 preset pickers and corresponding palettes where libraries are used. To learn more about the Preset Manager, see pages 438–440.

To save a new preset:

1. Customize a brush to your liking.

2. Click the Brush Preset picker arrowhead or thumbnail on the options bar, then click the New Preset button.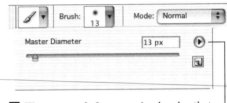
   or
   On the Brushes palette, click the New Brush button.

3. In the Brush Name dialog box, type a name for the preset, then click OK.

1 *The commands for managing brushes that appear on the* **Brush Preset** *picker menu…*

Newly saved presets aren't automatically added to the current brush preset library. This means if the current brush preset library is replaced, your new presets will be discarded. By **saving** your customized brush **presets** into a **library** as per the instructions below, you'll be able to access and use them at any time in the future in any Photoshop document. Brush presets that are saved and loaded as a library display as presets on the Brush Presets pane of the Brushes palette.

2 *…are also found on the* **Brushes palette** *menu.*

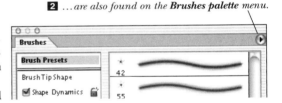

To save brush presets in a new library:

1. Choose Save Brushes from the Brush Preset picker menu **1** or the Brushes palette menu **2**.

2. Enter a Name for the set. Keep the default extension for the brush library (.abr).

3. Choose a location in which to save the set, then click Save (Enter/Return). If you want the new brush library to display at the bottom of the Brushes palette menu, store the library in Adobe Photoshop CS/Presets/Brushes, then relaunch Photoshop.

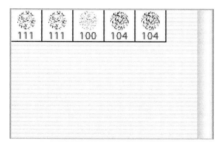

1 *Dry Media Brushes*

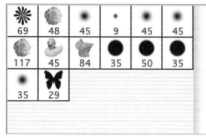

2 *Special Effect Brushes*

(image)

3 *Thick Heavy Brushes*

(image)

4 *Wet Media Brushes*

Photoshop supplies 12 specialty **brush preset libraries** in addition to the default presets, and they can be loaded onto the Brushes palette at any time. The libraries are listed on and accessed from the lower portion of the Brushes palette menu when any tool that uses brushes, such as the Brush tool, is chosen **1**–**4**. Once loaded, the presets can be chosen from either the Brushes palette or the Brush Preset picker.

To load a brush preset library:

1. Do one of the following: Click Brush Presets at the top of the Brushes palette; or click the arrowhead on the right side of the Brushes palette (or on the Brushes tab if the palette is in the Dock); or click the arrowhead on the Brush Preset picker on the options bar.

2. Choose any library from the lower portion of the menu.

3. When the prompt appears, click Append to add the additional brushes to the current picker.
   or
   Click OK to replace the current brushes on the picker with those in the library.

TIP If you need to locate and open a brush library that isn't in one of the default locations (the Adobe Photoshop CS/Presets/Brushes folder or the Adobe Photoshop Only folder inside the Brushes folder), choose Load Brushes from the Brush Preset picker menu or the Brushes palette menu, locate the library you want to load, then click Load.

The presets that are on the Brush Preset picker and the Brushes palette when you exit/quit Photoshop will still be there when you relaunch the application. Follow these instructions if you want to restore the default presets.

To restore the default brush presets:

Choose Reset Brushes from the Brush Preset picker menu or the Brushes palette menu, then click OK (or click Append to add them to the presets already on the palette).

There's also another method for customizing brushes: **tool presets.** You'll choose a tool, choose (and customize) a preset for it, and then save that tool/preset combo as a tool preset—with the added bonus of being able to associate a Foreground color with the tool. Tool presets that you create for a particular tool can be chosen from the **Tool Preset picker** (options bar) or the **Tool Presets palette** when that tool is chosen. It's worth your while to create tool presets even for seemingly minor variations, as it saves time in the long run.

To preserve your tool presets for future use in any document, you can save them to a tool presets library. Saved preset libraries can be loaded via the Tool Preset picker menu or the Tool Presets palette menu.

If you check **Current Tool Only** on the Tool Presets palette or on the Tool Preset picker, only those tool presets that were created for the currently chosen tool will display on the palette and picker. With Current Tool Only unchecked, the tool presets for all tools will display; if you then click a tool preset, the tool to which it applies will become selected.

To make a brush preset into a tool preset:

1. Choose a tool that uses the Brushes palette.

2. Customize a brush by using Brushes palette options.

3. *Optional:* Choose a Foreground color to be saved with the preset.

4. On the options bar, click the Tool Preset picker thumbnail or arrowhead **1**.
   or
   Display the Tool Presets palette **2**.

5. Check Current Tool Only to display only presets for the current tool.

6. Click the New Tool Preset button ▣ on the picker or on the Brushes palette.

1 *Click the thumbnail or arrowhead to open the* **Tool Preset** *picker.*

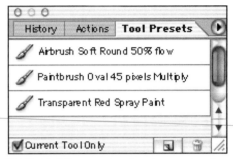

2 *The* **Tool Presets** *palette has the same function as the Tool Preset picker.*

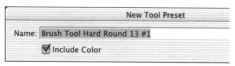

3 *Check* **Include Color** *in the* **New Tool Preset** *dialog box to save the current Foreground color with the preset.*

7. *Optional:* Change the brush name **3**, if desired. Check Include Color, if available, to save the current Foreground color with the preset.

8. Click OK. The new tool preset will appear on the Tool Preset picker and palette (not on the Brush Preset picker or Brushes palette).

TIP To preview the Brush tool preset that's currently selected on the Tool Presets palette, display the Brushes palette and look at the stroke preview at the bottom of the palette.

Tool presets can also be saved in a **library**.

To save tool presets to a library:

1. From the Tool Preset picker menu or the Tool Presets palette menu, choose Save Tool Presets.

2. Enter a name (keep the .tpl extension), choose a location for the library, then click Save. If you want the tool preset library to still display at the bottom of the Tool Preset picker menu and the Tool Presets palette menu when you relaunch Photoshop, save the preset file in the Adobe Photoshop CS/Presets/Tools folder.

TIP Use Load Tool Presets to load a tool preset library onto the palette or picker.

Tool Presets to a Library

In these instructions, you'll use the **Define Brush Preset** command to create a brush from existing imagery. You can have some fun with this!

To create a brush preset from an image:

1. Choose the Rectangular Marquee tool (M or Shift-M).

2. Marquee an area of a picture (maximum 1,000 by 1,000 pixels; look at the W and H values on the Info palette). Try using a distinct shape on a white background . Shift-drag if you want to create a square marquee.

3. Choose Edit > Define Brush Preset.

4. Enter a Name for the new preset 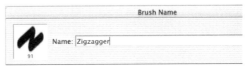, then click OK.

5. Deselect the selection (Ctrl-D/Cmd-D), then choose any tool that uses the Brushes palette. The new preset will be the last one on the Brush Preset picker and on the Brushes palette . Adjust any of the settings for the preset via the Brushes palette (e.g., increase the Spacing under Brush Tip Shape or increase the Opacity and Flow Jitter under Other Dynamics).

Deleting a brush preset has no effect on any existing strokes in the image.

To delete a brush preset:

On the Brush Preset picker, click the brush preset you want to delete, choose Delete Brush from the picker menu, then click OK.
or
On the Brushes palette, click Brush Presets at top left, click the brush preset you want to delete, choose Delete Brush from the palette menu, then click OK.
or
On the Brushes palette or the Brush Preset picker, right-click/Control-click the brush preset you want to delete, choose Delete Brush from the context menu, then click OK.

1 *Select an area of an image.*

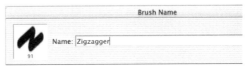
2 *Type a Name for the new brush preset.*

3 *A custom brush used with the Brush tool at various opacities (Wet Edges checked)*

1 *The left side of the* **Smudge** *tool options bar*

2 *The right side of the* **Smudge** *tool options bar*

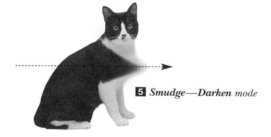

3 *The original image*

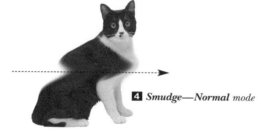

4 *Smudge—Normal mode*

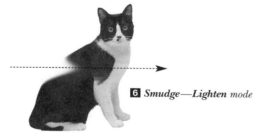

5 *Smudge—Darken mode*

6 *Smudge—Lighten mode*

Other painting techniques

In this section, you'll learn how to use the Smudge and Paint Bucket tools.

To smudge colors:

1. Choose a layer. *Note:* The Smudge tool can't be used on an image in Bitmap or Indexed Color mode.

2. Choose the Smudge tool (R or Shift-R).

3. On the Smudge tool options bar **1**–**2**, do the following:

   Click the Brush Preset picker arrowhead, then click a **brush preset;** or click a brush preset on the Brushes palette.

   Choose a blending **Mode.** Try Normal to smudge all shades or colors, Darken to push dark colors into lighter colors, or Lighten to push light colors into darker colors.

   Choose a **Strength** value to control how forcefully the stroke smudges pixels.

4. Check Use All Layers on the options bar to start the smudge using colors that the tool detects on all the currently visible layers (uncheck Finger Painting if you use this option). Or uncheck Use All Layers to smudge using only colors from the active layer. In either case, pixels will actually be smudged on only the currently active layer.

5. To start the smudge with the Foreground color, check Finger Painting on the options bar. Or uncheck Finger Painting to have the smudge start with the color under the pointer where the stroke begins. The higher the Strength percentage when Finger Painting is on, the more the Foreground color is applied.

   TIP Hold down Alt/Option to toggle the Finger Painting option on or off.

6. Drag across any area of the image **3**–**6**. Pause between strokes, if necessary, to let the screen redraw.

Smudge Colors

The **Paint Bucket** tool replaces pixels with the Foreground color or a pattern, and fills areas of a similar shade or color within a specified Tolerance range. You can use this tool without creating a selection.

To fill an area using the Paint Bucket tool:

1. Choose a layer. If you don't want to fill transparent areas on the layer, click the Lock Transparent Pixels button.
   Note: The Paint Bucket tool won't work on an image in Bitmap color mode.

2. Choose the Paint Bucket tool (G or Shift-G). It's on the Gradient tool pop-out menu.

3. On the Paint Bucket tool options bar **1**–**2**, do the following:

   Choose Fill: **Foreground** to fill with a solid color. Or choose **Pattern,** then click a pattern on the Pattern Preset picker.

   Choose a blending **Mode** (you can press Shift + [plus] or Shift - [minus] to cycle through the modes). Try Multiply, Soft Light, or Color Burn.

   Choose an **Opacity** percentage.

   Enter a **Tolerance** value (0–255). The higher the Tolerance, the wider the range of colors the Paint Bucket can fill. Try a low number first.

   Check **Anti-aliased** to smooth the edges of the fill area.

   Check **Contiguous** to permit only areas that are contiguous to the one you click on to be filled, or uncheck this option to allow noncontiguous areas to be filled.

   Check **All Layers** to have the Paint Bucket fill areas on the active layer based on colors the tool detects on all the currently visible layers, instead of just the colors it detects on the current layer.

4. Choose a Foreground color.

5. Click on the image **3**–**4**. The little black spill is the active part of the tool pointer.

> ### Defining a pattern
> To apply a custom pattern, create a rectangular selection on a layer, choose Edit > **Define Pattern,** enter a name, click OK, then deselect. The custom pattern will appear as the last swatch in the Pattern Preset picker.

1 *The left side of the **Paint Bucket** tool options bar*

2 *The right side of the **Paint Bucket** tool options bar*

PHOTO: PAUL PETROFF

3 *The original image*

4 *After clicking with the **Paint Bucket** tool, pixels that fall within the specified Tolerance range are recolored.*

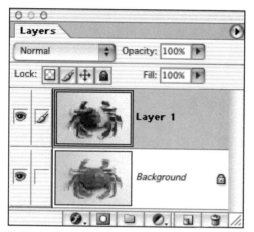

1 *The color tints are on Layer 1. The original Background image still looks like it's grayscale, even though the image is now in RGB Color mode.*

Here's a nice technique for applying **tints** to a grayscale image. By drawing colored strokes on a separate layer, you'll have the flexibility to change the blending mode or opacity for your painting tool or for the color layer, or to erase or dodge here or there—all without changing the underlying grayscale image one iota.

To apply tints to a grayscale image:

1. Open a Grayscale mode image and convert it to RGB Color mode (Image > Mode > RGB Color). You can use the "Ranch House" file in the Samples folder in the Photoshop application folder.

2. Alt-click/Option-click the New Layer button 🔳 at the bottom of the Layers palette to add a new layer above the grayscale imagery, choose Mode: Overlay or Color for the new layer, then click OK.

3. Choose the Brush tool (B or Shift-B). 🖌

4. Choose a Foreground color.

5. From the Brush tool options bar, do the following:

   Choose a **brush preset** from the Brush Preset picker.

   Choose Mode: **Normal.**

   Choose an **Opacity** percentage below 100%. Choose a low opacity for a subtle tint. You can change opacities between strokes, and you can also lower the opacity of the whole layer at any time via the Layers palette.

   Choose a **Flow** percentage.

   Optional: Click the Airbrush button. 🖌

6. Paint strokes on the new layer **1**. Gorgeous!

7. *Optional:* Use the Eraser tool to remove areas of unwanted color, then repaint, if desired. Or use the Dodge tool at a low Exposure percentage to gently lighten the tints.

8. *Optional:* Try a different blending mode for the color layer, such as Multiply, Soft Light, Color Burn, or Hard Mix, or use the Channel Mixer to apply colors.

Tint a Grayscale Image

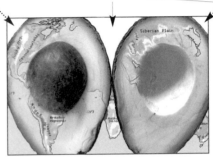

The **Eraser** tool options bar

Erasing

To erase part of a layer:

1. Choose a layer 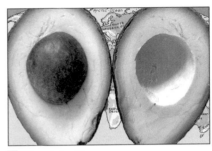. If you use the Eraser tool on a layer with the Lock Transparent Pixels option ▦ on (or use it on the Background of an image), the erased area will be replaced with the current Background color. If Lock Transparent Pixels is off for the layer, the erased area will be replaced with transparency. Decide which way you want to go.

2. Choose the Eraser tool (E or Shift-E). ⬗

3. On the Eraser tool options bar ❶, do the following:

    Click the Brush Preset picker arrowhead, then click a **brush preset** in the picker; or click a preset on the Brushes palette.

    Choose **Mode:** Brush, Pencil, or Block (square eraser).

    Choose an **Opacity** percentage.

    If you chose the Brush mode, you can choose a **Flow** percentage. The lower the Flow percentage, the rougher the erasure stroke.

    Click the Airbrush button ✎ on or off.

4. If you're going to erase the Background of the image, or if Lock Transparent Pixels is on, choose a Background color.

5. Click on or drag across any part of the layer ❸–❹.

TIP To restore areas on the current layer from a history state, move the History source icon 🗒 to the desired state on the History palette, then use the Eraser tool with Erase to History checked on the options bar (or Alt-drag/Option-drag to turn on the Erase to History function temporarily). The Erase to History option won't be available if you added a new layer or changed the number of pixels in (resampled) the file after using the eraser.

2 The original image

3 After **erasing** part of the avocados layer to reveal the map underneath it (Airbrush option on, 55% opacity) and erasing part of the map layer to white (Brush option, 100% opacity)

4 A detail of the **partially erased** map layer

Eraser

1 *The **Background Eraser** tool options bar*

2 *With **Find Edges** chosen from the **Limits** pop-up menu on the **Background Eraser** tool options bar, the tool successfully erased the background area on this image.*

The **Background Eraser** tool erases to transparency or to the current Background color by dragging. This tool's strength is that you can control several criteria, such as whether the tool erases contiguous or noncontiguous pixels. And by choosing your tool settings carefully, you can control how large the erasure will be and how soft the edges of the erased area will be.

To use the Background Eraser tool:

1. Choose the Background Eraser tool (it has a scissors icon)(E or Shift-E).

2. To control where the erasure occurs, from the Limits pop-up menu on the options bar **1**, choose one of the following:

    Discontiguous to erase all pixels within the current Tolerance range, whether or not they are next to one another. If you choose this option, also choose Once from the Sampling pop-up menu (see step 5).

    Contiguous to erase only adjacent pixels within the current Tolerance range that match the first pixel that you click on.

    Find Edges to erase contiguous pixels while preserving object edges (high-contrast borders) **2**.

3. Click the Brush Preset picker thumbnail or arrowhead on the options bar to open the pop-up palette, then modify the tip size and/or shape.

4. Choose a **Tolerance** percentage to control how much the colors to be erased can differ from the first color you clicked on.

5. From the Sampling pop-up menu on the options bar, choose:

    Continuous to erase to transparency all the pixels you drag across within the current Tolerance range.

(Continued on the following page)

Background Eraser

Once to erase to transparency only the pixels that closely match the first pixel you drag across. To erase only one color, choose Once and make the Tolerance 1%.

Background Swatch to erase only pixels that match the current Background color. Choose a Background color now. Use a low Tolerance with this option.

6. *Optional:* To protect a particular color from erasure, check Protect Foreground Color and make sure Once is chosen from the Sampling pop-up menu. Make the Foreground color square active on the Color palette, hold down Alt/Option, and then, in the image window, click to sample the color that you want to protect.

7. If you're using a pressure-sensitive tablet, you can set the brush size and tolerance to respond to pen pressure. Click the Brush Preset picker thumbnail, then set these options using the pop-up palette.

8. Choose the layer that you want to erase pixels from.

9. Drag across the area of the image that you want to erase **1**–**2**. The active part of the tool is the crosshair.

If you're unhappy with the results, either invoke the Undo command or click on an earlier history state, change any of the parameters described in steps 2–5 starting on the previous page, then try again. For example, if you want to widen or narrow the range of colors that the tool erases, change the Tolerance value on the Background Eraser tool options bar.

1 *The original image*

Find Edges, Once, Tolerance 18, Brush size 45

Contiguous, Once, Tolerance 40, Brush size 65

2 *After using the* **Background Eraser** *tool with various options bar settings*

Contiguous, Once, Tolerance 18, Brush size 45

Background Eraser

1 *The **Magic Eraser** tool options bar*

2 *The original image*

3 *After clicking on the rightmost leaf with the **Contiguous** option **off** on the **Magic Eraser** tool options bar*

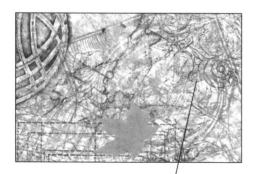

4 *After clicking with the **Magic Eraser** tool on the rightmost leaf in the original image with the **Contiguous** option **on:** the three dark leaves disappear.*

The **Magic Eraser** tool allows you to erase by clicking with the mouse—not by dragging. It erases pixels that are similar in color to the pixel you click on, within a defined Tolerance range. It works like the Paint Bucket tool, except it removes, rather than adds, pixels from a layer. Used with an Opacity setting below 100%, the Magic Eraser tool can be used to make target areas of a layer partially transparent.

To use the Magic Eraser tool:

1. Choose the Magic Eraser tool (E or Shift-E).

2. On the Magic Eraser tool options bar **1**, do the following:

Choose a **Tolerance** value. The higher the Tolerance, the wider the range of colors that will be erased. Enter a low Tolerance if you want to erase only colors that are very similar to the color you click on. Enter 0 to erase only one color.

Check **Anti-aliased** to slightly soften the edges of the erased area.

Check **Contiguous** to erase only pixels that are next to one another, or uncheck this option to erase similarly colored pixels throughout the layer **2**–**4**.

Check **Use All Layers** to erase areas on the active layer based on colors the tool detects on all the currently visible layers. With this option unchecked, the tool will detect colors on only the currently active layer. In either case, only pixels on the currently active layer will be erased.

Choose an **Opacity** percentage. Enter 100% to erase to transparency or a lower opacity to perform a partial erasure.

(Continued on the following page)

Magic Eraser

3. Choose the layer that you want to erase pixels from.

4. In the image window, carefully position the tool on the area that you want to erase, then click.

If the erasure is too large or too small, undo, change the Tolerance value on the Magic Eraser tool options bar, then try clicking again on the image **1**–**3**.

1 *The original image*

2 *Clicking on the sky with the Magic Eraser tool, Tolerance of 30*

3 *Clicking on the sky on the original image with the Magic Eraser tool, Tolerance of 10*

PHOTOGRAPHY 13

1 *The **Lens Blur** filter was used to change the focal point in this image.*

2 *These images will to be united into a panorama using the **Photomerge** command*

Match Color

For instructions on using the **Match Color** command, visit the Peachpit Press website (go to peachpit.com, click "chapters & articles," then click "Adobe").

IN **THIS** **CHAPTER** we cover a number of new features that will be of keen interest to photographers, such as the ability to open and work with Camera Raw (digital camera) files in Photoshop **1**. Other new features include a Shadow/Highlight command for salvaging overexposed or underexposed images; the Photo Filter command for creating a colored lens effect; the Lens Blur filter for simulating depth of field **2**; the Photomerge command for blending multiple images into a panorama **3**; and the Color Replacement tool for replacing colors using a brush. Features from earlier versions of Photoshop that are also covered include the Replace Color command for replacing colors and the Healing Brush and Patch tools for making repairs.

Camera Raw NEW

The digital cameras used by amateurs and consumers automatically store images in the JPEG format, whereas the cameras used by pros and serious enthusiasts provide the option to work directly with **Camera Raw** image files, which have substantial advantages. (See our comparison of JPEG versus Camera Raw on page 241.) When a digital camera stores an image in a format other than Camera Raw, it also performs processing operations, such as sharpening and color adjustment. With Camera Raw, you get only the "raw" information that the lens captured on its light sensors, and so the initial image processing is under your control.

The Camera Raw dialog box in Photoshop allows you to open camera files directly, to correct inaccuracies caused by unsatisfactory shooting conditions, and to create and save custom settings and profiles for specific camera models. Once opened in Photoshop, copies of your Camera Raw files can be saved in any file format.

NEW **To open a Camera Raw file:**

1. Open the File Browser, then locate and click a Camera Raw image file (you can also use the File > Open command). Note that different digital cameras use different file extensions for Camera Raw files, such as .nef for Nikon and .crw for Canon. If you're unsure which files are Camera Raw, choose Camera Raw from the Files of Type/Show pop-up menu; non-Camera Raw file names will be dimmed. (Don't confuse the Camera Raw format with Photoshop Raw, a file format that's used for transferring image files among applications.)

2. The Camera Raw dialog box opens **1**. In the title bar across the top of the dialog box, you'll see information about your photo, such as the camera used; the file name; and the camera data (ISO, or film speed, shutter speed, f-stop, and focal length) settings that were used to take the photograph.

3. On the Adjust and Detail tabs, adjust any of the image attributes that need correction, such as the white balance, exposure, color, or sharpening. These options are discussed in depth on pages 237–239.

4. When you're satisfied with the image, click OK. Photoshop will process the image using your settings and open it as a new file. You can name and save it in any file format; the original Camera Raw file will be left untouched.

TIP Camera Raw image files can also be batch-processed using an action (see pages 411–412).

TIP Camera Raw files can be created only by a camera; you can't save a Photoshop file as Camera Raw.

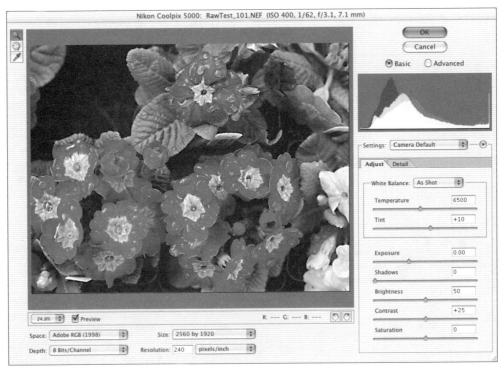

1 *The Camera Raw dialog box, showing the image preview, image attributes, histogram, and controls*

Is my camera supported?

There are many proprietary Camera Raw file formats. Some are unique to a particular manufacturer (e.g., Nikon, Canon) and some are unique to a particular camera model. For a complete listing of the Camera Raw formats that are supported by Adobe Photoshop CS (with support for new cameras added as they become available), visit the Adobe website.

Switcheroos

Hold down the following keys to change the function of buttons in the Camera Raw dialog box:

Alt/Option	Cancel becomes **Reset,** which restores the original dialog box settings
Alt/Option	OK becomes **Update,** which updates the image using the current settings without opening it in Photoshop
Shift	OK becomes **Skip,** which closes the current image and opens the next in a series of selected Camera Raw images
Alt/Option	Changes the Hand tool to a temporary **zoom out** tool
Ctrl/Cmd	Changes the Hand tool to a temporary **zoom in** tool
Spacebar	Changes the Zoom or White Balance tool into a temporary **Hand** tool

To change views in the preview window: NEW
Do any of the following:

Choose the **Zoom** tool (Z) in the toolbox in the upper left corner of the dialog box, then click the preview to zoom in or Alt-click/Option-click to zoom out.

Choose a preset zoom percentage from the **Zoom Level** pop-up menu (6–400%) below the image preview.

If the zoom level is higher than 100%, you can use the **Hand** tool (H) to drag the image in the preview window.

Click **Preview** to preview the current settings; uncheck to see the original image.

Click the button (L) to rotate the image 90° counterclockwise or the button (R) to rotate it 90° clockwise. The rotation will preview in the dialog box, and Photoshop will apply it automatically to the file when it's opened in Photoshop.

TIP Double-click the Zoom tool to change the view to 100% (actual pixels), or double-click the Hand tool to change the zoom level to Fit in View.

When you choose **image attributes** for a Camera Raw file, you'll be choosing settings for the image that will be opened in Photoshop, not the original file.

To change the image attributes for a NEW **Camera Raw file:**
Do any of the following in the Camera Raw dialog box:

1. From the **Space** pop-up menu, choose the color space profile you want the file to use in Photoshop: Adobe RGB (1998), Colormatch RGB, ProPhoto RGB, or sRGB IEC61966-1 (see pages 49–50).

2. If you're going to resize the image, you can make use of Camera Raw's algorithms. From the **Size** pop-up menu, choose from six preset sizes that match the proportions of your Camera Raw image. Choosing a size larger than the original will cause resampling.

(Continued on the following page)

Camera Raw Views, Attributes

3. As you pass the pointer across the image preview, note the RGB readouts below the preview window; these are the Red, Green, and Blue values of the pixel directly beneath the cursor.

4. From the **Depth** pop-up menu, choose a color depth of either 8 Bits/Channel or 16 Bits/Channel (see page 60).

5. Specify a **Resolution.**

NEW To change a Camera Raw image's basic settings:

1. Click Basic at the top of the Camera Raw dialog box.

The histogram **1** is a graph of the red, green, and blue channels, superimposed on one another, and is useful for monitoring how slider adjustments affect the image's tonal range (the tonal distribution of image pixels).

2. From the **Settings** pop-up menu, choose one of the following: Selected Image to use settings from the current file; Camera Default to use settings from the camera model that was used to take the photo; Previous Conversion to use settings from the last adjusted image; Custom; or a settings file that you've created and saved (see the next step).

3. When you open a Camera Raw file, Photoshop loads in the default settings from the camera used to take the photo. To change those settings, you can choose an option from the Camera Raw plug-in menu ⊙: Load Settings, Save Settings, Delete Current Settings, Set Camera Default, and Reset Camera Default.

For example, to correct multiple images using the same settings, first apply corrections to one of the images and choose Save Settings. Then, to apply those settings to another image, choose Load Settings. Or to use the currrent settings for other images that were produced by the same camera model, choose Set Camera Default.

Sticky settings

Settings in the Camera Raw dialog box are "sticky," meaning once you've applied settings to a Camera Raw file, they'll redisplay the next time you open that file, even if the file is renamed or moved. Those settings will also be used for the image thumbnail and preview in the File Browser. In fact, they're difficult to remove!

Individual file slider settings (but not other settings such as bit depth, color space, etc.) are stored in either in a Camera Raw database (in Windows, in C:\Documents and Settings\[username]\Application Data\Adobe; in Mac, in [username]/Library/ Preferences), or in a "sidecar" .xmp text file (with the same basic file name) in the same folder as the Camera Raw file. This sidecar file can also store metadata relevant to that file. (To change where these settings are stored, click Advanced in the Camera Raw dialog box, choose Preferences from the Camera Raw plug-in menu, ⊙ then choose from the "Save image settings in" pop-up menu.)

1 *The distribution of image pixels for each of the red, green, and blue color components is displayed as overlapping color graphs in the* **histogram** *window in the Camera Raw dialog box, with shadow pixels on the left and highlights on the right.*

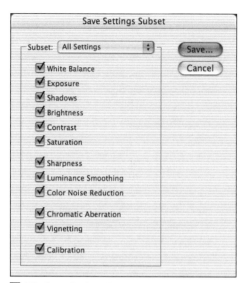

1 *The Save Settings Subset options dialog box*

Terms defined

The **white balance** is color temperature data from the camera, and it's used to reproduce the lighting conditions that were present when the photo was taken. If you want to preserve the white balance data, choose "As Shot" from the White Balance pop-up menu in the Adjust pane of the Camera Raw dialog box. Or choose different settings in the Adjust pane if you want to perfect the existing white balance or change it more dramatically to simulate different conditions.

Specular highlights are bright spots of light that appear on shiny, reflective surfaces.

Or if you want to selectively choose which settings are saved to a new settings file, click Advanced at the top of the dialog box, and choose Save Settings Subset from the Camera Raw plug-in menu. In the Save Settings Subset dialog box **1**, check which settings you want saved in the settings file. Finally, click Save, enter a name (leave the default location as is), then click Save again.

The **Adjust** pane in the Camera Raw dialog box lets you make image color and tonal adjustments. When doing so, we recommend choosing the Fit in View zoom setting for the preview.

To make global color adjustments to a (NEW) Camera Raw file:

1. Click Basic at the top of the dialog box, then click the Adjust tab (**1**, next page).

2. You can adjust the white balance of the photo to remove any undesirable color casts. There are three ways to do this:

   From the **White Balance** pop-up menu, choose the setting that best describes the lighting conditions when the photo was taken: As Shot, Auto, Daylight, Cloudy, Shade, Tungsten, Fluorescent, Flash, or Custom.
   or
   Choose the **White Balance tool** (I), then click on what you want to become a white or neutral light gray area in the photo—preferably a highlight area that has some detail, but not a specular highlight. Any color cast in the neutral tone will be removed, and the overall picture temperature will be adjusted accordingly. Photographers sometimes place a color chart next to the subject they're shooting and use the lighter tones in the chart to set the white balance.
   or
   Use the **Temperature** and **Tint** sliders in combination (this is an excellent way to set the white balance in the image

(Continued on the following page)

Camera Raw: Adjust

manually). Move the **Temperature** slider (values are shown in the Kelvin color temperature scale) to the left to add blue to cool the colors, or to the right to add yellow to warm them. Drag the **Tint** slider to adjust any green/magenta imbalances: to the left (–) to add green, or to the right (+) to add magenta.

3. Move the **Exposure** slider to the right to make the overall image lighter or to the left to make it darker (values display as f-stop settings). The Exposure option redistributes pixels to the shadow or highlight end of the tonal range.

4. Move the **Shadows** slider to control which image pixel levels will be output as black (this is similar to the black input slider in the Levels dialog box).

As you move the Exposure and Shadows sliders, watch on the histogram for highlight or shadow pixels that may be pushed to the edge of the graph, or "clipped." For Exposure, pixels in white areas will be clipped, and colored areas represent highlights; for Shadows, pixels in black areas will be clipped, and colored areas represent shadows. Your goal is to reduce areas of total white or black, respectively, to a minimum.

TIP Hold down Alt/Option as you move the two sliders to preview the effect on the image.

5. Now that you've adjusted the highlights and shadows, move the **Brightness** slider to make the image brighter or darker overall.

6. Move the **Contrast** slider to the left to reduce contrast in the image or to the right to increase contrast.

7. Move the **Saturation** slider. At +100 (far right), the Saturation slider will double the color saturation in an image; at –100 (far left), it will convert the image to grayscale. Don't raise the Saturation levels too much, or your image colors will exceed the gamut of the final output device (see page 465).

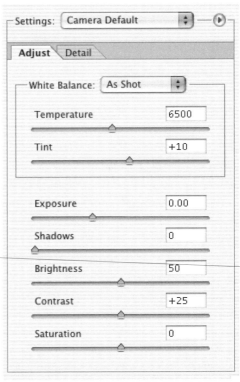

1 *The **Adjust** tab in the Camera Raw dialog box*

Camera Raw: Adjust

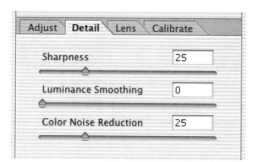

1 *Choose settings in the **Detail** tab of the Camera Raw dialog box. (Note: The Lens and Calibrate panes are available when the Advanced option is checked.)*

Use options on the **Detail** tab to make sharpness, smoothing, and noise adjustments (here, again, we recommend choosing Fit in View for the preview).

To make detail adjustments to a Camera Raw file:

1. Click the Detail tab in the Camera Raw dialog box **1**.

2. Use the **Sharpness** slider to control edge definition in the image. If you plan to do further editing in Photoshop, we recommend setting this slider to zero (no sharpening) and using the sharpening filters in Photoshop proper instead.

3. All digital cameras produce a certain amount of noise (visible artifacts, or stray pixels), with low-quality cameras and high ISO (film speed) settings producing the most. Noise should be removed before opening the file in Photoshop, as it can become accentuated by image editing. To reduce noise in the lights and darks of the overall image, move the **Luminance Smoothing** slider to the right.

4. And finally, if you're still awake, move the **Color Noise Reduction** slider to the right to eliminate color artifacts from the more solid-color areas in the image.

TIP The effect of the Luminance Smoothing and Color Noise Reduction sliders is more pronounced when the Sharpness value is increased.

TIP If you're not going to apply sharpening to your images here but you do want to preview sharpening, click Advanced, choose Preferences on the Camera Raw plug-in menu, ⊙ and in the Camera Raw Preferences dialog box, choose "Apply sharpening to: Preview images only."

Camera Raw: Detail

Now we'll show you, albeit reluctantly (some QuickStart, huh?), an advanced feature. Discrepancies can arise between a particular camera model's color profile and the built-in color profile that Camera Raw uses for that model. One way to compensate for these discrepancies is to go to the **Calibrate** tab of the Camera Raw dialog box and adjust the image's hue and saturation. Before doing so, once again, use the zoom level controls to display the whole image (Fit in View).

NEW To adjust Camera Raw's built-in camera profiles:

1. Click Advanced at the top of the Camera Raw dialog box, then click the Calibrate tab **1**.

2. Move the Shadow Tint slider to the left to add green to the shadow areas, or to the right to add magenta.

3. Use the Red Hue, Red Saturation, Green Hue, Green Saturation, Blue Hue, and Blue Saturation sliders to adjust the amount and saturation of each RGB component in the image. The farther any slider is moved away from zero, the more pronounced the changes in color and saturation.

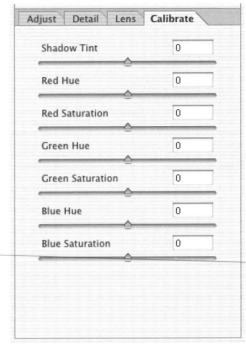

1 *The **Calibrate** tab in the Camera Raw dialog box*

Camera Raw: Calibrate

Camera Raw versus JPEG

To be fair, there are some advantages to working with JPEG files. JPEG file sizes are smaller, so more of them can be stored in a digital camera and they have shorter transfer speeds. It takes a camera less time to create and store a JPEG file while shooting than it does a Camera Raw file, which allows for faster shot sequencing. The JPEG format is also readable by almost any software, as it's used ubiquitously by Web designers and in the digital imaging industry.

One disadvantage to JPEG, however, is its lossy compression methods. This loss of image quality is less objectionable at moderate to low compression levels than at higher compression levels, where the undesirable side effects it produces, such as artifacts, banding, and loss of detail, become more pronounced. High compression methods can render photos unusable for high-end professional photographers.

Unlike JPEGs, Camera Raw employs lossless compression. Furthermore, Camera Raw files can be opened in 16-bit mode in Photoshop, which allows you to take advantage of the newly expanded range of editing features available for 16-bit images.

Finally, Camera Raw preserves the image's original pixel information, whereas cameras that process and save photos in the JPEG format perform image-processing operations and, in the process, alter the images' original data. Although you can reprocess and readjust your photos in Photoshop, you can't restore the original pixel information. And having to readjust images in Photoshop, especially when you're batch-processing a lot of them, can lower your productivity.

So all in all, there are some compelling reasons for using Camera Raw.

NEW Shadow and highlight adjustment

The **Shadow/Highlight** command is a welcome addition to Photoshop's assortment of image adjustment tools. It provides a very fast (but accurate) way to compensate for areas of overexposure and underexposure within RGB and Grayscale images, and it could prove helpful in alleviating unwanted effects from strong side- or backlighting. It's much faster than using other tools (e.g., using Curves or Levels in conjunction with layers or masks). Due to its speed and ease of use, we think it will also be very helpful for processing large numbers of images.

The Shadow/Highlight command works by increasing contrast in shadows and highlights without unduly altering other tonal areas of the image. It does this by adjusting the luminance of each individual pixel depending on the darkness or lightness of neighboring pixels. It's a "smart" feature that recognizes the tonal boundaries of individual objects within an image when making calculations.

This command works with RGB, LAB, Grayscale, and Duotone image files, and with 8-bit and 16-bit files, but not with CMYK, Bitmap, Indexed Color, or Multichannel mode files. Also, it can't be applied via an adjustment layer—at least not yet.

NEW To apply the Shadow/Highlight command:

1. Display the Histogram palette so you can monitor tonal range adjustments.

2. Choose Image > Adjustments > Shadow/Highlight .

3. For the **Shadows** 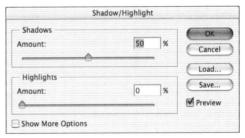, choose an Amount value to control how much you want each pixel to be lightened in the shadow areas. The default setting of 50% will compensate reasonably well for underexposure in the shadow areas of many images. Increase this value (up to 100%) for stronger shadow correction, such as

1 *The midtones and shadows in the bottom portion of this image are dark and murky; it's hard to see any details.*

2 *Choose settings in the **Shadow/Highlight** dialog box.*

Shadow/Highlight Command

1 *An adjustment of the shadows and highlights using the* **Shadow/Highlight** *command produced a better tonal range overall and restored details in the midtones and shadows.*

foreground subjects that are darkened by strong backlighting, and to extend those corrections into the midtones and highlight areas. A Shadow setting of 0%, like a straight line in the Curves dialog box, results in no change to the image.

4. For the Highlights, choose an Amount value to establish how much you want the highlight areas of the image to be darkened (0% produces no darkening).

5. Uncheck, then check, Preview to toggle between the original image and the adjusted image.

6. *Optional:* To save your Shadow/Highlight adjustment settings, click Save, enter a name (keep the .shh extension), choose a location, then click Save again. Or to load previously saved settings, click Load.

7. Click OK **1**.

TIP To restore the original settings in the dialog box while it's still open, hold down Alt/Option and click Reset.

TIP Click Show More Options in the Shadow/Highlight dialog box to access further options. To learn more about these features, see Photoshop Help.

Shadow/Highlight Command

Colored lens effect

The new **Photo Filter** command simulates the effect that a photographer achieves by using colored lens filters. When using this command, you can choose from the 18 preset filter colors or you can choose a color from the Color Picker.

NEW To apply the Photo Filter command:

1. Choose a layer or the Background.

2. Choose Image > Adjustments > Photo Filter.
   or
   Choose Photo Filter from the New Fill/ Adjustment Layer pop-up menu ⬤, at the bottom of the Layers palette.

3. Make sure Preview is checked 1.

4. Click Filter, then from the **Filter** pop-up menu, choose a warming or cooling filter or a preset filter color. The color you choose will appear in the swatch below the menu.
   or
   Click the color swatch to open the Color Picker, choose a color for the filter, then click OK.

5. Move the **Density** slider to choose an opacity for the effect. Of course, if you're using an adjustment layer for this command, the layer opacity can also be adjusted after you click OK.

6. Click **Preserve Luminosity** to preserve the image's overall brightness and tonal range.

7. Click OK.

TIP To restore the original settings in the dialog box while it's still open, hold down Alt/Option and click Reset.

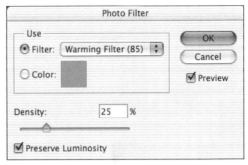

1 *The **Photo Filter** dialog box*

1 *The original image, entirely in focus*

2 *After applying the **Lens Blur** filter to blur the pumpkins in the background*

Lens Blur NEW

If you've ever snapped a photo and had it developed, you know that whether you like it or not, some parts of your subject matter remained in focus and some did not. If your camera has dials that you can fiddle with (as opposed to the point-and-shoot type of camera), you can use the f-stop to control the "depth of field" of the image, or how much of the image is in focus. Objects that fall outside (are in front of or behind) the depth of field will look blurry. The appearance of the blurred area will vary depending on the individual camera lens and camera model. For example, blurred white highlights, which photographers call specular highlights, can vary in shape and intensity.

The **Lens Blur** filter in Photoshop CS attempts to replicate the blurring that a camera lens produces **1**–**2**. What previously required the use of multiple channels, gradients, and editing steps can now be accomplished in one dialog box. All of this number crunching comes at a price, though: it can be slow when applied to large images. Also, it can't be applied to 16-bit images.

To apply the Lens Blur filter: NEW

1. Choose a layer in an image that's entirely in focus.

2. Create an alpha channel that contains a gradient (see page 308). Or for the selected layer, create a layer mask that contains a gradient (see page 278). The white part of the channel or mask gradient can be matched up with an area in the photo that you want to remain in focus. The white and black areas of the gradient can be switched from within the Lens Blur dialog box. Click back on the layer thumbnail. Later, you'll choose that alpha channel or layer mask as the Depth Map source.

Note: If these instructions seem overly complex, come back and visit after you're more comfortable using either gradients or masks.

(Continued on the following page)

Lens Blur Filter

Lens Blur Filter

1 *The **Lens Blur** dialog box. We clicked on the tip of the foreground pumpkin to make that the point in focus.*

2 *The original image contains a layer mask, which is composed of a gradient. This layer mask is chosen as the Depth Map source.*

When you click the dialog box preview, you're actually choosing a grayscale value from the layer mask. The grayscale value becomes the Blur Focal Distance value. Image pixels at the location you clicked remain in focus; all other image pixels become progressively more blurry (blurring at the same rate as the gradient transitions to black).

3. Choose Filter > Blur > Lens Blur. The Lens Blur dialog box opens (█, previous page). Choose Fit in View for the zoom level.

4. At any time while you're making adjustments, you can uncheck, then check Preview to toggle between the original image and the blurred image.

You can also change the zoom level for the preview by clicking the ⊞ or ⊟ zoom button in the lower left corner of the preview window or by choosing a preset zoom level from the zoom level pop-up menu.

5. The grayscale values in a Depth Map control where the blur is applied, mimicking the depth of field in a camera. In the Depth Map area:

From the **Source** pop-up menu, choose a source for the Depth Map (the grayscale values in the source will control what's in focus). Choosing None, or a source that is one overall value (such as a flat color background), will result in uniform blurring across the image.

Move the **Blur Focal Distance** slider to specify which grayscale value (0–255) in your Depth Map is to remain fully in focus. The higher the value, the shorter the depth of field. Values lighter or darker than this value will become progressively more blurred and will look as though they're either in front of or behind the areas that are in focus.

Or you can click in the preview on the area you want to keep in focus. Actually, what you're really doing is choosing a grayscale value that's located in that part of the chosen channel or mask (it's not visible, but it is aligned with the image) █.

Check **Invert** if you want to switch the white and black areas in the Depth Map.

6. Use the settings in the **Iris** area to specify the size and shape of the camera lens's iris, or aperture:

From the **Shape** pop-up menu, choose the number of blades that create the lens opening.

The **Radius** value controls the size of the iris opening and the amount of the blur. It has the most pronounced effect of any option in the dialog box.

Choose a **Blade Curvature** value for the curvature on the blade shapes.

Choose a **Rotation** value to rotate the iris opening.

As the number of blades and the blade curvature increase, the shape of the iris becomes more circular and the shape effect becomes harder to discern. The shape will be most noticeable in the specular highlights of an image.

If all of this seems overly complex, you can just experiment with different settings until you achieve the look you want without paying too much attention to the mechanics of how it works.

7. Blurring averages the values of neighboring pixels and tends to gray out white specular highlight areas. In the **Specular Highlights** area, you can use the **Brightness** slider to brighten highlight areas that have become blurred, and use the **Threshold** slider to control how many pixel levels are affected by the Brightness setting.

8. Blurring can also affect the film grain in an image, creating a nonuniform texture. To add **Noise** back to the blurred areas, do any of the following:

Move the **Noise:** Amount slider.

Click **Distribution:** Uniform or Gaussian.

Check **Monochromatic** if you want to limit the noise to just grayscale pixels instead of color pixels.

9. Click OK (█, page 245).

Replace colors

Using the **Replace Color** command, you can adjust the Hue, Saturation, or Lightness of colors in specific areas that you click on in the image window or in the dialog box—without using any selection tools. This command works best for adjusting soft-edged areas, such as in a landscape, that don't require a sharp-edged selection.

To use the Replace Color command:

1. *Optional:* For an RGB image, choose View > Proof Setup > Working CMYK to see a soft proof of the image and modifications to it in CMYK color.

   Once you've made a choice from the Proof Setup submenu, you can toggle it on or off while the Replace Color dialog box is open by pressing Ctrl-Y/Cmd-Y. Regardless of whether it's on or off, the Color and Result swatches in the Replace Color dialog box will display in RGB.

2. Choose a layer or the Background.

3. *Optional:* Create a selection to restrict color replacement to that area.

4. Choose Image > Adjustments > Replace Color.

5. Initially, the preview window will be solid black. In the preview window in the Replace Color dialog box or in the image window, click the color you want to replace **1**.

   Click Selection to preview the selection in the preview window, or click Image to display the entire image. In Mac, you can press/release Control to toggle between the two display modes.

6. Move the Fuzziness slider to the right to add related colors to the selection, or to the left to shrink the selection.
   or
   To add other color areas to the selection, choose the first eyedropper, 🖉 then Shift-click in the preview window or image window. Or choose the 🖉 eyedropper and click without holding down Shift.

1 *The white areas in the preview window in the* **Replace Color** *dialog box represent the areas that will be modified.*

1 *The original image*

2 *After a Lightness adjustment to the background using the **Replace Color** command*

7. If you've added colors to the selection and you want to subtract from it, with the first eyedropper, 🖋 Alt-click/ Option-click in the preview window or image window. Or choose the 🖋 eyedropper, then click without holding down Alt/Option.

8. Move the Hue, Saturation, or Lightness sliders to change the selected colors (only the Lightness slider will be available for a Grayscale image). The Result swatch will change as you move **NEW** the sliders.

or

Click the Result swatch, choose a color from the Color Picker, then click OK. All three sliders will adjust to reflect the new color's attributes.

Note: The Replacement sliders will stay in their current positions even if you click on a different area of the image.

9. Click OK **1**–**2**.

TIP The Result swatch color from the Replace Color dialog box will also display in the currently active square on the Color palette, and the Color palette sliders will reflect its individual components. If the gamut warning displays on the Color palette, it means the color is nonprintable. Note also that the Replacement sliders won't change the amount of Black (K) in a color for a CMYK image. That component is set by Photoshop's Black Generation function.

TIP To restore the original dialog box settings, hold down Alt/Option and click Reset.

1 *Choose options from the **Color Replacement** tool options bar.*

Like the Replace Color command, which we discussed on the previous two pages, the **Color Replacement** tool allows you to change color, hue, saturation, or luminosity values in select areas. But here, instead of using a dialog box, changes are applied manually using a brush. Also, unlike the plain ol' Brush tool, which applies flat colors, the Color Replacement tool tries to preserve the texture and shading of the original color. Catalogues and ad designers will enjoy using this tool to "recolor" merchandise.

NEW To use the Color Replacement tool:

1. Open or convert an image to RGB, CMYK, or Lab Color mode.

2. Choose the Color Replacement tool (J or Shift-J) (it's on the Healing Brush pop-out menu).

3. Choose a Foreground color, using the Color or Swatches palette, or Option-click with the tool to sample a color from the image (temporary Eyedropper). This is the color that will be applied.

4. From the options bar **1**, choose characteristics for the tool:

Click the **Brush Preset** picker arrowhead and choose brush attributes (diameter, hardness, spacing, etc.).

To control which color characteristics are altered, choose a blending **Mode:** Hue, Saturation, Color, or Luminosity (see "Blending modes" on pages 38–42).

Choose **Sampling: Continuous** to apply the current Foreground color to all pixels the brush passes over; **Once** to sample the first pixel the brush's crosshair clicks on and then apply the Foreground color only to pixels that match that initial sample (this option gives you the most control); or **Background Swatch**

1 *We used the **Color Replacement** tool on the baby's shirt…*

2 *…to replace the color with a darker color.*

to replace only colors that match the current Background color.

Choose **Limits: Discontiguous** to recolor pixels that the pointer is over that fall within the Sampling parameters; **Contiguous** to allow pixels to be recolored that are adjacent to the pixel under the pointer; or **Find Edges** to recolor pixels connected to color areas that match the sample color while preserving distinct shape edges.

To control the range within which a color can differ from the sampled color and still be recolored, enter or choose a **Tolerance** value (1–100%). Choose a high Tolerance to allow a wider range of colors to be recolored, or a low value to limit recoloring to only those pixels that closely match the sample color.

Optional: Check Anti-aliased to smooth the transitions between the existing colors and the replacement colors.

5. Drag the brush over areas of the image **1**–**2**. Only pixels that fall within the parameters of the tool's current Mode, Sampling, Limits, and Tolerance settings will be recolored. You can change any options bar settings between strokes to produce different results.

TIP This is the tool of choice for removing red-eye from an image. Set Sampling to Once, Limits to Contiguous, and the Tolerance to 30%. Choose a dark Foreground color, then paint out the red in each eye.

Color Replacement Tool

1 *The options bar for the **Healing Brush** tool*

Make repairs

The **Healing Brush** tool ("boo-boo brush"?) and the related Patch tool offer touch-up precision that the Clone Stamp and Pattern Stamp tools don't offer. Whereas the Stamp tools copy the source area's color to a target area, this pair of tools samples the source area's texture, applies that texture to the target area, and then matches it to the target area's surrounding color and brightness values. This makes it much easier to fix, say, a facial blemish in a photograph or a paper crinkle in a vintage photo and blend it seamlessly into the surrounding pixels. The Healing Brush is usually used in a free-hand manner, whereas with the Patch tool, changes are confined to preselected areas.

To repair areas using the Healing Brush tool:

1. Choose the Healing Brush tool (J or Shift-J).

2. On the Healing Brush tool options bar **1**, do all of the following:

Click the Brush Preset picker arrowhead, then click a **brush** that's appropriate for the area you want to sample. A small tip will give you the most control.

Choose Mode: **Replace** to have the grain, texture, and noise of the area surrounding the target be preserved. Choose a different mode if you don't care if those attributes are preserved.

Click Source: **Sampled.**

Check **Aligned** to maintain the same distance between the source point (which will change) and the target area that you drag across. Or uncheck Aligned to create repetitive strokes anywhere in the image using the sample from the same source point.

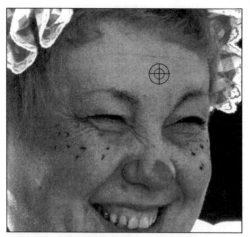

1 *With the **Healing Brush** tool, Alt-click/Option-click the area you want to use as **replacement** pixels...*

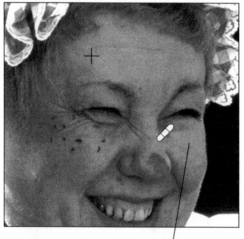

2 *...then drag across the area you want to **repair**.*

To allow the brush to sample pixels on all layers below the pointer, check **Use All Layers;** uncheck Use All Layers to allow the brush to sample pixels from only the current layer.

3. Choose a layer or the Background.

4. Alt-click/Option-click the area to be used as the source sample **1**.

5. Drag across the area you want to repair **2**. When you release the mouse, the source texture will be applied to the target area and will be blended with its surrounding pixels. It will render in two stages, though: at first a full clone will appear, and then the source color will disappear, leaving just the source texture. (Wow!)

TIP Shift-drag to constrain the stroke to the horizontal or vertical axis.

6. *Optional:* To establish a new source point for further repairs, Alt-click/Option-click a different area, then continue on your way.

TIP To confine the repair to a specific area and avoid picking up colors from surrounding areas, lasso the area you want to repair with the Lasso tool before using the Healing Brush.

TIP Before using the Healing Brush tool, duplicate the layer you're going to work on, or create a snapshot via the History palette. Then you'll be able to use the History Brush tool to selectively restore original pixels, if need be.

Healing Brush

1 *The options bar for the **Patch** tool*

Patch Tool

You can use the **Patch** tool to quickly repair tears, stains, and dust marks. Use this tool instead of the Healing Brush if you want to avoid sampling a particular color. This tool also lets you fine-tune and modify a selection (e.g., feather the edges) before applying the repair.

To use the Patch tool:

1. Choose the Patch tool (J or Shift-J).

2. Click Patch: Source on the Patch tool options bar **1**.

3. Drag a lasso-type marquee around the area you want to repair **2** (the Destination). You can Alt-click/Option-click to create a straight-edged selection.

4. *Optional:* Add to (Shift-drag) or subtract from (Alt-drag/Option-drag) the selection as needed, or use any Select menu commands to feather or otherwise modify the selection.

5. Drag from inside the selection to the area you want to sample **3**. The sampled area will update continuously within the selection. Release the mouse **4**. The patch will bounce back, and the sampled pixels will be applied automatically to the area you originally selected (see also **1**–**2** on the following page).

TIP You could also click Destination instead of Source for step 2 above, select the area you want to sample from, and then, for step 5, drag to the area you want to repair (the Destination). However, you'll have more control over which area is repaired if you do it in the reverse order, as in our instructions above.

TIP To patch (fill) the selection with a pattern, with the Patch tool chosen, on the options bar, click a pattern on the Pattern Preset picker, click Use Pattern, and also check Transparent if you want the fill to be semitransparent.

2 *Using the **Patch** tool, select the area you want to repair.*

3 *Drag from the selected area to the area that you want to **sample** pixels from…*

4 *…and the patch will be applied to the original **selected area**.*

1 *The original image*

2 *After using the **Patch** tool to repair the damaged area on the left side*

Photomerge

The new **Photomerge** feature combines a series of separate photos into one image .
You can either have the command blend the photos into one seamless view or you can opt to have the arranged images left intact as individual layers for later blending and editing by hand. As an added bonus, you can use the command to apply perspective, and then modify the vanishing points. This is one powerful command!

NEW **To collect images for Photomerge:**

1. *Optional:* Either collect a sequence of images and put them in their own folder, or open the files you want to use.

2. Choose File > Automate > Photomerge. A dialog box for choosing source files opens .

3. Choose Use: Folder, click Browse, locate and click the folder you organized in step 1, then click Choose.
   or
   Choose Use: Files, click Browse, multiple-select the files that you want to use, then click Open. You can keep clicking Browse to add more files.
   or
   Choose Use: Open Files to work with all the files that are open in Photoshop.

4. *Optional:* If you want to remove any files from the list, click the file name(s), then click Remove.

5. *Optional:* To have Photomerge try to arrange the images for you, check Attempt to Automatically Arrange Source Images. You can rearrange the photos once you get to the Photomerge dialog box proper.

6. Click OK, then follow the next set of instructions.

 *From these six image files, the **Photomerge** command created the seamless panorama shown at the bottom of the page.*

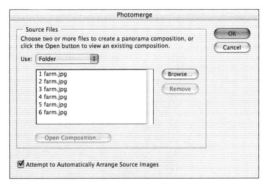

1 *Source Files are chosen for the Photomerge.*

PHOTOS ©NINA FULLER

Photomerge

After clicking OK in the last step on the previous page, sit tight as the Photomerge command opens and duplicates the source files, imports them into the **Photomerge** dialog box, and, if you checked the "Attempt to..." option, arranges them into a panorama.

To create a Photomerge montage: NEW

1. If you checked "Attempt to...," any images that Photoshop wasn't able to merge will be stored in the lightbox at the top of the Photomerge dialog box **1**. You can drag any image to or from the lightbox into the work area, and you can reposition any image in the work area.

2. In the **Navigator** area on the right side of the dialog box (**1**, next page), you'll see a red rectangle, which represents the overall border of the work area. You can drag the red rectangle to reposition the entire composition within the work area.

To change the zoom level of the composition, use the Zoom Out or Zoom In button or slider.

3. Use any of these tools to edit the images:

Drag with the **Select Image** tool (A) to reposition any individual image.

Drag with the **Rotate Image** tool (R) to rotate any individual image.

Click with the **Zoom** tool (Z) to zoom in, or Alt-click/Option-click to zoom out.

Drag with the **Hand** tool (H) to reposition the whole composite image.

4. Click **Settings: Normal** to create a flat collage, or click **Perspective** to apply perspective—as if the image were created using a wide-angle lens, with a fisheye effect at the edges. To change the vanishing point for the perspective, choose the **Vanishing Point** tool (V), then click in the work area.

(Continued on the following page)

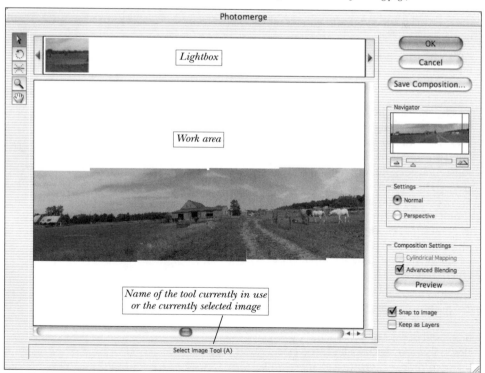

1 *The **Photomerge** dialog box has its own toolbox, a lightbox, a work area, and an assortment of controls.*

Photomerge

5. In the Composition Settings area **1**:

For the Perspective setting, click **Cylindrical Mapping** to make the Perspective appear to wrap around the viewer, without wide-angle distortion.

For the Normal or Perspective setting, click **Advanced Blending** to create the smoothest transitions between images. This option may increase the processing time and will flatten the Photoshop file when you exit the dialog box. (If Keep as Layers is checked, Advanced Blending is disabled.)

Click **Preview** to view the effects of the settings you've chosen; click **Exit Preview** to return to editing mode.

6. *Optional:* Click Snap to Image to snap the images to their original horizontal/vertical alignment (not available for the Perspective setting).

7. *Optional:* Click Keep as Layers to have each image appear on a separate layer in the final file, with no blending between them.

8. Click OK, then twiddle your thumbs as Photomerge creates a seamless image, ready to be edited and saved.
or
To save the current arrangement as a Photomerge (.pmg) file for later editing, click Save Composition, choose a location (preferably the same folder as the source images), then click Save. If you choose this option, when you're ready to reopen the Photomerge (.pmg) composition and its component files in Photoshop, choose Automate > Photomerge, click Open Composition, locate the desired .pmg file, then click Open. You can't reopen a Photomerge (.pmg) file using File > Open.

TIP To quickly remove all images from the work area and place them in the lightbox, hold down Alt/Option and click Reset. You can also use the Undo command to reverse individual changes while the dialog box is open.

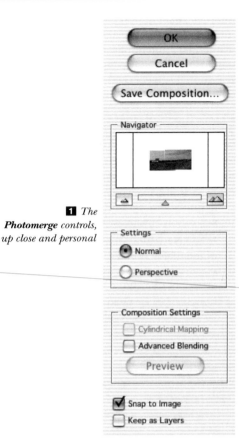

1 *The Photomerge controls, up close and personal*

Photomerge

GRADIENTS 14

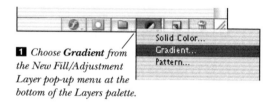

1 *Choose **Gradient** from the New Fill/Adjustment Layer pop-up menu at the bottom of the Layers palette.*

2 *In the **Gradient Fill** dialog box, click the gradient arrowhead, then choose from the Gradient Preset picker…*

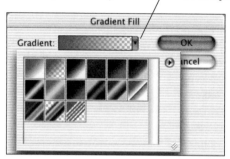

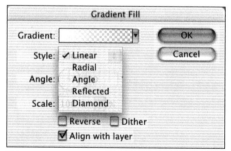

3 *…and choose gradient Style, Angle, and Scale percentages in the **Gradient Fill** dialog box.*

A **GRADIENT IS A GRADUAL** blend between two or more colors, and there are two ways to apply them. One way is to use the Gradient tool to apply a gradient directly to a normal layer. This tool is a good choice if you want to custom fit a gradient by hand in a particular area. You could also use this tool to apply a gradient to a layer mask in a fill or adjustment layer, creating a gradual masking effect.

A second option is to use a **gradient fill layer.** A gradient applied in this way appears in its own layer, with a layer mask that can be used to mask gradient layer pixels. This type of gradient is easier to edit.

To apply a gradient as a fill layer:

1. Choose a layer. The Gradient tool can't be used on an image in Bitmap or Indexed Color mode.

2. *Optional:* Select an area of a layer (see the sidebar on the next page). If nothing is selected, the gradient will fill the entire layer.

3. Choose Gradient from the New Fill/Adjustment Layer pop-up menu ⬤. at the bottom of the Layers palette **1**.

4. Click the gradient arrowhead at the top of the dialog box, choose a gradient preset from the picker, then click back in the dialog box **2**. (We'll show you how to create custom gradients later.)

5. Choose a gradient **Style:** Linear, Radial, Angular, Reflected, or Diamond **3**–**4**. and

(Continued on the following page)

Gradient Fill Layer

4 *The five basic gradient **styles***

Linear *gradient*

Radial *gradient*

Reflected *gradient*

Angle *gradient*

Diamond *gradient*

Choose an **Angle** by moving the dial or by entering a value.

and

Use the **Scale** slider or enter a value to scale the gradient relative to the layer. The higher the scale value, the more gradual the transition between gradient colors.

6. *Optional:* Drag in the image window to reposition the gradient in the image. Cool!

7. Do any of the following optional steps:

   Check/uncheck **Reverse** to reverse the order of colors in the gradient.

   Check **Dither** to minimize banding (stripes) in the gradient.

   Check **Align with layer** to have the length of the gradient fill be calculated based on either visible pixels on the layer or a current selection on the layer. Or uncheck this option to have the gradient stretch across the whole layer, whether or not the layer contains transparent pixels or a selection is present.

8. Click OK.

9. *Optional:* Use the Layers palette to change the gradient fill layer's opacity or blending mode. You can get some beautiful effects this way.

   Double-click a gradient fill layer to open the Layer Style dialog box, and apply a layer effect. Effects that spread outward from the edge of a layer will display only if the layer contains transparency.

   Note: To adjust any of the gradient settings, double-click the gradient fill layer thumbnail—the Gradient Fill dialog box reopens. This is what we meant before when we said this type of gradient is easy to edit.

TIP To hide a gradient fill layer, click the eye icon for the layer. To delete a gradient fill layer, drag it over the Delete Layer button. 🗑

Mask a gradient fill

If you create a selection before creating a gradient fill layer, the gradient will be limited to the selection area. The former selection will be displayed as a white area within the gradient fill layer mask thumbnail on the Layers palette **1**–**2**.

To reshape a gradient fill mask any time after creating the fill layer, click the layer mask thumbnail, then paint on the layer mask with white to enlarge the mask, black to remove parts of the mask, or gray to create a partial mask. You could also drag across a gradient fill layer with the Gradient tool to apply a black-to-white gradient to the layer mask.

1 *A **mask** on the gradient fill layer limits the fill effect.*

Gradient fill thumbnail

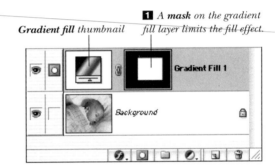

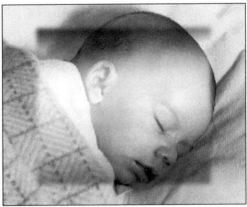

2 *The **gradient fill** is limited to the rectangular **mask**. We chose **Hard Light** blending mode for the gradient layer.*

Use the **Gradient tool** if you want to apply
a gradient by dragging. Each time you drag
with this tool, an additional gradient is
applied. Any additional gradient that you
create at less than 100% opacity will only
partially cover over the existing one(s).
Unlike a gradient fill layer, once this type of
gradient is applied, it can't be edited easily.

To apply a gradient using the Gradient tool:

1. Choose a layer or create a new layer.

2. If the layer already contains pixels, turn
on Lock Transparent Pixels if you want
to recolor only existing pixels, or turn
this option off to have the gradient fill
the entire layer. You could also select an
area on the layer.

3. Choose the Gradient tool (it shares a
pop-out menu with the Paint Bucket
tool) (G or Shift-G).

4. On the Gradient tool options bar **1**:

Click the Gradient Preset picker arrowhead, then click a gradient **preset.**
and
Click a gradient **style** button: Linear,
Radial, Angle, Reflected, or Diamond.

and
Choose a blending **Mode.**
and
Choose an **Opacity.**

5. *Do any of these optional steps:*

Check **Reverse** to reverse the order of
colors in the gradient.

Check **Dither** to minimize banding
(stripes) in the gradient.

Check **Transparency** to enable any transparency that was edited into the gradient
(see page 265). With Transparency off,
the gradient will be fully opaque.

6. For a Linear gradient, drag from one
side or corner of the image (or selection)
to the other. For any other gradient
style, drag from a center point outward.
Shift-drag to constrain the gradient to a
multiple of 45°. Drag a long distance to
produce a subtle transition area, or drag
a short distance to produce an abrupt
transition **2**–**4**. This works like the Scale
slider in the Gradient Fill dialog box.
(To delete a Gradient tool fill, remove
its state from the History palette.)

Gradient Tool

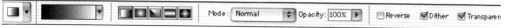

1 *The Gradient tool options bar*

2 *After dragging the Gradient tool from one edge to
the other. (This is a Linear gradient.)*

3 *After dragging the Gradient tool a **short** distance
in the middle using the same colors. Here the transitions are more abrupt.*

TOOL
TOOL

4 *The Gradient tool was used in different directions
to fill a rasterized type layer (with Lock Transparent
Pixels on).*

When you edit or delete a **preset** swatch, the actual gradient in the current gradient library isn't affected; you'll automatically be editing or deleting a copy of the preset.

To create or edit a gradient preset:

1. *Optional:* Open the Swatches palette if you're going to use it to choose colors for the gradient, and move it to the corner of your screen. Weirdly enough, you won't be able to move it around once the Gradient Editor is open.

2. Choose the Gradient tool (G or Shift-G),  then click the Gradient thumbnail **1** on the options bar to open the Gradient Editor.
   or
   Double-click an existing Gradient Fill layer thumbnail on the Layers palette, then click the gradient thumbnail at the top of the Gradient Fill dialog box.

3. In the Gradient Editor, click the preset swatch that you want to create a variation of. (When you edit a gradient, the Name changes to "Custom" automatically to ensure that you work on a copy of the gradient instead of the original.)

4. To choose a starting color, click the starting (left) color stop under the gradient bar **2**.

5. Click a color on the Swatches palette that you so conveniently stuck in a corner, or on the spectrum bar at the bottom of the Color palette, or in any open image window.
   or
   To create a gradient that will use the current Foreground and Background colors, click "Foreground to Background" in the presets area. A color stop that uses the Foreground color will have this checkerboard pattern: ▣; a color stop that uses the Background color looks like this: ▣.
   or
   Click the Color swatch at the bottom of the Gradient Editor, choose a color from the Color Picker, then click OK.

Click to edit the gradient

1 *Click the gradient **thumbnail** to open the Gradient Editor.*

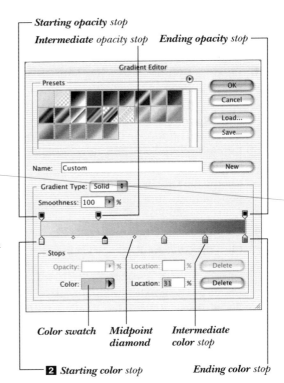

Starting opacity *stop*
Intermediate *opacity stop*   **Ending opacity** *stop*

Color swatch   Midpoint diamond   Intermediate color *stop*

2 *Starting color stop*   *Ending color stop*

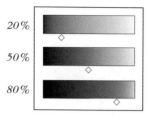

20%

50%

80%

1 *Three different* **Location** *settings*

Make noise!

For a more serendipitous approach, in the Gradient Editor, choose Gradient Type: **Noise 2**. Next, raise the Roughness to add colors to the gradient, or lower the Roughness to reduce colors in the gradient and produce smoother transitions. To define a color range for the gradient, choose a Color Model, then move the sliders. For Options, you can click Restrict Colors to remove oversaturated colors from the gradient; click Add Transparency to have transparent areas be added to the gradient. The gradient will be composed of randomly chosen colors within the parameters you've specified. You can click, and keep clicking, Randomize to cycle through some further options within those parameters. Fun!

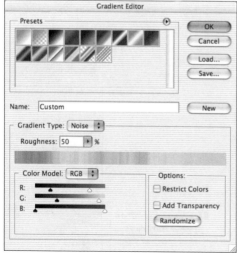

2 *The Gradient Editor with* **Noise** *chosen as the Gradient Type*

6. Click the ending (right) color stop under the gradient bar to set the ending color, then repeat the previous step.

7. *Do any of these optional steps:*

To **add** an intermediate color to the gradient, click below the gradient bar to produce a new stop, then choose a color for the new stop, as per step 5 on the previous page.

Move any color stop by dragging it or by changing its Location value (you can click the word "Location" and drag to the left or right).

To control the **abruptness** of a color transition, click a color stop, then drag a midpoint diamond on either side of it. The diamond marks the point where the two colors it's between are evenly blended (50% of each color). Clicking the diamond, then changing its Location percentage does the same thing **1**. 0% is for the far left, 100% is for the far right.

To **remove** a color, drag its stop downward off the bar.

Use Ctrl-Z/Cmd-Z to undo the previous operation.

8. Don't click OK yet. To create a preset from your custom gradient, enter a name in the Name field, then click New.

9. Now you can click OK. The new gradient preset is now available for use on the Gradient Preset picker.

To save the presets currently on the Gradient Preset picker to a file for future use in any document, see the instructions on the following page.

TIP To rename a gradient preset, double-click it in the Gradient Editor (the Gradient Name dialog box opens), change the Name, then click OK.

TIP To delete a preset, Alt-click/Option-click it in the Gradient Editor (scissors pointer).

Create or Edit a Gradient Preset

By **saving** your current (and custom) **presets** to a library file, you'll be able to reuse them.

To save the current gradient presets to a file:

1. To open the Gradient Editor, choose the Gradient tool (G or Shift-G), then click the gradient thumbnail on the options bar. Or double-click the thumbnail for an existing Gradient Fill layer on the Layers palette, then click the gradient thumbnail at the top of the Gradient Fill dialog box.

2. Click Save, enter a name (keep the .grd extension), leave the default location as is (in Windows it's Program Files\Adobe\Photoshop CS\Presets\Gradients; in Mac it's Applications/Adobe Photoshop CS/Presets/Gradients), then click Save. All the gradients currently displayed in the Presets panel will be saved in this new file, and the file name will appear on the Gradient Preset picker menu after you relaunch Photoshop. (Read about the Preset Manager on pages 438–440.)

3. Click OK to close the Gradient Editor (and also the Gradient Fill dialog box, if it's open).

To use alternate gradient preset libraries:

1. Open the Gradient Editor (see step 1 in the previous set of instructions).
   or
   Click the gradient arrowhead to open the Gradient Preset picker.

2. Click the arrowhead in the circle at the top of the palette, then choose a gradient preset library from the bottom of the picker menu **1**. Custom libraries saved as per the previous set of instructions on this page will appear on this menu along with the Adobe Photoshop libraries.

3. Click Append to add the selected library to the bottom of the current presets.
   or
   Click OK to replace the current presets with the library you've chosen.

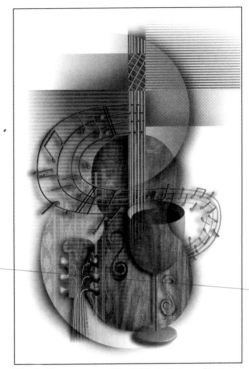

*Wendy Grossman combined Photoshop gradients and Illustrator patterns to produce this **Guitar with Wine** image.*

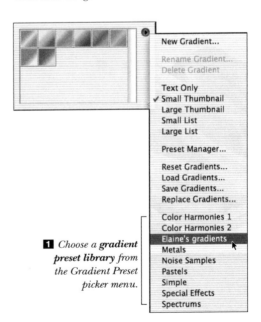

1 *Choose a **gradient preset library** from the Gradient Preset picker menu.*

1 *Click an* **opacity** *stop.*

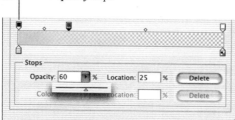

Restore Default Gradients; Gradient Opacity

To restore the default gradient presets:

1. Click the arrowhead in the circle in the Gradient Editor or on the Gradient Preset picker and choose Reset Gradients.

2. Click Append to append the default gradient presets to the exisiting presets on the picker.
   or
   Click OK to replace all presets on the picker with the default presets. Click Save to save any new presets before proceeding, or click Don't Save to remove them.

To change the opacity of gradient colors:

1. To open the Gradient Editor, choose the Gradient tool (G or Shift-G), then click the gradient thumbnail on the options bar. Or double-click the thumbnail for an existing Gradient Fill layer on the Layers palette, then click the thumbnail at the top of the Gradient Fill dialog box.

2. Click the gradient you want to edit.

3. Click an opacity stop, located above the gradient bar **1**.

4. Choose or enter an Opacity percentage. Look at the gradient bar to see a preview of the transparency effect.

5. *Do any of the following optional steps:*
   For each opacity level stop that you want to **add,** click just above the gradient bar, then choose an opacity percentage.

   To **delete** a stop, drag it upward off the bar.

   To **move** a stop, drag it or change its Location percentage.

   To adjust the location of the opacity **midpoint,** drag one of the diamonds above the transparency bar or click a diamond, then change the Location percentage.

6. Enter a Name, then click New.

7. Click OK **2**. On the following page, you'll learn how to apply semitransparent gradients by using multiple gradient fill layers.

2 *Two gradients, on separate layers, were applied to this image. The middle of the gradients fade to a 20% opacity to allow the balloons on an underlying layer to peek through.*

These steps describe how to use multiple Gradient Fill layers to apply a **multicolor wash.**

To create a multicolor wash:

1. Choose a layer.

2. *Optional:* Select an area of the layer.

3. Choose Gradient from the New Fill/ Adjustment Layer pop-up menu ⬤, at the bottom of the Layers palette.

4. In the Gradient Fill dialog box, click the gradient thumbnail to open the Gradient Editor.

5. In the Gradient Editor, either choose an existing gradient preset that fades to (finishes with) transparency or create a new gradient that fades to transparency (0% Opacity), then click OK.

6. In the Gradient Fill dialog box, choose a Style, Angle, and Scale for the gradient fill layer, then click OK.

7. Create another gradient fill layer, then repeat steps 4–6. Try out different Style, Angle, and Scale settings, or drag with the Gradient tool in the image window **1**–**2**.

8. *Optional:* Using the Layers palette, change the opacity or blending mode for, or restack, the gradient fill layers.

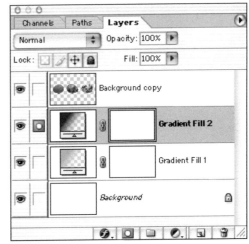

1 *You can create a painterly effect by placing translucent gradient washes on separate* **layers.**

2 *A diamond gradient and a linear gradient*

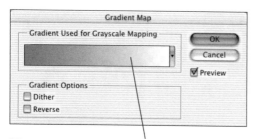

1 *Click the gradient **thumbnail** in the **Gradient Map** dialog box.*

The **Gradient Map** command applies (maps) a gradient based on luminosity levels (lights and darks) in the layer below it. This command can be used to colorize a grayscale image or re-render a color image in new tonalities, and the result can be anywhere from subtle to Day-Glo. If you apply the gradient map via an adjustment layer, it will be fully re-editable.

The starting (left) color of the selected gradient is applied to the shadow areas of the layer. The ending (right) color of the gradient is applied to the highlight areas of the layer. Any color stops that are added to the gradient are applied to the midtone areas of the layer. The number of color transitions in the resulting layer will be based on the number of color stops in the selected gradient.

To apply a gradient map to a layer:

1. Choose a layer.

2. Choose Gradient Map (not Gradient) from the New Fill/Adjustment Layer pop-up menu ●, at the bottom of the Layers palette.

Note: You can also apply a gradient map directly to a layer via the Image > Adjustments > Gradient Map command, but a gradient map applied this way can't be re-edited or removed the way an adjustment layer can, and so is less flexible.

3. Click the arrowhead to open the Gradient Preset picker, then click a preset.

4. Click the gradient thumbnail **1** to open the Gradient Editor.

5. *Do any of the following optional steps:*

Change the starting and/or ending stop **colors**.

Add more color stops to the middle of the gradient ramp to add color to the midtone areas of the image. As an example, if a gradient contains four color stops, the layer will contain four major color transition areas.

(Continued on the following page)

Gradient Map

Move any of the color stops to change the distribution of colors within the layer's tonal range.

6. Click OK.

7. *Optional:* Check Dither to have random noise be added to color transitions in the layer to help prevent color banding.

8. *Optional:* Check Reverse to reverse the direction of the gradient colors. This will reverse the color distribution in the layer.

9. Click OK **1**–**3**. To reedit a gradient map at any time, double-click the gradient map layer thumbnail on the Layers palette (the thumbnail on the left).

TIP To heighten the contrast in the colors produced from a gradient map adjustment layer, create an adjustment layer for the Posterize command, enter 4, 5, or 6 for the number of Levels, then restack the posterize adjustment layer between the image layer and the gradient map layer.

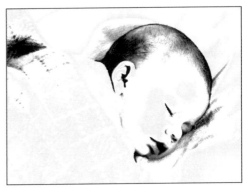

1 *Gradient map effect*

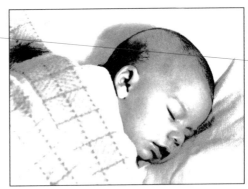

2 *Gradient map effect*

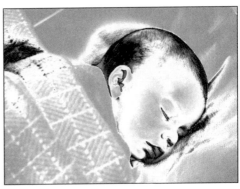

3 *Gradient map effect*

Gradient Map

LAYERING LAYERS 15

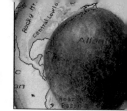

In this chapter

Change layer opacity or fill

Blend pixels between layers

Use layer comps

Create and use layer masks

Create and use clipping masks

Link layers

Align and distribute layers

Transform layers

IN THIS CHAPTER, you will learn about Photoshop's intermediate and advanced layers features. Be sure to read Chapter 5, Layer Basics first, to learn about basic layer operations. (Adjustment layers are discussed on pages 168–171.)

Layer opacity and fill

To change a layer's opacity or fill percentage:

Choose an Opacity or Fill percentage from the Layers palette (drag across the word, **NEW** enter a value, or use the slider) **1**. The lower the Opacity or Fill, the more pixels from the layer below will show through the active layer **2**–**3**. You can't change the Opacity or Fill of the Background.

or

Choose a tool other than a painting tool, then press 1 on the keyboard to change the Opacity of the active layer to 10%, 2 to change the Opacity to 20%, and so on. Or type both digits quickly (e.g., 15, for 15%). Hold down Shift using this method to change the Fill of the active layer.

Note: The Fill percentage changes the opacity of user-created pixels or shapes, but not the opacity of layer effects.

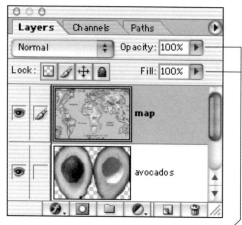

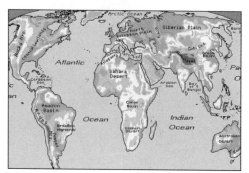

1 *Each layer can have a different **Opacity** and/or **Fill** percentage.*

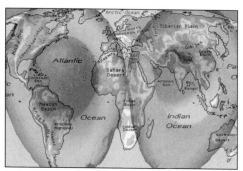

2 *The map layer, 100% Opacity, on top of the avocados layer*

3 *The opacity of the map layer reduced to 50%*

Blending layers

The layer blending modes

The layer blending mode you choose for a layer affects how that layer's pixels blend with pixels in the layer directly below it. Some modes produce subtle effects (e.g., Soft Light), whereas others produce dramatic color shifts (e.g., Difference). Normal is the default mode. The blending modes are discussed in detail and illustrated on pages 38–42.

There are three ways to choose a blending mode for a layer:

- From the mode pop-up menu in the top left corner of the Layers palette **1**–**3**.

- By pressing Shift + (plus) or Shift - (minus). This shortcut cycles through the modes for the currently active layer (don't have a painting tool selected when you do this).

- By double-clicking the layer, then choosing a Blend Mode under Blending Options in the Layer Style dialog box.

Blending Modes

Behind and Clear

You can choose **Behind** mode for the Brush, Paint Bucket, Pencil, History Brush, Clone Stamp, Pattern Stamp, or Gradient tool from the options bar, but not for a layer. In Behind mode, it will appear as if you're painting on the back of the current layer.

For the Paint Bucket or Brush tool, or for any shape tool with the Fill Pixels button ▢ clicked on the options bar, you can choose **Clear** mode. This mode works like an eraser.

To access Behind and Clear modes, make sure neither the Lock Image Pixels button ▨ nor the Lock Transparent Pixels button ▨ is selected on the Layers palette.

2 *The original image*

1 *A blending mode can be chosen from the pop-up menu on the Layers palette.*

3 *After choosing Color Burn mode for the top layer*

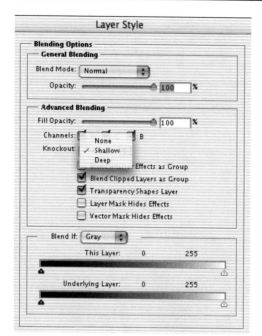

1 *The **Blending Options** settings in the **Layer Style** dialog box*

2 *Blend Interior Effect as Group unchecked:* Linear Dodge was chosen as the blending mode for the Inner Glow effect, and Difference was chosen as the blending mode for the Gradient Overlay effect. Both of these layer effects are more visible than the layer's blending mode (Difference).

3 *Blend Interior Effect as Group checked:* The Inner Glow and Gradient Overlay effects have the same blending modes as in the previous figure, but those modes are less obvious because the layer's blending mode (Difference) now controls the overall blending with underlying layers.

Using the Blend If sliders in the **Blending Options** section of the Layer Style dialog box, you can control which pixels in the current layer will remain visible and which pixels from the underlying layer will show through the current layer.

To fine-tune the blending between two layers:

1. Double-click a layer on the Layers palette, then click Blending Options at the top left side of the dialog box.

2. *Optional:* In the General Blending area, modify the current layer's Blend Mode or Opacity **1**.

3. Check Preview on the right side of the dialog box.

4. In the Advanced Blending section, do any of the following:

To control the opacity of user-created layer pixels without affecting pixels in any layer effects, adjust the **Fill Opacity** (this has the same function as the Fill option on the Layers palette).

Uncheck any **Channels** that you don't want blended with the underlying layer.

5. The first two check box options control how single layers or layers in a clipping mask blend with underlying layers (more about clipping masks on pages 283–284).

If **Blend Interior Effect as Group** is unchecked (the default setting) for a layer that has a blending mode other than Normal, the layer's interior effects (e.g., Inner Glow, Satin, Color Overlay, Pattern Overlay, or Gradient Overlay) will be used to blend the layer with the underlying layers, and the layer's overall blending mode will be less evident.

With Blend Interior Effect as Group checked, the layer's interior effects will blend first with the layer's own blending mode, then the whole blended collection of layers will blend with the underlying layers, thus diminishing the visual impact of the interior effects **2**–**3**.

(Continued on the following page)

Blending Options

For the Blend Clipped Layers as Group option, see Photoshop Help.

6. *Do any of these optional steps:*

    Check **Transparency Shapes Layer** (it's checked by default) to prevent effects from being visible in transparent areas of the layer. Uncheck this option to permit effects to cover the whole layer, including any transparent areas. Layer effects are discussed in the next chapter.

    Check **Layer Mask Hides Effects** to hide portions of layer effects that fall outside the layer mask shape.

    Check **Vector Mask Hides Effects** to hide portions of layer effects that fall outside the vector mask shape.

7. To set the blend range for each channel one at a time, choose a channel from the **Blend If** pop-up menu; to work on all the channels simultaneously, leave Gray as the choice on this pop-up menu. The current image mode (e.g., RGB or CMYK) determines which channels are available.

    Do any of the following:

    Move the leftmost Blend If: This Layer slider to the right to remove shadow areas from the active layer.

    Move the rightmost This Layer slider to the left to remove highlights from the active layer.

    Move the leftmost Underlying Layer slider to the right to restore shadow areas from the layer directly below the active layer.

    Move the rightmost Underlying Layer slider to the left to restore highlights from the layer directly below the active layer.

8. Click OK 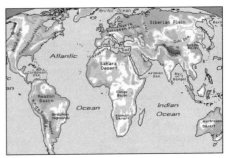–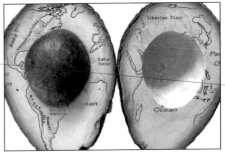.

TIP To adjust the midtones independently for either slider, Alt-drag/Option-drag the slider (it will divide in two).

1 *The map layer is above the avocados layer.*

2 *The same image after dividing and moving the white **This Layer** slider and the black **Underlying** slider under Blending Options in the **Layer Style** dialog box*

None

Shallow

Deep

1 *Our "sand" layer belongs to a layer set. Shallow knocks out to the layer below the set, whereas Deep knocks out all the way to the Background.*

2 *None has no knockout. The layer doesn't change.*

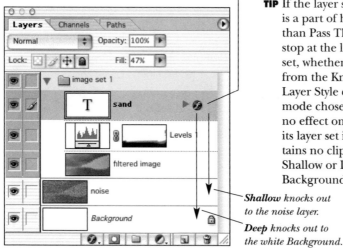

Shallow knocks out to the noise layer.

Deep knocks out to the white Background.

You can control how many layers down a chosen layer will **knock out** (cut away) underlying pixels: Either all the way to the Background or just down to a default stopping point among the layers below it.

To choose a knockout option for a layer:

1. On the Layers palette, arrange layers into the desired stacking order, or put them into a layer set.

2. Double-click a layer, then click Blending Options at the left side of the dialog box.

3. Make sure Preview is checked.

4. In the Advanced Blending area, choose from the Knockout pop-up menu **1**–**2**:

None for no knockout.

Shallow to knock out down to the default stopping point for a layer. The default stopping point will either be the layer directly below the layer set that the knockout layer is a part of or, if Blend Clipped Layers as Group is checked, the bottommost layer in a clipping mask.
or
Deep to knock out all the way down to the Background.

5. *Optional:* In the General Blending area of Blending Options, choose a blending mode other than Normal.

6. Click OK.

TIP If the layer set that the knockout layer is a part of has a blending mode other than Pass Through, the knockout will stop at the layer directly below the layer set, whether Shallow or Deep is chosen from the Knockout pop-up menu in the Layer Style dialog box. The blending mode chosen for other layer sets has no effect on how a knockout layer and its layer set interact. If the image contains no clipping masks or layer sets, Shallow or Deep will knock out to the Background.

In these instructions, a filter is applied to a duplicate layer and then the original and duplicate layers are blended using Layers palette **opacity** and **mode** controls. Use this technique to soften the effect of an image-editing command, such as a filter, or to experiment with various blending modes or adjustment commands. You can also use a layer mask to limit the area of an effect. If you don't like the results, you can just delete the duplicate layer and start over.

To blend a modified layer with the original layer:

1. Choose a layer .

2. Right-click/Ctrl-click the layer, choose Duplicate Layer from the context menu, then click OK.

3. Modify the duplicate layer (e.g., apply a filter or other image-editing command).

4. On the Layers palette, adjust the Opacity to achieve the desired degree of transparency between the original layer and the modified, duplicate layer  and/or choose a different blending mode.

5. *Optional:* Create a layer mask to partially hide pixels on the duplicate layer (see pages 278–282). You could also add a gradient to the layer mask to gradually fade the blend effect.

TIP To create a beautiful textural effect, duplicate a layer in a color image (not a solid white layer), click the new layer, and choose Image > Adjustments > Desaturate (Ctrl-Shift-U/Cmd-Shift-U) to make it grayscale. Next, apply the Artistic > Film Grain, Noise > Add Noise, or Texture > Grain filter . And finally, lower the opacity of, and try out different blending modes for, the new layer via the Layers palette.

TIP You could also click different channels in the Layer Style dialog box to control which channels in the duplicate layer blend with the underlying layer.

1 *The original image*

2 *After applying the Mezzotint filter to the duplicate layer, then lowering the opacity of the duplicate layer*

3 *Blended layers, with the Grain filter applied*

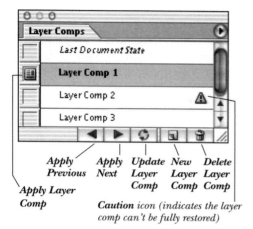

Apply   Apply   Update New   Delete
Previous   Next   Layer Layer Layer
                     Comp   Comp   Comp

*Apply Layer
Comp*   **Caution** *icon (indicates the layer
                   comp can't be fully restored)*

1 *The Layer Comps palette is used for saving, storing, applying, updating, and deleting layer comps.*

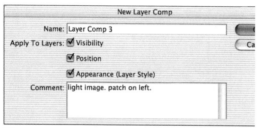

2 *In the **New Layer Comp** dialog box, name the layer comp, decide which characteristics you want saved in the comp, and enter comments, if desired.*

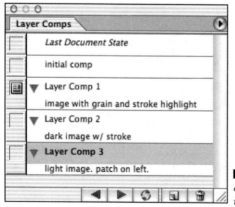

3 *The list for each comp expanded to reveal comments*

Layer Comps NEW

A **layer comp** (short for "composition") is a set of layer characteristics, such as visibility, position, and appearance (layer style). The purpose of layer comps is to enable multiple versions of the same image to coexist in one Photoshop or ImageReady file, for easy presentation to clients.

Layer comps are saved to the Layer Comps palette **1** and are applied to a whole image simply by clicking the apply layer comp square on the palette. They're saved only with the image in which they're created. Whereas histories affect all editing done to an image, layer comps remember and apply only specific layer options and settings.

To create a layer comp: NEW

1. Create all the layers to be used in the image. Then choose visibility, position, and appearance (Layer Style) settings for each layer.

2. Click the New Layer Comp button at the bottom of the Layer Comps palette.

3. In the New Layer Comp dialog box **2**, enter a Name for the comp, then check which types of layer settings you want saved in the comp. Visibility is whether the layer is hidden or visible; Position is its horizontal/vertical position in the image; and Appearance is any layer styles that are currently applied to the layer.

4. *Optional:* Enter descriptive information in the Comment field. It will display on the palette when the layer comp's list is expanded **3** (click the gray triangle).

5. Click OK. To create more layer comps, repeat steps 2–5.

TIP To bypass the New Layer Comp dialog box when creating a new layer comp, Alt-click/Option-click the New Layer Comp button.

Create Layer Comp

NEW To apply a layer comp to an image:

On the Layer Comps palette, click in the left column for a comp to select it. The Apply Layer Comp icon 🔳 will appear.

or

To cycle through a series of comps, click the Apply Next ▶ or Apply Previous ◀ button at the bottom of the palette **1**–**2** (and **1**–**2**, next page).

After applying layer comps, you can **restore** the image to its last state.

NEW To restore the last document state:

On the Layer Comps palette, click the Apply Layer Comp button 🔳 next to Last Document State.

or

Choose Restore Last Document State from the palette menu.

If you've changed the visibility, position, or layer style of any layers in your image, you can **update** any existing layer comp to incorporate those characteristics, in effect editing the comp.

To update a layer comp: NEW

1. Choose the layer settings (visibility, position, layer style) you want the current layer comp to be updated with.

2. Click the Update Layer Comp button 🔄 at the bottom of the Layer Comps palette.

Some edits, such as deleting, merging, or converting layers or changing image modes, will make a layer comp incapable of being restored. When this is the case, a **caution icon** ⚠ appears next to the comp name.

NEW To respond to a layer comp warning:

You can ignore the warning, but be aware that the layer comps won't be up-to-date.

or

You can update the comp as per the previous set of instructions, or right-click/Control-click the caution icon and choose Clear Layer Comp Warning (or Clear All Layer Comp Warnings).

Apply, Update Layer Comps

Start with a comp

To preserve the original state of an image, create a layer comp from the original image before making any edits. Yes, snapshots on the History palette serve a similar purpose, but they don't save with the image, whereas layer comps do.

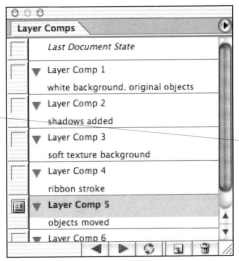

1 The **Layer Comps** palette for the images shown on this page and the next

2 **Layer Comp 1** (white background, original objects)

Duplicate comp

If you don't want to create a new layer comp from scratch, you can start from a **duplicate.** Drag a layer comp name over the New Layer Comp button ▣ at the bottom of the Layer Comps palette (or click a layer comp on the palette, then choose Duplicate Layer Comp from the palette menu). In the New Layer Comp dialog box, rename the comp, check which layer settings you want saved in the comp (Visibility, Position, or Appearance), then click OK.

1 *Layer Comp 2 (layer effects applied to two of the layers)*

2 *Layer Comp 5 (two additional layers visible; the butterfly layer in a new position)*

To change which characteristics a layer comp applies: **NEW**

1. Double-click a layer comp on the Layer Comps palette.

2. Change the layer comp Name, or check or uncheck Apply To Layers: Visibility, Position, or Appearance (Layer Styles).

3. Click OK.

TIP To change a layer comp name, double-click the name.

Deleting a **layer comp** has no effect on an image's appearance.

To delete a layer comp: **NEW**

1. On the Layer Comps palette, click the layer comp you want to delete.

2. Click the Delete Layer Comp button ▓ at the bottom of the palette.

You can use a predefined Photoshop script to automatically create a **multipage PDF** slide show and an onscreen PDF presentation of each layer comp in a Photoshop file.

To output layer comps as a multipage **NEW** PDF:

1. Open a Photoshop file that contains layer comps.

2. Choose File > Scripts > Layer Comps to PDF.

3. Click Browse, enter a file name, choose a location, then click Save.

4. *Optional:* Choose Slide Show Options to determine how each comp will sequentially display onscreen in the PDF viewing application.

5. Click Run. The script will output the images to a file and open Adobe Acrobat or Adobe Reader (whichever is installed). With the default script settings, the layer comps will display in Acrobat or Reader as a slide show. Press Esc at any time to stop the presentation.

Layer Comp Options; Delete Comp; Multipage PDF

Layer masks

A **layer mask** is an 8-bit grayscale channel that has white or black as its background color. By default, white areas on a layer mask permit pixels to be seen, black areas hide pixels, and gray areas partially mask pixels. You can use a mask to temporarily hide pixels on a layer so you can view the rest of the composite picture without them. Later, you can modify the mask, apply the mask effect to make it permanent, or discard the mask altogether.

1 *The trumpets **without layer masks***

An advantage of using a layer mask is that you can access it from both the Layers and Channels palettes. You'll see a thumbnail for the layer mask on the Layers palette and on the Channels palette when a layer that contains a mask is highlighted. Unlike an alpha channel selection, however, which can be loaded onto any layer, a layer mask can be turned on or off only for the layer or clipping mask (group of layers) with which it's associated.

Mask **link** icon · Layer mask **thumbnail**

2 *Add Layer Mask button*

The Layers palette, showing the three trumpet layers, each with its own layer mask

To create a layer mask:

1. Choose the layer or layer set to which you want to add a mask **1**.

2. *Optional:* Create a selection if you want to create a mask in that shape.

3. To create a white mask in which all the layer pixels are visible, choose Layer > Add Layer Mask > Reveal All, or click the Add Layer Mask button ▣ at the bottom of the Layers palette **2**–**3**.
   or
   To create a black mask in which all the layer pixels are hidden, choose Layer > Add Layer Mask > Hide All, or Alt-click/ Option-click the Add Layer Mask button on the Layers palette.
   or
   To reveal only layer pixels within an active selection, choose Layer > Add Layer Mask > Reveal Selection, or click the Add Layer Mask button on the Layers palette.
   or

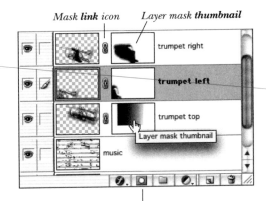

3 *The trumpets with layer masks: The topmost trumpet fades out due to a gradient in its layer mask, and portions of the middle and bottom trumpets are hidden via a black-and-white layer mask.*

Create Layer Mask

Other tools for modifying a mask

Try using the Eraser, Burn, Dodge, Sponge, Sharpen, Blur, Smudge, Paint Bucket, or Gradient tool. If you want to use any of the shape tools, you must first display the mask by itself (see step 3, at right).

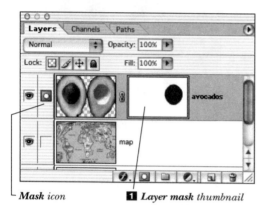

Mask *icon*   **1** **Layer mask** *thumbnail*

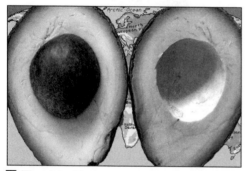

2 *The original image*

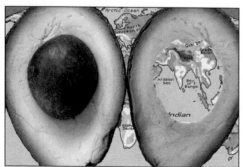

3 *The center of the avocado on the right is blocked by a* **layer mask.**

To hide layer pixels within the selection, choose Layer > Add Layer Mask > Hide Selection, or Alt-click/Option-click the Add Layer Mask button on the Layers palette.

To reshape a layer mask:

1. Choose the Brush tool (B or Shift-B).

2. On the options bar, click a brush on the Brush Preset picker, choose Mode: Normal, and choose 100% Opacity (or a lower opacity to partially hide layer pixels).

3. To reshape the layer mask while viewing the layer pixels, click the layer mask thumbnail (on the right) on the Layers palette **1**. The thumbnail will have a dark border, and a mask icon will appear for that layer.
   or
   To display the mask by itself in the image window, Alt-click/Option-click the layer mask thumbnail. (Alt-click/Option-click the layer mask thumbnail to redisplay the mask on the image.)

4. Paint on the picture with black as the Foreground color to enlarge the mask and hide pixels on the layer.
   and/or
   Paint with white as the Foreground color to reduce the mask and restore pixels on the layer.
   and/or
   Paint with gray as the Foreground color to partially hide pixels on the layer.

   Alt-Shift-click/Option-Shift-click the layer mask thumbnail to display the mask as an overlay on the image. (Alt-Shift-click/Option-Shift-click the thumbnail again to restore the normal display.)

5. When you're finished modifying the layer mask, click the layer thumbnail **2**–**3**.

TIP To invert the effect of a layer mask, click the layer mask thumbnail, then choose Image > Adjustments > Invert (Ctrl-I/ Cmd-I). Hidden areas will be revealed, and formerly visible areas will be hidden.

By default, a layer and its layer mask are linked and move in unison. If you want to **unlink** them so they can be moved independently of one another, follow these steps.

To move layer pixels or a layer mask independently:

1. On the Layers palette, click the link icon 🔗 between the layer thumbnail and the layer mask thumbnail **1**. The link icon will disappear.

2. Click the layer thumbnail or the layer mask thumbnail.

3. Choose the Move tool (V). ▸⊕

4. Drag in the image window.

5. Click again between the layer and layer mask thumbnails to relink them.

To duplicate a layer mask:

1. Click the layer you want the duplicate mask to appear on.

2. From another layer, drag the thumbnail of the layer mask you want to duplicate over the Add Layer Mask button ▣ at the bottom of the palette.
   or
   To have the hidden and revealed areas be switched in the duplicate, Alt-drag/ Option-drag the thumbnail of the layer mask you want to duplicate over the Add Layer Mask button.

On the previous page, we showed you how to display the mask overlay with the image (Alt-Shift-click/Option-Shift-click the layer mask thumbnail). If you like, you can change the **color** of the overlay to make it contrast more effectively with colors in the image, and you can also change its **opacity.**

To choose layer mask display options:

1. Double-click a layer mask thumbnail.

2. Click the Color square, then choose a different overlay color.
   and/or
   Change the Opacity percentage **2**.

3. Click OK.

1 *Click the **link** icon.*

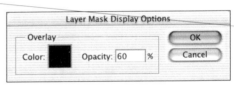

2 *In the **Layer Mask Display Options** dialog box, you can change the Overlay Color and/or Opacity for a layer mask.*

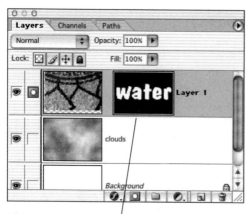

1 *This is the **layer mask** thumbnail. Layer 1 pixels are revealed through the white areas in the layer mask.*

2 *In this image, the water layer is visible only through the letter shapes of the **layer mask**.*

To fill type with imagery using a layer mask:

1. Activate a layer (not the Background) that contains little or no transparency.

2. Choose the Horizontal Type Mask tool (T or Shift-T).

3. Choose a font and other type specifications, then click on the image. The image will temporarily display in Quick Mask mode.

   Type the desired letters. *Note:* If Color Indicates: Masked Areas is chosen in the Quick Mask options dialog box (double-click the Quick Mask button on the Toolbox to open it), the mask will cover the whole image; if Selected Areas is chosen, the mask will cover only the letters.

4. When you're ready to turn the type into a selection, click the ✔ on the options bar, or press Enter (on the keypad), or choose any other tool.

5. *Optional:* Reposition the type selection using the Rectangular Marquee tool. (Don't use the Move tool to move the selection—that would remove image pixels from the current layer.)

6. Choose Layer > Add Layer Mask > Reveal Selection to reveal layer pixels within the selection.
   or
   Choose Layer > Add Layer Mask > Hide Selection to hide layer pixels within the selection.

   The type will display as white or black pixels in the layer mask thumbnail **1**–**2**. (To switch the mask function between hide and reveal, click the layer mask thumbnail, then press Ctrl-I/Cmd-I.)

TIP To reposition the type area within the layer mask, first unlink the layer mask from the layer (click the link icon to make the icon disappear), use the Move tool (V) to drag within the layer mask in the image window, then relink the mask to the layer.

Fill Type with Imagery

To temporarily deactivate a layer mask:

Shift-click the layer mask thumbnail on
the Layers palette (the thumbnail won't
become selected). A red "X" will appear
over the thumbnail and the entire layer
will be visible **1**. (Shift-click the layer mask
thumbnail again to remove the "X" and
restore the mask effect.)

Layer masks take up storage space, so you
should **discard** any that you no longer need.

To apply or discard the effects of a layer mask:

1. On the Layers palette, click the thumbnail of the layer mask you want to apply
or discard **2**.

2. Click the Delete Layer button. To
make the mask effect permanent, click
Apply **3**, or to remove the mask without
applying its effect, click Discard.
or
Right-click/Ctrl-click the layer mask
thumbnail and choose Discard Layer
Mask or Apply Layer Mask.

Clip it

Image layer pixels can also be masked using a **vector**
mask that you create using the Pen tool or a shape
tool (see page 328).

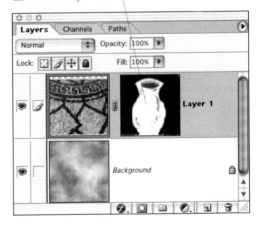

1 *Shift-click the layer mask thumbnail.*

2 *Click the layer mask thumbnail.*

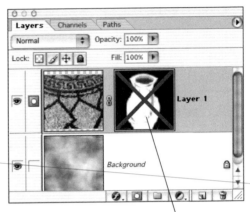

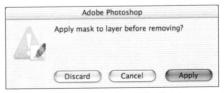

3 *Click Apply to make the mask effect permanent.*

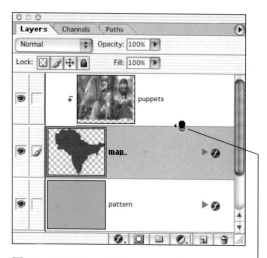

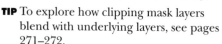

1 *Alt-click/Option-click between two layers to create a **clipping mask**. A dotted line will appear, and the base layer will be underlined.*

2 *The map of India is **clipping** (limiting) the view of the puppets.*

3 *You can also use a clipping mask to fill type with imagery.*

Clipping masks

The bottommost layer of a **clipping mask** of layers (the base layer) clips (limits) the display of pixels and, by default, controls the mode and opacity of the layers above it. Only pixels within the group of layers that overlap pixels on the base layer are visible. You can achieve very artful effects using this feature. Try it on various kinds of imagery.

To create a clipping mask:

1. Click a layer name in a multilayer image.

2. Alt-click/Option-click the line between that layer name and the name just above it (the pointer will be two overlapping circles) **1–3**. *Note:* The layers to be used for the clipping mask must be listed consecutively on the palette. A clipping mask can be formed using layers within a layer set, but not using layers from both inside and outside a set.

3. *Optional:* Repeat the previous step to add more layers to the clipping mask.

   The base layer name will be underlined, and the thumbnails for the other layers in the group will be indented above it.

TIP To create a clipping mask from linked layers, choose Layer > Create Clipping Mask from Linked (Ctrl-G/Cmd-G). **(NEW)**

TIP To explore how clipping mask layers blend with underlying layers, see pages 271–272.

Create Clipping Mask

When you **release** a layer from a clipping mask, any masked layers above the one you're unmasking are also released.

To release a layer from a clipping mask:

Alt-click/Option-click the line below the layer that you want to release **1**. The layer will no longer be indented.

or

Click the name of the layer you want to release, then choose Layer > Release Clipping Mask (Ctrl-Shift-G/Cmd-Shift-G).

To release an entire clipping mask:

1. Click the base layer in the group.
2. Choose Layer > Release Clipping Mask (Ctrl-Shift-G/Cmd-Shift-G) **2**.

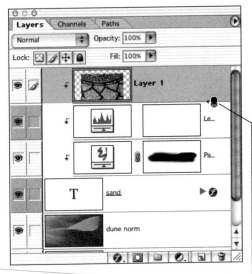

1 *Alt-click/Option-click below a layer to release it from a clipping mask.*

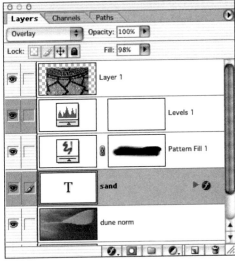

2 *Choose Layer > Release Clipping Mask to remove all layers from a clipping mask.*

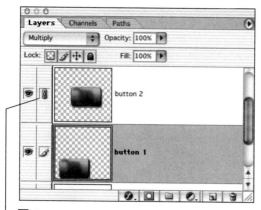

1 *Click to display the* **link** *icon in the second column on the Layers palette for any layers you want to link to the active layer. In this illustration, the button 1 and button 2 layers are linked.*

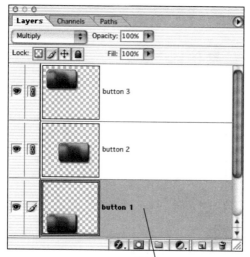

2 *Click a* **linked** *layer.*

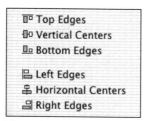

3 *Choose an option from the Layer >* **Align Linked** *submenu...*

4 *...or click an* **alignment** *button on the* **options** *bar.*

Linking layers

Linking is used to secure the position of multiple layers in relationship to one another. Once layers are linked together, they can be moved as a unit in the image window or drag-copied to another image, and they can be distributed or aligned. You can also transform linked layers. In fact, transforming multiple layers all at once helps to preserve image quality, as resampling will occur only once rather than for individual transformations.

To link layers (and move them as a unit):

1. On the Layers palette, click one of the layers that you want to link.

2. Click in the second column for any other layer that you want to link to the layer you chose in the previous step. The layers you link don't have be consecutive. The link icon will appear next to any nonactive, linked layers **1**.

3. *Optional:* Choose the Move tool (V), then drag the linked layers in the image window.

TIP To unlink a layer, click the link icon.

The **Align Layers** command is used to align the pixel edges of linked layers.

To align two or more linked layers:

1. Choose a layer that one or more other layers are linked to **2**. The layer you choose will be the reference position that the other linked layers will align to.

2. Choose Layer > Align Linked > Top Edges, Vertical Centers, Bottom Edges, Left Edges, Horizontal Centers, or Right Edges **3** (and **1**–**2**, next page).
   or
   Choose the Move tool (V), then click any alignment button on the options bar **4**.

To align the pixel edge of a layer with a selection:

1. Create a selection.

2. Click a layer to be aligned with the selection.

3. Choose an align command from the Layer > Align To Selection submenu.
or
Choose the Move tool (V), ⊹ then click an alignment button on the options bar.

TIP Any layers that were linked to the chosen layer will also be aligned.

You can distribute the pixel areas in linked layers by using any of the **Distribute Linked** commands.

To distribute three or more linked layers:

1. Choose a layer to which two or more other layers are linked (not the Background).

2. Choose Layer > Distribute Linked > Top Edges, Vertical Centers, Bottom Edges, Left Edges, Horizontal Centers, or Right Edges.
or
Choose the Move tool (V), ⊹ then click a distribute button on the options bar **1**.

The layers will be distributed evenly between the two layers that are farthest apart **2**–**4**.

TIP If you don't like the results and you want to apply a different align or distribute command, undo the last command before applying a new one!

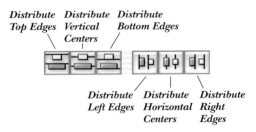

Distribute Top Edges   *Distribute Vertical Centers*   *Distribute Bottom Edges*

Distribute Left Edges   *Distribute Horizontal Centers*   *Distribute Right Edges*

1 *Distribute buttons on the Move tool options bar*

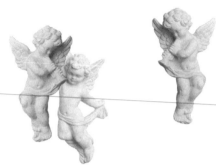

2 *The original image*

3 *The layers aligned: Bottom (see the instructions on the previous page)*

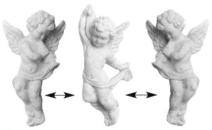

4 *The layers distributed: Horizontal Centers*

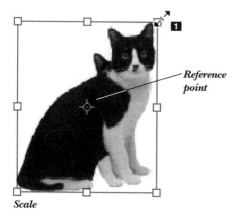

Reference point

Scale

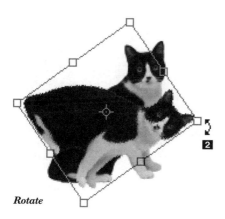

Rotate

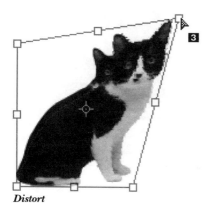

Distort

Transform layers

The transform commands are **scale, rotate, skew, distort,** and **perspective.**

To transform a layer using its bounding box:

1. On the Layers palette, activate the layer that you want to transform. Any layers that are linked to the active layer will also be transformed. You can transform **NEW** a 16-bits-per-channel image.

Optional: Create a selection to limit the transformation to those pixels.

2. Choose Edit > Transform > Scale, Rotate, Skew, Distort, or Perspective. A bounding box will appear around the opaque part of the layer or the selection.

3. *Optional:* To transform the layer or selection from a location other than its center, move the reference point (you can move it outside the bounding box) **1**.

4. *Note:* If you're going to perform multiple transformations, to save time and preserve image quality, after performing this step for the first command, choose and then perform additional transform commands, and then accept them all at once (step 5).

To **Scale** the layer horizontally and vertically, drag a corner handle **1**. To scale only the horizontal or vertical dimension, drag a side handle. Shift-drag to scale proportionately; Alt-drag/Option-drag to scale from the reference point.

For **Rotate,** position the pointer near a bounding box handle, either just inside or just outside the box (the pointer will become a double-headed arrow), then drag in a circular direction **2**. Shift-drag to constrain the rotation to a multiple of 15°.

For **Skew,** drag along an edge of the bounding box to skew along the horizontal or vertical axis. Alt-drag/Option-drag to skew symmetrically from the reference point.

(Continued on the following page)

Transform Commands

For **Distort,** drag a corner handle to freely reposition just that handle (**3**, previous page), or drag a side handle to distort the side of the bounding box along the horizontal and/or vertical axis. Alt-drag/Option-drag to distort symmetrically from the center of the layer. Distort can be more drastic than Skew.

For **Perspective**, drag a corner handle along the horizontal or vertical axis to create one-point perspective along that axis **1**–**2**. The adjacent corner will move in unison. Or drag a side handle to skew along the current horizontal or vertical axis.

5. To accept the transformation, double-click inside the bounding box or click the ✔ on the options bar (Enter/Return). To cancel the transformation, click the ⊘ (Esc).

TIP To undo the last handle modification, choose Edit > Undo.

TIP To move the entire layer (or selection), drag inside the transform bounding box.

TIP Choose the Measure tool (I or Shift-I), drag in the image window to define an angle, then with the Measure tool still selected, choose Edit > Transform > Rotate. The layer will rotate automatically along the angle you just defined.

Transform tips

- Choose an interpolation method for the transform commands in Edit (Photoshop, in Mac) > Preferences > General (Ctrl-K/Cmd-K). The Bicubic methods, albeit slower, cause the least degradation to the image. Use Bicubic Smoother when enlarging imagery, Bicubic Sharper when reducing.

- To repeat the last transformation, choose Edit > Transform > Again (Ctrl-Shift-T/Cmd-Shift-T).

- In addition to transforming a layer, you can also transform an alpha channel, a selection border (see page 135), a path (see page 321), or an unlinked, active layer mask.

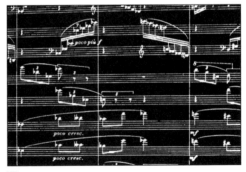

1 *The original image*

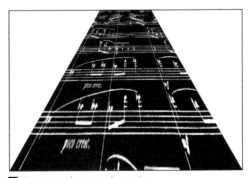

2 *A **perspective** transformation*

What's left?

If you transform a **layer** (or a selection on a layer), any empty space remaining after the transformation will become **transparent.**

If you transform the **Background,** any empty space remaining after the transformation will be filled with the current **Background color.**

Once you're acquainted with the individual Transform commands, you'll probably want to start using the **Free Transform** command, especially if you want to perform a series of transformations. With Free Transform, the various commands are accessed using keyboard shortcuts—you don't have to choose each command individually from a menu. And best of all, image data is resampled only once, when you accept the changes.

To free-transform a layer:

1. Click a layer on the Layers palette. Any layers that are linked to it will also be transformed. You can transform a 16-bits- **NEW** per-channel image.

    To transform the Background, you must create a selection. For a layer, you can create a selection or not, as you wish.

2. Choose Edit > Free Transform (Ctrl-T/ Cmd-T).
    or
    Choose the Move tool (V) and check Show Bounding Box on the options bar.

3. Follow step 4 on pages 287–288, with these exceptions:

    To **Skew**, Ctrl-Shift-drag/Cmd-Shift-drag.

    To **Distort**, Ctrl-drag/Cmd-drag.

    To apply **Perspective**, Ctrl-Alt-Shift-drag/ Cmd-Option-Shift-drag a corner handle.

    The transformation will automatically occur from the current reference point, which is chosen on the options bar (see step 3 on the next page).

4. To accept the transformation, double-click inside the bounding box or click the ✔ on the options bar (Enter/Return). To cancel the transformation, click the ⊘ (Esc). You must either accept or cancel to return to normal editing.

TIP As you transform a layer or a selection, note the width (W), height (H), rotation angle (A), and horizontal skew (H) or vertical skew (V) readout(s) on either the options bar or the Info palette.

Follow these instructions if you'd rather transform a layer by entering exact numeric values than by dragging the mouse. The controls for **numeric transforms** display on the options bar whenever a transform function is chosen.

To transform a layer by entering numeric values:

1. On the Layers palette, activate the layer that you want to transform. Any layers that are linked to it will also be transformed. To transform the Background, you must create a selection. For a layer, you can create a selection or not.

2. Choose Edit > Free Transform (Ctrl-T/ Cmd-T).

3. On the options bar **1**–**2**, choose the reference point location for the move, rotate, and flip transformations by clicking one of the nine little reference point squares.
   or
   In the image window, drag the reference point to the desired location.
   or
   Click the "Use relative positioning for reference point" button $\triangle$ to set the X

and Y fields to 0; otherwise those values will reflect the absolute position of the reference point as measured from the upper left corner of the layer. (Click the icon again to turn off the option. To change the measurement units, right-click/Ctrl-click either value.)

4. Do any of the following:

   To **move** the layer, enter new X and Y values.

   To **scale** the layer, enter W (width) and/or H (height) values. (Right-click/ Ctrl-click either value to choose different units from the pop-up menu.) Click the Maintain Aspect Ratio button to preserve the current width-to-height ratio.

   To **rotate** the layer, enter a rotation angle.

   To **skew** the layer, enter a horizontal (H) and/or vertical (V) skew angle (the amount of slant).

5. To accept the transformation, double-click inside the bounding box or click the ✔ on the options bar (Enter/Return). To cancel the transformation, click the ⊘ (Esc).

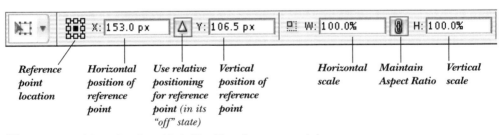

Reference point location   *Horizontal position of reference point*   *Use relative positioning for reference point* (in its "off" state)   *Vertical position of reference point*   *Horizontal scale*   *Maintain Aspect Ratio*   *Vertical scale*

1 *The left side of the options bar with the **Free Transform** command chosen*

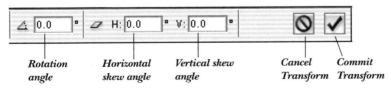

Rotation angle   *Horizontal skew angle*   *Vertical skew angle*   *Cancel Transform*   *Commit Transform*

2 *The right side of the options bar with the **Free Transform** command chosen*

LAYER EFFECTS 16

1 *A **Drop Shadow** layer effect*

*Click an effect name to switch to that pane so you can choose **custom settings** (the box will become checked automatically).*

IN THIS CHAPTER, you'll learn about layer effects, which are special effects that can easily be applied to any layer; hidden, redisplayed, or removed at any time; and edited at any time using a wide assortment of options. More than one layer effect can be applied to a layer. The layer effects that you can choose from are Drop Shadow **1**, Inner Shadow, Outer Glow, Inner Glow, Bevel and Emboss, Satin, Color Overlay, Gradient Overlay, Pattern Overlay, and Stroke.

Layer effects are applied via the Layer Style dialog box **2**; the options in the dialog box change depending on which effect is currently chosen. Starting on the next page, you'll find general instructions for applying layer effects. Following that are instructions for applying individual effects.

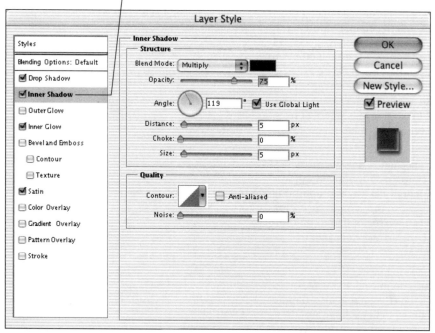

2 *Use the **Layer Style** dialog box to choose or change the settings for multiple layer effects.*

Applying layer effects

Layer effects can be applied to any layer, even an editable type layer, and individual effects can be turned on or off for a layer at any time. Layer effects automatically affect all the visible pixels on a layer and will update instantly if pixels are added, modified, or deleted from the layer.

TIP A style is a combination of one or more layer effects (see pages 530–531).

All the layer effects are applied and edited via one comprehensive dialog box—the Layer Style dialog box—and they're displayed on the Layers palette as indented (nested) layers below the name of the layer to which they're applied. Layer effects are attached to, and move with, the layer that they're applied to. They can't be applied to the Background of an image. Before we get into the individual effects, here are some general pointers:

■ To **apply** an effect to a layer, double-click the layer (or for an image layer—not a type layer—you can double-click the thumbnail). The Layer Style dialog box opens. Click an effect **name** on the left side (**2**, previous page), then choose settings; repeat to apply additional effects to the same layer. Be sure to check **Preview** to preview the effect in the image window. You can also apply an effect by choosing a layer and then choosing an effect from the **Add Layer Style** pop-up menu 🍩 at the bottom of the Layers palette **1**.

■ On the Layers palette, any layer to which a layer effect is currently applied will have an 🍩 icon. Click the right-pointing arrowhead next to this icon to view a list of the effects that are applied to that layer. (Click the arrowhead again to collapse the list.)

■ To **edit** an existing layer effect (or add another one), double-click the 🍩; or double-click the effect name nested under the layer name; or click a layer and then choose an effect from the Add Layer

The "f" icon indicates that one or more layer effects are applied to that layer.

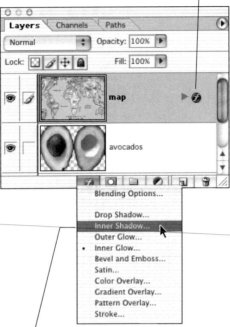

1 *Choose an effect name from the **Add Layer Style** pop-up menu. A bullet next to an effect signifies that that effect is applied to the currently active layer. Effects can also be applied via the **Layer > Layer Style** submenu.*

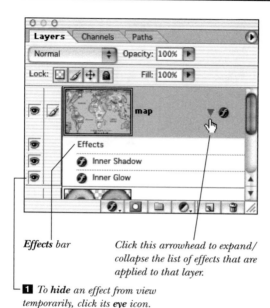

Effects *bar*

Click this arrowhead to expand/collapse the list of effects that are applied to that layer.

1 *To* **hide** *an effect from view temporarily, click its* **eye** *icon.*

Style pop-up menu at the bottom of the Layers palette.

- To **hide** one layer effect, expand the effects list for the layer in question, then click the eye icon for the effect you want to hide **1**. (Click in the eye column again to redisplay the effect.) To hide all the effects from one layer, click the eye icon for the Effects bar.

TIP To temporarily hide all effects from all layers and speed performance, choose Layer > Layer Style > Hide All Effects. Choose Show All Effects to redisplay them.

To remove a layer effect:

Drag an individual effect name over the Delete Layer button 🗑 at the bottom of the Layers palette. Or drag the Effects bar over the Delete Layer button to remove all effects from the layer.

TIP If you recheck an effect that was turned off or deleted, the last-used options for that effect will redisplay.

TIP Alt-click/Option-click Reset in the Layer Style dialog box to restore the last-used settings in all panes in the dialog box.

To copy layer effects from one layer to another:

Click the layer that contains the effect or effects you want to copy, right-click/Ctrl-click and choose Copy Layer Style, choose another layer, then right-click/Ctrl-click and choose Paste Layer Style.
or
Expand the effects list for a layer, then drag an individual effect name over another layer name or over another layer's Effects bar.
or
To copy multiple effects from one layer to another, expand the effects list for a layer, then drag the Effects bar over another layer or another layer's Effects bar. With this method, the duplicate effect(s) will replace any existing effects on the target layer!

Being able to create realistic **drop shadows** with a few clicks of the mouse is a great timesaver!

To apply the Drop Shadow or Inner Shadow effect:

1. Double-click a layer.

2. Click Drop Shadow or Inner Shadow.

3. Change any of the following settings 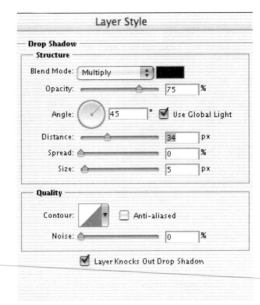:

   Choose a **Blend Mode** from the pop-up menu.

   To choose a different **shadow color,** click the color swatch, choose a color from the Color Picker (the new color will preview immediately), then click OK.

   Choose an **Opacity** percentage for the transparency of the shadow.

   Choose an **Angle** for the angle of the shadow relative to the original layer shapes. Check Use Global Light to use the angle that was entered in the Layer > Layer Style > Global Light dialog box. Uncheck this option if you want to use a unique angle setting for this particular effect. *Note:* If you readjust the Angle for an individual effect while Use Global Angle is checked, all effects that utilize the Global Angle option will also be modified. This option helps to unify the lighting across multiple layer effects.

   Choose a **Distance** for the distance (in pixels) of the drop shadow from the original layer shapes, or for the width of an inner shadow . We usually like to increase the Distance a bit.

   TIP You can drag the actual shadow in the image window while the dialog box is open, but this will also move all effects that use the Global Light option.

   For a Drop Shadow, choose a **Spread** (mask enlargement width, before blurring) for the shadow. For an Inner Shadow, choose a **Choke** (mask reduction) value for the shadow.

1 *Choose settings in the **Drop Shadow** or **Inner Shadow** pane of the **Layer Style** dialog box.*

2 *Drop Shadow*

3 *Inner Shadow (with a Drop Shadow, too)*

(sidebar) Drop Shadow, Inner Shadow

1 *The original layer with a **Drop Shadow***

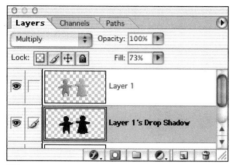

2 *Choosing the new **Drop Shadow** layer*

3 ***Distorting** the Drop Shadow*

4 *The final image*

Choose a **Size** for the shadow.

In the Quality area, click the arrowhead, then choose a preset **Contour** from the Contour Preset picker for the edge profile of the shadow (see also page 300). The profiles can change the shadow dramatically.

Check **Anti-aliased** to soften the jagged edges between the shadow and other parts of the image.

Set the **Noise** level to adjust the amount of speckling in the shadow.

For a Drop Shadow, check **Layer Knocks Out Drop Shadow** to prevent the shadow from showing through any layer pixels that have a low fill opacity.

4. Click OK.

To transform a Drop Shadow effect:

1. Apply the Drop Shadow effect (see the previous instructions) **1**, and keep the layer selected.

2. Choose Layer > Layer Style > Create Layer(s), then click OK. This transfers the shadow effect to its own layer.

3. Click the new shadow layer **2**.

4. Choose Edit > Transform > Distort, drag the handles of the bounding box to achieve the desired shape, then press Enter/Return **3**–**4**.

5. *Optional:* Change the luminosity of the shadow via an adjustment layer, or choose a different blending mode or opacity for the shadow layer. Turn on the Lock Transparent Pixels option **☒** on the Layers palette to limit any painting or fill changes to just the shadow shape.

TIP Link the shadow layer and its original object layer to move them in unison.

To create a drop shadow without using an effect:

1. Create a selection to become the shadow shape. To select a silhouetted object, Ctrl-click/Cmd-click the object's layer. *Note:* To use a type mask selection for these steps, save the active selection to a channel first, and then load the channel as a selection. You can save any active selection as a channel for later use.

2. Choose Select > Feather (Ctrl-Alt-D/ Cmd-Option-D), enter a Feather Radius above zero, then click OK.

3. Choose Select > Transform Selection or right-click/Ctrl-click the image and choose Transform Selection from the context menu, transform and/or move the selection marquee, then press Enter/Return.

4. Click the New Layer button at the bottom of the Layers palette, then restack the new layer directly below the layer that contains the silhouetted object.

5. Choose Edit > Fill; choose Fill: Black, Mode: Normal or Multiply, and Opacity: 75%; click OK; then deselect (Ctrl-D/ Cmd-D).

6. Choose the Move tool (V), then drag the shadow layer to the desired position in the image window. You can also change its blending mode or opacity.

To apply an Outer or Inner Glow effect:

1. Display the Swatches palette.

2. Double-click a layer.

3. Click Outer Glow or Inner Glow.

4. Choose **Structure** settings **1**:

   Choose a **Blend Mode** (see "Blending modes" on pages 38–42).

   Choose an **Opacity** for the transparency level of the glow.

   Set the **Noise** level for the amount of speckling in the glow.

   To change the glow **color,** click the color square in the Structure area, choose a color from the Color Picker (or, while

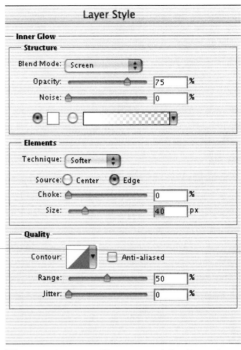

1 *Choose Structure, Elements, and Quality settings for an **Inner Glow** effect in the **Layer Style** dialog box.*

1 *Inner Glow (Center, with a Drop Shadow, too)*

2 *Outer Glow*

the picker is open, from the Swatches palette). Choose a color that contrasts with the background color. It might be hard to see a light Outer Glow color against a light background color. The new color will preview on the image. Click OK.

or

To create a glow using a **gradient,** click the arrowhead to choose a gradient from the Gradient Preset picker; or click the gradient thumbnail to edit one of the presets or create a new gradient (see pages 262–263).

5. Choose **Elements** settings:

Choose Softer or Precise from the **Technique** pop-up menu to control how closely the mask follows the contours of areas that contain pixels.

For an Inner Glow, click Source: **Center** to create a glow that spreads outward from the center of the layer pixels **1**. (Suggestion: Try this on type.) Or click **Edge** to create a glow that spreads inward from the inside edges of the layer pixels.

For an Outer Glow, set the **Spread** to define the width of the glow (a mask, actually) before it starts to blur **2**. For an Inner Glow, adjust the **Choke** to define the width of the glow before it starts to blur.

Choose a **Size** for the glow.

6. Choose **Quality** settings:

Click the arrowhead to choose a preset **Contour** from the Contour Preset picker for the edge profile of the glow (see page 300).

Choose a **Range** to control the placement of the contour along the width of the glow.

If the glow contains a gradient, choose a **Jitter** value to control how randomly colors are distributed in the gradient.

7. Click OK.

TIP To apply a layer effect to type, make the type large, and don't track it tightly.

Outer or Inner Glow

The **Bevel and Emboss** command creates an illusion of depth by adding a highlight and a shadow to layer shapes.

To apply the Bevel or Emboss effect:

1. Display the Swatches palette.

2. Double-click a layer on the Layers palette. It can be a type layer.

3. Click Bevel and Emboss.

4. Choose **Structure** settings **1**:

   Choose a **Style:** Outer Bevel **2**, Inner Bevel **3**, Emboss, Pillow Emboss (**1**–**2** next page), or Stroke Emboss.

   From the **Technique** pop-up menu, choose Smooth, Chisel Hard, or Chisel Soft.

   Choose a **Depth** for the amount the highlight and shadow are offset from the layer shapes.

   Click the **Up** or **Down** button to switch the highlight and shadow positions.

   Choose a **Size** for the bevel or emboss effect.

   Raise the **Soften** value to soften the shadows and highlights along the edge.

5. Choose **Shading** settings:

   Choose an **Angle** and an **Altitude** to change the location of the light source. These settings will in turn affect the highlight and shadow. Check Use Global Light to use the current Angle and Altitude settings from the Layer > Layer Style > Global Light dialog box. Or uncheck this option to use a unique setting for this particular style. *Beware!* If you readjust an individual style's Angle or Altitude while Use Global Light is checked, all other styles that utilize the Global Light option will update, too.

   Click the **Gloss Contour** arrowhead, then choose from the Contour Preset picker (see page 300).

   Choose a **Highlight Mode** and **Opacity** and a **Shadow Mode** and **Opacity** for

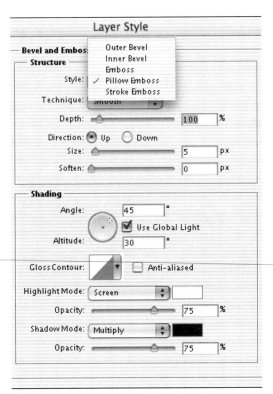

1 *Settings for the **Bevel and Emboss** layer effect*

2 *Outer Bevel*

3 *Inner Bevel (with a Drop Shadow, too)*

EMBOSS

1 *Emboss*

EMBOSS

2 *Pillow Emboss*

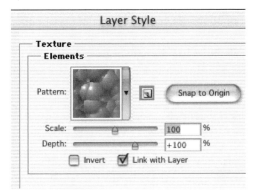

3 *The* **Texture** *options for the* **Bevel and Emboss** *layer effect*

4 *Adobe's Tie Dye* **texture** *used with the* **Bevel and Emboss** *layer effect (Style: Emboss)*

image highlight and shadow areas (see "Blending modes" on pages 38–42).

To change the highlight or shadow **color,** click either color swatch, then choose a color from the Color Picker (or, while the picker is open, choose from the Swatches palette). The color will preview on the image. Click OK.

6. To add a **Contour** to the edges of the bevel or emboss, click Contour at the left side of the dialog box, below Bevel and Emboss. Click the Contour arrowhead, then click a preset contour in the picker (see page 300). This can dramatically change the appearance of the effect.

Check **Anti-aliased** to soften the hard edges between adjoining areas.

Set the **Range** to control the placement of the contour along the width of the glow. The Range option affects only the Bevel style options.

7. To add a texture to a bevel or emboss, click **Texture** at the left side of the dialog box, click the Texture arrowhead, choose a pattern from the picker, then do any of the following **3**–**4**:

Adjust the **Scale** of the pattern.

Change the **Depth** to adjust the contrast of shadows and highlights in the pattern.

Check **Invert** to flip the shadows and highlights. This has the same effect as changing the Depth percentage from negative to positive, or vice versa.

Check **Link with Layer** to ensure that the texture and the layer move in unison.

Drag in the image window to reposition the texture within the effect. Click **Snap to Origin** to realign the pattern to the upper left corner of the image.

If you've changed settings for the current pattern, click the New Preset button to add it as a new preset.

8. Click OK.

Bevel or Emboss

For all the layer effects except the Overlay effects and the Stroke effect, you can choose a preset edge style, or **contour,** or you can create a custom contour. The contours control such elements as the fade on a drop shadow or a highlight on a bevel.

To change the profile of a contour:

1. Double-click a layer or an effect name to open the Layer Style dialog box. For the Bevel and Emboss effect only, also click Contour at the left side of the dialog box.

2. Click the Contour thumbnail (not the arrowhead).

3. *Optional:* In the Contour Editor **1**, choose a preset contour from the preset pop-up menu to use as a starting point.

4. When you do any of the following, the name "Custom" automatically appears on the Preset pop-up menu:

   Click on the graph to add points.

   Drag points to adjust the graph.

   To delete a point, drag it off the graph.

   To convert the currently selected point into a corner point, check Corner.

5. To save the custom graph as a preset contour, click New, enter a name, then click OK. The custom contour will be listed on the Contour Preset picker.

6. *Optional:* To save the custom graph as a file for reuse, click Save, enter a file name, then click Save again. Click Load to retrieve it.

7. Click OK to close the Contour Editor.

TIP To delete a contour, open the Contour Preset picker, Alt-click/Option-click the contour you want to delete, then close the picker. *Note:* The contour will be deleted only from the current picker— not from the actual preset library.

TIP To restore the default contour library, open the Contour Preset picker, choose Reset Contours from the Contour Preset picker menu, then click OK. If an alert dialog box appears, click Save, enter a

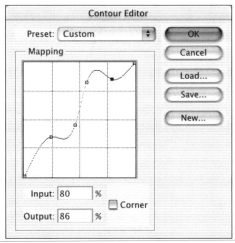

1 *Customize a contour using the **Contour Editor.***

Pick from the picker

The profile thumbnails in the **Contour Preset** picker illustrate different edge styles **2**. The gray areas in the profile represent opaque pixels; the white areas represent transparency. To close the picker, double-click a contour; or click the Contour arrowhead; or click somewhere outside the picker in the Layer Style dialog box.

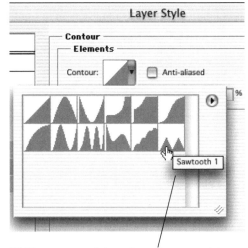

2 *You can use tool tips to learn the **names** of the various contours in the **Contour Preset** picker.*

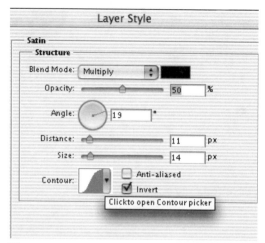

1 *Options for the **Satin** layer effect*

2 *The **Satin** layer effect applied to editable type*

3 *The **Satin** layer effect (with **Invert** unchecked)*

name, then click Save again. To open a different library, choose a library name from the bottom of the Contour Preset picker menu (click Append, or click OK to replace).

To apply the Satin effect :

1. Double-click a layer on the Layers palette.

2. Click Satin.

3. Do any of the following **1**:

Change the **Blend Mode** (see "Blending modes" on pages 38–42).

To change the overlay **color,** click the color swatch, then choose a color from the Color Picker.

Adjust the **Opacity** of the effect.

Change the **Angle** of the effect. This angle is independent of the Global Light settings.

Set the **Distance** and the **Size** of the effect. You can also drag in the image window to adjust the distance.

Click the **Contour** arrowhead, then choose from the Contour Preset picker for the edge profile of the effect.

Check **Anti-aliased** to soften the hard boundary between the effect and the underlying shape.

Check **Invert** to swap the shadows and highlights.

4. Click OK **2**–**3**.

Satin

301

To apply the Color Overlay effect :

1. Double-click a layer on the Layers palette.

2. Click Color Overlay.

3. Do any of the following :

   Choose a **Blend Mode.**

   Click the color swatch, then choose a different **color** for the overlay.

   Adjust the **Opacity** of the overlay.

4. Click OK.

To apply the Gradient Overlay effect:

1. Double-click the layer on the Layers palette.

2. Click Gradient Overlay.

3. Do any of the following 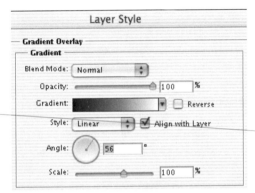:

   Choose a **Blend Mode.**

   Adjust the **Opacity** of the overlay.

   Click the **Gradient** arrowhead, then choose a preset gradient from the Gradient Preset picker.

   Check **Reverse** to change the direction of the gradient.

   Choose a **Style** (Linear, Radial, Angle, Reflected, or Diamond).

   Check **Align with Layer** to align the gradient with visible pixels in the layer. If this option is off, the gradient will align with the full canvas.

   Set the **Angle** of the gradient.

   Choose a **Scale** percentage for the placement of the midpoint of the gradient.

   You can also drag in the image window to reposition the gradient.

4. Click OK 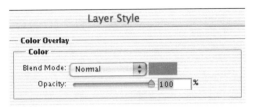. Read more about gradients in Chapter 14.

1 *Options for the Color Overlay layer effect*

2 *Options for the Gradient Overlay layer effect*

3 *Gradient Overlay (Style: Reflected, Reversed)*

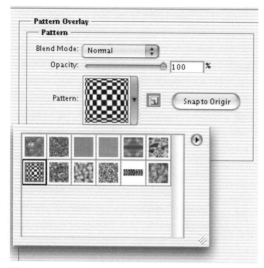

1 *Options for the **Pattern Overlay** layer effect*

2 *The **Pattern Overlay** effect applied to a shape layer object*

To apply the Pattern Overlay effect:

1. Double-click a layer on the Layers palette.
2. Click Pattern Overlay.
3. Do any of the following **1**:

   Choose a **Blend Mode.**

   Adjust the **Opacity** of the overlay.

   Click the **Pattern** arrowhead, then choose a preset pattern from the picker.

   Click **Snap to Origin** to align the pattern with the upper left corner of the image. You can also drag in the image window to reposition the pattern.

   Choose a **Scale** percentage for the pattern.

   Check **Link with Layer** to link the pattern to the layer.

   If you've changed settings for the current pattern, click the New Preset button ⃞ to add it as a new preset.
4. Click OK **2**.

To apply a Stroke effect:

1. Double-click a layer on the Layers palette.

2. Click Stroke.

3. Do any of the following :

   Choose a **Size** (width) for the stroke.

   From the **Position** pop-up menu, choose whether you want the stroke to be Outside, Inside, or Centered on the edges of shapes in the layer.

   Choose a **Blend Mode.**

   Choose an **Opacity** percentage.

   Choose a **Fill Type** (Color, Gradient, or Pattern), and choose options using the controls that become available. See the Color Overlay and Gradient Overlay information on page 302, or the Pattern Overlay information on the previous page.

4. Click OK 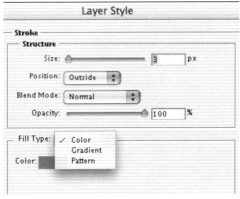.

1 *Options for the* **Stroke** *layer effect*

2 *The* **Stroke** *effect applied to a shape layer object*

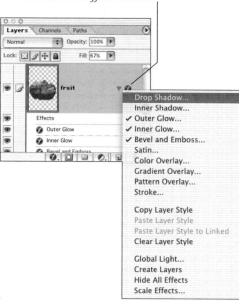

1 *Right-click/Ctrl-click a layer's **effects** icon and choose an effects command.*

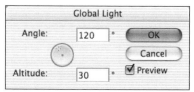

2 *In the **Global Light** dialog box, choose an Angle and Altitude to be applied to all effects for which the Use Global Light option is on.*

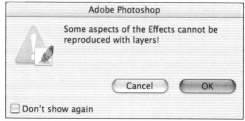

3 *This prompt may appear when you choose the Create Layer(s) command.*

Other effects commands

The effects commands that are discussed in this section can be accessed either by right-clicking/Ctrl-clicking an existing effects icon ✦ for a layer on the Layers palette **1** or via the Layer > Layer Style submenu.

Copy Layer Style copies all effects from a selected layer so they can be pasted into another layer.

Paste Layer Style pastes effects onto the current layer in the same document or in a different document; **Paste Layer Style to Linked** (layers) pastes effects onto any layers that are linked to the currently selected layer. For both paste commands, the pasted effects will replace any existing effects.

Clear Layer Style eliminates all styles from the selected layer. It also restores the Blending Options to their default settings.

Global Light establishes a common Angle and Altitude for all current and future effects for which the Use Global Light option is on. (A dialog box will open from which you can choose settings **2**.) And conversely, if you change the Angle or Altitude of any individual layer effect when Use Global Light is on, all the other effects that have a Global Light option will update, as will the Angle and Altitude in the Global Light dialog box. Using a Global Light helps to unify lighting across multiple effects.

If more than one effect has been applied to a layer and you choose **Create Layer(s),** each effect will be placed on its own layer. The image won't look substantially different after this command is chosen, but the effects will no longer be editable via the Layer Style dialog box, and they will no longer be associated with the layer that they were originally applied to. You may get a warning that effects may not completely carry over to the layers **3**. You don't have much choice, though, if you want to proceed.

(Continued on the following page)

After you apply the Create Layer(s) command, any layer effect that's inside a shape (an inner glow, or a highlight or a shadow for a bevel or an inner emboss) will be placed on a new, separate layer, but it will be joined with the original shape layer in a clipping mask, with the original layer being the base layer of the mask. Any effect that's outside a shape (a drop shadow, an outer glow, or a shadow for a bevel or an outer emboss) will be converted into separate layers below the original shape layer.

TIP After Effects 5 and later can import a layered Photoshop file, with the option of preserving individual layers, layer masks, and layer effects. Use Create Layer(s) before exporting a layered file to a multimedia program that can't import Photoshop layer effects.

Hide All Effects temporarily hides layer effects for all the layers in the document. To redisplay them, choose Show All Effects.

Scale Effects opens a dialog box **1** that allows you to increase or decrease the size of all the effects currently applied to the selected layer (not the layer imagery). Only parameters defined in pixels (not those defined by a percentage) are affected.

Save it!

Layer effects (or combinations thereof) can be saved as styles on the **Styles** palette in ImageReady or Photoshop. See pages 530–531 to learn how to save effects as a style, and how to apply a style to a layer.

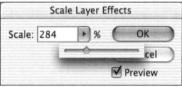

1 *Using the Scale Layer Effects dialog box, you can scale all the effects on the currently selected layer in one fell swoop.*

The composite color channel

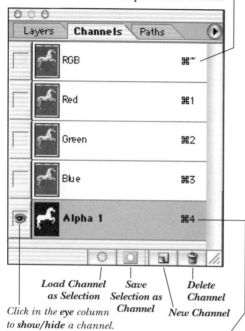

1 *Noncolor channels are called* **alpha channels.**

Load Channel
as Selection

Save
Selection as
Channel

Delete
Channel

New Channel

Click in the **eye** *column to* **show/hide** *a channel.*

2 *The active (selected) area is clear, the* **Quick Mask** *is semitransparent.*

THIS CHAPTER COVERS two special methods for saving and reshaping selections: alpha channels and Quick Mask mode.

If you save a selection to a user-created grayscale channel, called an alpha channel, you can load the selection onto the image at any time. A selection that has an irregular shape that would be difficult to reselect would be a logical candidate for this operation. A file can contain up to 56 channels, though from a practical standpoint, because each channel increases a picture's storage size (depending on the size of the selection area), you should be judicious about adding alpha channels. Alpha channels are accessed via the Channels palette **1**, and are saved or loaded onto an image via Select menu commands or the Channels palette. Only the currently highlighted channel or channels can be edited. (To create vector masks as an alternative to alpha channels in order to conserve file storage space, see page 328.)

Using Photoshop's **Quick Mask** mode **2**, the selected or unselected areas of an image can be covered with a semitransparent colored mask, which can then be reshaped using any editing or painting tool. Masked areas are protected from editing. Unlike an alpha channel, a Quick Mask can't be saved, but when you return to standard (non-Quick Mask) mode, the mask will turn into a selection, which can be saved.

Note: If you're unfamiliar with Photoshop's basic selection tools, read Chapter 6 before reading this chapter.

Layer masks are covered in Chapter 15.

Masks

Alpha channels

A selection that's **saved** in an alpha channel
can be loaded onto any image whenever
it's needed.

To save a selection to a channel using the current options settings:

1. Create a selection .

2. Click the Save Selection as Channel
   (second) button ⬛ at the bottom of
   the Channels palette **2**.

TIP To convert an alpha channel into a spot
color channel, see page 209.

1 *Select an area on a layer.*

To choose options as you save a selection to a channel:

1. Create a selection. It can be a type mask
   selection. *Optional:* Also choose a layer
   if you want to create a layer mask for it.

2. Choose Select > Save Selection.
   or
   Right-click/Ctrl-click and choose Save
   Selection from the context menu.

3. Leave the Document setting as the current file, or choose Document: New to
   save the selection to an alpha channel
   in a new, separate document **3**.

4. *Optional:* Choose Channel: [layer name]
   Mask to turn the selection into a layer
   mask for the current layer. Pixels will
   be visible only where the selection was.

5. Type a Name for the selection.

6. *Optional:* Choose an Operation option
   to combine the current selection with an
   existing alpha channel that you choose
   from the Channel pop-up menu. (The
   Operation options are illustrated on
   page 310.)

7. Click OK. The selection will remain
   active.

   Note: You can save an alpha channel with
   an image in the Photoshop, TIFF, or
   Photoshop PDF format. To save a copy of
   a file without alpha channels, uncheck
   Alpha Channels in the Save As dialog
   box, if it's available.

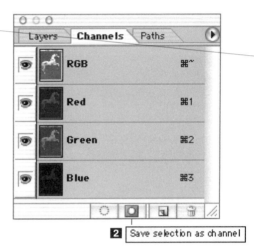

2 Save selection as channel

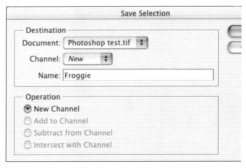

3 *In the Save Selection dialog box, choose Document and Channel options and give the channel a Name.*

(sidebar) **Save Selection to Channel**

Load channel to another image

Make sure the source and destination images have the same dimensions and resolution, activate the destination image, then follow steps 2–6 at below right, choosing the source document in the **Load Selection** dialog box. To load a layer mask selection, activate that layer first in the source image.

Just the pixels, please

To select only **nontransparent** pixels on an active layer, choose Channel: [layer name] Transparency in the Load Selection dialog box. Or Ctrl-click/ Cmd-click the layer thumbnail on the Layers palette.

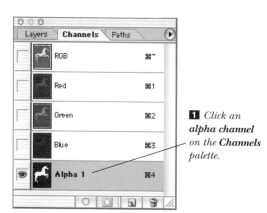

1 *Click an alpha channel on the Channels palette.*

2 *An alpha channel displayed in the image window: the selected area is white, the protected area is black.*

You can **display** an alpha channel without loading it onto the image as a selection.

To display a channel selection:

1. Click an alpha channel name on the Channels palette **1**. The selected area will be white, the protected area black **2**.

2. To restore the normal image display, click the top (composite) channel name on the palette (Ctrl-~/Cmd-~).

TIP If the selection has a Feather radius above zero, the feathered area will be gray, and will be only partially affected by editing.

TIP Reshape the mask with any painting tool, using black, gray, or white "paint."

To load a channel selection onto an image using the current options:

On the Channels palette, Ctrl-click/ Cmd-click the name of the alpha channel that you want to load.

To choose options as you load a channel selection onto an image:

1. If the composite image isn't displayed, click the top channel name on the Channels palette. You can combine the channel selection with an existing selection in the image (see the next page).

2. Choose Select > Load Selection.
   or
   If you didn't create a selection, you can right-click/Ctrl-click in the image window and choose Load Selection from the context menu.

3. Choose the alpha channel name from the Channel pop-up menu **3**.

4. To combine the channel with an existing selection in the image, click an Operation option (see the next page).

5. *Optional:* Check Invert to switch the selected and unselected areas in the loaded selection.

6. Click OK.

3 *Choose an alpha channel from the Channel pop-up menu.*

Save Selection Operations

When saving a selection, you can choose from these Operation options in the **Save Selection** dialog box:

Channel and selection to be saved   *Resulting channel*

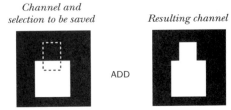

ADD

New Channel saves the current selection in a new channel.

Shortcut: Click the Save Selection as Channel button on the Channels palette.

Add to Channel adds the new selection to the channel.

Channel and selection to be saved   *Resulting channel*

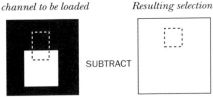

SUBTRACT

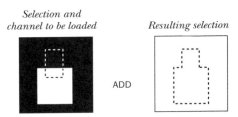

INTERSECT

Subtract from Channel removes white or gray areas that overlap the new selection.

Intersect with Channel preserves only white or gray areas that overlap the new selection.

Load Selection Operations

If a channel is loaded while an area of a layer is selected, you can choose from these Operation options in the **Load Selection** dialog box:

Selection and channel to be loaded   *Resulting selection*

ADD

New Selection: The channel becomes the current selection.

Shortcut: Ctrl-click/Cmd-click the channel name or drag the channel name over the Load Channel as Selection button. ⬚

Add to Selection adds the channel selection to the current selection.

Shortcut: Ctrl-Shift-click/Cmd-Shift-click the channel name.

Selection and channel to be loaded   *Resulting selection*

SUBTRACT

INTERSECT

Subtract from Selection removes areas of the current selection that overlap the channel selection.

Shortcut: Ctrl-Alt-click/Cmd-Option-click the channel name.

Intersect with Selection preserves only areas of the current selection that overlap the channel selection.

Shortcut: Ctrl-Alt-Shift-click/Cmd-Option-Shift-click the channel name.

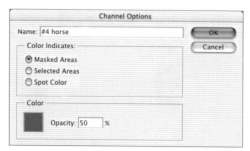

1 *Channel Options dialog box*

2 *The horse is the selected area.*

3 *The horse is still the selected area, but it's now **black** instead of white.*

4 *Delete Channel*

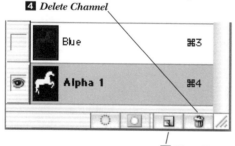

5 *New Channel*

6 *Choose **Duplicate Channel** from the context menu.*

To rename an alpha channel:

Double-click an existing alpha channel name on the palette, then type a new name.

Normally, the selected areas of an alpha channel are white and the protected areas are black or colored. You can **reverse** these colors without changing which area is actually selected.

To reverse the black and white areas in an alpha channel:

1. Double-click next to an alpha channel name on the Channels palette. (You could also click next to an alpha channel name, then choose Channel Options from the palette menu.)

2. In the Channel Options dialog box, click Color Indicates: Selected Areas **1**–**3**. (You can also change the channel name.)

3. Click OK.

TIP To change the size of the thumbnails on the Channels palette, choose Palette Options from the palette menu, then click a different thumbnail size.

To delete a channel:

On the Channels palette, click the channel you want to delete, then drag it over the Delete Channel button. 🗑
or
Click the channel you want to delete, click the Delete Channel button at the bottom of the palette **4**, then click Yes. Or Alt-click/Option-click the Delete Channel button to bypass the prompt.
or
Right-click/Ctrl-click the Channel name, then choose Delete Channel.

To duplicate a channel:

Drag the name of the channel you want to duplicate over the New Channel button or into another image window **5**.
or
Right-click/Ctrl-click the Channel name, choose Duplicate Channel from the context menu, change the name, if desired, then click OK **6**.

You can superimpose an alpha channel selection as a colored mask over an image, and then **reshape** the mask.

To reshape an alpha channel mask:

1. Make sure there is no selection on the image.

2. Click an alpha channel on the Channels palette. An eye icon will appear next to it **1**.

3. Click in the left column at the top of the palette (an eye icon will appear). A mask will cover the whole image except for where the white areas in the alpha channel are. Keep the alpha channel as the only highlighted channel **2**.

4. Choose the Pencil or Brush tool (B or Shift-B).

5. On the options bar, do all of the following:

   Click the Brush Preset picker arrowhead, then click a **brush** on the picker.

   Choose Mode: **Normal.**

   Choose 100% **Opacity** and 100% **Flow** to create a full mask or a lower Opacity and/or Flow to create a partial mask.

6. To enlarge the masked (protected) area, stroke on the edge of the mask with black as the Foreground color **3**. You can click the Switch Colors button on the Toolbox (X) to swap the Foreground and Background colors **4**.

   To enlarge the unmasked area, stroke on the mask with white as the Foreground color **5**.

7. To hide the mask, click the alpha channel's eye icon or choose a layer on the Layers palette.

1 *Click an **alpha channel** on the **Channels** palette.*

2 *Click in the **left** column at the top of the palette. Make sure the alpha channel stays highlighted.*

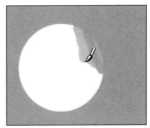

3 *Enlarge the **masked** area by stroking on the cutout with **black** as the Foreground color.*

5 *Enlarge the **unmasked** area by stroking on the mask with **white** as the Foreground color.*

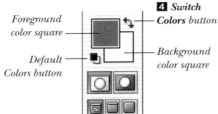

Foreground color square
4 *Switch Colors button*
Background color square
Default Colors button

1 *Select an area on a layer.*

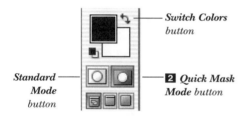

Switch Colors button

Standard Mode button

2 *Quick Mask Mode button*

3 *The unselected area is covered with a **mask**.*

Quick masks

If you choose **Quick Mask** r͏̶
area of a layer is selected, a sem͏̶
tinted mask will cover the unselecte͏̶
and the selected areas will be revealed ͏̶
cutout. You'll still be able to see the image
under the mask. The cutout (mask) can be
reshaped using the Brush or Pencil tool.

Note: You can't save a Quick Mask to a channel, but you can save it as a selection via the
Select > Save Selection command once you
return to the standard screen display mode.

To reshape a selection using Quick Mask mode:

1. Select an area of a layer **1**.

2. Click the Quick Mask Mode button on
the Toolbox (Q) **2**. A mask will cover
the unselected part of the picture **3**. (If
it doesn't, double-click the Quick Mask
Mode button, click Color Indicates:
Masked Areas in the Quick Mask
Options dialog box, then click OK.)

3. Choose the Pencil or Brush tool.
To use airbrush behavior, click the
Airbrush button on the options bar.

4. On the options bar, do all of the
following:

Click the Brush Preset picker arrowhead,
then click a **brush** on the picker.

Choose Mode: **Normal.**

Move the **Opacity** and **Flow** sliders to
100%.

5. Stroke on the cutout with black as the
Foreground color to enlarge the **masked**
(protected) area.
or
Stroke on the mask with white as the
Foreground color to enlarge the
unmasked area. You can click the Switch
Colors button on the Toolbox (X) to
swap the Foreground/Background colors.
or
Stroke with gray or a brush with an
Opacity below 100% (options bar) to

(Continued on the following page)

Quick Mask

create a partial mask. When you edit the layer, that area will be partially affected by modifications.

6. "Quick Mask" will be listed on the Channels palette and on the image window title bar while the image is in that mode. Click the Standard Mode button on the Toolbox (Q) when you're ready to turn off Quick Mask mode 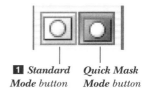. The non-masked areas will turn into a selection.

7. Now if you modify the layer, only the un-masked (selected) area will be affected.

In these instructions, you'll create a **mask without** first creating a selection.

To create a Quick Mask without using a selection:

1. Choose the Pencil or Brush tool, and choose options for the tool as per step 4 on the previous page.

2. Double-click the Quick Mask Mode button on the Toolbox.

3. Click Selected Areas, then click OK.

4. Stroke with black on the layer **2**. The selected areas (not the protected areas) will be covered with a mask; you'll be creating what will become the selection. Press Q to return to standard mode.

The **Quick Mask options** affect only how a Quick Mask looks on screen—not how it functions.

To choose Quick Mask options:

1. Double-click the Quick Mask Mode button on the Toolbox.

2. Do any of the following: **3**

   Choose whether Color Indicates: Masked Areas or Selected Areas.

   Click the Color swatch, then choose a new color for the Quick Mask.

   Change the Opacity of the mask color.

3. Click OK.

1 *Standard   Quick Mask*
Mode button   Mode button

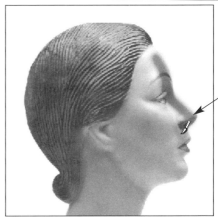

2 *Painting a mask on an image in* **Quick Mask** *mode*

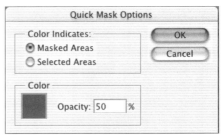

3 *In the* **Quick Mask Options** *dialog box, choose whether Color Indicates: Masked Areas or Selected Areas; click the Color swatch to choose a different mask color.*

PATHS AND SHAPES 18

1 *The **pen** tools and path **reshaping** tools*

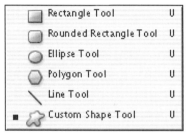

2 *The **shape** tools*

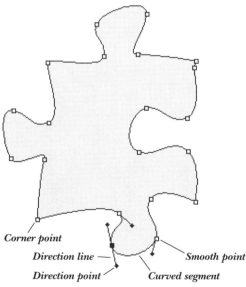

Corner point

Direction line

Direction point

Smooth point

Curved segment

3 *This is a **path.** To reshape a path or shape, you can drag, add, or delete a **point** or move a **segment.** A curved line segment can also be reshaped by adjusting its **direction lines.***

PHOTOSHOP'S PEN TOOLS **1** and shape tools **2** create precise vector shapes, called **paths.** Paths are made up of anchor points connected by curved or straight line segments **3**. Before drawing a path, you'll decide whether to click the first button on the options bar ⬜ for your pen tool to create a **shape layer** or click the second button ⬛ to create a **work path.** Both kinds of paths can be reshaped and filled.

Paths created by the Pen and Freeform Pen tools are displayed, activated, deactivated, restacked, saved, and deleted using the Paths palette **4**. Multiple path shapes can be saved under one name.

Shapes automatically show up as layers on the Layers palette, along with a vector mask that controls which part of the layer will be visible and which areas will be hidden.

Vector masks work like layer masks, but with an added bonus: they have sharp, precise path edges and take up far less storage space than channels. The contour of the vector mask is defined using a clipping path (a pen path or shape). A vector mask can be used on any fill, type, or image layer.

4 *The **Paths** palette*

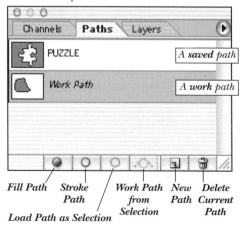

Fill Path   Stroke   Work Path   New   Delete
**   Path   from   Path   Current**
**   Selection   Path**

Load Path as Selection

A saved path

A work path

Creating paths

Before delving into the pen tools, we'll show you how to create a **path** using a **selection** as a starting point. Once a selection has been converted into a path, you can precisely reshape it and then use it either as a standard path or as a vector mask. You can also convert it back into a selection, if need be.

To convert a selection into a path:
Method 1

1. Select an area of an image . *Note:* When the selection is converted into a path, any feathering on the selection is removed.

2. Alt-click/Option-click the Work Path from Selection button at the bottom of the Paths palette.
   or
   Choose Make Work Path from the Paths palette menu.

3. Enter a Tolerance value (0.5–10) 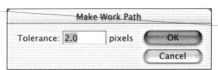. At a low Tolerance value, many anchor points will be created and the path will conform precisely to the selection marquee, but a low Tolerance could cause a printing error. At a high Tolerance value, fewer anchor points will be created and the path will be smoother, but it will conform less precisely to the selection. Try 4 or 5.

4. Click OK ▇–▇. The new work path name will appear on the Paths palette. Don't leave it as a temporary work path, though! Save the path by double-clicking the path name, entering a name, then clicking OK.

Method 2

To use the current Make Work Path tolerance setting, create a selection, then click the Work Path from Selection button at the bottom of the Paths palette. Now to save the path, double-click the path name, type a name, then click OK.

TIP You can export a Photoshop path to Adobe Illustrator, where it can also be used as a path (see page 327).

1 *The original selection*

2 *In the **Make Work Path** dialog box, enter a Tolerance value.*

3 *The selection converted into a **path: Tolerance 2.** (This shows our path after we clicked on it with the Path Selection tool.)*

4 *The selection converted into a **path: Tolerance 6***

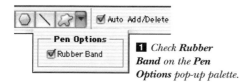

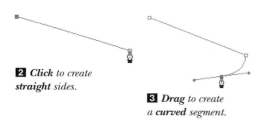

1 *Check* **Rubber Band** *on the* **Pen Options** *pop-up palette.*

2 *Click to create* **straight** *sides.*

3 *Drag to create a* **curved** *segment.*

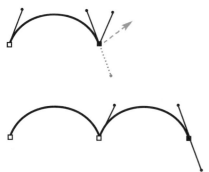

4 *Drag in the direction you want the curve to follow. Place anchor points at the* **ends** *of a curve, not at the peak of a curve. The fewer the anchor points, the more graceful the curves.*

5 *To draw curves that are connected by corner points, Alt-drag/Option-drag from the last anchor point in the direction you want the next curve to follow. Both direction lines will be on the same side of the curve segment.*

To draw a path using the Pen tool:

1. Choose the Pen tool (P or Shift-P). ✒

2. Deselect all paths on the Paths palette.

3. On the options bar:
   Click the Paths button. 🔳
   and
   To preview the line segments as you draw them, click the Geometry options arrowhead on the right side of the shape tools area, then check Rubber Band **1**.

4. Click in the image window, move the mouse, then click again to create a straight segment (Shift-click to draw the line at a multiple of 45°) **2**.
   or
   Drag to create a curved segment. Direction lines will appear **3**–**4**.
   or
   To create a nonsmooth point, starting from on top of the last anchor point, Alt-drag/Option-drag in the direction you want the next curve to follow, release Alt/Option and the mouse, then drag in the direction of the new curve **5**.

   TIP As you draw, press Esc once to erase the last created anchor point, or twice to delete the entire path.

5. Repeat the previous step as many times as necessary to complete the shape.

6. To end the path but leave it open, Ctrl-click/Cmd-click outside the path or click any tool.
   or
   To close the path, click the starting point (a small circle appears in the pointer).

7. To save the new work path, double-click the path name on the Paths palette, enter a name, then click OK. Deselect the path or the path name if you don't want the next path you draw to share that name. To reshape the path, see pages 324–325.

   TIP To add the new path to the existing name, click the name of a saved path before using the Pen. Or to start off with a saved path (instead of a work path), click the New Path button 🔳 on the Paths palette before drawing a new path.

Pen Tool

When the **Freeform Pen** tool is used with its **Magnetic** option on, it creates a path automatically as you move or drag the pointer along areas of high contrast. The path snaps to the nearest distinct shade or color edge that defines a shape.

To draw a magnetic Freeform Pen path:

1. Hide any layers you don't want to trace.

2. Choose the Freeform Pen tool (P or Shift-P).

3. Deselect all paths on the Paths palette.

4. On the Freeform Pen tool options bar, click the Paths button and check Magnetic. To choose Magnetic options, see the following page.

5. Click to begin the path, then slowly move the mouse—with or without pressing the mouse button—along the edge of the shape that you want the path to describe **1**. As you move or drag, the path will snap to the edge of the shape. Don't move the mouse too quickly— the tool might not keep pace with you.

6. If the path snaps to any neighboring shapes that you *don't* want to select, click on the edge of the shape that you *do* want to select to manually create an anchor point, and then continue to move or drag to finish the path.

7. To **close** the path **2**:

   Double-click anywhere over the shape to close with magnetic segments, or Alt-double-click/Option-double-click to close with a straight segment.
   or
   Click the starting point (a small circle appears next to the tool pointer).
   or
   Ctrl-click/Cmd-click anywhere over the shape.

   To end the path but leave it **open,** press Enter/Return.

TIP Press Esc to cancel an incomplete path.

> ### Drawing straight lines
> To draw straight segments with a temporary Pen tool while the Freeform Pen is chosen, **Alt-click/ Option-click,** and continue clicking. Release Alt/Option to return to the Freeform Pen.

1 *Using the **Freeform Pen** tool with the **Magentic** option, click to start the path, then move the mouse around the object you want to select.*

2 *The completed path*

Magnetic Path

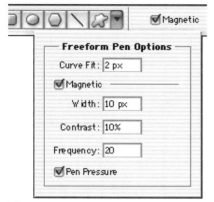

1 *When Magnetic is checked on the options bar for the Freeform Pen tool, you can choose settings from the Freeform Pen Options palette.*

The Freeform Pen Options pop-up palette **1**

Click the arrowhead in the shape tools area of the options bar to open the Freeform Pen Options palette (the tool tip says "Geometry options").

Curve Fit (0.5–10 pixels) controls how closely your Freeform Pen path will match the movement of your mouse. The higher the Curve Fit, the fewer the points, and thus the smoother the shape.

With Magnetic checked, the following options can be set:

The **Width** (1–256) is the width in pixels under the pointer that the tool considers when placing points. Use a wide Width for a high-contrast image that has clear delineations between shapes. For more exact line placement in a low-contrast image that contains subtle gradations or closely spaced shapes, use a narrow Width.

TIP To have the Magnetic Freeform Pen pointer display as a circle in the current Width, click Other Cursors: Precise in File > Preferences > Display & Cursors, or press Caps Lock to turn this option on temporarily.

TIP To decrease the Width incrementally while creating a path, press [. To increase the Width, press].

Contrast (0–100%) is the degree of contrast needed between shapes for the tool to discern an edge. At a low Contrast setting, even edges between low contrast areas are discerned.

Frequency (0–100) controls how quickly Photoshop places fastening points as you draw a path. The lower the Frequency, the more frequently fastening points are placed and the more anchor points are created.

Check **Pen Pressure** if you have a stylus tablet and want to control the pen width using pen pressure. As you apply more pressure, the width decreases.

With the **Freeform Pen** tool, you create a path by dragging. Anchor points will appear automatically when you release the mouse.

To draw a path using the Freeform Pen:

1. Choose the Freeform Pen tool (P or Shift-P). Deselect all paths on the Paths palette.

2. On the Freeform Pen tool options bar, click the Paths button and uncheck Magnetic.

3. Draw a path in a freehand style.

TIP To draw straight segments, Alt-click/ Option-click. To resume freehand drawing, release Alt/Option when the mouse button is down.

4. To **close** the path:

Keep the mouse button down, and drag back over the starting point **1**–**2**. A small circle will display next to the Freeform Pen tool pointer.
or
Hold down Ctrl/Cmd and release the mouse to close the path with a final straight segment.

To end the path but leave it **open,** just release the mouse.

Working with paths

In this section, you will learn how to move, add to, transform, copy, save, display/hide, select, reshape, delete, and deselect a path; convert a path into a selection; and finally, export a path to a drawing application.

To move a path:

1. On the Paths palette, click a path name.

2. Choose the Path Selection tool (A or Shift-A).

3. In the image window, drag inside the path **3**.

Beware!

As long as you don't click the blank area of the Paths palette, any additional paths you create will be part of the same work path. If you deselect all paths and draw again without saving the existing work path, however, the new work path will **replace** the old one! To save a path so it's not replaced, see page 322. Multiple paths can be saved under the same name.

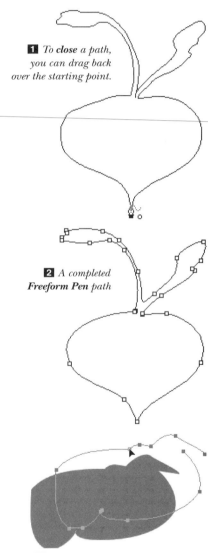

1 *To close a path, you can drag back over the starting point.*

2 *A completed* **Freeform Pen** *path*

3 *A path is moved using the Path Selection tool.*

Freeform Pen; Move Path

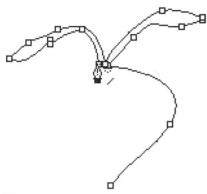

1 *To* **add** *to a path, drag from an* **endpoint** *using the* **Pen** *or* **Freeform Pen** *tool.*

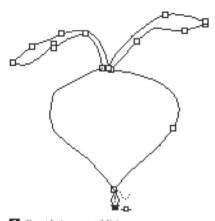

2 *Completing an addition*

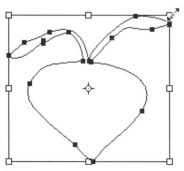

3 *Scaling a path*

To add to an existing, open path:

1. Choose the Freeform Pen tool 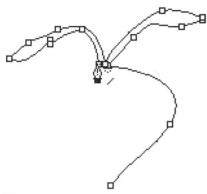 or Pen tool (P or Shift-P).

2. On the Paths palette, click the name of an open (not closed) path.

3. Drag from either endpoint of the path **1**–**2**. To end the path, follow step 4 in the first set of instructions on the previous page.

To transform an entire path:

1. Choose the Path Selection tool (A or Shift-A).

2. Click a path name on the Paths palette, then click inside the path in the image window.

3. Choose Edit > Transform Path > Scale, Rotate, Skew, Distort, or Perspective; or right-click/Ctrl-click and choose Free Transform Path (Ctrl-T/Cmd-T).
   or
Check Show Bounding Box on the options bar, then transform the path using the bounding box handles, as you would use the handles on the Free Transform box.

4. Follow the instructions on pages 287–290 to perform the transformation.

TIP To repeat the transformation, choose Edit > Transform Path > Again (Ctrl-Shift-T/Cmd-Shift-T).

To transform points on a path:

1. Choose the Direct Selection tool (A or Shift-A), then select one or more individual points on a path (marquee or Shift-click multiple points).

2. Choose Edit > Transform Points > Scale, Rotate, or Skew (the Distort and Perspective commands won't be available); or right-click/Ctrl-click and choose Free Transform Points (Ctrl-T/Cmd-T).

3. Follow the instructions on pages 287–290 to perform the transformation **3**.

To copy a path in the same image:

To have the copy appear under a **separate** path name, on the Paths palette, Alt-drag/Option-drag the path name over the New Path button ⬛ at the bottom of the palette, enter a Name **1**, then click OK. Or to copy the path without naming it, drag the path name without holding down Alt/Option.

To copy a path outline under the same name:

To copy a path outline under the **same** name, click a path on the Paths palette, choose the Path Selection tool (A or Shift-A), ▸ then Alt-drag/Option-drag the path outline in the image window **2**. The original and duplicate path outlines will share the same listing on the palette.

To drag and drop a path to another image:

1. Open the source and target images, and click in the source image window.

2. Drag the path name from the Paths palette into the target image window.
   or
   Choose the Path Selection tool, ▸ click the path in the source image window, then drag it into the target image window.
   or
   Click the path name on the Paths palette, choose Edit > Copy (Ctrl-C/Cmd-C), click in the target image window, then choose Edit > Paste (Ctrl-V/Cmd-V).

TIP You can also copy and paste a vector mask that you've created for an image layer or shape layer.

When you create a new path with the Pen tool, it's labeled "Work Path" automatically, and it saves with your file. The next work path you create, however, will replace it. Follow the instructions below if you want to **save a path** so it's not replaced by the next work path. Once a path is saved, it's resaved automatically each time it's modified.

To save a work path:

On the Paths palette, double-click "Work Path," enter a Name **3**, then click OK.

Quick-save a work path

Drag the work path name over the **New Path** button ⬛ at the bottom of the Paths palette. Photoshop will assign a default name to it. To rename it at any time, double-click the path name, then type a new name.

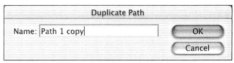

1 *Type a Name in the **Duplicate Path** dialog box.*

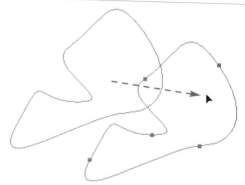

2 *To copy a path outline manually, Alt-drag/Option-drag it with the **Path Selection** tool.*

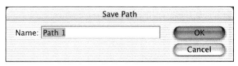

3 *Type a name in the **Save Path** dialog box.*

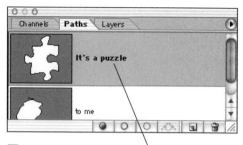

1 *To display a path, click its name on the **Paths** palette.*

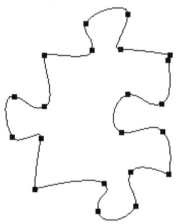

2 *Click with the **Path Selection** tool to select **all** the points on a path.*

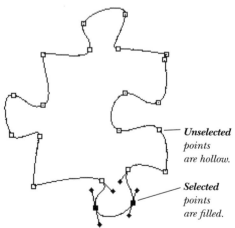

Unselected points are hollow.

Selected points are filled.

3 *Click with the **Direct Selection** tool to select **individual** points on a path.*

To display a path:

Click the path name or thumbnail on the Paths palette **1**.

TIP To change the size of the palette thumbnails, choose Palette Options from the Paths palette menu, then click a Thumbnail Size. (You can also turn off the thumbnail display altogether.)

To hide a path:

Shift-click the path name on the Paths palette.
or
Click below all the path names on the Paths palette.

To select anchor points on a path:
Method 1

1. Click a path name on the Paths palette.
2. Choose the Path Selection tool (A or Shift-A).
3. Click the path in the image window or draw a marquee around it. All the anchor points on the path will become selected **2**.

Method 2

1. Click a path name on the Paths palette.
2. Choose the Direct Selection tool (A or Shift-A).
3. Click the path or subpath, then click an anchor point **3**. Shift-click to select additional anchor points. Direction lines will be visible.
   or
   To select all the anchor points on the path, Alt-click/Option-click the path or subpath or draw a marquee around it. An entire path can be moved when all its points are selected. Direction lines won't be visible.

TIP To change the stacking position of a path, drag the path name up or down on the Paths palette. The work path will always remain at the bottom.

TIP Hold down Ctrl/Cmd to use the Direct Selection tool while any Pen tool is chosen.

To **reshape** a path, you can move, add, or delete an anchor point, or move a segment. To modify the shape of a curved line segment, you can move a direction line toward or away from its anchor point or rotate it around its anchor point.

To reshape a path:

1. On the Paths palette, click the name of the path you want to reshape.

2. Choose the Direct Selection tool (A or Shift-A). ▶ Or to turn another pen tool into a temporary Direct Selection tool, press Ctrl/Cmd.

3. Click a path in the image window.

4. Do any of the following:

   Drag an anchor **point** or a **segment** 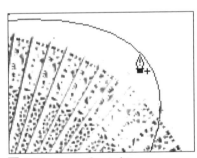. To select a segment, drag a marquee that includes both of the segment's endpoints. Shift-drag to marquee additional segments (or subpaths).

   Drag or **rotate** a **direction line** 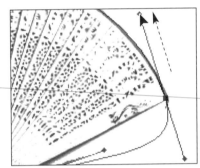. If you move a direction line on a smooth point, the two segments that are connected to that point will also move. If you move a direction line on a corner point, on the other hand, only one curve segment will move.

   To **add** an anchor **point,** choose the Add Anchor Point tool, ✎⁺ then click a line segment (the pointer will be a pen icon with a plus sign when it's over a segment) 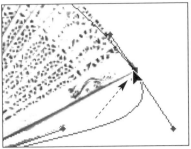–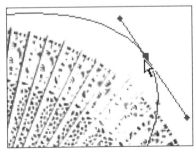.

   TIP If Auto Add/Delete is checked on the options bar, the Pen tool will turn into the Add Anchor Point tool when it's over a segment, or into the Delete Anchor Point tool when it's over a point. To turn this function off temporarily, hold down Shift.

1 *Dragging an anchor point*

2 *Pulling a direction line*

3 *Adding an anchor point*

4 *The new anchor point*

Reshape Path

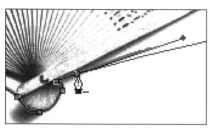

1 *Deleting an anchor point*

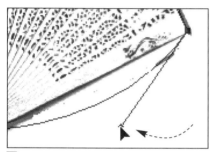

2 *Converting a direction line*

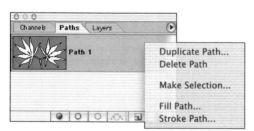

3 *To delete a path, right-click/Control-click the path name, then choose **Delete Path** from the context menu.*

Fill or stroke

To fill or apply a stroke to a path using default dialog box settings, click the path name, then click the Fill Path Color button ● or Stroke Path button ○ at the bottom of the Paths palette. For a shape layer, use the Stroke effect or an Overlay effect to fill or stroke the shape.

To **delete** an anchor **point,** choose the Delete Anchor Point tool, 🖊 then click the anchor point (the pointer will be a pen icon with a minus sign when it's over a point) **1**.

To **convert** a **smooth point** into a **corner point,** choose the Convert Point tool ▶ (or hold down Ctrl-Alt/Cmd-Option if the Direct Selection tool is chosen or Alt/Option if a pen tool is chosen), then click the anchor point (deselect the Convert Point tool by choosing another tool). To **convert** a **corner point** into a **smooth point,** choose the Convert Point tool, then drag away from the anchor point.

Use the Convert Point tool ▶ to rotate one direction line in a pair independently of the other **2**. Once the Convert Point tool has been used on part of a direction line, you can use either the Convert Point tool or the Direct Selection tool to move its partner.

5. Click outside the path to deselect it.

If the path you want to **delete** is a work path, simply drawing a new path with the Pen tool will cause it to be replaced with the new work path. If the path you want to delete isn't a work path, follow these instructions.

To delete a path:

1. On the Paths palette, activate the path you want to delete.

2. Right-click/Control-click the path name, then choose Delete Path from the context menu **3**.
or
Alt-click/Option-click the Delete Path button 🗑 on the Paths palette.
or
Click the Delete Path button, 🗑 then click Yes.
or
Drag the path name over the Delete Path button. 🗑

Is that enough options for ya?

Delete Path

To deselect a path:

1. Choose the Direct Selection tool or the Path Selection tool (A or Shift-A).

2. Click outside the path in the image window. The path will still be visible in the image window, but its anchor points and direction lines will be hidden.

To convert a path into a selection:

1. *Optional:* Create a selection if you want to add, delete, or intersect the new path selection with it.

2. On the Paths palette, Ctrl-click/Cmd-click the **path** that you want to convert into a selection.

   or

   Click the path that you want to convert into a selection, then click the **Load Path as Selection** button at the bottom of the palette. The last used Make Selection settings will apply.

   or

   To choose options as you load a path as a selection, right-click/Control-click the path name and choose **Make Selection** from the context menu. The Make Selection dialog box opens. You can apply a **Feather Radius** to the selection (try a low number to soften the edge slightly). If you check Anti-aliased, make the Feather Radius 0. You can also add, subtract, or intersect the path with an existing selection on the image by clicking an **Operation** option. The Operation shortcuts are listed in the sidebar on this page. Click OK.

3. On the Layers palette, choose the layer you created the selection for.

2 *Choose options for a selection in the* **Make Selection** *dialog box.*

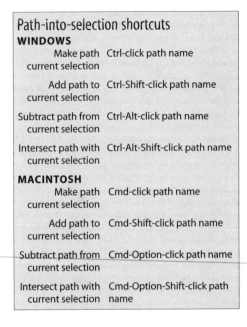

Path-into-selection shortcuts

WINDOWS

Make path current selection	Ctrl-click path name
Add path to current selection	Ctrl-Shift-click path name
Subtract path from current selection	Ctrl-Alt-click path name
Intersect path with current selection	Ctrl-Alt-Shift-click path name

MACINTOSH

Make path current selection	Cmd-click path name
Add path to current selection	Cmd-Shift-click path name
Subtract path from current selection	Cmd-Option-click path name
Intersect path with current selection	Cmd-Option-Shift-click path name

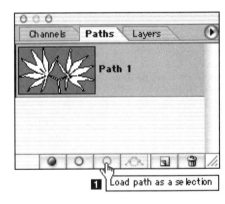

1 Load path as a selection

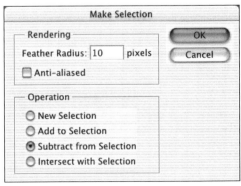

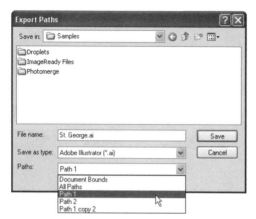

1 *In Windows, choose a path from the **Paths** drop-down menu.*

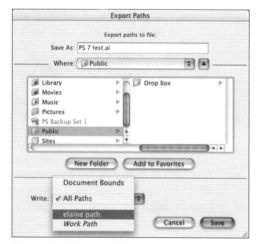

2 *In Mac, choose a path from the **Write** pop-up menu.*

You can create a path in Photoshop, **export** it to Adobe Illustrator or Macromedia FreeHand, and use it as an editable path in that program. You can even make a round trip—reopen the path in Photoshop using the Place or Open command.

Note: As an alternative to the method described below, you can use the Path Selection tool to copy and paste or drag and drop an active path to another application (or into another open Photoshop image).

To export a path to Illustrator or FreeHand:

1. With an image open, choose File > Export > Paths to Illustrator.

2. *Optional:* Change the name in the File Name/Save As field.

3. Choose a location in which to save the path file using the Save In pop-up menu in Windows, or the scroll windows in Mac.

4. From the Paths **1**/Write **2** pop-up menu:

Choose an individual path name.
or
Choose All Paths to export all the paths in the image as one file. Document crop marks will be included in the export file.
or
Choose Document Bounds to export only crop marks for the current file.

5. Click Save. The path can now be opened in Macromedia FreeHand or opened as an Adobe Illustrator file in Illustrator.

TIP To ensure that the path fits when you reimport it into Photoshop, don't alter its crop marks in Illustrator.

TIP You may have to choose Outline view in Illustrator to see the exported path, because it won't have a stroke.

TIP You can also follow the instructions above to export a shape layer's vector mask (to create a vector mask, see the next page). *Note:* To make a vector mask available on the Write pop-up menu, choose that layer before performing step 1 in the instructions above.

Vector masks

A **vector mask** works like a layer mask in that it hides pixels on a layer, except in this case a vector path shape is used to delineate the visible and masked areas in the current layer. The vector mask produces a clean, sharp-edged shape.

The path that will be used for the mask can be created using the Pen tool, Freeform Pen tool, or a shape tool, or it can be created from a selection that you convert into a path. You can reshape the path that's used for the mask or discard the mask at any time.

A vector mask displays as a gray thumbnail on the Layers palette, and also on the Paths palette when the layer that contains the mask is selected. As with layer masks, each vector mask is associated with only one layer.

1 *A layer with strokes that will be clipped*

To create a vector mask:

Method 1

1. On the Layers palette, choose the layer that you want to add a vector mask to **1**.

2. To create a mask in which all the layer pixels are visible, choose Layer > Add Vector Mask > Reveal All, or Ctrl-click/ Cmd-click the Add Vector Mask button [O] on the Layers palette.
   or
   To create a mask in which all the layer pixels are hidden, choose Layer > Add Vector Mask > Hide All or Ctrl-Alt-click/ Cmd-Option-click the Add Vector Mask button [O] on the Layers palette.

3. Choose the Pen tool, Freeform Pen tool, or a shape tool (Rectangle, Rounded Rectangle, Ellipse, Polygon, or Custom Shape), then create a clipping path in the desired shape **2**–**3**.

2 *A vector mask is added using the **Hide All** option, and the Pen tool is used to shape the path.*

Method 2

1. On the Layers palette, choose the layer that you want to add a vector mask to.

2. To reveal only layer pixels within a selected, existing path, click a path on the Paths palette, then choose Layer > Add Vector Mask > Current Path.

3 *The effect of the **vector mask** on the layer imagery*

EPS clipping paths—a new way

If you save a file that contains a vector mask as a Photoshop EPS for import into another program (e.g., InDesign or QuarkXPress), the masking effect of the vector mask will be preserved in the other program. Just make sure **Include Vector Data** stays checked in the EPS Options dialog box.

Note: To import a Photoshop file that contains a vector mask into Adobe Illustrator CS, use the Place command (Link option unchecked) or the Open command in Illustrator, and choose the option that converts layers to objects.

The **pathfinder** buttons are used to create add-ons to, or cutouts from, an existing path, or to create a separate path.

To combine a new path with an existing path:

1. Click the vector mask thumbnail for a layer that contains a vector mask.
2. Choose the Pen tool, Freeform Pen tool, or a shape tool (Rectangle, Rounded Rectangle, Ellipse, Polygon, or Custom Shape).
3. On the options bar, click one of the four pathfinder buttons **1**.
4. Draw another path in the image window **2**–**3**.

If you **reshape** a vector mask, the masking effect in the image will change accordingly.

To reshape a vector mask:

1. Choose the Direct Selection tool (A or Shift-A).
2. Click a vector mask thumbnail on the Layers palette. The vector mask should now be visible in the image window.
3. Click the edge of the vector mask to reveal and select its anchor points.
4. Follow the steps on pages 324–325 to reshape the path.

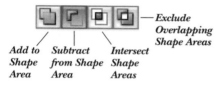

Add to Shape Area   Subtract from Shape Area   Intersect Shape Areas   — Exclude Overlapping Shape Areas

1 *The Pathfinder buttons on the options bar*

2 *The Pen tool and the Add to Shape Area button were used to add a second vector mask to a layer that already contains a vector mask.*

3 *Now two vector mask shapes are displayed in the vector mask thumbnail.*

Combine Paths; Reshape Vector Mask

A vector mask can be **moved** independently of its layer pixels at any time. It will stay on its designated layer.

To reposition a vector mask:

1. Choose the Path Selection tool (A or Shift-A).

2. On the Layers palette, click a vector mask thumbnail.

3. Drag the vector mask to a new location in the image window. A different area of layer pixels will now be visible inside the path **1**.

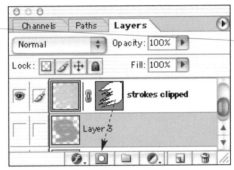

1 *The vector mask is **moved**, and now a different area of layer pixels is visible inside it.*

To duplicate a vector mask:

1. Choose the layer you want the duplicate to appear on.

2. From another layer, drag the vector mask thumbnail you want to duplicate over the Add Vector Mask button **2**–**3**. The duplicate vector mask will appear on the active layer.

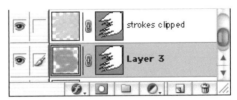

2 *Drag the vector mask thumbnail over the **Add Vector Mask** button.*

To deactivate a vector mask:

Shift-click the vector mask thumbnail on the Layers palette. A red X will appear over the thumbnail, and the entire layer will now be visible **4** (the vector mask thumbnail won't become selected).

You can Shift-click the vector mask thumbnail again at any time to remove the X and restore the masking effect.

3 *A **copy** of the vector mask appears on the active layer (in this case, Layer 3).*

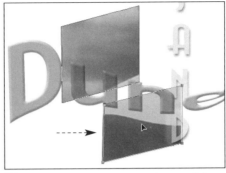

4 *The vector mask is **deactivated**.*

1 *Select a vector mask.*

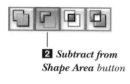

2 *Subtract from Shape Area button*

3 *The hidden and visible areas are reversed.*

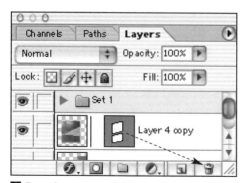

4 *Drag the vector mask thumbnail over the Delete Layer button.*

To reverse the visible and hidden areas in a vector mask:

1. Choose the Path Selection tool (A or Shift-A).

2. On the Layers palette, click a vector mask thumbnail. The vector mask will be highlighted in the image window.

3. Click the vector mask in the image window. Its anchor points and segments will become selected **1**.

4. Click the Subtract from Shape Area (second) button on the options bar **2**–**3**, or press the – (minus) key.

To switch the revealed and hidden areas again, click the Add to Shape Area (first) button on the options bar, or press the + (plus) key.

You can **delete** any vector masks that you no longer need, though you won't recoup any file storage space by doing so.

To discard a vector mask:

1. On the Layers palette, click the thumbnail for the vector mask that you want to remove.

2. Click the Delete Layer button, 🗑 then click OK.
or
Drag the vector mask thumbnail over the Delete Layer button **4**.
or
Choose Layer > Delete Vector Mask, then click OK.

Reverse, Discard Vector Mask

Should you decide that you want a hard-edged mask to define an image layer, you can **convert** a layer mask into a vector mask.

To convert a layer mask into a vector mask:

1. Ctrl-click/Cmd-click a layer mask thumbnail on the Layers palette.

2. On the Paths palette, click the Make Work Path from Selection button. Leave the path selected.

3. Choose Layer > Add Vector Mask > Current Path ■.

4. *Optional:* To remove the layer mask, drag the layer mask thumbnail (first thumbnail) to the Delete Layer button on the Layers palette, then click Discard, or choose Layer > Remove Layer Mask > Discard. The vector mask will remain.

To create an adjustment layer that uses a vector mask:

1. Create a new shape layer (see page 334).

2. Choose a command from the Layer > Change Layer Content submenu.

3. Make the desired adjustments in the dialog box, then click OK.

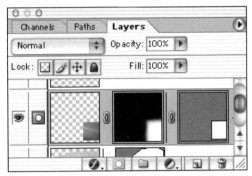

1 *The selection from a **layer mask** becomes the path for a **vector mask**. The layer shown here now has two mask thumbnails.*

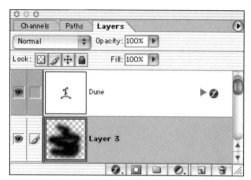

1 *Choose a* **type** *layer.*

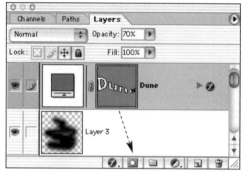

2 *Convert the type layer into a* **shape** *layer, select another layer, then drag the vector mask thumbnail over the* **Add Vector Mask** *button.*

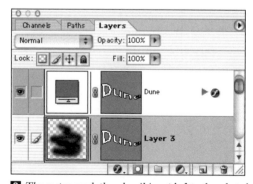

3 *The vector mask thumbnail is* **copied** *to the selected layer (Layer 3, in our example). (Any layer effects on the original layer can also be copied by dragging them over the selected layer.)*

You can fill **type** shapes with imagery using a vector mask.

To create a vector mask from type:

1. Create a type layer, and keep it active **1**.

2. Choose Layer > Type > Convert to Shape.

3. Choose the layer you want the new vector mask to appear on (the layer shouldn't already contain a vector mask).

4. Drag the vector mask thumbnail that was created in step 2 over the Add Vector Mask button 🔘 on the Layers palette **2**. A new vector mask will be created for the active layer **3**.

5. Delete or hide the type shape layer.

TIP In addition to the steps listed above, try doing any of the following:

Duplicate the original type layer before converting it so it will be available for future type edits, and thus future vector masks. Hide the duplicate type layer.

To reposition the vector mask within the layer, choose the Path Selection tool, drag a marquee around all the character shapes, then drag.

To reverse what's revealed and what's hidden on the layer, choose the Path Selection tool, drag a marquee across all the character shapes in the image window, then either click the Subtract from Shape Area button 🔲 on the options bar or press the – (minus) key.

Type into Vector Mask

Shapes

A shape is a precise geometric or custom-shaped clipping path that occupies its own layer and reveals a solid-color, gradient, or pattern fill within its contour **1**. At any time, shapes can be repositioned, transformed, or reshaped; their fill content can be modified or changed to a different type; and the usual layer styles, effects, blending modes, opacity settings, and fill settings can be applied to them.

Unlike the main Photoshop image, which is a bitmap, shape layers are composed of vector data (think Adobe Illustrator or Macromedia FreeHand). This means that shapes always look sharp and precise, whether they're printed on a PostScript printer, saved in PDF format, or imported into a vector drawing program; in other words, they're resolution-independent.

Creating a **shape layer** involves drawing a vector path, just as you would in an illustration program.

To create a shape layer:

1. Choose a layer on the Layers palette. The new shape layer will be created above this layer. *Note:* If the layer you choose has a vector mask, the shape will become part of the vector mask. To prevent this from happening, make sure the vector mask thumbnail is deselected.

2. Choose a Foreground color for the shape's color fill. (You'll learn how to fill a shape with a gradient or pattern later.)

3. Choose a shape tool (U or Shift-U) on the Toolbox **2**. Once a shape tool is selected, you can switch to any other shape tool by clicking one of the six shape tool buttons on the options bar **3**.

Effects on a clipping path

Apply **layer effects** (Inner Glow, Bevel, etc.) to a shape layer or to a layer that has a vector mask to enhance edges, add a shadow, etc. If you apply the Stroke effect or any of the Overlay effects to stroke or fill the vector mask, you'll be able to modify the stroke or fill at any time.

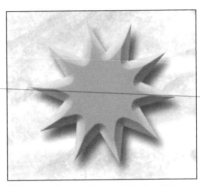

1 *A star **shape** with a solid-color fill*

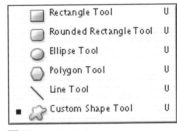

2 *The **shape** tools*

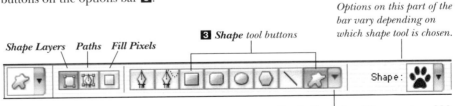

3 ***Shape** tool buttons*

Shape Layers   Paths   Fill Pixels

Options on this part of the bar vary depending on which shape tool is chosen.

Shape :

*For the **Geometry** options, see page 338.*

Photoshop versus ImageReady

	PHOTOSHOP	IMAGEREADY
Pen tools	**yes**	no
Polygon tool	**yes**	no
Custom Shape tool	**yes**	no
Create and edit shape layers	**yes**	create (with limitations), but not edit
Create and edit vector masks	**yes**	no
Edit shapes	**yes**	transform or move, but not edit

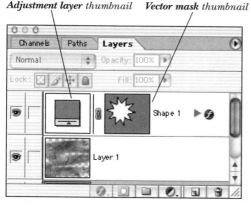

1 *A* **shape** *created using the* **Custom Shape** *tool*

Adjustment layer *thumbnail*   **Vector mask** *thumbnail*

2 *The* **shape** *layer appears on the Layers palette.*

4. On the shape tool options bar:

If you're using the Rounded Rectangle tool, choose a Radius value; for the Polygon tool, choose a number of Sides; for the Line tool, choose a Weight; or for the Custom Shape tool, choose a shape from the Custom Shape Preset picker.
and
Click the Shape Layers (first) button.

5. Drag in the image window to create the shape. While dragging, you can hold down Alt/Option to draw from the shape's center or Shift-drag to constrain a rectangle to a square, an ellipse to a circle, or a line to a multiple of 45°.
Note: In Windows, to draw from the center, the procedure is to click, hold down Alt, then drag.

6. When the mouse is released, the shape will display **1**. A new Shape 1 layer will be listed on the Layers palette. It will have an adjustment layer thumbnail that controls its fill content and a vector mask thumbnail that controls its contour and location **2**. You can choose layer style, blending mode, opacity, and fill settings for the new layer.

TIP When the Custom Shape tool is chosen, you can right-click/Ctrl-click the image to open an "on-the-fly" shape picker.

TIP If the link icon next to the Style thumbnail on the Shape Tool options bar is selected (visible in Windows, dark in Mac), style and color changes will apply to the current shape layer. If the link icon isn't selected (hidden/light), style and color changes will apply to the next shape layer you create.

The shape tools can be used to create a temporary **work path.**

To create a work path using a shape tool:

1. Follow steps 1–3 on page 334.

2. Click the Paths button on the options bar .

3. Deselect any existing paths (click the blank area of the Paths palette).

4. Drag in the image window to create the path shape **2**. You can Alt-drag/ Option-drag to draw from the center or Shift-drag to constrain a rectangle to a square, an ellipse to a circle, or a line to a multiple of 45°.

   The new work path will be listed on the Paths palette **3**. To learn more about work paths, see page 320.

5. The next time you use a shape tool with the Paths button chosen, the existing work path will be replaced! To save your new work path so it can't be replaced, double-click Work Path on the Paths palette, then click OK.

1 *Click the **Paths** button on the options bar.*

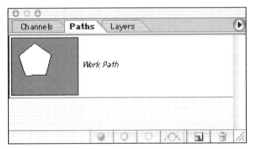
2 *A pentagonal **work path***

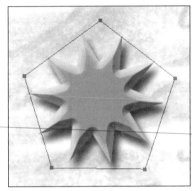
3 *The **work path** appears on the Paths palette.*

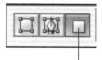

1 *Click the* **Fill Pixels** *button on the options bar.*

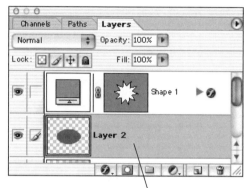

2 *On the Layers palette, the area created by the* **Fill Pixels** *command appears on a standard rasterized layer, not on a shape layer.*

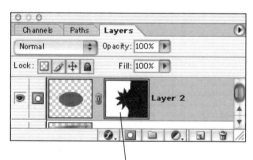

3 *You can use a shape tool with the* **Fill Pixels** *button clicked to add a geometric area to an existing* **layer mask.**

You can use any of the shape tools to quickly create a **geometric** or precisely drawn area of pixels on a standard layer without having to use a selection marquee.

To create a geometric area of pixels:

1. On the Layers palette, click a standard image layer or the Background, or create a new layer. You can't use a vector (shape or type) layer for this task.

2. Choose a Foreground color.

3. Choose a shape tool (U or Shift-U). Once a shape tool is chosen, you can click a different shape tool button on the options bar.

4. On the options bar, do all of the following:

   Click the **Fill Pixels** button 🔲 **1**.

   If you're using the Rounded Rectangle tool, choose a **Radius** value; for the Polygon tool, choose a number of **Sides;** for the Line tool, choose a **Weight;** or for the Custom Shape tool, choose a **shape** from the Custom Shape Preset picker. Shape: ♣▾

   Choose **Layer Style, Mode, Opacity,** and **Fill** settings.

5. Drag across the image window to create the shape. A pixel area will be created **2**. Use brushes, editing tools, filters—whatever—to modify the pixels. It's just a regular ol' layer.

TIP To create a geometric pixel area within a layer mask, click an existing layer mask thumbnail on the Layers palette, choose a shape tool, click the Fill Pixels button on the options bar, choose black as the Foreground color to add to the mask or white to take away from the mask, then drag in the image window **3**.

Geometric Area of Pixels

You can **customize** each shape tool so it will behave a certain way each time you use it.

To choose geometric options for a shape tool:

1. Choose a shape tool (U or Shift-U). Once the tool is chosen, you can click a different shape tool button on the options bar.

2. Click the Geometry Options arrowhead on the options bar 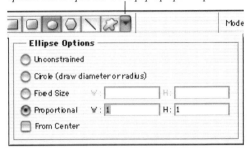.

3. Options on the pop-up palette will vary depending on which tool is chosen. For the Ellipse tool, for example, you can click Unconstrained, Circle, Fixed Size, or Proportional. For Fixed Size or Proportional, enter W and H values. To have the tool draw from the center, check From Center.

4. If you chose the Custom Shape tool, click the Custom Shape Preset picker arrowhead or thumbnail 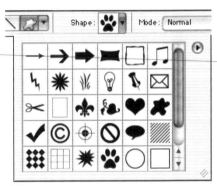, then click a shape on the picker. You can use the picker menu to load in other shape libraries.

5. To close the pop-up palette or picker, click the arrowhead again or click outside it.

Because a shape layer contains vector data, you can **modify** a shape's vector mask at any time, and its crisp edge will stay crisp.

To move a shape layer's vector mask:

1. Choose the Path Selection tool (A or Shift-A).

2. Click a shape in the image window.
   or
   Click a shape layer on the Layers palette.

3. Drag the vector mask in the image window . The vector mask thumbnail will update to reflect the new position 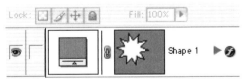.

TIP If you click a vector mask thumbnail on the Layers palette, the vector mask will become highlighted in the image window (this won't cause the path itself to become selected).

1 *Click the **Geometry** options arrowhead on the options bar to open the tool's pop-up options palette.*

2 *These are the default choices on the **Custom Shape Preset** picker. Other libraries are available.*

3 *Drag the **vector mask** in the image window.*

4 *The shape's vector mask thumbnail updates to reflect the shape's new location. Compare with **2** on the previous page.*

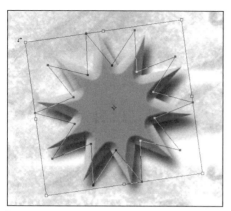

1 *Use the **Path Selection** tool with the Show Bounding Box option checked (or use the **Free Transform** command) to display the bounding box handles on a shape layer's vector mask, then drag a handle to transform it.*

2 *Use the **Direct Selection** tool to drag an anchor point on the vector mask for a shape layer.*

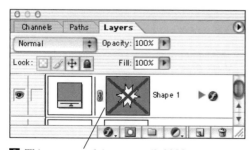

3 *This vector mask is temporarily **hidden.***

To transform a shape layer:

1. Choose the Path Selection tool (A or Shift-A).
2. Click a shape in the image window.
   or
   Click a shape layer thumbnail on the Layers palette.
3. Click the highlighted shape to display its anchor points (and its bounding box, too, if Show Bounding Box is checked on the options bar) **1**.
4. Follow the instructions on pages 287–290 to transform the shape.

To modify the contour of a shape layer:

1. Choose the Direct Selection tool (A or Shift -A).
2. Click a shape in the image window.
   or
   Click a shape layer thumbnail on the Layers palette.
3. Click the edge of the highlighted shape to display its anchor points **2**.
4. Follow the instructions on pages 324–325 to reshape the path.

To deactivate a shape layer's vector mask:

Shift-click the vector mask thumbnail for the shape layer on the Layers palette. An X will appear over the thumbnail **3** and the entire layer's fill contents will display.

(If you want to restore the masking effect, Shift-click the vector mask thumbnail again to remove the X.)

To paste a path object from Illustrator into Photoshop as a shape layer:

1. In Adobe Illustrator, copy a vector object.

2. In Photoshop, choose Edit > Paste. In the Paste dialog box, click Paste As: Shape Layer, then click OK **1**. The shape layer will be filled with the current Foreground color, but it won't have a stroke. You have pasted only the vector mask outline for the shape layer.

To use pathfinder options to add to or subtract from a shape:

1. Create a shape layer.

2. Leave the vector mask thumbnail for the new shape layer selected.

3. Make sure a shape tool is chosen and the Shape Layers button 🞔 is selected on the options bar.

4. Click a pathfinder button on the options bar **2**.

5. Drag partially across the existing shape. A new shape path will be created that either extends or subtracts from the existing shape, depending on which pathfinder button you clicked **3**.

TIP To reverse what a vector mask shape clips and reveals, select the mask with the Path Selection tool, then on the options bar, click the Subtract from Shape Area button **4**; click the Add to Shape Area button **5** to restore the original clipping setup.

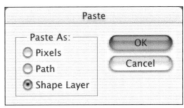

1 *Click Paste As: **Shape Layer** in the **Paste** dialog box.*

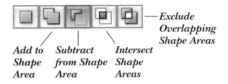

Add to Shape Area — Subtract from Shape Area — Intersect Shape Areas — Exclude Overlapping Shape Areas

2 *Click a **pathfinder** button on the options bar. We chose Subtract from Shape Area.*

3 *The new shape path **subtracts** (cuts out) from the existing shape area.*

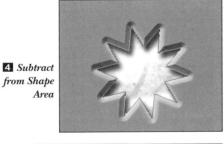

4 *Subtract from Shape Area*

Subtract from shape area (-)

5 *Add to Shape Area*

Add to shape area (+)

Quick switcheroo

To change the fill contents of a selected shape layer to a gradient or pattern fill, or to change the command in a selected adjustment layer (e.g., Hue/Saturation to Levels), choose from the Layer > **Change Layer Content** submenu.

1 *Create a custom shape.*

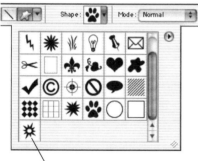

2 *The new shape appears on the Custom Shape Preset picker.*

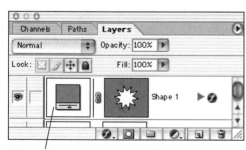

3 *The shape layer thumbnail*

If you've altered the contour of a preset shape or pasted in a shape from Adobe Illustrator, you can then add that new shape to the **Custom Shape Preset** picker so you can use it again.

To save a shape as a preset:

1. Customize a shape **1**.
   or
   Create a new shape layer from an Illustrator object that you've pasted into Photoshop.

2. Make sure the vector mask thumbnail for the shape layer on the Layers palette is selected.

3. Choose Edit > Define Custom Shape, enter a Name in the Shape Name dialog box, then click OK. The new custom shape will appear at the bottom of the Custom Shape Preset picker **2**, and it will stay on the picker even if you exit/quit and relaunch Photoshop. It will be removed from the picker, however, if you click Replace as you load in another shape library or the default shape library.

The **fill** contents of a shape layer can be changed at any time.

To change the fill contents of a shape layer:

1. Double-click the shape layer thumbnail on the Layers palette (it has a slider icon) **3**.
   or
   Choose a shape layer, then choose Layer > Layer Content Options.

2. Choose a new color from the Color Picker, then click OK.

Before you can perform pixel edits on a shape layer (e.g., apply brush strokes or a filter) or change a shape's vector mask into a (pixel) layer mask, the shape layer must be **rasterized.**

To rasterize a shape layer:

1. Choose a shape layer **1**.

2. From the Layer > Rasterize submenu, choose:

Shape to convert the shape layer into a filled pixel shape on a transparent layer, without a vector mask. You can now paint or edit the layer **2**.

Fill Content to convert the shape layer's fill content into a pixel area clipped by the existing vector mask. You can now paint or edit the layer **3**.

Vector Mask to convert the vector mask into a pixel-based layer mask in the exact same shape and position as the vector mask. The fill content is still an editable solid-color fill. The layer mask can be repositioned within the layer **4**.

Layer converts a shape layer into a filled pixel shape, or converts a vector mask into a layer mask **5**.

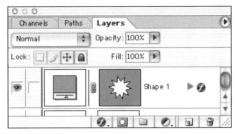

1 *The original shape layer on the Layers palette*

2 *The Rasterize > **Shape** command removed the clipping path and the adjustable fill.*

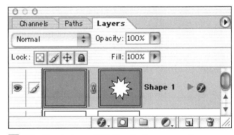

3 *The Rasterize > **Fill Content** command converted the adjustable fill into a normal pixel area.*

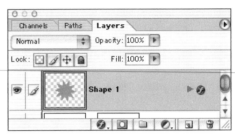

4 *The Rasterize > **Vector Mask** command converted the vector mask into a layer mask.*

5 *The Rasterize > **Layer** command produced the same results as in figure **2**, above.*

TYPE 19

How will it look?

Editable type that you create in Photoshop consists of pixels in the same resolution as the image. Photoshop (and ImageReady) use a typeface's vector outlines when resizing editable type and when outputting it to PDF, EPS, or a PostScript printer. Vector type has sharp edges and outputs at the printer's resolution.

Vector

1 *This is sharp,* **editable** *vector type.*

Pixels

2 *This type was* **rasterized** *and then filters were applied to it.*

3 *Click the palette button* 📋 *on the options bar to show/hide the* **Character/ Paragraph** *palettes.*

IN THIS CHAPTER you'll learn how to create different kinds of editable type; select type; change character and paragraph attributes; change paragraph type to point type and vice versa; transform, move, and warp type; rasterize a type layer into pixels; produce special effects, such as screened back type; fill type with imagery; create type selections; create a type mask for an adjustment layer; create type in a spot color channel; and use word processing commands (Find and Replace Text and Check Spelling).

Creating type

Different kinds of type

When type is created in Photoshop using the Horizontal Type tool or Vertical Type tool **1**, it appears instantly in the image window, and a new layer is created automatically for it. It's also fully **editable.** Not only can you change its attributes (e.g., font, style, point size, color, kerning, tracking, leading, alignment, and baseline shift), you can also transform it, apply layer effects to it, change its blending mode, or change its opacity.

What can't be done to an editable type layer? You can't apply filters or paint strokes to it or fill it with a gradient or a pattern. In order to apply those kinds of edits, you have to **rasterize** the type layer into pixels (Layer > Rasterize > Type) **2**. But you can't have your cake and eat it, too. Once type is rasterized, its typographic attributes (e.g., font, style) can't be changed.

Attributes are chosen for type using the Character palette **3**, the Paragraph palette, and the options bar **4**.

(Continued on the following page)

Editable vs. Rasterized Type

4 *The* **options bar** *for the* **Type** *tool*

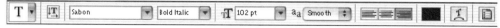

Using the Horizontal or Vertical Type Mask tool, you can create a selection in the shape of characters on any layer. You can then convert the type selection into a layer mask (see page 278), save it as an alpha channel, or save it as a shape layer for later use (see page 334).

Because **editable type** (as opposed to type that's created as a selection) automatically appears on its own layer, it can be edited, moved, transformed, restacked, or otherwise modified without affecting any other layer. You can be very casual about where you position editable type initially, and about which typographic attributes you choose for it, since it's so easy to edit afterward.

Note: Type that's created in a Bitmap, Indexed Color, or Multichannel image will appear on the Background, not on a layer, and can't be edited.

To create an editable type layer:

1. Choose the Horizontal Type tool or Vertical Type tool (T or Shift-T) **1**.

2. To create point type, click to define an insertion point (see the sidebar).
   or
   To create paragraph type, drag a marquee to define the boundaries of the bounding box for the text to fit into.

3. From the options bar, do any of the following:
   Choose a **font** family **2**.
   Choose a font **style.**
   Choose or enter a **size** (.10 to 1296 pt.).
   Choose an **Anti-aliasing** method 🅰️ **3**: Sharp (sharpest), Crisp (somewhat sharp), Strong (heavier), or Smooth (smoothest). Photoshop will smooth the edges of the type by introducing partially transparent pixels along its edges. With anti-aliasing off (None), type will have jagged edges (**1**–**4**, next page).

   Click an **Alignment** button to align point type relative to its original insertion point, or to align paragraph type to the

---

Point or paragraph?

Point type is created when you click in the image window with the Horizontal Type tool or Vertical Type tool, and then type some characters. This kind of type keeps on going, disappearing off the edge of the image, until you press Enter/Return. Use this method if you want to control hyphenation and line breaks manually in just a few lines of text.

Paragraph type is created when you drag in the image window with the Horizontal or Vertical Type tool to define an area for type to fit into before typing your characters. It's better suited for larger text blocks. From the Paragraph palette menu, you can choose between two algorithms for paragraph type—**Adobe Single-line Composer** and **Adobe Every-line Composer**—that control how Photoshop flows type to the next line when the type reaches the edge of the text bounding box. The differences between the two algorithms are subtle.

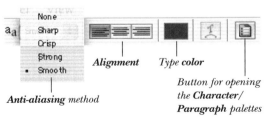

1 *The first two* **type** *tools create editable type; the second two create a type selection.*

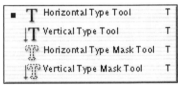

Font family   Font style   Font size

2 *The left side of the* **Horizontal Type** *tool options bar*

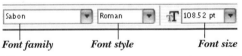

Anti-aliasing *method*   Alignment   Type color   Button for opening the **Character/ Paragraph** palettes

3 *The right side of the* **Horizontal Type** *tool options bar*

1 *No anti-aliasing*

2 *Crisp anti-aliasing*

3 *Strong anti-aliasing*

4 *Smooth anti-aliasing*

5 *The **Alignment** buttons control where paragraph type is positioned within its bounding box (or where point type is positioned relative to the insertion point).*

left edge, right edge, or center of its bounding box **5**.

Choose a **color** for the type by clicking the swatch, then choosing a color from the Color Picker (or from the Swatches palette or Color palette).

If the Character and Paragraph palettes aren't already open, click the palettes button, 🖼 then adjust any of the settings on either palette (you'll learn about these palettes throughout this chapter).

4. Type the text into the image window.

5. Press Enter on the keypad or click the ✔ on the options bar to accept the new text. (To cancel it, press Esc or click the ⊘ button.)

TIP Each time type is created using the Horizontal or Vertical Type tool, a new layer is created **6**. If you tend to create type by trial and error, and the layers start to overpopulate, you can periodically delete any layers you don't need.

Create a preset!

After styling your type, click the Tool Preset picker thumbnail or arrowhead ⊤▾ on the left side of the options bar, click the **New Tool Preset** button, 🔲 enter a name, then click OK. This is like creating a style sheet. You can then choose this tool preset from either the Tool Preset picker or the Tool Presets palette any time you create type.

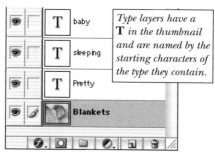

*Type layers have a **T** in the thumbnail and are named by the starting characters of the type they contain.*

6 *For the greatest flexibility, place individual words or characters on separate layers. Then they can be moved around independently.*

NEW **To add type on or inside a path:**

1. Create a path, as per the instructions on pages 316–320. The path can be open or closed.

2. Click a path on the Paths palette.

3. Choose the Horizontal Type tool T or Vertical Type tool |T (T or Shift-T).

4. Click on the outside or inside of the path, then start typing **1**. You could also copy type from another object and paste it onto or into the path.

5. *Optional:* If you place type on the edge of a path, you can drag it along the path or to the other side of the path using the Path Selection tool.

TIP To shift type upward or downward from the edge of a path, select the type you want to shift, then drag the baseline shift icon A$^a_+$ on the Character palette to the left or right.

TIP If you want to draw standard paragraph or point text and the pointer is near a path, you can disable the path type feature by Shift-clicking.

Editing text

In order to edit text, you first need to **select** it. You can select a single character, a word, or all the characters on a type layer. You can also select the bounding box for a whole block of text.

To select all or some characters on a type layer:

1. Choose the Horizontal Type tool T or Vertical Type tool |T (T or Shift-T), click in the type to create an insertion point, then drag across one or more characters or words to select them **2**. Or double-click a word to select the whole word; or double-click a word, then drag to select multiple words; or drag downward to select multiple lines.
   or
   With any kind of tool selected, double-click the T icon for the type layer on

Editable type from Illustrator

You can export type from Illustrator CS and then import it into Photoshop CS, where it will remain editable. To perform this magical feat, in Illustrator, make sure the type is on its own layer and has a stroke color of None. Next, use Illustrator's **Export** command to save the file in Photoshop (.psd) format (check Write Layers and Preserve Text Editability). Now you can open the file in Photoshop.

1 *Type is entered **inside** a **path** using the Horizontal Type tool.*

2 *Drag across the characters you want to **select.***

Selecting type with a type tool

Select text **string**	Drag across it. Or click at beginning of the text string, then Shift-click at the end.
Select **word**	Double-click
Select **line**	Triple-click
Select **paragraph**	Quadruple-click
Select **all**	Double-click the thumbnail on the Layers palette; or click in the text, then press Ctrl-A/Cmd-A

the Layers palette. All the text on that layer will become selected, and the appropriate type tool will become selected automatically.

2. After performing the text edits, to take the text tool out of edit mode and commit to the editing changes, click the ✔ on the options bar, or press Enter on the keypad, or click any other tool, or click a different layer.

(If you need to cancel your editing changes before committing to them, click the ⊘ on the options bar or press Esc.)

TIP To apply layer effects to a type layer (or to edit an existing effect), double-click the layer on the Layers palette (not the layer name). This opens the Layer Style dialog box.

TIP If you want to see the bounding box for a block of text, choose the Move tool (V), click the type layer on the Layers palette, and check Show Bounding Box on the options bar.

To convert paragraph type to point type:

1. Click the type layer in the Layers palette.

2. Choose Layer > Type > Convert to Point Text. A carriage return will be added at the end of every line of type except the last line.

To convert point type to paragraph type:

1. Click the type layer in the Layers palette.

2. Choose Layer > Type > Convert to Paragraph Text. To reshape the resulting bounding box, choose a type tool, click the converted text, then drag any of the handles on the bounding box (you may need to enlarge the image window to locate the handles). Also delete any unwanted hyphens.

To resize characters uniformly by number, change the **point size** on the options bar or the Character palette.

To resize type by choosing a value:

1. On the Layers palette, click the layer that contains the type you want to resize.

2. Choose the Horizontal or Vertical Type tool, then select the characters or words you want to scale.
   or
   To resize all the characters in the layer, don't select anything.

3. On the options bar, drag the font size **NEW** icon 𝕋 to the left or right (Alt-drag/ Option-drag for finer increments) **1**; or enter a value (0–1000%); or choose from the pop-up menu **2**. You can also change point sizes via the Character palette **3**.

Type can also be **scaled interactively**.

To resize type manually:

1. Click the type layer on the Layers palette.

2. Choose the Move tool (V) and check Show Bounding Box on the options bar.

3. Drag a corner handle to scale the height and width simultaneously, or drag a side handle to scale just the height or width.
   or
   Shift-drag a corner handle to preserve the proportions of the type as you scale it **4**.

4. To commit to the scale change, click the ✔ on the options bar, or double-click the text block. (To cancel the scale change before committing to it, click the ⊘ on the options bar or press Esc.)

TIP To change the Vertical Scale or Horizontal Scale via the Character palette, see the sidebar on page 351.

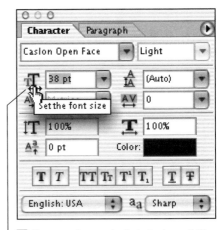

1 *Drag the font size icon to the left or right on the options bar...*

2 *...or enter a value, or choose a point size from the pop-up menu.*

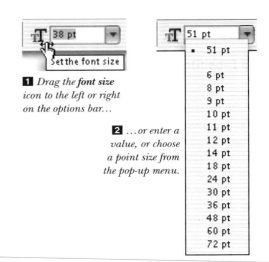

3 *You can also use the font size icon, field, or pop-up menu on the Character palette to change point sizes.*

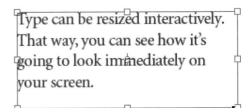

4 *Shift-drag a corner handle to resize type interactively while preserving its proportions.*

Opening the Character palette

Choose the Horizontal Type tool T or Vertical Type tool ⏐T (T or Shift-T), then click the ▤ button on the options bar (or choose Window > Character).

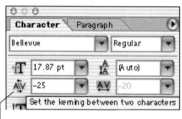

1 *The **kerning** icon, field, and pop-up menu on the Character palette*

Kern
Kern

2 *Use a negative kerning value (–100, in this case) to tighten the spacing **between** characters.*

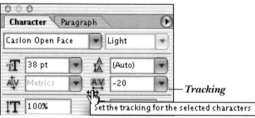

3 *The **Character** palette has some features that aren't found on the options bar.*

T R A C K I N G   T I P S

Tracking can help or hinder readability, depending on how high the tracking values are. Try not to overdo it!

4 *Occasionally we'll spread out **little bits** of text, as in the headline in this illustration—but never whole paragraphs.*

Kerning affects the spacing between a pair of text characters.

To apply kerning:
Method 1

1. On the Layers palette, click a type layer.

2. Choose the Horizontal or Vertical Type tool, then click to create an insertion point between two characters.

3. Open the Character palette (see the sidebar).

4. Choose Metrics from the Kerning pop-up menu on the Character palette to apply the font's built-in kerning, or choose Optical to have Photoshop control the kerning.
   or
   Drag the kerning icon 🅰🆅 **1** to the left **NEW** or right; or enter a value (–1000 to 1000); or choose a value from the pop-up menu. A negative value moves characters closer together **2**, a positive value spreads them apart. (See page 551 for kerning and tracking shortcuts.)

Method 2

With a type tool chosen and the cursor inserted between two characters, press Alt/Option plus the left or right arrow key.

Tracking is like kerning, except it affects multiple characters instead of just a pair.

To apply tracking:

1. On the Layers palette, click a type layer.

2. *Optional:* Choose the Horizontal or Vertical Type tool, then select some text. Don't do this if you want to apply tracking to all the type on the layer.

3. Open the Character palette (see the sidebar).

4. Drag the tracking icon 🅰🆅 **3** to the **NEW** left or right; or enter a value in the field (–1000 to 1000); or choose a value from the pop-up menu. A negative value moves characters closer together, a positive value spreads them apart **4**.
   or
   If type is selected, you can press Alt/Option and the left or right arrow key.

349

Leading is the space that separates each line of text from the one above it. Each character can have its own leading value; the highest value in a line controls that line. Consequently, if you apply different leading values to different lines of paragraph text and then edit the text so as to cause it to reflow, the spacing between lines may change as a result.

We can't guarantee that your readers will find your writing interesting, but if you use an adequate amount of leading between the lines, at least it won't be a strain to read. So let the type eat up a bit more space on the page—at least your reader's eyes won't tire.

P.S. To create a bulky amount of paragraph type, use a layout or Web design program rather than Photoshop.

To adjust leading in horizontal type:

1. On the Layers palette, click a type layer.

2. *Optional:* Using the Horizontal Type tool, highlight the line or lines of text that you want to apply leading values to. To apply leading to point type, select the whole line. If you don't highlight text, all the type on the layer will be affected. Leading doesn't affect the first line in a paragraph.

3. Drag the leading icon **1**–**2** to the left or right (Alt-drag/Option-drag for finer increments); or enter a value in the field (.01 to 5000 pt.); or choose a value from the pop-up menu.

TIP Auto leading is calculated as a percentage of the font size. The ratio is set in the Justification dialog box, which is opened from the Paragraph palette menu. The default value is 120% of the font size. The Auto leading amount for 30 pt. type, for example, would be 36 pt.

TIP To adjust the vertical spacing between characters in vertical type, highlight the characters you want to adjust, then change the Tracking value on the Character palette.

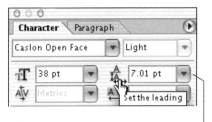

1 *The **leading** area on the **Character** palette*

It will be well, however, always to bear in mind, that cake of every sort is to be partaken of as a luxury, not eaten for a full meal. Those who attend evening parties several times a week, can hardly take too small a quantity of the sweet and rich preparations. Many a young lady loses her appetite bloom and health by indulgence in these tempting but pernicious delicacies; and dyspeptic complaints frequently are aggravated, if not originated, by the absurd fashion of making our evening circles places for eating and drinking, rather than social and mental enjoyment. They manage these things better in Paris. —*Sara Josepha Hale, 1841*

It will be well, however, always to bear in mind, that cake of every sort is to be partaken of as a luxury, not eaten for a full meal. Those who attend evening parties several times a week, can hardly take too small a quantity of the sweet and rich preparations. Many a young lady loses her appetite bloom and health by indulgence in these tempting but pernicious delicacies; and dyspeptic complaints frequently are aggravated, if not originated, by the absurd fashion of making our evening circles places for eating and drinking, rather than social and mental enjoyment. They manage these things better in Paris. —*Sara Josepha Hale, 1841*

2 *The type in both paragraphs illustrated above has the same point size but different **leading**. Leading affects both the overall look of a page and the readability of the text.*

Adjust Leading

Stretch it out

Use the Horizontal Scale or Vertical Scale command to make characters wider or narrower **1**. First, with the Horizontal or Vertical Type tool, select the characters or words you want to scale; or if you want to scale all the characters in the layer, don't select anything. Then drag the vertical scale $\downarrow$T or horizontal scale **T** icon on the Character palette to the left or the right (0–1000%). **NEW**

stretch *Horizontal scale 50%*

stretch *Horizontal scale 100% (normal)*

stretch *Horizontal scale 200%*

stretch *Vertical scale 300%*

1 *Type can be **scaled** horizontally, vertically, or uniformly (both).*

You can change the **orientation** of existing horizontal type to vertical, or vice versa.

To change type orientation:

1. On the Layers palette, click a type layer **2**.

2. Choose a type tool, then click the Change Text Orientation button $\boxed{\text{T}}$ on the options bar **3**.
   or
   Choose Change Text Orientation from the Character palette menu.
   or
   Choose Layer > Type > Horizontal or Vertical.

   You may need to reposition the type after applying either command.

TIP To rotate vertical type a different way, double-click its layer thumbnail (or highlight just the characters you want to rotate, if you don't want to rotate them all), then choose Standard Roman Vertical Alignment from the Character palette menu to uncheck the command **4**. This command isn't available for horizontal type.

2 *The original **vertical** type*

3 *The same type after clicking the **Change Text Orientation** button on the options bar*

4 *The original vertical type after unchecking **Standard Roman Vertical Alignment** on the Character palette menu.*

Change Type Orientation

351

To style type using the Character palette:

1. Select the type to be modified with a type tool, or to modify a whole type layer, click the layer.

2. Click any style button on the Character palette **1** (use tool tips to identify them) or choose any of these styles from the Character palette menu **2**:

   Faux Bold simulates the bold style; **Faux Italic** simulates the italic style. Faux Bold isn't available for warped text.

   All Caps converts all letters to uppercase.

   Small Caps converts lowercase characters to small caps.

   Superscript shrinks type and raises it above the baseline; **Subscript** shrinks type and lowers it below the baseline.

   NEW **Underline Left** and **Underline Right** produce underlines in vertical type.

   Strikethrough produces a horizontal line through horizontal type or a vertical line through vertical type.

   Fractional Widths allows Photoshop to use fractions of pixels for type spacing for optimal appearance (it applies to the entire layer). Uncheck this option only for small type to be output online.

   System Layout allows you to preview text as it would appear in the current operating system. Use this for designing interfaces, such as dialog boxes or menus.

   No Break forces the currently selected words to stay on the same line (e.g., to keep the words "Mr. Smith" together).

   Note: The options from Oldstyle through Fractions are available only for type set in an OpenType or other font that contains the desired characters.

   NEW **Oldstyle** numerals **3** are shorter than standard numerals. Some old-style numerals descend below the baseline.

   NEW **Ordinals** substitutes specially formatted superscript characters (e.g., 8th, 3rd).

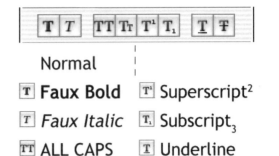

1 *The **style** buttons on the Character palette*

2 *The **Character** palette menu*

3 *Old-style numerals are beautiful!*

> You are cordially invited
> to attend the wedding
> of
> Mopsy and Flopsy
> ❖
> Saturday, November 3rd, 2003
> at
> 3195-34 Old Hill Lane
> Springfield, Pennsylvania
> RSVP 119-356-7889

Character Palette Options

Ersatz

If you're using a font for which no actual bold (or italic) font is installed on your system and you turn on the **Faux Bold** (or **Faux Italic**) option, Photoshop whips up an ersatz bold (or italic) version of that font for you. Type purists (ourselves included) will notice that the faux style doesn't quite match the grace and shape of the authentic font.

1 *A swash glyph*

2 *A titling capital*

3 *Some ornaments in the Minion Pro font.*

4 *The baseline shift area of the Character palette*

+20 pts

0 pts

Normal baseline

−20 pts

5 *A positive baseline shift value raises characters upward; a negative value moves them downward. Note: To shift whole lines of type, use leading—not baseline shift.*

NEW **Swash 1** substitutes swash glyphs, which are stylized characters with extended strokes.

NEW **Titling 2** substitutes special capital letters.

NEW **Contextual Alternates** are glyphs that provide better character joining for some letter pairs.

NEW **Stylistic Alternates** substitutes ornate characters for some letters.

NEW **Ornaments 3** are decorative symbols (use for borders or paragraph dividers).

Ligatures are combinations of the characters fi, fl, ff, ffi, and ffl, which are joined together (they look better!).

Discretionary Ligatures substitutes special characters for some letter pairs, such as "ct," "st," and "ft."

NEW

Fractions substitutes preformatted fraction characters. Type in the numerator, a slash, and the denominator, select them all, then choose this command—presto!

Reset Character resets the selected characters to the default Character palette settings.

The Standard Vertical Roman Alignment and Change Text Orientation commands are discussed on page 351.

Use the **baseline shift** feature to shift a character or two, or to shift type on a path.

To shift characters above or below the normal baseline:

1. On the Layers palette, click the layer that contains the type you want to shift.

2. Choose the Horizontal or Vertical Type tool (T or Shift-T), then select the characters you want to shift. Otherwise, all the characters on the layer will be shifted.

3. On the Character palette, drag the baseline shift icon to the left or the right (Alt-drag/Option-drag for finer increments); or enter a baseline shift value **4**. A positive value shifts characters above the normal baseline **5**; a negative value shifts them below the baseline.

Paragraph settings

For paragraph type, Photoshop offers a range of formatting options. By foregoing the manual control you have with point text, you get a pretty sophisticated layout tool. The Paragraph palette lets you choose settings for justification, alignment, indents, and paragraph spacing, and the palette menu allows you to fine-tune those options.

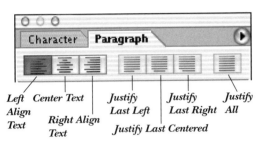

Left Align Text   Center Text   Justify Last Left   Justify Last Right   Justify All
Right Align Text   Justify Last Centered

1 The **alignment** and **justification** buttons at the top of the **Paragraph** palette, for horizontal type

To set paragraph alignment and justification for horizontal type:

1. On the Layers palette, click a type layer.

2. If you want to modify all the paragraphs in the layer, don't select any text.
   or
   To modify one or more paragraphs, choose the Horizontal Type tool T (T or Shift-T), then click in one paragraph or select a series of consecutive paragraphs.

3. If the Paragraph palette isn't open, click the 🗎 button on the options bar, then click the Paragraph tab.

4. Click an alignment and/or justification button at the top of the palette **1**:

   The buttons in the first group—**Left Align Text, Center Text,** and **Right Align Text**—align type to an edge or the center of the text bounding box **2**. (These options can be used on point type.)

   The buttons in the second group— **Justify Last Left, Justify Last Centered,** and **Justify Last Right**—justify the type, forcing all but the last line to fill the space between the margins **3**.

   The last button, **Justify All,** forces *all* the lines to fill the space, even the last line.

5. Check Hyphenate at the bottom of the palette to enable automatic hyphenation. Be sure to check this option for justified text to help eliminate large, unsightly gaps between words.

TIP To change the alignment and/or justification for vertical type, the procedure is the same as outlined above, except the buttons have different labels.

Left Align Text

Whoever you are holding me now in hand
Whoever you are holding me now in hand,
Without one thing all will be useless,
I give you fair warning before you attempt me further,
I am not what you supposed, but far different…

Center Text

Whoever you are holding me now in hand
Whoever you are holding me now in hand,
Without one thing all will be useless,
I give you fair warning before you attempt me further,
I am not what you supposed, but far different…

Right Align Text

Whoever you are holding me now in hand
Whoever you are holding me now in hand,
Without one thing all will be useless,
I give you fair warning before you attempt me further,
I am not what you supposed, but far different…
Walt Whitman

2 Paragraph **alignment** options

Justify Last Left

Civilization is the encouragement of differences. Civilization thus becomes a synonym of democracy. Force, violence, pressure, or compulsion with a view to conformity, is both uncivilized and undemocratic. —*Mohandas Gandhi*

Justify Last Centered

Civilization is the encouragement of differences. Civilization thus becomes a synonym of democracy. Force, violence, pressure, or compulsion with a view to conformity, is both uncivilized and undemocratic. —*Mohandas Gandhi*

Justify Last Right

Civilization is the encouragement of differences. Civilization thus becomes a synonym of democracy. Force, violence, pressure, or compulsion with a view to conformity, is both uncivilized and undemocratic. —*Mohandas Gandhi*

Justify All

Civilization is the encouragement of differences. Civilization thus becomes a synonym of democracy. Force, violence, pressure, or compulsion with a view to conformity, is both uncivilized and   undemocratic.   —*Mohandas   Gandhi*

3 Paragraph **justification** options

Alignment and Justification

Good values

To enter a value in a nondefault unit on the Paragraph palette, type the unit after the value: **in** for inches, **pt** for points, **mm** for millimeters, **cm** for centimeters, **px** for pixels, or **pica** for picas. The value will be converted automatically to the unit currently chosen in Edit (Photoshop, in Mac) > Preferences > Units & Rulers > Units: Type.

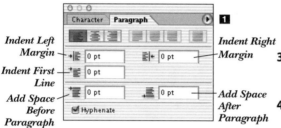

Indent Left Margin
Indent First Line
Add Space Before Paragraph
Indent Right Margin
Add Space After Paragraph

1

Civilization is the encouragement of differences. Civilization thus becomes a synonym of democracy. Force, violence, pressure, or compulsion with a view to conformity, is both uncivilized and undemocratic. —*Mohandas Gandhi*

Indents of 0 (zero)

Civilization is the encouragement of differences. Civilization thus becomes a synonym of democracy. Force, violence, pressure, or compulsion with a view to conformity, is both uncivilized and undemocratic. —*Mohandas Gandhi*

Indent 2 picas right and left

Civilization is the encouragement of differences. Civilization thus becomes a synonym of democracy. Force, violence, pressure, or compulsion with a view to conformity, is both uncivilized and undemocratic. —*Mohandas Gandhi*

Indent 16 pt. first line

2 *Examples of indents*

Civilization is the encouragement of differences.

Civilization thus becomes a synonym of democracy.

Force, violence, pressure, or compulsion with a view to conformity, is both uncivilized and undemocratic.

3 *Add Space Before Paragraph (7 pt.)*

The paragraph **indent** and **spacing-between-paragraph** controls let you shape your paragraphs for improved readability.

To adjust paragraph indents and spacing for horizontal type:

1. On the Layers palette, click the type layer you want to modify.

2. If you want to modify all the paragraphs in the layer, don't select any text.
   or
   To modify one or more paragraphs, choose the Horizontal Type tool **T** (T or Shift-T), then click in one paragraph or select a series of consecutive paragraphs.

3. If the Paragraph palette isn't open, click the ▣ button on the options bar, then click the Paragraph tab.

4. Change the **Indent Left Margin, Indent Right Margin,** or **Indent First Line** value **1**–**2**. Use an Indent First Line value to make text more readable if you don't have room to add space between paragraphs. Don't apply an Indent First Line value above zero *and* add space between paragraphs (bad typesetting!). You can use a combination of left and right indentation values to make a pull quote or bulleted list stand out.
   and/or
   Enter **Add Space Before Paragraph 3** and **Add Space After Paragraph** values.

TIP To change the alignment and/or justification for vertical type, the procedure is the same as above, except the fields have different labels.

TIP When you choose a type tool and a type layer containing paragraph type and click the type in the image window, the bounding box for the type becomes visible. If you drag any handle on the bounding box, the type will reflow. If you want to reshape the bounding box while scaling the type horizontally and/or vertically, Ctrl-drag/Cmd-drag any handle (this works like a temporary Move tool).

Paragraph Indents and Spacing

These are some of the **paragraph settings** that can make the difference between okay-looking type and professional-looking type.

To fine-tune paragraph settings:

1. Select a paragraph or paragraphs, as per steps 1–2 on the previous page.

2. From the **Paragraph** palette menu, choose any of the following:

   Roman Hanging Punctuation to have Photoshop nudge punctuation marks that fall at the beginning and end of lines outside the type bounding box.

   Justification and **Hyphenation** to specify the limits within which the Photoshop algorithms can operate as they adjust text to optimize its appearance —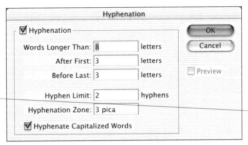. (In the Justification dialog box, you can also set the Auto Leading value as a percentage of the type size.) Enter a Glyph Scaling value above the default 100% in the Justification dialog box to allow Photoshop to adjust the widths of characters (glyphs) in order to optimize how the text fits inside the bounding box.

   Adobe Single-line Composer ❸ or **Adobe Every-line Composer** ❹ for the method Photoshop will use to evaluate potential word breaks (hyphenation) in a paragraph, factoring in letter and word spacing values, in an attempt to minimize hyphenation. The Adobe Single-line Composer does this line by line; the Adobe Every-line Composer does it by evaluating the appearance of the paragraph as a whole. Every-line Composer can change the word breaks at the beginning of a paragraph in order to create more visually appealing word breaks toward the end of the paragraph. We like Every-line Composer.

   Reset Paragraph to reset all the currently selected paragraphs to their default settings.

❶ *In the **Justification** dialog box, choose Minimum, Desired, and Maximum values for Photoshop to adhere to when adjusting line widths in justified text.*

❷ *In the **Hyphenation** dialog box, choose settings for word breaks created in paragraph type.*

> Civilization is the encouragement of differences. Civilization thus becomes a synonym of democracy. Force, violence, pressure, or compulsion with a view to conformity, is both uncivilized and undemocratic.
> —*Mohandas Gandhi*

❸ *Adobe Single-line Composer goes through paragraphs line by line as it hyphenates words and adjusts the spacing between them.*

> Civilization is the encouragement of differences. Civilization thus becomes a synonym of democracy. Force, violence, pressure, or compulsion with a view to conformity, is both uncivilized and undemocratic.
> —*Mohandas Gandhi*

❹ *Every-line Composer considers each paragraph as a whole as it strives to optimize its appearance.*

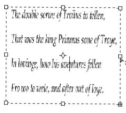

The double sorwe of Troilus to tellen,

That was the king Priamus sone of Troye,

In lovinge, how his aventures fellen

Fro wo to wele, and after out of Ioye,

1 *The original type*

2 *A **Scale** transformation changes the shape of the bounding box and **distorts** the type (also true for Skew). The type remains editable.*

3 *Skew*

4 *Rotate: Unlike Scale and Skew, the Rotate transformation doesn't distort the characters.*

The double sorwe

of Troilus to

tellen,

That was the king

Priamus sone of

Troye,

5 *Here the Horizontal Type tool was used to transform the **bounding box** for paragraph type. The characters don't change in shape or scale.*

Special effects with type

The transform commands, which we discussed in Chapter 15, reshape type and its bounding box. Editable type can be moved, scaled, rotated, and skewed. You can do the same to rasterized type, plus apply perspective and distortion. You can transform a whole block of type, but not individual characters.

Another way to transform a block of point or paragraph type is to choose the Move tool (V), choose a type layer on the Layers palette, check Show Bounding Box on the options bar, then move any of the handles on the type's bounding box using the same techniques as for Free Transform.

And finally, a block of point or paragraph type can also be transformed by choosing the type layer on the Layers palette, then choosing Edit > Free Transform. Move the handles to transform the type. This method works when any tool except a pen tool, shape tool, or path selection tool is chosen.

To transform a type bounding box and the type inside it:

Follow the instructions for Free Transform on pages 287–290.
or
On the Layers palette, double-click the type layer thumbnail for paragraph type, then hold down Ctrl/Cmd and use the shortcuts for Free Transform (see page 289) **1**–**4**.

Follow these instructions if you want to modify the overall shape of a **block** of type without distorting the characters inside it.

To transform a type bounding box but not the type:

1. On the Layers palette, double-click the type layer thumbnail for paragraph type.
2. Position the cursor over a handle, pause, then drag to scale the bounding box. The type will reflow **5**.
   or

(Continued on the following page)

Position the cursor outside one of the corners of the box (curved, double-arrow pointer), then drag to rotate the box
or
Ctrl-drag/Cmd-drag in the box to move the whole type block.

3. To accept the changes, press Enter on the keypad or click the ✔ on the options bar. (To cancel, press Esc or click the ⊘ on the options bar.)

The **Warp Type** command, with its various style choices (arc, flag, arch, shell, wave, fish, etc.) transform the bounding box that contains type and distort the type accordingly. Warped type is fully editable.

To warp type on an editable layer:

1. On the Layers palette, click the text layer you want to warp.

2. To open the Warp Text dialog box **1**:
Choose Layer > Type > Warp Text.
or
Choose the Horizontal or Vertical Type tool (T or Shift-T), then click the Warp Text button ⬆ on the options bar.

3. Choose a transform option from the Style pop-up menu **2**.

4. Click Horizontal or Vertical as the overall orientation for the distortion.

5. Move the Bend, Horizontal Distortion, and Vertical Distortion sliders. Pause for the type to redraw onscreen, then readjust any of the sliders, if you like.

6. Click OK. The warped text icon will appear in the layer thumbnail **3**. With the type selected, you can reopen the Warp Text dialog box at any time and choose a different style or adjust the sliders.

TIP To scale or reshape warped type to make it fit into a specific area of a composition, click the warped type layer, choose the Move tool (check Show Bounding Box on the options bar), then reshape the bounding box. Pause, if necessary, for the type to redraw.

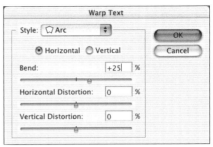

1 *The **Warp Text** dialog box*

Arc (horizontal)

This is a selection of paragraph type and it can be can be twisted and warped in a wide variety of ways. Have fun with it!

The snail walked slowly to the supermarket, where he ran into the bluebird family. Hello, he said, how's the birdseed selection? Mr.
Shell Upper *Bluebird said, Why would you care?*

Flag (horizontal)

This is a selection of paragraph type and it can be can be twisted and warped in a wide variety of ways. Have fun with it!

2 *Three of the **Warp Text** styles*

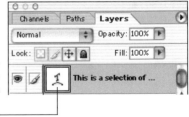

3 *A layer that contains **warped text** has this distinctive thumbnail icon.*

Warp Type

Missing fonts

If a font is missing (not available or installed) when you open a file that contains editable type, an alert box will display **1**, and an alert triangle will appear on the thumbnail of the offending layer on the Layers palette **2**. If you then try to edit a layer in which that font is used, another alert dialog box will appear. For each affected layer, you can either open the required font outside of Photoshop or elect to have font substitution occur.

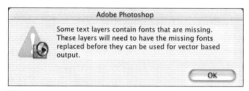

1 *The missing fonts alert dialog box*

2 *The missing fonts alert triangle on the Layers palette*

The Pattern Overlay effect The Pattern Overlay and
Gradient Overlay effects

3 *Editable type with effects applied*

A pattern Fill and the   A pattern Fill and the
Fresco filter   Palette Knife filter

4 *Rasterized type with filters applied*

To move a type layer:
Method 1
1. Choose the Move tool (V).
2. Right-click/Control-click on the type in the image window, and choose the name of the layer you want to move.
   or
   On the Layers palette, click the name of the layer you want to move.
3. Drag the type in the image window.
   or
   Press any arrow key.

Method 2
1. Double-click the type layer thumbnail (the T).
2. Ctrl-drag/Cmd-drag the type in the image window.

To rework type shapes using a filter, a tool (such as the Brush, Blur, Eraser, or Smudge tool), or the Transform > Distort or Perspective command, you must first convert the **type** into **pixels,** a process that's called rasterization **3**–**4**. Remember this important fact, though: Once type is converted to pixels, its typographic attributes can't be changed, period.

To rasterize type into pixels:
1. On the Layers palette, click the layer you want to rasterize. Or if you want to preserve this editable layer for later use, duplicate it and keep the duplicate selected.

2. Choose Layer > Rasterize > Type. The ways in which rasterized type can be dressed up are almost limitless—just use your imagination. Here's just one little idea: Turn on Lock Transparent Pixels on the Layers palette, fill the rasterized type with a pattern, apply a filter to it, turn off Lock Transparent Pixels, then use the Smudge tool to smudge the edges of the type shapes.

To paint within the confines of the rasterized type, choose the Brush tool and a Foreground color, turn on Lock

(Continued on the following page)

Move Type; Rasterize Type

Transparent Pixels for the type layer, then draw brushstrokes in the image window. To paint behind the type, do it on the layer directly below the type layer **1**.

TIP If you drag and drop, copy and paste, or place an editable type object from Adobe Illustrator into Photoshop, it will be rasterized into pixels automatically. Editable type (without a stroke) can be exported in Photoshop format from Adobe Illustrator and opened in Photoshop (see the sidebar on page 346).

Printing dark text on top of a picture can be tricky. The picture has to be **light** enough to allow the text to be readable, yet visible enough to be interpreted as an image.

To screen back an image behind type:

1. Choose the background image on the Layers palette. In our example, we will lighten the background behind a text layer.

2. Choose Layer > New Adjustment Layer > Levels, then click OK.
   or
   Choose Levels from the New Fill/Adjustment Layer pop-up menu , at the bottom of the Layers palette.

3. Check Preview.

4. Move the gray Input slider a little to the left.
   and
   Move the black Output slider a little to the right.

5. Click OK **2**–**3**.

TIP To further adjust levels, try a different blending mode (e.g., Screen or Lighten) or opacity for the Levels adjustment layer.

TIP To have the adjustment layer affect only the layer immediately below it, Alt-click/Option-click the line between the two layers on the Layers palette.

Try this!

To make an editable type layer look painterly without rasterizing it into pixels, make the type layer the base layer in a **clipping mask** (see page 283), and then draw brush strokes on the layer directly above the type layer. An advantage of using this method is that you can repaint, reposition, or delete the strokes without affecting the type layer.

1 *We painted on the rasterized type and on the layer below it.*

2 *We applied the **Levels** command to an adjustment layer over an image Background (Input Levels 0, .95, and 255, and Output Levels 92 and 255).*

3 *We selected the adjustment layer mask thumbnail, then filled the adjustment layer with a black-to-white gradient by dragging with the **Gradient** tool from the upper right corner to the lower left corner. This masked out the Levels effect in the upper right corner.*

Screen Image Behind Type

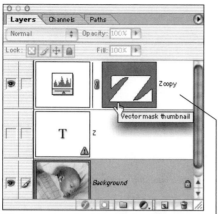

1 *A vector mask with a Levels adjustment layer*

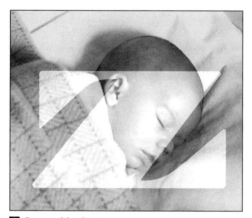

2 *Screened back type*

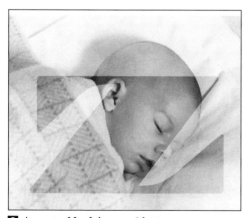

3 *A screened back image with type*

In these instructions, instead of screening back the image, as in the instructions on the previous page, you'll be **screening** back the **type,** thus allowing the image to be visible inside it.

To screen back type:

1. Create a type layer above an image layer.

2. Duplicate the type layer by dragging it over the New Layer button at the bottom of the Layers palette. Hide the original type layer by clicking its eye icon (keep it for future type edits).

3. With the duplicate layer chosen, choose Layer > Type > Convert to Shape. The type layer will be converted into a shape layer with a vector mask. The original type shapes will be preserved, but their typographic attributes will no longer be editable.

4. Choose Layer > Change Layer Content > Levels **1**. The clipping effect won't be visible until you perform the next step.

5. Move the gray Input (midtones) slider to the left to lighten the midtones in the type. You can also move the Input highlights slider.
   and
   Move the Output shadows slider to the right to reduce the contrast in the type.

6. Click OK **2**. Click back on the background image layer.

TIP Change the blending mode for the adjustment layer to restore some of the color to the background (try Overlay, Color Burn, or Hard Light mode). Lower the layer's opacity to lessen the Levels effect. You can also apply layer effects to the adjustment layer.

TIP To screen back an image with type, follow steps 1–4 above. For step 5, adjust the sliders to darken the type, remove any opacity or blending mode changes, then create an adjustment layer to lighten the imagery below the type layer (see the steps on the previous page) **3**.

Screen Back Type

To create fading type:

1. Create type, and leave the type layer active. It can be editable or rasterized.

2. Click the Add a Mask button 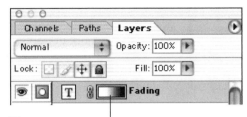 at the bottom of the Layers palette. A layer mask thumbnail will appear next to the layer name **1**.

3. Choose the Gradient tool (G or Shift-G).

4. On the options bar: Click the Gradient Preset picker arrowhead, then click the Foreground to Background swatch in the picker; click the Linear gradient button; choose Mode: Normal; and choose Opacity: 100%.

5. Drag in the image window from top to bottom or left to right, at least halfway across the type. The type layer mask will fill with a white-to-black gradient. Type will be hidden where black is present in the layer mask **2**.

TIP Click the type layer thumbnail or next to the layer name to modify the type or the layer; click the layer mask thumbnail to modify the layer mask. (Read more about layer masks in Chapter 15.)

Layer effects can be applied to editable type layers. (Read more about layer effects in Chapter 16.)

To apply layer effects to semitransparent type:

1. Create type on an editable type layer.

2. Double-click next to the type layer name.

3. Click one or more of the layer effect names on the left side of the Layer Style dialog box (e.g., Drop Shadow, Inner Shadow, Inner Glow, or Bevel & Emboss), and choose settings for each effect **3**–**5**. Apply the Satin effect to darken the contents of a type layer; use Color Overlay or Gradient Overlay to apply a tint; use Pattern Overlay to fill with a pattern.

4. Click Blending Options on the top left side of the Layer Style dialog box. For

1 *Layer mask thumbnail*

2 *Fading type*

3 *The type layer shapes were used to create the mask for the Paste Into layer.*

4 *A combination of layer effects applied to type*

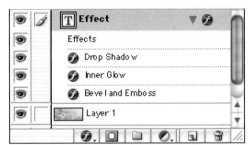

5 *More layer effects applied to type*

How to fill type with imagery

Use a **clipping mask** (see page 283); use the **Paste Into** command (see page 146); use a **layer mask** (see page 278); or use a **vector mask** (see page 328).

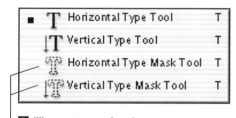

1 *A layer effect **Stroke** (Fill Type: Gradient) applied to editable type*

2 *The two **type mask** tools*

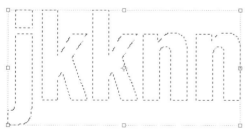

3 *A **type mask** selection*

Advanced Blending, drag the Fill Opacity slider to 0%. The fill opacity can also be adjusted on the Layers palette. It doesn't affect layer effects.

5. Click OK.

TIP To reposition the type with its effect, choose the type layer, choose the Move tool, then drag in the image window.

TIP To modify a layer effect, double-click the layer or the ✪ icon. This opens the Layer Style dialog box.

To apply a stroke to type:

1. Click a type layer on the Layers palette.

2. From the Add Layer Style pop-up menu ✪. at the bottom of the Layers palette, choose Stroke.

3. Choose a stroke Size, Position (Outside, Inside, or Center), Blend Mode, Opacity, Fill Type, and Color **1**.

4. Click OK.

Using the type mask tools

The **Type Mask** tools create a selection in the shape of type characters. You might want to do this to copy layer imagery in the shape of letters; to mask (limit) an adjustment layer's effect to a type selection; or to add a layer mask using type characters as the mask shapes (Reveal Selection or Hide Selection).

To create a type selection:

1. Activate the layer that you want the type selection to appear on (preferably not a type layer).

2. Choose the Horizontal Type Mask or Vertical Type Mask tool (T or Shift-T) **2**.

3. Click in the image window where you want the selection to appear. A Quick Mask will display temporarily.

4. Create and style the type **3**.

5. Click the ✔ on the options bar to accept the selection.

TIP Save a type selection to a new channel (click the Save Selection as Channel

(Continued on the following page)

Move Type Selection

button  at the bottom of the Channels palette) **1**. It can then be viewed on the Channels palette and loaded onto any layer or layer mask at any time.

Note: Editable text can extend outside the image area, and it can be moved back within the image area at any time. But once a type mask selection is saved and deselected, any parts of characters that extend outside the image area will be lost. If you want to reposition a type mask, do so before deselecting it.

To move a type selection:

1. Choose the Rectangular Marquee tool (M or Shift-M)—not the Move tool!

2. Click the New Selection button on the options bar.

3. Drag from inside the selection in the image window.
or
Press an arrow key. Hold down Shift and press an arrow key to move the type selection 10 screen pixels at a time.

TIP *Beware!* If you drag a type selection using the Move tool, you'll cut away and move pixels inside the letter shapes from the active layer **2**.

TIP To deselect a selection, choose Select > Deselect (Ctrl-D/Cmd-D).

TIP To copy pixels from within a type selection, first position the type selection over the desired pixels. Next, choose Edit > Copy to copy pixels from only the active layer, or choose Edit > Copy Merged to copy pixels from all visible layers below the selection.

TIP To paste imagery into a type selection **3**, select and copy an area of pixels from another layer or another image, create a type selection on the target image, then choose Edit > Paste Into. The type selection will be deselected and a new layer will be created.

> **Line 'em up**
>
> To align or distribute multiple type layers, link them together (click in the second column on the Layers palette), then choose from the Layer > **Align Linked** or Layer > **Distribute Linked** submenu.

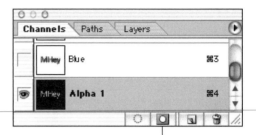

1 *To save a type mask selection to an alpha channel so you can reload it at any time, click the Save Selection as Channel button on the Channels palette.*

2 *When you use the Move tool to move a type selection, pixels inside the selection move within the type outline.*

3 *Imagery pasted into a type selection*

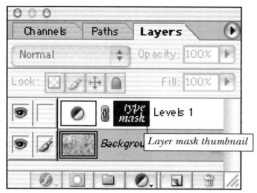

1 *The **type mask selection** functions as a **mask** for the **adjustment layer**.*

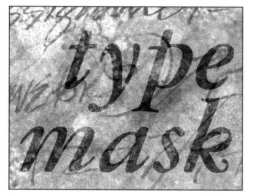

2 *Only pixels **below** the character shapes are affected by the **adjustment layer**.*

To create a type mask for an adjustment layer:

1. Choose the Horizontal Type Mask tool ⊤ or Vertical Type Mask tool ⊤ (T or Shift-T), then click in the image window where you want the type to appear.

2. Choose type attributes, enter characters, then click the ✔ on the options bar. Leave the type selection active.

3. Click the layer above which you want the new adjustment layer to appear.

4. Choose an adjustment command from the New Fill/Adjustment Layer pop-up menu ●, at the bottom of the Layers palette **1**. Choose adjustment options, then click OK. The type character shapes will be used as a mask for the adjustment layer. Only pixels directly below the character shapes will be affected by the adjustment **2**.

TIP You can also use an existing type layer to create a selection. First hide the type layer. Next, Ctrl-click/Cmd-click the type layer thumbnail on the Layers palette to turn the type into a selection. Finally, perform step 4, above.

TIP Alt-click/Option-click the layer mask thumbnail (thumbnail on the right) to display just the mask. Alt-click/Option-click it again to restore the full image.

TIP With the adjustment layer selected, choose Image > Adjustments > Invert (Ctrl-I/Cmd-I) to swap the black and white areas in the adjustment layer mask.

TIP Use the Move tool with Auto Select Layer unchecked on the options bar to reposition a mask on a selected adjustment layer.

Type Mask for Adjustment Layer

Type in a spot channel

To create type in a spot channel:

1. Create an editable type layer so you'll be able to modify it later on.

2. Follow steps 1–6 on page 208 to create a new spot channel.

3. Choose the type layer, then Ctrl-click/Cmd-click the type layer name or thumbnail to select only the visible parts of the layer (the character shapes).

4. Hide the type layer (click the eye icon).

5. On the Channels palette, choose the spot color channel name, and make sure its eye icon is showing.

6. Choose Edit > Fill, choose Use: Black, Normal mode, choose an Opacity value that matches the tint (density) value of the spot color ink to be used on press, then click OK. The selection will fill with the spot channel color at 100%.

7. Choose Select > Deselect –**3**.

TIP To move the type in the spot color channel, choose that channel, choose the Move tool (V), then drag in the image window. To adjust the tint, see the sidebar on page 209.

TIP You can't actually **edit** type in a spot channel. Instead, you have to remove the existing spot channel, edit the type in the type layer, then redo steps 2–7 above.

Don't lose your pixels
To deselect a selection, be sure to use Select > **Deselect** (Ctrl-D/Cmd-D). Don't press Delete or choose Edit > Clear—those commands will remove pixels from inside the selection!

1 *Type in a spot channel*

2 *A type mask selection in a spot channel displays on the image in the current Ink Characteristics: Color (see the figure below).*

3 *You can change the **Solidity** value to view an onscreen-only simulation of a spot color ink tint. The Solidity value has no effect on actual print output.*

(sidebar, left margin) **Type in Spot Channel**

Word processing

You can **find** and **replace** text in your Photoshop file, and you can check the spelling of your text on all visible type layers.

To find and replace text:

1. *Optional:* Click with the Horizontal Type or Vertical Type tool to create an insertion point from which to start your search. If you don't do this, the search will begin from the most recently created object.

2. Choose Edit > Find and Replace Text.
   or
   Choose the Horizontal Type or Vertical Type tool, then right-click/Ctrl-click in the image window and choose Find and Replace Text from the context menu.

3. Enter a search word or phrase in the Find What field **1**.

4. Enter a replacement word or phrase in the Change To field **2**.

5. *Do any of these optional steps:*
   Check **Search All Layers** to find text on any type layer, not just the currently active layer.

   Check **Case Sensitive** to find only those instances that exactly match the uppercase/lowercase configuration of the Find What text. With this option unchecked, case will be ignored as a criterion in the search.

Check **Forward** to search from the current cursor position to the end of the text. Leave this option unchecked to search backward from the current cursor position. If Search All Layers is checked, the cursor position is irrelevant.

Check **Whole Word Only** to find the Find What text only if it appears as a complete word—not as part of a larger word (e.g., "for" but not "forward").

6. Click **Find Next** to search for the first instance of the Find What text in the document, if Forward is unchecked, or the first instance following the current cursor position, if Forward is checked **3**.

7. Click **Change** to replace only the current instance of the Find What text.
   or
   Click **Change All** to replace all instances of the Find What text at once **4**.
   or
   Click **Change/Find** to replace the current instance of the Find What text and search for the next instance.

8. Click Done at any time to end the search, or if a summary of the search appears onscreen, click OK.

1 *Enter text to be searched for in the **Find What** field.*

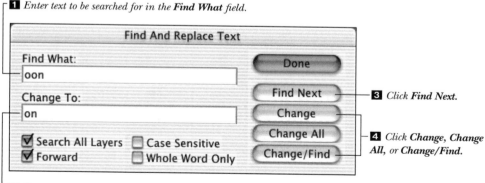

3 *Click **Find Next**.*

4 *Click **Change**, **Change All**, or **Change/Find**.*

2 *Enter replacement text in the **Change To** field.*

The **Check Spelling** command checks spelling on a single type layer or in an entire document using a built-in dictionary, to which you can add entries. As far as we know, you can't edit the dictionary afterward.

To check spelling:

1. Choose Edit > Check Spelling.
   or
   Choose the Horizontal Type or Vertical Type tool (T or Shift-T), then right-click/Ctrl-click and choose Check Spelling Text from the context menu. A type layer doesn't have to be selected.

   The first word the dictionary doesn't recognize will appear in the Not in Dictionary field **1**. The dictionary's best guess for a replacement word will appear in the Change To field, and other possible replacements will be listed in the Suggestions window.

2. *Optional:* Check Check All Layers to have Photoshop search through every type layer in the document, not just the current layer.

3. For each word that appears, do one of the following:

   If the Change To word is incorrect but the correct word appears on the **Suggestions** list, click the correct word to make it appear in the **Change To** field; if the correct word doesn't appear on the Suggestions list, type it in the Change To field yourself. Next, click **Change** to change only the current instance of the word or click **Change All** to change all instances of the word.

   Click **Ignore** to skip over only this instance of the word, or click Ignore All to skip over all instances of the word.

   Click **Add** to add the unrecognized word, as is, to the dictionary and also leave it unchanged in the image.

4. Click Done at any time to end the spelling check, or if a summary of the spelling check appears onscreen, click OK.

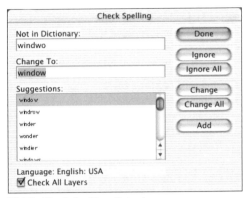

1 *The **Check Spelling** dialog box*

Check spelling in Spanish?
Use the **Language** pop-up menu **2** on the Character palette to choose which dictionary Photoshop will use.

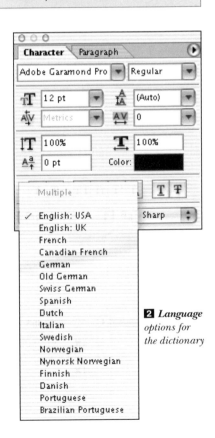

2 *Language options for the dictionary*

FILTERS 20

Filter	
Last Filter	⌘F
Extract...	⌥⌘X
Filter Gallery...	
Liquify...	⇧⌘X
Pattern Maker...	⌥⇧⌘X
Artistic ▶	Colored Pencil...
Blur ▶	Cutout...
Brush Strokes ▶	Dry Brush...
Distort ▶	Film Grain...
Noise ▶	Fresco...
Pixelate ▶	Neon Glow...
Render ▶	Paint Daubs...
Sharpen ▶	Palette Knife...
Sketch ▶	Plastic Wrap...
Stylize ▶	Poster Edges...
Texture ▶	Rough Pastels...
Video ▶	Smudge Stick...
Other ▶	Sponge...
	Underpainting...
Digimarc ▶	Watercolor...

1 *Filters are grouped into submenu categories under the* **Filter** *menu.*

The **Groucho** *filter...okay, the joke's getting old.*

PHOTOSHOP'S FILTERS produce a myriad of special effects, ranging from slight sharpening to wild distortion. For example, you could apply the Sharpen or Blur filter for subtle retouching; the Lighting Effects filter to apply illumination; one or more of the filters on the Artistic, Brush Strokes, Sketch, or Texture submenu to make your image look hand-rendered; or for a very dramatic change, apply one of the filters on the Stylize or Distort submenu. The filters are grouped into 13 submenu categories under the Filter menu **1**.

This chapter has three sections: techniques for applying filters; an illustrated compendium of all the filters; and step-by-step instructions for using some of the filters, such as Lighting Effects and Pattern Maker.

Filter basics
How filters are applied

A filter can be applied to a whole layer or to a selection on a layer. For a soft transition between the filtered and nonfiltered areas, feather the selection before applying a filter.

Some filters are applied in one step, with no dialog box opening. Other filters are applied either via the Filter Gallery or via the filter's own dialog box. Choose Filter > **Last Filter** [last filter name] (**Ctrl-F/Cmd-F**) to reapply the last-used filter using the same settings. To open the dialog box or Filter Gallery for the last-used filter, with its last-used settings displayed, press **Ctrl-Alt-F/Cmd-Option-F**. To reapply a filter using different settings, choose it from its submenu or from the Filter Gallery.

All the filters are available for an image in RGB Color or Multichannel mode; not all filters are available for an image in CMYK, Grayscale, or Lab Color mode, or for an image that has 16 bits per channel. No filters are available for an image in Bitmap or Indexed Color mode.

(Continued on the following page)

The **Filter Gallery** dialog box (**1**, next page) houses most of the Photoshop filters under one roof. You can show/hide each filter effect that you've previewed and also change the sequence in which they're applied. This way, you can judge which filters you want to apply, and in which sequence, all before exiting the dialog box or altering any image pixels. Using the Filter Gallery, you avoid having to make multiple trips to the Filter menu to try out individual filters, and it's easier to gauge the effect that one filter or a sequence of filters will have on your image before making a commitment to them.

To use the Filter Gallery:

1. With an image open, choose Filter > Filter Gallery. *Note:* If a filter is included in the Filter Gallery, the Filter Gallery dialog box opens automatically when that filter is chosen from the Filter menu.

2. In the middle panel, click a chevron/arrowhead to expand one of the six filter categories, then click a filter effect thumbnail to preview that filter in the dialog box.

3. Choose settings for the filter from the panel on the right side. The filter name you've chosen will display on the scroll list at the bottom of the right panel.

4. *Optional:* To add another filter effect to the image, click the New Effect Layer button, click another filter thumbnail in the same category or expand another category and click a thumbnail, then choose settings for the filter.

   or

   To replace one existing filter effect with another, leave the existing filter effect name selected on the scroll list (don't click the New Effect Layer button), click a new filter effect thumbnail, then choose settings.

5. *Do any of the following optional steps:*

   Repeat the previous step to add or replace other filter effects. The most recently applied effect will be listed at the top of the list on the right panel.

   On the filter effects name scroll list, click the eye icon to hide that filter effect; click again to redisplay it.

   Drag a filter name up or down on the list to change the sequence in which it's applied—a different sequence will produce a different result in the image.

   Click the Delete Effect Layer button to remove the currently selected filter effect from the list.

6. Click OK.

TIP You can also choose any Filter Gallery effect from the alphabetical listing on the pop-up menu on the right side of the dialog box.

Use the scroll bars or arrows or drag the preview to move the image in the preview window.

Click the chevron/arrowhead to hide the thumbnail panel and expand the preview window to two panels wide; click again to redisplay the thumbnail panel.

Choose settings for the currently chosen filter here.

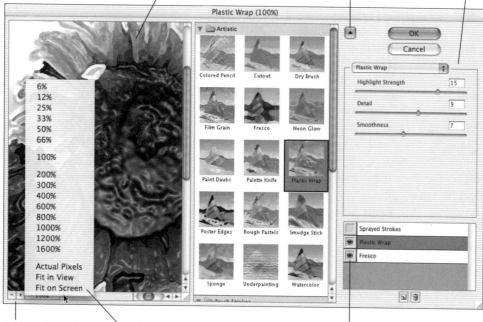

Click the Zoom Out or Zoom In button...

...or choose a zoom level from the pop-up menu.

Click in the eye column to hide/show that filter effect preview. Alt-click/Option-click to hide/show all the previews.

1 The **Filter Gallery** dialog box has three panels: a preview on the left; filter categories with thumbnails in the middle; and on the right, filter settings and a list of the filters effects you've previewed.

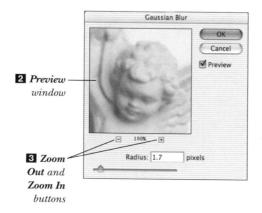

2 *Preview window*

3 *Zoom Out and Zoom In buttons*

Individual filter dialog boxes

Some individual filter dialog boxes have a **preview** window **2**. Drag in the preview window to move the image inside it. With some filter dialog boxes open, the pointer becomes a square when it's passed over the image window; you can click that area of the image to preview it. (Check Preview to preview the effect in the dialog box and the image window.)

Click the + button to zoom in on the image in the preview window, or click the – button to zoom out **3**. A line will blink on and off below the preview percentage while a filter is rendering in the preview window.

Lessening a filter's overall effect

The **Fade** command can be used to lessen the effect of a filter, the Extract or Liquify command, an Image > Adjustments command, or any paint, eraser, or editing tool stroke. After applying a filter, choose Edit > Fade (Ctrl-Shift-F/Cmd-Shift-F), change the Opacity (you can drag across the word "Opacity") and/or blending Mode, if you like, then click OK **1**–**3**.

To lessen a filter's effect with the option to test out various **blending modes,** do the following:

1. Duplicate the layer that you're going to apply the filter to.

2. Apply the filter to the duplicate layer.

3. On the Layers palette:

   Lower the layer's Opacity or Fill percentage to lessen (fade) the filter's effect.
   and
   Choose a different blending mode (**1**–**2**, next page).

   At any time, you can change the blending mode or opacity of the filter effect layer to blend it differently with the original layer, or create a layer mask for the duplicate layer to hide portions of the filter effect, or discard the filter layer entirely. When the image is finalized, merge the duplicate layer with the original layer.

Another way to soften a filter's effect is to modify pixels in one of the image's color components. To do this, choose a layer, click a **channel** color name on the Channels palette, apply a filter (Add Noise is a nice one to experiment with), then click the top channel on the palette (Ctrl-~/Cmd-~) to redisplay the composite image.

And finally, you can selectively reduce a filter effect using the **History Brush** tool. Set the History Brush icon to a prior state on the History palette, then draw strokes on the image (**3**, next page).

1 *Filter > Texture > **Mosaic Tiles** applied to an image*

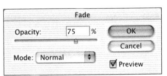

2 *Use the **Fade** command to lessen the effect of the most recent edit.*

3 *After using the **Fade** command in **Overlay** mode to lessen the filter effect on the overall image*

1 *The original image*

2 *After applying the **Find Edges** filter to a dupli-cate of the original layer, lowering the opacity of the duplicate layer, and choosing Hard Light blending mode (also try Overlay, Color Dodge, or Difference)*

3 *After applying the **Poster Edges** filter to an image and then using the **History Brush** tool to restore the angel's face and tummy to its original state*

Cool edges

Use one of the "canned" frame effects from a third-party supplier, such as PhotoFrame from Extensis **4**.

4 *A **Camera** edge from **PhotoFrame***

Restricting the area a filter affects

Before applying a filter, create a **selection** on a layer; the filter will affect pixels only within the selection. To create a soft-edged transition between the filtered and nonfil-tered areas, go one step further and **feather** the selection before applying the filter.

You can also use a **layer mask** to limit the effect of a filter. The edge between the white and black areas of a layer mask can be soft, hard, or painterly, depending on the type of brush strokes you use to paint the black areas of the mask. Applying a filter to the layer mask causes the filter effect to be visible where the white areas of the mask are.

Another option is to create a black-to-white **gradient** in the layer mask and then apply a filter to the layer imagery (click the layer thumbnail, not the layer mask thumbnail). The filter will apply fully to the image where

(Continued on the following page)

Filter Techniques

the mask is white and fade to nil in areas where the mask is black **1**–**3**.

Making filter effects look less artificial

Use the Filter Gallery to apply **more than one** filter—the effect will look less canned. If the imagery you're creating lends itself to experimentation, try concocting your own formulas. And use the sliders in the dialog box to test different variables. If you come up with a sequence that you'd like to reuse, you can save it in an action. And remember, if you get carried away and apply too many filters, you can always revert to an earlier state or snapshot using the History palette.

Maximizing a filter's effect

Pumping up a layer's **brightness** and **contrast** values before applying a filter can help intensify the filter's effect (choose Image > Adjust > Levels, move the black Input slider to the right and the white Input slider slightly to the left, then click OK).

To **recolor** a layer after applying a filter that strips color (e.g., the Charcoal filter), use Image > Adjustments > Hue/Saturation (check Colorize).

TIP The Sketch filters (with the exception of Water Paper) reduce a layer's colors to just white and the current Foreground color, so choose a Foreground color before using any of those filters.

Texture mapping using a filter

And finally, in lieu of choosing a preset pattern in filter dialog boxes that offer a pattern option (e.g., Conté Crayon, Glass, Lighting Effects, Rough Pastels, and Texturizer) for the filter to apply as a texture, you can load in another image for the filter to use. Lights and darks from the image you load in will be used to create peaks and valleys in the texture (it's called "texture mapping"). The image you load in must be saved in the Photoshop file format. If the filter dialog box has a Texture pop-up menu, click the ⊙ and choose Load Texture, locate a color or grayscale image file in the Photoshop (.psd) format, then click OK.

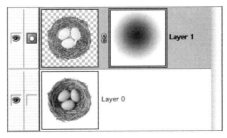

1 *A **radial gradient** in the **layer mask**…*

2 *…is diminishing the Stamp filter effect in the center of the nest.*

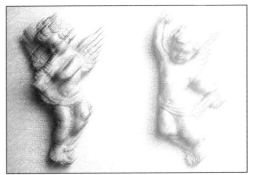

3 *The Rough Pastels filter is applied to the whole layer, but a linear gradient in the **layer mask** is diminishing the filter's impact on the right side.*

All the filters illustrated

Artistic filters

Original image

Colored Pencil

Cutout

Dry Brush

Film Grain

Fresco

Neon Glow

Paint Daubs

Palette Knife

Artistic Filters

Artistic filters

Original image

Plastic Wrap

Poster Edges

Rough Pastels

Smudge Stick

Sponge

Watercolor

Underpainting

Artistic Filters

Blur filters

Original image

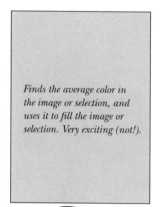

Finds the average color in the image or selection, and uses it to fill the image or selection. Very exciting (not!).

Average **NEW**

Blur More

Gaussian Blur

Lens Blur **NEW**
See pages 245–247.

Motion Blur

Radial Blur

Smart Blur (Normal)

Smart Blur (Overlay Edge)

Blur Filters

Brush Strokes filters

Original image

Accented Edges

Angled Strokes

Crosshatch

Dark Strokes

Ink Outlines

Spatter

Sprayed Strokes

Sumi-e

Distort filters

Original image

Diffuse Glow

Displace

Glass

Ocean Ripple

Pinch

Polar Coordinates

Ripple

Shear

Distort Filters

Distort filters

Spherize

Twirl

Wave (Type: Square)

Wave (Type: Sine)

ZigZag

Noise filters

Original image

Add Noise

Median

Distort Filters; Noise Filters

Pixelate filters

Original image

Color Halftone

Crystallize

Facet

Fragment

Mezzotint (Short Strokes)

Mezzotint (Medium Dots)

Mosaic

Pointillize

Render filters

Original image

Clouds

Difference Clouds

Fibers **NEW**

Lens Flare

For the Lighting Effects filter, see pages 390–392.

Sharpen filters

Sharpen Edges

Sharpen More

Unsharp Mask

Render Filters; Sharpen Filters

Sketch filters

Original image

Bas Relief

Chalk & Charcoal

Charcoal

Chrome

Conté Crayon

Graphic Pen

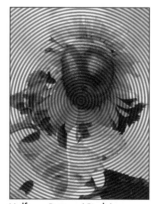

Halftone Pattern (Circle)

Halftone Pattern (Dot)

Sketch Filters

Sketch filters

Sketch Filters

Original image

Note Paper

Photocopy

Plaster

Reticulation

Stamp

Torn Edges

Water Paper

Stylize filters

Original image

Diffuse

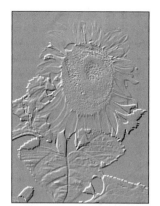

Emboss

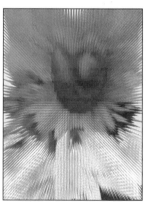

Extrude

Find Edges

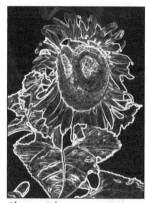

Glowing Edges

Solarize

Tiles

Tiles, then Fade (Overlay mode)

Stylize filters

Original image

Trace Contour

Wind

Texture filters

Craquelure

Grain (Horizontal)

Mosaic Tiles

Patchwork

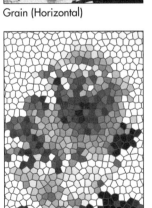

Stained Glass

Texturizer

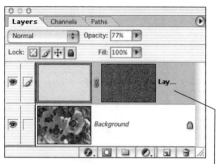

1 *A filter is applied to a **layer mask**.*

2 *A filter applied via a **layer mask***

3 *The original image*

4 *The final image (see the following page).*

Filters in action

In the instructions on this page and the next two pages, you'll learn how to apply multiple filters to the same image, and how to use such features as masks, layer opacity, and blending modes to modify the result. Feel free to try out your own combinations and techniques!

In these instructions, you'll add a black or gray **texture** to a layer mask via a filter. Black areas in the layer mask will hide pixels in the layer, revealing imagery from the layer below it.

To apply a texture using a layer mask:

1. Create a new layer and fill it with white, or choose an existing layer.

2. Create a layer mask for the layer by clicking the Add Layer Mask button ▣ on the Layers palette, and leave the layer mask thumbnail active.

3. Apply Filter > Noise > Add Noise to the layer mask.

4. Apply another filter or series of filters to the layer mask **1**–**2**. Try a Texture filter (e.g., Craquelure, Grain, Mosaic Tiles, Patchwork). For Grain, experiment with different Grain Types. Or try the Artistic > Dry Brush (small brush size), Palette Knife (small stroke size), Sponge, or Watercolor filter.

5. *Do any of the following optional steps:*

   To intensify a filter's effect, apply the Distort > Ripple or Twirl, or Stylize > Wind filter.

   To fade a filter effect, use Edit > Fade.

   Adjust the opacity of the layer that contains the layer mask; or change blending modes (try Overlay, Soft Light, or Hue).

   To limit texture blending to some image channels, double-click the new layer. In the Layer Style dialog box, click Blending Options, and in the Advanced Blending area, uncheck any channel to prevent it from blending with the underlying image. You can also change the Blend Mode and Opacity in this dialog box.

Texture Using Layer Mask

Turn a photograph into a painting or a drawing:

1. Open an image, right-click/Ctrl-click a layer on the Layers palette and choose Duplicate Layer from the context menu, then click OK.

2. Choose Filter > Stylize > Find Edges.

3. With the duplicate layer still active, click the Add Layer Mask button ☐ at the bottom of the Layers palette.

4. Choose the Brush tool and paint with black at below 100% opacity (Normal mode) on the layer mask to reveal parts of the layer below (**3**–**4**, previous page).

5. *Optional:* Lower the opacity of the duplicate layer.

6. *Optional:* For a dramatic effect of colors on a dark background, click the layer thumbnail, then choose Image > Adjustments > Invert (Ctrl-I/Cmd-I).

TIP To produce a magic marker drawing, in lieu of step 2, above, apply Filter > Stylize > Trace Contour, then apply Filter > Other > Minimum (Radius of 1 or 2).

1 *The original image*

In these instructions, you'll turn a photograph into a **watercolor** using the Median Noise and Minimum filters. Compare it to Photoshop's Watercolor filter. This is but one of the infinite ways you can apply multiple filters to the same image.

Our watercolor filter:

1. Duplicate the layer that you want to turn into a watercolor.

2. With the duplicate layer active, choose Filter > Noise > Median.

3. Move the Radius slider to between 2 and 8, then click OK.

4. Choose Filter > Other > Minimum.

5. Move the Radius slider to 1, 2, or 3, then click OK **1**–**3**.

6. Choose Filter > Sharpen > Unsharp Mask, choose high Amount and Radius values, then click OK.

2 *The **Watercolor** filter*

3 *Our watercolor*

1 *Select an object.*

To create an illusion of motion, you'll select an object that you want to remain stationary, copy it to a new layer, and then apply the **Motion Blur** filter to the original background.

To apply a motion blur to part of an image:

1. Select the imagery that you want to remain stationary **1**.

2. Choose Select > Feather (Ctrl-Alt-D/ Cmd-Option-D), enter a number between 5 and 8 in the Feather Radius field, then click OK.

3. Press Ctrl-J/Cmd-J to copy the selected imagery to a new layer **2**.

4. Click the original layer that contains the background imagery.

5. Choose Filter > Blur > Motion Blur.

6. Choose or enter an Angle between –360 and 360 **3**. (We used –17 for our image.) *and*
Choose a Distance (1–999) for the amount of blur. (We entered 50 for our image.)

7. Click OK **4**.

2 *Copy the **selection** to a **new layer**.*

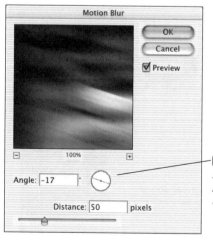

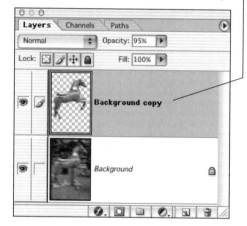

3 *Choose an Angle in the **Motion Blur** dialog box.*

4 *The completed **motion blur***

Lighting effects

The **Lighting Effects** filter produces a tremendous variety of lighting effects. You can place up to 16 light sources in your image, and you can assign a different color, intensity, and angle to each source. *Note:* For optimal use of this filter, allocate as much RAM as you can possibly spare to Photoshop.

To cast a light on an image:

1. Make sure your image is in RGB Color mode .

1 *The original RGB image*

2. Choose a layer. *Optional:* Select an area on the layer to limit the filter's effect.

3. Choose Filter > Render > Lighting Effects.

2 *Choose from the Style pop-up menu in the **Lighting Effects** dialog box.*

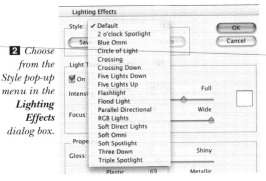

4. From the Style pop-up menu, choose Default or one of the preset lighting effects **2**.

5. For Light Type **3**:

   Check **On** to preview the lighting effect in the dialog box.

   Choose from the **Light Type** pop-up menu. Spotlight, for example, produces a narrow, cone-shaped beam.

   Move the **Intensity** slider to adjust the brightness of the light. Full Intensity creates the brightest light **4**; Negative removes light from the scene.

   For the Spotlight Light Type, you can move the **Focus** slider to adjust the size of the beam that fills the ellipse (**1**–**2**, next page). The spotlight's highest intensity falls where the radius touches the edge of the ellipse.

   To change the **color** of the light, click the color swatch, then choose a color from the Color Picker.

6. Do any of the following in the preview window:

   Drag the center point to move the entire light.

3 *Choose Light Type options.*

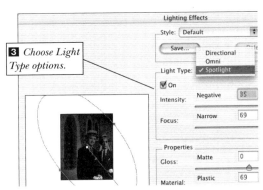

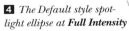

4 *The Default style spotlight ellipse at **Full Intensity***

(sidebar) **Lighting Effects Filter**

1 *The Default spotlight ellipse with a **Wide Focus:** The light is strongest at the sides of the ellipse.*

2 *The Default spotlight ellipse with a **Narrow Focus***

3 *The Default spotlight ellipse after dragging the **end** and **side points** inward to narrow the light beam*

4 *The spotlight ellipse **rotated** to the left by dragging a side point*

5 *The spotlight ellipse after dragging the **radius** inward to make the light beam more round*

Drag either endpoint toward the center point to make the light more intense **3**.

For an ellipse, drag either side point to change the direction of the light, or to widen or narrow it **4**–**5**.

7. Move the Properties sliders to adjust the surrounding light conditions on the active layer:

    Gloss controls the amount of surface reflectance on the lighted surfaces.

    Material adjusts the relative amount of color that emanates from the light source (Plastic) or from the image (Metallic).

    Exposure lightens or darkens the whole layer **6**–**7**.

    Ambience controls the balance between the light source and the overall light in the image **8**–**9**. Move this slider in small increments.

    Click the Properties color swatch to choose a different **color** from the Color Picker for the ambient light around the spotlight.

8. *Do any of these optional steps:*

    To add the current configuration of settings to the Style pop-up menu so you can choose it again, click **Save,** enter a name, then click OK.

    (Continued on the following page)

Lighting Effects Filter

6 *The spotlight ellipse with the **Exposure Property** set to **Over***

7 *The spotlight ellipse with the **Exposure Property** set to **Under***

8 *The spotlight ellipse with a **Positive Ambience Property***

9 *The spotlight ellipse with a **Negative Ambience Property***

To **add** another light source, drag the light bulb icon 💡 into the preview window 1.

To **delete** a light source, drag its center point over the trash icon. 🗑 One light source must remain.

To **duplicate** a light source, Alt-drag/ Option-drag its center point.

9. Click OK.

Note: The last-used settings of the Lighting Effects filter will remain in the dialog box until you change them or exit/quit Photoshop. To restore the default settings, choose Default from the Style menu. To remove the currently selected style from the pop-up menu, Click Delete, then click Delete again.

TIP To create a textured lighting effect, choose a channel that contains a texture from the Texture Channel pop-up menu, and move the Height slider to adjust the height of the texture. This works best with the Spotlight Light Type.

TIP An Omni light creates a circular light source 2. Drag an edge point to adjust its size.

TIP Shift-drag the side points on an ellipse to resize the ellipse while keeping its angle constant. Ctrl-drag/Cmd-drag the angle line to change the angle or direction of the ellipse while keeping its size constant.

TIP To create a pin spot, choose Light Type: Spotlight, move the Intensity slider to around 55, move the Focus slider to around 30, and drag the side points of the ellipse inward to narrow the ellipse. To cast light on a different part of the image, move the whole ellipse by dragging its center point.

TIP If the background of an image was darkened too much from a previous application of the Lighting Effects filter, apply Image > Adjustments > Shadow/ Highlight at a high Shadow percentage to restore it.

1 *Dragging a* **new light source** *into the preview window*

2 *The default* **Omni** *light is spherical, like a bare light bulb shining over a photograph.*

Lighting effects by example

To produce **3**, we used a Spotlight with a wide Focus, rotated and reshaped the ellipse, moved the Exposure Property slider slightly toward Over to brighten the light source, and moved the Ambience Property slider slightly to the left to darken the background of the image. Next, we Alt-dragged/Option-dragged the ellipse to duplicate the light and illuminate the face on the right. Finally, we added a low-intensity light to illuminate the background **4**.

3 *The* **final** *image*

4 *These three ellipses show the light source positions that were used to produce the image above.*

Lighting Effects Filter

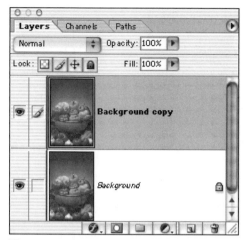

1 *Click a **layer** to use for the **pattern tile** (or select an area of a layer and choose Edit > Copy).*

Pattern Maker

The **Pattern Maker** filter allows you to generate multiple patterns from imagery on a layer or imagery that has been copied to the Clipboard. Instead of utilizing the imagery exactly, though, Photoshop jumbles pixels slightly in order to create an assortment of different pattern tiles. You can use this feature simply to fill a layer with a pattern once, or you can save your favorite pattern tiles as a pattern preset to use with any tool or command that uses pattern presets, such as Pattern Overlay in Layer Style, the Healing Brush tool, the Pattern Stamp tool, or the Fill command.

The sample that you use for a tile can range from an area just a few pixels square to a whole layer. If the tile is smaller than the layer it's generated from, it will be repeated in a grid formation to fill up the layer. If the tile is the same size as the current layer, just a single tile will fill the whole layer. Any type of imagery will work for this, as it will become quite distorted by the filter.

Note: The Pattern Maker filter can be used only on 8-bit images in RGB Color, CMYK Color, Lab Color, and Grayscale image modes.

To generate a pattern:

1. Click the layer that contains the imagery that you want to use for the pattern **1**. This layer will be replaced by the pattern, so we suggest you duplicate it and then click the original or duplicate layer.
    or
    To generate a pattern in a new layer or file, select the area of imagery that you want to use for the pattern, then either add a layer or create a new file that has the dimensions that you want the final image to have (don't Paste).

    Note: If you create a nonrectangular selection, the filter will automatically square it off using the bounding box for the selected area.

2. Choose Filter > Pattern Maker (Ctrl-Alt-Shift-X/Cmd-Option-Shift-X). If the

(Continued on the following page)

dialog box is gobbling up your whole screen, you can resize it by dragging the lower right corner.

3. To generate a pattern in the current layer, choose the Rectangular marquee tool in the dialog box,⬚ then marquee the area you want to use as the pattern **1**. You can drag the selection marquee to a different spot.

or

To generate a pattern in a new layer or file based on the selection you put on the Clipboard for step 1, check Use Clipboard as Sample (don't worry if the preview window is blank).

4. To specify the dimensions of tiles in the generated pattern:

Enter or choose a Width value and a Height value.

or

Using the preview

Do any of the following in the Pattern Maker dialog box:

■ To magnify the preview, choose the **Zoom** tool (Z) 🔍 in the dialog box, then click the preview image. To zoom out, Alt-click/Option-click the preview image. The current zoom level will be listed in the lower left corner of the dialog box.

■ To move the pattern in the preview window, choose the **Hand** tool (H) 🖑 in the dialog box or hold down the Spacebar, then drag in the preview window. To move the pattern, the zoom level must be above 100%.

■ If you're curious to know where the nonprinting tile boundaries are, check Preview: **Tile Boundaries**. To choose a different color for the boundaries to make them contrast better with the imagery, click the color swatch, then choose a color from the Color Picker.

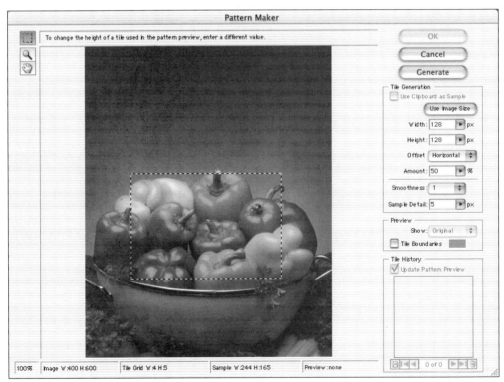

1 *In the **Pattern Maker** dialog box, either marquee the area to be used for the tile, using the **Rectangular marquee** tool, or click **Use Clipboard** to create a tile based on the current contents of the Clipboard.*

Click Use Image Size to have the tile size match the current image size. This option creates a pattern using one large tile instead of multiple tiles.

5. From the Offset pop-up menu, choose the direction in which tiles will be offset in the generated pattern (None, Horizontal, or Vertical), then enter or choose an offset Amount (0–99%). The tiles will be offset from each other by a percentage of the tile's dimensions in the chosen direction.

6. Click Generate (Ctrl-G/Cmd-G). The tiled pattern will display in the preview area **1** (see the sidebar on the previous page).

   TIP If the tile takes time to process, a progress bar will appear. You can press Esc to cancel the generation in midstream.

7. Click Generate Again to have additional randomized patterns be generated using the same options, or change any of the options, such as the Width and/or Height, then click Generate Again.

   TIP To switch between the original image and the generated pattern in the preview window, choose Original or Generated from the Show pop-up menu in the Preview area.

To use a different part of the image for the pattern, choose Show: Original in the Preview area, move or redraw the sample marquee, then click Generate Again.

8. Once the pattern preview is to your liking, the next step is to delete any tiles you don't want and save any tiles that you may want to use later. For this, keep the Pattern Maker dialog box open and follow the instructions on the next page.

TIP If the current layer's transparent pixels are locked, the pattern will replace only nontransparent pixels.

TIP The default Smoothness and Sample Detail settings work well for most samples, and higher values will cause the pattern to generate more slowly, so we don't recommend raising them unless you need to. However, if the pixels in the sample lack contrast, Photoshop may oversharpen the edges when it generates the pattern. In this case, you can raise the Smoothness to reduce the prominence of edges within the tiles or raise the Sample Detail value to produce a more abstract pattern, with more deviation from the original imagery.

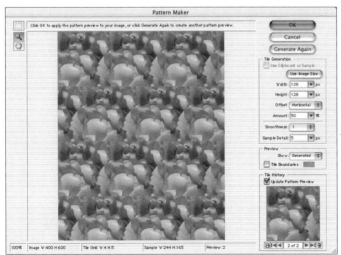

1 *Click **Generate** to have the filter generate a pattern using the tile. Click **Generate Again** to create more tile variations.*

Using the **Tile History** area of the Pattern Maker dialog box, you can navigate through the patterns that have been generated, delete any pattern tiles that you don't need, and save any tile as a pattern preset for future use.

To navigate through pattern tiles:

In the Tile History area of the Pattern Maker dialog box, click the First Tile, Previous Tile, Next Tile, or Last Tile button ▉.

or

Highlight the current tile number, type the number of the tile you want to view, then press Enter/Return.

When you **delete** a tile from the Tile History, its preview is discarded, too.

To delete a pattern tile:

1. Use the navigation buttons to locate the tile that you want to delete.

2. Click the Delete Tile from History button. 🗑 You can't undo this.

When a tile is **saved** as a preset pattern, it becomes a swatch on the Pattern Preset picker and is available for any command or tool that the picker is normally used with. Only the single tile will be saved, not the full, generated pattern.

To save a tile as a pattern preset:

1. Use the navigation buttons to locate the tile that you want to save.

2. Click the Save Preset Pattern button. 💾

3. Type a Name for the preset ▉, then click OK. To create and manage preset libraries, use the Preset Manager (see pages 438–440). *Note:* Canceling out of the Pattern Maker dialog box won't delete the tile that you've saved as a preset.

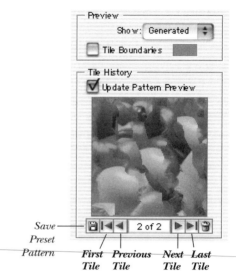

Save Preset Pattern · *First Tile* · *Previous Tile* · *Next Tile* · *Last Tile*

1 *Use the* **Tile History** *buttons to* **navigate** *through tile variations.*

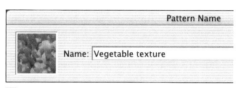

2 *Type a name for the preset in the* **Pattern Name** *dialog box.*

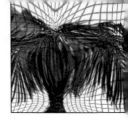

LIQUIFY **21**

THE **LIQUIFY COMMAND** lets you twist, warp, stretch, and otherwise distort all or part of an image layer. Like the Extract command, Liquify gives you a full-size preview right in the dialog box **1**. You can apply the distortion (or reconstruction) with an assortment of Liquify tools, use a brush to freeze parts of the image to protect them from distortion, and undo the havoc you have wrought, partially or completely, with the Reconstruct tool. The edits are applied to the image when you click OK.

1 The **Liquify** dialog box, after applying the Twirl Clockwise tool to the image preview

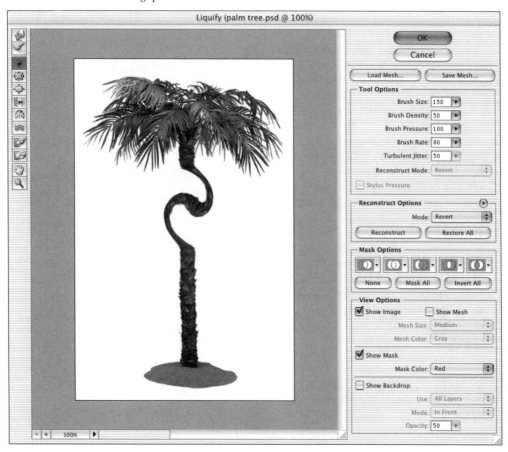

The instructions for using the **Liquify** dialog box below are long-winded, but you don't have to follow them to the letter—you can choose among the various options **1**.

This command works only on 8-bit images in RGB Color, CMYK Color, Lab Color, Grayscale, and Duotone image modes. Also, it can't be applied to an editable type or shape layer.

To apply distortion using the Liquify command:

1. Choose a layer or select part of an image layer. If you want to use a rectangular selection as a mask, save the selection as an alpha channel. Also, we suggest you make a snapshot of the current image state using the History palette.

2. Choose Filter > Liquify (Ctrl-Shift-X/ Cmd-Shift-X). The dialog box is resizable. If you created a rectangular selection, only the selected portion will appear in the dialog box. If the selection is nonrectangular or is feathered, and View Options: Show Mask is checked in this dialog box, the unselected part of the layer will be masked. This is akin to using the Freeze Mask tool (see step 6).

3. The settings you choose in the **Tool Options** area (except for Brush Rate and Turbulent Jitter) will apply to all the Liquify tools:

   Enter or choose a **Brush Size** (1–600 pixels) for the brush width; a **Brush Density** (0–100%) to control edge feathering (similar to brush hardness on the Brushes palette); and a **Brush Pressure** (1–100%) to control how quickly distortion is applied when a tool is dragged.

   For the Reconstruct, Twirl, Pucker, Bloat, **NEW** or Turbulence tool, choose a **Brush Rate** (0–100%) to control how much distortion is applied when you click rather than drag with the tool.

   If you're using a graphics tablet, check Stylus Pressure to control the brush pressure using your stylus.

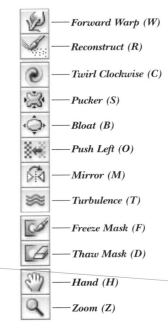

Forward Warp (W)
Reconstruct (R)
Twirl Clockwise (C)
Pucker (S)
Bloat (B)
Push Left (O)
Mirror (M)
Turbulence (T)
Freeze Mask (F)
Thaw Mask (D)
Hand (H)
Zoom (Z)

NEW **1** *Many of the names and shortcuts for tools in the* **Liquify** *dialog box have changed.*

2 *After applying the* **Forward Warp** *tool in the direction shown by the arrow*

1 *After applying the **Pucker** tool with the brush held stationary at the top of the tree*

2 *After using the **Mirror** tool to pick up pixels from the right side of the stroke*

4. Choose any of the following Liquify tools (type a tool shortcut to switch to that tool), then drag across areas of the image in the preview window:

The **Forward Warp** tool (W) 🖐 pushes pixels in the direction the brush is dragged (**2**, previous page).

The **Reconstruct** tool (R) 🖌 restores distorted pixels to their undistorted state. Choices on the Tool Options: Reconstruct Mode pop-up menu control how the reconstruct effect is applied (see page 402).

The **Twirl Clockwise** (C) 🌀 tool rotates pixels as long as you hold down the mouse button or drag (**1**, page 397). **NEW** Alt-click/Option-click to rotate pixels counterclockwise. The higher the Brush Pressure, the faster the rotation.

The **Pucker** (S) 🔳 **1** and **Bloat** (B) 💠 tools push pixels toward or away from the center of the brush for as long as you hold down the mouse button or drag. The higher the Brush Pressure when you drag with either tool, the faster pixels will move.

The **Push Left** tool (O) 🔳 moves pixels at right angles to the direction the brush is moved. Alt-drag/Option-drag to move pixels to the opposite side of the brush's direction. This tool can make an object look as if it's coming forward or receding.

The **Mirror** tool (M) 🔳 copies pixels from the area to the right of your brush and applies a mirror image of them to the area the brush passes over **2**. The tool picks up pixels on the right side of an upward stroke or on the left side of a downward stroke. Alt-drag/Option-drag to copy pixels from the opposite side of the brush.

TIP Before using the Mirror tool, freeze the area that you're going to apply the reflection to (see step 6).

(Continued on the following page)

Liquify Command

The **Turbulence** tool (T) 〰 jumbles pixels, creating a crumbly effect **1**. Adjust the Tool Options: Turbulence Jitter value (0–100%) to control the tightness of the effect.

5. To move the image in the preview window, drag with the **Hand** tool (H). 🖐 Or to access this tool without selecting it, Spacebar-drag.

   To change the **Zoom** level of the preview image, choose the Zoom tool (Z), 🔍 then click or drag in the preview window. Alt-click/Option-click to zoom out. Or choose a preset zoom level from the pop-up menu at the bottom left of the dialog box. Double-click the Zoom tool to reset the preview to 100%.

   TIP You can invoke the Undo/Redo command (Ctrl-Z/Cmd-Z) and the Step Backward/Step Forward commands (Ctrl-Alt-Z/Cmd-Option-Z) while using any Liquify tool or reconstruction controls.

6. *Optional:* To paint a mask to protect areas of the image from distortion (or to add to an existing mask), choose the **Freeze Mask** tool (F), 🖌 choose tool options, then paint on the preview image. The higher the Brush Pressure, the stronger the freeze effect. If the Brush Pressure is below 100%, you can drag again across the same spot to intensify the effect.

   To remove protection from frozen areas, choose the **Thaw Mask** tool (D), 🖌 choose Tool Options, then paint on the preview image.

1 *After applying the* **Turbulence** *tool with the brush held stationery at the top of the tree*

NEW *Optional:* To create a mask based on an existing nonrectangular selection, layer transparency, layer mask, or alpha channel in the original image (**1**, next page), choose from one of the Mask Options pop-up menus **2**: **Replace** Selection to use the selection, transparency, layer mask, or alpha channel as a mask; **Add** to Selection or **Subtract** from Selection to add to or subtract from the mask shape; **Intersect** with Selection to intersect the current mask shape with your menu choice; or **Invert** Selection to invert the mask.

7. *Optional:* Use the Mask Options buttons **NEW** to make additional changes to the mask. To unmask the entire image (make all pixels editable again), click **None.** To mask the entire image, click **Mask All.** To reverse what's masked and what isn't, click **Invert All.**

   To hide (but not disable) the mask, uncheck View Options: **Show Mask.**

   Choose a different overlay color for the frozen area from the View Options: **Mask Color** pop-up menu.

8. Though the Liquify command modifies only the currently active layer in your image, other visible layers can be viewed as a "Backdrop," either one at a time or all together as a composite image. To have only the active layer display in the preview window, uncheck View Options: **Show Backdrop.** Or to display the active layer along with the Backdrop, check Show Backdrop, and from the Use pop-up menu, choose All Layers for the

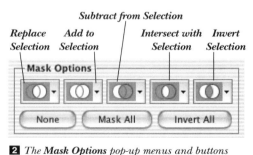

2 *The* **Mask Options** *pop-up menus and buttons*

1 *At left is the original image, with a selection that was saved as an **alpha channel**. At right is the image after applying the Liquify command using the alpha channel as a mask. Only the unmasked area was altered.*

2 *Both the **image** and the **mesh** are visible.*

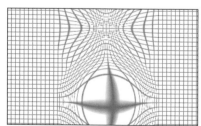

3 *The **mesh** is visible, but the image is not (Show Image is unchecked).*

composite, or choose any individual layer.

Make a choice from the **Mode** pop-up **NEW** menu to control how the Backdrop interacts with the active layer: **In Front** places the Backdrop in front of the active layer; **Behind** places it behind the active layer; **Blend** lets you combine the two.

Set the **Opacity** slider from 0–100% to reveal more or less of the layer chosen on the Use pop-up menu.

Note: When using the Show Backdrop option, keep the Opacity value below 100% so you'll be able to see the changes on the active layer.

9. *Optional:* To partially or completely undo the Liquify changes, read about the Reconstruct Options on the following page. When you're done using the Liquify dialog box, click OK.

To help gauge the extent of your Liquify command edits, you can superimpose a **mesh** over the image. The mesh gridlines display the same pattern of distortion as the image itself. The mesh comes in handy if parts of your image lack a distinct pattern. You can adjust the size and color of the mesh.

To display the Liquify mesh:

1. In the Liquify dialog box, check View Options: Show Mesh. A regularly spaced set of gridlines displays **2**.

2. *Do any of the following optional steps:*

Choose a size from the **Mesh Size** pop-up menu.

Choose a color from the **Mesh Color** pop-up menu.

To hide the image, uncheck View Options: **Show Image 3**. Now distortion patterns in the mesh will be more evident.

TIP You can save a mesh and then apply it to other images. Click Save Mesh, type a name for the mesh, choose a location for it, then click Save (Photoshop saves Mesh files with the .msh extension). To load in a mesh, click Load Mesh.

Liquify Mesh

After appling distortion to your image, you can use the **Reconstruct** Options, together with the Reconstruct tool, to undo some or all of the distortion.

To remove all distortion from the preview:

In the Reconstruct Options area of the Liquify dialog box, click Restore All. The entire preview image will return to the state it was in when you originally opened the Liquify dialog box.

or

Alt-click/Option-click Cancel to reset the preview to its unaltered state and also reset all tools and options to their default settings.

To reverse distortion in all unfrozen areas:

1. In the Reconstruct Options area of the Liquify dialog box, choose Mode: Revert, Rigid, Stiff, Smooth, or Loose (see the sidebar). Revert, the default mode, reverses all changes without introducing additional distortion.

2. Click the Reconstruct button several times. Unfrozen parts of the preview image will reverse incrementally to the state they were in when you opened the dialog box; frozen areas won't change. The number of reverse steps depends on which Reconstruct mode you chose.

   or

   From the palette menu in the Reconstruct Options area, choose a

   NEW Reconstruct mode. In the dialog box that opens, move the slider to specify the desired amount of reconstruction for that mode, then click OK.

To return individual unfrozen areas to their initial state:

1. In the Liquify dialog box, choose Reconstruct Mode: Revert from the pop-up menu in the Tool Options area.

2. Choose the Reconstruct tool (R), then click and hold on, or drag over, the areas that you want to restore. The restoration will happen more quickly at the center of the brush cursor.

The Reconstruct modes

You can choose the **Revert, Rigid, Stiff, Smooth,** or **Loose** mode for the Reconstruct tool or as a Reconstruct option. Each mode reverses the distortion in its own fashion. Some modes extend distortion from frozen areas into unfrozen areas, with the result being part restoration and part distortion. Rigid and Stiff both produce sharp transitions between the frozen and nonfrozen areas; both Smooth and Loose produce additional distortion, with a more gradual transition between the frozen and nonfrozen areas; and Revert reverses all changes without introducing additional distortion.

For an explanation of Displace, Amplitwist, and Affine modes, which can be chosen for the Reconstruct tool in the Tool Options area, see Photoshop Help.

AUTOMATE 22

*An **included** command has a black check mark; an excluded command doesn't.* *An **action***

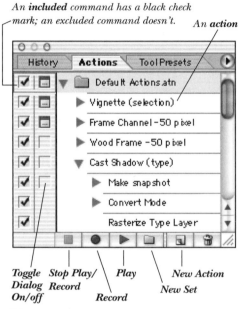

Toggle Dialog On/off · **Stop Play/Record** · **Play** · **Record** · **New Action** · **New Set**

1 *With the Actions palette in **list** (edit) mode, you can exclude a command, toggle a dialog box pause on or off, rearrange the order of commands, record additional commands, rerecord a command, delete a command, or save actions and/or sets to an actions file. This is the default (start-up) mode.*

Wood Frame – 50 pixel	
Cast Shadow (type)	F1
Water Reflection (type)	F2
Custom RGB to Grayscale	F3
Molten Lead	F4
Make Clip Path (selection)	F5
Sepia Toning (layer)	F6

2 *This is the Actions palette in **button** mode. Any button colors and function keys chosen in the Action Options dialog box are displayed.*

AN ACTION IS A recorded sequence of menu commands, tool operations, or other image-editing functions that can be played back on a single file, a handful of files, or a folder full (batch) of files. Actions can execute anything from one simple editing step to a complex sequence of commands that trigger still other actions. They can be used to accomplish multiple tasks, such as applying a series of adjustment commands or filters, performing a sequence of "pre-flight" steps to prepare multiple images for print output, or converting images to a different format or image mode.

Actions can help you achieve consistent editing results on multiple images, and they can help you save seconds or hours of work time, depending on how they're used. Start by recording a few simple actions. You'll be programming more complex processes and boosting your productivity in no time. (Bonus: At the end of this chapter, we'll show you how to use some of the commands on the File > Automate submenu.)

Actions can be created in Photoshop or ImageReady. The Actions palette is used to record, play back, edit, delete, save, store, and load actions **1**–**2**. Each action can be assigned its own keyboard shortcut for quick access. Actions can also be triggered via droplets—small applications that are created from actions. Dragging a file or folder full of files onto a droplet icon activates the action.

The Actions palette can be displayed in list or button mode. To turn button mode on or off, choose Button Mode from the Actions palette menu.

TIP With the Action Palette in list (edit) mode, Alt-click/Option-click a right-pointing triangle to expand (or collapse) all the steps in an action or to expand all the steps of all the actions contained in an actions set.

Actions

Actions

As you **create** an action, the commands you use are recorded. When you're finished recording, the commands will appear as a list in indented (nested) format on the Actions palette.

To record an action:

1. Open an image or create a new one. Just to be on the safe side, copy the image using File > Save As.

2. Click the New Action button 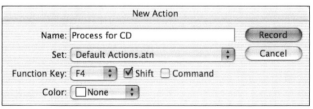 at the bottom of the Actions palette, or choose New Action from the Actions palette menu.

3. In the New Action dialog box, enter a Name for the action **1**. For this first try, you can ignore the Set pop-up menu (see the following page).

4. *Optional:* Assign a keyboard shortcut Function Key and/or display Color to the action. These options will display on the Actions palette when it's in button mode.

5. Click Record.

6. Execute the commands that you want to record as you would normally apply them to any image. When you enter values in a dialog box and then click OK, those settings will be recorded (unless you click Cancel). See the list of recordable commands on the following page.

7. Click the Stop button ■ or press Esc to stop recording.

8. The action will now be listed on the Actions palette. With the palette in list

It's all relative

Position-related operations (e.g., using a selection tool, or the Slice, Gradient, Magic Wand, Path, or Notes tool) are recorded based on the current ruler units. The units can be **actual** (e.g., inches or picas) or **relative** (e.g., percentages). An action that's recorded when an actual measurement unit is chosen can be played back on an image that's smaller than the dimensions used in the original recorded action, provided there's enough canvas area to execute the action. An action that's recorded when a relative unit is chosen will work in any other relative space and on an image of any dimensions. To change the units, go to Edit (Photoshop, in Mac) > Preferences > Units & Rulers, then choose a unit, or choose "percent" from the Units: Rulers pop-up menu.

mode, you can click the arrowhead next to the new action name to collapse or expand its list of commands.

TIP Alt-click/Option-click the New Action button to create a new action without using a dialog box. It will be assigned a name automatically (e.g., "Action 1").

TIP To rename an action, double-click its name (press Enter/Return when done).

TIP Record the Save and Save As commands in an action with caution. Be especially careful not to change any file names. You may want to make your action pause in the Save dialog box to prevent existing files from being overwritten (see page 414). To delete a command from an action, see page 410.

1 *Use the **New Action** dialog box to assign a name, set, function key, and color to your action.*

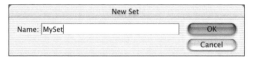

1 *Enter a **Name** for the new set.*

Actions are saved in **sets** on the Actions palette. Sets are a convenient way of organizing task-related actions.

To create an actions set:

1. Click the New Set button at the bottom of the Actions palette.

2. Type a Name for the set **1**, then click OK.

TIP Alt-click/Option-click the New Set button to create a new set without naming it yourself. It will be assigned a name automatically.

What can (or can't) be recorded in an action NEW

TOOLS							PALETTES	
Marquee tools	YES		Path Selection		NO		Actions	SOME
Move	YES		Direct Selection		NO		Brushes	YES
Lasso tools	YES		Type Tools	YES			Channels	YES
Magic Wand	YES		Pen		NO		Character	YES
Crop	YES		Anchor Point Tools		NO		Color	YES
Slice tools	YES		Shape Tools	YES			File Browser	NO
Healing Brush		NO	Notes		YES		Histogram	NO
Patch		NO	Audio Annotation	YES			History	YES
Color Replacement		NO	Eyedropper	YES			Info	NO
Brush		NO	Color Sampler	YES			Layer Comps	YES
Pencil		NO	Measure		NO		Layers	YES
Clone Stamp		NO	Hand		NO		Navigator	NO
Pattern Stamp		NO	Zoom		NO		Options	NO
History Brush		NO	QuickMask Mode	YES			Paragraph	YES
Art History		NO	Screen Mode		NO		Paths	YES
Eraser		NO					Styles	YES
Background Eraser		NO	**MENU COMMANDS**				Swatches	YES
Magic Eraser	YES		File commands	MOST			Tool Options	NO
Gradient	YES		Edit commands	MOST			Tool Presets	YES
Paint Bucket	YES		Image commands	MOST			Tools	NO
Blur		NO	Layer commands	MOST				
Sharpen		NO	Select commands	MOST				
Smudge		NO	Filter commands	MOST				
Dodge		NO	View > Proof setup	YES				
Burn		NO	View commands		NO			
Sponge		NO	Window commands	SOME				
			Help commands		NO			

You can insert a variety of commands into an action. For example, you can insert a **stop** into an action that will interrupt the playback, at which point the user can manually perform a nonrecordable operation, such as using the Brush or Clone Stamp tool. When the manual operation is finished, the user resumes the playback by clicking the Play button again. A stop can also be used to allow an informative alert message to display at a designated pause.

To insert a stop in an action:

1. As you're creating an action, pause at the point at which you want the stop to appear. For an existing action, click the command name on the Actions palette after which you want the stop to appear.

2. Choose Insert Stop from the Actions palette menu.

3. Type an instructional or alert message for the user who's going to replay the action 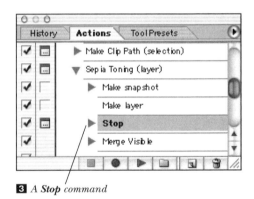. It's a good idea to specify in your stop message that after performing a manual step, the user should click the Play button or action name on the Actions palette to resume the playback. If the Actions palette is in button mode, the Play button isn't accessible; instead, the user will need to click the action name, displayed in red, to resume the playback.

4. *Optional:* Check Allow Continue to include a Continue button in the stop alert box **2**. This allows the user to choose to continue the action without performing any manual tasks. *Note:* If Allow Continue isn't checked, the user will still be able to click Stop at that point in the action playback and then click the Play button (or the action name) on the palette to resume playing back the action.

5. Click OK.

6. The stop will be inserted below the command you highlighted in step 1 **3**.

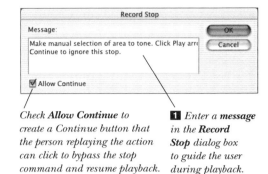

*Check **Allow Continue** to create a Continue button that the person replaying the action can click to bypass the stop command and resume playback.*

1 *Enter a **message** in the **Record Stop** dialog box to guide the user during playback.*

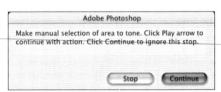

2 *The **Continue** button lets the user continue an action without performing manual tasks.*

3 *A **Stop** command*

The **Insert Menu Item** command allows you to add nonrecordable menu commands to an action. No values for the commands are recorded, but during playback, the dialog box for each command in the action sequence will open onscreen, allowing the user to choose custom settings.

To insert a menu item in an action:

1. In an existing action, click the command name after which you want the new menu command to be inserted.

2. Choose Insert Menu Item from the Actions palette menu ■.

3. From the Photoshop menu bar, choose the command that you want to add to the action. The command name will be listed in the Insert Menu Item dialog box ■.

4. Click OK. The menu command you chose is now added to the action ■. The ability to toggle the dialog box open or closed (called "modal control") is disabled for the inserted command (see also page 414).

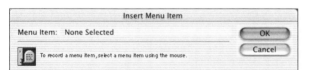

■ *When **Insert Menu Item** has been chosen, the dialog box tells you to choose a menu item.*

■ *We chose the Fill command from the Photoshop menu bar; it then is listed automatically in the dialog box.*

■ *The **inserted menu item***

A **path** can also be inserted into an action, just as if you copied and pasted it from another document or application. Because the path is saved in the action, you can place it in as many files as you want. What's more, after the path is placed, you can have your action transform and/or manipulate it.

Note: Adding paths to actions requires significant memory. If you need to increase the memory allotted to Photoshop, see page 436.

To insert a path in an action:

1. Create the path that you want to use in an action (see pages 316–320), and leave Work Path selected on the Paths palette.

2. Start recording the action, and pause at the point in your action at which you want the path to be inserted. Or for an existing action, click the command name after which you want the path to be inserted, then click the Record button. ●

3. Choose Insert Path from the Actions palette menu. The command "Set Work Path" will be added to the action **1**.

4. Choose Save Path from the Paths palette menu, then click OK to accept the default name.

5. Finish recording your action, including any transformations of the path.

TIP If percent is the current ruler unit, the action will draw the path in proportion to the size of the document the action is being played back on. For example, if you create a path, insert that path into an action using an 8.5″ x 11″ document, and then play the action back in a document half that size, the path will be drawn at 50% of its original size.

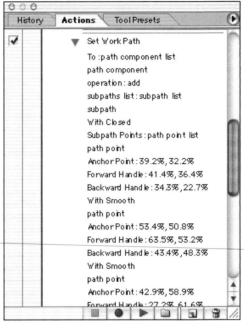

1 *The **work path** you created appears in the action, along with a list of the path's anchor points and related attributes. More information than you ever wanted.*

Insert Path

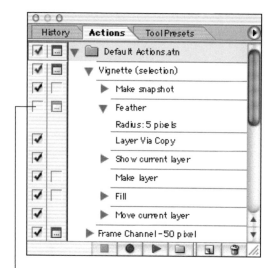

1 *The "Vignette" action is expanded on the Actions palette, and the Feather step is unchecked to **exclude** it from playback.*

To exclude a command from playback:

1. Make sure the Actions palette is in list—not button—mode. (In button mode, you can execute only an entire action, and previously excluded commands won't play back.)

2. Make sure the list for the action you want to edit is expanded. Click the right-pointing triangle next to the action name to expand the list, if necessary.

3. Click in the leftmost column to remove the check mark and exclude that command from playback **1**.

   (You can click in the same spot again at any time to restore the check mark and include the command.)

To play back an action on an image:

1. Open the image that you want to play back the action on.

2. If the Actions palette isn't in list mode, choose Button Mode from the palette menu to uncheck the command.

3. Click an action name on the palette.

4. Click the Play button ▶ on the palette.
   or
   Create a droplet from the desired action, then drag files onto the droplet icon (to make your own droplets, see page 413).

TIP Make a snapshot of your image before running an action on it. That way, you can quickly restore its pre-action state without having to undo any individual action steps.

Exclude/Include Command; Play Back Action

To add commands to an action:

1. On the Actions palette, click the right-pointing triangle next to an action name to expand the list, if it's not already expanded, then click the command name after which you want the new command to appear.

2. Click the Record button. ●

3. Perform the steps required to record the command(s) that you want to add. *Note:* A command that's available only under certain conditions (e.g., the Feather command, which requires an active selection) can't be added to an action unless the creation of those conditions is also included as steps in the action.

4. Click the Stop button ■ to stop recording.

TIP To copy a command from one action to another, expand both action lists, then Alt-drag/Option-drag the command you want to copy from one list to the other. If you don't hold down Alt/Option while dragging, you'll cut the command from the original action. Be careful if you copy any Save commands—they may contain info that's specific to the original action.

You can **delete** individual commands from an action. *Note:* To save the current list of actions as a set for later use, before deleting any items from the Actions palette, follow the instructions on page 416.

To delete a command from an action:

1. Click the name of the command that you want to delete. Shift-click to highlight additional commands, if desired.

2. Click the Delete button 🗑 at the bottom of the Actions palette, then click OK.
   or
   Drag the command to the Delete button.

The ability to play an action using the **Batch** command is one of the most powerful features of actions.

To play an action on a batch of images:

1. Make sure all the files to be batch-processed are located in the same folder. That is, make sure the destination folder actually exists! Or you can select files in the File Browser for the batch.

2. Choose File > Automate > Batch, or **NEW** choose Batch from the Automate menu in the File Browser.

3. Choose a set from the **Set** pop-up menu and choose an action from the **Action** pop-up menu **1**.

4. For **Source,** choose Folder, click Browse/Choose, and locate the folder that contains the files to be processed; or if files were selected in the File Browser, you can choose File Browser.

   If the action contains an Open command and you want to deactivate it, check Override Action "Open" Commands. This will ensure that only images in the Source location designated above will be batch-processed.

5. Check Suppress File Open Options Dialogs and/or check Suppress Color **NEW** Profile Warnings to have batch processing bypass those alerts or other dialog

boxes that may appear onscreen as source files are opened.

6. From the Destination pop-up menu, choose one of the following options:

   None to have the files stay open after processing.

   Save and Close to have the files save over their originals and then close.

   Folder to have the files save to a new folder. Click Browse/Choose, then choose a destination folder. Also check Override Action "Save As" Commands to save images to the destination folder instead of the location listed in the action. The chosen action must contain a Save or Save As command; otherwise files won't be saved.

7. *Optional:* By default, Photoshop will end the batch process when it encounters an error message. To have the batch play through instead and keep track of the error messages in a text file, choose Log Errors to File from the Errors menu, click Save As, type a name, choose a location, then click Save. Now, if errors are encountered, you'll be alerted via a prompt that errors were logged into the designated error log file.

   For information about the File Naming options, see the following page.

8. Click OK. The batch processing begins.

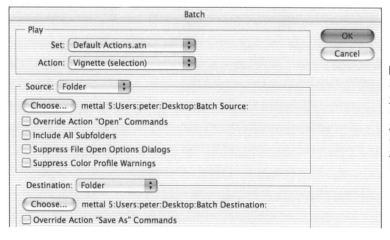

1 *In the **Batch** dialog box, choose the action you want to Play, locate the files you want to process (the Source), and specify where you want the processed files to be saved (the Destination).*

When Folder is chosen as the destination for batch files, many options are available for **naming** the resulting files. For example, the files can be named sequentially using serial numbers or letters so they don't replace each other in the new folder. There are also options for ensuring that the file names are compatible with various operating systems.

To choose file naming options:

1. Follow the batch-processing instructions on the previous page to create a folder for saving the processed files, choose File > Automate > Batch, and choose Destination: Folder for the processed files.

2. Choose options from the pop-up menus in the File Naming area **1**, or simply type in any text you want to include in the name.

3. Make sure the Example name exhibits the naming convention that you chose.

4. If you chose a naming option that uses **NEW** sequential (serial) numbers, enter up to a four-digit starting number in the Starting serial# field.

5. Check any file name Compatibility boxes: Windows, Mac OS, or Unix.

Playback options

Four options for playback control are available in the Playback Options dialog box, which can be opened from the Actions palette menu when the palette is in list mode.

Accelerated: The fastest option.

Step by Step: The action's list expands on the Actions palette and each command or edit name become highlighted on the list as it's executed.

Pause for [   ] seconds: This option works like Step by Step, plus a user-defined pause is inserted at each step.

Pause for Audio Annotation: The playback pauses until an audio annotation, if included, has completed.

More playback options

■ To play an action starting from a specific command in the action, click that command name, then click the Play button or choose Play from the Actions palette menu.

■ To play one command in a multicommand action, click the command name, then Ctrl-click/ Cmd-click the Play button or Ctrl-double-click/ Cmd-double-click the command.

1 *File Naming options in the **Batch** dialog box*

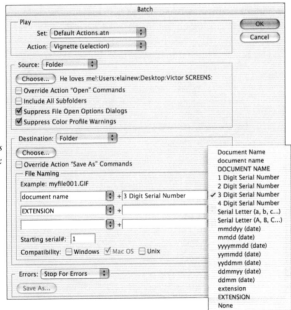

Back and forth

To make a droplet that was created in Windows usable in Macintosh (Mac OS-ready), drag the Windows droplet onto the Macintosh Photoshop CS **application** icon. To make a Mac-made droplet usable in Windows, add the extension **.exe** at the end of the droplet name. *Note:* References to file names and paths within an action aren't supported between operating systems.

An action can be turned into its own little mini-application, called a **droplet,** which sits out on the desktop or in a folder, waiting to be triggered. If you drag a file or a folder full of files onto the droplet icon, Photoshop CS will launch automatically, if it's not already open, and the action that the droplet represents will be applied to those files. Droplets can be given to other users and used on other computers.

To create a droplet for an action:

1. Choose File > Automate > Create Droplet.

2. Click Choose **1**. A Save dialog box opens. Enter a name in the Save As field, choose a location for the droplet, then click Save.

3. Back in the Create Droplet dialog box, choose a set from the Set pop-up menu, then choose the action you want saved as a droplet from the Action pop-up menu.

4. Check any Play options that you want included in the droplet (see page 411).

5. Choose Destination and Errors options for the processed files (see steps 6–7 on page 411).

6. Click OK **2**. The droplet will appear in the designated location.

TIP In ImageReady, you can create a droplet simply by dragging an action to the Desktop.

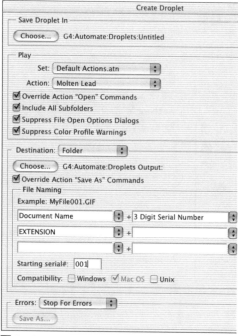

1 *In the* ***Create Droplet*** *dialog box, choose a location for saving the droplet.*

2 *A* ***droplet*** *icon*

A **modal control** is a pause in an action. A modal control can be toggled on or off for any command that uses a dialog box or any tool that requires pressing Enter/Return in order to be executed. If users encounter a modal control upon playing back an action, they can either enter different settings in the dialog box or click OK to proceed with the settings that were originally recorded for the action.

To add a modal control to an action:

1. Make sure the Actions palette is in list mode (not button mode).

2. On the Actions palette, click the right-pointing triangle next to the action name to expand the list, if it's not already expanded.

3. Click in the second column from the left; a dialog box icon should appear 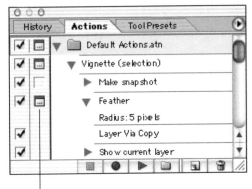. When the action is played back and the modal control is encountered, the action will pause and the dialog box for that command will appear onscreen. The user can then enter new values, accept the existing values (click OK), or click Cancel. The playback will resume after the dialog box is closed. (To remove a modal control, click the dialog box icon.)

TIP You can also click the dialog box icon next to an action name to turn on/off all the modal controls for that action.

Keep in mind that if you change the **order** of commands in an action, the revised action may produce different results than the original.

To change the order of commands:

1. Work on a duplicate action, or at least save the set before proceeding (see page 416).

2. On the Actions palette, click the right-pointing triangle next to an action name to expand the list, if it's not already expanded.

3. Drag a command upward or downward on the list **2**. Simple as that.

1 *The **dialog box** icon. This icon displays in red if the modal control for one or more commands in the action has been turned off.*

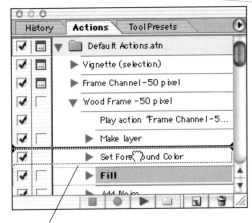

2 *The Fill command is being **moved upward** on the list.*

Modal Control; Change Command Order

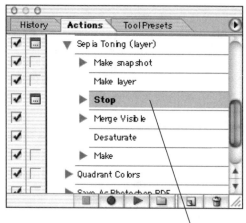

1 *Double-click the command you want to rerecord.*

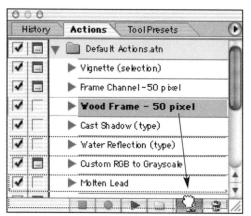

2 *To duplicate an action, drag the action name over the New Action button.*

To rerecord an action using different dialog box settings:

1. Click the name of the action that you want to revise.

2. Choose Record Again from the Actions palette menu. The action will play back, stopping at any command that uses a dialog box.

3. When each dialog box opens, enter new settings, if desired, then click OK. When the dialog box closes, the rerecording will continue.

4. To stop the rerecording, click Cancel in a dialog box, or click the Stop button ■ at the bottom of the Actions palette.

To rerecord a single command in an action:

1. On the Actions palette, double-click the command that you want to rerecord **1**.

2. Enter new settings.

3. Click OK. (Click Cancel to have any revisions be disregarded.)

If you want to experiment with an action or add to it without messing around with the original, work on a **duplicate.**

To duplicate an action:

Click an action, then choose Duplicate from the Actions palette menu.

or

Drag an action over the New Action button ▣ at the bottom of the Actions palette **2**.

TIP To duplicate a command in an action, click the command name, then choose Duplicate from the palette menu. Or drag the command over the New Action button at the bottom of the Actions palette.

To delete an action:

1. Click the action you want to delete.

2. Click the Delete button 🗑 at the bottom of the Actions palette, then click OK.

or

Alt-click/Option-click the Delete button.

Rerecord, Duplicate, Delete Action

Actions are stored automatically in actions sets (a set can contain one or more actions). Follow these instructions to save an actions set to a **separate file** for use on another computer or as a backup to prevent accidental or inadvertent loss.

To save an actions set to a file:

1. Click the actions set that you want to save.

2. Choose Save Actions from the Actions palette menu.

3. In the File name/Save As field, type a name for the actions set file, and choose a location in which to save it.

4. Click Save. The new file will be regarded as one set, irrespective of the number of actions it contains.

TIP To copy an action from one set to another, Alt-drag/Option-drag it into the target set.

To load a set onto the Actions palette:

1. Click the set name that you want the loaded set to appear below.

2. Choose Load Actions from the Actions palette menu, locate and highlight the actions set file that you want to append, then click Load.
   or
   Choose an actions set name from the bottom of the Actions palette menu.

To replace the current actions set with a different set:

1. Choose Replace Actions from the Actions palette menu.

2. Locate and click the actions set file that you want to replace the existing sets with.

3. Click Load.

Where are actions stored?

In Mac, the actions that are visible on the Actions palette list are stored in the **Actions Palette** file in Users/[UserName]/Library/Preferences/Adobe Photoshop CS Settings. They'll live there until they're replaced or the file is trashed. To keep a set from being inadvertently removed, save it as a separate file! (In Windows, the storage location of the action files isn't visible to the user.)

For easy access, save your actions sets in Presets/ **Photoshop Actions** inside the application folder. The sets you save will be listed at the bottom of the Actions palette menu.

To save a **text** version of an actions set, hold down Ctrl-Alt/Cmd-Option while choosing Save Actions from the Actions palette menu. This file can't be imported back into Photoshop.

Actions and AppleScript

Although Photoshop actions can be real time-savers because they let you record and play back a series of commands, they do have some limitations. They can't use **conditional logic,** meaning you can't tell an action to perform one command if one situation exists and another command if it doesn't exist. (ImageReady actions do allow for limited conditional logic.) Also, you can control only Photoshop files with an action, not files in other programs.

Fortunately, you can get around these limitations by controlling Photoshop with scripts written in any of these widely known languages: AppleScript on the Mac platform, Visual Basic on Windows, and JavaScript for cross-platform scripting.

An introduction to scripting is beyond the scope of this book, but the standard Photoshop CS installation provides a good bit of information, as well as the sample scripts that are located in the Adobe Photoshop CS/Scripting Guide folder. There you'll find the Photoshop Scripting Guide, plus substantial guides to each of the scripting languages.

Save, Load, Replace Actions Set

1 *Click the command **after** which you want the additional action to appear, click the Record button...*

2 *...then click the action to be added.*

You can make an action run **within** another action.

To run one action in another action:

1. Open a file, or better yet, duplicate the file, as the action that you'll be adding will run through all of its commands, and thus will affect the currently open image!

2. With the Actions palette in list mode, click the right-pointing triangle next to the action name to expand the list, if it's not already expanded, then select the command after which you want the additional action to appear **1**.

3. Click the Record button. ●

4. Click the action to be added **2**.

5. Click the Play button ▶ to record it into the other action (double-clicking the action won't do the job here). The added action will run through its commands. The new command on the actions list will have this name: "Play action [action name] of set [set name]."

6. Click the Stop button ■ when the action you added is finished playing.

TIP An action can include multiple actions, but careful planning ahead of time is essential. The actions you need may be moved or modified in the interim or may be unavailable the next time you call upon them. Spending some time organizing your actions and sets now and backing up often will save you time in the long run.

Run One Action in Another

Other automate commands

In addition to the Batch and Create Droplet commands on the Automate submenu, there are other commands that work like actions on steroids: PDF Presentation, Conditional Mode Change, Contact Sheet II, Crop and Straighten Photos (new), Fit Image, Multi-Page PDF to PSD, Picture Package, Web Photo Gallery, and Photomerge (also new). These commands combine many complex command sequences into one dialog box setting. *Note:* The Crop and Straighten command is discussed on page 99, Photomerge on pages 256–258. For the PDF Presentation command, see Photoshop Help.

The PDF Presentation, Contact Sheet II, Picture Package, Web Photo Gallery, and Photomerge commands can also be activated via the Automate menu in the File Browser. Be sure to select the thumbnails for the files you want to use before choosing a command.

By adding the **Conditional Mode Change** command to an action, you can ensure that all the images being processed by the action are in the desired image mode. The following instructions show you how the command works.

To perform a conditional image mode change:

1. With an image open, choose File > Automate > Conditional Mode Change.

2. In the Source Mode area, check which image modes you'll permit the command to work with ◼.

3. From the Target Mode: Mode pop-up menu, choose the image mode you want the image converted to.

4. Click OK. If the file's original image mode doesn't match any of the source modes that you checked in step 2, an alert dialog box will appear ◼. Respond by clicking OK.

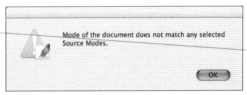

◼ *Choose Source Mode and Target Mode options in the **Conditional Mode Change** dialog box.*

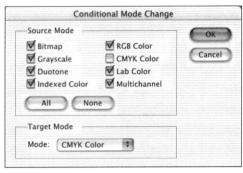

◼ *This alert dialog box will appear if the image mode of the processed file doesn't match any of the chosen source modes.*

A **contact sheet** is an arrangement of image thumbnails on a page, all with the same size bounding box, with or without captions.

To create a contact sheet:

1. Depending on which source option you're going to choose (see step 3, below), you can either put files in a folder or go to the File Browser and select all the images that you want placed on the contact sheet. The command can locate files in a folder as well as any nested subdirectories/subfolders within that folder. Also make sure that all the files you want on the contact sheet are saved in a format that Photoshop can read.

2. Choose File > Automate > Contact Sheet II.

3. In the Source Images area, choose **NEW** Current Open Documents, Folder, or Selected Images from File Browser for your source images. If you chose Folder, click Browse/Choose, highlight the folder that contains the images for the contact sheet, then click Choose **1**.

   Optional: Check Include All Subdirectories/Subfolders to have the command process files in the designated folder and in any subdirectories/subfolders inside it.

4. In the Document area, do the following:

   Choose a measurement unit from the **NEW** **Units** pop-up menu, then enter overall **Width** and **Height** values for the contact sheet.

   Choose a **Resolution** and **Mode** for the contact sheet.

   Optional: Check Flatten All Layers to have all images (and captions, if chosen) **NEW** appear on a single layer, or uncheck this option to have each image and caption pair appear on a separate layer.

   (Continued on the following page)

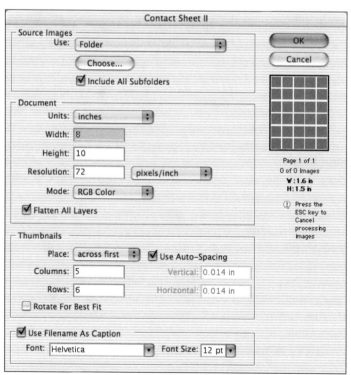

1 *In the* **Contact Sheet II** *dialog box, locate the images to be put on a contact sheet and also choose layout options for the sheet.*

5. In the Thumbnails area:

   Choose a **Place** option for the direction in which the images are to be arranged.

   Enter the desired number of **Columns** and **Rows** for the contact sheet.

   NEW Check **Use Auto-Spacing** to have Photoshop automatically calculate the spacing between thumbnails, or uncheck this option and enter the desired spacing value between thumbnails in the Vertical and Horizontal fields.

   Optional: Check Rotate for Best Fit to have Photoshop automatically orient each thumbnail to fit on the sheet.

   NEW The contact sheet will preview on the right side of the dialog box, and information about the current page, image, and thumbnail size will also be listed.

6. *Optional:* Check Use Filename As Caption to have a caption with the file's name appear under each thumbnail. If you choose this option, also choose a Font and Font Size for the captions.
7. Click OK **1**. Save the contact sheet file that appears onscreen. (To cancel the command in progress, press Esc.)

Be forewarned: The **Fit Image** command resamples an image (changes its pixel count) as it changes its dimensions in order to keep the resolution constant.

To fit an image to width and/or height dimensions:

1. Open a file.
2. Choose File > Automate > Fit Image.
3. Enter the desired Constrain Within: Width and Height dimensions **2**. The command will fit the image to the smaller of the two dimensions. For example, say your source image is 210 x 237 pixels and you enter 275 in the Height field and 1500 in the Width field. The image will be fit to the 275-pixel dimension at the original aspect ratio (with a long dimension of 310 pixels).
4. Click OK.

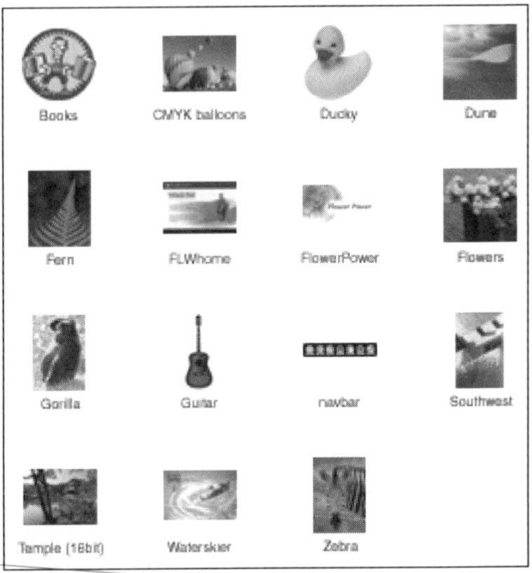

1 *A **contact sheet** with **filename captions***

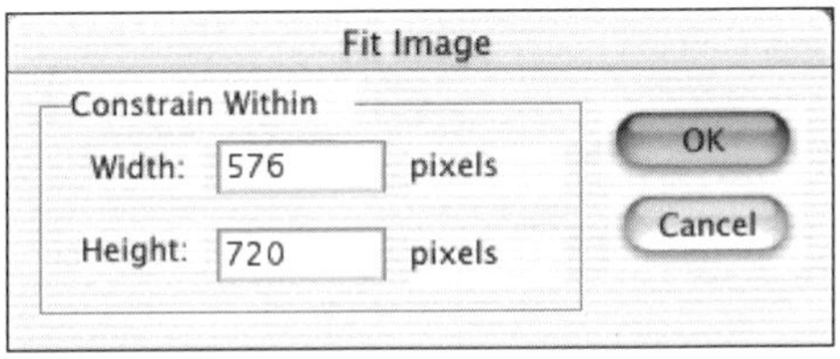

2 *Enter the desired dimensions in the **Fit Image** dialog box.*

Use the **Multi-Page PDF to PSD** command to import a multi-page Acrobat PDF (.pdf) file into Photoshop. Each page of the PDF file is converted and saved as an individual Photoshop .psd file. To learn more about PDF, see pages 80–82, 84, and 459.

To convert a multipage PDF to Photoshop format:

1. Choose File > Automate > Multi-Page PDF to PSD.

2. Under Source PDF, click **Browse/ Choose,** locate and select the PDF file that you want to convert, then click Open ◼.

3. Click **Page Range:** All, or click From and enter a page range. It helps to be familiar with the source file, because you won't see a preview of the source PDF file here.

4. In the Output Options area, enter a **Resolution.** 250 ppi is the minimum suggested resolution for an image that contains type that will be output to print, in order for the type to rasterize well; 72 ppi is sufficient for Web output.

5. Choose a **Mode** (you can change the image mode later in Photoshop).

Optional: Check Anti-aliased to slightly smooth the edges of type characters (this also thins out the characters a bit).

6. In the Destination area:

Leave the **Base Name** as is or enter a new base name for the converted files. The name will be followed by "0001.psd," "0002.psd," and so on, to identify the source pages.

Next, click **Browse/Choose,** locate and click a destination folder for the converted files, then click Choose.

Optional: Check Suppress Warnings to prevent any alert dialog boxes from appearing during the conversion.

7. Click OK. Image windows will quickly display and close onscreen as they're being processed. The converted files will be placed in the designated folder and can be modified like any other Photoshop files.

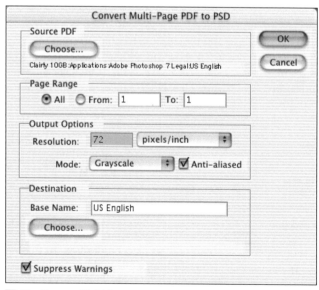

◼ *The **Convert Multi-Page PDF to PSD** dialog box*

The **Picture Package** command arranges multiples of the same image in various sizes on one sheet, like the layouts produced by traditional photo studios. You can use preset or custom sizes and configurations.

Note: If you're going to select images via the File Browser, do so before opening the Picture Package dialog box.

To create a picture package:

1. Choose File > Automate > Picture Package.

2. For Source Images (**1**, next page), choose Use:

   File, click Browse/Choose, locate the image that you want to use, then click Open.
   or
   Folder, click Browse/Choose, locate a folder of images that you want to use, then click Open to create a Picture Package for each of the images in the folder.
   or
   Frontmost Document to use the currently open, active image.
   or
   NEW **Selected Images from File Browser.**

3. In the Document area, choose a **Page Size** for the overall picture package.
   and
   Choose a **Layout** option for the size (in inches) of the images that will appear on the page. The layout will preview in the Layout area.
   and
   Choose a **Resolution** and an image **Mode.**

   Optional: Check Flatten All Layers to have all images (and labels, if chosen) appear on one layer. Uncheck this option to have each image and label pair appear on a separate layer.

4. In the Label area, if you want each file to be labeled, choose a **Content** type. If you chose Custom Text, enter the desired label in the Custom Text field. Labels for

other Content types will be extracted, if available, from information found in File > File Info.
and
Choose a **Font, Font Size, Color,** and **Opacity** for the labels.
and
Choose a **Position** for each label, relative to the image.
and
Choose a **Rotate** option or leave it on the default setting of None.

5. *Optional:* To customize the layout, click **NEW** Edit Layout on the right side of the dialog box. The Picture Package Edit Layout dialog box opens (**2**, next page) Do any of the following:

   Enter a **Name** for the new layout.

   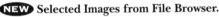

   Choose a preset size from the **Page Size** pop-up menu, or enter custom **Width** and **Height** settings in the currently chosen Units.

   Click **Add Zone** to add a new thumbnail or placeholder box.

   Click a thumbnail or placeholder box and drag a handle to **resize** it, or drag inside it to **reposition** it.

   Click **Delete Zone** to delete a selected thumbnail or placeholder box.

   Click **Save** when done, enter a file name, then click Save again. (Or click Cancel, then click No to cancel any Edit Layout changes you've made.)

   For other options, see Photoshop Help.

6. Click OK. Sit by idly while the command processes. (Press Esc, if need be, to stop the command during processing.)

7. Save the new picture package file in a format of your choosing.

TIP To use more than one image in a picture **NEW** package, in the Layout area, click a thumbnail or placeholder box. In the Select an Image File dialog box, locate a file, then click Open. The newly chosen image will display in the selected box.

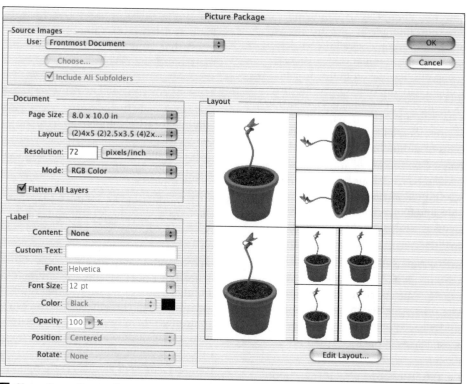

1 *Choose Source Images, Document, and Label options in the* **Picture Package** *dialog box. This is the* (2) 4 x 5 & (2) 2.5 x 3.5 & (4) 2 x 2.5 layout. Many other layout options are available.

NEW

2 *Use the* **Picture Package Edit Layout** *dialog box to further customize your settings.*

Using the **Web Photo Gallery** command, you can export multiple images directly as a website—Photoshop does all the work for you! You'll get, automatically, a gallery home page with its index.htm file, which can be opened in any Web browser for previewing; individual JPEG image pages inside an images subfolder; HTML page files inside a pages subfolder; and JPEG thumbnail images inside a thumbnails subfolder.

Note: When you're ready to upload your Web gallery to a server, ask your Internet service provider (ISP), domain host, or Webmaster which file- and folder-naming conventions to use, and also ask them for uploading instructions.

To create a Web gallery:

1. Make sure all the images you want to use for the website are contained in one folder or are selected in the File Browser (don't select a folder there).

2. Choose File > Automate > Web Photo Gallery.

3. From the Styles pop-up menu **1**, choose a layout style for the website. A tiny preview of each chosen Style will appear in the dialog box.

4. *Optional:* Enter an Email address to serve as a contact address for the gallery.

5. For Source Images, choose Use:
   Folder, click Browse/Choose, locate the folder that contains the images that you want to use, then click Choose.
   or
   Selected Images from File Browser. **NEW**

   Optional: Check Include All Subdirectories/Subfolders to have the command process images in any subdirectories/subfolders inside the designated folder, in addition to any images on the top level.

6. Click Destination, locate the folder that you want to save the resulting files in, then click Choose.

7. When you choose different categories on the Options pop-up menu, the dialog box options change accordingly, and they also will vary depending on which style you chose in step 3. You can go through them one by one to specify such settings as image size, resolution, font, file naming, and link colors.

   Choose **General** to choose HTML options for your website: choose an Extension for the HTML files; click Use UTF 8 Encoding if you want Unicode™ file names; click Add Width and Height Attributes for Images to display image

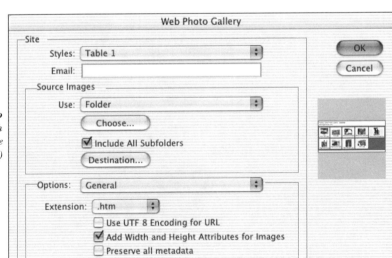

1 *The Web Photo Gallery dialog box (with General chosen on the Options pop-up menu)*

1 *With **Banner** chosen on the Options pop-up menu in the **Web Photo Gallery** dialog box*

2 *With **Large Images** chosen on the Options pop-up menu in the **Web Photo Gallery** dialog box*

3 *With **Thumbnails** chosen on the Options pop-up menu in the **Web Photo Gallery** dialog box*

4 *With **Custom Colors** chosen on the Options pop-up menu in the **Web Photo Gallery** dialog box*

sizes; click Preserve All Metadata to **NEW** maintain file metadata information.

Choose **Banner 1**, then enter information that is to appear on every gallery page, such as Site Name, Photographer, Contact Info, and Date, and choose a Font and Font Size for the banner text (if available for the chosen Style).

Choose **Large Images 2** to set options for the large image previews used on gallery pages. *Optional:* Check Add Numeric Links to include a number **NEW** sequence to aid in navigating between previews; check Resize Images to enable the options for changing the size of the previews. Choose a preset size from the pop-up menu or enter a size in pixels. Choose a Constrain option to resize the images' width, height, or both. Choose a preset JPEG Quality, enter a value (0–12), or move the File Size slider. The higher the JPEG Quality, the larger the file size. Enter a Border Size in pixels (0–99). If available, check any Titles Use options (to be extracted from File > File Info), and finally (Phew!) choose Font and Font Size settings for the titles text.

Choose **Thumbnails 3** to set options for pictures on the home page of the Web gallery. Choose the thumbnail image Size, and choose any of the available thumbnail layout settings (Columns, Rows, and Border Size). If available, check Titles Use options (to be extracted from the File > File Info dialog box), and choose Font and Font Size settings.

Choose **Custom Colors 4** to choose colors for Background, Banner, Text, and Links spaces. Click a color swatch to change it via the Color Picker (remember to use Web-safe colors, if possible). This isn't available for all the Styles.

Choose **Security** (**1**, next page) to display text over your images as an antitheft measure. Choose a type of Content. For Custom Text, type the desired text in the Custom Text field. The other options are

(Continued on the following page)

Web Photo Gallery

extracted automatically, if available, from File > File Info.

Choose a Font, Font Size (the default is 36 pt.), Color (remember to use Web-safe colors, if possible), and Opacity for the text. Choose a Position for the text relative to the image, and finally, choose a Rotate option (for no rotation, choose the default setting of None).

8. Click OK. Photoshop will create the following files: at least one home page named "index"; HTML files for the other pages of the site bearing the extension chosen in Options: General; and JPEG files for the images and thumbnails.

The gallery will display in your default Web browser. If you click a thumbnail or caption in the Web browser, an enlarged view of that image will appear **2**. There may also be navigation arrows to enable the viewer to navigate to the previous picture, next picture, or home page.

TIP To preserve the links, keep all the gallery files and folders in the same folder.

TIP Extra gallery templates are found in the Goodies/Web Photo Gallery Template folder on the Photoshop CS Installation CD. To make these templates accessible from the Styles pop-up menu in the Web Photo Gallery dialog box, drag any or all of the template folders from the CD into the Photoshop CS/Presets/Web Photoshop Gallery folder.

TIP For more information about this feature, see "Creating Web photo galleries" in Photoshop Help.

TIP Web Photo Gallery templates can be restrictive as far as choice of colors, fonts, and, in particular, large image size options. And when many image files are used, navigating between previews can be time-consuming. Try running tests with a few moderately sized images and simple font and color schemes.

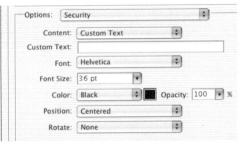

1 *With **Security** chosen on the Options pop-up menu in the **Web Photo Gallery** dialog box*

2 *This is a finished **Web Photo Gallery** home page. Clicking a thumbnail image or name on the home page links you to an enlarged image view page, complete with navigation arrows for viewing the preview or the next enlarged picture, or returning to the home page.*

PREFERENCES 23

Back to the defaults

To reset all the preferences to their **default** values, hold down Ctrl-Alt-Shift (Win)/Cmd-Option-Shift (Mac) when launching Photoshop, then click Yes to delete the Photoshop Settings file. Do the same thing at startup for ImageReady.

PREFERENCES ARE SETTINGS that apply to the application as a whole, such as which ruler units are used, or if channels display in color. Most preference changes take effect immediately; a few take effect only upon relaunching (we've noted those exceptions). All preference changes are saved when you exit/quit Photoshop.

To access the **Preferences** dialog box **1** the fast-and-easy way, press Ctrl-K/Cmd-K. From there, you can cycle through the various panes by using the shortcuts listed on the pop-up menu or by clicking Prev or Next. You can also open the Preferences dialog box by choosing Edit (Photoshop, in Mac) > Preferences.

In addition to the preferences, the **Preset Manager** is also covered in this chapter.

Preferences

✓ General ⌘1	OK
File Handling ⌘2	Cancel
Display & Cursors ⌘3	Prev
Transparency & Gamut ⌘4	Next
Units & Rulers ⌘5	
Guides, Grid & Slices ⌘6	
Plug–Ins & Scratch Disks ⌘7	
Memory & Image Cache ⌘8	☐ Beep When Done
File Browser ⌘9	☑ Dynamic Color Sliders
☑ Zoom Resizes Windows	☑ Save Palette Locations
☐ Auto–update open documents	☑ Show Font Names in English
☐ Show Asian Text Options	☑ Use Shift Key for Tool Switch
	☑ Use Smart Quotes

☐ History Log

Save Log Items To: ⊙ Metadata
⃝ Text File [Choose...]
⃝ Both

Edit Log Items: [Sessions Only]

[Reset All Warning Dialogs]

1 *The* **Preferences** *dialog box*

The Preferences dialog boxes

General Preferences

Choose the Adobe **Color Picker** to access the application's own Color Picker.

Choose an **Image Interpolation** option for commands that involve resampling or transforming: Nearest Neighbor (Faster) is the fastest but least precise (use for hard-edged graphics); Bilinear is medium quality; Bicubic is the highest quality (creates the smoothest gradations) but also the slowest; Bicubic Smoother is appropriate for enlarging images; and Bicubic Sharper is appropriate for reducing images but may cause oversharpening.

Enter the maximum number of **History States** that can be listed on the History palette at a time (1–1000).

Check **Export Clipboard** to have the current Clipboard contents stay on the Clipboard when you exit/quit Photoshop.

Check **Show Tool Tips** to permit the function and name of whichever tool, button, or palette feature the pointer is currently over (mouse button up) to pop up onscreen.

Uncheck **Zoom Resizes Windows** to prevent the image window from resizing when the view size is changed via the Ctrl/Cmd- + (plus) or Ctrl/Cmd- - (minus) shortcut.

Check **Auto-update open documents** to have documents save automatically when jumping between Photoshop and ImageReady. Documents always update after jumping, whether this option is on or off.

Check **Show Asian Text Options** to display and choose options for Chinese, Japanese, and Korean type on the Character and Paragraph palettes.

Check **Beep When Done** to have a beep sound when any command that takes time to process (has a progress bar) is finished processing.

With **Dynamic Color Sliders** checked, colors above the sliders on the Color palette will update as the sliders are moved. Turn this option off to speed performance.

With **Save Palette Locations** checked, palettes that are open when you exit/quit Photoshop will appear in their same location when you relaunch the application.

With **Show Font Names in English** checked, font names on the Font pop-up menu will display in English, regardless of the native language being used in the program.

With **Use Shift Key for Tool Switch** checked, tools that share the same pop-out menu can be accessed using Shift and the letter assigned to them (e.g., press Shift-R to cycle through the Blur, Sharpen, and Smudge tools).

Check **Use Smart Quotes** to have typographically correct curly quotation marks inserted automatically when text is created, instead of straight (foot and inch) marks.

Check **History Log** to choose options for when a log of image edits is saved to the Metadata section of a file, to a separate Text File, or to Both. From the Edit Log Items pop-up menu, choose Sessions Only to log when Photoshop was launched and exited/quit and which files were opened; or Concise to log Sessions information plus a list of edits, as displayed on the History palette; or Detailed, which is like Concise plus a list of the options and parameters used in each editing step.

Click **Reset All Warning Dialogs** to reenable any and all warning prompt messages that you disabled by choosing the Don't Show Again option in individual message dialog boxes.

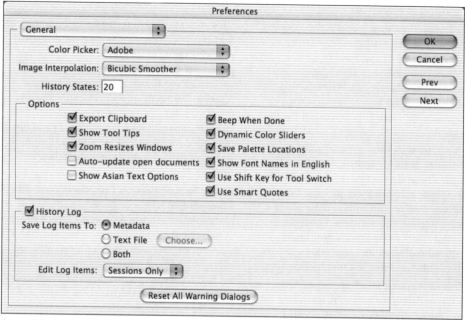

General Preferences in Macintosh

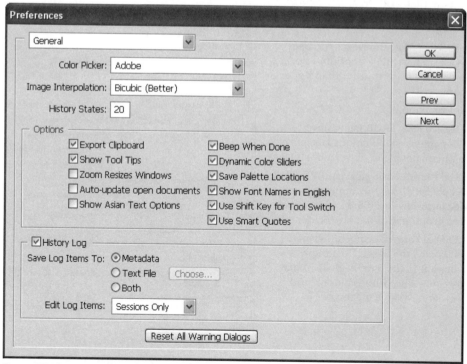

General Preferences in Windows

File Handling Preferences

Choose **Image Previews**: Never Save to save files without a thumbnail preview for the desktop; or choose Always Save to have an updated preview save with files whenever they're saved; or choose Ask When Saving to decide whether to include a preview on a case-by-case basis when files are saved for the first time.

Mac: Check Icon to have a thumbnail of an image display as its file icon on the Desktop and in the Open dialog box. Check Full Size to include a 72-ppi PICT preview for applications that require this option when importing non-EPS files. Check Macintosh Thumbnail and/or Windows Thumbnail to have a thumbnail of an image display when its name is highlighted in the Open dialog box.

Mac: Choose **Append File Extension:** Always or Ask When Saving to have a three-letter abbreviation of the file format (e.g., .tif for TIFF) be included when a Macintosh file is saved. This is helpful when converting files for Windows, and essential when saving files for the Web.

In Windows and Mac, choose/check **Use Lower Case** to have file extensions appear in lowercase characters rather than upper-case characters.

For File Compatibility:

NEW Check **Ignore EXIF sRGB tag** to have Photoshop ignore sRGB color space information when opening digital camera images.

Check **Ask Before Saving Layered TIFF Files** to have an alert dialog box appear when an image is saved as a TIFF, giving you the option to proceed with the save or not.

NEW Check **Enable Large Document Format (.psb)** to enable the Large Document Format option in the Save As dialog box. Currently, only Photoshop can save and open files larger than 2 gigabytes.

Choose a **Maximize PSD File Compability** **NEW** option to maximize file compatibility with previous versions of Photoshop and other programs (e.g., to include a flattened version of the image so all programs can read it). We recommend choosing Ask to force an alert dialog box to open when you save an image, at which point you can check or ignore the option. Including a flattened version with an image produces a larger file size.

Check **Enable Version Cue Workgroup File Management** when you need to share and manage files among Adobe CS applications. When checked, you can click the Version **NEW** Cue button in Photoshop's Open or Save dialog box to see a list of all the currently available CS documents. See the Photoshop Help file for more information about this feature.

In the **Recent file list contains [ ] files** field, enter the maximum number of files that can be listed on the File > Open Recent submenu (0–30).

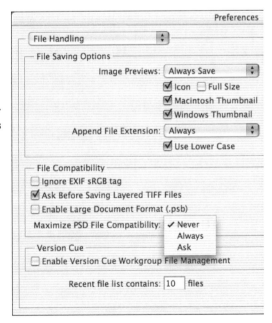

Display & Cursors Preferences

Check **Color Channels in Color** to have individual RGB or CMYK channels display in color on the Channels palette and in the image window. With this option off, channels will display as grayscale.

When using a monitor that's set to 8-bit color, check **Use Diffusion Dither** to have Photoshop use a dithering method to improve color simulation.

Check **Use Pixel Doubling** to speed up preview redraws by having a low-resolution preview display first. This affects only redraw, not "actual" pixels.

For the **Painting Cursors** (Eraser, Pencil, Brush, Clone Stamp, Pattern Stamp, Smudge, Blur, Sharpen, Dodge, Burn, Sponge, Healing Brush, Patch, Color Replacement, and Paint Bucket tools), click Standard to have the cursor be an icon of

the tool being used; or click Precise to have it be a crosshair icon; or click Brush Size to have it be a round icon the exact size of the brush tip (up to 999 pixels) .

For the nonpainting tools (the marquees, the lassos, the Magic Wand, Crop, Slice, Eyedropper, Pen, Freeform Pen, Measure, and Color Sampler), click **Other Cursors:** Standard or Precise.

TIP Depending on the current Preferences setting, pressing the Caps Lock key will turn Standard cursors to Precise, Precise to Brush Size, or Brush Size to Precise.

Standard *cursor*   ***Precise*** *cursor*   ***Brush Size*** *cursor*

1 *Painting cursors*

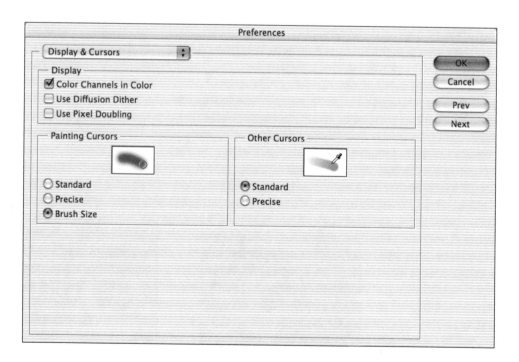

Transparency & Gamut Preferences

Photoshop uses a checkerboard grid to represent transparent areas on a layer (areas that don't contain pixels). You can choose a different **Grid Size.**

Change the **Grid Colors** for the transparency checkerboard by choosing Light, Medium, Dark, Red, Orange, Green, Blue, or Purple. Or choose Custom, then choose a color from the Color Picker **2**.

Check **Use video alpha (requires hardware support)** if you use a 32-bit video card that allows chroma keying for video editing. You'll be able to see through certain parts of the video image.

To change the color used to mark out-of-gamut colors on an image when View > **Gamut Warning** is on, click the Color square, then choose a color from the Color Picker. You can also lower the Opacity of the Gamut Warning color to make it easier to see the image color underneath.

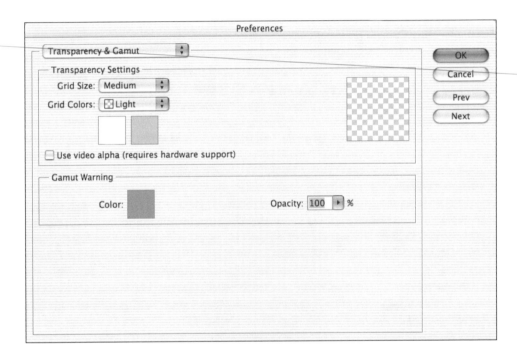

2 *Grid Size: Large; Grid Colors: Medium*

Units & Rulers Preferences

Choose a unit of measure from the Units: **Rulers** pop-up menu for the horizontal and vertical rulers that display in the image window. (Choose View > Rulers to show/hide the rulers.)

Choose a unit for **Type** (as shown on the Character palette).

Note: If you change the measurement units for the Info palette **1**, the ruler units will also change here in this dialog box, and vice versa.

TIP You can also change ruler units by right-clicking/Ctrl-clicking either ruler in the image window and choosing a unit from the context menu. Or to open the Preferences dialog box and get right to the Units & Rulers pane, double-click either ruler.

Enter **Column Size** Width and Gutter values to allow the Image Size and Canvas Size commands to fit images for a specific column width in a layout program.

Values entered in the New Document Preset Resolutions: **Print Resolution** and **Screen Resolution** fields will display in the New dialog box when a preset print or screen size is chosen. The default settings are 300 ppi for print and 72 ppi for onscreen display.

For **Point/Pica Size**, click PostScript (the default) to have Photoshop use the PostScript value for calculating the points-to-inch ratio, or click Traditional to use the pre-desktop publishing value.

Units symbols	
Pixels	**px**
Inches	**in** or **"**
Centimeters	**cm**
Millimeters	**mm**
Points	**pt**
Picas	**p**
Percent	**%**

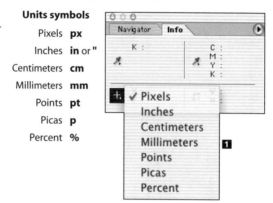

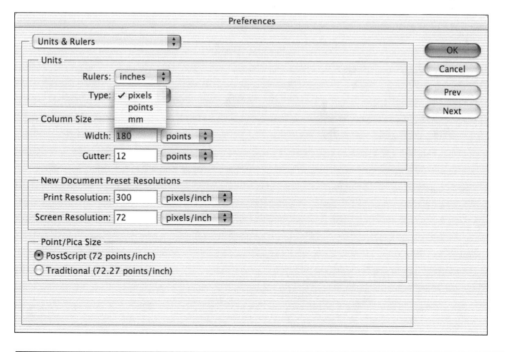

Guides, Grid & Slices Preferences

Note: Changes in this dialog box preview immediately in the image window.

For **Guides,** choose a ready-made color for the removable ruler guides from the Color pop-up menu, or click the color square and choose a color from the Color Picker. (Choosing Custom also opens the Color Picker.) Choose Lines or Dashed Lines for the Guides Style **1**.

For the **Grid,** choose a ready-made color for the nonprinting Grid from the Color pop-up menu, or click the color square and choose a color from the Color Picker. Choose Lines, Dashed Lines, or Dots for the Grid Style.

To have gridlines appear at specific unit-of-measure intervals, choose a unit of measurement from the drop-down menu, then enter a value in the **Gridline every** field. If you choose percent from the drop-down menu, gridlines will appear at those percentage intervals of the overall image, starting from the left edge of the image. For the gridlines between the thicker gridline increments chosen in the "Gridline every" field, enter a number in the **Subdivisions** field.

For Slices, choose a preset **Line Color** for the lines that are used to mark slices. Check **Show Slice Numbers** to have a slice number display in the upper left corner of every slice.

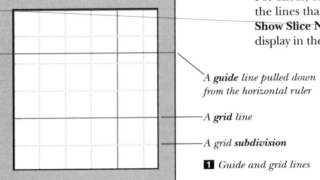

*A **guide** line pulled down from the horizontal ruler*

*A **grid** line*

*A grid **subdivision***

1 *Guide and grid lines*

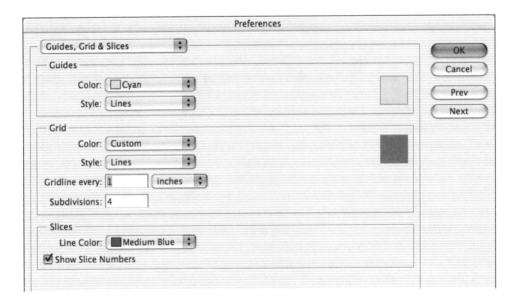

Plug-ins & Scratch Disks Preferences

Note: For changes made in this dialog box to take effect, you must relaunch Photoshop.

Check **Additional Plug-Ins Folder,** then click Choose if you need to relocate or use another plug-ins folder. Photoshop needs to know where to find this folder in order to access third-party plug-ins. *Note:* Don't move Photoshop's internal Plug-Ins module out of the Photoshop folder unless you have a specific reason for doing so. Moving it could inhibit access to filters; the Import, Export, and Effects commands; and some file formats under the save commands.

Some third-party plug-ins that are installed for earlier versions of Photoshop may require the pre-CS version serial number in order to run properly. Enter this number in the **Legacy Photoshop Serial Number** field.

The **First** (and optional Second, Third, or Fourth) **Scratch Disk** is used when available RAM is insufficient for processing or storage. Choose an available hard drive from the First pop-up menu. Startup is the default.

As an optional step, choose an alternative **Second, Third,** or **Fourth** hard drive to be used as extra work space when necessary. If you have only one hard drive, of course, you'll have only one scratch disk.

TIP If you hold down Ctrl-Alt/Cmd-Option when launching Photoshop, the Scratch Disk Preferences dialog box will open (this is a different dialog box from the Plug-Ins & Scratch Disks Preferences).

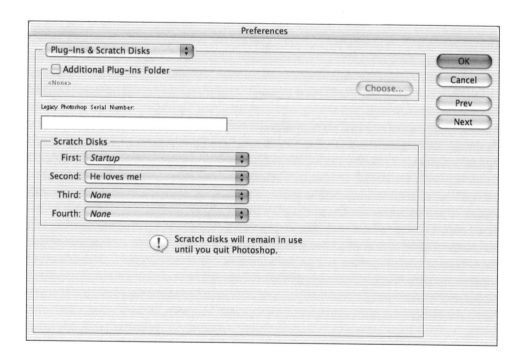

Memory & Image Cache Preferences

Note: For changes made in this dialog box to take effect, you must relaunch Photoshop.

The image cache is designed to help speed up screen redraw when you're editing or color-adjusting high-resolution images. Low-resolution versions of the image are saved in individual cache buffers and are used for updating the onscreen image. The higher the **Cache Levels** value (1–8), the more buffers are used and the speedier the redraw. The Histogram palette also uses the current Cache Levels value to calculate pixel values based on cached data rather than actual data.

Check **Use cache for histograms in Levels** for faster, but slightly less accurate, histogram display in the Levels dialog box.

In the **Maximum Used by Photoshop** field, specify the maximum percentage of RAM to be used by Photoshop.

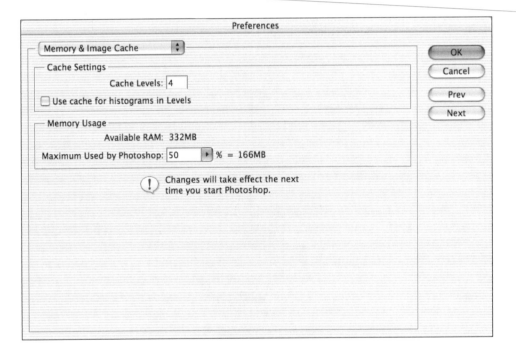

File Browser Preferences **NEW**

In the **Do Not Process Files Larger than** field, enter the maximum file size (0–2047 MB) that you will permit the File Browser to process. Processing large files slows down the browser. The default maximum size is 200 MB.

For **Display: [ ] Most Recently Used Folders in Location Popup,** enter the maximum number of folders (0–30) that can be listed on the location pop-up menu in the Recent Folders section at the top of the main window in the File Browser.

Enter the **Custom Thumbnail Size,** in pixels, to be used in the thumbnails pane when Custom Thumbnail Size is chosen from the View menu in the File Browser.

In the Options area:

Check **Allow Background Processing** to have the program process the data for the display of thumbnails and metadata info as a background operation.

Check **High Quality Previews** to have higher-quality previews display in the browser. The cache files that store File Browser thumbnails will become larger when this option is checked.

Check **Render Vector Files** to have the File Browser generate thumbnails of vector files (e.g., Adobe Illustrator files).

Check **Parse XMP Metadata from Non-image Files** to see and edit metadata from nonimage files (such as text files) in the Metadata pane in the File Browser.

Check **Keep Sidecar Files with Master Files** if you want the option to move, copy, delete, and rename the XMP and THM files that accompany Camera Raw image files, which contain metadata. Other applications use sidecar files in order to work with and process image files.

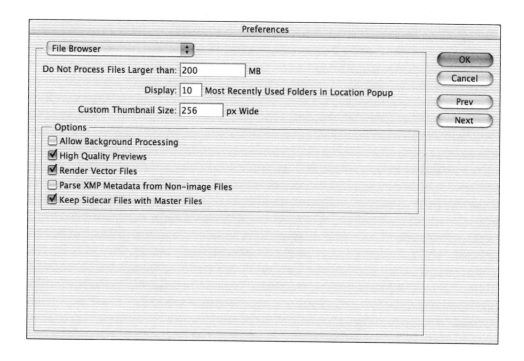

File Browser Preferences

Managing presets

No doubt you've already become acquainted with many of the preset pickers, such as the Brush and Gradient Preset pickers. The Swatches palette also functions as a preset picker. Each picker item is called a **preset,** and each collection of presets is called a **library.** You can use the **Preset Manager** to organize, append, replace, and reset which items are loaded onto each of the preset pickers, or you can make those changes in any of the individual preset pickers. Changes made in an individual preset picker will be reflected in the Preset Manager, and vice versa.

To use the Preset Manager:

1. Choose Edit > Preset Manager.
or
With any palette or preset picker pop-up palette open (e.g., the Brush Preset picker or Gradient Preset picker), choose Preset Manager from the palette menu.

2. *Optional:* Click the arrowhead in the circle ● at the top of the dialog box and choose a different view for the Preset Manager: Text Only, Small Thumbnail, Large Thumbnail, Small List, or Large List. For Brushes, you can also choose Stroke Thumbnail to see a sample of the brushstroke alongside the brush thumbnail.

3. Choose a category of presets from the Preset Type pop-up menu (or use the appropriate Ctrl/Cmd shortcut) **1**.

4. *Do any of the following:*

Click the arrowhead in the circle and choose a library name from the bottom of the menu. Click Append to add that library to the current library, or click OK to replace the current library with the new one.

Click Load, then locate a library to append to the current library.

Click a preset you want to delete (or click, then Shift-click a series of them or Ctrl-click/Cmd-click nonconsecutive presets), then click Delete. The default presets can be deleted, and they can also be restored at any time.

5. Click Done. The edited picker will update.

TIP Preset libraries can be shared among Photoshop users. Nice to know.

TIP Each preset library type has its own file extension and default folder, which is located in Adobe Photoshop CS/Presets. The default preset libraries aren't listed on the preset picker menu or on the Preset Manager menu.

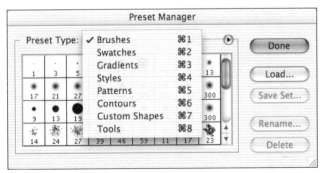

1 *Choose a category from the Preset Type pop-up menu in the **Preset Manager.***

A preset by any other name

To rename a preset, double-click the preset **thumbnail** in the Preset Manager, then change the name in the dialog box that opens. Or if the Preset Manager is in Text Only view or a List view, double-click the preset **name,** then change it right there. You can also select multiple presets, then click **Rename.** In this case, the naming dialog boxes will open one by one in succession.

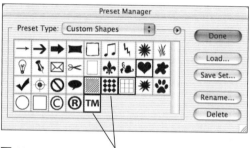

1 *Shift-click the presets you want to save in a **set.***

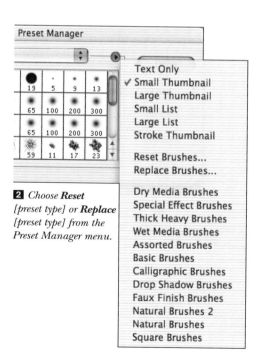

2 *Choose **Reset** [preset type] or **Replace** [preset type] from the Preset Manager menu.*

Via the Preset Manager, you can save a selected group of presets into a **library** for future access and use.

To save selected presets to a new library:

1. Choose Edit > Preset Manager or choose Preset Manager from any picker or palette menu.

2. From the Preset Type pop-up menu, choose the category of presets that you want to save as a set.

3. Shift-click or Ctrl-click/Cmd-click the presets that you want saved in a set **1**.

4. Click Save Set, leave the location as the default preset folder, then enter a name for the new library.

5. Click Save, then click Done to close the Preset Manager dialog box.

TIP You can select multiple presets in the Preset Manager, but you can select only one preset at a time in any of the preset pickers.

To reset or replace presets:

1. Choose Edit > Preset Manager or choose Preset Manager from any preset picker or palette menu.

2. From the Preset Type pop-up menu, choose the category of presets that you want to reset or replace.

3. *Optional:* Any unsaved presets on the list will be deleted, so we recommend saving the current library before proceeding (see the previous set of instructions).

4. From the Preset Manager menu **2**:

   Choose **Reset** [preset type] to restore the default library for the chosen type, then click Append to append the default presets to the current library, or click OK to replace the current library with the default presets (click Cancel if you change your mind).
   or
   Choose **Replace** [preset type], locate a library to replace the current library with, then click Load.

If you define a new brush, pattern, or custom shape via the Edit menu, add a new swatch to the Swatches palette, add a new style to the Styles palette, create a new gradient in the Gradient Editor dialog box, or create a new contour in any Contour picker, that new preset will display on the appropriate tool's preset picker on the options bar. It will also display when its Preset Type is chosen in the Preset Manager.

New presets are saved in the Adobe Photoshop Preferences file temporarily and will display in the appropriate preset picker even after you relaunch Photoshop—provided you don't open another library of the same category (e.g., another brush library), or reset the individual preset picker, or reset the preset picker category via the Preset Manager. If you do any of the above, the new item will be discarded. Don't despair, though, because there's a way to preserve all your hard work. The following method **saves** all the **presets** in the current picker, whereas in the instructions on the previous page, you could pick and choose.

To save the presets in the current picker to a new library:

1. Customize whichever presets you want to customize (as described in the first paragraph above), then from the menu on whichever preset palette or picker you're using, choose Save [preset type].

2. Enter a name, leave the default extension and location as is, then click Save.

Note: In order for the newly created library to appear on the palette or preset picker menu and on the Preset Type pop-up menu in the Preset Manager **1**, you have to relaunch Photoshop.

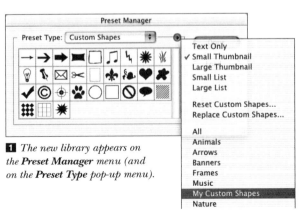

1 *The new library appears on the **Preset Manager** menu (and on the **Preset Type** pop-up menu).*

Resolution of output devices

PostScript b&w laser printer	600 or 1200 dpi
Color ink-jet printer	1440 x 720, 2880 x 1440 dpi
IRIS	600 dpi (looks like 1600 dpi)
Color Laser/Fiery	600 x 600 dpi
Epson Stylus Color/ Photo ink-jet	2880 x 720, 5760 x 720 dpi
Large format ink-jet printer	600 x 600 dpi
Linotronic imagesetter	1200–4000 dpi

100%	Doc: 502.0K/0 bytes

*Press and hold on the status bar in the lower left corner of the application window (Win)/image window (Mac) to display the **page preview**—a thumbnail of the image relative to the paper size.*

Width: 504 pixels (7 inches)
Height: 340 pixels (4.722 inches)
Channels: 3 (RGB Color)
Resolution: 72 pixels/inch

*Alt-press/Option-press and hold on the status bar to display **file information.***

AN IMAGE CAN be printed from Photoshop to a laser printer, to a color printer (e.g., ink-jet, dye sublimation), or to an imagesetter. A Photoshop image can also be imported into and then printed from a drawing application, such as FreeHand or Illustrator; a layout application, such as QuarkXPress or InDesign; or a multimedia application, such as Director or After Effects. And of course your file can also be prepared for viewing online (for that, see the next chapter).

This chapter contains instructions for choosing print options in Photoshop, applying trapping, preparing an image for other applications, saving a file in the EPS, DCS, TIFF, and PDF formats, creating duotones, and creating a percentage tint of a PANTONE color. The last part of the chapter is devoted to color reproduction basics. (To print a spot color channel, see page 210.)

Printing from Photoshop

Getting a good print from an image, especially a color image, is more art than science. It's not accomplished simply by twiddling Photoshop's dials and knobs alone but requires a thorough understanding of the settings available on your printing device, as well as the color management software that's built into your computer's operating system. Here, we can provide only the basics for printing from Photoshop. You'll also need to refer to the Photoshop Help file, which contains a wealth of specialized technical information, as well as the documentation for your specific printer. If you're preparing images for an output service provider, be sure to consult the experts there before setting up your image for printing.

(Continued on the following page)

Print

Your printer drivers and operating system determine what print options are available. You can choose from these options in the Page Setup and Print dialog boxes.

■ To choose Photoshop-specific options, including color management options, **NEW** use the **Print with Preview** command (Ctrl-Alt-P/Cmd-Option-P).

■ The basic **Print** command is activated by our old friend, the shortcut Ctrl-P/ Cmd-P.

■ Even more direct is the **Print One Copy** command (Ctrl-Alt-Shift-P/Cmd-Option-Shift-P).

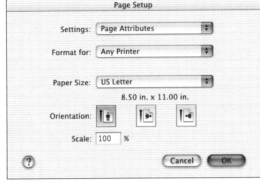

1 *The **Page Setup** dialog box in **Mac***

The first step for any kind of print job is to tell Photoshop what type of **printer** and **paper size** you're using.

To choose a paper size and orientation:

1. Choose File > Page Setup (Ctrl-Shift-P/ Cmd-Shift-P) **1**–**2**.

2. From the Paper Size pop-up menu, choose the paper size you want the file to print on.

3. Click one of the Orientation buttons to have Photoshop print the image parallel to the length or width of the paper.

4. *Windows:* From the Source pop-up menu, choose the tray that holds the paper you want to print on. Click the Printer button to choose printer-specific options.

5. *Mac:* Leave the Scale value at 100%. If you need to change the scale, it's better to do it in File > Print with Preview, where you can preview the results.

   Choose the desired printer from the "Format for" pop-up menu, then use the Settings menu to switch to other panels for printer-specific options.

6. Click OK.

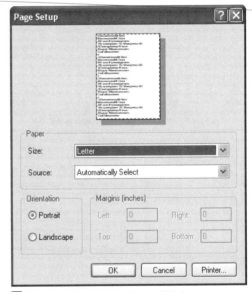

2 *The **Page Setup** dialog box in **Windows***

Page Setup

Resolution overkill?

If your image resolution is greater than two and a half times the screen frequency (much higher than you need) you'll get a warning prompt when you send the image to print. If this occurs, copy the file using File > Save As with As a Copy checked, lower the image resolution using Image > Image Size, then print again.

In Photoshop CS, the simple **Print** command takes you directly to the Print dialog box that's specified in your printer's driver, bypassing all Photoshop-specific options.

To print using the basic Print command:

1. Choose File > Print (Ctrl–P/Cmd–P). The default Print dialog box for your printer opens **1**–**2**.
2. Choose the number of copies to be printed.
3. Choose the printer-specific options that are appropriate for your document.
4. Click OK/Print.

TIP Only the currently visible layers and channels will print.

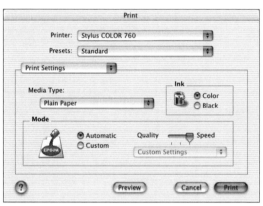

1 *The* **Print** *dialog box for a* **color,** *non-PostScript, ink-jet printer in* **Mac,** *showing the Print Settings panel*

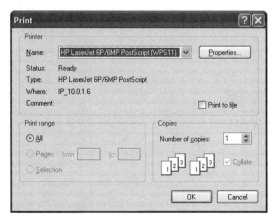

2 *The* **Print** *dialog box for a* **black-and-white** *PostScript printer in* **Windows**

Pressing Ctrl-Alt-P/Cmd-Option-P (the **Print with Preview** command) takes you to a Print dialog box, where you'll see a preview of the image on the printed page, along with other options for adjusting position, print size, color management, and output settings. This is the command that we prefer to use for printing.

To print using the Print with Preview command:

 1. Choose File > Print with Preview (Ctrl-Alt-P/Cmd-Option-P) **1**.

2. Do any of the following:

Check **Center Image** to position your image in the center of the page, or uncheck this option and enter new Top and Left values to move the image on the page.

Change the Scaled Print Size: **Scale** percentage or enter specific **Height** and **Width** values to reduce or enlarge the image for printing purposes only. The Scale, Height, and Width options are interdependent; changing any one option will cause the other two to change.

Check **Scale to Fit Media** to have the image fit automatically to the paper size chosen in File > Page Setup.

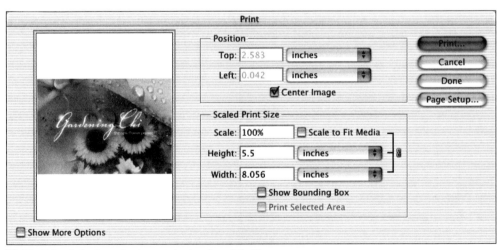

1 *The* **Print** *dialog box, showing a print preview of the file*

Print with Preview

Quick print

If you're in a hurry, and if you've already configured your print options to your liking, you can skip all print-related dialog boxes by choosing File > **Print One Copy** (Ctrl-Alt-Shift-P/Cmd-Option-Shift-P).

The hidden buttons

In the Print with Preview dialog box, pressing Alt/Option changes the functions of these buttons:

Print becomes **Print One.** One copy of the document will print immediately, without the printer's Print dialog box opening.

Done becomes **Remember.** Your custom settings will be saved for the current document, and the dialog box will stay open.

Cancel becomes **Reset.** All settings in the dialog box will be restored to their default values.

Check **Show Bounding Box** to display the image boundary in the preview window. Pull a handle or side of the box to scale your image (for printing purposes only). If Center Image isn't checked, you can drag the whole bounding box to change the position of the image on the printed page. *Note:* Show Bounding Box won't print a border around an image. To print a border, see page 448.

If a rectangular selection is currently active in the image, check **Print Selected Area** to print only that selected portion (the selection won't preview).

3. Check Show More Options to display and choose Color Management and Output settings (see the next page).

4. If you haven't yet chosen page setup settings, click Page Setup. Clicking OK in the Page Setup dialog box will get you back to Print with Preview.

5. When you're done choosing the above-mentioned options, click Print to access your printer's Print dialog box (see page 443), then click Print.
or
Press Alt-click/Option-click and click Print One. One copy of the document will print immediately, without the printer's Print dialog box opening.

You can also click Done to close the dialog box without printing; your custom settings will be saved with the document. *Note:* If you click Cancel to close the dialog box, you'll lose all your custom settings—Ouch!

To print using color management:

1. Choose File > Print with Preview (Ctrl-Alt-P/Cmd-Option-P). **NEW**

2. Check Show More Options and choose Color Management from the pop-up menu (**1**, next page):

3. Choose your **Source Space.** We recommend that you choose the Document option, which uses the color profile of your image (for the specifics of color management, see pages 43–56). It will list whichever profile is currently assigned (tagged) to the document. The Proof Setup option uses the color profile of whichever proof is chosen in View > Proof Setup > Custom.

4. From the Profile pop-up menu in the Print Space area:

Choose **Same As Source** to print using the Source Space profile. No color conversion will occur during the printing process.

or

NEW Choose **Printer Color Management** to let the chosen output printer driver handle color management. All of the file's color information will be sent along with the Source Space profile to the printer, and the printer, not Photoshop, will manage the color conversion.

> **TIP** The only way to determine the best Print Space setting is to run multiple test prints. Try out various color profile settings and decide which one gives you the best print results.

5. Choose Relative Colormetric for the rendering **Intent,** if that pop-up menu is available. As noted in Chapter 2, Intent determines how the color conversion will render when sent to any Print profile other than Same As Source.

6. Check **Use Black Point Compensation** (if available) if you're printing the image in RGB mode, but consult your print shop before checking it for a CMYK image that will be printed on a device that uses a non-CMYK profile.

TIP To print an individual layer or channel, make it the sole visible layer or channel before choosing File > Print or File > Print with Preview.

TIP Our output service provider has advised us not to choose Lab Color for the image mode or for the profile from the Print Space Profile menu. Apparently, few folks calibrate their monitors or edit images in Lab Color mode; also, files sent in Lab Color mode to dye sublimation and IRIS printers tend to exhibit banding and color shifts. Our output service provider recommends saving files in CMYK mode instead. But don't just take our word for it; ask your output service provider for advice.

7. Check Show More Options, choose **Output** from the pop-up menu (**1**, page 448), then:

To print a colored background around the image, click **Background,** then choose a color.

(Instructions continue on page 448)

Desktop ink-jet printers

When printing to a desktop ink-jet printer, leave your image in RGB mode. Even though such printers print using CMYK inks (with some using six or more process ink colors), their drivers expect to receive RGB data and then perform the conversion to CMYK internally. Usually, the printer driver installation program installs a set of profiles for the printer for printing on different kinds of paper.

When the time comes to print, choose File > Print with Preview (Ctrl-Alt-P/ Cmd-Option-P), check Show More Options, and choose Color Management from the pop-up menu. In the Print Space area of the dialog box, choose the profile for your printer and paper type from the Profile pop-up menu.

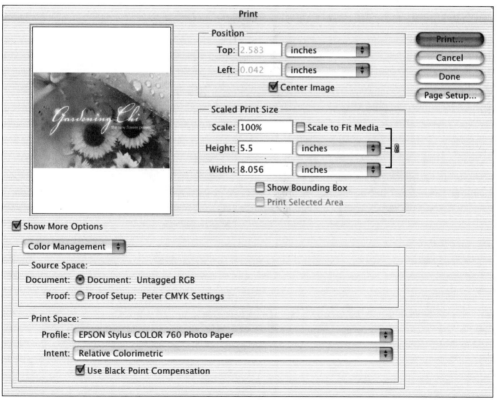

1 *The **Print** dialog box with **Show More Options** checked and **Color Management** chosen from the pop-up menu*

To print a black border around an image, click **Border,** choose a measurement unit, then enter a Width (0–10 pt.).

Click **Bleed** to specify a Width (distance) inward from the edge of the canvas area for the placement of crop marks (0–9.01 pt.).

Click the **Screen** button to open the Halftone Screens dialog box, where you can change the halftone screen settings, including the dot shape (see page 451).

Click **Transfer** to open the Transfer Functions dialog box, which allows you to adjust dot gain values to compensate for a miscalibrated imagesetter.

Check any of the following options:

Interpolation reduces jaggies when outputting to some PostScript Level 2 (or higher) printers.

Calibration Bars creates a grayscale and/or color calibration strip outside the image area.

Registration Marks creates marks that a print shop uses to align color separations.

Corner Crop Marks and **Center Crop Marks** create short little lines that a print shop uses to trim the final printed page.

Description (formerly called Caption) prints, outside the image area, whatever information was entered in the Description heading of File > File Info.

Labels prints the file's name and mode and the current channel name on each page, outside the image area.

For film output, ask your print shop whether you should check **Emulsion Down** and/or **Negative.**

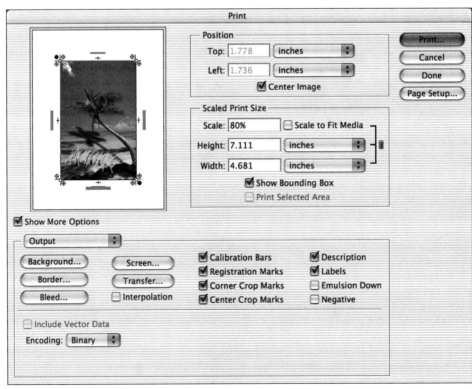

1 *The **Print** dialog box with **Show More Options** checked and **Output** chosen from the pop-up menu*

Check **Include Vector Data** to have the edges of any vector objects (e.g., type or shapes) print at the printer's full resolution, not the document's resolution.

Choose an **Encoding** method from the pop-up menu if you're using a PostScript printer. Binary is the default method. JPEG encoding (available only on PostScript Level 2 or higher printers) compresses image files and speeds up the transfer of data to the printer but results in a lower image quality. If you run into problems with your print spooler or printer driver, use ASCII85 encoding (a new, more compact method). Both ASCII options double the size of print files, slowing down the printing process accordingly. For most purposes, you should use ASCII85 in Windows and Binary encoding in Mac.

8. Click Print or, for information about the buttons below Print, see step 5 and the sidebar on page 445 ■.

Print Using Color Management

■ *A printout showing various **Output** options*

Label

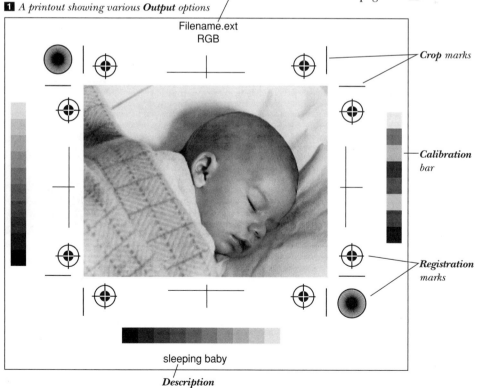

Filename.ext
RGB

Crop marks

Calibration bar

Registration marks

sleeping baby

Description

Photoshop's **Trap** command slightly overlaps solid-color areas in an image to help prevent gaps that may occur due to plate misregistration or paper shift. Trapping is necessary only when two distinct, adjacent color areas share less than two of the four process colors. You don't need to trap a continuous-tone or photographic image.

Unlike applications that use both the spread and choke methods for trapping, Photoshop uses only the spread method. Photoshop's Trap command also flattens all layers. Consult with your press shop before using this command. If you do decide to use it, apply it to a copy of your image, and store your original image without traps.

1 *Open the image to which you want to apply trapping.*

To apply trapping:

1. Open the image to which you want to apply trapping **1**, and make sure it's in CMYK Color mode.

2. Choose Image > Trap.

3. If a prompt appears regarding flattening layers, click OK.

4. Enter the Width that your press shop recommends **2**–**3**.

5. Click OK.

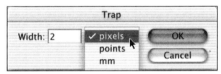

2 *Choose a* **Trap Width**.

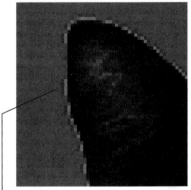

3 *This detail of the kitty's ear shows that the command added extra pixels along color edges where trapping was needed.*

Printing Color Separations

Convert the image to CMYK Color mode, then choose File > Print with Preview. Check Show More Options, then choose Color Management from the pop-up menu. Under Source Space, choose Document. It should say U.S. Web Coated (SWOP) v2, unless you've chosen a different option in the Color Settings dialog box. Under Print Space, choose Separations for the Profile, click Print, then click Print again.

Also, in the Output pane of the Print with Preview dialog box, you can check one or more of the Calibration Bars, Registration Marks, Corner Crop Marks, Center Crop Marks, or Labels options. Some of these options may not be available on a non-PostScript printer.

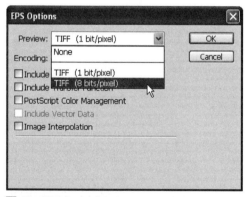

1 *The EPS Options dialog box in Windows*

Screens

For a PostScript Level 2 (or higher) printer, click Screen in the Print with Preview dialog box, uncheck Use Printer's Default Screens, then check Use Accurate Screens **2** (don't change the Ink angles). The Halftone Screens options will take effect if you print directly from Photoshop to a PostScript printer or if you save the file in the Photoshop EPS or Photoshop DCS 2.0 format and print to a PostScript printer from another application.

Before printing your file, save your image at the resolution that your output service provider says is appropriate for the **color printer** or **imagesetter** you're going to use.

To prepare a file for an IRIS or dye sublimation printer, or an imagesetter:

1. To print on a PostScript Level 2 (or higher) printer, choose File > Print with Preview (Ctrl-Alt-P/Cmd-Option-P), check Show More Options, and choose Output from the pop-up menu. Click Screen, uncheck Use Printer's Default Screens, check Use Accurate Screens, click OK, and then click Done.

2. Choose Image > Mode > CMYK Color, if the document isn't already in that mode.

3. Choose File > Save As (Ctrl-Shift-S/Cmd-Option-S) and check the As a Copy option.

4. Choose Format: Photoshop EPS.

5. Choose a location in which to save the file, then click Save.

6. In the EPS Options dialog box, choose a Preview option **1**, and choose Encoding: ASCII85 in Windows, Binary in Mac.

7. If you've changed the screen settings in the Halftone Screens dialog box (as per your output service provider's instructions, of course), check Include Halftone Screen.

8. Click OK.

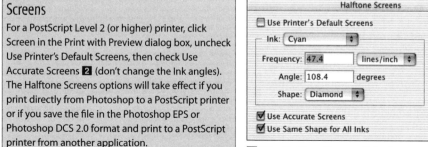

2 *The Halftone Screens dialog box*

Preparing files for other applications

Photoshop to QuarkXPress

To color-separate a Photoshop image in QuarkXPress, you can convert it to CMYK Color mode before importing it into QuarkXPress. Different imagesetters require different formats, so ask your output service provider if you should save your image as a single- or multilayer file in the TIFF file format (see pages 458–459) or the PDF file format (see page 459), or as a single-layer file in the EPS file format (see pages 455–456) or either of the two DCS formats (see page 457). QuarkXPress can also read an embedded profile and convert an RGB TIFF into a CMYK TIFF. Ask your output service provider which program you should use for the conversion.

Photoshop to InDesign

InDesign can separate Photoshop PDFs (RGB or CMYK), and it can import PSD files directly. It can also read any ICC profile that's embedded in a Photoshop file.

Photoshop to After Effects

You can import a layered Photoshop image into Adobe After Effects 5 and later and position it in the Time Layout window to create animated effects over time for video or QuickTime output.

Import a layered Photoshop file into After Effects using the Composition option. Photoshop layers and adjustment layers, layer effects, blending modes, and alpha channels will be preserved. Editable type layers will render correctly in After Effects (you don't need to prerender them). Layer masks and vector masks will also import into, and render correctly in, After Effects.

A Photoshop clipping mask will import into After Effects as a composition. As such, it can be placed and manipulated as a unit. The separate layers of the clipping mask will display in the Time Layout window in After Effects.

> ## Keeping a background transparent
>
> To preserve the transparent background of a Photoshop image, before importing it into a drawing or page layout application, save it with a vector mask (see page 328).

Photoshop to Quark, InDesign, After Effects

452

Check your preferences

If you want the ability to open a Photoshop (.psd) file in another application, find out if the target application requires File Compatibility: **Maximize PSD Compatibility** to be checked in Edit (Photoshop, in Mac) > Preferences > File Handling. This option saves a composite preview with the layered version for applications that don't support layers. It also saves a rasterized copy of any vector art for those applications that don't support vector data. Checking this option will result in lengthier saving times and larger file sizes.

Some applications also require the Image Previews options to be checked. For Web output, however, uncheck Image Previews to save a few extra bytes of storage size and speed up the transfer time.

Keep your slices NEW

If you place a Photoshop CS file that contains slices into Adobe Illustrator CS with the Link option unchecked, a slice group will show up on the Layers palette in Illustrator.

Photoshop to Illustrator

Photoshop CS and Adobe Illustrator CS are highly compatible. If you drag and drop a Photoshop selection or layer into Illustrator, the image will appear on the Layers palette in Illustrator as a group containing a generic clipping path layer and an image layer. Opacity and blending mode settings will be ignored; a layer or vector mask will be applied to its layer.

You can use the Path Selection tool to drag and drop a selected path for a vector shape or a path for a vector mask from a Photoshop image window into an Illustrator image window. Or you can use Photoshop's File > Export > Paths to Illustrator command to export a saved path, then open the saved path file in Illustrator. In either case, the path will become an editable vector object in Illustrator, with no fill or stroke.

If you copy and paste a layer from Photoshop into Illustrator, any layer masks and vector masks will be ignored.

If you place a Photoshop image into Illustrator using Illustrator's Place command with the Link option checked, the image will appear on the Layers palette on a single image layer. The image will be properly masked, but some blending modes may produce strange effects.

If you embed a Photoshop image as you place it into Illustrator (uncheck the Link option), or open it via the Open command in Illustrator, you'll have the option to choose whether layers are to be converted into objects or flattened into one layer. If you opt to convert Photoshop layers into objects, each object will appear on its own nested layer within an image layer group, and the Background will also be a separate, opaque layer. Any layer can be deleted or modified in Illustrator. All transparency values and blending modes will be preserved and will be listed as editable appearances in Illustrator. Layer masks will become opacity masks, vector masks will become clipping paths, and shape layers will become editable

(Continued on the following page)

vector objects. Any clipping paths that were saved to the Paths palette in the Photoshop file will remain in effect.

The presence of layer effects on any layer in a Photoshop image may prevent Photoshop layers from becoming individual layers in Illustrator. You can either apply the effects to the layers in Photoshop before opening/placing the image in Illustrator or use Illustrator effects to achieve similar results.

If you opt to flatten Photoshop layers into one layer, all transparency, blending modes, and layer mask effects will be preserved visually, but they won't be editable in Illustrator. Any clipping paths from the Paths palette in the Photoshop file, on the other hand, will remain in effect.

The resolution of any Photoshop TIFF, EPS, or PSD image that's opened or placed in Illustrator will remain intact, but the Photoshop image will adopt the color mode of the Illustrator file. Illustrator raster filters, raster effects, and some vector effects can be applied to the imported image.

Photoshop to CorelDRAW 11

Save the file in the EPS, TIFF, JPEG, BMP, PSD (Photoshop), PDF, PICT, GIF, or PNG format, and in RGB Color or CMYK Color image mode, then place it into a CorelDRAW file. Alternatively, you could drag and drop a layer or copy and paste a layer or selection from Photoshop into a CorelDRAW window. Note, however, that all vector data, such as shapes and type, will be turned into bitmaps. CorelDRAW 11 can read a layered Photoshop image; each layer will become a separate object. You can use the Export Paths to Illustrator command to export a Photoshop path to a file, and then open that file in CorelDRAW.

Once imported into CorelDRAW, a bitmap image can be moved around; you can perform some bitmap edits on it; you can apply a filter to it; you can convert it to a different color mode or change its color depth; and you can resample it by changing its image size and/or resolution.

Photoshop to a film recorder

Color transparencies, also called chromes, are widely used as a source for high-quality images in the publishing industry. Photoshop files can be output to a film recorder to produce chromes. Although the output settings for each film recorder may vary, to output to any film recorder, the pixel count for the height and width of the image file must conform to the pixel count that the film recorder requires for each line it images.

If the image originates as a scan, the pixel count should be taken into consideration when choosing the scan resolution, dimensions, and file storage size.

For example, let's say you need to produce a 4 x 5-inch chrome on a Solitaire film recorder. Your output service provider advises you that to output on the Solitaire, you can create a 4K image at 4096 pixels x 3276 pixels, at a resolution of 819 dpi; an 8K image at 8192 pixels x 6553 pixels, at a resolution of 1638 dpi; or a 16K image at 16,384 pixels x 13,107 pixels, at a resolution of 3276 dpi. (Other film recorders may require different resolutions.) Choose File > New, enter the desired dimensions and resolution, and choose RGB Color mode. Click OK to produce the image entirely within Photoshop, or note the resolution and dimensions and ask your output service provider to match those values when they scan your image.

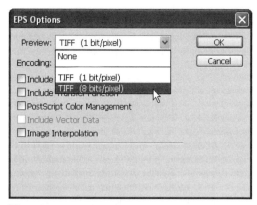

1 *In the* ***EPS Options*** *dialog box in Windows, choose a Preview option.*

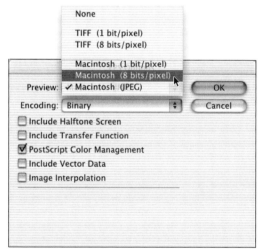

2 *In the* ***EPS Options*** *dialog box in Macintosh, choose a Preview option.*

The **EPS** format is a good choice for importing a Photoshop image into an illustration program or into a page layout program (e.g., QuarkXPress, PageMaker, or InDesign). Printing an EPS file requires a PostScript or PostScript-emulation printer. When you save a file in the EPS format, layers are flattened, and alpha channels and spot channels are discarded. The EPS format is available for an image in any image mode except Multichannel and 16-Bits/Channel.

To save an image as an EPS:

1. If the image is going to be color-separated by another application, choose Image > Mode > CMYK Color (to preview the image mode change).

2. Choose File > Save As (Ctrl-Shift-S/ Cmd-Shift-S).

3. Enter a name.

4. Choose Format: Photoshop EPS, then choose a location in which to save the file.

5. *Optional:* Check ICC Profile/Embed Color Profile to have Photoshop embed a color profile that tags the image with your working color space. Check Use Proof Setup to include a "soft proof" with your file (an onscreen preview of how your image will look when it's printed on a specifc type of printer). For more on color management, see pages 43–56.

   Click Save. Note that any layers will be flattened. The EPS Options dialog box opens.

6. From the Preview pop-up menu **1** (Win)/**2** (Mac), choose a 1-bit/pixel option to save the file with a black-and-white preview or choose an 8-bits/pixel option to save the file with a grayscale or color preview. Mac users, choose a TIFF preview option only if you're planning to open the file in a Windows application.

7. On a Mac, choose Encoding: Binary, the default method used by PostScript

(Continued on the following page)

Save as EPS

printers, as Binary encoded files are smaller and process more quickly than ASCII files. In Windows, and for some applications, PostScript printers, or printing utilities that can't handle Binary files, you'll have to choose ASCII or ASCII85. JPEG is the fastest encoding method, but it causes some data loss. A JPEG file can print only on a PostScript Level 2 or higher printer.

8. If you've changed the frequency, angle, or dot shape settings in the Halftone Screens dialog box, check Include Halftone Screen. (In case you're wondering, to get to the Halftone Screens dialog box, you choose File > Print with Preview, click Show More Options, choose Output from the pop-up menu, then click Screen.)

9. The PostScript Color Management Option converts the file's color data to the printer's color space. Don't choose this option if you're going to import the file into another color-managed application, as unpredictable color shifts may occur!

10. If your page contains vector elements, such as shapes or type, check Include Vector Data. Saved vector data in EPS files is available to other applications, but, as a warning dialog box will tell you when you reopen the file in Photoshop, the vector data will be rasterized.

11. Check Image Interpolation to enable other applications to resample image pixels in an effort to reduce jagged edges on low-resolution printouts.

12. Click OK.

Multichannel

You can save a Multichannel mode image in the Photoshop DCS 2.0 format as a single file or as multiple files, with or without grayscale or color composites. The DCS 2.0 format preserves channels. A Multichannel image can't be saved as a Photoshop EPS for composite (single-page) printing.

When an RGB or CMYK image is converted to Multichannel mode, all layers are flattened, the channels are converted to cyan, magenta, and yellow (with no composite channel), and the black channel and any spot color channels (if present) are preserved.

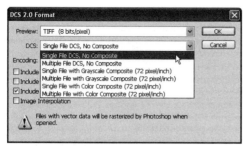

1 *Choose a DCS option in the DCS 2.0 Format dialog box (Windows).*

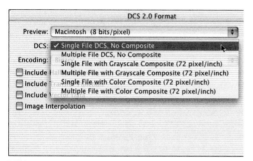

2 *Choose a DCS option in the DCS 2.0 Format dialog box (Mac).*

The DCS (Desktop Color Separation) formats are relatives of the EPS format. The DCS 1.0 format preseparates the image and produces five related files, one for each CMYK channel and one for the combined, composite CMYK channel. The newer **DCS 2.0** format preserves color channels and any spot color channels, and also offers the option to save the combined channels into one file or as multiple files. A DCS file can be printed only on a PostScript printer.

To save an image in DCS 2.0 format:

1. Choose Image > Mode > CMYK Color (to preview the mode change). Choose File > Save As, enter a name, choose Format: Photoshop DCS 2.0, then choose a location in which to save the file.

Optional: Check Use Proof Setup or ICC Profile/Embed Color Profile (see step 5 on page 455).

2. Click Save. The DCS 2.0 Format dialog box opens.

3. From the Preview pop-up menu, choose a 1 bit/pixel option (for a black-and-white preview) or choose an 8 bits/pixel option (for a grayscale or color preview). In Windows, choose any TIFF preview.

4. Choose a DCS option: Single File (all the separations together in one file) or Multiple File (one file for each separation), with No Composite, a Grayscale Composite, or a Color Composite preview **1** (Win)/**2** (Mac).

5. Choose Encoding: Binary, ASCII, ASCII85, or a JPEG option (see page 449).

6. Leave both Include Halftone Screen and Include Transfer Function unchecked. Let your output service provider choose settings for these options.

7. Check Include Vector Data if the file contains vector graphics (e.g., type).

8. Check Image Interpolation to enable other applications to resample image pixels in an effort to reduce jagged edges on low-resolution printouts.

9. Click OK.

Save as DSC 2.0

A **TIFF** file can be imported by most applications, including QuarkXPress, PageMaker, and InDesign. Color profiles are recognized by, and color management options are available for, this format. QuarkXPress, PageMaker, and InDesign can color-separate a CMYK TIFF.

To save an image as a TIFF:

1. Choose Image > Mode > CMYK Color (to preview the mode change), choose File > Save As, then enter a name 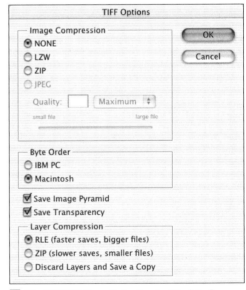. Choose Format: TIFF, and choose a location for the file.

2. You can check Layers to preserve any layers in your file, but note that few image or layout programs can work with a layered TIFF, and those that don't will flatten a TIFF upon import. You can also choose to save any spot color channels, alpha channels, or annotations.

3. *Optional:* Check Embed Color Profile to include the currently embedded color profile with the file. For more on color management, see pages 43–56.

4. Click Save.

5. In the TIFF Options dialog box, choose an Image Compression method 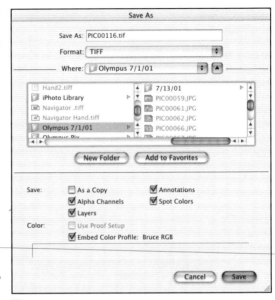 to reduce the file's storage size. Some programs can't open a TIFF that's saved with JPEG or ZIP compression. LZW is a non-lossy method. For a layered TIFF, click a Layer Compression method at the bottom of the dialog box. For files that are going to be color-separated, output service providers recommend clicking None (no compression).

6. For Byte Order, click IBM PC or Macintosh for the platform the file will be exported to.

7. Check Save Image Pyramid to create a file that contains multiple resolutions of the image. Photoshop doesn't currently offer options for opening image pyramids; Adobe InDesign does.

   If your file contains transparency and you want it to be preserved, check Save

1 *The **Save As** dialog box in **Macintosh***

2 *The **TIFF Options** dialog box in **Macintosh***

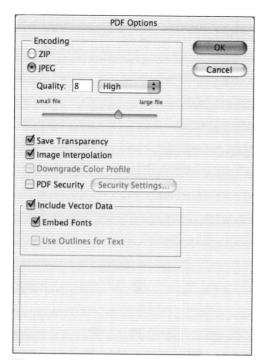

1 *In the* **PDF Options** *dialog box, choose an encoding option, and check any other exporting options.*

Transparency. To access this option, the bottom layer in the file must be a layer—not the Background.

Note: The Transparency option is automatically checked for a layered TIFF.

8. Click OK.

A **PDF** (Portable Document Format) file can be opened in either Windows or Mac applications. The format preserves image layout, fonts, and vector data from a Photoshop file. An image in any color mode except Multichannel can be saved as a PDF.

To save an image as a PDF:

1. Choose File > Save As.

2. Enter a name for the file, choose Format: Photoshop PDF, and choose a location for the PDF file.

3. Check any available options (e.g., Alpha Channels, Layers, Spot Colors, Annotations, ICC Profile/Embedded Profile) that you want saved in the file, then click Save.

4. Choose an encoding method for compressing the file **1**. For JPEG, choose a quality setting (see pages 484–485).

5. Check Save Transparency to preserve any transparency in the image when the file is opened in other applications.

6. Check Image Interpolation to enable other applications to resample image pixels in an effort to reduce jagged edges on low-resolution printouts.

7. Check PDF Security to attach security options (such as password protection for opening, editing, and printing) to the file (see Photoshop Help for more info).

8. Check Include Vector Data to preserve any shape or type objects as resolution-independent objects for smoother edges on printouts. With this option checked, check Embed Fonts to include fonts used in the file, or check Use Outlines for Text to save text as clipping path outlines.

9. Click OK.

Save as PDF

Producing duotones

Up to approximately 50 shades of a single ink color can be printed from one plate, so to extend an image's tonal range and give it added depth and richness, print shops are sometimes asked to add midtones or highlights to a grayscale image by using two or more plates instead of one. The additional plates can be gray or color tints. Using the **Duotone Options** dialog box in Photoshop, you can create a duotone (two plates), tritone (three plates), or quadtone (four plates).

To produce a duotone:

1. Choose Image > Mode > Grayscale. An image with medium to high contrast will work best, an image with low contrast not as well.

2. Choose Image > Mode > Duotone. The Duotone Options dialog box opens.

3. Check Preview to see a live preview of your curve changes in the image window.

4. Choose Type: Duotone **1**.

5. Leave the Ink 1 color as Black. Click the Ink 2 color square. The Custom Colors dialog box opens.

6. Ink 1 will be the darkest of the two ink colors. The highest ink number (Ink 2, in this case) should be the lightest of the two ink colors.

   To choose a matching system color, such as PANTONE color, choose from the Book pop-up menu, then type a color number or click a swatch. Subtle colors tend to look better in a duotone than bright ones.
   or
   To choose a process color, click Picker, then enter C, M, Y, and K percentages.

7. Click OK.

8. For a process color, enter a name next to the color square. For a custom color, leave the name as is.

9. Click the Ink 2 curve.

It's not easy

Printing a tritone (three inks) or a quadtone (four inks) requires specifying the order in which the inks will print on press, so be sure to ask your commercial printer for advice. A duotone effect can't be proofed on a PostScript color printer, though; only a press proof offers reliable feedback.

If you're a novice at producing duotones, try using one of the duotone, tritone, or quadtone curve presets that are provided by Photoshop. You can load them in to use as is or adapt them for your own needs. To do this, go to Image > Mode > Duotone, click Load, make a choice in Adobe Photoshop CS/Presets/Duotones, then click Open.

*Click a **curve** to modify it.* *Click a **color square** to choose a color.* *Don't change the spot color name.*

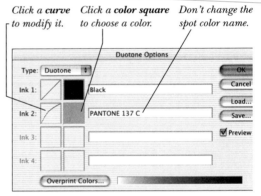

1 *In the **Duotone Options** dialog box, choose Type: **Duotone**, then click the **Ink 2** color square.*

Nice curves!

Reshaping the duotone curve for an ink color affects how that color is distributed among an image's highlights, midtones, and shadows. Using the curve shape shown in the screen shot on the previous page, Ink 2 will tint the image's midtones. To produce a pleasing duotone, try to distribute Ink 1 and Ink 2 in different tonal ranges.

Here's an example. Use black as Ink 1 in the shadow areas, somewhat in the midtones and a little bit in the highlights . Then use an Ink 2 color in the remaining tonal ranges—more in the midtones and light areas and less in the darks.

The image's *The image's* *The image's*
highlights **midtones** **shadows**

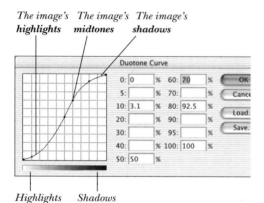

Highlights *Shadows*

1 *A duotone curve*

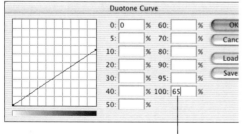

2 *This is the **Duotone Curve** dialog box for a monotone print. The 100% value has been lowered to the desired PANTONE tint percentage.*

10. Click to create data points or drag existing points in the graph in the Duotone Curve dialog box **1**. To produce a pleasing duotone, the Ink 1 curve should be different from the Ink 2 curve.

11. Click OK.

12. Click the Ink 1 curve, then repeat steps 10 and 11.

13. *Optional:* Click Save to save the current settings for use with other images.

14. Click OK to close the dialog box.

15. Save the file in the Photoshop EPS format.

TIP To reduce black ink in the highlights, for the black ink (Ink 1) curve, enter 10 in the 0% field. To reduce color in the shadows, for the color ink (Ink 2) curve, enter 85 in the 100% field.

TIP The Duotone dialog box opens with the last-used settings. If you change the duotone Type and then decide you want to restore the last-used settings, hold down Alt/Option and click Reset.

Here's a low-budget—but effective—way to expand the tonal range of a grayscale image. It will print as a **monotone** (from one plate).

To print a grayscale image using a PANTONE tint:

1. Open a grayscale image.

2. Choose Image > Mode > Duotone.

3. Choose Monotone from the Type pop-up menu.

4. Click the Ink 1 color square, click Custom, choose a PANTONE color, then click OK.

5. In the Duotone Options dialog box, click the Ink 1 curve.

6. In the 100% field, enter the desired tint percentage value **2**. Leave the 0% field at 0 and all the other fields blank, then click OK.

7. Click OK to close the dialog box.

8. Save the file in the Photoshop EPS format.

Color reproduction basics

A computer monitor displays additive colors by projecting red, green, and blue (RGB) light, whereas an offset press prints subtractive colors using CMYK and/or spot color inks. Obtaining good CMYK color reproduction from an offset press is an art. But before you get to that stage in the process, you'll want to carefully calibrate your monitor so the onscreen image closely resembles what comes off the press (see pages 44–47). For online imaging issues, see the next chapter!

Settings in the Color Settings dialog boxes in Photoshop control the conversion of images from RGB to CMYK mode as well as the CMYK mode preview. We'll discuss some of these dialog boxes in this section.

These are the major steps in color separation:

■ Choose color settings.

■ Obtain a color proof using those settings.

■ Match the onscreen preview to the proof.

Now, to get down to the nitty-gritty.

To enter custom CMYK settings:

1. Choose Edit (Photoshop, in Mac) > Color Settings (Ctrl-Shift-K/Cmd-Shift-K).

2. From the Working Spaces: CMYK pop-up menu, choose one of the U.S. prepress defaults that matches your chosen press and paper type (that is, unless the file will be printed in Japan or Europe).
   or
   If you want to control the various CMYK settings, choose Custom CMYK from the CMYK menu. Name your setting 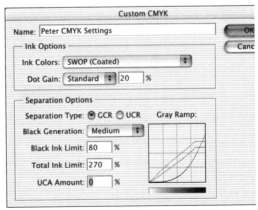 and choose or enter the Ink Options for the offset press, such as the Ink Colors and Dot Gain. Ask your print shop about these settings.

   Other characteristics of the offset press are entered in the Separation Options area. These settings are particular to each press, so ask your commercial printer for this information. In short, the Separation Type tells Photoshop about the type of press used: Does the press use the GCR (gray component

What to ask your commercial printer

As we said a second ago, color separation is an art. Start by asking your print shop the questions below so you'll be able to choose the correct scan resolution and settings in the Custom CMYK dialog box:

What lines-per-inch setting is going to be used on the press for my job? Knowing this value will help you choose the appropriate scanning resolution.

What is the dot gain for my choice of paper stock on the press? Allowances for dot gain can be made using the Custom CMYK dialog box.

Which printing method will be used on the press—UCR or GCR? GCR produces better color printing and is the default choice in the Custom CMYK dialog box. (GCR stands for gray component replacement, UCR stands for undercolor removal.)

What is the total ink limit and the black ink limit for the press? These values can also be adjusted in the Custom CMYK dialog box.

Note: Change the dot gain, GCR or UCR method, and ink limits before you convert your image from RGB Color mode to CMYK Color mode. If you change any of these values after the conversion, you must convert the image back to RGB Color mode, readjust the values, then reconvert it to CMYK Color mode.

In which file format should the file be saved? Save the image in the requested format.

1 *In this screen shot of the **Custom CMYK** dialog box, the **Black Ink Limit** and the **Total Ink Limit** values have been changed as per a commercial printer's recommendation. The graph maps the current values.*

CMYK Setup

Total readout

To display total ink coverage percentages on the Info palette for the pixels currently under the pointer, click the eyedropper on the palette and choose **Total Ink 1**. This readout is based on the current CMYK settings.

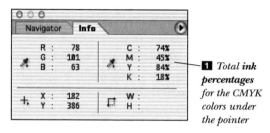

1 *Total ink percentages for the CMYK colors under the pointer*

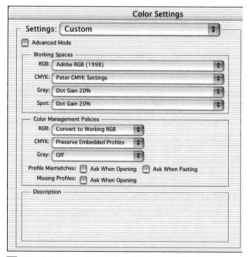

2 *The left side of the Color Settings dialog box*

Another option

To save your custom CMYK settings as just a profile rather than as a full set of color settings, from the CMYK pop-up menu in the Working Spaces area of the Color Settings dialog box, choose Save CMYK. Leave the name, extension, and file location as is, then click Save. You can access this profile by choosing Load from the same CMYK pop-up menu.

replacement) or UCR (undercolor removal) method?

The Black Generation amount controls how much black ink is used when the RGB components of light are translated into CMY inks. Black is substituted for a percentage of CMY inks to prevent the inks from becoming muddy when they're mixed together. How much black is substituted is determined by the Black Generation amount.

Finally, each press shop uses its own amount of ink coverage on individual separation plates; some use less than 100% coverage for each plate. Ask your press shop for its Total Ink Limit settings.

Follow these remaining three steps.

Instead of reentering this information every time you need to convert files from RGB to CMYK, you can save your Custom CMYK and all other settings as a **preset.**

To save a Color Settings preset with your custom CMYK settings:

1. Once you've entered your CMYK settings in the Custom CMYK dialog box, enter a name, then click OK (for an alternate option, read the sidebar at lower left).

2. Choose other Working Spaces options, click Save **2**, name the file, leave the default location (the Settings folder) as is, then click Save again.

3. In the Description area of the Color Settings Comment dialog box, enter any notes, then click OK twice. The next time you output to that particular press situation, open the Color Settings dialog box and choose your saved preset from the Settings pop-up menu. *Note:* These settings apply only when converting from RGB Color to CMYK Color mode. If you subsequently readjust any settings in the Custom CMYK dialog box, you'll have to reconvert your image from RGB to CMYK again to apply the new settings. Always reserve a copy of your image in RGB Color mode for possible reconversion!

The Proof Colors and Proof Setup commands provide a way to soft-proof an image based on the **custom** CMYK profile you set up in the previous steps, or based on the color profile for output devices available on your system (e.g., a desktop ink-jet). Soft proofs provide a fairly accurate preview of how an image will look when printed to a specific output device.

To create a custom proof setup:

1. Choose View > Proof Setup > Custom.

2. From the Profile pop-up menu, choose the custom CMYK profile you created on the previous pages **1**. If Color Settings has been set to the custom CMYK profile (as explained on the previous page), the profile should be the current working CMYK space on the list. If not, locate your custom CMYK profile near the bottom of the menu.

3. Choose an Intent. Ask your print shop for advice on this. Read more about Intents on page 52.

4. Click the Save button, enter a name, leave the location and extension as is, click Save, then click OK.

5. Make sure View > Proof Colors (Ctrl-Y/ Cmd-Y) has a check mark. The proofing profile you saved will be listed at the bottom of the View > Proof Setup submenu.

TIP When Proof Colors is on (checked), the name of the proofing profile being used is listed on the document's title bar.

The big squeeze

To reduce the storage size of an image, use a compression program such as **WinZip** or **PKZip** (Win) or **Stuffit** (Mac). Compression using this kind of software is non-lossy, meaning it doesn't cause data loss.

If you don't have compression software, choose File > Save As, and choose **TIFF** from the Format pop-up menu. If you want to save the file without alpha channels, also uncheck Alpha Channels. Click Save. Check the LZW or ZIP Compression option in the TIFF Options dialog box. *Note:* LZW and ZIP compression are non-lossy, but not all programs can import files in these formats. Some programs will import an LZW or ZIP TIFF only if it doesn't contain any alpha channels.

Although **JPEG** offers substantially more file compression than LZW or ZIP TIFF, it's a better choice for Web output than for print output, as JPEG compression causes additional image data loss with each compression. This may not be noticeable onscreen, but it's very noticeable in high-resolution output.

TIP Proof Colors needs to be turned on for each image that's opened. When it's on, the onscreen soft proof of each RGB image will reflect the profile chosen on the Proof Setup submenu (in this case, the custom CMYK settings profile), but the actual image information will be changed only if the image is converted to CMYK Color mode using the current Color Settings.

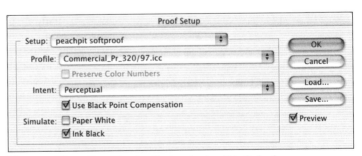

1 *Choose View > **Proof Setup** > **Custom** to open this dialog box.*

Desaturate another way

Instead of using the Sponge tool, you can use Image > Adjustments > **Hue/Saturation** on a layer to correct out-of-gamut colors in individual color categories. To desaturate colors, move the Saturation slider to the left.

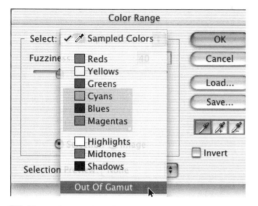

1 *Choose Select:* ***Out Of Gamut*** *in the* ***Color Range*** *dialog box.*

2 *For illustration purposes,* ***out-of-gamut*** *colors in this image are shown in white instead of the usual gray.*

If you convert an image to CMYK Color mode, its colors are automatically forced into printable gamut. In certain cases, however, you may want to see which areas are out-of-gamut (nonprintable) in RGB Color mode first, and then bring some of them into the **printable gamut** manually.

Note: CMYK color equivalents are generated based on the current CMYK settings in the Color Settings dialog box, so you should adjust those settings first (see page 462).

To correct out-of-gamut colors:

1. Open your RGB Color image.

2. Choose View > Gamut Warning (Ctrl-Shift-Y/Cmd-Shift-Y).

3. *Optional:* To select and restrict color changes to only the out-of-gamut areas, choose Select > Color Range, choose Select: Out Of Gamut **1**, then click OK. Out-of-gamut colors in the image will become selected.

4. Choose the Sponge tool (O or Shift-O).

5. On the Sponge tool options bar, choose a tip from the Brush Preset picker, choose Desaturate from the Mode pop-up menu, and choose a Flow percentage.

6. Choose a layer.

7. Drag across the gray, out-of-gamut areas **2**. As they become desaturated, they'll redisplay in color (this may take a few passes). Don't desaturate colors too much, though, or they'll become dull.

TIP To preview the image in CMYK, choose View > Gamut Warning again to uncheck the command. Next, make sure Working CMYK is chosen on the View > Proof Setup submenu (this proof option will reflect your CMYK settings from the Color Settings dialog box). Make sure View > Proof Colors is checked.

TIP When the pointer is over an out-of-gamut pixel, exclamation points will appear next to the CMYK readout on the Info palette.

Color correction: A first glance

Such a complex process as color correction is beyond the scope of this QuickStart Guide. It involves using many commands, such as Levels, Curves, Color Balance, and Unsharp Mask. You can get some assistance from the books listed at right. Just by way of introduction, though, these are the basic steps in the color correction process:

- Calibrate your monitor.
- Scan, acquire, or open an image in Photoshop from a Photo CD, digital camera, or scanner.
- Limit tonal values to determine where the darkest shadow and lightest highlight areas are in the image, and then limit the highest and lowest tonal values to the range that your print shop specifies. (Areas outside this range won't print well.)
- Adjust the color to correct any undesirable color cast in the image. You can correct the overall color balance or the neutral gray component of the image.
- Unsharp Mask to resharpen the image.
- Print a CMYK proof, and then analyze the proof with color-reading instruments to determine the exact color characteristics of the output.
- Readjust the Photoshop image, then print and analyze yet another proof.

For onscreen output, do all your color correction in RGB Color mode. Proof it by viewing it on other monitors or in different Web browsers.

For print output, if you're working with a CMYK scan, do all your correction in CMYK Color mode. For an image that's going to be color-separated, Adobe recommends working in RGB Color mode and then converting it to CMYK Color mode using the appropriate Color Settings options.

For ink-jet printer output, make the image mode RGB Color.

> **Continue your studies**
>
> From Peachpit Press:
>
> **Real World Adobe Photoshop CS** by David Blatner and Bruce Fraser
>
> **Real World Color Management** by Bruce Fraser, Chris Murphy, and Fred Bunting

Color Correction: First Glance

*The Peachpit Press website: **http://www.peachpit.com***

THIS CHAPTER covers the preparation of Photoshop images for the World Wide Web (online) using **ImageReady,** Photoshop's sister application, which is designed specifically for preparing images for the Web. You'll learn how to optimize files in the GIF, JPEG, and PNG file formats; control dithering; create layer slices and user slices; create and use layer styles; and create image maps, rollovers, and GIF animations—to name but a few topics!

The basics

When you're preparing graphics to be viewed online (as opposed to in print), issues of storage and transmission of data are especially important. All of these issues come into play during **optimization,** the process by which a file is saved within specific format, storage size, and color parameters. The overall goal for each image is to preserve its quality but compress it enough so that it downloads quickly on the Web. You want to reduce the file size just until the image quality reaches its reduction limit (starts to degrade). Keep this goal in mind as you choose optimization settings.

Although you can optimize your images using Photoshop's File > Save for Web command (a one-stop optimize dialog box), we recommend using ImageReady instead because its optimization controls and options are, as they say in computer parlance, more "robust."

Before you plunge into ImageReady, though, you need to familiarize yourself with some general concepts, such as file formats, image compression, and color depth—all of which affect how successfully images download on the Web. Then, once the groundwork is laid, you'll follow step-by-step instructions for optimizing your images.

(Continued on the following page)

The Basics

You'll be jumping back and forth between ImageReady and Photoshop for the instructions in this chapter. If Photoshop is already launched, and you want to go to ImageReady (or go back to Photoshop from ImageReady), click the **Edit in** button at the bottom of the Toolbox **1** or press **Ctrl-Shift-M/ Cmd-Shift-M**.

ImageReady's Optimize palette is illustrated below, with two different file formats chosen (GIF and JPEG) **2**–**3**.

1 *The Edit in ImageReady/ Photoshop button*

Why not use Photoshop?

Many of ImageReady's file optimization features have counterparts in Photoshop's File > **Save for Web** dialog box (e.g., Original, Optimized, 2-Up, and 4-Up preview tabs at the top of the main window; a Color Table palette; and format, matte, quality, and other options). Photoshop also has a Preview menu and a Preview in [default browser] button. So once you learn how to use ImageReady, you can either stick with that program (as we do), or you can use the Save for Web dialog box, which is illustrated on page 534.

Photoshop's **Save a Copy** command can also be used to save copies of a file in the GIF, JPEG, or PNG format, but we prefer to use ImageReady for saving files in these formats because it offers more optimization variables and preview features.

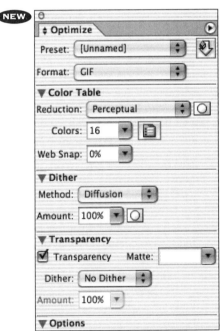

2 *ImageReady's **Optimize** palette, with **GIF** chosen as the format: Choose GIF for images that contain sharp-edged elements (e.g., flat-color shapes, line art, text). The PNG-8 format is similar to GIF and uses the same Optimize palette options.*

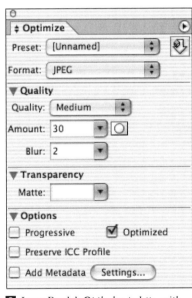

3 *ImageReady's **Optimize** palette, with **JPEG** chosen as the format: This format is appropriate for continuous-tone, photographic images.*

Optimize Palette

Golden rules for Web output

- Let the content of the image—whether it be flat colors or continuous tones—determine which file **format** you choose.

- Use an image as **low** in **file size** as is practical, balancing file size and image quality.

- For flat-color images, choose colors using the Web color sliders and the **Web Safe** color ramp on the Color palette, and Web-shift any existing flat-color areas.

- Try to **reduce** the number of colors in the image's color table.

- View your Web image through a Web **browser** on computers other than your own, so you can see how quickly it actually downloads and how good (or bad) it looks.

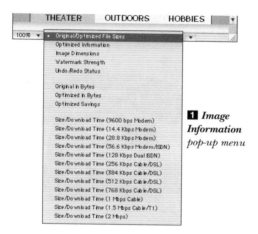

1 *Image Information pop-up menu*

2 *We chose **Original/Optimized File Sizes** from the **Image Information** pop-up menu on the right to view the size readouts for our file.*

The basic formula for outputting an image for online viewing may seem straightforward: Design the image in Photoshop (RGB Color mode), save it, click the **Edit in** button on the Toolbox, then optimize the file for Web output. But how do you know if you've been successful? If the image downloads quickly in the browser and looks okay, you chose the right optimization settings for it. If the image looks overly dithered (grainy), was subject to unexpected color substitutions, or takes too long to view on the Web page, it's not outputting well.

Next, we'll discuss four important issues that you'll need to address for online output: the image's pixel size, color palette, color depth, and file format (GIF, JPEG, or PNG).

Image size

Your first task is to calculate the appropriate image size, but it's not hard to figure out. Normally, you'll be designing images for an 800 x 600-pixel viewing area, the most common browser window size, and for a 56 Kbps modem, the most common modem speed. Your maximum image size will occupy only a portion of the browser window—about 10 inches wide (740 pixels) by 7.5 inches high (550 pixels). The image resolution needs to be just a mere 72 ppi.

To determine the file storage size of an image, don't rely on the Document Sizes readout on the image window status bar in Photoshop. Instead, go to ImageReady (click the "Edit in" button on the Toolbox), click the Optimized tab, make sure **Original/ Optimized File Sizes** is chosen from either of the Image Information pop-up menus at the bottom of the image window **1**, and note the file size information **2**. Saving a file in the GIF, JPEG, or PNG file format reduces its storage size significantly because these formats have built-in compression schemes. We'll discuss them in depth shortly.

(Continued on the following page)

Image Size

Compression

Compression

If you know the exact file size of the compressed image, you can then calculate how long it will take to transmit over the Web. Better still, choose a **Size/Download Time** from ImageReady's Image Information pop-up menu at the bottom of the image window for various modem speeds, and look at the readouts **1**. Just by way of example, a 70K file traveling on a 56 Kbps modem will take about 14 seconds to download.

The degree to which the GIF, JPEG, or PNG file format compresses depends on how compressible the image is **2**–**3**. Both the GIF and JPEG formats cause a small reduction in image quality, but it's worth the size-reduction trade-off because they'll allow your image to download faster on the Web. ImageReady offers weighted optimization, which helps finesse that trade-off by letting you selectively compress different areas of an image (see page 481).

A document with a solid background color and a few solid-color shapes will compress a great deal. A large document (over 100K) with many color areas, textures, or patterns (e.g., an Add Noise texture covering most of the image) won't compress nearly as much.

Continuous-tone, photographic images may compress less than flat-color images when saved in the GIF format. If you reduce the color table of a continuous-tone image down to somewhere between 8 and 16 colors, the resulting GIF file size will be similar to that of a flat-color image, but you will have lost the continuous color transitions in the bargain. So that leaves JPEG as the best format choice for a photographic-type image.

To summarize, if an image has to be large (say, 500 x 400 pixels or larger), it should ideally contain only a handful of large, flat-color shapes. An image that has intricate shapes and colors should be restricted in size to only a portion of the Web browser window. Another option is to divide it into slices (much more about that later!).

Browser window layer
Take a screen shot of your browser window, open the file in Photoshop, and paste it into a document as your bottommost layer. Now you can design your layout for the dimensions of that browser window.

1 *Choose a **Size/Download Time** from one of the **Image Information** pop-up menus.*

2 *A **20K GIF**, from an image with a reduced color table...*

3 *...as compared with a **120K GIF**, from a **continuous-tone** image*

__GIF__ is a suitable optimization format for this image because it contains flat colors (and thus fewer colors).

__GIF__ is a good format choice for this __hybrid__ image, too, because it contains both sharp-edged elements (the type) and continuous-tone elements (the ducky).

TIP A pattern that fills the background of a browser window is usually created by using a tiling method in a Web-page creation program or by using HTML code, but you can also use ImageReady to create the code for, and generate, background tiling (see pages 532–533).

GIF

GIF is an 8-bit file format, meaning it saves up to 256 colors. This format is appropriate for images that contain flat-color areas or shapes with well-defined edges (e.g., type) where color fidelity is important. These images contain fewer colors to begin with than continuous-tone images, so a color restriction won't have a negative impact.

To save an image in the GIF format, and to see how it will actually look when it's viewed via the browser, you can either use File > Save for Web in Photoshop or optimize and save it in ImageReady (see page 477).

Your color choices for a GIF image should be based on the equipment your Web viewers are using. 8-bit monitors can display a maxiumum of 256 colors, whereas 16-bit monitors can display thousands or millions of colors. Colors that a monitor doesn't display are simulated by dithering, a technique that juxtaposes color pixels.

To prevent unexpected dithering, one approach is to optimize your image using ImageReady's Web palette. Another option is to Web Snap most of the image colors in ImageReady and manually Web-shift any flat-color areas where color fidelity is crucial (and substitutions would be objectionable). A third option is to use the weighted optimization feature to fine-tune the dithering and color reduction. You'll learn these methods in this chapter.

TIP If you want to apply a gradient fill to a large area of an image, and you're going to use the GIF format, create a top-to-bottom gradient, which will produce a smaller file size than a left-to-right or diagonal gradient.

(Continued on the following page)

GIF

Color depth

An image's color depth is the amount of color information that's available for each of its pixels. If you lower an image's color depth, you'll be reducing the actual number of colors it contains. That, in turn, will reduce its file size and speed up its download time on the Web. Color reduction may produce dithered (grainy) edges and duller colors, but you'll achieve the necessary reduction in file size.

You can reduce the number of colors in an 8-bit image to fewer than the 256 colors it originally contained by using Photoshop's Save for Web dialog box or ImageReady's Optimize palette. Both features provide options that will give you the opportunity to preview how your image will look with fewer available colors.

TIP To evaluate its color quality, preview your image at 100% view.

JPEG

The JPEG format will do a better job than GIF of preserving color fidelity if your image is continuous-tone (contains gradations of color or is photographic) and will be viewed on 24-bit monitors, which can display millions of colors. Another advantage of JPEG is its compression power: It can take a 24-bit image and make it as small as the GIF format can make an 8-bit image.

The JPEG format does have some short-comings. Unlike GIF files, JPEG files are decompressed when they're downloaded for viewing on a Web page, which takes time.

Second, the JPEG compression methods tend to produce artifacts along the well-defined edges of flat-color images and type, so it's not a good format for images that contain such elements.

On 8-bit monitors, JPEG images are subject to dithering. This is more noticeable in flat-color areas than in continuous-tone areas. You can preview what an image will look like in an 8-bit setting by choosing View > Preview > Browser Dither in ImageReady.

Color depth	
Number of colors	**Bit depth**
256	8
128	7
64	6
32	5
16	4
8	3
4	2
2	1

JPEG *optimization is suitable for this* ***continuous-tone*** *image.*

*JPEG isn't a great choice for optimizing **sharp-edged** imagery. Note the artifacts around the type.*

*The word "duck" looks crisper in this **GIF**.*

If it doesn't contain type or objects with sharp edges, a JPEG image will probably survive a conversion to 8-bit. *Note:* Nowadays, most Web users have 24-bit monitors, so this issue is rapidly becoming moot.

JPEG format files can also be optimized as **Progressive JPEG,** which is supported by both the Netscape Navigator and Internet Explorer browsers. A Progressive JPEG displays in increasing detail as it downloads onto a Web page.

If you choose JPEG as your output format, you can experiment in ImageReady or in Photoshop's Save for Web dialog box by optimizing an image, then using the 4–Up option to preview several versions of it in varying degrees of compression. Decide which degree of compression is acceptable by weighing the file size versus the diminished image quality. In ImageReady (or in Photoshop), you can save the optimized file separately, leaving the original file intact for potential future revision.

Each time an image is optimized using the JPEG format, some image data is lost. The greater the degree of compression, the greater the data loss. To prevent such data loss, first edit and save your image in Photoshop. Next, click the "Edit in" button. Perform further edits, if desired, optimize the file, and finally, use File > Save Optimized to output the file in the JPEG format. Don't panic—we'll break it down into steps for you!

PNG-8 and PNG-24

The two PNG formats, PNG-8 and PNG-24, can save partially transparent pixels (e.g., soft, feathered edges) using a method called alpha transparency. With alpha transparency, a pixel can have any one of 256 levels of opacity, ranging from totally transparent to totally opaque. The PNG-8 format is limited to a maximum of 256 colors in the optimized image and is similar to the GIF format. The PNG-24 format allows for millions of colors in the optimized image and

(Continued on the following page)

PNG-8, PNG-24

473

is more similar to the JPEG format. The compression method used by both PNG formats is lossless, meaning it doesn't cause data loss. PNG is supported directly by the two major Web browsers: Internet Explorer versions 4.0 and later directly support PNG, as does Netscape Navigator 6 and later.

Are there any drawbacks to PNG? For one thing, you can't save animations in the PNG format (whereas you can with GIF files), and PNG-24 files have larger file sizes than (don't compress as much as) equivalent JPEGs.

Dithering

Dithering is the juxtaposition of two or more palette colors to create the impression of a third color. It's used to make images that contain a limited number of colors (256 or fewer) appear to have a greater range of colors and shades. Dithering is usually applied to continuous-tone images to increase their tonal range, but—argh, life is full of compromises—it can also make them look grainy **1**–**2**.

Dithering usually doesn't produce aesthetically pleasing results in flat-color images. This is because the browser palette will dither pixels to re-create any color that the palette doesn't contain. You're better off creating flat colors in Photoshop or ImageReady using the Web Color sliders and the Web Safe color ramp on the Color palette. Any existing flat-color areas should be selected and Web-shifted to bring them into the Web-safe gamut.

As for continuous-tone imagery, it already contains a wider mixture of colors, and will look okay on both 8-bit and 24-bit monitors. If you reduce the number of colors on the color table of a continuous-tone image, however, you'll increase the likelihood of banding. Banding can be prevented by applying dithering, but do it at a low value. Choose a dither method and amount value either in ImageReady or in Photoshop's Save for Web dialog box. Keep in mind that the higher the dither value, the more seamless

1 *A closeup of an image with a **small** amount of dithering*

1 *The same image with a **lot** of dithering*

Dithering

Halos nobody wants

Here's a way to prevent halos when copying anti-aliased objects to other programs. Ctrl-click/Cmd-click a layer name in Photoshop to select an object on its layer without its anti-aliased edge, then zoom in (at least 200% view) so you can see the object's edge clearly. Use Select > Modify > **Contract** to contract the selection by 1 or 2 pixels in order to remove the anti-aliased edge **1**, copy the object selection, and then paste it into your other program.

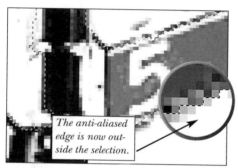

The anti-aliased edge is now outside the selection.

1 *After using the Magic Wand tool to select the white background around the signpost and then inversing the selection, some of the original anti-aliased edge remained. Select > Modify > **Contract** (by 1 pixel) was then used to shrink the selection inward.*

2 *These two signposts were pasted into an image in another program. The signpost on the left was copied without contracting the selection in Photoshop, whereas the signpost on the right was copied after contracting the selection in Photoshop in order to remove its halo.*

the color transitions, but the more grainy the image.

One more consideration: Dithering adds noise and additional colors to a file, so compression is less effective when dithering is turned on than when it's off. So, with dithering enabled, you may not be able to achieve your desired degree of file compression. As is the case with most Web output, you'll have to strike an acceptable balance between aesthetics and file size. (Dithering is discussed further on page 487.)

Anti-aliasing

Anti-aliasing blends the edges of an object with its background by adding pixels with progressively less opacity along the object's edges. When imagery is composited or montaged in Photoshop, anti-aliasing helps to smooth the transitions between shapes. With anti-aliasing off, the edges of an object will look sharp because its edge pixels won't be blended with the background color.

One potential problem to keep in mind is that if you create a selection using a tool with anti-aliasing on, a fringe of pixels may be picked up in the selection from the background of the original image. If you copy and paste this type of shape onto a flat-color background, the fringe may become painfully visible **2**. To prevent this from happening, before creating your selection, uncheck Anti-aliased on the options bar for your marquee, lasso, or Magic Wand tool.

You can also use the Matte option on ImageReady's Optimize palette to control how partially transparent pixels (the kind of pixels that are created by anti-aliasing) are treated in GIFs and JPEGs. Both Photoshop and ImageReady also provide options for controlling the amount of anti-aliasing on type. These options can be chosen in, and will transfer correctly between, the two programs. The matting and anti-aliasing controls both help to eliminate unwanted halos.

Anti-aliasing

The ImageReady Toolbox

As we said at the beginning of this chapter, if Photoshop is launched, and you want to go to ImageReady (or vice versa), click the **Edit in** button at the bottom of the Toolbox or press **Ctrl-Shift-M/Cmd-Shift-M.**

The ImageReady Toolbox **1** looks similar to Photoshop's, but it contains a few additional Web-related tools for creating image maps, viewing image maps, viewing slices, previewing rollovers and animation effects, and switching to a Web browser.

Like Photoshop, ImageReady has a context-sensitive tool options bar, which changes depending on which tool is currently chosen **2**–**3**. You can drag the bar's left edge to move it anywhere on the desktop.

TIP *Release the mouse on the downward-pointing arrowhead to create a standalone, tearoff* **palette.**

Click here to go to the Adobe website

Marquee **M**

Slice **K**

Rectangle Image Map Tool P
Circle Image Map Tool P
Polygon Image Map Tool P

Type **T**

Line **S**

Crop **C**

Hand **H**

Move **V**

Slice Select **O**

Image Map Select **J**

Paintbrush **B**

Rectangle **U**

Tab Rectangle **R**

Eyedropper **I**

Zoom **Z**

Foreground color square

Default colors **D**

Toggle Image Maps Visibility **A**

Preview Document **Y**

Switch Foreground/ Background colors **X**

Background color square

Toggle Slices Visibility **Q**

Preview in [default browser] (Ctrl-Alt-P/ Cmd-Option-P)

Edit in Photoshop (Ctrl-Shift-M/Cmd-Shift-M)

1 *The* **ImageReady Toolbox**

ImageReady Toolbox

Fixed Size Width: Height: Style: Mode: Normal Opacity: 100%

2 *The options bar with the* **Rectangle** *tool chosen*

T T Helvetica Medium T 17.28 px a Sharp

3 *The options bar with the* **Type** *tool chosen*

Color-reduction methods

Note: ImageReady's tool tip calls the Reduction pop-up menu "color reduction algorithm" (huh?).

Perceptual
Generates a color table based on the colors currently in the image, with particular attention paid to how people actually perceive colors.

Selective
Generates a color table based on the colors currently in the image, with a bias toward preserving flat colors, Web-safe colors, and overall color integrity.

Adaptive
Generates a color table based on the part of the color spectrum that represents most of the colors in the image. This choice produces a slightly larger optimized file.

TIP If you switch among the Perceptual, Selective, or Adaptive options, most of the Web-safe colors that are currently on the Color Table palette will be preserved.

Restrictive (Web)
Generates a color table by shifting image colors to colors that are available in the standard Web-safe palette. (The Web-safe palette contains only the 216 colors that the Windows and Mac OS browser palettes have in common.) This choice produces the least number of colors and thus the smallest file size—but not necessarily the best image quality.

To optimize an image in the GIF or PNG-8 format:

1. If you're working in Photoshop, save your file, then click the "Edit in" button at the bottom of the Toolbox (Ctrl-Shift-M/ Cmd-Shift-M). ImageReady will launch, if it isn't already open, and the image will open in that application.
or
In ImageReady, choose File > Open, locate an image, then click Open.

2. Click the 2-Up tab at the top of the image window to display both the original and optimized previews of the image simultaneously **1**.

3. Display the Optimize palette (Window > Optimize) **2**.

4. Choose a named, preset combination of optimize settings from the Settings pop-up menu. Leave the preset as is, and save your file.
or
Follow the remaining steps to choose custom optimization settings.

5. From the Format pop-up menu, choose GIF or PNG-8.

6. From the Reduction pop-up menu in the Color Table pane, choose a color **reduction** method (algorithm) (see the sidebar at left).

(Continued on the following page)

1 *2-Up view in* **ImageReady**

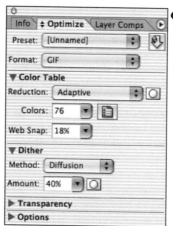

2 **ImageReady's** *Optimize palette*

Perceptual, Selective,  and **Adaptive** render the optimized image using colors from the original image.

Restrictive (Web) shifts all the image colors to Web-safe colors .

Custom optimizes image color based on a palette you have previously saved in Photoshop or ImageReady.

Mac OS and **Windows** optimize image color based on the Standard palette for each particular operating system.

1 *The **Selective** palette produces a **smoother** optimization.*

7. Choose the maximum number of **Colors** to be generated in the color table by choosing a standard setting from the pop-up menu or by entering an exact number in the field. Auto (available for the Restrictive [Web] reduction method only) sets the number of colors in the color table automatically to either the number of colors used in the image or to 216, whichever number is lower.

2 *The **Web** palette produces a **dithered** optimization.*

8. Choose or enter a **Web Snap** percentage to establish the range of colors that will automatically snap to their Web-safe equivalents. The higher the Web Snap, the fewer the number of colors in the image and the smaller the file size, but also the more dithered or posterized the image will become.

9. In the Dither pane, choose a **Dither** method from the **Method** pop-up menu: No Dither, Diffusion, Pattern, or Noise. Dithering simulates image colors for 8-bit display (you won't be able to see this on the palette), and it increases a file's size. Diffusion produces the most subtle results, with the least increase in file size.

3 *Selective palette with a **high Dither** value*

Also choose the **Amount** of dither **3**–**4**. A high dither amount will produce more color simulation and a larger file size. (To modify dithering using a channel, see page 481.)

10. In the Transparency pane, check **Transparency** to have ImageReady preserve any transparent pixels in the

4 *The **Web** palette with a **high Dither** value produces, as one would expect, a lot of **dithering**.*

Fading away redux

Another way to have your GIF or JPEG image fade into a flat-color background is to create two layers in your Photoshop or ImageReady document: a lower layer that contains a flat color filled with the Web-safe color that will be used on the Web page, and an upper layer that contains the image element with a soft edge or an effect such as Drop Shadow or Outer Glow.

1 *A GIF image with **Transparency** checked and **Matte** set to **a color**, resulting in a thin line of that color along the edge of each shape*

2 *A GIF image with **Transparency** checked and **Matte** set to **None**. There's a hard edge along each shape.*

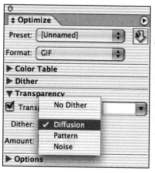

3 *To apply transparency dithering, check **Transparency**, then choose from the **Transparency Dither** pop-up menu.*

image (areas on a layer where the checkerboard pattern shows). The GIF format doesn't allow for partially transparent pixels; the PNG-8 format does. Transparency permits the creation of nonrectangular image borders. With Transparency unchecked, transparent pixels will be filled with the current Matte color.

11. To control how partially transparent pixels along the edge of an image blend with the background of a Web page (as on the edges of anti-aliased elements), choose a **Matte** option. Set the Matte color to the color of the Web page background, if you happen to know what that color is **1**. Any soft-edged effect (such as a Drop Shadow) on top of transparent areas will fill with the current Matte color. If the backgound color is unknown, set Matte to None, which will result in a hard, jagged edge **2**.

Another option is to choose Matte: None and then, in the Transparency pane, check Transparency and choose one of three options from the **Dither** pop-up menu **3**. These effects will look the same on any background. Diffusion applies a random pattern to partially transparent pixels and diffuses it across adjacent pixels. This is often the least noticeable of the three dither patterns, and it's the only one that lets you set the dithering amount. Pattern applies a halftone pattern to the partially transparent pixels. Noise applies a pattern similar to Diffusion, but it doesn't affect adjacent pixels. All four Dither options in the Transparency pane eliminate halo effects along the edge of an image when it's displayed on the Web.

12. In the Options pane, check **Interlaced** to have the GIF or PNG image display in successively greater detail as it downloads on the Web page. This option causes the file size to increase slightly.

(Continued on the following page)

Optimize as GIF or PNG-8

13. *Optional:* For a GIF only, you can adjust the **Lossy** value to further reduce the file size of the optimized image. As the name "Lossy" implies, some image data will be discarded, but the slight reduction in image quality may be justified by the savings in file size. (To modify lossiness using a channel, see the following page.)

14. Save the file (see pages 490–491).

TIP To save a current (Unnamed) set of palette options, choose Save Settings from the palette menu. Enter a name (in Windows, use the .irs extension), locate and open the Adobe Photoshop CS > Presets > Optimize Settings folder (the default), then click Save. Your saved set will display on the Settings pop-up menu in ImageReady and in the Save for Web dialog box in Photoshop.

ImageReady's **master palettes** offer a way to ensure that every image in a group uses an identical palette, and this can help you save storage space.

To create a master palette for optimized images in ImageReady:

1. In ImageReady, choose Image > Master Palette > Clear Master Palette, if a Master Palette already exists.

2. Open an image whose colors you want to use in building a master palette.

3. Choose Image > Master Palette > Add to Master Palette ∎.

4. Repeat steps 2 and 3 to add the colors of any other images to the master palette.

5. Once you've added all the desired images, choose Image > Master Palette > Build Master Palette.

6. Finally, choose Image > Master Palette > Save Master Palette.

7. Type a name for the palette, then click Save. The palette can now be applied to other images (see the next page).

How to treat a hybrid

For a hybrid image that contains both flat-color areas or type and photographic imagery, the best choice for optimization may be the GIF format using the Perceptual, Selective, or Adaptive palette (not the Web palette). This combination will strike a good balance between keeping the flat-color areas Web safe and rendering the continuous-tone areas pretty well.

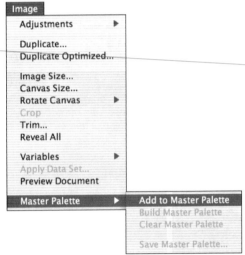

∎ *Choose Image > Master Palette > Add to Master Palette to add the colors from the currently open image to a master palette.*

Master Palette

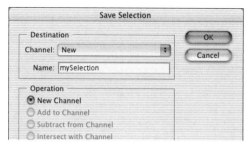

1 *Enter a* ***Name*** *in the* ***Save Selection*** *dialog box.*

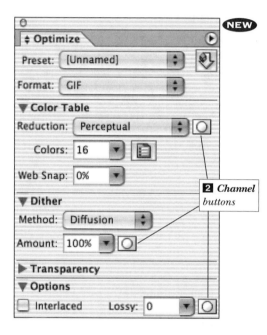

2 ***Channel*** *buttons*

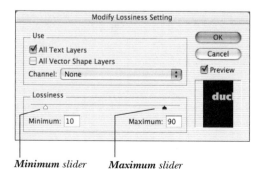

Minimum *slider*   ***Maximum*** *slider*

3 *Use a text or vector shape mask or an alpha channel to control where optimization is applied.*

To apply a master palette to an image:

1. Open an image within ImageReady.

2. For a GIF or PNG-8, from the Reduction pop-up menu in the Color Table pane on the Optimize palette, choose the master palette that you've saved.

Using a technique called **weighted optimization,** you can apply different optimization settings to different areas of an image. You'll create an alpha channel and then apply maximum-quality optimization settings to the channel's white areas inside the selection and minimum-quality settings to the black areas outside the selection. You can choose limits for color reduction, dithering, lossiness, and overall quality.

To use weighted optimization:

1. Create an alpha channel mask by selecting an area in the image and choosing Select > Save Selection. Leave the Channel pop-up menu set to New **1**, enter a name in the Name field, then click OK. Then, on the Optimize palette, click a channel button next to the Reduction pop-up menu, the Lossy field (GIF only), or the Amount field for a GIF or PNG **2**, or next to the Quality field for a JPEG.

    Text and vector shapes have masks that are made automatically for them, which can be accessed via the Modify Setting dialog box in the next step.

2. In the Modify [Lossiness, Dither, or Quality] Setting dialog box **3**, check All Text Layers and/or All Vector Shape Layers to use the text or shape masks to control where optimization settings are applied. For all other areas, choose your new channel mask from the Channel pop-up menu.

    Also choose Minimum and Maximum limits for the image quality. The black slider controls what level of optimization is applied to black areas of a mask; the white slider controls white areas of a mask.

3. Click OK.

To use the ImageReady previews:

Click the 4-Up tab on the image window to see an original view and three previews simultaneously. ImageReady will use the current Optimize palette settings to generate the first preview (to the right of the original), and then automatically generate ("autopopulate") the two other previews as variations on the current optimization settings. You can click on any preview and change the Optimize palette settings for just that preview.

The Optimized preview(s) will update every time a value or setting is changed on the Optimize palette. If you need to stop the preview from updating, click the Stop button on the image window progress bar **1**. A halted preview button (triangle with an exclamation point) will display in the lower right corner of any halted preview **2**. If you change a setting on the Optimize palette or click the alert triangle, the preview will update automatically.

TIP The File > Save Optimized command saves the image using the currently chosen Optimize palette settings.

Edit in

Leave both Photoshop and ImageReady open so you can quickly make changes to the same file in either program. To go back and forth, click the **Edit in** button on the toolbox, or press **Ctrl-Shift-M/Cmd-Shift-M**.

NEW The two programs will automatically close, open, and update your file when you switch from one to the other. If you start working on an image in ImageReady, go to Photoshop to perform some edits, then go back to ImageReady, the Photoshop edits will be identified on the History palette in Image-Ready as a single history state named **Update From Photoshop.** Similarly, Photoshop's History palette will list an **Update From ImageReady** history state when a change is made in ImageReady. You can click an earlier state at any time to undo an edit made in the other program!

Revert is a state

The **Revert** command is recorded as a **state** on the History palette in Photoshop and ImageReady, and it won't wipe out the existing states. This means you can undo a Revert.

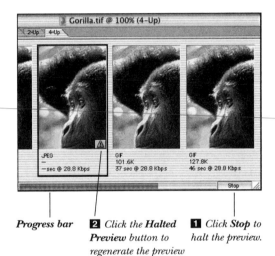

Progress bar   **2** *Click the Halted Preview button to regenerate the preview (it's not easy).*   **1** *Click Stop to halt the preview.*

Calling all auto-updates!

Regardless of whether you check or uncheck **Auto-Update Files** in General Preferences in ImageReady or **Auto-update open documents** in Photoshop, files will update automatically in both programs.

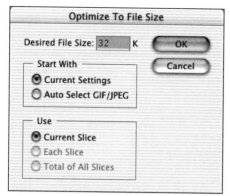

1 *Using the **Optimize To File Size** dialog box, you can let ImageReady make the optimization calculations for you.*

2 *Click the **Droplet** button on the **Optimize** palette, or drag it to the Desktop.*

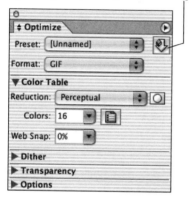

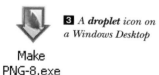

3 *A **droplet** icon on a Windows Desktop*

Make
PNG-8.exe

4 *A **droplet** icon on a Mac Desktop*

Make JPEG (quality 60)

Why not let ImageReady make all the decisions **for you?** All you need to decide is how large you want the optimized image to be.

To quick-optimize:

1. *Optional:* Click a slice (see pages 495–497) to optimize just that area of the image.

2. Choose Optimize to File Size from the Optimize palette menu.

3. Enter a Desired File Size value for the final optimized file size. **1**

4. Click Start With: Current Settings to use the current settings on the palette.
   or
   Click Auto Select GIF/JPEG to let ImageReady pick the optimize method.

5. Click Use: Current Slice, or click Each Slice or Total of All Slices, if available.

6. Click OK. Presto—ImageReady will choose all the Optimize palette settings for you and generate an optimized file based on your designated file size.

A **droplet** is a tiny but powerful application that remembers the Optimize palette settings that are in effect when it's created. When you drag a file over a droplet, ImageReady launches automatically and optimizes the file based on the instructions contained in the droplet.

To create and apply a droplet:

1. Choose Optimize palette settings.

2. Click the Droplet button 🔱 on the Optimize palette **2**, choose a location in which to save it, then click Save.
   or
   Drag the Droplet button 🔱 from the Optimize palette to the Desktop.

3. To optimize a file or a whole folder of files using the droplet and its settings, drag the file or folder icon over the droplet icon on the Desktop **3**–**4**. An optimized version of the file(s) will be saved in the same location as the droplet.

JPEG is the format of choice for optimizing continuous-tone imagery (photographs, paintings, gradients, or blends) for display on the Web. If you optimize to this format, the file's 24-bit color depth will be preserved, and these colors will be seen and enjoyed by any Web viewer whose monitor is set to millions of colors (24-bit depth). Keep in mind, however, that JPEGs are optimized using a lossy compression method that causes image data to be eliminated.

The **PNG-24** format is similar to JPEG, except that PNG allows for multiple levels of transparency along edges and employs a lossless compression method. PNG-24 files are larger than equivalent JPEGs.

To optimize an image in the JPEG or PNG-24 format:

1. If you're working in Photoshop, save your file, then click the "Edit in" button at the bottom of the Toolbox. ImageReady will launch, if it isn't already open.
   or
   In ImageReady, choose File > Open, locate the image, then click Open.

2. Click the 2-Up tab at the top of the image window to display the original and optimized previews of the image simultaneously.

3. Display the Optimize palette (Window > Optimize) **1**.

4. From the **Preset** pop-up menu, choose JPEG High **2**, JPEG Low, JPEG Medium, or PNG-24. Leave this preset setting as is, then save your file.
   or
   Follow the remaining steps to choose custom settings.

5. Choose JPEG as the format from the Format pop-up menu.

6. From the **Quality** pop-up menu in the Quality pane, choose Low, Medium, High, or Maximum as the resulting quality level for the optimized image (**1**–**2**, next page).
   or

JPEGs and Web-safe colors

JPEG compression adds compression artifacts to an image. Because of this, Web-safe colors in a JPEG image are rendered un-Web-safe after compression, but this is acceptable because the JPEG format is usually used to optimize continuous-tone images, and on these type of images, browser dither isn't objectionable. Don't try to match a color area in a JPEG file to a color area in a GIF file, or on the background of a Web page, though, because the JPEG color will shift and become dithered when the image is compressed.

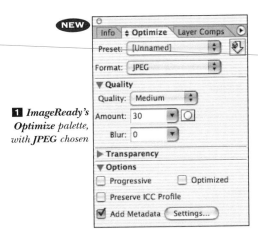

1 *ImageReady's Optimize palette, with JPEG chosen*

2 *A JPEG optimized with **High** Quality*

Optimize as JPEG or PNG-24

1 *A JPEG optimized with **Medium** Quality*

2 *A JPEG optimized with **Low** Quality. Note how pixelated the image has become.*

Move the **Amount** pop-up slider to an exact level of compression. Watch the adjacent Quality pop-up menu setting change as you change the Amount value. (To vary the compression using a selection channel, see page 481.)

Always remember, the lower the compression, the higher the quality—and the larger the file size.

7. Increase the **Blur** value to lessen the visibility of JPEG artifacts that arise from the JPEG compression method and also to reduce the file size. Be careful not to overblur the image, though, or the details will soften too much. The Blur setting can be lowered later to reclaim some of the diminished sharpness.

8. In the Transparency pane, choose a **Matte** color to be used for areas of transparency in the original image. If you choose None, transparent areas will appear as white.

   Note: The JPEG format doesn't support transparency. To have the Matte color simulate transparency, use the same solid color as the background of the Web page, if that color is known.

9. In the Options pane, check **Progressive** to have the optimized image display on the Web page in successively greater detail.

10. *Optional:* Check ICC Profile to embed an ICC Profile in the optimized image. To utilize this option, the original image must have had a profile embedded into it in Photoshop. See the sidebar on this page.

11. *Optional:* Check Optimized to produce the smallest file size. Check Add Metadata if you imported the file from a digital camera and want camera settings, caption, and keyword information to be saved with the file.

12. Save the file (see pages 490–491).

TIP To save the current settings as a named preset, see page 480.

Optimize as JPEG or PNG-24

Let's say you've got an image that you're going to optimize in the GIF format using the Perceptual, Selective, or Adaptive palette, but it contains flat-color areas that aren't **Web-safe.** Before outputting it online, you can make the flat-color areas Web-safe.

To make flat-color areas Web-safe:

1. Open the image in ImageReady and optimize it in the GIF format.

2. Choose the Eyedropper tool (I). ✐

3. Click on a flat-color area to be made Web-safe ∎.

4. On the Optimize palette, click the Show Color Table Palette button 🗒 to open the Color Table palette. The color you just clicked on will be the highlighted swatch ∎.

5. Click the Shift Selected Colors to Web Palette button 🔲 at the bottom of the palette. A diamond with a diagonal line will appear on the selected swatch, signifying that the color was shifted to its Web-safe equivalent. The swatch will also become locked (see the next step).

6. *Optional:* Click the Lock Selected Color button 🔒 at the bottom of the palette, to have the currently selected swatch be preserved even if the number of colors in the GIF palette is reduced.

TIP Shift-click with the Eyedropper tool on other areas in the image to select more than one color, then shift all the selected colors to the Web palette at once. Or use the Magic Wand tool or a lasso or marquee tool to create a selection or selections in the image, choose the Select All From Selection command from the Color Table palette menu, then click the Shift Selected Colors to Web Palette button 🔲 at the bottom of the Color Table palette.

TIP To assign transparency to a particular color in the Color Table, click the color swatch, then click the Map Selected Colors to Transparent button. ▨ To unassign the color, click the button again.

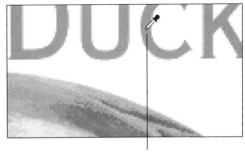

∎ *Click on a **flat-color** area with the **Eyedropper** tool.*

A **diamond** *signifies that the swatch was made Web-safe via the Optimize palette.*

A **small square** *signifies that a swatch is locked.*

*A diamond with a **diagonal line** signifies that the swatch was made Web-safe via the Shift Selected Colors to Web Palette button.*

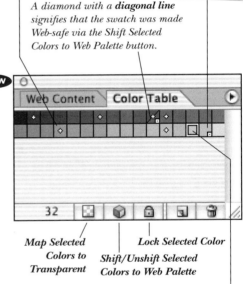

Map Selected Colors to Transparent

Lock Selected Color

Shift/Unshift Selected Colors to Web Palette

∎ *The color you click on will become the highlighted swatch on the **Color Table** palette in ImageReady.*

1 *An image optimized as a JPEG in ImageReady with **Browser Dither** turned **off***

2 *The same image optimized as a JPEG, but with Preview > **Browser Dither** turned **on**. The image's millions of colors are reduced to the browser's 8-bit color palette.*

Using various preview methods in ImageReady, you can get a pretty reliable idea of how optimized images will look when they're viewed online. This will help you choose appropriate settings as you optimize your images.

8-bit monitors (which very few Web viewers use nowadays) can display up to 256 colors, whereas Macintosh and Windows browsers use a color palette of 216 colors. The browsers use a technique called **dithering** to simulate colors in an image that the browser palette lacks.

To preview potential browser dither in an optimized image:

1. Open the image in ImageReady, and display at least one optimized preview in the image window.

2. Right-click/Ctrl-click and choose Display Preview > Browser Dither; or choose View > Preview > Browser Dither; or press Ctrl-Shift-Y/Cmd-Shift-Y) **1**–**2**.

Controlling dithering

When you use ImageReady to optimize an image, the application applies dithering to simulate colors that were in the original image but that won't appear on the color palette of the optimized image. You can control the amount of this type of dithering via options in the Dither pane on the Optimize palette. If you raise the Amount value, colors in the optimized image will more closely match colors in the original—but with the drawback of a slightly larger file size.

The Web Snap value on the Optimize palette also affects the amount of browser dither in an image. The higher the Web Snap value, the less the optimized image will be dithered, and the smaller its file size.

Setting the palette's Dither Amount to a high value will make the color transitions in the optimized image smoother. Some degree of dithering is acceptable in continuous-tone imagery, though, and it's more pleasing than the color banding that a high Web Snap value can cause.

Preview Browser Dither

Because the Windows operating system uses a higher gamma value than the Macintosh operating system, the same image will appear darker in Windows than on a Mac. When creating Web graphics for cross-platform use, it's important to **preview** your image in, and adjust it for, both platforms.

To preview Windows and Mac gamma values:

With an optimized preview showing in ImageReady, choose View > Preview > Standard Macintosh Color to simulate the Mac gamma value, or Standard Windows Color to simulate the Windows gamma value.

Choose View > Preview > Uncompensated Color to preview the image without gamma compensation. Choose Use Embedded Color Profile to match the ImageReady preview (based on the monitor RGB) with the profile assigned to, or embedded in, the image in Photoshop. This option will be grayed out if the image lacks a profile.

You can compensate for differences in **gamma** between operating systems for an individual file.

To change the gamma for an optimized file:

1. With an optimized preview showing for an image in ImageReady, choose Image > Adjustments > Gamma.

2. Click Windows to Macintosh to change the gamma to the Mac gamma value. The image will look darker on a Mac **1**–**2**.
or
Click Macintosh to Windows to change the gamma to the Windows gamma value. The image will look lighter on a Mac **3**.

3. Click OK.

TIP You can also use the slider to manually choose a gamma value in between the button choices, or to set a gamma value for another platform. The gamma setting is relative, meaning if you set a value, close the dialog box, and then reopen it, the gamma setting will be back at 1.

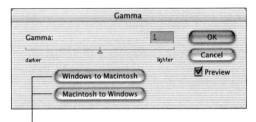

1 *Click either of these buttons in the **Gamma** dialog box to preview the other platform's gamma values.*

2 *An image after clicking the **Windows to Macintosh** button: The lower gamma value has caused the image to look darker.*

3 *The same image after clicking the **Macintosh to Windows** button: The image looks lighter.*

Keep the code

There are two methods for copying source code from ImageReady into an HTML-editing program. You can drag through the source code that's displayed at the bottom of the browser window to select it **3** and then copy and paste it into the HTML-editing or Web-page creation program. Or in ImageReady, you could choose Edit > Copy HTML Code > For All Slices for the current file and then paste the source code into an HTML-editing or Web-page creation program.

1 *Click this button to **preview** your optimized image in the default **browser**.*

Preview in Internet Explorer (Cmd+Option+P)

For a more definitive simulation of online viewing for an optimized image, use ImageReady's **Preview in [default browser]** feature. You can choose from any of the browsers that are currently installed on your system.

Note: This preview feature won't test the actual download time for an image over an actual Web connection, and it will display a preview for your monitor type only—not for any other monitor type. Nevertheless, it's still very useful.

To preview an optimized image in a browser on your system:

1. With an optimized image opened in ImageReady, click the Preview in [default browser] button on the Toolbox (Ctrl-Alt-P/Cmd-Option-P) **1**, or click the Preview in [default browser] button and choose a browser from the submenu.

2. The browser will launch and the image will load into the browser window **2**. You can preview any GIF animations or rollovers that you created in ImageReady.

3. Exit/quit the browser, if desired, then click back on any ImageReady palette or window to switch back to ImageReady.

   Note: Be sure to preview your final files by actually uploading them to the Web. Do this on both computer platforms and, ideally, on a spectrum of monitor types.

TIP If your monitor's color depth setting is higher than 8-bit and you want to see how an image will look in an 8-bit browser, set your system to 256 colors first, then launch your browser. We've seen only minor differences between this method and choosing View > Preview > Browser Dither (in ImageReady).

3 *The **HTML source code** from ImageReady*

2 *An image being viewed in Microsoft's **Internet Explorer***

To save a file in ImageReady:

1. Make sure you're in ImageReady and the file you want to save is open, then choose File > Save (Ctrl-S/Cmd-S).

2. Enter a file name and leave the file extension for the Photoshop format (.psd) as is. Choose a location, then click Save. The saved file won't contain optimization settings.

Follow these instructions to save a file as an **optimized** file according to the settings currently chosen on the Optimize palette.

To save an optimized file in ImageReady:

1. Choose File > Save Optimized (Ctrl-Alt-S/Cmd-Option-S).

2. To control how the file will be saved, choose one of the following from the **Save as Type/Format** pop-up menu 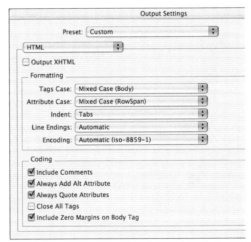:

   HTML and Images to create an HTML file and save the image slices in a separate folder of files.

   Images Only to save just the image slices.

   HTML Only to create an HTML file without saving the optimized image files. It will have the .htm or .html extension and will be saved in the location you'll chose in step 6.

3. *Optional:* To choose additional options, choose Other from the Settings pop-up menu. The **Output Settings** dialog box opens.

   To choose HTML preferences for formatting and coding, choose **HTML** from the second pop-up menu 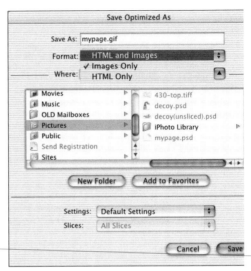. Use these options to establish consistency between the HTML in ImageReady and other HTML-editing applications.

   Click OK now, or follow the next step before clicking OK.

4. Choose **Saving Files** from the second pop-up menu.

1 *Choose from the **Format** pop-up menu in the **Save Optimized As** dialog box.*

2 *The **Output Settings** dialog box, with custom settings chosen in the **HTML** pane*

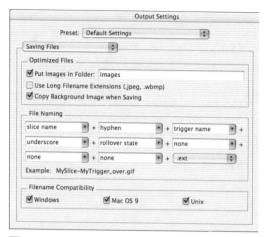

1 *Choose options for saving files in the **Saving Files** pane of the **Output Settings** dialog box.*

Check any **Optimized Files** options **1**. Enter the name of the folder you want to save the autogenerated optimized files in.

Choose **File Naming** conventions for any autogenerated files, such as slices or rollover frames, to be saved with the optimized file and used in the HTML page. Consult with your HTML specialist before making changes in these fields. If the naming convention seems confusing, leave the default settings as is.

Check any platform **Filename Compatibility** options.

5. Click OK to exit the Output Settings dialog box.

6. Type a file name, choose a location, then click Save.

TIP Use the Save As or Save Optimized As command to save a version of a file under a different name.

TIP To attach a URL or an Alt tag to an image, use the Slice palette (see page 507).

TIP You can also open the Output Settings dialog box by choosing from the File > Output Settings submenu.

To update an HTML file:

If you have modified an optimized file and you want to update the HTML file that's associated with it, choose File > Update HTML, locate the HTML file for that image, then click Open. Click Replace, if an alert box appears. Click OK when the update is finished. Any HTML code generated for the optimized file will be updated, even if the code was already copied and pasted into a larger HTML file, or that larger file contains tables from other image files.

You can use the **File Info** dialog box to modify the page title for the browser window and embed metadata and copyright information into the optimized HTML file. Metadata and the Web page document title help categorize your document. Providing keywords and descriptions to categorize your page makes it easier for a viewer to locate your page when using a Web search engine. This is a way to embed information into a page that doesn't need to be seen by the average Web viewer.

NEW **To change a Web page title and embed metadata:**

1. With the image open in ImageReady, choose File > File Info (Ctrl-Alt-I/Cmd-Option-I).

2. Change the page title in the Document Title field **1**. This title will display on the title bar of the browser window (the text between the HTML <TITLE> tags). The default title is the title of the current file for the image.

3. Enter descriptive metadata in the Author, Description, Description Writer, or Keywords fields. This information will

Color matching between applications

If you try to mix a color in Photoshop using the same RGB values as a color used in another application, you probably won't be able to achieve an exact match, because other applications use the Windows Color Picker or Apple Color Picker (depending on the platform) to determine R, G, and B component color values, whereas Photoshop, by default, uses its own color picker.

If you ask Photoshop to use the Windows or Apple Color Picker instead, the colors you mix using the RGB sliders on the Color palette in Photoshop will match the colors used in other applications. To switch pickers, choose Edit (Photoshop, in Mac) > Preferences > General, choose Color Picker: Windows/Apple, then click OK. Remember to reset this preference to the Photoshop Color Picker when you're done.

be added to the header section of the HTML file, and will make it easier for search engines to locate the page.

4. *Optional:* Choose a Copyright Status, enter a Copyright Notice, and enter a Copyright Info URL.

5. Click OK.

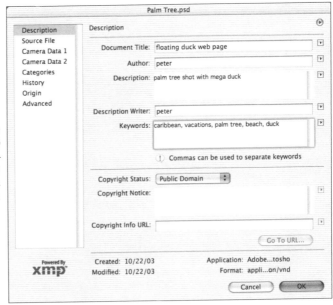

1 *Use the **File Info** dialog box to modify the page (document) title for your HTML file for display in the browser window, and to embed copyright information into your optimized HTML file.*

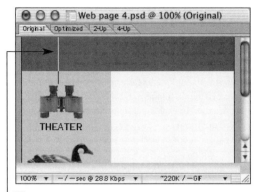

1 *Click with the **Type** tool to create an insertion point, then start typing.*

2 *The type is entered.*

As in Photoshop, **type** in **ImageReady** is entered directly on the image, and it can be styled using the options bar, the Character palette, or the Paragraph palette. To learn how to create type in ImageReady, read Chapter 19.

Furthermore, in ImageReady, as in Photoshop, type automatically appears on its own layer and remains editable until or unless you rasterize its layer. You can apply any layer effect or style to editable type and it will remain editable. When type is optimized in ImageReady, whether it's rasterized or not, it becomes bitmapped, like the overall image.

Note: Editable type in a file that's exported to the Flash (SWF) format will remain as vector shapes unless you use layer effects (such as Drop Shadow, Outer Glow, or Emboss), which create soft outer edges.

Some significant differences should be noted, though: Unlike type in Photoshop, type in ImageReady can't be created as a selection, converted to a work path, or converted to shapes.

To create type in ImageReady:

1. Make sure the Original view is chosen for the image in the image window.

2. Choose the Type tool (T or Shift-T). T

   Optional: On the options bar, click the Text orientation button 🔳 to switch the type's orientation.

3. Click in the image window where you want the type to start. A flashing insertion point will appear **1**.

4. Create point or paragraph type (see pages 344–345) **2**.

Creating display type for Web pages

- All type layer attributes and anti-aliasing options are preserved for editable and rasterized type, whether you use Photoshop or ImageReady to edit the file.

(Continued on the following page)

Create Type: Type for Web Pages

- Anti-aliasing can be applied to type in Photoshop or ImageReady, but because it adds colors to type edges, it also adds colors to a file's color table and slightly increases its storage size. Some people are of the opinion that anti-aliasing should be applied to small type if it's being created for onscreen output; we think small type looks better without it. Use ImageReady's preview features to decide for yourself.

- To help make online type more legible, choose a slightly larger point size for it than you would choose for print output.

  Note: The same type size on a Web page will display differently on a Mac screen than on a Windows screen due to the ppi resolution difference between Macintosh and Windows monitors (e.g., 72 for the former, 96 for the latter). Just one more discrepancy to worry about. Be sure to test your page(s) on both platforms.

- You can toggle the Faux Bold and Faux Italic styles on or off via ImageReady's Character palette menu. These type styles are designed for use with font families that lack a true bold or italic style.

- Remember to make your type colors Web-safe to prevent dithering. To make a color Web-safe in ImageReady, choose the Eyedropper tool (I), click on a type character in an optimized preview, then shift the color to the Web palette using the Color Table palette (see page 486).

  To make a non-Web-safe color Web-safe in Photoshop, double-click the T thumbnail on the type layer, then click the Color swatch on either the options bar or the Character palette. In the Color Picker, either click the non-Web color alert icon 🔲 to have Photoshop substitute the closest Web-safe equivalent or check Only Web Colors, then click OK.

Mixed optimization

Hybrid images, which contain both continuous-tone imagery and flat-color areas (such as type), pose a special challenge **1**. You can use the slicing feature in Photoshop or ImageReady to frame off different areas of a hybrid image, and then apply a different optimization to each area. To facilitate slicing for mixed optimization, whenever possible, position the type so it doesn't overlap any continuous-tone areas. Optimize type slices as GIF and continuous-tone areas as JPEG. (For more information about slicing, see pages 495–507.)

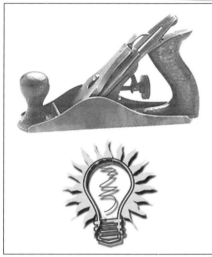

1 *This image would be considered a hybrid because it contains both continuous-tone imagery and flat-color areas.*

Behind the scenes

In HTML, a table can be used as a grid system to control the layout of graphics and text on a Web page. Table cells can be coded to display separate images and data or portions of a large, sliced graphic. Frames function like separate windows within the larger browser window. A frame can display an HTML graphic, page, or site independently from the other frames on the same Web page. To learn more about HTML tables and frames, see:

designing web graphics.4: the definitive guide to web design & development, by Lynda Weinman and Ali Karp (Pearson Education)

creative html design.2, by Lynda Weinman and William Weinman (Pearson Education)

HTML for the World Wide Web with XHTML and CSS: Visual QuickStart Guide, by Elizabeth Castro (Peachpit Press)

HTML and XHTML: The Definitive Guide, by Chuck Musciano and Bill Kennedy (O'Reilly & Associates)

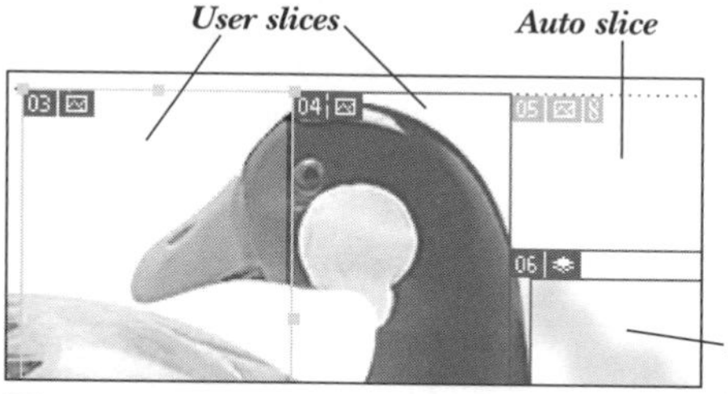

1 *All three types of slices can be combined in the same image. Every document starts out with a default auto slice that's the size of the entire image. It has a light gray label and is numbered "01."*

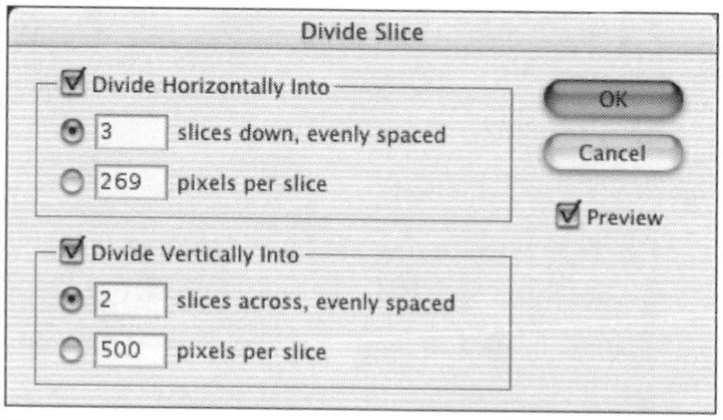

2 *Use the **Divide Slice** dialog box to divide an image into slices using a command, rather than manually.*

Slicing

Slicing is a process by which an image is divided into distinct **zones.** A group of small slices will download more quickly than a whole, large image. The browser assembles the slices into the overall image in sequence, using HTML tables and frames.

There are three types of slices, and each type has its own icon **1**:

- Slices that are created manually using the Slice tool are called **user slices** (this page and the next).
- **Layer-based slices** (page 497) resize automatically to include all the visible pixels within the currently selected layer.
- Whatever's left of the image after you've created user slices and/or layer-based slices is divided automatically into **auto slices** (lighter gray label).

Slices can be created, selected, edited, and displayed in Photoshop or ImageReady, but we prefer to use ImageReady because it offers more options for slicing. To show the Slice palette in ImageReady, choose Window > Slice or click the palette toggle button on the Slice Select tool options bar. In Photoshop, you can click Slice Options on the Slice Select tool options bar to view the Slice Options dialog box.

To slice an image using a command:

1. In an image that contains just the single default slice, choose Slices (or right-click/Ctrl-click) > Promote to User Slice, then choose Slices > Divide Slice. Check Preview.
2. Check **Divide Horizontally Into** to create horizontal slices **2**, then enter the desired number of slices in the "slices down, evenly spaced" field, or enter the desired number of "pixels per slice" for the height of each horizontal slice.
   and/or
   Check **Divide Vertically Into** to create vertical slices, then enter the desired number of slices in the "slices across,

(Continued on the following page)

evenly spaced" field, or enter the desired number of "pixels per slice" for the width of each vertical slice.

3. Click OK **1**. A label will appear in the upper left corner of each slice, bearing the slice number. Numbering begins at "01" and proceeds from left to right, and from top to bottom.

TIP After the Divide Slice command is used, all the slices will be selected. To highlight only one slice, choose the Slice Select tool, 🗡 then click the slice.

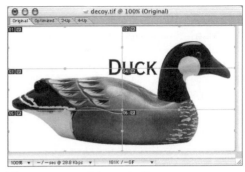

1 *An image divided into six **slices***

Using the **Slice tool,** you can control manually where the slice divisions occur. And unlike auto slices, the user slices that this tool creates can be resized, repositioned, restacked, and optimized separately.

To slice an image manually:

1. Choose the Slice tool (K). 🗡

2. Drag diagonally across part of the image to define the first slice **2**–**3**. A label with a number will appear in the upper left corner of the slice zone, and a thin highlight (frame) with resizing handles will appear around the new slice. ImageReady will divide the rest of the image into auto slices.

2 *Drag to create a slice using the **Slice tool.***

3. *Optional:* Draw additional user slices with the Slice tool. Each new slice will be assigned a label and a number, and ImageReady will continue to redivide and renumber the rest of the image into auto slices as it sees fit.

4. *Optional:* To divide a slice into smaller user slices, choose the Slice Select tool (NEW) (O), 🗡 click a user slice or auto slice, choose Slices > Divide Slice, enter values, then click OK. Each new slice will be assigned its own number.

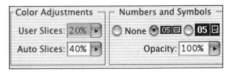

3 *A **new slice** is created.*

TIP Selected slices display normally; unselected slices are dimmed. To control how dimmed they get, in ImageReady, go to Edit (ImageReady, in Mac) > Preferences > Slices, and in the Color Adjustments area, choose or enter User Slices and/or Auto Slices percentages **4**.

4 *A portion of the **Slices** pane in the **Preferences** dialog box*

Plot your slices

If the techniques discussed here seem more laborious than using the Slice tool, stick with using the tool.

To plot your slice areas before creating them, display the rulers (Ctrl-R/Cmd-R); drag guides from the rulers, releasing them where you want the slice borders to occur; then choose Slices > **Create Slices from Guides.**

Beware! This command deletes all previous slices. Also, because guides always extend from one edge to the other of the whole image, you'll be able to produce a checkerboard of similarly sized slices, but not a more irregular arrangement.

To resize the resulting slices, choose the Slice Selection tool, then drag any handle on the slice border. To combine two or more selected slices, choose Slices > Combine Slices.

1 *Use the* **Table** *palette to enter the ID for the table, the Dimensions of the table, choose an Auto Slicing method, and enter Cell Options.*

The borders between **layer-based** slices automatically update whenever you transform, move, or add layer effects to the layer. Layer-based slices are especially useful when creating rollovers that contain effects (such as a Drop Shadow) that might enlarge the layer.

To create a layer-based slice:

Click a layer on the Layers palette, then choose Layer > New Layer Based Slice. Simple as that.

To convert an auto slice or a layer-based slice into a user slice:

1. Choose the Slice Select tool (O).
2. Click the slice you want to convert.
3. Choose Slices > Promote to User Slice.

TIP For an auto slice, you can right-click/ Ctrl-click and choose Promote to User Slice.

To delete slices:

1. Choose the Slice Select tool (O).
2. To delete one slice, click on it; to delete multiple slices, Shift-click all the slices you want to delete. Then choose Delete Slice(s) from the Slices menu or the Slice palette menu, or press Backspace/ Delete.
   or
   To delete all the slices in an image, choose Slices > Delete All.

To use the Table palette: **NEW**

An HTML table is produced when an ImageReady file is divided into slices. The **Table** palette **1** lets you control the following table attributes:

- Enter a Table **ID,** so you can easily locate the table code in the HTML page code.

- For **Table Dimensions,** to create a fixed-size table, choose Pixels from the pop-up menu, then enter W and H values. Or choose Percentage, then make the W and H 100% to have the table fill the whole Web page automatically, whatever its size.

(Continued on the following page)

Layer-Based Slices; Delete Slices; Table Palette

- For the **Auto Slicing** Method, choose As Column (rowspan) or As Row (colspan) to determine how auto slices are formatted. (If you're not sure what these options do, select one and watch how the auto slices reformat in the image window.) Choose the option that will best maintain consistency with other tables in your Web pages. The Default option maintains the current auto slice layout.

- Enter **Cell Options** for a Border (any frame around the whole table or an individual cell), Pad (the space between cell content and cell edges), and Space (the distance between cells).

> ## Hide/show slice borders and labels
>
> In ImageReady, click the **Toggle Slice Visibility** button on the Toolbox **1** (or press Q) to toggle between hiding and showing slices.
>
> Or in ImageReady or Photoshop, hide or show slices by choosing View > **Show** > **Slices.**

1 *The **Toggle Slice Visibility** button on the Toolbox*

Resize User Slices

If you make a user **slice smaller,** ImageReady automatically generates and renumbers the auto slices that surround it in order to fill in the exposed gaps.

If you **enlarge** a slice, it may obscure other slices behind it. The hidden slices can be removed manually, or you can ignore them for now because any overlapping or hidden slice frames (or table cells) will be eliminated automatically when you save an optimized file. To see what's hiding behind a slice, you can use any of the buttons for restacking slices on the Slice Select tool options bar to assist you (see page 500).

To resize user slices:

1. Choose the Slice Select tool (O). Slice borders will display automatically.

2. Click the user slice you want to resize.

3. Drag a side handle to resize the slice along one axis, or drag a corner handle to resize along two axes **2**–**3**.

2 *To **resize** a user slice, drag a handle with the **Slice Select** tool.*

3 *The **auto slices** around the resized slice will reconfigure **automatically.***

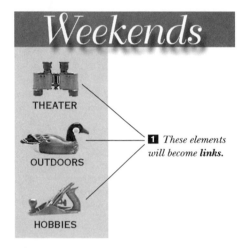

1 *These elements will become links.*

2 *A slice is created for each element that will become a link.*

3 *Enter the destination Web address in the URL field.*

You can attach a URL **link** to a slice on a Web page. When a viewer clicks on that slice, they're taken automatically to the Web page associated with that URL address. Slices with links are usually created over prominent or conspicuous graphic elements (buttons, words, or icons) so the viewer can identify them easily.

In ImageReady, you can create multiple slices in a single image, and you can assign a different URL address to each slice.

To slice an image into multiple links:

1. Open or create a document that contains imagery that you want to use as links, such as buttons, thumbnails, or icons **1**. A series of links arranged in a column or row is called a navigation bar.

2. Choose the Slice tool (K).

3. Drag diagonally to create a slice over each individual portion of the image that you want to use as a link **2**.

4. Choose the Slice Select tool (O).

5. Click on a slice. The selected slice will display as a thumbnail on the Slice palette. (Choose Window > Slice if the palette isn't displayed.)

6. Enter the destination Web address in the URL field **3**.

7. *Optional:* The Target field becomes available when information is entered into the URL field. Target info tells the browser which HTML frame to load the link contents into and which existing HTML frames to preserve. Press Tab to move to this area of the palette, then choose one of the following from the pop-up menu: _blank to have a new browser window open for the link contents; _self to have the new link contents load into the HTML frame for the current slice;

(Continued on the following page)

Slice into Multiple Links

_parent to have the new link contents replace the current HTML frames; and _top to have the new link contents load into the entire browser window (this is similar to the _parent option).

8. Repeat steps 5–7 for any other slices you want to designate as links.

TIP If the image has only one slice (the default auto slice for the image), you can attach a link address to the entire image via the URL field on the Slice palette.

User slices and layer-based slices are displayed and numbered based on the order in which they were created. You can rearrange the **stacking** order of these slices at any time. User slices are displayed in their current stacking order on the Web Content palette (formerly called the Rollovers palette, and boasting some new features).

To change the stacking position of a slice:

1. Choose the Slice Select tool (O), 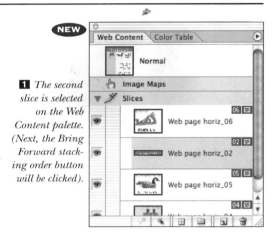 then click a slice in the image (not an auto slice).
   or
   Click a slice name on the Web Content palette **1**.

2. Click a stacking order button on the options bar **2**–**3** (unavailable stacking options will be dimmed).

By **aligning user slices** along a common edge or by distributing them evenly along the same axis, you can create smaller HTML files that will download more quickly. You can't align or distribute layer-based slices, because their position is tied to their layers.

To align user slices along a common edge:

1. Choose the Slice Select tool (O), 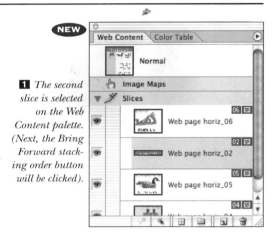 then Shift-click all the slices you want to align.

2. Click one of the six alignment buttons in the options bar **4**. The slices will align, but not the imagery inside them.

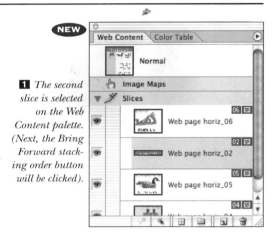

1 *The second slice is selected on the Web Content palette. (Next, the Bring Forward stacking order button will be clicked).*

Bring to Front   Bring Forward   Send Backward   Send to Back

2 *The **stacking order** buttons on the **Slice Select** tool options bar*

3 *Slice 02 is now in **front** of the slices adjacent to it.*

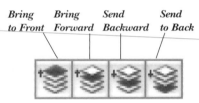

4 *To align multiple slices, click an **alignment** button on the **Slice Select** tool options bar.*

Slice Stacking Order; Align Slices

1 *Click a* **distribution** *button on the* **Slice Select** *tool options bar.*

2 *This image, because it contains overlapping elements, is a good candidate for encoding as an* **image map** *using the Layer Options palette.*

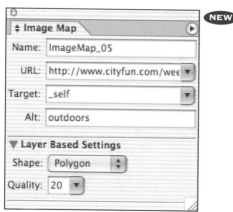

3 *Choose a* **Shape** *and enter the* **URL** *address on the* **Image Map** *palette.*

To evenly distribute user slices along a common axis:

1. Choose the Slice Select tool (O), 📐 then Shift-click the slices you want to distribute.

2. Click one of the six distribution buttons on the options bar **1**.

An **image map** is an image that contains designated image hotspots, each with its own URL link **2**. A viewer can click a hotspot to link to another page. Use this method if your hotspot shape is nonrectangular, or if you'd rather use a single image file instead of the multiple files that slices would create.

ImageReady lets you create layer-based or tool-based image maps. **Layer-based** maps include nontransparent pixel areas in a layer and are automatically updated when the layer is edited.

Tool-based maps can be aligned to a common edge or distributed along a common axis. You can also duplicate a tool-based map's dimensions and settings. And finally, you can easily change a layer-based map to a tool-based one.

To create a layer-based image map:

1. On the Layers palette, choose a layer that contains transparent areas.

2. Choose Layer > New Layer Based Image Map Area. A rectangular image map will surround the layer's nontransparent areas.

3. On the Image Map palette **3**, enter a URL address (including the "http://" prefix). A hand icon will appear to the right of the layer name on the Layers palette (**1**, next page).

4. *Optional:* The Target field becomes available once a URL is entered. The Target info tells which HTML frame to load the link contents into and which existing HTML frames to preserve.

(Continued on the following page)

Distribute Slices; Layer-Based Image Map

5. *Optional:* In the Alt field, enter the word or words you want displayed if the user's Web browser doesn't display images (see page 507).

6. From the Shape pop-up menu in the Layer Based Settings pane, choose a shape for the hotspot (Rectangle, Circle, or Polygon).

7. Repeat steps 1–6 for any other layers.

TIP You can change a layer-based image map's shape by choosing the Image Map Select tool (J), , clicking the image map, then choosing from the Shape pop-up menu on the Image Map palette.

TIP When using a Polygon, you can adjust how tightly the image map follows the outline of the imagery by using the Quality field or slider. To generate smaller HTML files, try to limit the complexity of any polygonal image maps you use.

To create a tool-based image map:

1. Choose the Rectangle Image Map, , Circle Image Map, , or Polygon Image Map , tool (P or Shift-P).

2. Draw a rectangle or circle over an area in the image window. (Shift-drag to create a square. Alt-drag/Option-drag to draw a rectangle or circle from its center.)
   or
   Create a straight-sided polygon by clicking a starting point, then clicking for each subsequent corner until you surround the area. Double-click anywhere, and the shape will close automatically .

3. Enter a URL address (including the "http://" prefix) on the Image Map palette.

4. *Optional:* The Target field becomes available when you enter a URL. The Target info identifies the HTML frame into which the link contents will be loaded and the existing HTML frames that will be preserved (see pages 499–500).

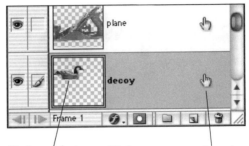

*Pixel areas (not transparent areas) will become **hotspots** for the image map.*

1 *Once you create a Layer-based image map, a hand icon appears near the layer name, indicating the presence of an image map.*

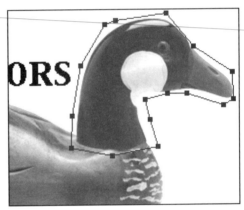

2 *Double-click to have an image map shape close automatically.*

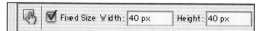

1 *On the options bar, you can enter exact dimensions for an* **image map**.

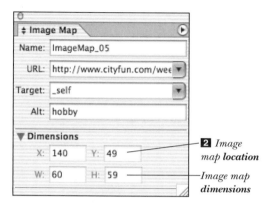

2 *Image map* **location**

Image map **dimensions**

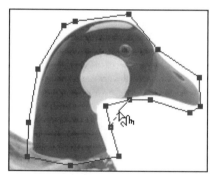

3 *You can* **resize** *an image map* **manually**.

4 *The* **Image Map Visibility** *button on the Toolbox*

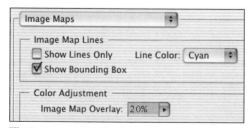

5 *The* **Image Maps Preferences** *pane in ImageReady*

5. *Optional:* In the Image Map palette's Alt field, enter the word or words you want displayed if the user's Web browser doesn't display images.

6. Repeat steps 1–5 for any other image maps you want to create.

TIP To specify the exact dimensions of a rectangular or circular image map before drawing it, check Fixed Size on the options bar, then enter Width and Height values **1**.

TIP To precisely reposition a rectangular or circular image map after drawing it, change the X and Y values on the Image Map palette. To resize an image map, change the W and H values **2**; or choose the Image Map Select tool, 🖑 then drag any of the handles on the image map **3**.

To change an image map from layer based to tool based:

1. Choose the Image Map Select tool (J), 🖑 then click the layer-based image map you want to convert.

2. From the Image Map palette menu, choose Promote Layer Based Image Map Area.

To hide/show image maps:

To toggle between the hide and show settings for all image maps in the document, click the Image Map Visibility button on the Toolbox **4** or press A.

or

Choose View > Show > Image Maps.

TIP You can change the display characteristics for image maps (such as whether the line and/or the bounding box are visible) in Edit (ImageReady, in Mac) > Preferences > Image Maps **5**.

To select an image map:

1. Make sure the image maps are visible, and choose the Image Map Select tool (J). 🖐

2. Click an image map in the image window (Shift-click to select more than one image map, if desired).

To delete an image map:

Select an image map, then press Backspace/ Delete.

or

From the Image Map palette menu, choose Delete Image Map Area.

To align tool-based image maps along a common edge:

1. Choose the Image Map Select tool (J), 🖐 then Shift-click the image maps you want to align.

2. Click one of the six alignment buttons on the options bar.

To evenly distribute tool-based image maps along a common axis:

1. Choose the Image Map Select tool, 🖐 then Shift-click the image maps you want to distribute.

2. Click one of the six distribution buttons on the options bar **1**.

1 *Select multiple image maps, then click a* ***distribution*** *button on the* ***Image Map Select*** *tool options bar.*

> ## Client or server?
>
> ImageReady codes an image map in HTML either as **client-side** or **server-side.** To choose between these two options, choose File > Output Settings > Image Maps, then click an option in the Type area **2**.

Select, Delete, Align, Distribute Image Maps

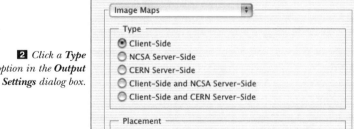

2 *Click a* ***Type*** *option in the* ***Output Settings*** *dialog box.*

1 *The continuous-tone element (the plane) in this hybrid image should be optimized as a JPEG; the vector element (lightbulb) should be optimized as a GIF.*

If the image you're working with is a hybrid, meaning it contains both sharp-edged elements (e.g., type or linework) and continuous-tone areas, you can draw a separate slice around each of those areas, then **optimize** each **slice** separately using settings that are appropriate for that type of imagery **1**.

To optimize an individual slice:

1. Choose the Slice Select tool (O).

2. Click a slice.

3. Choose Optimize palette settings. Use the GIF format to optimize sharp-edged areas, the JPEG format for continuous-tone areas.

TIP If you select two or more slices that have different Optimize palette settings, the palette will display only the settings that the selected slices have in common. If you change any of the available settings, however, the new settings will apply to all the currently selected slices.

TIP If you later decide you want to optimize all the slices in the same way, choose the Slice Select tool, choose Select > All Slices, then choose settings on the Optimize palette. If you choose Select > Deselect Slices, the Optimize palette will go blank.

2 *Drag the **Droplet** button from the **Optimize** palette over any unselected slice.*

This technique for **copying optimization** settings is speedy and efficient.

To copy optimization settings from one slice to another:

1. Choose the Slice Select tool (O).

2. Click a slice that has the desired optimization settings.

3. Drag the Droplet button from the Optimize palette over any unselected slice. The current palette settings will be applied to that slice **2**.

Slices that are **linked** share the same optimization settings. Linked slices that are optimized in the GIF format also share the same color table and dither pattern, which helps to disguise any edge seams.

To link slices:

1. Choose the Slice Select tool (O).

2. Click a slice, then Shift-click one or more additional slices **1**.

3. Right-click/Ctrl-click and choose Link
NEW Slice for Optimization.
or
Choose Slices > Link Slices for Optimization. The linked slices will now be assigned a link icon with a unique group color **2**, which will display next to the linked slices' labels in the image and on the Web Content palette.

TIP To add a slice to a group of already linked slices, select the slice you want to add, plus one of the slices already in the group, then choose Slices > Link Slices for Optimization.

To unlink slices:

To unlink one slice, click on it with the Slice Select tool (O), then right-click/Ctrl-click and choose Unlink Slice, or choose Slices > Unlink Slice.
or
To unlink a group of slices, click one of the linked slices with the Slice Select tool, then right-click/Ctrl-click and choose Unlink
NEW Shared Links, or choose Slices > Unlink Shared Links.
or
To unlink all the slices in the image, right-click/Ctrl-click and choose Unlink All, or choose Slices > Unlink All.

Note: Auto slices created by ImageReady are already linked. If you unlink an auto slice, it becomes a user slice.

Link/Unlink Slices

1 *Three slices are **selected**.*

2 *The **linked** slices have the same colored link icon.*

Slice Sets NEW

In ImageReady CS, you can create **slice sets,** which can be used to contain slicing for one particular layout arrangement in your image. If you create a different layout arrangement (say, when creating layer comps), you can hide the first slice set, create slices that fit the new arrangement, then gather the new slices into a new set. When you save an optimized file, only the currently visible slice set(s) will be saved to the HTML file. To create a slice set, Shift-select existing slices on the Web Content palette, then click the **New Slice Set** button on the palette ■.

Older, nongraphic Web browsers (or any browser for which the Show Pictures preference is turned off) display text but not Web graphics. In order to display an image as a generic icon with text for browsers that can't or won't display graphics, Web designers attach a unique HTML **Alt tag** to each graphic. Then, if the image displays in the browser only as the Alt tag text, any attached URL links will still be able to link the viewer to the designated site. Alt tags also help visually impaired people use text browsers that "speak" the link, a legal requirement for some websites in order to meet accessibility standards (www.section508.gov). Here's how you can attach an Alt tag to a slice in ImageReady.

To attach an Alt tag to a slice or to an entire image:

1. Show the Slice palette.

2. *Optional:* Click a slice using the Slice Select tool (O).

3. In the Alt field on the Slice palette, enter the word or words that you want used as a substitute for the image ■.

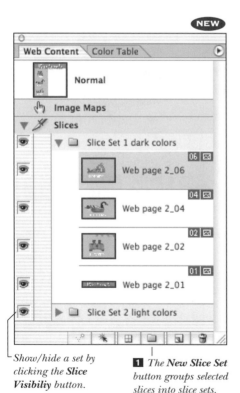

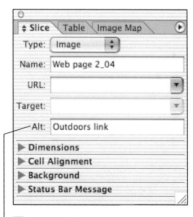

*Show/hide a set by clicking the **Slice Visibiliy** button.*

■ *The **New Slice Set** button groups selected slices into slice sets.*

■ *In the **Alt** field on the **Slice** palette, enter the word or words that you want used as a substitute for the image.*

Attach Alt Tag

Rollovers

Now that you understand something about slices, you're ready to create another kind of hotspot: a **rollover.** A rollover is a screen event that occurs when a user's mouse moves over or clicks on an area of a Web page that has a built-in modification. Rollovers are like the voice of a Web page, causing a visual change in the dynamic parts of a page, and they make Web pages more entertaining. Three basic types of rollovers can be created:

- A **change** in an image area (e.g., a color changes, a layer effect appears)
- The **substitution** of one image for another
- Text or a **remote** graphic that appears in another area of the browser window when the mouse is over a button, keyword, or icon

To create a **rollover,** first you need to divide the image into **slices.** (So go back and read the section on slices first—no cheating!) In **NEW** ImageReady, rollovers are created by using the Web Content palette, and by displaying and hiding layers on the Layers palette. When ImageReady previews the rollover, it turns different layers on or off, as per your built-in instructions. Onscreen, one image will be substituted for another.

To create a rollover for a slice:

1. Select a layer, choose the Slice tool (K), then marquee the area to be used for the rollover.

2. If the imagery you want to use for the rollover isn't already on its own layer, choose Select > Create Selection from Slice, then choose Layer > New > Layer via Copy (Ctrl-J/Cmd-J).
   or
   If the imagery in the slice is already on its own layer, duplicate that layer now via the Layers palette.

3. Leave both the new layer and its associated slice selected.

Three basic rollovers

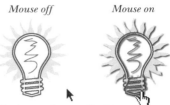

Mouse off   Mouse on

*The **image changes** (in this case, a Drop Shadow layer effect appears).*

Mouse off

Mouse on

*A **new image** is substituted for the current image.*

Mouse off

Mouse on

__Remote__ text (or an image) appears in another area of the image.

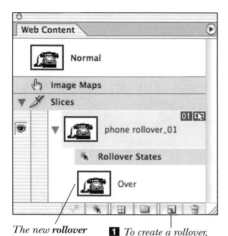

The new rollover thumbnail

1 *To create a rollover, click the **Create Rollover State** button.*

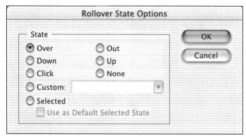

2 *To change a rollover state, double-click its thumbnail, then choose an option in the **Rollover State Options** dialog box.*

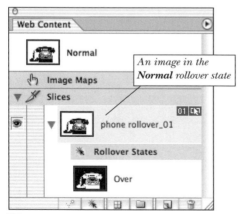

3 *A duplicate layer of the same image was inverted for the **Over** rollover state.*

4. Display the Web Content palette. The NEW currently selected slice will appear as a thumbnail on the palette.

5. Click the Create Rollover State button at the bottom of the Web Content palette **1**. A rollover state will appear as a new nested thumbnail on the palette.

6. *Optional:* ImageReady automatically assigns a rollover state to thumbnails in this default sequence: Over, Down, Click. If you want to override this default sequence, double-click the new rollover thumbnail, and in the Rollover State Options dialog box, choose the rollover state that you want to be the initiator (triggering event) for the rollover you'll create in the remaining steps **2**:

   For **Over,** the mouse must be over the slice area but not pressed down.

   For **Down,** the mouse button must be down when it's over the slice. Some Web designers like to have a special graphic appear when the mouse button is down.

   For **Click,** the mouse must be clicked (button pressed and released) when it's over the slice. When the slice is clicked, the browser tries to link to any URL that's attached to it.

   Click OK.

7. Modify the imagery on the separate or duplicate layer (that you created in step 2) to make it look different from the original layer. A few suggestions: Invert the layer's color or luminosity (Image > Adjustments > Invert) **3**; apply a texture or distort filter to the layer; change the layer's hue or saturation (see also page 513); or paste in new imagery. The imagery on the original layer won't change.

8. Select the slice on the Web Content palette that contains the nested rollover state. On the Layers palette, hide the duplicate layer, and show the original layer on the Layers palette. Next, select

(Continued on the following page)

Create a Rollover

the Over state on the Web Content palette, show the duplicate layer, and hide the original layer, if necessary, from which the duplicate was created .

9. Click back and forth between the original slice and rollover thumbnail on the Web Content palette, and compare them in the image window. The Web Content palette tracks which layers are visible or hidden, as well as other changes on the Layers palette, as each rollover thumbnail is selected. Make sure the correct layers are visible or hidden for each Rollover state.

For a more realistic preview, you can click the Preview in [default browser] button 🌐 on the Toolbox. Or try using ImageReady's preview function (see page 514). Roll the mouse over or click where the rollover is to see the effect.

Beware! Always take note of which thumbnail is currently selected on the Web Content palette as you modify a layer. Each thumbnail should have, and produce, a different look. Rollover effects created via painting, filters, transformations, or image substitutions require a separate layer for each state. In order to display each rollover state, you'll need to hide or show the different layers.

TIP To create a rollover using a layer effect, see page 511. To create a remote rollover, see page 515.

TIP Choose Palette Options from the Web Content palette menu to choose a different Thumbnail Size for the Web Content palette.

TIP To create a rollover in which supplemental imagery is added to an existing image, create new imagery on a new layer, making sure to match the size and location of the imagery on the original layer –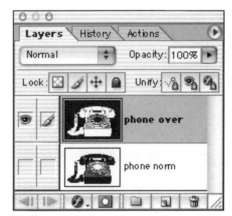. In this case, the original layer should always remain visible.

TIP To add a third state to the selected slice, click the Create Rollover State button again on the Web Content palette.

1 *When the Over thumbnail is chosen, the inverted layer becomes visible and the normal layer is hidden.*

2 *An image in the Normal rollover state*

3 *In the Over rollover state, a layer with a hand-drawn glow effect becomes visible below the bulb layer.*

1 *The image in the **Normal** rollover state*

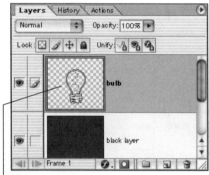

2 *Choose a layer that contains some* ***transparent*** *areas.*

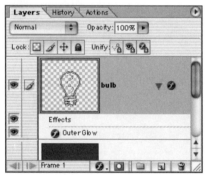

3 *The image in the **Over** rollover state: An Outer Glow **effect** that was added to the layer becomes visible on the Layers palette...*

4 *...and in the image.*

A great advantage to using **layer effects** to produce a **rollover** is that because different layer effects can be applied to (or turned off for) the same layer for each rollover state, you don't have to duplicate a layer to achieve a visible change between rollover states.

To create a rollover using a layer effect:

1. Choose the Slice Select tool, ⬩ then click a slice.

2. Click the Create Rollover State button ⬩ at the bottom of the Web Content palette.

3. *Optional:* Double-click the new rollover thumbnail and choose a different rollover state.

4. Choose a layer that contains transparent areas **1**–**2**.

5. Choose and apply an effect from the Add Layer Style pop-up menu at the bottom of the Layers palette. ⬩ You could try Inner Shadow to recolor the inner edges of the layer image or Outer Glow to recolor the area behind the layer imagery.

6. *Optional:* To intensify an effect, increase the Size, Spread, Distance, Depth, or Opacity. If you're using the Bevel and Emboss effect to make a button look convex, you could click the opposite Direction (e.g., Up versus Down) to reverse the lighting direction and make the rollover version look concave (see page 298). Try applying the Color Overlay effect at a low opacity to apply a tint and enhance a concave effect.

7. Click OK. The layer effect will be visible on the Layers palette **3** (and in the image **4**) only when the rollover state thumbnail that it's assigned to is selected.

8. Preview the rollover (instructions on page 514).

TIP You can use the predefined layer effects (or combinations of effects) on the Styles palette in ImageReady (see page 530).

TIP To remove a layer effect, see page 293.

The **Create Layer-based Rollover** button automatically makes the current layer a layer-based slice and creates a new rollover state using that slice. *Note:* The only way you can produce changes between rollover states when creating a rollover using this method is by adding layer effects to each rollover state.

To create a layer-based rollover:

1. Choose a layer (not the Background).

2. Click the Create Layer-based Rollover button ![icon] at the bottom of the Web Content palette. An icon indicating that the slice is layer based ![icon] will display next to the layer name on the Web Content palette, an icon indicating that the layer contains a layer-based slice ![icon] will appear for the layer on the Layers palette, and a star icon will display in the icon in the slice.

Normally, changes made to the currently active layer affect only the current rollover state or animation frame. ImageReady CS's **Unify** buttons, however, let you control whether changes to the active layer's position, visibility, style, or a combination thereof will be applied to all the states or frames, thus unifying layer-based effects across a rollover or animation.

Beware! Any preexisting layer style effects are deleted when the Unify command is chosen.

To use the Unify buttons to apply changes from the active layer:

1. On the Web Content palette, click the state you want to use, and on the Layers palette, click the layer you want to change **1**.

2. On the Layers palette, click one, two, or all three of the Unify buttons **2**.

3. Depending on your choice, an alert box will appear **3**, asking if you want to match the current layer's position, visibility, style, or a combination thereof with the other rollover states or animation frames. Click **Match** to unify those

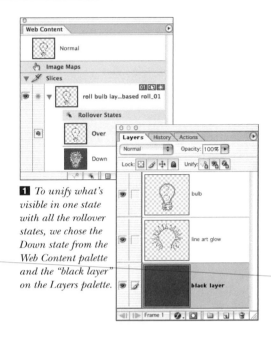

1 *To unify what's visible in one state with all the rollover states, we chose the Down state from the Web Content palette and the "black layer" on the Layers palette.*

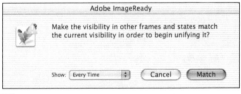

2 *The Unify buttons on the Layers palette in ImageReady*

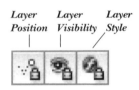

3 *This alert box will appear, asking if you want to match an attribute from the current layer.*

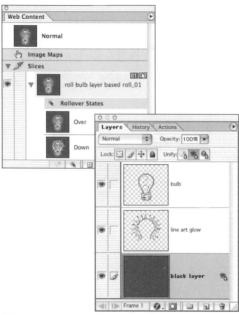

1 *After clicking the **Layer Visibility** button for the selected "black layer" on the Layers palette, and clicking Match, that layer became visible in all the rollover states.*

states or frames with any current and future changes in the selected layer **1**.

TIP To turn off a Unify command, click the layer, then click the highlighted Unify button again.

TIP To automatically apply any changes in the Normal state or Frame 1 to all the other states or frames, choose Propagate Frame 1 Changes from the Layers palette menu.

More rollover ideas

Here are some further suggestions for creating visually interesting rollover effects. Use these ideas when modifying a duplicated layer that will become a rollover state (as in step 7 on page 509):

To produce a rollover in which imagery enlarges and contracts, scale the duplicate layer up a bit using Edit > Transform > Scale, or use Filter > Blur > Radial Blur to stretch the shape **2**–**3**, or use Filter > Distort > Pinch (with a negative Amount) to bulge it out **4**.

To make a button or image area look like it's flipping, use Edit > Transform > Flip Horizontal or Flip Vertical (see the ducky on page 508).

2 *The **original** button*

3 *After applying the **Radial Blur** filter*

4 *After applying the **Pinch** filter to the original image using a negative Amount*

This button changes sizes for a rollover, so it's a good choice for a layer-based slice. The slice will resize based on the largest area of imagery on the layer.

You can **preview** a **rollover** within ImageReady or, if you prefer, stick with the tried-and-true Web browser-based preview. Take ya pick.

To preview a rollover in ImageReady:

1. Click the Preview Document button 🖑 on the Toolbox (Y).

2. Move your cursor over the image within the image window to see the rollover in action. To stop the action, click the Preview Document button again.

To preview a rollover in a Web browser:

1. Save your ImageReady file.

2. Choose a currently installed browser from the File > Preview in submenu.
or
Click the Preview in [default browser] button 🌐 on the Toolbox (Ctrl-Alt-P/ Cmd-Option-P).

3. In the browser, roll the mouse over (Over), press the mouse down on (Down), or click on (Click) the area of the image that contains the rollover.

Note: You can verify a URL address of an image map even if you're not online. Pass the mouse over the image map area, and the attached URL address will appear at the bottom of the browser window.

Note: You won't be able to preview the Down state in any pre-4.0 browser version of Navigator or Explorer. In these earlier browser versions, the mouse action will open a browser context menu instead.

1 *For this layout, we created a column of small images and then sliced each one of them individually. A larger version of each slice image was created to become separate remote images.*

NEW

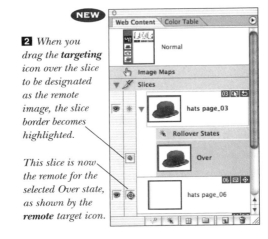

2 *When you drag the **targeting** icon over the slice to be designated as the remote image, the slice border becomes highlighted.*

*This slice is now the remote for the selected Over state, as shown by the **remote** target icon.*

3 *The remote image is now **hidden** for the selected slice's normal state.*

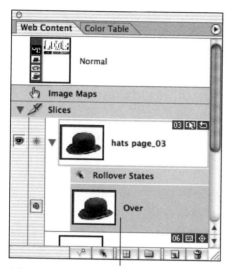

1 *When the* ***Over*** *thumbnail is selected...*

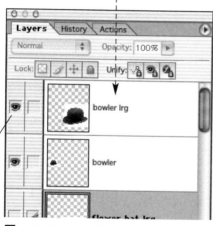

2 *...the "bowler lrg" layer becomes* ***visible.***

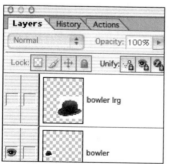

3 *When the* ***slice*** *(that contains the nested Over state) is selected, our "bowler lrg" layer is* ***hidden*** *(eye icon is off).*

In a **remote rollover,** as the viewer moves the mouse over a keyword, image, or button, supplementary text or imagery appears. When the viewer moves the mouse away from the keyword or image, the supplementary info disappears. Remote rollovers help to reduce visual clutter because they reduce what initially appears on a Web page.

To create a remote rollover:

1. Create a new layer, then create the supplementary image or text on that layer to become the remote image.

2. Choose the Move tool, then drag the new remote layer imagery to the location in the image where you want it to appear.

3. Choose the Slice tool (K), and draw a slice around the remote layer image (**1**, previous page). The slice will appear as a new thumbnail on the Web Content palette. Hide that image layer on the Layers palette.

4. On the Web Content palette, select the slice that will trigger the remote rollover, then click the Create Rollover State button at the bottom of the palette. A rollover state for the triggering slice will appear as a nested thumbnail on the palette **1**.

5. With the new Over state on the Web Content palette still selected, drag the targeting icon from the palette to the slice that contains the hidden remote imagery (**2**, previous page). The slice border will highlight. Make the remote image layer visible on the Layers palette **2**. The targeted slice now has a remote target icon on the Web Content palette and in its label, and the slice that triggers the rollover has an "affects remote" icon.

6. Click the slice thumbnail the rollover state is nested under. The new remote image layer should be hidden for the normal state **3** (and **3**, previous page). *Don't* hide the layer containing the image that will trigger the rollover. This layer should be visible for all the states.

NEW

Remote Rollover

To create a button for a Web page:

1. Click the Normal state on the Web Content palette.

2. Choose a shape tool: Rectangle ▢, Rounded Rectangle ▢, Ellipse ○ **NEW** (U or Shift-U), Tab ▢ (R), or Pill ○ (R).

3. On the shape tool options bar, click the Create New Shape Layer button.▢

4. Choose a Foreground color, then drag diagonally to draw a shape **1**. The shape will appear on its own layer automatically. Add a text layer, if desired.

To add rollover states to the button:

To quickly apply a predefined rollover effect to the button, display the Styles palette, choose the Rollover Buttons library from the Styles palette menu, then click Replace when asked if you want to replace the current styles. Click on any of the listed styles, and the Web Content palette will automatically display that style's button states and generate a layer-based slice for the shape **2**. You can also drag a style name or swatch from the Styles palette over the shape in the image window. Your button rollover is done.
or
Choose the Slice tool, ✐ then draw a slice around the new button for the normal rollover state. The new slice will appear as a thumbnail on the Web Content palette. Now follow steps 2–9, starting on page 508, to create a rollover state for the button.

Using three new tools on the **Move** tool options bar, you can select and/or move layers in the image window with ease; they behave like objects in a drawing program. As you drag layer "objects," blue smart guides display, which you can use to help you align objects along their edges or centers.

NEW ### To use the Move tool modifiers:

1. Choose the Move tool.

2. Do any of the following:

    Choose the Layer Select tool on the options bar **3**, then click a layer object in the image window; its layer will become selected on the Layers palette.

1 *The new* **shape**

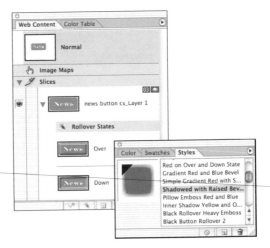

The predefined style for the Over state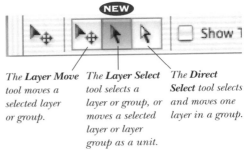

2 *Styles for the button's* **Normal, Over,** *and* **Down** *states are automatically created using a predefined rollover button style from the* **Styles** *palette. (We chose the Shadowed with Raised Bevel style in the Rollover Buttons style library.)*

NEW

The **Layer Move** *tool moves a selected layer or group.*   *The* **Layer Select** *tool selects a layer or group, or moves a selected layer or layer group as a unit.*   *The* **Direct Select** *tool selects and moves one layer in a group.*

3 *Tools on the* **Move** *tool options bar*

Shift-click or drag-select multiple layer objects in the image, then align them using the align buttons on the Move tool options bar.

To create a layer group that can be moved as a unit, click the Layer Select tool, select multiple layer objects in the image, then choose Layer > Group Layers.

GIF animations

In ImageReady, you can create **GIF animations** in which multiple image frames play back in a specified sequence. Animation effects that you can create for a Web page include text or graphics that move, fade in or out, or undergo some other kind of change or transformation.

To produce an animation in ImageReady, you'll create multiple image frames via the Animation palette. Then you'll modify individual layers via the Layers palette for each frame (each frame has its own unique Layers palette setup). And finally, you'll save the sequence of frames as a single GIF file, ready for online viewing.

We'll provide the instructions for creating two basic animation effects: moving a layer element and fading a layer element in or out. Once you've mastered these basics, you'll be ready to try other, more complex animation projects.

The Animation palette

The currently selected frame

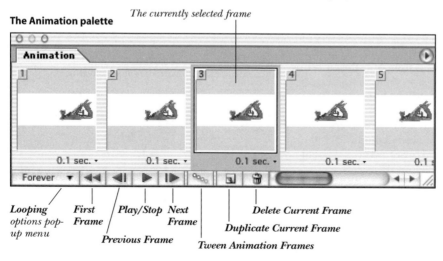

Looping options pop-up menu *First Frame* *Play/Stop* *Next Frame* *Delete Current Frame* *Duplicate Current Frame* *Previous Frame* *Tween Animation Frames*

To move layer imagery across an image via animation:

1. Open or create an image that contains imagery silhouetted on transparency (see pages 138–140 and 228–230) and a Background or layer behind it .

2. Display the Animation palette (choose Window > Animation).

3. Choose a layer on the Layers palette.

4. Choose the Move tool and drag the layer element to one side of the image window **2**. The current thumbnail on the Animation palette will update to reflect this new position.

5. Click the Duplicate Current Frame button ▣ at the bottom of the Animation palette. Both the duplicate frame and the layer chosen for step 3 should now be selected.

6. Choose the Move tool (V), then drag the layer element to the opposite side of the image window **3**. The current thumbnail on the Animation palette will update to reflect this change **4**. Leave this layer selected!

7. Click the Tween button ◷◌ on the Animation palette. (Tweening adds frames in between selected frames.)

8. Click Layers: **All Layers** to copy pixels from all layers to the new frames—even layers that weren't modified (**1**, next page). (Also choose this option to record changes that occur simultaneously in two or more layers.) Or click **Selected Layer** to copy pixels from only the currently selected layer to the new frames. All other layers will be hidden.
   and
   Check which layer **Parameters** the in-between frames will modify: Position, Opacity, and/or Effects (read about layer effects in Chapter 16).
   and
   From the **Tween With** pop-up menu, choose to add the in-between frames between the currently selected frame

1 *This document has an image layer and a back-ground layer.*

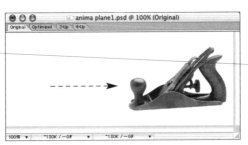

2 *Drag the layer element to one side of the image window.*

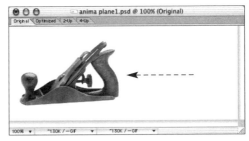

3 *Drag the same layer element to the opposite side of the image window for the duplicate animation frame.*

4 *The original (start) and duplicate (end) frames*

More animation options

■ Click, then Shift-click, to **select** a range of frames. Drag to **move** one frame or a selected range of frames.

■ To flatten each frame into a layer, choose **Flatten Frames into Layers** from the Animation palette menu. Any preexisting layers will remain.

■ To reverse the frame sequence, choose **Reverse Frames** from the Animation palette menu. This is equivalent to playing the animation backward.

■ To redo a tween, modify the sequence's start and end frames, Shift-click to select all the frames that were added by the tween, then click the **Tween** button. You could also delete all the tweened frames and redo the whole operation.

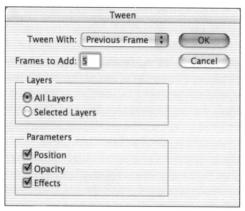

1 Use the **Tween** command to add in-between frames to an animation.

and the Previous Frame. (Note: If you select two or more frames before opening the Tween dialog box, only the Selection option will be available on this pop-up menu.)

and

In the **Frames to Add** field, specify how many frames are to be added in total (1–100). The greater the number of frames, the smoother (less choppy) the animation, but also the larger the file size and the longer its download time.

9. Click OK **2**. Now preview the animation (see page 521).

TIP You can use an editable or rasterized type layer for an animation. You can make type fade in or out or move across the image, or use it in any other layer animation effect.

TIP If you want your animations to download and play back quickly, keep them small (approximately 200 x 200 pixels or less).

2 The Animation palette after **tweening**. When the animation is played back, the layer element moves smoothly from one side of the image window to the other.

Move Layer Imagery via Animation

To make imagery fade in or out:

In order to make stationary or moving imagery fade in or out on a Web page, you'll need to adjust the opacity of the imagery instead of, or in addition to, its position. For this, follow the instructions starting on page 518, but choose an Opacity value (and position, if desired) for the starting layer for step 4 **1**, then choose an Opacity value (and position, if desired) for the ending layer for step 6 **2**. Also make sure Opacity is checked in the Tween dialog box (step 8) **3**.

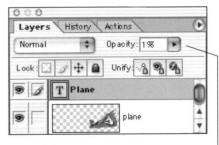

1 *The **Opacity** setting for the type layer for the **first** animation frame*

To remove frames from an animation:

To remove one frame from an animation, click the frame, then choose Delete Frame from the Animation palette menu or drag the frame over the Delete Current Frame button (this can be undone).

or

To delete the entire animation except for the first frame, choose Delete Animation from the Animation palette menu, then click Delete.

TIP Both of these Delete commands are accessible from the Web Content palette menu.

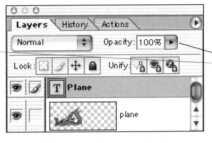

2 *The **Opacity** setting for the type layer for the **second** animation frame*

To choose options for animation playback:

Beware! Don't jump to or click on another program or choose Preview in [default browser] while an animation is playing. If you do so, the animation will continue to play in the background and will steal processing time from the application you clicked on or jumped to.

Choose a **Looping** option from the pop-up menu in the lower left corner of the Animation palette to specify whether the animation will play back Once or play back Forever (loop continuously) (**2**, next page). Or choose Other and enter the specific number of playback times for the animation, then click OK. Resist creating an endlessly looping animation—they're tedious to watch, and are a turnoff for Web viewers.

3 *After tweening, the tool moves to the left and the word "Plane" fades in.*

What you can tween

An animation can involve a change in a layer element's **position** (as in the steps on pages 518–519), a change in a layer's **opacity,** or a transition from one layer **effect** to another. Or you can simply tween between a layer effect that's turned **on** and the same effect turned **off.** Since these types of modifications are created via Layers palette options, they don't affect actual layer pixels. (The animation effect discussed on the next page does actually change layer pixels.)

Using each frame's **Delay Value** pop-up menu, you can specify how long it will be displayed during playback. Each frame can have a different delay setting.

To choose a delay value for a frame:

Click a frame on the Animation palette, then choose a **delay value** from the Delay Time pop-up menu below the frame ■. The "No delay" option equals 0 seconds. You can also choose Other, enter a custom delay time (0–240 seconds), then click OK.

The looping and frame delay settings will save with the file and control the animation playback when the Web page is viewed in a browser.

To preview an animation:

1. Click the Original or Optimized tab in the image window.

2. If the first frame isn't selected, click the Select First Frame button ◄◄ at the bottom of the Animation palette.

3. Click the Play button. ► The animation will play back at a slower pace than normal (for a more realistic speed, see step 5).

4. Click the square Stop button ■ to stop the animation (the Play button turned into a square Stop button).

5. Save the file, then click the Preview in [default browser] button 🔲 on the Toolbox. Click back in ImageReady when you're finished previewing. If the animation won't play properly in the browser, see page 528.

■ *The default frame **delay time** is No delay (0 seconds). You can choose a different delay time for any individual frame in the animation from the pop-up menu below the frame. A delay time of 0.1 second will be slightly slower than the default.*

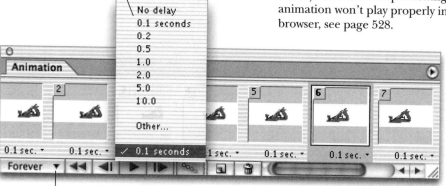

■ *Choose a **looping** option for the animation (Once or Forever).*

In these instructions, you'll learn how to make a layer element **rock** back and forth. In this type of animation, actual pixels are modified and are copied to all the existing frames. You'll be creating a duplicate layer for each incremental stage (rocking position) of the animation.

To create a rocking animation:

1. Open an image, and display the Animation palette.

2. To create the animation frames, click the Duplicate Current Frame button at the bottom of the Animation palette 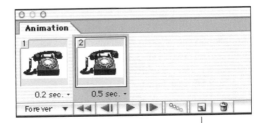. The duplicate frame will now be selected.

1 *Duplicate Current Frame*

3. Click the Tween button on the Animation palette, click Layers: All Layers, enter the desired number of Frames to Add to complete the animation, then click OK.

4. Click the animation frame where you want the rocking effect to start.

5. On the Layers palette, duplicate the layer that you want to be in motion.

6. On the duplicate layer, edit actual pixels (e.g., rotate the layer slightly, apply brush strokes, make color or tonal adjustments, or perform other modifications) **2**. Hide the original layer so you can see the change. The change will display inside the selected frame on the Animation palette. Reposition the imagery, if necessary.

2 *The "receiver left tilt" layer (our duplicate) is visible and the "receiver" layer is hidden. The handle rotates to the left.*

7. Click the next animation frame (or click the Next Frame button at the bottom of the Layers palette). Show the original layer and hide the duplicate, modified layer **3**.

8. Click the next consecutive frame. Show the duplicate, modified layer and hide the original, unmodified layer.

9. Continue to alternately hide, then show, the two layers for the remaining frames in the animation.

   To add to the animation, follow the steps on the next page.

3 *Now the "receiver" layer is visible and the "receiver left tilt" layer is hidden.*

Unify buttons

Changes in a layer's position, visibility, or style don't automatically copy to all animation frames, but such changes can be copied to all frames by using the Unify buttons in the Layers palette (see pages 512–513). *Note:* The Unify buttons remove any changes on the currently selected layer that were achieved through tweening. If you can't afford to lose such changes, edit your animation using the method described on the next page instead.

"Receiver left tilt" shows   *"Receiver" shows*   *"Receiver right tilt" shows*

1 *An animation sequence*

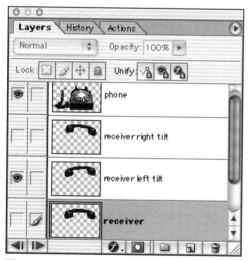

2 *For the animation sequence pictured above, to create three positions for the receiver, we used three layers, with each layer becoming visible in the order pictured.*

To make further pixel **edits** to our rocking motion that won't be copied automatically to all the animation frames, you need to create another duplicate layer.

To make further pixel edits to an animation object:

1. Select the original object's layer. Make another duplicate of that layer.

2. Edit the new duplicate layer. You now have an original layer and two duplicates.

3. Select the first animation frame, show the original layer, and hide the duplicates.

4. Select the next animation frame, show the first duplicate layer, and hide the original and second duplicate. Select the next animation frame, show the second duplicate layer, and hide the original and first duplicate, and so on **1**–**2**.

Layers palette edits and animations:

Layers palette changes (visibility, opacity, blend mode, or layer effects) or changes to a layer element's position affect only the frame they are applied to. They won't automatically be copied to other frames.

Parameters in the Tween dialog box (Position, Opacity, and Effects) are also Layers palette edits. Changing Parameters for one frame won't affect other frames.

These instructions expand an animation by adding all or part of the same animation in **reverse.** During playback, the animation will play forward and then backward in a smooth loop.

To make an existing animation reverse itself to the first frame:

1. Click the last frame on the Animation palette.

2. Click the Tween button.

3. Click Layers: All Layers; check all Parameters; choose Tween With: First Frame; then enter the desired number of Frames to Add.

4. Click OK.

Follow these steps if you created an animation effect for a layer and now want to **add** another animation effect to a different layer.

To apply a second animation effect to an existing animation:

1. Choose or create the layer that you want to apply the second animation to.

2. On the Animation palette, click any frame where you want the new animation effect to start 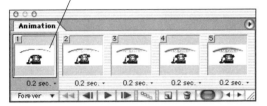.

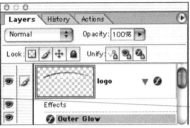

■ *The **starting** frame for the second animation effect*

3. For the frame you've chosen, position the layer imagery exactly where you want it, and adjust its opacity or effect(s), if desired **2**.

4. Click the frame where you want the new animation sequence to end.

5. For the end of this layer's animation sequence, modify the layer element's position or opacity, or remove or adjust any layer effects. Keep the layer selected!

6. If you chose the first and last animation frames for steps 2 and 4, respectively, choose Select All Frames from the Animation palette menu.

   or

   If you did *not* choose the first and last animation frames for steps 2 and 4, click the frame you chose for step 2, then Shift-click the frame you chose for step 4 to select a range of frames.

7. Click the Tween button on the Animation palette to tween without choosing options.

   or

   Choose Tween from the Animation palette menu, click Layers: Selected Layer, check the Parameters you've just modified (Position, Opacity, or Effects), then click OK **3**.

   The second animation effect will develop incrementally within the range of frames you selected in the previous step. Any preexisting animation effects on other layers will be preserved.

2 *We applied the Invert command to the "logo" layer to make the type white; the change was copied automatically to all the frames. An Outer Glow effect was also added, at a low opacity value for the first frame and a high opacity for the last frame.*

The first frame had an Outer Glow of 4% Opacity.

A tweened frame in the middle

3 *The completed animation*

The last frame had an Outer Glow of 100% Opacity.

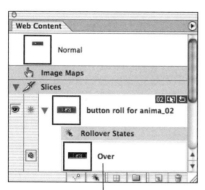

1 *Create a new rollover state for a slice.*

2 *With the rollover state selected, add frames to the animation via the Animation palette.*

3 *When you click the original slice name...*

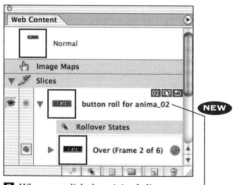

4 *...all the frames but the first one disappear from the* **Animation** *palette.*

It's easy to program a rollover state so it triggers an **animation** sequence—and it makes for a lively and entertaining Web page. To achieve this effect, you'll use your new rollover and animation skills.

To make a rollover trigger an animation sequence:

1. On the Web Content palette, create a new rollover state for a selected slice in an image, preferably using the Over state (see pages 508–509) **1**.

2. With the new rollover state selected on the Web Content palette (not the slice thumbnail), click on the Animation palette and create frames and events for the animation (see page 518) **2**. Or copy and paste frames from another animation file, using commands on the Animation palette menu.

   Imagery for the animation must be positioned within the slice area for the rollover image. Don't enlarge this slice too much—remember, the rollover is triggered when a viewer's pointer is over the slice area. (See the sidebar below.)

3. Click the name of the original slice that contains the nested rollover **3**. All the animation frames will temporarily disappear from the Animation palette **4**.

4. Save the file, and preview it by using the Preview in [default browser] button.

TIP To display animation frames as nested thumbnails for a state on the Web Content palette, choose Palette Options from the palette menu, check Include Animation Frames, then click OK.

Remote animation

To have animation occur in another area of an image, you need to target a remote slice (see page 515). Create a slice over the desired image area, select the Over state on the Web Content palette, then drag the triggering icon ⊕ over the new slice. This slice will now be the targeted remote for the Over state and will have a remote target icon. ⊕ Place your animation imagery into this slice area.

The **Warp Text** feature, which lets you apply any of 15 distortions, makes it easy to create text animations.

To create a warped type animation:

1. Open or create an image that has a Background, and also a layer that contains editable type that's surrounded by transparency.

2. Click the type layer **1**.

3. Display the Animation palette, click the first frame, then click the Duplicate Current Frame button. **3**

4. With the Type tool still selected, click the Create Warped Text button **T** on the Type options bar.

5. In the Warp Text dialog box, do the following:

   Choose a warp style from the Style pop-up menu **2**.

   Click Horizontal or Vertical to control the direction of the warp.

   Use the Bend, Horizontal Distortion, and Vertical Distortion sliders or fields to achieve the desired degree of "warpage." Your adjustments will preview in the image window.

6. Click OK **3**.

7. The current frame in the Animation palette will update to display the warp. With the second frame still selected, click the Tween button on the Animation palette. Click Layers: All Layers, check all Parameters, enter the desired number of Frames to Add, then click OK.

8. Choose a delay value for the frames, if desired, and click the Play button on the Animation palette to run the animation.

TIP Not all of ImageReady's animation features may be available for warped vertical type.

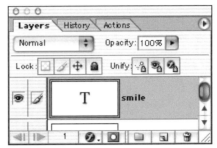

1 *Begin with a normal editable type layer.*

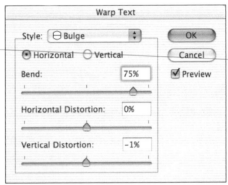

2 *Choose Style and Bend parameters in the **Warp Text** dialog box.*

3 *The finished warped type animation*

Warped Type Animation

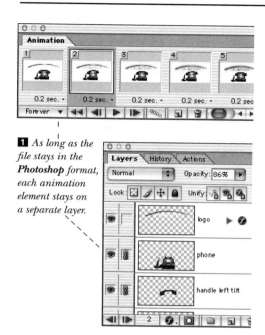

1 *As long as the file stays in the **Photoshop** format, each animation element stays on a separate layer.*

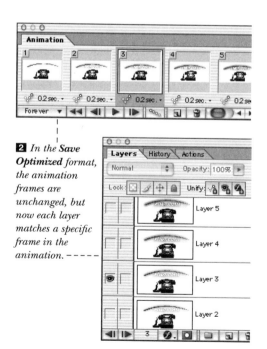

2 *In the **Save Optimized** format, the animation frames are unchanged, but now each layer matches a specific frame in the animation.*

To remove or adjust warped type:

1. Choose a warped type layer.

2. Choose the Type tool, then click the Create Warped Text button 工 on the Type tool options bar.

3. To remove the warp, from the Style pop-up menu, choose None.
or
To adjust the warp, choose a different Style; or click the opposite orientation button; or adjust the Bend, Horizontal Distortion, or Vertical Distortion settings.

TIP You can also click any frame on the Animation palette, then click the Create Warped Text button and adjust the warp for just that frame.

To save a GIF animation:

Use File > **Save** to save an animation as a Photoshop file; the GIF settings currently on the Optimize palette will be stored in the file. Choose the Perceptual, Selective, or Adaptive palette from the Optimize palette, and whichever Dither method you think will best smooth the transitions between frames. The Save command has no effect on the Layers palette (compare this with the Save Optimized command, which is discussed next) **1**. This is the file to keep in reserve for future editing.

When you use File > **Save Optimized** (Ctrl-Alt-S/Cmd-Option-S) to save an animation, the format is automatically set to GIF— not Photoshop. That is, with one exception: If the file contains a rollover that triggers an animation, the format will automatically be set to HTML instead of GIF. The Save Optimized command has a dramatic effect on layers. Instead of preserving the separate layer elements that make up the animation, Save Optimized matches each layer to a specific frame in the animation **2**. Watch what happens on the Layers palette when you reopen the Save Optimized file. Read more about the Save Optimized command on page 490.

To optimize an animation:

1. Choose Optimize Animation from the Animation palette menu.

2. Check Optimize By: Bounding Box to save the initial frame, as well as just the areas that are modified from one frame to the next **1**. This will reduce the file size, but it also may limit which other GIF editor applications can be used to edit it. *and/or*
Check Redundant Pixel Removal to remove any pixels in an object or a background that doesn't undergo a change, and thus doesn't need to be reloaded for each frame. This also helps to reduce the file size.

Ways to slim an animation down

The speed at which an animation plays back in a browser is determined by several factors, such as the speed of the Web viewer's CPU, the browser version, and the amount of RAM currently allocated to the browser.

If the animation you've created takes too long to download, there are a couple of remedies. You can lower its file size using the Image > Image Size command or lower its file size by cropping. Regardless of which method you use, be sure to work on a copy of the file (use File > Save As).

In addition to cropping, you can also reduce a file's size by reducing the number of layers or animation frames it contains, or by reducing the number of colors in its color table. Remember, a smaller file size makes for faster downloading. (Did we say that before?)

The **Animation Frames as Files** command creates files from individual animation frames. You can use any of the resulting files as an image in another project or in another application.

NEW To save animation frames as layers:

1. Open a file that contains an animation.

2. Choose File > Export > Animation Frames as Files.

Consider using SWF NEW

The **Macromedia Flash (SWF)** file format uses vector-based graphics in order to keep exported file sizes small. In ImageReady, you can create an SWF file via File > Export. To obtain the greatest size reduction using this format, try to use mostly vector-based graphics in your file—especially if you're going to use the file for animations. To keep text and shapes as vector objects, avoid applying layer effects that create soft outer edges (e.g., Drop Shadow, Outer Glow, Bevel, and Emboss) to them, as these effects will cause the objects to become pixel based in the SWF file.

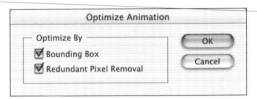

1 *The Optimize Animation dialog box*

Soft around the edges

Layer effects, which produce soft-edged shadows and colors, don't always optimize well, even in animations that are optimized in the GIF format. Bear this in mind as you create animations, and always remember to preview them using the Preview in [default browser] button.

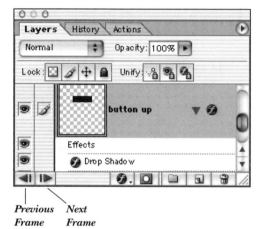

Previous Frame *Next Frame*

1 *Use these buttons on the Layers palette to navigate from frame to frame on the Animation palette.*

3. In the File Options area, enter a base name for the files, click Choose, locate a destination folder, then click OK/Choose.

4. In the Format Options area, choose a preset (if you've created one for the Optimize palette), or enter optimization options in the Format area. These options are also found on the Optimize palette.

5. Click OK.

Other layer features in ImageReady

■ **Layer effects** work the same way in ImageReady as they do in Photoshop (see Chapter 16). In brief, to apply a layer effect, choose from the Add Layer Effect pop-up menu *ƒ* at the bottom of the Layers palette or double-click a layer thumbnail. This opens the Layer Style dialog box.

■ One more reminder about applying image **edits** to animation frames. Changes made via the Layers palette (e.g., visibility, opacity, blend mode, or layer effects) don't apply automatically to other animation frames, nor does the repositioning of layer imagery. Changes made without using the Layers palette (except for repositioning) are applied automatically to other animation frames.

■ To help you navigate from frame to frame on the Animation palette, you can use the **Previous Frame** and **Next Frame** buttons on the Layers palette **1**.

■ To organize layers and effects, you can create layer **sets** or layer **groups,** and they can be shown or hidden as needed (see pages 108 and 113).

■ To protect layers and layer sets from editing, you can use the **lock** commands in ImageReady (see pages 113 and 115).

Other Layer Features

Applying styles

The **Styles palette** is a convenient place to store individual effects or combinations of effects. Once saved on the Styles palette, an effect or effects combo can be applied to any layer with a click of the mouse. The same styles are available in both ImageReady and Photoshop (they're stored in Adobe Photoshop CS > Presets > Styles).

In ImageReady, choose from three display modes for the Styles palette from the palette menu: Small Thumbnail , Small List, or Large Thumbnail (name and swatch) 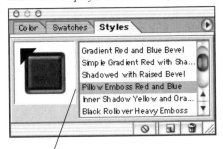.

(To save an effect as a style, see the following page.)

To apply a style to a layer:

Click a layer, then click a style on the Styles palette 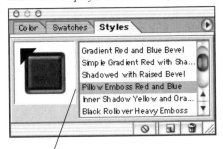.

or

Drag a style name or thumbnail over any selected or unselected layer on the Layers palette 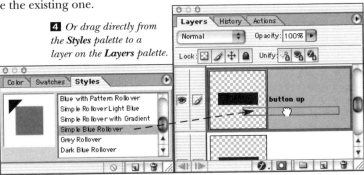.

or

Drag a style name or thumbnail over imagery in the image window.

or

In the Layer Style dialog box, click Styles, then click a style thumbnail to apply it to the selected layer (**1**, next page).

TIP An applied style's effects will replace any existing layer effects. Hold down Shift as you click or drag a style name to add the effects to any existing effects instead of replacing them. *Note:* If an effect of the same name already exists, the effect in the style will replace the existing one.

1 *This is the **Small Thumbnail** display mode on the **Styles** palette. Styles that contain rollovers have a triangle in the upper left corner.*

2 *This is the **Large Thumbnail** display mode on the **Styles** palette in ImageReady. (In Large Thumbnail mode in Photoshop, large thumbnails display without the text.)*

3 *After choosing a layer, **click** a thumbnail or style name on the **Styles** palette.*

4 *Or drag directly from the **Styles** palette to a layer on the **Layers** palette.*

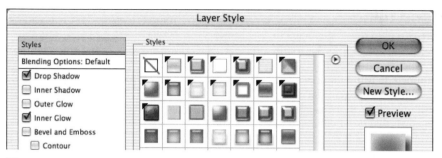

1 *Styles can also be applied from within the **Layer Style** dialog box. Click **Styles** at the top left of the dialog box, then click a style thumbnail to apply that style to the selected layer.*

Rollover styles

Rollover states can be stored in a style, along with layer effects. To do this, create a layer-based slice for an ImageReady layer, then create a rollover for that layer. Drag the layer name or the layer shape over the Styles palette, or select the layer name and choose New Style from the Styles palette menu, check Include Rollover States in the Style Options dialog box, then click OK.

Now you can drag the rollover style thumbnail (designated by the triangle in the upper left corner) from the Styles palette over a layer name or layer shape in the image window to apply that rollover. Or click the thumbnail to apply it to the currently active layer.

To save a layer effect as a style:

1. In Photoshop or ImageReady, display the Styles palette.

2. Drag one nested effect layer onto the Styles palette.
   or
   To preserve a combination of effects, drag the nested Effects bar from the Layers palette onto the Styles palette **2**.

   Regardless of which method you use, a New Style 1 will be created.

3. With the new style still selected, choose Style Options from the Styles palette menu, rename the style, then click OK.

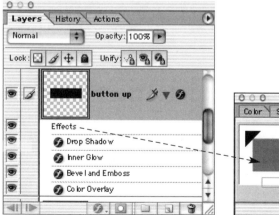

2 *Drag one effect or an Effects bar from the **Layers** palette to the **Styles** palette, then **rename** the new style.*

Background tiling

Tiling is the repetition of the same image in a horizontal/vertical pattern in order to fill (and decorate) the background of a Web page. One advantage to using tiling instead of one large background image is that a small tile file will download more quickly. Another advantage is that the tiled image will always fill the viewer's entire browser window, regardless of the current window size.

You can use ImageReady to convert an image into a repeating **tile** and then save the tile as an HTML file. Import this file into your Web-page creation program for use as a background. The tile effect can be previewed in ImageReady.

To create a tile for an HTML background:

1. In ImageReady, open an image to be used for the tile. To ensure that the imagery and the type that will be displayed on top of it are readable, we recommend using an image that has low contrast and soft, pale colors.

2. If there are any slices, right-click/Ctrl-click and choose Delete All Slices, or choose Slices > Delete All.

3. *Optional:* Crop the image if you want to use only part of it.

4. Choose Filter > Other > Tile Maker.

5. Click Blend Edges **1** to make each tile edge blend (overlap) with the next tile. Enter a Width percentage (1–20) for the amount of blending (overlap).

6. Check Resize Tile to Fill Image to make the tile size match the current image size. With this option unchecked, the tile will be reduced in size by the current Width amount (e.g., a Width of 10 will reduce the tile size by 10 percent).
   or
   Click Kaleidoscope Tile to have the filter generate an abstract image from the original.

Take a road more traveled

Although ImageReady can be used to produce HTML background tiling, there are advantages to attaching a tiled background to your Web page using a Web-page creation program, such as Adobe GoLive or Macromedia Dreamweaver. Ask your Web programmer or layout specialist how to import a tile file into a Web program.

Tiling tips

■ An image will be repeated, if necessary, to fit within the dimensions of the browser window. If you don't want the background image to repeat at all, use a large optimized image of around 800 x 800 pixels that contains few colors and shapes.

■ If the file you've chosen for the background image contains an animation, the animation will automatically play back repetitively across the browser page. Visually overwhelming, yes, but maybe the effect you're looking for.

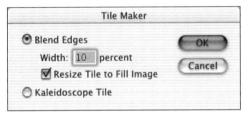

1 *Choose tiling options in the **Tile Maker** dialog box.*

1 *This image was tiled using the **Tile Maker** filter, with the Blend Edges, Width 10, and Resize options chosen. The tile edges blend together.*

2 *This image was optimized for use as a background image, but the Tile Maker filter **wasn't** used on it, so the tile edges don't blend together.*

7. Click OK **1**–**2**.

8. Choose File > Save Optimized (Ctrl-Alt-S/Cmd-Option-S), change the default name, choose a location in which to save the file, then click Save.

To preview an image as a tiled background:

1. In ImageReady, open the image you saved as a tile in the previous set of instructions.

2. Right-click/Ctrl-click and choose Delete All Slices.
   or
   Choose Slices > Delete All.

3. Choose File > Output Settings > Background.

4. Click View Document As: Background **3**.

5. Click OK.

6. To preview the background, click the Preview in [default browser] button 🌐 on the Toolbox, or click the button and choose from the available browsers on the list.

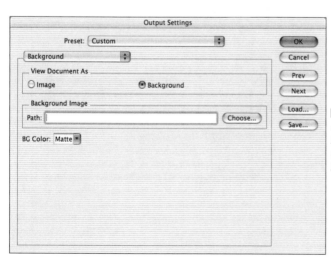

3 *The **Output Settings** dialog box, with the Background pane displayed and View Document As: Background chosen*

To use Photoshop's Save for Web dialog box:

Photoshop's Save for Web dialog box is like ImageReady Lite. ImageReady offers the same optimizing features as the Save for Web dialog box—and much, much more. If you want to learn more about the Save for Web optimizing features, use the page numbers in the callouts in the illustration below to direct yourself to the equivalent information about ImageReady.

TIP The shortcut for opening the Save for Web dialog box in Photoshop is Ctrl-Alt-Shift-S/Cmd-Option-Shift-S.

TIP In the Save for Web dialog box, choose Edit Output Settings from the Optimize menu to change the HTML and image output settings (see page 490).

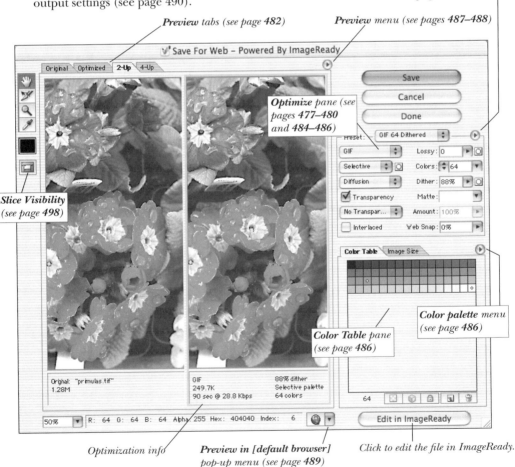

Save for Web Dialog Box in Photoshop

Optimize menu (see pages 480 and 483)

Preview tabs (see page 482)

Preview menu (see pages 487–488)

Optimize pane (see pages 477–480 and 484–486)

Slice Visibility (see page 498)

Color palette menu (see page 486)

Color Table pane (see page 486)

Optimization info

Preview in [default browser] pop-up menu (see page 489)

Click to edit the file in ImageReady.

SHORTCUTS **A**

	Windows	**Mac**
CREATING AND OPENING FILES		
New	Ctrl + N	Cmd + N
New, with last document size settings		Cmd + Option + N
Open	Ctrl + O	Cmd + O
Browse (File Browser)	Ctrl + Shift + O	Cmd + Shift + O
File Info	Ctrl + Alt + I	Cmd + Option + I
Color Settings	Ctrl + Shift + K	Cmd + Shift + K
Edit in ImageReady	Ctrl + Shift + M	Cmd + Shift + M
Open As	Ctrl + Alt + O	
In the File Browser		
Refresh	F5	F5
Open	Ctrl + O	Cmd + O
Close File Browser	Ctrl + W	Cmd + W
Select All	Ctrl + A	Cmd + A
Select All Flagged	Ctrl + Shift + A	Cmd + Shift + A
Deselect All	Ctrl + D	Cmd + D
Flag	Ctrl + ' (apostrophe)	Cmd + ' (apostrophe)
Rotate 90° CW	Ctrl +]	Cmd +]
Rotate 90° CCW	Ctrl + [	Cmd + [
SAVING FILES		
Save	Ctrl + S	Cmd + S
Save As	Ctrl + Shift + S	Cmd + Shift + S
Save A Copy	Ctrl + Alt + S	Cmd + Option + S
Save for Web	Ctrl + Alt + Shift + S	Cmd + Option + Shift + S
Revert	F12	F12
CLOSING AND QUITTING		
Minimize image window		Cmd + Control + M
Close	Ctrl + W	Cmd + W
Close All	Ctrl + Alt + W	Cmd + Option + W
Hide Photoshop		Cmd + Control + H
Hide Others		Cmd + Option + H
Exit/Quit	Ctrl + Q or Alt + F4	Cmd + Q

	Windows	**Mac**
GENERAL SHORTCUTS		
Accept crop, transform, or any dialog box	Enter	Return or Enter
Toggle Cancel to Reset in dialog box	Alt	Option
Cancel crop, transform, or any dialog box	Esc	Esc or Cmd + . (period)
Cancel out of pop-up slider (mouse button up)	Esc	Esc
Commits edit in pop-up slider (mouse button up)	Enter	Return or Enter
Activate button in alert dialog box	First letter of button (e.g., N = No)	First letter of button (e.g., C = Cancel)
Increase value in highlighted field by 1 or .1 (or .01, in Rotate Canvas)	Up Arrow	Up Arrow
Increase value in highlighted field by 10 or 1 (or .1, in Rotate Canvas)	Shift + Up Arrow	Shift + Up Arrow
Decrease value in highlighted field by 1 (or .01, in Rotate Canvas)	Down Arrow	Down Arrow
Decrease value in highlighted field by 10 (or .1, in Rotate Canvas)	Shift + Down Arrow	Shift + Down Arrow
Adjust angle in 15° increments	Shift + drag in angle wheel	Shift + drag in angle wheel
Help	F1	Help or Cmd-/
Adobe Online	Click identifier icon on Toolbox	Click identifier icon on Toolbox
PALETTES		
Show/hide all palettes, tools, and Toolbox	Tab	Tab
Show/hide all palettes	Shift + Tab	Shift + Tab
Show/hide Brushes	F5	F5
Show/hide Color	F6	F6
Show/hide Layers	F7	F7
Show/hide Info	F8	F8
Show/hide Actions	F9	Option-F9
Show options bar (if hidden)	Double-click tool, or press Enter if tool is selected	Double-click tool, or press Return or Enter if tool is selected
UNDO		
Undo	Ctrl + Z	Cmd + Z
Step Forward	Ctrl + Shift + Z	Cmd + Shift + Z
Step Backward	Ctrl + Alt + Z	Cmd + Option + Z
Fade	Ctrl + Shift + F	Cmd + Shift + F

	Windows	Mac

CHOOSING TOOLS
Choose a tool

To cycle through tools on same pop-out menu, press **Shift** plus the shortcut listed below. Except for the Rectangular Marquee and Pen tools, the shortcut selects whichever tool on the pop-out menu was used last.

	Windows	Mac
Rectangular Marquee, Elliptical Marquee (not Single Row Marquee or Single Column Marquee)	M	M
Move	V	V
Lasso, Polygonal Lasso, Magnetic Lasso	L	L
Magic Wand	W	W
Crop	C	C
Slice, Slice Select	K	K
Healing Brush, Patch, Color Replacement	J	J
Brush, Pencil	B	B
Clone Stamp, Pattern Stamp	S	S
History Brush, Art History Brush	Y	Y
Eraser, Background Eraser, Magic Eraser	E	E
Gradient, Paint Bucket	G	G
Blur, Sharpen, Smudge	R	R
Dodge, Burn, Sponge	O	O
Path Selection, Direct Selection	A	A
Horizontal Type, Vertical Type, Horizontal Type Mask, Vertical Type Mask	T	T
Pen, Freeform Pen (not Add Anchor Point, Delete Anchor Point, or Convert Point)	P	P
Rectangle, Rounded Rectangle, Ellipse, Polygon, Line, Custom Shape	U	U
Notes, Audio Annotation	N	N
Eyedropper, Color Sampler, Measure	I	I
Hand	H	H
Zoom	Z	Z

Toggle tools

	Windows	Mac
Move tool	Ctrl	Cmd
Precise cursors	Caps Lock	Caps Lock
Pencil to Eyedropper	Alt	Option
Line to Eyedropper	Alt	Option
Paint Bucket to Eyedropper	Alt	Option

	Windows	Mac
Blur to Sharpen; Sharpen to Blur	Alt	Option
Dodge to Burn; Burn to Dodge	Alt	Option
Hand tool	Spacebar	Spacebar
Zoom Out	Ctrl + - (minus)	Cmd + - (minus)
Zoom In	Ctrl + + (plus)	Cmd + + (plus)

TOOL BEHAVIOR

Tool opacity

	Windows	Mac
Change tool opacity in 10% increments	Number keys (2 = 20%, 3 = 30%)	Number keys (2 = 20%, 3 = 30%)
Change tool opacity in 1% increments	Number keys (2 + 3 = 23%)	Number keys (2 + 3 = 23%)

Constrain tools

	Windows	Mac
Constrain to horizontal or vertical axis (Eraser, Brush, Pencil, Blur, Sharpen, Smudge, Dodge, or Burn tool)	Shift + drag	Shift + drag
Draw, erase, etc. in straight lines (Eraser, Brush, Pencil, Blur, Sharpen, Smudge, Dodge, or Burn tool)	Shift + click	Shift + click
Constrain to 45° axis (Line, Gradients, (or Convert Point tool)	Shift + drag	Shift + drag

Move tool (V)

	Windows	Mac
Move constrained to 45°	Shift + drag	Shift + drag
Copy selection or layer	Alt + drag	Option + drag
Select layer by name	Right-click	Control + click
Select topmost visible layer	Ctrl + Alt + click	Control + Option + click
Link with topmost visible layer	Ctrl + Shift + click	Control + Shift + click
Nudge layer or selection 1 pixel	arrow key	arrow key
Nudge layer or selection 10 pixels	Shift + arrow key	Shift + arrow key

Lasso tool (L)

	Windows	Mac
Add to selection	Shift + click, then draw	Shift + click, then draw
Delete from selection	Alt + click, then draw	Option + click, then draw
Intersect with selection	Alt + Shift + click, then draw	Option + Shift + click, then draw
Temporary Polygonal Lasso	With mouse button down, hold down Alt, then click	With mouse button down, hold down Option, then click

Polygonal Lasso tool (L)

	Windows	Mac
Add to selection	Shift + click, then draw	Shift + click, then draw
Delete from selection	Alt + click, then draw	Option + click, then draw
Intersect with selection	Alt + Shift + click, then draw	Option + Shift + click, then draw
Temporary Lasso	Alt + drag	Option + drag
Constrain to 45° while drawing	Shift + drag	Shift + drag

	Windows	**Mac**
Magnetic Lasso tool (L)		
Add to selection	Shift + click, then draw	Shift + click, then draw
Delete from selection	Alt + click, then draw	Option + click, then draw
Intersect with selection	Alt + Shift + click, then draw	Option + Shift + click, then draw
Add point	Single click	Single click
Remove last point	Backspace or Delete	Delete key
Close path	Double-click or Enter	Double-click or Enter or Return
Close path using straight line segment	Alt + double-click	Option + double-click
Cancel operation	Esc	Esc or Cmd + . (Period)
Temporary Lasso	Alt + drag	Option + drag
Temporary Polygonal Lasso	Alt + click	Option + click
Increase width option	] (close bracket)	] (close bracket)
Decrease width option	[(open bracket)	[(open bracket)
Crop tool (C)		
Rotate crop marquee	Drag outside crop marquee	Drag outside crop marquee
Move crop marquee	Drag inside crop marquee	Drag inside crop marquee
Resize crop marquee	Drag crop corner handle	Drag crop corner handle
Maintain aspect ratio of crop box	Shift + drag handle	Shift + drag handle
Resize crop from center	Alt + drag handle	Option + drag handle
Constrain crop from center	Alt + Shift + drag handle	Option + Shift + drag handle
Apply crop	Enter	Enter/Return
Discard crop without applying	Esc	Esc
Slice tool (K)		
Toggle between Slice and Slice Select tool	Ctrl	Cmd
Draw square slice	Shift + drag	Shift + drag
Draw from center outward	Alt + drag	Option + drag
Draw square slice from center outward	Alt + Shift + drag	Option + Shift + drag
Reposition slice while drawing it	Spacebar + drag	Spacebar + drag
Eraser tool (E)		
Temporary History Eraser	Alt + drag	Option + drag
Smudge tool (R)		
Smudge using Foreground color	Alt	Option

	Windows	Mac
Burn and Dodge tools (O)		
Set Burn or Dodge to Shadows	Alt + Shift + S	Option + Shift + S
Set Burn or Dodge to Midtones	Alt + Shift + M	Option + Shift + M
Set Burn or Dodge to Highlights	Alt + Shift + H	Option + Shift + H
Sponge tool (O)		
Desaturate setting	Alt + Shift + D	Option + Shift + D
Saturate setting	Alt + Shift + S	Option + Shift + S
Path Selection tool (A)		
Duplicate path	Alt + drag	Option + drag
Temporary Direct Selection tool	Ctrl	Cmd
Direct Selection tool (A)		
Temporary Path Selection tool	Ctrl	Cmd or Option
Duplicate path	Alt + drag	Option + drag
Pen tool (P)		
Temporary Convert Anchor Point tool	Alt key (over anchor point)	Option key (over anchor point)
Temporary Direct Selection tool	Ctrl	Cmd
Freeform Pen tool (with Magnetic option enabled) **(P)**		
Add point	Single click	Single click
Remove last point	Backspace or Delete	Delete
Close path	Double-click or Enter	Double-click, Return, or Enter
Close path using straight line segment	Alt + double-click	Option + double-click
Cancel operation	Esc	Esc
Temporary Pen	Alt + click	Option + click
Temporary Freeform Pen	Alt + drag	Option + drag
Increase magnetic width	] (close bracket)	] (close bracket)
Decrease magnetic width	[(open bracket)	[(open bracket)
Eyedropper tool		
Choose Background color	Alt + click	Option + click
Toggle to Color Sampler tool	Shift	Shift
Delete sampler	Alt + Shift + click on sampler	Option + Shift + click on sampler
Color Sampler tool		
Delete sampler	Alt + click on sampler	Option + click on sampler
Measure tool		
Measure constrained to 45° axis	Shift + drag	Shift + drag
Create protractor	Alt + click + drag end point	Option + click + drag end point

	Windows	**Mac**
Hand tool		
Temporary Zoom tool (zoom in)	Ctrl	Z
Toggle to zoom out	Alt	Option
Fit image on screen	Double-click Hand tool	Double-click Hand tool
Zoom tool		
Zoom out	Alt + click	Option + click
Actual pixels	Double-click Zoom tool	Double-click Zoom tool
DISPLAY		
Change zoom levels		
Zoom in	Ctrl + Spacebar + click or drag or Ctrl + Alt + + (plus)	Cmd + Spacebar + click or drag or Cmd + + (plus)
Zoom out	Ctrl + Alt + Spacebar + click or Ctrl + Alt + - (minus)	Cmd + Option + Spacebar + click or Cmd + - (minus)
Zoom to 100%	Double-click Zoom tool	Double-click Zoom tool
Zoom to fit in window	Double-click Hand tool	Double-click Hand tool
Fit on screen	Ctrl + 0	Cmd + 0
Actual pixels	Ctrl + Alt + 0	Cmd + Option + 0
Zoom in without changing window size	Ctrl + + (plus)	Cmd + Option + + (plus)
Zoom out without changing window size	Ctrl + - (minus)	Cmd + Option + - (minus)
Keep Zoom field highlighted after changing zoom percentage	Shift + Enter	Shift + Return
Switch screen modes		
Toggle Standard/Full Screen with Menu Bar/Full Screen modes	F	F
Toggle Menu Bar when in Full Screen mode with Menu Bar	Shift + F	Shift + F
Show/hide		
Show/Hide Extras	Ctrl + H	Cmd + H
Show/Hide Target Path	Ctrl + Shift + H	Cmd + Shift + H
Show/Hide Rulers	Ctrl + R	Cmd + R
Show/Hide Guides	Ctrl + ; (semicolon)	Cmd + ; (semicolon)
Show/Hide Grid	Ctrl + " (quote)	Cmd + " (quote)
Grid and guides		
Toggle Snap on/off	Ctrl + Shift + ; (semicolon)	Cmd + Shift + ; (semicolon)
Lock Guides	Ctrl + Alt + ; (semicolon)	Option + Cmd + ; (semicolon)
Snap guide to ruler	Shift + drag guide	Shift + drag guide
Toggle guide orientation (H/V)	Alt + drag guide	Option + drag guide

	Windows	Mac
NAVIGATE		
Move image in window		
Scroll up one screen	Page up	Page up
Scroll up 10 units	Shift + page up	Shift + page up
Scroll down one screen	Page down	Page down
Scroll down 10 units	Shift + page down	Shift + page down
Scroll left one screen	Ctrl + page up	Cmd + page up
Scroll left 10 units	Ctrl + Shift + page up	Cmd + Shift + page up
Scroll right one screen	Ctrl + page down	Cmd + page down
Scroll right 10 units	Ctrl + Shift + page down	Cmd + Shift + page down
Move view to upper left corner	Home key	Home key
Move view to lower right corner	End key	End key
Navigator palette		
Scroll viewable area of image	Drag view box	Drag view box
Move view to new portion of image	Click in preview area	Click in preview area
View new portion of image	Ctrl + drag in preview area	Cmd + drag in preview area
Keep Zoom field highlighted after changing Zoom percentage	Shift-Enter	Shift-Return
SELECTIONS		
All	Ctrl + A	Cmd + A
Deselect	Ctrl + D	Cmd + D
Reselect	Ctrl + Shift + D	Cmd + Shift + D
Inverse	Ctrl + Shift + I	Cmd + Shift + I
Feather	Ctrl + Alt + D	Cmd + Option + D
Nudge selection marquee 1 pixel	Arrow key	Arrow key
Nudge selection marquee 10 pixels	Shift + arrow key	Shift + arrow key
CLIPBOARD		
Cut	Ctrl + X	Cmd + X
Copy	Ctrl + C	Cmd + C
Copy Merged	Ctrl + Shift + C	Cmd + Shift + C
Paste	Ctrl + V	Cmd + V
Paste Into	Ctrl + Shift + V	Cmd + Shift + V
LAYERS		
Creating layers		
New Layer	Ctrl + Shift + N	Cmd + Shift + N
New Layer without dialog box	Ctrl + Alt + Shift + N	Cmd + Option + Shift + N

	Windows	**Mac**
Layer via Copy	Ctrl + J	Cmd + J
Layer via Cut	Ctrl + Shift + J	Cmd + Shift + J

Layers palette

	Windows	**Mac**
Show/hide layer	Click in eye column	Click in eye column
Toggle show all layers/show just this layer	Alt + click on eye column	Option + click on eye column
Show/hide multiple layers	Click + drag thru eye column	Click + drag thru eye column
Link layer to current target layer	Click in link column	Click in link column
Turn on/off linking for multiple layers	Click + drag thru link column	Click + drag thru link column
Create new, empty layer	Click New Layer button	Click New Layer button
Create new, empty layers with Layer Options dialog box	Alt + click New Layer button	Option + click New Layer button
Duplicate layer	Drag layer to New Layer button	Drag layer to New Layer button
Delete layer using warning alert	Click Delete Layer button	Click Delete Layer button
Delete layer, bypass warning alert	Alt + click Delete Layer button	Option + click Delete Layer button
Change layer opacity in 10% increments	Number keys (2 = 20%, 3 = 30%)	Number keys (2 = 20%, 3 = 30%)
Change layer opacity in 1% increments	Number keys (2 + 3 = 23%)	Number keys (2 + 3 = 23%)
Toggle last chosen Lock button for target layer on/off	/ (forward slash)	/ (forward slash)
Load layer pixels as selection	Ctrl + click layer thumbnail	Cmd + click layer thumbnail
Add layer pixels to selection	Ctrl + Shift + click layer thumbnail	Cmd + Shift + click layer thumbnail
Subtract layer pixels from selection	Ctrl + Alt + click layer thumbnail	Cmd + Option + click layer thumbnail
Intersect layer pixels with selection	Ctrl + Alt + Shift + click layer thumbnail	Cmd + Option + Shift + click layer thumbnail
Activate top layer	Shift + Alt +]	Shift + Option +]
Activate next layer (up)	Alt +]	Option+]
Activate previous layer (down)	Alt + [	Option + [
Activate bottom layer	Shift + Alt + [	Shift + Option + [
Edit layer style	Double-click layer	Double-click layer

Merge layers

	Windows	**Mac**
Merge Down/Linked/Layer Set	Ctrl + E	Cmd + E
Merge Visible	Ctrl + Shift + E	Cmd + Shift + E
Merge down a copy of current layer into layer below	Ctrl + Alt + E	Cmd + Option + E
Merge a copy of all visible layers into current layer	Ctrl + Alt + Shift + E	Cmd + Option + Shift + E
Merge a copy of linked layers into current layer	Ctrl + Alt + E	Cmd + Option + E

	Windows	**Mac**
Arrange layers		
Bring to Front	Ctrl + Shift +]	Cmd + Shift +]
Bring Forward	Ctrl +]	Cmd +]
Send to Back	Ctrl + Shift + [	Cmd + Shift + [
Send Backward	Ctrl + [	Cmd + [
Clipping masks		
Create Clipping Mask	Ctrl + G	Cmd + G
Release Clipping Mask	Ctrl + Shift + G	Cmd + Shift + G

BLENDING MODES
Layer blending modes

Set layer to next blend mode	Shift + + (plus)	Shift + + (plus)
Set layer to previous blend mode	Shift + - (minus)	Shift + - (minus)

Blending modes for layers, and tools that have a Mode pop-up menu

Normal	Alt + Shift + N	Option + Shift + N
Dissolve	Alt + Shift + I	Option + Shift + I
Darken	Alt + Shift + K	Option + Shift + K
Multiply	Alt + Shift + M	Option + Shift + M
Color Burn	Alt + Shift + B	Option + Shift + B
Linear Burn	Alt + Shift + A	Option + Shift + A
Lighten	Alt + Shift + G	Option + Shift + G
Screen	Alt + Shift + S	Option + Shift + S
Color Dodge	Alt + Shift + D	Option + Shift + D
Linear Dodge	Alt + Shift + W	Option + Shift + W
Overlay	Alt + Shift + O	Option + Shift + O
Soft Light	Alt + Shift + F	Option + Shift + F
Hard Light	Alt + Shift + H	Option + Shift + H
Vivid Light	Alt + Shift + V	Option + Shift + V
Linear Light	Alt + Shift + J	Option + Shift + J
Pin Light	Alt + Shift + Z	Option + Shift + Z
Hard Mix	Alt + Shift + L	Option + Shift + L
Difference	Alt + Shift + E	Option + Shift + E
Exclusion	Alt + Shift + X	Option + Shift + X
Hue	Alt + Shift + U	Option + Shift + U
Saturation	Alt + Shift + T	Option + Shift + T
Color	Alt + Shift + C	Option + Shift + C

	Windows	**Mac**
Luminosity	Alt + Shift + Y	Option + Shift + Y
Behind (Brush tool only)	Alt + Shift + Q	Option + Shift + Q

HISTORY
History palette

Step forward	Shift + Ctrl + Z	Cmd + Shift + Z
Step backward	Alt + Ctrl + Z	Cmd + Option + Z
Duplicate history state (other than current)	Alt + click state	Option + click state
Create new snapshot	Click Create new snapshot button	Click Create new snapshot button
Create new document from state/snapshot	Click Create new document button	Click Create new document button

History brush tool

Constrain to horizontal or vertical axis	Shift + drag	Shift + drag
Paint straight lines	Shift + click	Shift + click

ADJUSTMENT COMMANDS

Levels	Ctrl + L	Cmd + L
Auto Levels	Ctrl + Shift + L	Cmd + Shift + L
Auto Contrast	Ctrl + Alt + Shift + L	Cmd + Option + Shift + L
Auto Color	Ctrl + Shift + B	Cmd + Shift + B
Color Balance	Ctrl + B	Cmd + B
Desaturate	Ctrl + Shift + U	Cmd + Shift + U
Invert	Ctrl + I	Cmd + I

Adjustment layers

Edit adjustment layer	Double-click layer thumbnail (on the left)	Double-click layer thumbnail (on the left)

Reopen dialog box

Levels, with last settings	Ctrl + Alt + L	Cmd + Option + L
Curves, with last settings	Ctrl + Alt + M	Cmd + Option + M
Color Balance, with last settings	Ctrl + Alt + B	Cmd + Option + B
Hue/Saturation, with last settings	Ctrl + Alt + U	Cmd + Option + U

Hue/Saturation dialog box

Hue/Saturation	Ctrl + U	Cmd + U
Move color range to new location	Click in image	Click in image
Add to range	Shift + click/drag in image	Shift + click/drag in image
Subtract from range	Alt + click/drag in image	Option + click/drag in image
Edit master	Ctrl + ~ (tilde)	Cmd + ~ (tilde)
Edit individual colors	Ctrl + 1–6	Cmd + 1–6
Slide color spectrum	Ctrl + drag on ramp	Cmd + drag on ramp

	Windows	Mac
Curves dialog box		
Curves	Ctrl + M	Cmd + M
Add color as new point on curve	Ctrl + click in image	Cmd + click in image
Add color as individual points for each curve	Ctrl + Shift + click	Cmd + Shift + click
Move curve point 2 points	Arrow keys	Arrow keys
Move curve points in multiples of 15 points	Shift + arrow keys	Shift + arrow keys
Add point	Click in grid	Click in grid
Delete point	Ctrl + click on point	Cmd + click on point
Deselect all points	Ctrl + D	Cmd + D
Toggle grid between fine and coarse	Alt + click in grid	Option + click in grid
Select next control point	Ctrl + Tab	Cmd + Tab
Select previous control point	Ctrl + Shift + Tab	Cmd + Shift + Tab
Select multiple control points	Shift + click	Shift + click

COLORS

	Windows	Mac
Color buttons on Toolbox		
Swap Foreground/Background colors	X	X
Reset to default colors	D	D
Proofing colors		
Proof Colors	Ctrl + Y	Cmd + Y
Gamut Warning	Ctrl + Shift + Y	Cmd + Shift + Y
Fill		
Open Fill dialog box	Shift + Backspace	Shift + Delete or Shift F5
Fill with Foreground color	Alt + Delete/Backspace	Option + Delete
Fill with Foreground color, Preserve Transparency on	Shift + Alt + Delete/Backspace	Shift + Option + Delete
Fill with Background color	Ctrl + Delete/Backspace	Cmd + Delete
Fill with Background color, Preserve Transparency on	Shift + Ctrl + Delete/Backspace	Shift + Cmd + Delete
Fill from previous history state	Ctrl + Alt + Backspace	Cmd + Option + Delete
Color palette		
Cycle through color bars	Shift + click on color bar	Shift + click on color
Swatches palette		
Add Foreground color as a new swatch	Click in empty slot	Click in empty slot
Choose swatch as Foreground color	Click on swatch	Click on swatch
Choose swatch as Background color	Ctrl + click on swatch	Cmd + click on swatch
Delete swatch	Alt + click on swatch	Option + click on swatch

	Windows	**Mac**
BRUSHES		
Select first brush	Shift + , (comma)	Shift + , (comma)
Select previous brush	, (comma)	, (comma)
Select next brush	. (period)	. (period)
Select last brush	Shift + . (period)	Shift + . (period)
Increase brush size	]	]
Decrease brush size	[	[
Increase brush hardness	Shift +]	Shift +]
Decrease brush hardness	Shift + [	Shift + [
Delete brush from Brush Presets	Alt + click	Option + click
Rename brush in Brush Presets	Double-click on stroke thumbnail	Double-click on stroke thumbnail
QUICK MASK		
Toggle Quick Mask on/off	Q	Q
Invert Quick Mask mode	Alt + click Quick Mask button	Option + click Quick Mask button
Open Quick Mask Options dialog box	Double-click Quick Mask button	Double-click Quick Mask button
LAYER MASKS		
Create layer mask with Reveal All/ Reveal Selection	Click Add Layer Mask button	Click Add Layer Mask button
Create layer mask with Hide All/ Hide Selection	Alt + click Add Layer Mask button	Option + click Add Layer Mask button
Link/unlink layer and layer mask	Click Link layer mask icon	Click Link layer mask icon
Open Layer Mask Display Options dialog box	Double-click layer mask thumbnail (on the right)	Double-click layer mask thumbnail (on the right)
Toggle layer mask on/off	Shift + click layer mask thumbnail (on the right)	Shift + click layer mask thumbnail (on the right)
Toggle rubylith mode on/off	\	\
Toggle viewing layer mask/composite	Alt + click layer mask thumbnail	Option + click layer mask thumbnail
Toggle create clipping mask on/off	Alt + click line between layers	Option + click line between layers
CHANNELS PALETTE		
Target individual channels	Ctrl + [1–9]	Cmd + [1–9]
Target composite channel	Ctrl + ~ (tilde)	Cmd + ~ (tilde)
Show or hide channel	Click in eye column	Click in eye column
Add/remove channel to selected channels	Shift + click channel	Shift + click channel
Create new channel	Click New Channel button	Click New Channel button
Create new channel with New Channel dialog box	Alt + click New Channel button	Option + click New Channel button

SHORTCUTS

	Windows	**Mac**
Duplicate channel	Drag channel to New Channel button	Drag channel to New Channel button
Delete channel using warning alert	Click Delete Channel button	Click Delete Channel button
Delete channel bypassing warning alert	Alt + click Delete Channel button	Option + click Delete Channel button
Create new spot color channel	Ctrl + click New Channel button	Cmd + click New Channel button
Create new channel from selection	Click Save Selection as Channel button	Click Save Selection as Channel button
Create new channel from selection, with New Channel dialog box	Alt + click Save Selection as Channel button	Option + click Save Selection as Channel button
Load channel as selection	Click Load Channel as Selection button or Ctrl + click channel thumbnail	Click Load Channel as Selection button or Cmd + click channel thumbnail
Add channel to selection	Shift + click Load Channel as Selection button or Ctrl + Shift+ click channel thumbnail	Shift + click Load Channel as Selection button or Cmd + Shift + click channel thumbnail
Subtract channel from selection	Alt + click Load Channel as Selection button or Ctrl + Alt + click channel thumbnail	Option + click Load Channel as Selection button or Cmd +Option + click channel thumbnail
Intersect channel with selection	Alt + Shift + click Load Channel as Selection button or Ctrl + Alt + Shift + click thumbnail	Option + Shift + click Load Channel as Selection button or Cmd +Option + Shift + click thumbnail
Edit Channel Options	Double-click alpha channel name	Double-click alpha channel name

LAYER EFFECTS

Toggle show/hide effect	Show/hide layer effect eye icon	Show/hide layer effect eye icon
Edit layer effect options	Double-click layer effect name	Double-click layer effect name
Copy effect to another layer	Drag effect on Layers palette	Drag effect on Layers palette

In Layer Style dialog box

Drop Shadow	Ctrl + 1	Cmd + 1
Inner Shadow	Ctrl + 2	Cmd + 2
Outer Glow	Ctrl + 3	Cmd + 3
Inner Glow	Ctrl + 4	Cmd + 4
Bevel and Emboss	Ctrl + 5	Cmd + 5
Satin	Ctrl + 6	Cmd + 6
Color Overlay	Ctrl + 7	Cmd + 7
Gradient Overlay	Ctrl + 8	Cmd + 8
Pattern Overlay	Ctrl + 9	Cmd + 9
Stroke	Ctrl + 0	Cmd + 0

	Windows	Mac
PATHS		
Paths palette		
Create new path	Click New Path button	Click New Path button
Create new path, with New Path dialog box	Alt + click New Path button	Option + click New Path button
Duplicate path	Drag path to New Path button	Drag path to New Path button
Delete path using warning alert	Click Delete Path button	Click Delete Path button
Delete path, bypass warning alert	Alt + click Delete Path button	Option + click Delete Path button
Save work path into path item	Drag Work Path onto New Path button	Drag Work Path onto New Path button
Paths and selections		
Convert selection into work path	Click Make Work Path button	Click Make Work Path button
Convert selection into work path, with Make Work Path dialog box	Alt + click Make Work Path button	Option + click Make Work Path button
Convert path into selection	Click Load Path as Selection button	Click Load Path as Selection button
Convert path into selection, with Make Selection dialog box	Alt + click Load Path as Selection button	Option + click Load Path as Selection button
Load path as selection	Ctrl + click path thumbnail	Cmd + click path thumbnail
Add path to selection	Ctrl + Shift + click path thumbnail	Cmd + Shift + click path thumbnail
Subtract path from selection	Ctrl + Alt + click path thumbnail	Cmd + Option + click path thumbnail
Intersect path with selection	Ctrl + Alt + Shift + click thumbnail	Cmd + Option + Shift + click thumbnail
Stroke/fill path		
Stroke path with Foreground color	Click Stroke Path with Brush button	Click Stroke Path with Brush button
Stroke path with Stroke Path dialog box	Alt + click Stroke Path button	Option + click Stroke Path button
Fill path with Foreground color	Click Fill Path with Foreground Color button	Click Fill Path with Foreground Color button
Fill path using Fill Path dialog box	Alt + click Fill Path with Foreground Color button	Option + click Fill Path with Foreground Color button
TRANSFORM		
Transform Again	Ctrl + Shift + T	Cmd + Shift + T
Transform Again, with duplication	Ctrl + Alt + Shift + T	Cmd + Option + Shift + T
Free Transform		
Free Transform	Ctrl + T	Cmd + T
Free Transform, with duplication	Ctrl + Alt + T	Cmd + Option + T

	Windows	Mac
Transform, constrain proportions	Shift + drag handle	Shift + drag handle
Transform from center	Alt + drag handle	Option + drag handle
Transform from center, constrain proportions	Ctrl + Shift + drag handle	Option + Shift + drag handle
Distort	Ctrl + drag handle	Cmd + drag handle
Skew	Ctrl + drag side handle	Cmd + drag side handle

TYPE
Type tools

	Windows	Mac
Designate type origin	Click or click + drag	Click or click + drag
Designate type origin while over existing type	Shift + click or click + drag	Shift + click or click + drag
Re-edit existing type	Click on type in image	Click on type in image
Edit Type Options	Double-click type thumbnail	Double-click type thumbnail
Reposition type while typing	Ctrl + drag type in image	Cmd + drag type in image
Faux Bold	Ctrl + Shift + B	Cmd + Shift + B
Faux Italic	Ctrl + Shift + I	Cmd + Shift + I
All Caps	Ctrl + Shift + K	Cmd + Shift + K
Small Caps	Ctrl + Shift + H	Cmd + Shift + H
Superscript	Ctrl + Shift + + (plus)	Cmd + Shift + + (plus)
Subscript	Ctrl + Shift + Alt + + (plus)	Cmd + Shift + Control + + (plus)
Underline	Ctrl + Shift + U	Cmd + Shift + U
Strikethrough	Ctrl + Shift + /	Cmd + Shift + /

Alignment

	Windows	Mac
Left (or Top)	Ctrl + Shift + L	Cmd + Shift + L
Center	Ctrl + Shift + C	Cmd + Shift + C
Right (or Bottom)	Ctrl + Shift + R	Cmd + Shift + R

Size

	Windows	Mac
Increase point size by 2 pts.	Ctrl + Shift + >	Cmd + Shift + >
Decrease point size by 2 pts.	Ctrl + Shift + <	Cmd + Shift + <
100% Horizontal Scale	Ctrl + Shift + X	Cmd + Shift + X

Leading

	Windows	Mac
Increase leading by 2 pts.	Alt + Down Arrow	Option + Down Arrow
Increase leading by 10 pts.	Ctrl + Alt + Down Arrow	Cmd + Option + Down Arrow
Decrease leading by 2 pts.	Alt + Up Arrow	Option + Up Arrow
Decrease leading by 10 pts.	Ctrl + Alt + Up Arrow	Cmd + Option + Up Arrow

	Windows	**Mac**
Justification		
Justify paragraph, left align last line	Ctrl + Shift + J	Cmd + Shift + J
Justify paragraph, force last line	Ctrl+ Shift + F	Cmd + Shift + F
Hyphenation		
Toggle paragraph hyphenation on/off	Ctrl + Alt + Shift + H	Cmd + Option + Shift + H
Toggle single/every-line composer	Ctrl + Alt + Shift + T	Cmd + Option + Shift + T
Kerning/tracking		
Increase kern/track $^{20}/_{1000}$ em space	Alt + Right Arrow	Option + Right Arrow
Increase kern/track $^{100}/_{1000}$ em space	Ctrl + Alt + Right Arrow	Cmd + Option + Right Arrow
Decrease kern/track $^{20}/_{1000}$ em space	Alt + Left Arrow	Option + Left Arrow
Decrease kern/track $^{100}/_{1000}$ em space	Ctrl + Alt + Left Arrow	Cmd + Option + Left Arrow
Set tracking to 0	Ctrl + Shift + Q	Cmd + Control + Shift + Q
Baseline shift		
Increase baseline shift by 2 pts.	Alt + Shift + Up Arrow	Option + Shift + Up + Arrow
Increase baseline shift by 10 pts.	Ctrl + Alt + Shift + Up Arrow	Cmd + Option + Shift + Up Arrow
Decrease baseline shift by 2 pts.	Alt + Shift + Down + Arrow	Option + Shift + Down Arrow
Decrease baseline shift by 10 pts. Arrow	Ctrl + Alt + Shift + Down Arrow	Cmd + Option + Shift + Down
Move insertion point		
Move to the right one character	Right arrow	Right arrow
Move to the left one character	Left arrow	Left arrow
Move up one line	Up arrow	Up arrow
Move down one line	Down arrow	Down arrow
Move to the right one word	Ctrl + Right Arrow	Cmd + Right Arrow
Move to the left one word	Ctrl + Left Arrow	Cmd + Left Arrow
Select		
Select word	Double-click	Double-click
Select one character to the right	Shift + Right Arrow	Shift + Right Arrow
Select one character to the left	Shift + Left Arrow	Shift + Left Arrow
Select one word to the right	Ctrl + Shift + Right Arrow	Cmd + Shift + Right Arrow
Select one word to the left	Ctrl + Shift + Left Arrow	Cmd + Shift + Left Arrow
Select one line	Triple-click	Triple-click
Select one line above	Shift + Up Arrow	Shift + Up Arrow
Select one line below	Shift + Down Arrow	Shift + Down Arrow
Select one paragraph	Quadruple-click	Quadruple-click

	Windows	Mac
Select all characters	Ctrl + A	Cmd + A
Select characters from insertion point	Shift + click	Shift + click

Horizontal Type Mask and Vertical Type Mask tools

	Windows	Mac
Add to selection	Shift + click, then draw	Shift + click, then draw
Designate type origin	Click + drag	Click + drag

FILTERS

	Windows	Mac
Reapply last filter	Ctrl + F	Cmd + F
Reapply filter with the last settings	Ctrl + Alt + F	Cmd + Option + F
Extract	Ctrl + Alt + X	Cmd + Option + X
Liquify	Ctrl + Shift + X	Cmd + Shift + X
Pattern Maker	Ctrl + Alt + Shift + X	Cmd + Option + Shift + X

In Lighting Effects dialog box

	Windows	Mac
Clone light in preview area	Alt + drag light	Option + drag light
Adjust light footprint without changing angle	Shift + drag handle	Shift + drag handle
Adjust light angle without changing footprint	Ctrl + drag handle	Cmd + drag handle

PRINTING FILES

	Windows	Mac
Page Setup	Ctrl + Shift + P	Cmd + Shift + P
Print with Preview	Ctrl + Alt + P	Cmd + Option + P
Print	Ctrl + P	Cmd + P
Print One Copy	Ctrl + Alt + Shift + P	Cmd + Option + Shift + P

PREFERENCES

	Windows	Mac
General	Ctrl + K	Cmd + K

In Preferences dialog box

	Windows	Mac
File Handling	Ctrl + 2	Cmd + 2
Display & Cursors	Ctrl + 3	Cmd + 3
Transparency & Gamut	Ctrl + 4	Cmd + 4
Units & Rulers	Ctrl + 5	Cmd + 5
Guides, Grid & Slices	Ctrl + 6	Cmd + 6
Plug-Ins & Scratch Disks	Ctrl + 7	Cmd + 7
Memory & Image Cache	Ctrl + 8	Cmd + 8
File Browser	Ctrl + 9	Cmd + 9

KEYBOARD SHORTCUTS

	Windows	Mac
Keyboard Shortcuts dialog box	Ctrl-Alt-Shift-K	Cmd-Option-Shift-K

16-bits-per-channel mode, 60

A

Accented Edges filter, 378
actions, 403–417
  AppleScript and, 416
  assignment, 404
  commands, adding, 410
  commands, changing order of, 414
  commands, deleting, 410
  commands, playback exclusion, 409
  defined, 403
  deleting, 415
  droplet creation for, 413
  duplicating, 415
  file naming options, 412
  menu item, inserting, 407
  modal control, adding, 414
  path, inserting, 408
  playback, on images, 409
  playback options, 412
  playing, on batch of images, 411
  recording, 404
  recording, single command, 415
  recording, with different settings, 415
  recording guidelines, 405
  renaming, 404
  running, in actions, 417
  saving command sequences in, 32
  stop, inserting, 406
  storage location, 416
  uses, 403
action sets
  creating, 405
  defined, 405
  loading, 416
  replacing, 416
  saving, 416
Actions palette, 403–417
  button mode, 403
  defined, 14
  Delete button, 410, 415
  dialog box icon, 414
  illustrated, 14, 403
  list mode, 403, 409, 417
  menu
    Duplicate command, 415
    Insert Menu Item command, 407
    Insert Path command, 408
    Insert Stop command, 406
    Load Actions command, 416
    Record Again command, 415
    Replace Actions command, 416
    Save Actions command, 416
  New Action button, 404
  New Set button, 405
  Play button, 406, 409, 417
  Record button, 410, 417
  Stop button, 410, 417
Add Anchor Point tool
  defined, 9
  illustrated, 9
  using, 324
additive primaries, 33
Add Noise filter, 274, 380, 387
adjustment commands, 167–182
  application methods, 168, 191
  Auto Contrast, 172
  basics, 167
  different, choosing, 170
  effects, reducing, 167
  Invert, 173
  previews, 167, 191
  resetting, 167
  settings comparison, 171
  shortcuts, 545–546
  Threshold, 173
  thumbnails, 168
adjustment layers, 114
  blending options, 169
  choosing different command for, 170
  copying, 169
  creating, 168
  defined, 29
  deleting, 170
  effect, limiting, 171, 179
  effect, removing, 171
  effect, restoring, 179
  merging, 170
  modifying, 168
  pixel-based layer mask default, 179
  restacking layers above, 171
  restricting, 179
  selecting, 170
  using, 31, 171
  See also layers
Adobe Every-line Composer, 344, 356
Adobe Gamma dialog box, 46–47
Adobe Single-line Composer, 344, 356
After Effects, file preparation for, 452

Index

airbrushing, 212, 313
aligning
  gradients, 260
  layers to selection marquee, 142
  linked layers, 285
  paragraphs, 354
  point type, 344
  tool-based image maps, 504
  type layers, 364
  user slices, 500
alpha channels
  accessing, 307
  black/white area reversal, 311
  clicking on, 309
  converting, to spot color channels, 209
  defined, 32, 35, 307
  deleting, 311
  as Depth Map source, 245
  displaying, 309
  double-clicking, 209
  duplicating, 311
  illustrated, 35
  loading, 309
  mask, reshaping, 312
  renaming, 311
  saving, 308
  saving selections to, 308
Alt tags, 507
anchor points
  adding, 324
  converting, 325
  corner, 317, 325
  deleting, 325
  dragging, 324
  non-smooth, 317
  selecting, 323
  smooth, 325
Angled Strokes filter, 378
angular gradient, 259
Animation palette (ImageReady), 517–529
  Delay Time pop-up menu, 521
  Duplicate Current Frame button, 522
  illustrated, 517
  Looping option, 520
  menu
    Delete Animation command, 520
    Delete Frame command, 520
    Flatten Frames into Layers command, 519
    Optimize Animation command, 528
    Tween command, 524
  opening, 519
  Play button, 521
  in Save Optimized format, 527
  Select First Frame button, 521
  Stop button, 521
  Tween button, 518, 522, 523, 524, 526

animations, 517–529
  cropping, 528
  defined, 517
  frames, as nested thumbnails, 525
  frames, delay value, 521
  frames, removing, 520
  frames, saving as layers, 528–529
  imagery, fading, 520
  Layers palette edits and, 523
  looping, 520
  optimizing, 528
  options, 519
  pixel edits, 523
  playback options, 520
  previewing, 521
  remote, 525
  reversing to first frame, 523
  rocking, 522
  rollovers triggering, 525
  saving, 527
  second effects, 524
  sequence illustration, 523, 524
  slimming down, 528
  warped type, 526
anti-aliasing, 125, 475
  applying, to type, 494
  defined, 475
  halos and, 475
Art History Brush tool
  defined, 9, 166
  illustrated, 9
  options bar, 166
  using, 166
Assign Profile dialog box, 54
Audio Annotation tool, 9, 10
Auto Color Correction Options dialog box, 205
Auto Contrast command, 172
Auto Resolution dialog box, 62
auto slices
  converting, 497
  defined, 495
  linked, 506
  multiple, combining, 499
  See also slices
Average filter, 377

B

Background
  converting, into layer, 111
  converting layers into, 111
  double-clicking, 111
  moving, 110
  selecting, 123
  transforming, 289
Background colors, 183
  choosing, 183

converting, to grayscale, 203
defined, 29–30
display, 183
gradient use of, 262
See also color(s); Foreground colors
Background Eraser tool
Contiguous option, 229
defined, 8
Discontiguous option, 229
Find Edges option, 229
illustrated, 8
Limits pop-up menu, 229
options bar, 229
Sampling pop-up menu, 230
Tolerance percentage, 229
using, 229–230
baseline shift, 353
Bas Relief filter, 383
Batch dialog box, 411–412
Behind mode, 42, 270
Bevel effect, 298–299
applying, 298–299
Inner Bevel, 298
Outer Bevel, 298
Shading settings, 298–299
Structure settings, 298
Texture options, 299
Bitmap mode, 36
Black Generation function, 249
blending
fine-tuning, 271–272
layers, 270–274
modified layers, 274
blending modes, 38–42
adjustments, 169
Behind, 42, 270
choosing, 270
Clear, 42, 270
Color, 42
Color Burn, 39, 270
Color Dodge, 39
cycling through, 42
Darken, 38
Difference, 41
Dissolve, 38
Exclusion, 41
Hard Light, 40
Hard Mix, 41
Hue, 42
Lighten, 39
Linear Burn, 39
Linear Dodge, 39
Linear Light, 41
Luminosity, 42
Multiply, 38
Normal, 38

Overlay, 40
Pin Light, 40
Saturation, 42
Screen, 39
selecting, 38
shortcuts, 544–545
smudging and, 225
Soft Light, 40
Vivid Light, 41
Blur More filter, 377
Blur tool
defined, 7, 148
illustrated, 7
options bar, 148
using, 148
Border Selection dialog box, 131
brightness
adjustment, 175
adjustment, with Levels dialog box, 176
defined, 30
filter effects and, 374
monitor, 44, 46
preserving, 244
Brightness/Contrast dialog box, 175
browser window layer, 470
brushes
custom, 224
organization, 220
shortcuts, 547
Brushes palette, 213–219
Airbrush option, 217
Angle Jitter option, 215
Angle option, 214
Both Axes option, 215
Brightness Jitter value, 216
Brush Presets button, 214
Brush Tip Shape option, 214
categories, 213
Color Dynamics category, 216, 218
Control pop-up menus, 215, 218–219
Count Jitter value, 215
Count value, 215
defined, 15, 213
Depth Jitter value, 216
Diameter option, 214
Direction command, 219
docking, 213
Dual Brush option, 216
Fade command, 218
Flow Jitter value, 217
Foreground/Background Jitter value, 216
Hardness option, 214
Hue Jitter value, 216
illustrated, 15, 213, 218
Initial Direction command, 219
Invert option, 216

lock icon, 217
Maximum roundness value, 215
menu
    Clear Brush Controls command, 219
    Copy Texture to Other Tools command, 219
    Delete Brush command, 224
    Expanded View command, 213
    Save Tool Presets, 222
Minimum Diameter value, 215
Mode option, 216
Noise option, 217
Opacity Jitter value, 217
opening, 213, 218
options, 213
Other Dynamics category, 217, 218
panes, 213
Pen Pressure command, 218
Pen Tilt command, 218
Protect Texture option, 217
Purity value, 216
Roundness Jitter option, 215
Roundness option, 214
Saturation Jitter value, 216
Scale option, 216
Scatterer value, 215
Scattering category, 218
Shape Dynamics category, 215, 218
Size Jitter option, 215
Smoothing option, 217
Spacing option, 214, 215
Stylus Wheel command, 219
Texture category, 215, 218
Texture Each Tip option, 216
using, 213
Wet Edges option, 217
brush libraries, 220, 221
Brush Preset picker, 153
closing, 11, 15
defined, 15
opening, 11, 15, 211
brush presets
angle, 214
converting, to tool presets, 222
creating, from images, 224
default, restoring, 221
deleting, 224
editing, 214–217
hardness, 212, 214
library, loading, 221
locking, 217
master diameter, 212
naming, 224
roundness, 214
saving, 217, 220
saving, in new library, 220
selecting, 211, 214, 221

size, 214
size variation, 215
spacing, 214, 215
temporary changes to, 212
tools using, 212
working with, 220–224
brush tips
choosing, 15
shape, 214
shape options, 219
shape variation, 215
Brush tool, 211–212
Airbrush option, 212
Brush Preset picker arrowhead, 211
defined, 7
Fill option, 202
Flow percentage, 211, 227
illustrated, 7
Mode option, 179, 209, 211, 227
Opacity option, 179, 202, 209, 211, 227
options bar, 11, 227
for reshaping layer masks, 279
using, 211–212
Burn tool
darkening with, 178
defined, 10
illustrated, 10
options bar, 178
shortcuts, 540
buttons (Web page), 516

C

cache files, 77
calibration, 44–47, 240
Camera Raw dialog box, 233–241
Adjust tab, 234, 238
Advanced option, 240
Basics option, 237
Blue Hue/Blue Saturation sliders, 240
button functions, switching, 235
Calibrate pane, 240
Camera Raw plug-in menu, 236
Color Noise Reduction slider, 239
Contrast slider, 238
defined, 233
Depth pop-up menu, 236
Detail tab, 234, 239
Exposure slider, 238
Green Hue/Green Saturation sliders, 240
histogram window, 236, 238
illustrated, 234
Luminance Smoothing slider, 239
opening, 234
preview window, changing, 235
preview window, dragging images to, 235
Red Hue/Red Saturation sliders, 240

Resolution setting, 236
Saturation slider, 238
Settings pop-up menu, 236
Shadows slider, 238
Shadow Tint slider, 240
Sharpness slider, 239
Size pop-up menu, 235
Space pop-up menu, 235
sticky settings, 236
Temperature slider, 237–238
Tint slider, 237–238
views, changing, 235
White Balance pop-up menu, 237
Camera Raw files
basic settings, changing, 236
batch processing, 234
camera support, 235
global color adjustments, 237–238
image attributes, changing, 235–236
JPEG vs., 241
lossless compression, 241
opening, 234, 236
pixel information preservation, 241
proprietary formats, 235
saving, 233
working with, 233
Camera Raw Preferences dialog box, 239
canvas
enlarging, with Crop tool, 101
rotating, 103
size, changing, 98
Canvas Size dialog box, 98
Chalk & Charcoal filter, 383
Channel Mixer dialog box, 180
Channel Options dialog box, 209, 311
channels, 34–35
adjusting, 204–205
alpha, 32, 35, 209, 307, 308–312
default, 34
spot color, 35, 208–210
storage size and, 35
channel selections
displaying, 309
loading, 309
operations, load, 310
operations, save, 310
saving, 308
See also alpha channels
Channels palette, 308–312
defined, 16
Delete Channel (trash) button, 311
eye icon, 16, 312
illustrated, 16
menu
Channel Options command, 311
Merge Spot Channel command, 210

New Channel button, 311
Save Selection as Channel button, 308, 364
shortcuts, 547–548
spot color channels in, 208
thumbnails, 311
Character palette
Baseline Shift icon, 353
defined, 17
Font Size icon, 348
Horizontal Scale icon, 351
illustrated, 348
Kerning icon, 349
Leading area, 350
menu
All Caps command, 352
Change Text Orientation command, 351
Contextual Alternates command, 353
Discretionary Ligatures command, 353
Faux Bold command, 352
Faux Italic command, 352
Fractional Widths command, 352
Fractions command, 353
Ligatures command, 353
No Break command, 352
Old Style command, 352
Ordinals command, 352
Ornaments command, 353
Reset Characters command, 353
Small Caps command, 352
Strikethrough command, 352
Stylistic Alternates command, 353
Subscript command, 352
Superscript command, 352
Swash command, 353
System Layout command, 352
Titling command, 353
Underline Left/Right commands, 352
opening, 349
Style buttons, 352
Tracking icon, 349
Vertical Scale icon, 351
Charcoal filter, 383
Check Spelling dialog box, 368
Chrome filter, 383
chromes, 454
Clear mode, 42, 270
Clipboard
basics, 143
contents, pasting, 143
purging, 143
shortcuts, 542
clipping masks, 283–284
creating, 283
defined, 283
EPS, 329
from linked layers, 283

releasing, 284
releasing layers from, 284
shortcuts, 544
Clone Stamp tool
Airbrush button, 153, 156
Aligned option, 153, 156
Brush Preset picker arrowhead, 153
defined, 7
Flow percentage, 153, 156
illustrated, 7
Mode option, 153, 156
Opacity percentage, 153, 154, 156
options bar, 153, 156
Use All Layers option, 153, 154
cloning, 153–156
areas in same image, 153–154
with Clone Stamp tool, 153–154
from image to image, 156
with Pattern Stamp tool, 155
Close button, 2
Clouds filter, 382
CMYK Color mode, 33–34
converting to, 35–36
corrections in, 466
curves, 206
defined, 37
illustrated, 37
Working Spaces settings, 49
CMYK custom settings, 462–463
Color Balance dialog box, 200
Color Burn mode, 39, 270
color depth, 472
Color Dodge mode, 39
colored lens effect, 244
Colored Pencil filter, 375
Color Halftone filter, 381
color management, 43–56
benefits, 43
calibration and, 44–47
color profiles, 54–55
controls, 43
conversion options, 52–53
policies, customizing, 51
predefined settings, 43, 48–50
printing with, 446–449
proofing, 55–56
for RGB/CMYK color files, 43
settings synchronization, 43
Color Overlay effect, 302
Color palette
Background color square, 184, 185, 186
choosing colors with, 186
defined, 18
Foreground color square, 184, 185, 186
grayscale mode, 209
icons, 184

menu, 186
Copy Color As HTML command, 190
Grayscale Slider command, 202
out-of-gamut indicator, 34
sliders, 186
Color Picker
choosing colors with, 184
icons, 184
illustrated, 30, 184
opening, 18, 184
color profiles
available, 66
changing, 54
converting, 54–55
deleting, 54
reassigning, 54
Color Range dialog box, 130, 465
Color Replacement tool, 250–251
defined, 7
illustrated, 7
Limits option, 251
options bar, 250
for red-eye removal, 251
Sampling option, 250–251
Tolerance value, 251
color(s)
adding, 187
adjustments, 34
amount, increasing/decreasing, 204
auto correction options, 205
basics, 33–42
choosing, 183–190
choosing, from Swatches palette, 187
choosing, with Color palette, 186
choosing, with Color Picker, 184
choosing, with Eyedropper tool, 189
combining grays with, 203
copying, 190
custom, 185
custom, choosing, 185
deleting, 187
desaturating, 201
display, 33
document-specific, 49
heightening, 202
hexadecimal values, 190
matching, 492
opposites, 206
out-of-gamut, correcting, 465
pasting, 190
process, 184, 185
proofing, with custom settings, 56
proofing, with preset settings, 55
replacing, 250–251
saturating, 201
shortcuts, 546

silhouetting, 202
smudging, 225
spot, 185, 208
type, 345
Web-safe, 184
See also Background colors; Foreground colors
color samplers, 198–199
Color Sampler tool
  defined, 10, 198
  illustrated, 10
  Info palette with, 199
  options bar, 199
  shortcuts, 540
  using, 198–199
Color Settings dialog box, 48–53, 462–463
  Advanced Mode option, 52
  CMYK pop-up menu, 462
  Color Management Off setting, 48
  Color Management Policies area, 51
  ColorSync Workflow setting, 48
  Conversion options, 52–53
  Convert to Working option, 51
  defined, 462
  Description area, 48
  Emulate Acrobat 4 setting, 48
  Emulate Photoshop 4 setting, 48
  Engine option, 52
  illustrated, 48, 52
  Intent option, 52–53
  Missing Profiles option, 51
  North American General Purpose Defaults
    setting, 48
  opening, 43, 48
  Photoshop 5 Default Spaces setting, 48
  Preserve Embedded Profiles option, 51
  Profile Mismatches options, 51
  RGB Working Spaces, 49–50
  Save button, 53
  Settings pop-up menu, 48
  Use Black Point Compensation option, 53
  Use Dither (8-bit/channel images) option, 53
  U.S. Prepress Defaults setting, 48
  Web Graphics Defaults setting, 49
Color Table palette (ImageReady), 486
color tints, 204
  adding, to layers, 180
  applying, to grayscale image, 227
  illustrated, 227
  spot channel, 209
color transparencies, 454
commercial printers, 462
compression
  dithering and, 475
  image quality and, 470
  programs, 464
  Web graphics, 470–472

Conditional Mode Change dialog box, 418
Contact Sheet II dialog box, 419–420
  Document area, 419
  illustrated, 419
  Source Images area, 419
  Thumbnails area, 420
  Use Filename As Caption option, 420
contact sheets
  creating, 419–420
  defined, 419
  with filename captions, 420
Conté Crayon filter, 383
context menus, 32
Contour Editor, 300
Contour picker, 300
contours, 300
contrast
  adjustment, 175
  adjustment, with Levels dialog box, 176
  auto, 172
  Camera Raw image, 238
  filter effects and, 374
  high, 173
  highlight, 242
  monitor, 44, 46
  shadow, 242
Convert Multi-Page PDF to PSD dialog box, 421
Convert Point tool
  defined, 9
  illustrated, 9
  using, 325
Convert to Profile dialog box, 54–55
copying, 142–147
  action commands, 410
  adjustment layers, 169
  colors, 190
  drag, 142
  drag-and-drop, 145
  layer effects, 293, 305
  layers, 116–118
  pasting and, 144–145
  paths, 322
  to spot color channels, 208
  textures, 219
CorelDRAW, file preparation for, 454
corner points, 317, 325
Craquelure filter, 386
Create Droplet dialog box, 413
Crop and Straighten Photos, 99
cropping
  animations, 528
  canceling, 100
  with Crop command, 102
  with Crop tool, 99, 101
  dimensions/resolution while, 100
  images, 99

layers, 99
  resharpening after, 100
  scanning and, 59
  with Trim command, 102–103
Crop tool
  defined, 7
  enlarging canvas with, 101
  illustrated, 7
  options bar, 99, 100
  shortcuts, 539
  using, 99
Crosshatch filter, 378
Crystallize filter, 381
Curves dialog box, 206–207
custom brushes, 224
Custom CMYK dialog box, 462, 463
custom colors, 185
  applied to layers, 210
  choosing, 185
Custom Colors dialog box, 184, 185
custom curves, 207
Custom Shape picker, 335, 341
Custom Shape tool
  Geometry Options, 338
  using, 335
  See also shape tools
Cutout filter, 375

D
Darken mode, 38
Dark Strokes filter, 378
DCS files, 84
  defined, 457
  saving as, 457
  saving Multichannel mode images as, 456
Defringe dialog box, 158
defringing, 158
Delete Anchor Point tool
  defined, 9
  illustrated, 9
  using, 325
Delete Workspaces dialog box, 13
diamond gradient, 259, 266
Difference Clouds filter, 382
Difference mode, 41
Diffuse filter, 385
Diffuse Glow filter, 379
digital cameras
  noise, 239
  support, 235
  See also Camera Raw files
dimensions
  changing, for onscreen output, 91
  changing, for print output, 92
  lowest, 31
  while cropping, 100

Direct Selection tool, 321, 323, 324, 326
  defined, 9
  illustrated, 9
  for point selection, 323
  for shape layer contour modification, 339
  shortcuts, 540
Displace filter, 379
Display & Cursors preferences, 112, 431
Dissolve mode, 38
distorting
  drop shadows, 295
  free transform layers, 289
  layers, 288
  with Liquify command, 398–401
  paths, 321
distort transformation, 287
dithering, 474–475
  compression and, 475
  with continuous-tone imagery, 474
  controlling, 487
  defined, 474
  illustrated effect, 474
  method selection, 478
  previewing, 487
Divide Slice dialog box, 495
document presets, 67
document-specific color, 49
Dodge tool
  defined, 7
  illustrated, 7
  lightening with, 178
  options bar, 178
  shortcuts, 540
drag-and-drop copying, 145
droplets
  applying, 483
  creating, 483
  creating, for actions, 413
  defined, 413
Drop Shadow effect
  applying, 294–295
  illustrated, 291, 294
  transforming, 295
drop shadows
  creating, with Drop Shadow effect, 294–295
  creating, without an effect, 296
  distorting, 295
  luminosity, 295
Dry Brush filter, 375
DS 2.0 Format dialog box, 457
Duotone Curve dialog box, 461
Duotone mode, 36
Duotone Options dialog box, 460–461
duotones
  defined, 460
  producing, 460–461

Duplicate command, 85
Duplicate Layer dialog box, 116
Duplicate Path dialog box, 322
duplicating
  actions, 415
  alpha channels, 311
  history states, 161
  layer comps, 277
  layer masks, 280
  layers, 107
  vector masks, 330

E

edges
  blurring, 148
  pixels beyond, removing, 147
  sharpening, 148
editable type, 344
  applying layer effects to, 362–363
  beyond image area, 364
  with effects, 359
  Illustrator, 360
  See also type
Edit menu
  Check Spelling command, 368
  Clear command, 132
  Color Settings command, 48, 51, 52, 462
  Copy command, 144, 322
  Copy Merged command, 146
  Cut command, 132
  Define Brush Preset command, 224
  Define Custom Shape command, 341
  defined, 4
  Define Pattern command, 155
  Fade command, 31, 167, 372
  Fill command, 165, 179, 193, 296, 366
  Find and Replace Text command, 367
  Free Transform command, 289, 290
  illustrated, 4
  Keyboard Shortcuts command, 553
  Paste command, 143, 144, 190, 322, 340
  Paste Into command, 143, 363, 364
  Preferences submenu
    Display & Cursors command, 6, 113
    File Handling command, 79
    General command, 13, 184, 186, 288
    Transparency & Gamut command, 115
  Preset Manager command, 438, 439
  Proof Colors command, 55
  Proof Setup submenu, 55
  Purge submenu, 32
    Clipboard command, 143
    Histories command, 160
  Stroke command, 195
  Transform Path submenu, 321
  Transform Points submenu, 321

  Transform submenu, 287
    Again command, 288
    Distort command, 288, 295
    Flip Horizontal command, 109, 513
    Flip Vertical command, 109, 513
    Perspective command, 288
    Rotate command, 287, 288
    Scale command, 287, 513
    Skew command, 287
  Undo command, 31, 109, 127, 178, 288
Ellipse tool
  defined, 10
  Geometry Options, 338
  illustrated, 10
  See also shape tools
Elliptical Marquee tool, 131
  defined, 8
  Feather field, 137
  illustrated, 8
  options bar, 124
elliptical selections, 124
Emboss effect, 298–299
Emboss filter, 385
EPS files
  clipping paths, 329
  format choice, 455
  opening, 80
  placing, 82
  saving, 85, 455
EPS Options dialog box, 451, 455–456
  Encoding options, 455–456
  Include Vector Data option, 329
  Preview pop-up menu, 455
Eraser tool
  for color removal, 227
  defined, 7
  Eraser to History option, 228
  illustrated, 7
  with Lock Transparent Pixels option, 115
  options bar, 228
  shortcuts, 539
  using, 228
erasing, 228–232
  with Background Eraser tool, 229–230
  with Eraser tool, 228
  with Magic Eraser, 231–232
  part of layer, 228
Exclusion mode, 41
exporting
  File Browser cache, 77
  files, 84
  paths, 327
  spot color channels, 210
Export Paths dialog box, 327
Extract dialog box, 138–140
  Brush Size option, 138

Index

Cleanup tool, 140
Display option, 140
Edge Highlighter tool, 138
Edge Touchup tool, 140
Eraser tool, 139
Fill colors, 139
Fill tool, 139
Highlight colors, 138
opening, 138
Show Fill option, 140
Show Highlight option, 140
Show option, 140
Textured Image option, 139
Extrude filter, 385
Eyedropper tool
    choosing colors with, 189
    copying colors with, 190
    defined, 7
    illustrated, 7
    options bar, 189
    Sample Size option, 189
    shortcuts, 540
    using, 189–190

F

Facet filter, 381
Fade dialog box, 372
fading
    imagery, 520
    type, 362
feathering, 157
Fibers filter, 382
File Browser, 31, 68–77
    Automate menu, 71, 94
    cache, exporting, 77
    closing, 71
    customizing, 70
    defined, 19, 68
    Edit menu, 71, 73
    file deletion, 76
    File menu, 71
        Add Folder to Favorites command, 73
        Delete command, 76
        Export Cache command, 77
        illustrated, 71
        New Folder command, 76
        Open command, 72
        Purge Cache command, 77
        Purge Entire Cache command, 77
        Search command, 74
    file renaming, 76
    file search in, 74
    Flag File button, 73
    folder creation, 76
    Folders palette, 69, 72
    illustrated, 19, 68
    Keywords palette, 69, 77
    main window, 69
    Metadata palette, 69
    opening, 68, 71
    opening files via, 72
    preferences, 437
    Preview palette, 69
    Rotate Clockwise button, 73
    Rotate Counter-Clockwise button, 73
    settings, saving, 70
    Sort menu, 71, 75
    Toggle Expanded View button, 70
    updating, 72
    Up One Level button, 72
    View menu, 71, 73
file formats
    layers and, 106
    saving (Mac), 57
    saving (Windows), 57
    selecting, 85
    See also specific formats
File Handling preferences, 84, 430
File Info dialog box (ImageReady), 492
File menu
    Automate submenu, 71
        Batch command, 411, 412
        Conditional Mode Change command, 418
        Contact Sheet II command, 419
        Create Droplet command, 413
        Crop and Straighten Photos command, 99
        Fit Image command, 147, 420
        Multi-Page PFD to PSD command, 421
        Photomerge command, 256
        Picture Package command, 422
        Web Photo Gallery command, 424
    Browser command, 68
    Close command, 90
    defined, 4
    Exit command, 90
    Export submenu
        Animation command, 528
        Paths to Illustrator command, 327
    illustrated, 4
    Import command, 61
    New command, 23, 65, 67
    Open command, 78, 80, 234
    Page Setup dialog box, 442
    Place command, 82
    Print command, 442, 443
    Print One Copy command, 445
    Print with Preview command, 92, 444, 446, 451
    Revert command, 84, 161
    Save As command, 84, 85, 119, 404, 455
    Save command, 83, 84
    Save for Web command, 467, 468
    Scripts submenu, 277

Index

file preparation, 452–454
  After Effects, 452–453
  CorelDRAW, 454
  film recorder, 454
  Illustrator, 453–454
  InDesign, 452
  QuarkXPress, 452
files
  Camera Raw, 233–241
  closing, 90
  deleting, 76
  exporting, 84
  information, 441
  opening, in Windows/Mac, 79
  opening, with File Browser, 72
  opening, with Open command, 78
  preparation for other applications, 452–459
  ranking, 75
  renaming, 76
  reopening, 79
  saving, 83–85
  searching for, 74
  shortcuts, 535
  sorting, 75
Fill dialog box
  Blending options, 194
  Opacity percentage, 296
  Use: Black option, 366
  Use: Color option, 193
  Use: Foreground Color option, 179
  Use: History option, 165, 193
  Use: Pattern option, 193
fill layers, 114
  with color, 193
  defined, 192
  gradient, 259–260
  with history, 193
  with layer effects, 194
  shortcuts, 192
Film Grain filter, 274, 375
film recorders, 454
Filter Gallery dialog box, 370–371
Filter menu
  Artistic submenu, 274
  Blur submenu
    Gaussian Blur command, 97
    Lens Blur command, 247
    Motion Blur command, 389
    Radial Blur command, 513
  defined, 5
  Distort submenu
    Pinch command, 513
    Ripple command, 387
    Twirl command, 387
  Extract command, 138
  Filter Gallery command, 370

  illustrated, 5
  Last Filter command, 369
  Liquify command, 398
  Noise submenu
    Add Noise command, 274, 387
    Median command, 388
  Pattern Maker command, 393
  Render submenu, 390
  Sharpen submenu
    Sharpen Edges command, 97
    Unsharp Mask command, 96, 388
  Stylize submenu
    Find Edges command, 388
    Trace Contour command, 388
    Wind command, 387
  Texture submenu
    Grain command, 274
    Mosaic Tiles command, 372
filters, 369–396
  Accented Edges, 378
  Add Noise, 274, 380, 387
  Angled Strokes, 378
  applying, 369
  applying multiple, 374
  area restrictions, 373
  Average, 377
  basics, 369–374
  Bas Relief, 383
  Blur More, 377
  Chalk & Charcoal, 383
  Charcoal, 383
  Chrome, 383
  Clouds, 382
  Colored Pencil, 375
  Color Halftone, 381
  Conté Crayon, 383
  Craquelure, 386
  Crosshatch, 378
  Crystallize, 381
  Cutout, 375
  Dark Strokes, 378
  defined, 369
  dialog boxes, 371
  Difference Clouds, 382
  Diffuse, 385
  Diffuse Glow, 379
  Displace, 379
  Dry Brush, 375
  effects, less artificial, 374
  effects, lessening, 372
  effects, maximizing, 374
  Emboss, 385
  exercises, 387–392
  Extrude, 385
  Facet, 381
  Fibers, 382

Film Grain, 274, 375
Find Edges, 385, 388
finding, 369
Fragment, 381
Fresco, 375
Gaussian Blur, 377
Glass, 379
Glowing Edges, 385
Grain, 274, 386
Graphic Pen, 383
Halftone Pattern, 383
Ink Outlines, 378
Lens Blur, 245–247, 377
Lens Flare, 382
Lighting Effects, 390–392
Median, 380, 388
Mezzotint, 381
Mosaic Tiles, 381, 386
Motion Blur, 377, 389
Neon Glow, 375
Note Paper, 384
Ocean Ripple, 379
Paint Daubs, 375
Palette Knife, 375
Patchwork, 386
Pattern Maker, 393–396
Photocopy, 384
Pinch, 379, 513
Plaster, 384
Plastic Wrap, 376
Pointillize, 381
Polar Coordinates, 379
Poster Edges, 376
previewing, 371
Radial Blur, 377
reapplying, 369
Reticulation, 384
Ripple, 379, 387
Rough Pastels, 374, 376
Sharpen Edges, 382
Sharpen More, 382
Shear, 379
shortcuts, 552
Smart Blur, 377
Smudge Stick, 376
Solarize, 385
Spatter, 378
Spherize, 380
Sponge, 376
Sprayed Strokes, 378
Stained Glass, 386
Stamp, 374, 384
Sumi-e, 378
texture mapping with, 374
Texturizer, 386
Tiles, 385

Torn Edges, 384
Trace Contour, 386, 388
Twirl, 380, 387
Underpinning, 376
Unsharp Mask, 96–97, 382, 388
Watercolor, 376
Water Paper, 384
Wave, 380
Wind, 386, 387
ZigZag, 380
Find And Replace Text dialog box, 367
Find Edges filter, 385, 388
Fit Image dialog box, 94, 420
flattening layers, 122
flipping layers, 109
folders
  creating, 76
  listing, 69
Foreground colors, 183
  black, 179
  choosing, 183
  copying, 190
  defined, 29
  display, 183
  gradient use of, 262
  mixing, 187
  in stroke, 216
  See also Background colors; color(s)
Forward Warp tool, 398, 399
Fragment filter, 381
frame selections, 131
Freeform Pen tool, 318–320
  Contrast option, 319
  Curve Fit option, 319
  defined, 9
  drawing paths with, 320
  Frequency option, 319
  illustrated, 9
  Magnetic option, 318, 319
  options bar, 318
  Options palette, 319
  Pathfinder buttons, 329
  Paths button, 318, 320
  Pen Pressure option, 319
  shortcuts, 540
  Width option, 319
FreeHand, exporting paths to, 327
free transform, 289
Freeze Mask tool, 400
Fresco filter, 375

G

gamma
  adjusting, 45, 46–47
  values, 488
Gamma dialog box (ImageReady), 488

Index

Gaussian Blur filter, 377
General preferences, 428–429
    Auto-update open documents option, 482
    Color Picker option, 184, 428
    Dynamic Color Sliders option, 186, 428
    Export Clipboard option, 143, 428
    History Log option, 428
    History States field, 428
    illustrated, 429
    Image Interpolation option, 428
    Options area, 429
    Reset All Warning Dialogs button, 428
    Save Palette Locations option, 13, 428
    Zoom Resizes Windows option, 87
    See also preferences
geometric pixel areas, 337
GIF format, 471
    animations, 517–529
    choosing, 471
    defined, 471
    image fading, 479
    optimizing images in, 477–480
    saving in, 471
Glass filter, 379
Global Light dialog box, 305
Glowing Edges filter, 385
Gradient Editor
    Color swatch, 262
    Gradient Type: Noise option, 263
    illustrated, 262, 263
    opacity stops, 265
    opening, 262, 264
Gradient Fill dialog box, 259–260
    Align with layer option, 260
    Angle slider, 260
    Dither option, 260
    illustrated, 259
    Reverse option, 260
    Scale slider, 260
    Style setting, 259
gradient fill layers, 114, 259–260
Gradient Map dialog box, 267
gradient maps
    applying, 267–268
    color contrast, heightening, 268
    color stops, 267–268
    defined, 267
    reediting, 268
    starting/ending colors, 267
Gradient Overlay effect, 302
Gradient Preset picker, 264, 267
gradient presets, 262–265
    creating, 262–263
    default, restoring, 265
    deleting, 262
    editing, 263

    ending color, 263
    libraries, alternate, 264
    saving, 264
    starting color, 262
gradients, 259–268
    aligning, with layer, 260
    angle, 260
    angular, 259
    applying, as fill layer, 259–260
    applying, with Gradient tool, 261
    banding, minimizing, 260
    colors, removing, 263
    colors, reversing, 260
    constraining, 261
    defined, 259
    diamond, 259, 266
    intermediate colors, 263
    linear, 259, 261, 266
    masking, 260
    opacity, 260, 265
    radial, 259
    reflected, 259
    scaling, 260
    settings, adjusting, 260
    styles, 259
    transition abruptness, 263
Gradient tool, 259–265
    applying gradients with, 261
    defined, 7
    Dither option, 261
    Gradient thumbnail, 262
    illustrated, 7
    options bar, 11, 261
    Transparency option, 261
Grain filter, 274, 386
Graphic Pen filter, 383
grayscale images
    applying color tints to, 227
    colorizing, 196
    printing, with Pantone tint, 461
Grayscale mode, 35, 36
grid
    defined, 150
    hiding/showing, 150
    illustrated, 150
    preferences, 434
    snapping to, 149, 150
guides
    creating, 151
    illustrated, 151
    orientation, switching, 151
    preferences, 434
    removing, 151
    snapping to, 151
Guides, Grid, & Slices preferences, 434

H

Halftone Pattern filter, 383
Halftone Screens dialog box, 451
Hand tool
  defined, 7
  illustrated, 7
  Liquify, 400
  moving images with, 88
  options bar, 89
  Shift key with, 89
  shortcuts, 540–541
Hard Light mode, 40
Hard Mix mode, 41
Healing Brush tool, 252–253
  Aligned option, 252
  before using, 253
  defined, 8, 252
  dragging, 253
  illustrated, 8
  options bar, 252
  Use All Layers option, 253
  using, 252–253
Help menu
  defined, 5
  illustrated, 5
  Photoshop Help command, 69
  Resize Image command, 95
hexadecimal values, 190
highlights
  adjusting, 243
  contrast, increasing, 242
  specular, 237
Histogram palette
  Cached Data Warning icon, 181
  defined, 20, 181
  illustrated, 20, 181
  reading, 182
  Uncached Refresh button, 181
  updating, 181
  using, 181–182
  views, 181
histograms, 182
History Brush tool
  defined, 7
  dragging, 164
  filter effect reduction with, 372
  illustrated, 7
  options bar, 164
  resampling and, 93
  for restoring areas, 31
  shortcuts, 545
  snapshot as source, 164
  using, 164–165
History Options dialog box
  Allow Non-Linear History option, 159, 161, 163

Automatically Create First Snapshot option, 160, 162
Automatically Create New Snapshot When Saving option, 162
History palette, 159–166
  clearing, 160
  defined, 20, 159
  Delete Current State button, 161, 163
  illustrated, 20, 159, 160
  linear mode, 20, 159
  menu
    Clear History command, 160
    Delete command, 163
    Step Backward command, 161
    Step Forward command, 161
  New document from Current State button, 163
  New Snapshot button, 31, 162
  nonlinear mode, 20, 159
  shortcuts, 545
History Source icon, 164, 166, 228
Horizontal Type Mask tool
  defined, 10
  illustrated, 10
  using, 281, 344, 363–365
Horizontal Type tool, 343–346
  Alignment buttons, 344
  Anti-aliasing option, 344
  defined, 7
  Font family option, 344
  Font Size option, 344, 348
  Font style option, 344
  illustrated, 7
  options bar, 343, 344
  selecting with, 346–347
  Type color, 344, 345
HSB Color mode, 34
Hue mode, 42
Hue/Saturation dialog box, 196–197
  Add to Sample eyedropper, 197
  adjustment slider, 197
  Colorize option, 196
  Hue slider, 196
  illustrated, 196
  Lightness slider, 196
  opening, 196
  Saturation slider, 196, 203
  Subtract from Sample eyedropper, 197
Hyphenation dialog box, 356

I

Illustrator
  editable type, 360
  exporting paths to, 327
  file preparation for, 453–454
  files, 80–81, 82
  pasting from, 81
  pasting path object from, 340

Image Map palette (ImageReady), 501–503
  Alt field, 502, 503
  Dimensions area, 503
  Shape pop-up menu, 502
  Target field, 501, 502
  URL field, 501, 502
image maps
  converting, 503
  defined, 501
  deleting, 504
  hiding/showing, 503
  layer-based, 501–502
  selecting, 504
  tool-based, 502–503
Image Map Select tool, 503, 504
Image menu
  Adjustments submenu, 167
    Auto Contrast command, 172
    Auto Levels command, 176
    Brightness/Contrast command, 175
    Channel Mixer command, 180
    Color Balance command, 200
    Curves command, 206
    Desaturate command, 203, 274
    Gradient Map command, 267
    Hue/Saturation command, 196, 201, 465
    Invert command, 173, 279, 365
    Levels command, 176, 177, 204, 374
    Photo Filter command, 244
    Posterize command, 174
    Replace Color command, 248
    Shadow/Highlight command, 242
    Threshold option, 173
  Canvas Size command, 98, 147
  Crop command, 102, 147
  defined, 4
  Duplicate command, 85, 147
  illustrated, 4
  Image Size command, 62, 91, 92, 93, 528
  Mode submenu
    Assign Profile command, 54
    CMYK Color command, 451, 455, 457
    Convert to Profile command, 54
    Duotone command, 461
    Grayscale command, 460
    RGB Color command, 227
  Rotate Canvas submenu, 103, 104
  Trap command, 450
  Trim command, 102
image modes, 35–37
  Bitmap, 36
  CMYK Color, 33–34, 35–36, 37
  conversions, 35
  Duotone, 36
  Grayscale, 36

  Indexed Color, 36
  Lab Color, 37
  Multichannel, 37
  RGB Color, 33–34, 35, 37
  types of, 35
  viewing in, 35–36
ImageReady, 467–534
  copying source code from, 489
  GIF animations, 517–529
  layer effects in, 529
  layer features, 529
  master palettes, 480–481
  Preview in Browser feature, 489
  previews, 482
  rollover preview, 514
  rollovers, 508–517
  saving files in, 490
  scanning into, 61
  slicing in, 495–507
  Toolbox, 476
  type in, 493
images
  brush preset creation from, 224
  closing, 90
  color depth, 472
  creating, 65–66
  cropping, 59
  displaying, in two windows, 89
  editing, 257
  file storage size, 469
  flipping, 103
  grayscale, 196
  hybrid, 480
  keyword categorization, 69
  montages, 256–258
  motion blurring, 389
  moving, in window, 88
  Multichannel mode, 456
  new window, 66
  opening, 79
  placing, 82
  resizing, automatically, 95
  resizing, to fit width/height, 94
  resolution, 58, 59
  resolution, decreasing, 93
  resolution, increasing, 93
  rotating, 104
  saving, 83, 84
  scaling, 59–60
  scanning, 57–61
  screened back, 361
  size calculation, 469
  storage size, 64
  storage size, reducing, 464
  tool tips, 69
  vignetting, 137

Image Size dialog box, 30
 Auto option, 62
 Constrain Proportions option, 91, 92
 illustrated, 91
 opening, 91
 Resample Image option, 91, 92, 93, 147
 Resolution setting, 91
 Scale Styles option, 91, 92
 settings, restoring, 92
 units of measure, 91, 92
image window (ImageReady)
 2-Up tab, 484
 4-Up tab, 482
 Optimized tab, 521
 Size/Download Time, 470
importing, PDF files, 421
InDesign, file preparation for, 452
Indexed Color mode, 36
Info Options dialog box, 21
Info palette
 Color Sampler tool with, 199
 defined, 21
 illustrated, 21
 out-of-gamut indicator, 34
 Palette Options command, 21
ink-jet printers, 447
Ink Outlines filter, 378
Inner Glow effect, 296–297
 applying, 296–297
 Elements settings, 297
 illustrated, 297
 Quality settings, 297
 Structure settings, 296–297
Inner Shadow effect, 294–295
Insert Menu Item dialog box, 407
Invert command, 173, 279

J

JPEG format, 472–473
 Camera Raw vs., 241
 choosing, 473
 compression, 464, 472
 defined, 472
 image fading, 479
 optimization illustrations, 484–485
 optimization with, 473
 optimizing images in, 484–485
 Progressive, 473
 Web-safe colors and, 484
Justification dialog box, 356

K

kerning, 349
Keyboard Shortcuts dialog box, 552, 553–554
keywords, 77
knockout layers, 273

L

Lab Color mode, 34, 84
 defined, 37
 illustrated, 37
Lasso tool
 defined, 7
 Feather field, 137
 illustrated, 7
 shortcuts, 538
layer-based image maps
 converting, 503
 creating, 501–502
 defined, 501
 See also image maps
layer-based rollovers, 512
layer-based slices
 borders between, 497
 creating, 497
 defined, 495
 See also slices
layer comps, 275–277
 applying, 275, 276
 characteristics, changing, 277
 creating, 275
 cycling through, 276
 defined, 22, 275
 deleting, 277
 duplicating, 277
 outputting, as multipage PDF, 277
 saving, 22
 updating, 276
 warning, responding to, 276
Layer Comps palette, 275–277
 Apply Layer Comp button, 276
 defined, 22
 Delete Layer Comp button, 277
 illustrated, 22, 275
 New Layer Comp button, 275, 277
 Update Layer Comp button, 276
layer effects, 291–306
 applying, 291, 292–306
 applying, to shape layer, 334
 applying, to type, 362–363
 applying, to type layer, 347
 applying strokes to, 195
 Bevel, 298–299
 clearing, 305
 Color Overlay, 302
 copying, 293, 305
 defined, 30
 display on Layers palette, 292
 Drop Shadow, 291, 294–295, 296
 editing, 292
 Emboss, 298–299
 filling layers with, 194
 Gradient Overlay, 302

hiding, 293, 306
in ImageReady, 529
Inner Glow, 296–297
Inner Shadow, 294–295
list, expanding, 293
Outer Glow, 296–297
pasting, 305
Pattern Overlay, 303
preserving, as styles, 531
removing, 293
rollovers with, 511
Satin, 301
scaling, 306
shortcuts, 548
Stroke, 304
temporarily hiding, 293
Layer Mask Display Options dialog box, 280
layer masks, 278–282
    advantages, 278
    applying textures with, 387
    black-to-white gradient in, 373
    converting, to vector masks, 332
    creating, 278
    deactivating, 282
    defined, 278
    as Depth Map source, 245
    display options, 280
    duplicating, 280
    effect, applying, 282
    effect, discarding, 282
    effect, inverting, 279
    filling type with imagery with, 281
    for hiding pixels, 31
    for limiting filter effects, 373
    modification tools, 279
    moving, 146, 280
    painting on, 146
    pixel-based, 179
    radial gradient in, 374
    reshaping, 279
    shortcuts, 179, 547
    thumbnails, 146, 281, 282
    type area, repositioning, 281
    vector, 179
Layer menu
    Add Layer Mask submenu
        Hide All command, 278
        Hide Selection command, 281
        Reveal All command, 278
        Reveal Selection command, 278, 281
    Add Vector Mask submenu, 328, 332
    Align Linked submenu, 285
    Align to Selection submenu, 142, 286
    Arrange submenu, 110
    Change Layer Content submenu, 170, 332, 341, 361
    Create Clipping Mask from Linked command, 283

defined, 4
Delete Vector Mask command, 331
Distribute Linked submenu, 286
illustrated, 4
Layer Content Options command, 168, 341
Layer Style submenu
    Create Layer(s) command, 295
    Hide All Effects command, 293
    Show All Effects command, 293
Matting submenu, 158
Merge Clipping Mask command, 121
Merge Visible command, 121
New Adjustment Layer submenu, 168, 171, 360
New Fill Layer command, 114
New Layer Based Slice command, 497
New submenu
    Background From Layer command, 81, 111
    Layer Set command, 113
Rasterize submenu
    Fill Content command, 342
    Layer command, 342
    Shape command, 342
    Type command, 343, 359
    Vector Mask command, 342
Release Clipping Mask command, 284
Type submenu
    Convert to Paragraph Text command, 347
    Convert to Point Text command, 347
    Convert to Shape command, 333, 361
    Horizontal command, 351
    Vertical command, 351
    Warp Text command, 358
Layer Palette Options dialog box, 31
layers, 105–122
    activating, 121, 287
    activating, with Move tool, 112
    active, 105, 120
    adjustment, 29, 31, 114, 168–171
    aligning, to selection marquee, 142
    applying gradient maps to, 267–268
    applying strokes to, 195
    basics, 105–109
    blending, 270–274
    browser window, 470
    building images with, 31
    in clipping masks, 106
    color tints to, 180
    converting, into Background, 111
    converting, to grayscale, 203
    converting Background into, 111
    copying, 116–118
    creating, 106–107
    cropping, 99
    defined, 29, 105
    defringing, 158
    deleting, 109

distorting, 288
distributed, 286
double-clicking, 109
dragging, 110
dragging/dropping, with Layers palette, 117
dragging/dropping, with Move tool, 118
duplicating, 107
erasing parts of, 228–230
file formats and, 106
fill, 114, 192
filling, with color, pattern, imagery, 193–194
filling, with history state, 165
flattening, 122
flipping, 109
gradient, 114
grayscale, 180
hiding, 108
knockout option, 273
layering, 269–290
linking, 121, 285–286
list, 105
locking, 113, 529
managing, 110–115
merging, 120
moving, 113
multiple, merging, 121
multiple, moving, 118
naming, 106, 107
number of, 106
opacity, 115, 269
opaque, 29
pattern, 114
pixels, moving, 112
recoloring, 374
releasing, from clipping mask, 284
renaming, 109
repositioning, 118
restacking, 110, 118
rotating, 287
saving, 84
scaling, 287
screening back, 177
selecting, 123
selections into, 107
shape, 315, 334–342
Shift-dragging, 118
shortcuts, 542–544
showing, 108
skewing, 287
solid color, 114
tools and, 115
transforming, 287–290
transparency, 23, 29
type, 344–345, 346–347, 364
types of, 23
vector, 31

layer sets
benefits, 113
copying, 116
creating, 113
defined, 113
deleting, 113
locking, 113, 529
Merge Visible command, 121
merging layers in, 121
Layers palette
Add a Mask button, 362
Add Layer Mask button, 278, 387
Add Layer Style pop-up menu, 292, 511
Add Vector Mask button, 330, 333
Clear Layer Styles command, 305
Copy Layer Style command, 305
defined, 23
Delete Layer button, 109, 170, 282, 293, 331
dragging/dropping layers with, 117
edits and animations, 523
effects commands, 305–306
eye icon, 107, 108
Fill percentage, 269
Global Light command, 305–306
Hide All Effects command, 306
illustrated, 23, 105
layer effects display, 292
layer list, 105
Linked command, 305
link icon, 280, 285
Lock All button, 113
Lock Position button, 113
Lock Transparent Pixels button, 38, 115, 154,
 193, 212
menu
 Flatten Image command, 122, 170
 Merge Down command, 120, 170
 Merge Linked command, 121
 Merge Visibles command, 121, 170
 New Layer command, 106
Merge Clipping Mask command, 121
missing fonts alert triangle, 359
New Fill/Adjustment Layer pop-up menu, 114,
 128, 168
 Brightness/Contrast command, 175
 Channel Mixer command, 180
 Curves command, 206
 Gradient command, 259, 266
 Gradient Map command, 267
 Hue/Saturation command, 203
 Invert command, 173
 Levels command, 176, 177, 204, 360
 Photo Filter command, 244
 Posterize command, 174
 Threshold command, 173
New Layer button, 106, 107, 202, 227, 296, 361

Index

New Set button, 113
Next Frame button, 522, 529
Opacity percentage, 115, 269, 274, 520
Paste Layer Style command, 305
Previous Frame button, 529
Scale Effects command, 306
shortcuts, 543
thumbnails, 107
Unify buttons, 512, 513, 523
Layers Palette Options dialog box, 106
Layer Style dialog box
  Advanced Blending options, 169
  Bevel effect settings, 298–299
  Blend If pop-up menu, 272
  Blending Options, 169, 270, 271
  Blend Interior Effect as Group option, 271
  Blend Mode, 169
  Channels option, 271
  Color Overlay options, 302
  Drop Shadow options, 294–295
  Emboss settings, 298–299
  Fill Opacity slider, 271
  General Blending area, 271
  Gradient Overlay options, 302
  illustrated, 291
  Inner Glow settings, 296–297
  Knockout pop-up menu, 273
  Layer Mask Hides Effects option, 272
  Opacity setting, 169
  opening, 260
  Pattern Overlay options, 303
  Satin options, 301
  Stroke options, 304
  Transparency Shapes Layer option, 272
  Underlying Layer slider, 272
  Vector Mask Hides Effects option, 272
leading, 350
Lens Blur filter, 245–247, 377
  applying, 245–247
  defined, 245
  dialog illustration, 246
  options, 247
Lens Flare filter, 382
Levels dialog box
  Auto button, 176, 204
  brightness/contrast adjustment, 176
  color channel adjustment with, 204–205
  Input highlights slider, 176, 177
  Input midtones slider, 176
  Options button, 205
  Output highlights slider, 176
  Output shadows slider, 176, 177
  screening back layers with, 177
Lighten mode, 39
Lighting Effects filter, 390–392
  Ambience controls, 391, 392

  circular light source, 392
  defined, 390
  by example, 392
  Exposure controls, 391, 392
  Gloss controls, 391
  light sources, 391–392
  Light Type options, 390, 392
  Material controls, 391
  Omni light, 392
  pin spot, 392
  Style pop-up menu, 390
  textured effect, 392
Linear Burn mode, 39
Linear Dodge mode, 39
linear gradient, 259, 261, 266
Linear Light mode, 41
Line tool
  defined, 10
  illustrated, 10
  Weight option, 335
  See also shape tools
linked layers, 285–286
  aligning, 285
  creating, 285
  defined, 285
  distributing, 286
  selecting, 285
  See also layers
linked slices, 506
Liquify filter, 397–402
  applying, 398–401
  Bloat tool, 399
  defined, 397
  dialog box, 397–402
  distortion, removing, 402
  Forward Warp tool, 398, 399
  Freeze Mask tool, 400
  Hand tool, 400
  Mask Options buttons, 400
  Mirror tool, 399
  Mode pop-up menu, 401
  Opacity slider, 401
  Pucker tool, 399
  Push Left tool, 399
  Reconstruct Mode option, 402
  Reconstruct Options area, 402
  Reconstruct tool, 399
  Show Backdrop option, 400
  Thaw Mask tool, 400
  Tool Options area, 398
  Turbulence tool, 400
  Twirl Clockwise tool, 399
  unfrozen areas, initial state, 402
  unfrozen areas, reversing distortion, 402
  View Options area, 401
Load Selection dialog box, 309, 310

Index

locking
    brush presets, 217
    layers/layer sets, 113, 529
luminosity
    drop shadow, 295
    preserving, 244
Luminosity mode, 42

M

Mac
    file save formats, 57
    gamma values, 488
    General preferences, 429
    image storage size display, 64
    launching Photoshop in, 1
    monitor calibration, 44–45
    opening images from, 79
    Photoshop screen, 2
    shortcuts, 535–552
Magic Eraser tool
    Anti-aliased setting, 231
    Contiguous setting, 231
    defined, 8, 231
    illustrated, 8
    Opacity option, 231
    options bar, 231
    Tolerance setting, 231
    undoing, 232
    Use All Layers option, 231
    using, 231–232
Magic Wand tool, 475
    Add to Selection button, 136
    Contiguous option, 126
    defined, 7
    illustrated, 7
    Intersect with Selection button, 136
    options bar, 126
    selecting by color with, 126
    Subtract from Selection button, 136
    Tolerance value, 126, 127
Magnetic Lasso tool
    defined, 8
    Feather option, 129
    Frequency option, 129
    illustrated, 8
    options bar, 129
    selecting with, 128–129
    shortcuts, 539
    Width option, 129
Make Selection dialog box, 326
Make Work Path dialog box, 316
marquees, 101
    repositioning, 99
    resizing, 99
    rotating, 99, 100
    selection, hiding, 134

    selection, modifying, 135
    selection, moving, 133
    selection, transforming, 135
masks, 307–314
    alpha channels, 307, 308–312
    clipping, 283–284
    Quick Mask, 307, 313–314
    vector, 315, 328–333
    See also layer masks
master palettes (ImageReady), 480–481
    applying, 481
    creating, 480
    defined, 480
Measure tool
    defined, 10
    illustrated, 10
    options bar, 152
    shortcuts, 540
    using, 152
Median filter, 380, 388
Memory & Image Cache preferences, 436
    Cache Levels option, 181
    Cache Settings area, 436
    illustrated, 436
    Maximum Used by Photoshop field, 436
    See also preferences
menu bar, 2
merging
    adjustment layers, 170
    layers, 121
Mezzotint filter, 274, 381
Minimize button, 2
Mirror tool, 399
missing fonts, 359
modal controls, 414
Modify Lossiness Setting dialog box, 481
monitors
    brightness, 44, 46
    calibrating (Mac), 44–45
    calibrating (Windows), 46–47
    contrast, 44, 46
Mosaic Tiles filter, 381, 386
Motion Blur filter, 377, 389
Move tool
    align buttons, 142, 285
    Auto Select Layer option, 365
    defined, 7
    Direct Select, 516
    distribute buttons, 286
    for drag-copying, 142
    dragging/dropping layers with, 118
    illustrated, 7
    layer activation with, 112
    Layer Move, 516
    Layer Select, 516

modifiers, 516
  for moving type selection, 364
  moving with, 141
  options bar, 112
  Shift-drag with, 145
  shortcuts, 538
  Show Bounding Box option, 145, 348
moving, 141–142
  Background, 110
  color samplers, 199
  layer masks, 146, 280
  layers, 113
  layers, with numeric values, 290
  layers/layer masks in unison, 146
  paths, 320
  placed images, 82
  selection contents, 141
  selection marquees, 133
  type selections, 364
  vector masks, 330
Multichannel mode, 37
multicolor wash, 266
Multiple mode, 38

N

navigation, 86–89, 541–542
Navigator palette
  defined, 24
  illustrated, 24, 86
  moving images with, 88
  shortcuts, 542
  view box outline color, 86
  Zoom in/out buttons, 86
  Zoom slider, 86
Neon Glow filter, 375
New Action dialog box, 404
New dialog box, 65–67
  Advanced options, 65–66
  Background Contents option, 65
  Color Mode menu, 65
  Contents: Transparent option, 23
  illustrated, 65
  Image Size display, 65
  opening, 65, 67
  Resolution field, 65
  Save Preset button, 67
  settings, matching, 66
  Width/Height fields, 65
New Document Preset dialog box, 67
New Guide dialog box, 151
New Layer Comp dialog box, 275
New Layer dialog box, 106–107, 111
  Mode option, 202
  Use Previous Layer to Create Clipping Mask
    option, 171
New Set dialog box, 405

New Snapshot dialog box, 162
New Spot Channel dialog box, 208, 366
Normal mode, 38
Note Paper filter, 384
Notes tool, 7, 10
numeric transforms, 290

O

Ocean Ripple filter, 379
opacity
  Brush tool, 179, 202, 209, 211, 227
  Clone Stamp tool, 153, 154, 156
  colored lens effect, 244
  Color Overlay effect, 302
  Eraser tool, 228
  fill, 296
  gradient, 260, 265
  Gradient Overlay effect, 302
  Gradient tool, 261
  Inner/Outer Glow effect, 296
  layers, 115, 269, 520
  Liquify filter, 401
  Magic Eraser tool, 231
  Paint Bucket tool, 226
  Pattern Overlay effect, 303
  Satin effect, 301
  spot color area, 210
  stops, 265
  stroke, 217
  Stroke effect, 304
  variance, 217
Open dialog box, 78
optimization
  animation, 528
  defined, 30, 467
  with droplets, 483
  GIF/PNG-8 formats, 477–480
  JPEG/PNG-24 formats, 484–485
  mixed, 494
  quick, 483
  slice, 505
  weighted, 481
Optimize Animation dialog box, 528
optimized images
  dither preview in, 487
  gamma, changing, 488
  GIF/PNG-8, 477–480
  JPEG/PNG-24, 484–485
  master palettes for, 480–481
  previewing, 489
  saving, 490–491
  updating, 491
Optimize palette (ImageReady)
  Blur value, 485
  Colors option, 478
  displaying, 477

Dither area, 478
Droplet button, 483, 505
Format pop-up menu, 477
with GIF chosen, 468
ICC Profile option, 485
Image Information pop-up menu, 469
with JPEG chosen, 468, 484
Matte option, 475, 479, 485
Options pane, 479–480, 485
Original/Optimized File Sizes option, 469
Preset pop-up menu, 484
Progressive option, 485
Quality pop-up menu, 484
Reduction pop-up menu, 477
Transparency pane, 479, 485
Web Snap percentage, 478, 487
Optimize to File Size dialog box (ImageReady), 483
options bar, 2, 11
Art History Brush tool, 166
Blur tool, 148
Brush tool, 11, 227
Burn tool, 178
Clone Stamp tool, 153, 156
Color Replacement tool, 250
Color Sampler tool, 199
Crop tool, 99, 100
defined, 11
Dodge tool, 178
Elliptical Marquee tool, 124
Eraser tool, 228
Eyedropper tool, 189
File Browser button, 68, 71
Freeform Pen tool, 318
Free Transform command, 290
Gradient tool, 11, 261
Hand tool, 89
Healing Brush tool, 252
History Brush tool, 164
Horizontal Type tool, 343, 344
Magic Eraser tool, 231
Magic Wand tool, 126
Magnetic Lasso tool, 129
Measure tool, 152
Mode option, 261
Move tool, 112
Paint Bucket tool, 226
Patch tool, 254
Pattern Stamp tool, 155
pop-up sliders, 13
Rectangle shape tool (ImageReady), 476
Rectangular Marquee tool, 11, 124
shape tools, 334
Sharpen tool, 148
Smudge tool, 225
Sponge tool, 201, 465
Toggle palette button, 12

tool settings, 6
Type tool (ImageReady), 476
type tools, 343
Zoom tool, 87
Outer Glow effect, 296–297
out-of-gamut colors, correcting, 465
Output Settings dialog box (ImageReady), 490–491, 504, 533
Overlay mode, 40

P

Page Setup dialog box, 442
Paint Bucket tool
defined, 9, 226
illustrated, 9
options bar, 226
using, 226
Paint Daubs filter, 375
painting, 211–232
on spot color channel, 209
techniques, 225–227
palette groups, 12
Palette Knife filter, 375
palettes, 2, 12–28
Actions, 14, 403–417
Animation (ImageReady), 517–529
Brushes, 15, 213–219
Channels, 16, 208, 308–312
Character, 17, 345, 352–353
Color, 18, 186
displaying, 12
docking, 12
File Browser, 19, 68–77
Histogram, 20, 181–182
History, 20, 159–166
Image Map (ImageReady), 501–503
Info, 21, 34, 199
Layer Comps, 22, 275–277
Layers, 23, 120–121, 170–177, 305–306, 511–554
locations, saving, 13
Navigator, 24
opening, 12
Optimize (ImageReady), 477–480, 484–485
Paragraph, 24, 345, 354–356
Paths, 25, 315–327
resizing, 12
separating, 12
shortcuts, 536
showing/hiding, 12
Slice (ImageReady), 499
Styles, 26, 530–531
Swatches, 27, 187–188
Table (ImageReady), 497–498
Tool Presets, 28, 222
using, 12–13
Web Content (ImageReady), 500, 509

palette well, 2
Paragraph palette, 354–356
   alignment buttons, 354
   defined, 24
   Hyphenate option, 354
   illustrated, 24
   indent controls, 355
   justification buttons, 354
   menu
      Adobe Every-line composer command, 344, 356
      Adobe Single-line Composer command, 344, 356
      Hyphenation command, 356
      Justification command, 356
      Reset Paragraph command, 356
      Roman Hanging Punctuation command, 356
   spacing controls, 355
paragraphs
   alignment options, 354
   indentation, 355
   justification options, 354
   settings, 354–356
   spacing, 355
paragraph type, 344
   algorithms, 344
   converting to, 347
Paste dialog box, 81, 340
pasting
   Clipboard and, 143
   colors, 190
   copying and, 144–145
   from Illustrator, 8
   into, 146
   into smaller image, 147
   into type selection, 364
   layer effects, 305
   layers into other images, 147
   selection size and, 144
Patch tool, 254–255
   before/after use photos, 255
   defined, 8
   dragging, 254
   illustrated, 8
   options bar, 254
   using, 254–255
Patchwork filter, 386
paths, 32, 316–327
   anchor points, selecting, 323
   applying strokes to, 195
   closing, 317, 320
   combining, 329
   converting, to selections, 326
   converting selections to, 316
   copying, 322
   creating, 316–320
   creating, with Freeform Pen tool, 320
   creating, with Pen tool, 317

   defined, 25
   deleting, 325
   deselecting, 326
   displaying, 323
   dragging-and-dropping, 322
   exporting, 327
   fills, 325
   hiding, 323
   illustrated, 315
   inserting, in actions, 408
   magnetic, with Freeform Pen tool, 318
   moving, 320
   open, adding, 321
   reshaping, 315, 324–325
   saving, 317
   scaling, 321
   shape, copying, 322
   shortcuts, 549
   stacking order, 323
   strokes, 325
   transforming, 321
   work, 315
   working with, 320–327
Path Selection tool, 320, 321, 323
   Alt-drag/Option-drag paths with, 322
   defined, 7
   dragging, 320
   illustrated, 7
   for point selection, 323
   shortcuts, 540
   Show Bounding Box option, 339
   Subtract from Shape Area button, 331, 333
Paths palette, 316–327
   defined, 25
   Delete Path (trash) button, 325
   Fill Path with Foreground Color button, 325
   illustrated, 25, 315
   Load Path as Selection button, 326
   Make Work Path from Selection button, 332
   menu
      Make Work Path command, 316
      Save Path command, 408
   New Path button, 322
   Stroke Path with button, 325
   Work Path from Selection button, 316
Pattern Fill dialog box, 114
Pattern layers, 114
Pattern Maker filter, 393–396
   defined, 393
   Delete Tile from History button, 396
   dialog box, 394
   Generate button, 395
   Offset pop-up menu, 395
   opening, 393
   Preview area, 394
   Sample Detail setting, 395

Save Preset Pattern button, 396
Smoothness setting, 395
Tile History section, 396
Width/Height values, 394
Pattern Name dialog box, 396
Pattern Overlay effect, 303
patterns
defining, 226
deleting, 396
generating, 393–395
navigating through, 396
previewing, 394
saving, 194, 396
tile dimensions, 394
working with, 194
Pattern Stamp tool
defined, 8
illustrated, 8
options bar, 155
Pattern Preset picker, 155
using, 155
PDF files, 84
defined, 459
importing, 421
opening, 80–81
placing, 82
saving as, 459
PDF Options dialog box, 459
PDF Page Selector dialog box, 80
Pencil tool, 9
Pen tool
Auto Add/Delete option, 324
defined, 7
drawing paths with, 317
illustrated, 7
options bar, 11
Pathfinder buttons, 329
Paths button, 317
shortcuts, 540
perspective transformation, 288, 289
Photocopy filter, 384
Photo Filter dialog box, 244
photography, 233–258
Photomerge, 256–258
Advanced Blending option, 258
Composition Settings area, 258
controls, 258
Cylindrical Mapping option, 258
defined, 256
dialog box, 256–258
illustrated, 257
image arrangement, 256
image collection, 256
image editing, 257
montage creation, 257–258
Navigator area, 257

preview, 258
Settings options, 257
source file selection, 256
starting, 256
vanishing point, 257
Photoshop
exiting/quitting, 90
file preparation, 452–454
launching (Mac), 1
launching (Windows), 1
printing from, 441–451
scanning into, 61
screen (Mac), 2
screen (Windows), 3
Picture Package dialog box, 422, 423
Picture Package Edit Layout dialog box, 423
Picture Package plug-in, 422–423
Pinch filter, 379, 513
Pin Light mode, 40
pixels, 33, 91–104
beyond edge, removing, 147
color breakdown, 21
defined, 29
dimensions, 30
distribution, 236
geometric area of, 337
hiding, 31
layer, moving, 112
lock transparent, 115
nontransparent, 115
opaque, 123
rasterizing type into, 359
resolution, 30
shadow, 238
transparent, 102
trimming, 102
Plaster filter, 384
Plastic Wrap filter, 376
Playback Options dialog box, 412
Plug-Ins & Scratch Disks preferences, 435
PNG-8 format, 473–474
defined, 473
optimizing images in, 477–480
PNG-24 format, 473–474
defined, 473, 474
optimizing images in, 484–485
Pointillize filter, 381
points. *See* anchor points
point type, 344, 347
Polar Coordinates filter, 379
Polygonal Lasso tool
defined, 8
illustrated, 8
selection creation with, 125
shortcuts, 538
See also shape tools

Polygon tool
   defined, 10
   illustrated, 10
   Sides option, 335
Poster Edges filter, 376
Posterize dialog box, 174
preferences, 427–438
   accessing, 427
   defined, 427
   Display & Cursors, 431
   File Browser, 437
   File Handling, 430
   General, 428–429
   Guides, Grid, Slices, 434
   Memory & Image Cache, 436
   Plug-Ins & Scratch Disks, 435
   shortcuts, 552
   Transparency & Gamut, 432
   Units & Rulers, 433
preset libraries
   current, saving presets into, 220, 440
   default, 438
   defined, 438
   directions to, 438
   new, saving presets into, 439
   sharing, 438
Preset Manager, 438–440
   defined, 220
   illustrated, 438
   Load button, 438
   opening, 438, 439
   Preset Type pop-up menu, 438, 439
   Replace command, 439
   Reset command, 439
   Save Set button, 439
   using, 438
presets
   accessing, 28
   defined, 30, 438
   document, 67
   gradient, 262–265
   managing, 438–440
   renaming, 439
   save location, 440
   saving, 28, 220
pressure-sensitive tablets
   brush size and, 230
   Jitter/Scatter attributes and, 219
   tolerance and, 230
previews
   adjustment, 167, 191
   animation, 521
   in browser, 489
   dither, 487
   extract, 139, 140
   filter, 371

   ImageReady, 482
   optimized image, 489
   page, 64
   pattern, 394
   Photomerge, 258
   print, 92, 444–445
   rollover, 514
   selection, 130
   thumbnail, 69
   tiled background, 533
printable gamut, 465
Print dialog box, 443
printers
   color separations, 451
   desktop ink-jet, 447
   dye sublimation, 451
   imagesetters, 451
   IRIS, 451
   resolution, 441
printing, 441–466
   with color management, 446–449
   duotones, 460–461
   grayscale images with Pantone tint, 461
   one copy, 445
   option availability, 442
   out-of-gamut colors and, 465
   page orientation, 442
   page size, 442
   from Photoshop, 441–451
   with Print command, 443
   with Print with Preview command, 444–445
   quadtone, 460
   quick, 445
   shortcuts, 552
   shortcuts list, 554
   spot color channels, 210
   tritone, 460
print output
   changing dimensions for, 92
   professional-quality, 58
   resolution calculation, 62–63
   resolutions, 58, 59
Print with Preview dialog box, 444–445
   Background button, 448
   Bleed button, 448
   Border button, 448
   Calibration Bars option, 448
   Center Image option, 444
   Color Management options, 447
   Crop Marks options, 448
   Emulsion Down option, 449
   Encoding pop-up menu, 449
   hidden buttons, 445
   illustrated, 444, 447, 448
   Include Vector Data option, 449
   Intent pop-up menu, 447

Interpolation option, 448
Labels option, 448
Negative option, 449
Output options, 448–449
Print Selected Area option, 445
Profile pop-up menu, 446
Registration Marks option, 448
Scaled Print Size options, 444–445
Screen button, 448, 451
Show Bounding Box option, 445
Show More Options option, 54, 446, 448
Source Space options, 447
Transfer button, 448
process colors, 184, 185
production techniques, 31–32
Progressive JPEG, 473
Proof Setup dialog box, 55–56
illustrated, 464
Intent pop-up menu, 464
opening, 55, 56
Preserve Color Numbers option, 56
Profile pop-up menu, 56, 464
Simulate options, 56
Use Black Point Compensation option, 56
PSB files, 84
PSD files, 84
Pucker tool, 399
Push Left tool, 399

Q

QuarkXPress, file preparation for, 452
Quick Mask dialog box, 281
Quick Mask mode, 32, 307, 313
Quick Mask Options dialog box, 314
Quick Masks, 313–314
creating, 314
defined, 307
options, 314
reshaping selections with, 313–314
saving and, 313
shortcuts, 547
quick-optimize, 483

R

Radial Blur filter, 377
radial gradient, 259
Rank Files dialog box, 75
Rasterize Generic PDF Format dialog box, 80–81
rasterizing
shape layers, 342
type layers, 343
Real World Adobe Photoshop, 207, 466
Real World Color Management, 466
Reconstruct tool, 399
Record Stop dialog box, 406
Rectangle tool, 7

Rectangular Marquee tool, 131
defined, 7
drawing with, 102
Feather field, 137
illustrated, 7
New Selection button, 364
options bar, 11, 124
rectangular selections, 124
red-eye removal, 251
reflected gradient, 259
remote animation, 525
remote rollovers, 515
repairs, 252–255
with Healing Brush tool, 252–253
with Patch tool, 254–255
Replace Color dialog box, 248–249
eyedroppers, 248, 249
Fuzziness slider, 248
Hue slider, 249
illustrated, 248
Lightness slider, 249
opening, 248
preview window, 248
Replacement sliders, 249
Result swatch, 249
Saturation slider, 249
resampling
defined, 91
History Brush tool and, 93
Reset All Tools command, 6
resetting, 167
Reset Tool command, 6
Resize Image Assistant, 95
resolution
allocating, 93
Camera Raw image, 236
cropping and, 100
decreasing, 93
file storage sizes and, 63
gray levels and, 63
image, increasing, 93–94
lowest, 31
output devices, 441
overkill, 443
print output, 62–63
scan, 58, 59
Web graphics, 62
Reticulation filter, 384
reverting, 84
RGB Color mode, 33–34
converting, 35
curves, 207
defined, 37
illustrated, 37
Working Spaces settings, 49–50
Ripple filter, 379, 387

Index

rocking animation, 522
rollovers, 508–517
 for buttons, 516
 Click state, 509
 creating, 508–510
 creating, with layer effects, 511
 defined, 30, 508
 Down state, 509
 ideas, 513
 layer-based, 512
 Normal state, 510, 511
 Over state, 510, 511, 514
 previewing, 514
 remote, 515
 states, 509, 510
 as styles, 531
 thumbnails, 510
 triggering animations, 525
 types of, 508
Rollover State Options dialog box (ImageReady), 509
Rotate Canvas dialog box, 104
rotate transformation, 287
rotating
 canvas, 103
 direction lines, 324
 images, by number specification, 104
 images, preset amount, 104
 layers, 287
 layers, with numeric values, 290
 marquees, 99, 100
 paths, 321
 placed images, 82
 points on paths, 321
 thumbnails, 73
 type, 351
 type bounding box, 357
Rough Pastels filter, 374, 376
Rounded Rectangle tool
 defined, 10
 illustrated, 10
 Radius value, 335
 See also shape tools
rulers
 hiding/showing, 149
 illustrated, 2
 opening, 2
 zero origin, changing, 149

S

sampling, colors, 189
Satin effect, 301
saturation
 Camera Raw image, 238
 defined, 30
Saturation mode, 42
Save As dialog box, 84, 85

Save for Web dialog box, 468, 534
Save Optimized As dialog box (ImageReady), 490
Save Path dialog box, 322
Save Selection dialog box, 308, 310, 481
 illustrated, 308
 opening, 308
 Operation options, 310
Save Settings subset dialog box, 237
saving, 416
 alpha channels, 308
 brush libraries, 220
 brush presets, 217
 Camera Raw files, 233
 color settings, 53
 custom CMYK settings, 463
 in DCS 2.0 format, 457
 effects, 84
 as EPS file, 455–456
 File Browser settings, 70
 file formats, 57
 files, 83–85
 GIF animations, 527
 in GIF format, 471
 gradient presets, 264
 in ImageReady, 490–491
 layer comps, 22
 layers, 84
 optimized images, 490–491
 paths, 317
 patterns, 194
 pattern tiles, 396
 as PDF file, 459
 presets, 28
 reverting and, 84
 saved images, 84
 selections to channels, 308
 swatches library, 188
 as TIFF file, 458
 tool preset libraries, 222
 tool presets, 222, 223
 type selections, 364
 unsaved images, 83
 vectors, 84
 work paths, 322
Scale Layer Effects dialog box, 306
scale transformation, 287
scaling
 gradients, 260
 layer effects, 306
 layers, 287
 layers, with numeric values, 290
 paths, 321
 points on paths, 321
 scanning and, 59–60
 type bounding box, 357
 warped text, 358

scanning, 57–61
  16-bits-per-channel mode, 60
  cropping and, 59
  device dialog box, 61
  device quality, 58
  into ImageReady, 61
  into Photoshop, 61
  original quality, 58
  preview, 58
  scaling and, 59–60
  scan mode, 59
  software, 58–60
scan resolution, 58–59
screening back type, 361
Screen mode, 39
scrolling, in multiple windows, 89
Search dialog box, 74
segments
  curved, 317
  dragging, 324
  straight, 317
selecting
  Background, 123
  border selections, 131
  brush presets, 211
  by color with Magic Wand tool, 126–127
  copying and pasting, 144–145
  dragging-and-dropping, 145
  image maps, 504
  layers, 123
  opaque pixels, 123
  selection intersections, 136
  text, 346
  vector masks, 331
selection marquees
  aligning layers to, 142
  hiding, 134
  modifying, 135
  moving, 133
  transforming, 135
selections, 123–140
  active, verifying, 134
  adding to, 136
  applying strokes to, 195
  border, selecting, 131
  channel, displaying, 309
  channel, loading, 309
  channel, saving, 308
  contents, moving, 141
  converting, into paths, 123, 316
  converting paths to, 326
  converting to layers, 107
  creating, 123–131
  creating, with Color Range command, 130
  creating, with Magnetic Lasso tool, 129
  creating, with Polygonal Lasso tool, 125

  defined, 30
  deleting, 132
  deselecting, 132
  drag-copying, 142
  dragging, on layers, 133
  elliptical, creating, 124
  feathering, 157
  filling, from history state, 165
  filling, with color, pattern, imagery, 193–194
  frame, 131
  freeform, creating, 125
  illustrated, 30
  intersection, selecting, 136
  pasting into, 146
  polygonal, creating, 125
  previewing, 130
  rectangular, creating, 124
  reselecting, 132
  shortcuts, 542
  smoothing, 133
  subtracting from, 136
  type mask, 363
  unselected area switching, 134
  width-to-height ratio, 124
  working with, 132–140
Select menu
  All command, 123, 147
  Color Range command, 130, 465
  defined, 5
  Deselect command, 132, 364, 366
  Feather command, 157, 296, 389
  Grow command, 126, 135
  illustrated, 5
  Load Selection command, 309
  Modify submenu, 127
    Border command, 131, 139
    Smooth command, 133, 135
  Save Selection command, 308, 481
  Transform Selection command, 296
Shadow/Highlight dialog box, 242–243
shadows
  adjusting, 243
  contrast, increasing, 242
  pixels, 238
shape layers, 315, 334–342
  applying layer effects to, 334
  contour, modifying, 339
  creating, 334–335
  fill contents, changing, 341
  pasting Illustrator path objects into, 340
  rasterizing, 342
  transforming, 339
  vector mask, deactivating, 339
  vector mask, moving, 338
Shape Name dialog box, 341

shapes, 334–342
  adding, to Custom Shape picker, 341
  adding/subtracting, 340
  color fill, 334
  with Custom Shape tool, 335
  defined, 334
shape tools
  Add to Shape Area button, 340
  Fill Pixels button, 337
  geometric options, 338
  Geometry Options arrowhead, 338
  link button, 335
  list of, 334
  options bar, 334
  Pathfinder buttons, 329
  Shape Layers button, 340
  Subtract from Shape Area button, 340
  work path creation with, 336
  See also specific shape tools
Sharpen Edges filter, 382
Sharpen More filter, 382
Sharpen tool
  defined, 8, 148
  illustrated, 8
  options bar, 148
  using, 148
Shear filter, 379
shortcuts, 535–554
  adjustment commands, 545–546
  blending modes, 544–545
  brushes, 547
  Channels palette, 547–548
  Clipboard, 542
  colors, 546
  creating, 553–554
  deleting, 554
  display, 541
  files, 535
  fill layer, 192
  filters, 552
  general, 536
  history, 545
  history states, 161
  layer effects, 548
  layer masks, 179, 547
  layers, 542–544
  memorizing, 31
  navigation, 541–542
  palettes, 536
  path-into-selection, 326
  paths, 549
  preferences, 552
  printing, 552
  printing list of, 554
  Quick Masks, 547
  restoring, 554

  selections, 542
  tool, 6, 537–541
  transformations, 549–550
  type, 550–552
  undo, 536
  zoom, 87
Show Extra Options dialog box, 134
Single Column Marquee tool, 8
Single Row Marquee tool, 8
skewing
  free transform layers, 289
  layers, 287
  layers, with numeric values, 290
  paths, 321
  points on paths, 321
  type bounding box, 357
Slice palette (ImageReady)
  Alt field, 507
  Target field, 499
  URL field, 499
slices, 495–507
  Alt tag, attaching, 507
  attaching URL links to, 499
  auto, 495, 497
  borders, 498
  defined, 495
  deleting, 497
  illustrated, 496
  keeping, 453
  layer-based, 495, 497, 512
  linking, 506
  optimizing, 505
  plotting, 497
  rollovers for, 508–510
  showing/hiding, 498
  stacking order, 500
  types of, 495
  unlinking, 506
  user, 495, 496, 498
Slice Select tool, 498, 499, 500, 505
  alignment buttons, 500
  defined, 9
  distribution button, 501
  illustrated, 9
  palette toggle button, 495
  using, 497
slice sets, 507
Slices Preferences dialog box, 496
Slice tool
  defined, 7
  illustrated, 7
  shortcuts, 539
  using, 496
slicing
  with commands, 495–496
  defined, 495

into multiple links, 499
manually, 496
Smart Blur filter, 377
Smudge Stick filter, 376
Smudge tool
defined, 8
illustrated, 8
options bar, 225
shortcuts, 539
using, 225
Snap features, 150
snapshots, 162–163
creating, 162
creating, from history state, 163
defined, 162
deleting, 163
as History Brush tool, 164
as latest state, 163
restoring from, 165
thumbnails, 162, 163
Soft Light mode, 40
Solarize filter, 385
Solid Color layers, 114
sorting, files, 75
Spatter filter, 378
specular highlights, 237
Spherize filter, 380
Sponge filter, 376
Sponge tool
defined, 10
Flow percentage, 465
illustrated, 10
Mode pop-up menu, 465
options bar, 201, 465
saturating/desaturating colors with, 201
shortcuts, 540
Spot Channel Options dialog box, 210
spot color channels, 208–210
active, 210
basics, 210
in Channels palette, 208
converting alpha channels to, 209
copying to, 208
creating, 208
defined, 208
exporting, 210
illustrated, 35
merging, 210
overprinting prevention, 210
painting on, 209
printing, 210
tint, lightening/darkening, 209
type in, 366
See also channels
spot colors
changing, in channel, 208

matching systems, 208
outputting, 185
Sprayed Strokes filter, 378
Stained Glass filter, 386
Stamp filter, 374
states
defined, 159
deleting, 161
duplicating, 161
earlier, 159
filling selections/layers with, 165
latest, snapshot of, 163
listed, number of, 160
maximum number of, 160
restoring, 161
Revert command as, 482
shortcuts, 161
snapshot creation, 162
snapshots of, 163
See also History palette
status bar, 2
displaying/hiding, 64
pop-up menu, 64
sticky settings, 236
stops, 406
Stroke dialog box, 195
Stroke effect, 304
strokes
applying, 195
applying, to paths, 325
applying, to type, 363
density, 215
edge pigment, 217
fill, 304
noise, 217
opacity, 217, 304
options, 195
pattern, 215–216
position, 304
size, 304
texture, 215–216
Style Options dialog box, 531
styles
applying, 530
preserving layer effects as, 531
rollover, 531
Styles palette, 531–532
defined, 26, 530
illustrated, 26, 530
Style Options command, 531
subtractive primaries, 33
Sumi-e filter, 378
swash glyphs, 353
swatches
adding, 27
deleting, 27

library, 188
renaming, 187
Swatches palette, 187–188
adding colors to, 187
choosing colors from, 187
default, restoring, 188
defined, 27
deleting colors from, 187
editing, 187
illustrated, 27, 187
menu, 188
New Swatch of Foreground Color button, 187
shortcuts, 546
Small List mode, 187
SWF file format, 528

T

Table palette (ImageReady), 497–498
text. *See* type
texture, 215–216
applying, with layer mask, 387
copying, 219
depth, 216
mapping, with filters, 374
patterns, 374
scale, 216
uniform, 217
Texturizer filter, 386
Thaw Mask tool, 400
Threshold dialog box, 173
thumbnails
adjustment, 168
arranging, manually, 75
Channels palette, 311
Contour, 300
creating, 79
dragging, 76
flag, 73
layer mask, 146
Layers palette, 107
nonconsecutive, selecting, 72
ranking, 75
rollovers, 510
rotating, 73
selecting, 72
snapshot, 162, 163
vector masks, 329, 339
TIFF files, saving as, 458
TIFF Options dialog box, 458
Tile Maker dialog box, 532
Tiles filter, 385
tiling, 532–534
background preview, 533
defined, 532
process, 532–533
tips, 532

tints. *See* color tints
title bar, 2
tool-based image maps
aligning, 504
converting to, 503
creating, 502–503
defined, 501
distributing, 504
See also image maps
Toolbox, 6–10
Background color square, 7, 183, 184, 185
Edit in ImageReady option, 7, 468
Foreground color square, 7, 183, 184, 185
Full Screen Mode button, 7, 88
Full Screen Mode with Menu Bar button, 88
illustrated, 2, 7–10
Quick Mask Mode button, 7, 313
showing/hiding, 2, 88
Standard Mode button, 7, 88, 314
See also tools
Toolbox (ImageReady)
illustrated, 476
Preview in [default browser] button, 489, 521
Toggle Slice Visibility button, 498
tool preset libraries
loading, 223
naming, 223
saving, 223
Tool Preset picker, 6
Current Tool Only option, 222
New Tool Preset button, 345
opening, 222
tool presets, 222
converting brush presets to, 222
saving, 222
saving, to library, 223
Tool Presets palette
defined, 28
illustrated, 28, 222
Include Color command, 222
tools
Add Anchor Point, 9, 324
Art History Brush, 9, 166
attributes, selecting, 6
Audio Annotation, 9, 10
Background Eraser, 8, 229–230
Blur, 7, 148
Brush, 7, 11, 211–212
Burn, 10, 178
Clone Stamp, 7, 153–154, 156
Color Replacement, 7, 250–251
Color Sampler, 10, 198–199
Convert Point, 9, 325
Crop, 7, 99–100
Custom Shape, 335, 338
Delete Anchor Point, 9, 325

Direct Selection, 9, 321, 323, 324, 326
Dodge, 7, 178
Ellipse, 10, 338
Elliptical Marquee, 8, 124, 131
Eraser, 7, 228
Eyedropper, 7, 189–190
Forward Warp, 398, 399
Freeform Pen, 9, 318–320
Freeze Mask, 400
Gradient, 7, 11, 259–265
Hand, 7, 88, 89, 400
Healing Brush, 8, 252–253
History Brush, 7, 31, 164–165
Horizontal Type, 7, 343–346
Horizontal Type Mask, 10, 281, 344, 363–365
Image Map Select, 503, 504
ImageReady, 476
incorrect use of, 6
Lasso, 7, 137, 538
layers and, 115
Line, 10, 335
Magic Eraser, 8, 231–232
Magic Wand, 7, 126, 127, 136, 475
Magnetic Lasso, 8
Measure, 10, 152
Mirror, 399
Move, 7, 141
Notes, 7, 10
Paint Bucket, 9, 226
Patch, 8, 254–255
Path Selection, 7, 320, 321, 323
Pattern Stamp, 8, 155
Pen, 7, 11, 317
Pencil, 9
pointers, 6
Polygon, 10, 335
Polygonal Lasso, 8, 125
Pucker, 399
Push Left, 399
Reconstruct, 399
Rectangle, 7
Rectangular Marquee, 7, 11, 102, 124, 131
resetting, 6
Rounded Rectangle, 10, 335
selecting, 6
Sharpen, 8, 148
shortcuts, 6, 537–541
Single Column Marquee, 8
Single Row Marquee, 8
Slice, 7, 496, 539
Slice Select, 9, 495, 496, 497, 505
Smudge, 8, 225
Sponge, 10, 201
Thaw Mask, 400
Turbulence, 400
Twirl Clockwise, 399

Vanishing Point, 257
Vertical Type, 10, 343–346
Vertical Type Mask, 10, 344, 363–365
Zoom, 7, 87, 89
tool tips, defined, 6
Torn Edges filter, 384
Trace Contour filter, 386, 388
tracking, 349
transformations, 287–290
    accepting, 289
    Background, 289, 290
    with bounding box, 287–288
    distort, 288
    Drop Shadow effect, 295
    free, 289
    with numeric values, 290
    path, 321
    perspective, 288
    rotate, 287
    scale, 287
    selection marquees, 135
    shortcuts, 549–550
    skew, 287
    tips, 288
    type bounding box, 357–358
Transform Selection command, 135
Transparency & Gamut preferences, 432
Trap dialog box, 450
Trim dialog box, 102
Turbulence tool, 400
Tween dialog box, 519
Twirl Clockwise tool, 399
Twirl filter, 380, 387
type, 343–368
    anti-aliasing, 494
    applying layer effects to, 362–363
    applying strokes to, 363
    baseline shift, 353
    bounding box, transforming, 357–358
    color, 345
    converting, 347
    creating, 343–346
    creating, for Web pages, 493–494
    editable, 344
    editing, 346–353
    fading, 362
    finding/replacing, 367
    importing from Adobe Illustrator, 346
    in ImageReady, 493
    kerning, 349
    leading, 350
    online, 494
    orientation, 351
    paragraph, 344, 347
    paragraph settings, 354–356
    point, 344, 347

rasterizing, 359–360
resizing, manually, 348
resizing, with values, 348
rotating, 351
screen back, 361
screen back images behind, 360
selecting, 346–347
shortcuts, 550–552
special effects, 357–362
spell check, 368
in spot channels, 366
stretching, 351
styling, 352–353
tracking, 349
types of, 343–344
vector mask creation from, 333
warping, 358
word processing, 367–368
type layers
aligning, 364
applying layer effects to, 347
editable, creating, 344–345
hiding, 366
moving, 359
rasterizing, 343
selecting on, 346
See also layers
type selections
for adjustment layer, 365
copying pixels within, 364
creating, 363–364
illustrated, 363
moving, 364
pasting into, 364
saving, 364
Type tool (ImageReady)
Create Warped Text button, 527
options bar, 476
using, 493
type tools. *See* Horizontal Type tool; Vertical Type tool

U
Underpinning filter, 376
undo, 31, 536
Units & Rulers preferences, 433
Unsharp Mask filter, 382, 388
Amount percentage, 96
applying, 96–97
defined, 96
user slices
aligning, 500
defined, 495
drawing, 496
evenly distributing, 501
resizing, 498
See also slices

V
values, changing, 13
Vanishing Point tool, 257
vector layers, 31
vector masks, 32, 328–333
adjustment layer use, 332
converting layer masks to, 332
creating, 328
creating, from type, 333
deactivating, 330
defined, 315, 328
discarding, 331
duplicating, 330
hidden/visible areas reverse, 331
for hiding pixels, 31
moving, 330
repositioning, 330, 333
reshaping, 329
selecting, 331
thumbnails, 329, 339
vectors
defined, 29
saving, 84
Vertical Type Mask tool
defined, 10
illustrated, 10
using, 344, 363–365
Vertical Type tool, 343–346
defined, 10
Font Size option, 348
illustrated, 10
options bar, 343
selecting with, 346–347
View menu
Clear Guides command, 151
defined, 5
Gamut Warning command, 465
illustrated, 5
New Guide command, 151
Print Size command, 92
Proof Colors command, 35, 464, 465
Proof Setup submenu, 35, 199
Custom command, 464
Working CMYK command, 32, 248
Rulers command, 2, 149
Show submenu, 150
Extras command, 150
Grid command, 133, 149, 150
Selection Edges command, 134
Show Extra Options command, 134
Snap To submenu, 150
All command, 150
Document Bounds command, 100, 150
Grid command, 133, 141, 149, 150
Guides command, 133, 141, 149, 150

None command, 150
Slices command, 150
Vivid Light mode, 41

W

warped type
animation, creating, 52
removing/adjusting, 527
Warp Text dialog box, 358, 526
Watercolor filter, 376
Water Paper filter, 384
Wave filter, 380
Web browsers
rollover preview in, 514
window layer, 470
Web Content palette (ImageReady), 500
Create Layer-based Rollover button, 512
Create Rollover State button, 509, 511
New Slice Set button, 507
Palette Options command, 510, 525
Web formats
GIF, 471
JPEG, 472–473
PNG-8/PNG-24, 473–474
Web output
anti-aliasing, 475
color depth, 472
compression, 470–471
dithering, 474–475
golden rules, 469
image size, 469
Web pages
buttons, 516
title, changing, 492
type, creating, 493–494
Web Photo Gallery dialog box, 424–426
Banner Options, 425
Custom Colors Options, 425
files, 426
General Options, 424
illustrated, 424
Large Images Options, 425
Security Options, 425–426
Source Images area, 424
Styles pop-up menu, 424
templates, 426
Thumbnails Options, 425
Web-safe colors, 184, 494
flat-color areas as, 486
JPEG and, 484
See also color(s)
weighted optimization, 481
white balance, 237

Wind filter, 386, 387
Window menu
Arrange submenu, 89
Brushes command, 213
defined, 5
File Browser command, 68
illustrated, 5
Status Bar command, 64
Workspace submenu, 13
Windows
droplets, 413
file save formats, 57
gamma values, 488
General preferences, 429
image storage size display, 64
launching Photoshop in, 1
monitor calibration, 46–47
only features, 3
opening images from, 79
Photoshop screen, 3
shortcuts, 535–552
windows, image
moving images in, 88
multiple, 32
two, displaying images in, 89
word processing, 367–368
work paths, 315
creating, 322
creating, with shape tools, 336
quick-save, 322
saving, 322
See also paths
workspaces, 13
saving File Browser settings as, 70

Z

zero origin, 149
ZigZag filter, 380
zoom
changing, with Navigator palette, 86
changing, with Zoom tool, 87
Liquify, 400
in multiple windows, 89
shortcuts, 87
Zoom button, 2
Zoom tool
defined, 7
illustrated, 7
options bar, 87
Shift key with, 89
shortcuts, 540
window resize with, 87
zooming in/out with, 87

Index